Christian Omnibus Vol. 3
Five Books on Reliance

TABLE OF CONTENTS

INTRODUCTION TO THE DEVOUT LIFE 3

THE PURSUIT OF GOD 141

HUMILITY 187

CALVIN'S BOOK ON THE CHRISTIAN LIFE 218

THE GOD OF ALL COMFORT 244

Introduction to the Devout Life

~ ※ ~

By *St. Francis of Sales*

The 1875 Edition

~ ※ ~

Preface by the Author

DEAR reader, I request you to read this Preface for your own satisfaction as well as mine.

The flower-girl Glycera was so skilled in varying the arrangement and combination of her flowers, that out of the same kinds she produced a great variety of bouquets; so that the painter Pausias,[1] who sought to rival the diversity of her art, was brought to a standstill, for he could not vary his painting so endlessly as Glycera varied her bouquets. Even so the Holy Spirit of God disposes and arranges the devout teaching which He imparts through the lips and pen of His servants with such endless variety, that, although the doctrine is ever one and the same, their treatment of it is different, according to the varying minds whence that treatment flows. Assuredly I neither desire, nor ought to write in this book anything but what has been already said by others before me. I offer you the same flowers, dear reader, but the bouquet will be somewhat different from theirs, because it is differently made up.

Almost all those who have written concerning the devout life have had chiefly in view persons who have altogether quitted the world; or at any rate they have taught a manner of devotion which would lead to such total retirement. But my object is to teach those who are living in towns, at court, in their own households, and whose calling obliges them to a social life, so far as externals are concerned. Such persons are apt to reject all attempt to lead a devout life under the plea of impossibility; imagining that like as no animal presumes to eat of the plant commonly called Palma Christi, so no one who is immersed in the tide of temporal affairs ought to presume to seek the palm of Christian piety.

And so I have shown them that, like as the mother-of-pearl lives in the sea without ever absorbing one drop of salt water; and as near the Chelidonian Isles springs of sweet water start forth in the midst of the ocean;[2] and as the firemoth[3] hovers in the flames without burning her wings; even so a true stedfast soul may live in the world untainted by worldly breath, finding a well-spring of holy piety amid the bitter waves of society, and hovering amid the flames of earthly lusts without singeing the wings of its devout life. Of a truth this is not easy, and for that very reason I would have Christians bestow more care and energy than heretofore on the attempt, and thus it is that, while conscious of my own weakness, I endeavour[4] by this book to afford some help to those who are undertaking this noble work with a generous heart.

It is not, however, my own choice or wish which brings this Introduction before the public. A certain soul, abounding in uprightness and virtue, some time since conceived a great desire, through God's Grace, to aspire more earnestly after a devout life, and craved my private help with this view. I was bound to her by various ties, and had long observed her remarkable capacity for this attainment, so I took great pains to teach her, and having led her through the various exercises suitable to her circumstances and her aim, I let her keep written records thereof, to which she might have recourse when necessary. These she communicated to a learned and devout Religious, who, believing that they might be

---

[1] Pausias of Sicyon (B.C. 368); see Plin. *Hist. Nat.* xxxv. 11-40. A portrait of Glycera, the young flower-girl whom he loved, with a garland of flowers, was one of his masterpieces. It was called the Stephane-plocos [Στεφανὴ - πλόκος], or garland wreather, and was purchased by L. Lucullus at Athens for two talents, or about 430 pounds.

[2] These islands are in the Mediterranean Sea, in the Gulf of Lycia.

[3] Πυραύστης

[4] Original spelling kept throughout.

profitable to others, urged me to publish them, in which he succeeded the more readily that his friendship exercised great influence upon my will, and his judgment great authority over my judgment.

So, in order to make the work more useful and acceptable, I have reviewed the papers and put them together, adding several matters carrying out my intentions; but all this has been done with scarce a moment's leisure. Consequently you will find very little precision in the work, but rather a collection of well-intentioned instructions, explained in clear intelligible words, at least that is what I have sought to give. But as to a polished style, I have not given that a thought, having so much else to do.

I have addressed my instructions to Philothea,[5] as adapting what was originally written for an individual to the common good of souls. I have made use of a name suitable to all who seek after the devout life, Philothea meaning one who loves God. Setting then before me a soul, who through the devout life seeks after the love of God, I have arranged this Introduction in five parts, in the first of which I seek by suggestions and exercises to turn Philothea's mere desire into a hearty resolution; which she makes after her general confession, by a deliberate protest, followed by Holy Communion, in which, giving herself to her Saviour and receiving Him, she is happily received into His Holy Love. After this, I lead her on by showing her two great means of closer union with His Divine Majesty; the Sacraments, by which that Gracious Lord comes to us, and mental prayer, by which He draws us to Him. This is the Second Part.

In the Third Part I set forth how she should practise certain virtues most suitable to her advancement, only dwelling on such special points as she might not find elsewhere, or be able to make out for herself. In the Fourth Part I bring to light the snares of some of her enemies, and show her how to pass through them safely and come forth unhurt. And finally, in the Fifth Part, I lead her apart to refresh herself and take breath, and renew her strength, so that she may go on more bravely afterwards, and make good progress in the devout life.

This is a cavilling age, and I foresee that many will say that only Religious and persons living apart are fit to undertake the guidance of souls in such special devout ways; that it requires more time than a Bishop of so important a diocese as mine can spare, and that it must take too much thought from the important duties with which I am charged.

But, dear reader, I reply with S. Denis that the task of leading souls towards perfection appertains above all others to Bishops, and that because their Order is supreme among men, as the Seraphim among Angels, and therefore their leisure cannot be better spent. The ancient Bishops and Fathers of the Primitive Church were, to say the least, as devoted to their duties as we are, yet they did not refuse to undertake the individual guidance of souls which sought their help, as we see by their epistles; thereby imitating the Apostles, who, while reaping the universal world-harvest, yet found time to gather up certain individual sheaves with special and personal affection. Who can fail to remember that Timothy, Titus, Philemon, Onesimus, Thekla, Appia, were the beloved spiritual children of S. Paul, as S. Mark and S. Petronilla were of S. Peter (for Baronius and Galonius have given learned and absolute proof that S. Petronilla was not his carnal but spiritual

---

[5] The address to Philothea by name has been omitted, as being somewhat stiff and stilted, and the term child or daughter used instead, but the omission in no way alters the sense or application of any sentence.

daughter). And is not one of S. John's Canonical Epistles addressed to the "elect lady" whom he loved in the faith?

I grant that the guidance of individual souls is a labour, but it is a labour full of consolation, even as that of harvesters and grape-gatherers, who are never so well pleased as when most heavily laden. It is a labour which refreshes and invigorates the heart by the comfort which it brings to those who bear it; as is said to be the case with those who carry bundles of cinnamon in Arabia Felix. It is said that when the tigress finds one of her young left behind by the hunter in order to delay her while he carries off the rest of her cubs, she takes it up, however big, without seeming over-weighted, and speeds only the more swiftly to her lair, maternal love lightening the load. How much more readily will the heart of a spiritual father bear the burden of a soul he finds craving after perfection—carrying it in his bosom as a mother her babe, without feeling weary of the precious burden?

But unquestionably it must be a really paternal heart that can do this, and therefore it is that the Apostles and their apostolic followers are wont to call their disciples not merely their children, but, even more tenderly still, their "little children."

One thing more, dear reader. It is too true that I who write about the devout life am not myself devout, but most certainly I am not without the wish to become so, and it is this wish which encourages me to teach you. A notable literary man has said that a good way to learn is to study, a better to listen, and the best to teach. And S. Augustine, writing to the devout Flora,[6] says, that giving is a claim to receive, and teaching a way to learn.

Alexander caused the lovely Campaspe,[7] who was so dear to him, to be painted by the great Apelles, who, by dint of contemplating her as he drew, so graved her features in his heart and conceived so great a passion for her, that Alexander discovered it, and, pitying the artist, gave him her to wife, depriving himself for love of Apelles of the dearest thing he had in the world, in which, says Pliny, he displayed the greatness of his soul as much as in the mightiest victory. And so, friendly reader, it seems to me that as a Bishop, God wills me to frame in the hearts of His children not merely ordinary goodness, but yet more His own most precious devotion; and on my part I undertake willingly to do so, as much out of obedience to the call of duty as in the hope that, while fixing the image in others' hearts, my own may haply conceive a holy love; and that if His Divine Majesty sees me deeply in love, He may give her to me in an eternal marriage. The beautiful and chaste Rebecca, as she watered Isaac's camels, was destined to be his bride, and received his golden earrings and bracelets, and so I rely on the boundless Goodness of my God, that while I lead His beloved lambs to the wholesome fountain of devotion, He will take my soul to be His bride, giving me earrings of the golden words of love, and strengthening my arms to carry out its works, wherein lies the essence of all true devotion, the which I pray His Heavenly Majesty to grant to me and to all the children of His Church—that Church to which I would ever submit all my writings, actions, words, will and thoughts.

ANNECY, S. Magdalene's Day, 1608

---

[6] This is probably the person mentioned as "our most religious daughter Flora" in S. Augustine's Treatise "On care to be had for the Dead", addressed to his fellow Bishop Paulinus. See *Library of the Fathers, S. Augustine's Short Treatises*, p. 517.

[7] Plin. *Hist. Nat.* l. xxv. c. 10.

PART I.
COUNSELS AND PRACTICES SUITABLE FOR THE SOUL'S
GUIDANCE FROM THE FIRST ASPIRATION AFTER A
DEVOUT LIFE TO THE POINT WHEN IT ATTAINS A
CONFIRMED RESOLUTION TO FOLLOW THE SAME.

Chapter I: What true Devotion is.

YOU aim at a devout life, dear child, because as a Christian you know that such devotion is most acceptable to God's Divine Majesty. But seeing that the small errors people are wont to commit in the beginning of any under taking are apt to wax greater as they advance, and to become irreparable at last, it is most important that you should thoroughly understand wherein lies the grace of true devotion;—and that because while there undoubtedly is such a true devotion, there are also many spurious and idle semblances thereof; and unless you know which is real, you may mistake, and waste your energy in pursuing an empty, profitless shadow. Arelius was wont to paint all his pictures with the features and expression of the women he loved, and even so we all colour devotion according to our own likings and dispositions. One man sets great value on fasting, and believes himself to be leading a very devout life, so long as he fasts rigorously, although the while his heart is full of bitterness;—and while he will not moisten his lips with wine, perhaps not even with water, in his great abstinence, he does not scruple to steep them in his neighbour's blood, through slander and detraction. Another man reckons himself as devout because he repeats many prayers daily, although at the same time he does not refrain from all manner of angry, irritating, conceited or insulting speeches among his family and neighbours. This man freely opens his purse in almsgiving, but closes his heart to all gentle and forgiving feelings towards those who are opposed to him; while that one is ready enough to forgive his enemies, but will never pay his rightful debts save under pressure. Meanwhile all these people are conventionally called religious, but nevertheless they are in no true sense really devout. When Saul's servants sought to take David, Michal induced them to suppose that the lifeless figure lying in his bed, and covered with his garments, was the man they sought; and in like manner many people dress up an exterior with the visible acts expressive of earnest devotion, and the world supposes them to be really devout and spiritual-minded, while all the time they are mere lay figures, mere phantasms of devotion.

But, in fact, all true and living devotion presupposes the love of God;—and indeed it is neither more nor less than a very real love of God, though not always of the same kind; for that Love one while shining on the soul we call grace, which makes us acceptable to His Divine Majesty;—when it strengthens us to do well, it is called Charity;—but when it attains its fullest perfection, in which it not only leads us to do well, but to act carefully, diligently, and promptly, then it is called Devotion. The ostrich never flies,—the hen rises with difficulty, and achieves but a brief and rare flight, but the eagle, the dove, and the swallow, are continually on the wing, and soar high;—even so sinners do not rise towards God, for all their movements are earthly and earthbound. Well-meaning people, who have not as yet attained a true devotion, attempt a manner of flight by means of their good actions, but rarely, slowly and heavily; while really devout men rise up to God frequently, and with a swift and soaring wing. In short, devotion is simply a spiritual activity and liveliness by means of which Divine Love works in us, and causes us to work briskly and lovingly; and just as charity leads us to a general practice of all God's Commandments, so devotion leads us to practise them readily and diligently. And therefore we cannot call him who neglects to observe all God's Commandments either good or devout, because in order to be good, a man must be filled with love, and to be devout, he must further be very ready and apt to perform the deeds of love. And forasmuch as devotion consists in a high degree of real love, it not only makes us ready, active, and diligent in following all God's Commands, but it also excites us to be ready and loving in performing as many good works as possible, even such as are not enjoined upon us, but are only matters of counsel or inspiration. Even as a man just recovering from illness, walks only so far as he is obliged to go, with a slow and weary step, so the converted sinner journeys along as far as God commands him but slowly and wearily, until he attains a true spirit of devotion, and then, like a sound man, he not only gets along, but he runs and leaps in the way of God's Commands, and hastens gladly along the paths of heavenly counsels and inspirations. The difference between love and devotion is just that which exists between fire and flame;—love being a spiritual fire which becomes devotion when it is fanned into a flame;—and what devotion adds to the fire of love is that flame which makes it eager, energetic and diligent, not merely in obeying God's Commandments, but in fulfilling His Divine Counsels and inspirations.

Chapter II: The Nature and Excellence of Devotion.

THOSE who sought to discourage the Israelites from going up to the Promised Land, told them that it was "a land which eateth up the inhabitants thereof;"[1] that is, that the climate was so unhealthy that the inhabitants could not live long, and that the people thereof were "men of a great stature," who looked upon the new-comers as mere locusts to be devoured. It is just so, my daughter, that the world runs down true devotion, painting devout people with gloomy, melancholy aspect, and affirming that religion makes them dismal and unpleasant. But even as Joshua and Caleb protested that not only was the Promised Land a fair and pleasant country, but that the Israelites would take an easy and peaceful possession thereof, so the Holy Spirit tells us through His Saints, and our Lord has told us with His Own Lips, that a devout life is very sweet, very happy and very loveable.

The world, looking on, sees that devout persons fast, watch and pray, endure injury patiently, minister to the sick and poor, restrain their temper, check and subdue their passions, deny themselves in all sensual indulgence, and do many other things which in themselves are hard and difficult. But the world sees nothing of that inward, heartfelt devotion which makes all these actions pleasant and easy. Watch a bee hovering over the mountain thyme;—the juices it gathers are bitter, but the bee turns them all to honey,—and so tells the worldling, that though the devout soul finds bitter herbs along its path of devotion, they are all turned to sweetness and pleasantness as it treads;—and the martyrs have counted fire, sword, and rack but as perfumed flowers by reason of their devotion. And if devotion can sweeten such cruel torments, and even death itself, how much more will it give a charm to ordinary good deeds? We sweeten unripe fruit with sugar, and it is useful in correcting the crudity even of that which is good. So devotion is the real spiritual sweetness which takes away all bitterness from mortifications; and prevents consolations from disagreeing with the soul: it cures the poor of sadness, and the rich of presumption;

---

[1] Numb. xiii. 32.

it keeps the oppressed from feeling desolate, and the prosperous from insolence; it averts sadness from the lonely, and dissipation from social life; it is as warmth in winter and refreshing dew in summer; it knows how to abound and how to suffer want; how to profit alike by honour and contempt; it accepts gladness and sadness with an even mind, and fills men's hearts with a wondrous sweetness.

Ponder Jacob's ladder:—it is a true picture of the devout life; the two poles which support the steps are types of prayer which seeks the love of God, and the Sacraments which confer that love; while the steps themselves are simply the degrees of love by which we go on from virtue to virtue, either descending by good deeds on behalf of our neighbour or ascending by contemplation to a loving union with God. Consider, too, who they are who trod this ladder; men with angels' hearts, or angels with human forms. They are not youthful, but they seem to be so by reason of their vigour and spiritual activity. They have wings wherewith to fly, and attain to God in holy prayer, but they have likewise feet wherewith to tread in human paths by a holy gracious intercourse with men; their faces are bright and beautiful, inasmuch as they accept all things gently and sweetly; their heads and limbs are uncovered, because their thoughts, affections and actions have no motive or object save that of pleasing God; the rest of their bodies is covered with a light shining garment, because while they use the world and the things of this life, they use all such purely and honestly, and no further than is needful for their condition—such are the truly devout. Believe me, dear child, devotion is the sweetest of sweets, the queen of virtues, the perfection of love. If love is the milk of life, devotion is the cream thereof; if it is a fruitful plant, devotion is the blossom; if it is a precious stone, devotion is its brightness; if it is a precious balm, devotion is its perfume, even that sweet odour which delights men and causes the angels to rejoice.

Chapter III: Devotion is suitable to every Vocation and Profession.

WHEN God created the world He commanded each tree to bear fruit after its kind;[2] and even so He bids Christians,—the living trees of His Church,—to bring forth fruits of devotion, each one according to his kind and vocation. A different exercise of devotion is required of each—the noble, the artisan, the servant, the prince, the maiden and the wife; and furthermore such practice must be modified according to the strength, the calling, and the duties of each individual. I ask you, my child, would it be fitting that a Bishop should seek to lead the solitary life of a Carthusian? And if the father of a family were as regardless in making provision for the future as a Capucin, if the artisan spent the day in church like a Religious, if the Religious involved himself in all manner of business on his neighbour's behalf as a Bishop is called upon to do, would not such a devotion be ridiculous, ill-regulated, and intolerable? Nevertheless such a mistake is often made, and the world, which cannot or will not discriminate between real devotion and the indiscretion of those who fancy themselves devout, grumbles and finds fault with devotion, which is really nowise concerned in these errors. No indeed, my child, the devotion which is true hinders nothing, but on the contrary it perfects everything; and that which runs counter to the rightful vocation of any one is, you may be sure, a spurious devotion. Aristotle says that the bee sucks honey from flowers without damaging them, leaving them as whole and fresh as it found them;—but true devotion does better still, for

---

[2] Gen. i. 12.

it not only hinders no manner of vocation or duty, but, contrariwise, it adorns and beautifies all. Throw precious stones into honey, and each will grow more brilliant according to its several colour:—and in like manner everybody fulfils his special calling better when subject to the influence of devotion:—family duties are lighter, married love truer, service to our King more faithful, every kind of occupation more acceptable and better performed where that is the guide.

It is an error, nay more, a very heresy, to seek to banish the devout life from the soldier's guardroom, the mechanic's workshop, the prince's court, or the domestic hearth. Of course a purely contemplative devotion, such as is specially proper to the religious and monastic life, cannot be practised in these outer vocations, but there are various other kinds of devotion well-suited to lead those whose calling is secular, along the paths of perfection. The Old Testament furnishes us examples in Abraham, Isaac and Jacob, David, Job, Tobias, Sarah, Rebecca and Judith; and in the New Testament we read of St. Joseph, Lydia and Crispus, who led a perfectly devout life in their trades:—we have S. Anne, Martha, S. Monica, Aquila and Priscilla, as examples of household devotion, Cornelius, S. Sebastian, and S. Maurice among soldiers;—Constantine, S. Helena, S. Louis, the Blessed Amadaeus,[3] and S. Edward on the throne. And we even find instances of some who fell away in solitude,—usually so helpful to perfection,—some who had led a higher life in the world, which seems so antagonistic to it. S. Gregory dwells on how Lot, who had kept himself pure in the city, fell in his mountain solitude. Be sure that wheresoever our lot is cast we may and must aim at the perfect life.

Chapter IV: The Need of a Guide for those who would enter upon and advance in the Devout Life.

WHEN Tobias was bidden to go to Rages, he was willing to obey his father, but he objected that he knew not the way;—to which Tobit answered, "Seek thee a man which may go with thee:"[4] and even so, daughter, I say to you, If you would really tread the paths of the devout life, seek some holy man to guide and conduct you. This is the precept of precepts, says the devout Avila,—seek as you will you can never so surely discover God's Will as through the channel of humble obedience so universally taught and practised by all the Saints of olden time. When the blessed Teresa read of the great penances performed by Catherine of Cordova, she desired exceedingly to imitate them, contrary to the mind of her Confessor, who forbade her to do the like, and she was tempted to disobey him therein. Then God spoke to Teresa, saying, "My child, thou art on a good and safe road:—true, thou seest all this penance, but verily I esteem thy obedience as a yet greater virtue:"—and thenceforth S. Teresa so greatly loved the virtue of obedience, that in addition to that due to her superiors, she took a vow of special obedience to a pious ecclesiastic, pledging herself to follow his direction and guidance, which proved an inexpressible help to her. And even so before and after her many pious souls have subjected their will to God's ministers in order the better to submit themselves to Him, a practice much commended by S. Catherine of Sienna in her Dialogues. The devout Princess S. Elisabeth gave an unlimited obedience to the venerable Conrad; and one of the parting counsels given by S. Louis to his son ere he died was, "Confess thyself often,—choose a single-minded, worthy

---

[3] It is probable that S. Francis here means to indicate Amadeo IX., Duke of Savoy, who died 1472.
[4] Tob. v. 3.

confessor, who is able wisely to teach thee how to do that which is needful for thee."[5] "A faithful friend," we are told in Holy Scripture, "is a strong defence, and he that hath found such an one hath found a treasure;"[6] and again: "A faithful friend is the medicine of life; and they that fear the Lord shall find him."[7] These sacred words have chiefly reference, as you see, to the immortal life, with a view to which we specially need a faithful friend, who will guide us by his counsel and advice, thereby guarding us against the deceits and snares of the Evil One:—he will be as a storehouse of wisdom to us in our sorrows, trials and falls; he will be as a healing balm to stay and soothe our heart in the time of spiritual sickness,—he will shield us from evil, and confirm that which is good in us, and when we fall through infirmity, he will avert the deadly nature of the evil, and raise us up again.

But who can find such a friend? The Wise Man answers:—"He that feareth the Lord:"[8] that is to say, the truly humble soul which earnestly desires to advance in the spiritual life. So, daughter, inasmuch as it concerns you so closely to set forth on this devout journey under good guidance, do you pray most earnestly to God to supply you with a guide after His Own Heart, and never doubt but that He will grant you one who is wise and faithful, even should He send you an angel from Heaven, as He sent to Tobias.

In truth, your spiritual guide should always be as a heaven-sent angel to you;—by which I mean that when you have found him, you are not to look upon him, or trust in him or his wisdom as an ordinary man; but you must look to God, Who will help you and speak to you through this man, putting into his heart and mouth that which is needful to you; so that you ought to hearken as though he were an angel come down from Heaven to lead you thither. Deal with him in all sincerity and faithfulness, and with open heart; manifesting alike your good and your evil, without pretence or dissimulation. Thus your good will be examined and confirmed, and your evil corrected and remedied;—you will be soothed and strengthened in trouble, moderated and regulated in prosperity. Give your guide a hearty confidence mingled with sacred reverence, so that reverence in no way shall hinder your confidence, and confidence nowise lessen your reverence: trust him with the respect of a daughter for her father; respect him with the confidence of a son in his mother. In a word, such a friendship should be strong and sweet; altogether holy, sacred, divine and spiritual. And with such an aim, choose one among a thousand, Avila says;— and I say among ten thousand, for there are fewer than one would think capable of this office. He must needs be full of love, of wisdom and of discretion; for if either of these three be wanting there is danger. But once more I say, ask such help of God, and when you have found it, bless His Holy Name; be stedfast, seek no more, but go on simply, humbly and trustfully, for you are safe to make a prosperous journey.

Chapter V: The First Step must be Purifying the Soul.

"THE flowers appear on the earth,"[9] says the Heavenly Bridegroom, and the time for pruning and cutting is come. And what, my child, are our hearts' flowers save our good desires? Now, so soon as these begin to appear, we need the pruning-hook to cut off all

---

[5] "Confesse-toi souvent, eslis un confesseur idoine, qui soit prudhomme, et qui te puisse seurement enseigner a faire les choses qui te seront necessaires."

[6] Ecclus. vi. 14.

[7] Ecclus. v. 16.

[8] Ecclus. vi. 17.

[9] Cant. ii. 12.

dead and superfluous works from our conscience. When the daughter of a strange land was about to espouse an Israelite, the law commanded her to put off the garment of her captivity, to pare her nails, and to shave her head;[10] even so the soul which aims at the dignity of becoming the spouse of Christ, must put off the old man, and put on the new man, forsaking sin: moreover, it must pare and shave away every impediment which can hinder the Love of God. The very first step towards spiritual health is to be purged from our sinful humours. S. Paul received perfect purification instantaneously, and the like grace was conferred on S. Magdalene, S. Catherine of Genoa, S. Pelagia, and some others, but this kind of purgation is as miraculous and extraordinary in grace as the resurrection of the dead in nature, nor dare we venture to aspire to it. The ordinary purification, whether of body or soul, is only accomplished by slow degrees, step by step, gradually and painfully.

The angels on Jacob's ladder had wings, yet nevertheless they did not fly, but went in due order up and down the steps of the ladder. The soul which rises from out of sin to a devout life has been compared to the dawn, which does not banish darkness suddenly, but by degrees. That cure which is gradually effected is always the surest; and spiritual maladies, like those of the body, are wont to come on horseback and express, while they depart slowly and on foot. So that we must needs be brave and patient, my daughter, in this undertaking. It is a woeful thing to see souls beginning to chafe and grow disheartened because they find themselves still subject to imperfection after having made some attempt at leading a devout life, and well-nigh yielding to the temptation to give up in despair and fall back; but, on the other hand, there is an extreme danger surrounding those souls who, through the opposite temptation, are disposed to imagine themselves purified from all imperfection at the very outset of their purgation; who count themselves as full-grown almost before they are born, and seek to fly before they have wings. Be sure, daughter, that these are in great danger of a relapse through having left their physician too soon. "It is but lost labour to rise up early and late take rest," unless the Lord prosper all we do.

The work of the soul's purification neither may nor can end save with life itself;—do not then let us be disheartened by our imperfections,—our very perfection lies in diligently contending against them, and it is impossible so to contend without seeing them, or to overcome without meeting them face to face. Our victory does not consist in being insensible to them, but in not consenting to them. Now to be afflicted by our imperfections is certainly not to consent thereto, and for the furtherance of humility it is needful that we sometimes find ourselves worsted in this spiritual battle, wherein, however, we shall never be conquered until we lose either life or courage. Moreover, imperfections and venial sins cannot destroy our spiritual life, which is only to be lost through mortal sin; consequently we have only need to watch well that they do not imperil our courage. David continually asks the Lord to strengthen his heart against cowardice and discouragement; and it is our privilege in this war that we are certain to vanquish so long as we are willing to fight.

Chapter VI: The First Purification, namely, from Mortal Sin.

THE first purification to be made is from sin;—the means whereby to make it, the sacrament of penance. Seek the best confessor within your reach, use one of the many

---

[10] Deut. xxi. 12.

little books written in order to help the examination of conscience.[11] Read some such book carefully, examining point by point wherein you have sinned, from the first use of your reason to the present time. And if you mistrust your memory, write down the result of your examination. Having thus sought out the evil spots in your conscience, strive to detest them, and to reject them with the greatest abhorrence and contrition of which your heart is capable;—bearing in mind these four things:—that by sin you have lost God's Grace, rejected your share in Paradise, accepted the pains of Hell, and renounced God's Eternal Love. You see, my child, that I am now speaking of a general confession of your whole life, which, while I grant it is not always necessary, I yet believe will be found most helpful in the beginning of your pursuit after holiness, and therefore I earnestly advise you to make it. Not unfrequently the ordinary confessions of persons leading an everyday life are full of great faults, and that because they make little or no preparation, and have not the needful contrition. Owing to this deficiency such people go to confession with a tacit intention of returning to their old sins, inasmuch as they will not avoid the occasions of sin, or take the necessary measures for amendment of life, and in all such cases a general confession is required to steady and fix the soul. But, furthermore, a general confession forces us to a clearer selfknowledge, kindles a wholesome shame for our past life, and rouses gratitude for God's Mercy, Which has so long waited patiently for us;—it comforts the heart, refreshes the spirit, excites good resolutions, affords opportunity to our spiritual Father for giving the most suitable advice, and opens our hearts so as to make future confessions more effectual. Therefore I cannot enter into the subject of a general change of life and entire turning to God, by means of a devout life, without urging upon you to begin with a general confession.

Chapter VII: The Second Purification, from all Sinful Affections.

ALL the children of Israel went forth from the land of Egypt, but not all went forth heartily, and so, when wandering in the desert, some of them sighed after the leeks and onions,—the fleshpots of Egypt. Even so there are penitents who forsake sin, yet without forsaking their sinful affections; that is to say, they intend to sin no more, but it goes sorely against them to abstain from the pleasures of sin;—they formally renounce and forsake sinful acts, but they turn back many a fond lingering look to what they have left, like Lot's wife as she fled from Sodom. They are like a sick man who abstains from eating melon when the doctor says it would kill him, but who all the while longs for it, talks about it, bargains when he may have it, would at least like just to sniff the perfume, and thinks those who are free to eat of it very fortunate. And so these weak cowardly penitents abstain awhile from sin, but reluctantly;—they would fain be able to sin without incurring damnation;—they talk with a lingering taste of their sinful deeds, and envy those who are yet indulging in the like. Thus a man who has meditated some revenge gives it up in confession, but soon after he is to be found talking about the quarrel, averring that but for the fear of God he would do this or that; complaining that it is hard to keep the Divine rule of forgiveness; would to God it were lawful to avenge one's self! Who can fail to see that

---

[11] S. Francis suggests Grenada, Bruno, Arias, Augez, authors little known now, though we have the substance of their teaching in numerous valuable helps for those who are preparing for confession: such as "Pardon through the Precious Blood," "Helps for Confirmation and First Communion" (Masters), "Manual for Confession," "Repentance," (Rev. T. T. Carter), "Hints to Penitents" (Palmer), Brett's "Guide to Faith and Piety," Crake's "Bread of Life" (Mowbray), "Paradise of the Christian Soul," etc.

even if this poor man is not actually committing sin, he is altogether bound with the affections thereof, and although he may have come out of Egypt, he yet hungers after it, and longs for the leeks and onions he was wont to feed upon there! It is the same with the woman who, though she has given up her life of sin, yet takes delight in being sought after and admired. Alas! of a truth, all such are in great peril.

Be sure, my daughter, that if you seek to lead a devout life, you must not merely forsake sin; but you must further cleanse your heart from all affections pertaining to sin; for, to say nothing of the danger of a relapse, these wretched affections will perpetually enfeeble your mind, and clog it, so that you will be unable to be diligent, ready and frequent in good works, wherein nevertheless lies the very essence of all true devotion. Souls which, in spite of having forsaken sin, yet retain such likings and longings, remind us of those persons who, without being actually ill, are pale and sickly, languid in all they do, eating without appetite, sleeping without refreshment, laughing without mirth, dragging themselves about rather than walking briskly. Such souls as I have described lose all the grace of their good deeds, which are probably few and feeble, through their spiritual languor.

Chapter VIII: How to effect this Second Purification.

THE first inducement to attain this second purification is a keen and lively apprehension of the great evils resulting from sin, by means of which we acquire a deep, hearty contrition. For just as contrition, (so far as it is real,) however slight, when joined to the virtue of the Sacraments, purges away sin; so, when it becomes strong and urgent, it purges away all the affections which cling around habits of sin. A moderate, slight hatred makes men dislike its object and avoid his society; but when a violent, mortal hatred exists, they not only abhor and shun the person who excites it, but they loathe him, they cannot endure the approach of his relations or connexions, nor even his likeness or anything that concerns him. Just so when a penitent only hates sin through a weakly although real contrition, he will resolve to avoid overt acts of sin; but when his contrition is strong and hearty, he will not merely abhor sin, but every affection, every link and tendency to sin. Therefore, my daughter, it behoves us to kindle our contrition and repentance as much as we possibly can, so that it may reach even to the very smallest appearance of sin. Thus it was that the Magdalen, when converted, so entirely lost all taste for her past sin and its pleasures, that she never again cast back one thought upon them; and David declared that he hated not only sin itself, but every path and way which led thereto. This it is which is that "renewing of the soul" which the same Prophet compares to the eagle's strength.[12]

Now, in order to attain this fear and this contrition, you must use the following meditations carefully; for if you practise them stedfastly, they (by God's Grace) will root out both sin and its affections from your heart. It is to that end that I have prepared them: do you use them one after another, in the order in which they come, only taking one each day, and using that as early as possible, for the morning is the best time for all spiritual exercises;—and then you will ponder and ruminate it through the day. If you have not as yet been taught how to meditate, you will find instructions to that purpose in the Second Part.

---

[12] Ps. ciii. 5, Bible version.

Chapter IX: First Meditation.

Of Creation.

Preparation.

1. PLACE yourself in the Presence of God.
2. Ask Him to inspire your heart.

Considerations.

1. Consider that but a few years since you were not born into the world, and your soul was as yet non-existent. Where wert thou then, O my soul? the world was already old, and yet of thee there was no sign.

2. God brought you out of this nothingness, in order to make you what you are, not because He had any need of you, but solely out of His Goodness.

3. Consider the being which God has given you; for it is the foremost being of this visible world, adapted to live eternally, and to be perfectly united to God's Divine Majesty.

Affections and Resolutions.

1. Humble yourself utterly before God, saying with the Psalmist, O Lord, I am nothing in respect of Thee—what am I, that Thou shouldst remember me? O my soul, thou wert yet lost in that abyss of nothingness, if God had not called thee forth, and what of thee in such a case?

2. Give God thanks. O Great and Good Creator, what do I not owe Thee, Who didst take me from out that nothingness, by Thy Mercy to make me what I am? How can I ever do enough worthily to praise Thy Holy Name, and render due thanks to Thy Goodness?

3. Confess your own shame. But alas, O my Creator, so far from uniting myself to Thee by a loving service, I have rebelled against Thee through my unruly affections, departing from Thee, and giving myself up to sin, and ignoring Thy Goodness, as though Thou hadst not created me.

4. Prostrate thyself before God. O my soul, know that the Lord He is thy God, it is He that hath made thee, and not thou thyself. O God, I am the work of Thy Hands; henceforth I will not seek to rest in myself, who am nought. Wherein hast thou to glory, who art but dust and ashes? how canst thou, a very nothing, exalt thyself? In order to my own humiliation, I will do such and such a thing,—I will endure such contempt:—I will alter my ways and henceforth follow my Creator, and realise that I am honoured by His calling me to the being He has given; I will employ it solely to obey His Will, by means of the teaching He has given me, of which I will inquire more through my spiritual Father.

Conclusion.

1. Thank God. Bless the Lord, O my soul, and praise His Holy Name with all thy being, because His Goodness called me forth from nothingness, and His Mercy created me.

2. Offer. O my God, I offer Thee with all my heart the being Thou hast given me, I dedicate and consecrate it to Thee.

3. Pray. O God, strengthen me in these affections and resolutions. Dear Lord, I commend me, and all those I love, to Thy neverfailing Mercy. OUR FATHER, etc.

At the end of your meditation linger a while, and gather, so to say, a little spiritual bouquet from the thoughts you have dwelt upon, the sweet perfume whereof may refresh you through the day.

Chapter X: Second Meditation.

Of the End for which we were Created.

Preparation.

1. PLACE yourself before God.
2. Ask Him to inspire your heart.

Considerations.

1. God did not bring you into the world because He had any need of you, useless as you are; but solely that He might show forth His Goodness in you, giving you His Grace and Glory. And to this end He gave you understanding that you might know Him, memory that you might think of Him, a will that you might love Him, imagination that you might realise His mercies, sight that you might behold the marvels of His works, speech that you might praise Him, and so on with all your other faculties.

2. Being created and placed in the world for this intent, all contrary actions should be shunned and rejected, as also you should avoid as idle and superfluous whatever does not promote it.

3. Consider how unhappy they are who do not think of all this,—who live as though they were created only to build and plant, to heap up riches and amuse themselves with trifles.

Affections and Resolutions.

1. Humble yourself in that hitherto you have so little thought upon all this. Alas, my God, of what was I thinking when I did not think of Thee? what did I remember when I forgot Thee? what did I love when I loved Thee not? Alas, when I ought to have been feeding on the truth, I was but filling myself with vanity, and serving the world, which was made to serve me.

2. Abhor your past life. I renounce ye, O vain thoughts and useless cogitations, frivolous and hateful memories: I renounce all worthless friendships, all unprofitable efforts, and miserably ungrateful self-indulgence, all pitiful compliances.

3. Turn to God. Thou, my God and Saviour shalt henceforth be the sole object of my thoughts; no more will I give my mind to ideas which are displeasing to Thee. All the days of my life I will dwell upon the greatness of Thy Goodness, so lovingly poured out upon me. Thou shalt be henceforth the delight of my heart, the resting-place of all my affections. From this time forth I will forsake and abhor the vain pleasures and amusements, the empty pursuits which have absorbed my

time;—the unprofitable ties which have bound my heart I will loosen henceforth, and to that end I will use such and such remedies.

Conclusion.

1. Thank God, Who has made you for so gracious an end. Thou hast made me, O Lord, for Thyself, that I may eternally enjoy the immensity of Thy Glory; when shall I be worthy thereof, when shall I know how to bless Thee as I ought?

2. Offer. O Dearest Lord, I offer Thee all my affections and resolutions, with my whole heart and soul.

3. Pray. I entreat Thee, O God, that Thou wouldest accept my desires and longings, and give Thy Blessing to my soul, to enable me to fulfil them, through the Merits of Thy Dear Son's Precious Blood shed upon the Cross for me. OUR FATHER, etc. Gather your little spiritual bouquet.

Chapter XI: Third Meditation.

Of the Gifts of God.

Preparation.

1. PLACE yourself in the Presence of God.
2. Ask Him to inspire your heart.

Considerations.

1. Consider the material gifts God has given you—your body, and the means for its preservation; your health, and all that maintains it; your friends and many helps. Consider too how many persons more deserving than you are without these gifts; some suffering in health or limb, others exposed to injury, contempt and trouble, or sunk in poverty, while God has willed you to be better off.

2. Consider the mental gifts He has given you. Why are you not stupid, idiotic, insane like many you wot of? Again, God has favoured you with a decent and suitable education, while many have grown up in utter ignorance.

3. Further, consider His spiritual gifts. You are a child of His Church, God has taught you to know Himself from your youth. How often has He given you His Sacraments? what inspirations and interior light, what reproofs, He has given to lead you aright; how often He has forgiven you, how often delivered you from occasions of falling; what opportunities He has granted for your soul's progress! Dwell somewhat on the detail, see how Loving and Gracious God has been to you.

Affections and Resolutions.

1. Marvel at God's Goodness. How good He has been to me, how abundant in mercy and plenteous in loving-kindness! O my soul, be thou ever telling of the great things the Lord has done for thee!

2. Marvel at your own ingratitude. What am I, Lord, that Thou rememberest me? How unworthy am I! I have trodden Thy Mercies under foot, I have abused Thy Grace, turning it against Thy very Self; I have set the depth of my ingratitude against the deep of Thy Grace and Favour.

3. Kindle your gratitude. O my soul, be no more so faithless and disloyal to thy mighty Benefactor! How should not my whole soul serve the Lord, Who has done such great things in me and for me?

4. Go on, my daughter, to refrain from this or that material indulgence; let your body be wholly the servant of God, Who has done so much for it: set your soul to seek Him by this or that devout practice suitable thereto. Make diligent use of the means provided by the Church to help you to love God and save your soul. Resolve to be constant in prayer and seeking the Sacraments, in hearing God's Word, and in obeying His inspirations and counsels.

Conclusion.

1. Thank God for the clearer knowledge He has given you of His benefits and your own duty.

2. Offer your heart and all its resolutions to Him.

3. Ask Him to strengthen you to fulfil them faithfully by the Merits of the Death of His Son. OUR FATHER, etc. Gather the little spiritual bouquet.

Chapter XII: Fourth Meditation.

On Sin.

Preparation.

1. PLACE yourself in the Presence of God.

2. Ask Him to inspire your heart.

Considerations.

1. Consider how long it is since you first began to commit sin, and how since that first beginning sin has multiplied in your heart; how every day has added to the number of your sins against God, against yourself and against your neighbour, by deed, word, thought and desire.

2. Consider your evil tendencies, and how far you have followed them. These two points will show you that your sins are more in number than the hairs of your head, or the sand on the seashore.

3. Apart from sin, consider your ingratitude towards God, which is in itself a sin enfolding all the others, and adding to their enormity: consider the gifts which God has given you, and which you have turned against the Giver; especially the inspirations you have neglected, and the promptings to good which you have frustrated. Review the many Sacraments you have received, and see where are their fruits. Where are the precious jewels wherewith your Heavenly Bridegroom decked you? with what preparation have you received them? Reflect upon the ingratitude with which, while God sought to save you, you have fled from Him and rushed upon destruction.

Affections and Resolutions.

1. Humble yourself in your wretchedness. O my God, how dare I come before Thine Eyes? I am but a corrupt being, a very sink of ingratitude and wickedness. Can it be that I have been so disloyal, that not one sense, not one

faculty but has been sullied and stained;—not one day has passed but I have sinned before Thee? Was this a fitting return for all my Creator's gifts, for my Redeemer's Blood?

2. Ask pardon;—throw yourself at the Lord's Feet as the prodigal son, as the Magdalene, as the woman convicted of adultery. Have mercy, Lord, on me a sinner! O Living Fountain of Mercy, have pity on me, unworthy as I am.

3. Resolve to do better. Lord, with the help of Thy Grace I will never again give myself up to sin. I have loved it too well;—henceforth I would abhor it and cleave to Thee. Father of Mercy, I would live and die to Thee.

4. In order to put away past sin, accuse yourself bravely of it, let there not be one sinful act which you do not bring to light.

5. Resolve to make every effort to tear up the roots of sin from your heart, especially this and that individual sin which troubles you most.

6. In order to do this, resolve stedfastly to follow the advice given you, and never think that you have done enough to atone for your past sin.

Conclusion.

1. Thank God for having waited till now for you, and for rousing these good intentions in your heart.

2. Offer Him all your heart to carry them to good effect.

3. Pray that He would strengthen you.

Chapter XIII: Fifth Meditation.

Of Death.

Preparation.

1. PLACE yourself in the Presence of God.

2. Ask His Grace.

3. Suppose yourself to be on your deathbed, in the last extremity, without the smallest hope of recovery.

Considerations.

1. Consider the uncertainty as to the day of your death. One day your soul will quit this body—will it be in summer or winter? in town or country? by day or by night? will it be suddenly or with warning? will it be owing to sickness or an accident? will you have time to make your last confession or not? will your confessor or spiritual father be at hand or will he not? Alas, of all these things we know absolutely nothing: all that we do know is that die we shall, and for the most part sooner than we expect.

2. Consider that then the world is at end as far as you are concerned, there will be no more of it for you, it will be altogether overthrown for you, since all pleasures, vanities, worldly joys, empty delights will be as a mere fantastic vision to you. Woe is me, for what mere trifles and unrealities I have ventured to offend my God? Then you will see that what we preferred to Him was nought. But, on the other hand, all devotion and good works will then seem so precious and so sweet:—Why did I not tread that pleasant path? Then what you thought to be

little sins will look like huge mountains, and your devotion will seem but a very little thing.

3. Consider the universal farewell which your soul will take of this world. It will say farewell to riches, pleasures, and idle companions; to amusements and pastimes, to friends and neighbours, to husband, wife and child, in short to all creation. And lastly it will say farewell to its own body, which it will leave pale and cold, to become repulsive in decay.

4. Consider how the survivors will hasten to put that body away, and hide it beneath the earth—and then the world will scarce give you another thought, or remember you, any more than you have done to those already gone. "God rest his soul!" men will say, and that is all. O death, how pitiless, how hard thou art!

5. Consider that when it quits the body the soul must go at once to the right hand or the left. To which will your soul go? what side will it take? none other, be sure, than that to which it had voluntarily drawn while yet in this world.

Affections and Resolutions.

1. Pray to God, and throw yourself into His Arms. O Lord, be Thou my stay in that day of anguish! May that hour be blessed and favourable to me, if all the rest of my life be full of sadness and trial.

2. Despise the world. Forasmuch as I know not the hour in which I must quit the world, I will not grow fond of it. O dear friends, beloved ones of my heart, be content that I cleave to you only with a holy friendship which may last for ever; why should I cling to you with a tie which must needs be broken?

I will prepare for the hour of death and take every precaution for its peaceful arrival; I will thoroughly examine into the state of my conscience, and put in order whatever is wanting.

Conclusion.

Thank God for inspiring you with these resolutions: offer them to His Majesty: intreat Him anew to grant you a happy death by the Merits of His Dear Son's Death. Ask the prayers of the Blessed Virgin and the Saints. OUR FATHER, etc.

Gather a bouquet of myrrh.

Chapter XIV: Sixth Meditation.

On Judgment.

Preparation.

1. PLACE yourself in the Presence of God.
2. Intreat Him to inspire you.

Considerations.

1. When the time comes which God has appointed for the end of this world, and after many terrible signs and warnings, which will overwhelm men with fear,—the whole earth will be destroyed, and nothing then left.

2. Afterwards, all men, save those already risen, shall rise from the dead, and at the voice of the Archangel appear in the valley of Jehoshaphat. But alas, with what divers aspects! for some will be glorious and shining, others horrible and ghastly.

3. Consider the majesty with which the Sovereign Judge will appear surrounded by all His Saints and Angels; His Cross, the Sign of Grace to the good and of terror to the evil, shining brighter than the sun.

4. This Sovereign Judge will with His awful word, instantly fulfilled, separate the evil and the good, setting the one on His Right Hand, the other on His Left—an eternal separation, for they will never meet again.

5. This separation made, the books of conscience will be opened, and all men will behold the malice of the wicked, and how they have contemned God; as also the penitence of the good, and the results of the grace they received. Nothing will be hid. O my God, what confusion to the one, what rejoicing to the other! Consider the final sentence of the wicked. "Depart from Me, ye cursed, into everlasting fire, prepared for the devil and his angels." Dwell upon these awful words. "Go," He says—for ever discarding these wretched sinners, banishing them for ever from His Presence. He calls them "cursed:" O my soul, what a curse: a curse involving all other maledictions, all possible evil, an irrevocable curse, including all time and eternity; condemning them to everlasting fire. Think what that eternity of suffering implies.

6. Then consider the sentence of the good. "Come," the Judge says—O blessed loving word with which God draws us to Himself and receives us in His Bosom. "Blessed of My Father"—O blessing above all blessings! "inherit the Kingdom prepared for you from the beginning of the world." O my God, and that Kingdom will know no end!

Affections and Resolutions.

1. Tremble, my soul, at the thought. O God, who will be my stay in that hour when the pillars of the earth are shaken?

2. Abhor your sins, which alone can cause you to be lost when that fearful day comes. Surely I will judge myself now, that I be not judged;—I will examine my conscience, accuse, condemn, punish myself, that the Judge may not condemn me then. I will confess my faults, and follow the counsels given me.

Conclusion.

Thank God for having given you means of safety in that terrible Day, and time for repentance. Offer Him your heart, and ask for grace to use it well. OUR FATHER, etc.

Gather your bouquet.

Chapter XV: Seventh Meditation.

Of Hell.

Preparation.

1. PLACE yourself in God's Presence.

2. Humble yourself, and ask His Aid.

3. Picture to yourself a dark city, reeking with the flames of sulphur and brimstone, inhabited by citizens who cannot get forth.

Considerations.

1. Even so the lost are plunged in their infernal abyss;—suffering indescribable torture in every sense and every member; and that because having used their members and senses for sin, it is just that through them they should suffer now. Those eyes which delighted in impure vicious sights, now behold devils; the ears which took pleasure in unholy words, now are deafened with yells of despair;—and so on with the other senses.

2. Beyond all these sufferings, there is one greater still, the privation and pain of loss of God's Glory, which is for ever denied to their vision. If Absalom cared not to be released from exile, if he might not see his father's face,[13] how much sorer will it be to be deprived for ever of the blessed vision of God?

3. Consider how insupportable the pains of Hell will be by reason of their eternal duration. If the irritating bite of an insect, or the restlessness of fever, makes an ordinary night seem so long and tedious, how terrible will the endless night of eternity be, where nought will be found save despair, blasphemy and fury!

Affections and Resolutions.

1. Read the Prophet's descriptions of the terrors of the Lord,[14] and ask your soul whether it can face them—whether you can bear to lose your God for ever?

2. Confess that you have repeatedly deserved to do so. Resolve henceforth to act differently, and to rescue yourself from this abyss. Resolve on distinct definite acts by which you may avoid sin, and thereby eternal death.

Give thanks, offer yourself, pray.

Chapter XVI: Eighth Meditation.

On Paradise.

Preparation.

1. PLACE yourself in the Presence of God.
2. Invoke His Aid.

Considerations.

1. Represent to yourself a lovely calm night, when the heavens are bright with innumerable stars: add to the beauty of such a night the utmost beauty of a glorious summer's day,—the sun's brightness not hindering the clear shining of moon or stars, and then be sure that it all falls immeasurably short of the glory of Paradise. O bright and blessed country, O sweet and precious place!

---

[13] 2 Sam. xiv. 32.

[14] Isa. xxxiii. 14. "Who among us shall dwell with the devouring fire? who among us shall dwell with everlasting burnings?"

2. Consider the beauty and perfection of the countless inhabitants of that blessed country;—the millions and millions of angels, Cherubim and Seraphim; the glorious company of Apostles, martyrs, confessors, virgins, and saints. O blessed company, any one single member of which surpasses all the glory of this world, what will it be to behold them all, to sing with them the sweet Song of the Lamb? They rejoice with a perpetual joy, they share a bliss unspeakable, and unchangeable delights.

3. Consider how they enjoy the Presence of God, Who fills them with the richness of His Vision, which is a perfect ocean of delight; the joy of being for ever united to their Head. They are like happy birds, hovering and singing for ever within the atmosphere of divinity, which fills them with inconceivable pleasures. There each one vies without jealousy in singing the praises of the Creator. "Blessed art Thou for ever, O Dear and Precious Lord and Redeemer, Who dost so freely give us of Thine Own Glory," they cry; and He in His turn pours out His ceaseless Blessing on His Saints. "Blessed are ye,—Mine own for ever, who have served Me faithfully, and with a good courage."

Affections and Resolutions.

1. Admire and rejoice in the Heavenly Country; the glorious and blessed New Jerusalem.

2. Reprove the coldness of your own heart for having hitherto so little sought after that glorious abode. Why have I so long lingered indifferent to the eternal happiness set before me? Woe is me that, for the sake of poor savourless earthly things, I have so often forgotten those heavenly delights. How could I neglect such real treasures for mere vain and contemptible earthly matters?

3. Aspire earnestly after that blessed abode. Forasmuch, O Dear Lord, as Thou hast been pleased to turn my feet into Thy ways, never will I again look back. Go forth, my soul, towards thy promised rest, journey unweariedly to that hoped-for land; wherefore shouldest thou tarry in Egypt?

4. Resolve to give up such and such things, which hinder you on the way, and to do such others as will help you thitherwards.

Give thanks, offer, pray.

Chapter XVII: Ninth Meditation.

On the Choice upon to you between Heaven and Hell.

Preparation.

1. PLACE yourself in the Presence of God.
2. Humble yourself before Him, and ask His inspiration.

Considerations.

1. Imagine yourself alone with your good angel in an open plain, as was Tobit on his way to Rages. Suppose the Angel to set before you Paradise, full of delights and joys; and on the other hand Hell, with all its torments. Contemplate both, kneeling in imagination before your guardian Angel. Consider that you are most

truly standing between Hell and Paradise, and that both the one and the other are open to receive you, according to your own choice.

2. Consider that the choice you make in this life will last for ever in the next.

3. Consider too, that while both are open to receive you according to your choice, yet God, Who is prepared to give the one by reason of His Justice, the other by reason of His Mercy, all the while desires unspeakably that you should select Paradise; and your good Angel is urging you with all his might to do so, offering you countless graces on God's part, countless helps to attain to it.

4. Consider that Jesus Christ, enthroned in Heaven, looks down upon you in loving invitation: "O beloved one, come unto Me, and joy for ever in the eternal blessedness of My Love!" Behold His mother yearning over you with maternal tenderness— "Courage, my child, do not despise the Goodness of my Son, or my earnest prayers for thy salvation." Behold the Saints, who have left you their example, the millions of holy souls who long after you, desiring earnestly that you may one day be for ever joined to them in their song of praise, urging upon you that the road to Heaven is not so hard to find as the world would have you think. "Press on boldly, dear friend,"—they cry. "Whoso will ponder well the path by which we came hither, will discover that we attained to these present delights by sweeter joys than any this world can give."

The Choice.

1. O Hell, I abhor thee now and for ever; I abhor thy griefs and torments, thine endless misery, the unceasing blasphemies and maledictions which thou pourest out upon my God;—and turning to thee, O blessed Paradise, eternal glory, unfading happiness, I choose thee for ever as my abode, thy glorious mansions, thy precious and abiding tabernacles. O my God, I bless Thy Mercy which gives me the power to choose—O Jesus, Saviour, I accept Thine Eternal Love, and praise Thee for the promise Thou hast given me of a place prepared for me in that blessed New Jerusalem, where I shall love and bless Thee for ever.

2. Dwell lovingly upon the example set before you by the Blessed Virgin and the Saints, and strive to follow where they point you. Give yourself up to your guardian Angel, that he may be your guide, and gird up your courage anew to make this choice.

Chapter XVIII: Tenth Meditation.

How the Soul chooses the Devout Life.

Preparation.

1. PLACE yourself in the Presence of God.
2. Humble yourself before Him, and ask His Aid.

Considerations.

1. Once more imagine yourself in an open plain, alone with your guardian Angel, and represent to yourself on the left hand the Devil sitting on a high and mighty throne, surrounded by a vast troop of worldly men, who bow bareheaded before him, doing homage to him by the various sins they commit. Study the

countenances of the miserable courtiers of that most abominable king:—some raging with fury, envy and passion, some murderous in their hatred;—others pale and haggard in their craving after wealth, or madly pursuing every vain and profitless pleasure;—others sunk and lost in vile, impure affections. See how all alike are hateful, restless, wild: see how they despise one another, and only pretend to an unreal self-seeking love. Such is the miserable reign of the abhorred Tyrant.

2. On the other hand, behold Jesus Christ Crucified, calling these unhappy wretches to come to Him, and interceding for them with all the Love of His Precious Heart. Behold the company of devout souls and their guardian Angels, contemplate the beauty of this religious Kingdom. What lovelier than the troop of virgin souls, men and women, pure as lilies:—widows in their holy desolation and humility; husbands and wives living in all tender love and mutual cherishing. See how such pious souls know how to combine their exterior and interior duties;—to love the earthly spouse without diminishing their devotion to the Heavenly Bridegroom. Look around—one and all you will see them with loving, holy, gentle countenances listening to the Voice of their Lord, all seeking to enthrone Him more and more within their hearts.

They rejoice, but it is with a peaceful, loving, sober joy; they love, but their love is altogether holy and pure. Such among these devout ones as have sorrows to bear, are not disheartened thereby, and do not grieve overmuch, for their Saviour's Eye is upon them to comfort them, and they all seek Him only.

3. Surely you have altogether renounced Satan with his weary miserable troop, by the good resolutions you have made;—but nevertheless you have not yet wholly attained to the King Jesus, or altogether joined His blessed company of devout ones:—you have hovered betwixt the two.

4. The Blessed Virgin, S. Joseph, S. Louis, S. Monica, and hundreds of thousands more who were once like you, living in the world, call upon you and encourage you.

5. The Crucified King Himself calls you by your own name: "Come, O my beloved, come, and let Me crown thee!"

The Choice.

1. O world, O vile company, never will I enlist beneath thy banner; for ever I have forsaken thy flatteries and deceptions. O proud king, monarch of evil, infernal spirit, I renounce thee and all thy hollow pomp, I detest thee and all thy works.

2. And turning to Thee, O Sweet Jesus, King of blessedness and of eternal glory, I cleave to Thee with all the powers of my soul, I adore Thee with all my heart, I choose Thee now and ever for my King, and with inviolable fidelity I would offer my irrevocable service, and submit myself to Thy holy laws and ordinances.

3. O Blessed Virgin Mother of God, you shall be my example, I will follow you with all reverence and respect.

O my good Angel, bring me to this heavenly company, leave me not until I have reached them, with whom I will sing for ever, in testimony of my choice, "Glory be to Jesus, my Lord!"

Chapter XIX: How to make a General Confession.

SUCH meditations as these, my daughter, will help you, and having made them, go on bravely in the spirit of humility to make your general confession;—but I entreat you, be not troubled by any sort of fearfulness. The scorpion who stings us is venomous, but when his oil has been distilled, it is the best remedy for his bite;—even so sin is shameful when we commit it, but when reduced to repentance and confession, it becomes salutary and honourable. Contrition and confession are in themselves so lovely and sweet-savoured, that they efface the ugliness and disperse the ill savour of sin. Simon the leper called Magdalene a sinner,[15] but our Lord turned the discourse to the perfume of her ointment and the greatness of her love. If we are really humble, my daughter, our sins will be infinitely displeasing to us, because they offend God;—but it will be welcome and sweet to accuse ourselves thereof because in so doing we honour God; and there is always somewhat soothing in fully telling the physician all details of our pain.

When you come to your spiritual father, imagine yourself to be on Mount Calvary, at the Feet of the Crucified Saviour, Whose Precious Blood is dropping freely to cleanse you from all your sin. Though it is not his actual Blood, yet it is the merit of that outpoured Blood which is sprinkled over His penitents as they kneel in Confession. Be sure then that you open your heart fully, and put away your sins by confessing them, for in proportion as they are put out, so will the Precious Merits of the Passion of Christ come in and fill you with blessings.

Tell everything simply and with straightforwardness, and thoroughly satisfy your conscience in doing so. Then listen to the admonitions and counsels of God's Minister, saying in your heart, "Speak, Lord, for Thy servant heareth." It is truly God to Whom you hearken, forasmuch as He has said to His representatives, "Whoso heareth you, heareth Me."[16] Then take the following protest, as a summary of your contrition, having carefully studied and meditated upon it beforehand: read it through with as earnest an intention as you can make.

Chapter XX: A hearty Protest made with the object of confirming the Soul's resolution to serve God, as a conclusion to its acts of Penitence.

I, THE undersigned,—in the Presence of God and of all the company of Heaven, having considered the Infinite Mercy of His Heavenly Goodness towards me, a most miserable, unworthy creature, whom He has created, preserved, sustained, delivered from so many dangers, and filled with so many blessings: having above all considered the incomprehensible mercy and loving-kindness with which this most Good God has borne with me in my sinfulness, leading me so tenderly to repentance, and waiting so patiently for me till this—(present) year of my life, notwithstanding all my ingratitude, disloyalty and faithlessness, by which I have delayed turning to Him, and despising His Grace, have offended Him anew: and further, remembering that in my Baptism I was solemnly and happily dedicated to God as His child, and that in defiance of the profession then made in my name, I have so often miserably profaned my gifts, turning them against God's Divine Majesty:—I, now coming to myself prostrate in heart and soul before the Throne of His Justice, acknowledge and confess that I am duly accused and convicted of treason against

---

[15] S. Mark xiv. and S. Luke vii. 39.
[16] S. Luke x. 16.

His Majesty, and guilty of the Death and Passion of Jesus Christ, by reason of the sins I have committed, for which He died, bearing the reproach of the Cross; so that I deserve nothing else save eternal damnation.

But turning to the Throne of Infinite Mercy of this Eternal God, detesting the sins of my past life with all my heart and all my strength, I humbly desire and ask grace, pardon, and mercy, with entire absolution from my sin, in virtue of the Death and Passion of that same Lord and Redeemer, on Whom I lean as the only ground of my hope. I renew the sacred promise of faithfulness to God made in my name at my Baptism; renouncing the devil, the world, and the flesh, abhorring their accursed suggestions, vanities and lusts, now and for all eternity. And turning to a Loving and Pitiful God, I desire, intend, and deliberately resolve to serve and love Him now and eternally, devoting my mind and all its faculties, my soul and all its powers, my heart and all its affections, my body and all its senses, to His Will. I resolve never to misuse any part of my being by opposing His Divine Will and Sovereign Majesty, to which I wholly immolate myself in intention, vowing ever to be His loyal, obedient and faithful servant without any change or recall. But if unhappily, through the promptings of the enemy, or human infirmity, I should in anywise fail in this my resolution and dedication, I do most earnestly resolve by the grace of the Holy Spirit to rise up again so soon as I shall perceive my fall, and turn anew, without any delay, to seek His Divine Mercy. This is my firm will and intention,—my inviolable, irrevocable resolution, which I make and confirm without any reserve, in the Holy Presence of God, in the sight of the Church triumphant, and before the Church militant, which is my mother, who accepts this my declaration, in the person of him who, as her representative, hears me make it. Be pleased, O Eternal, All-Powerful, and All-Loving God,—Father, Son, and Holy Spirit, to confirm me in this my resolution, and accept my hearty and willing offering. And inasmuch as Thou hast been pleased to inspire me with the will to make it, give me also the needful strength and grace to keep it. O God, Thou art my God, the God of my heart, my soul, and spirit, and as such I acknowledge and adore Thee, now and for all eternity. Glory be to Jesus. Amen.

Chapter XXI: Conclusion of this First Purification.

HAVING made this resolution, wait attentively, and open the ears of your heart, that you may in spirit hear the absolution which the Lord of your soul, sitting on the throne of His Mercy, will speak in Heaven before the Saints and Angels when His Priest absolves you here below in His Name. Be sure that all that company of blessed ones rejoice in your joy, and sing a song of untold gladness, embracing you and accepting you as cleansed and sanctified. Of a truth, my daughter, this is a marvellous deed, and a most blessed bargain for you, inasmuch as giving yourself to His Divine Majesty, you gain Him, and save yourself for eternal life. No more remains to do, save to take the pen and heartily sign your protest, and then hasten to the Altar, where God on His side will sign and seal your absolution, and His promise of Paradise, giving Himself to you in His Sacrament, as a sacred seal placed upon your renewed heart. And thus, dear child, your soul will be cleansed from sin, and from all its affections. But forasmuch as these affections are easily rekindled, thanks to our infirmity and concupiscence (which maybe mortified, but which can never be altogether extinguished while we live), I will give you certain counsels by the practice of which you may henceforth avoid mortal sin, and the affections pertaining thereto. And as these counsels will also help you to attain a yet more perfect purification, before giving them, I would say somewhat concerning that absolute perfection to which I seek to lead you.

Chapter XXII: The Necessity of Purging away all tendency to Venial Sins.

AS daylight waxes, we, gazing into a mirror, see more plainly the soils and stains upon our face; and even so as the interior light of the Holy Spirit enlightens our conscience, we see more distinctly the sins, inclinations and imperfections which hinder our progress towards real devotion. And the selfsame light which shows us these blots and stains, kindles in us the desire to be cleansed and purged therefrom. You will find then, my child, that besides the mortal sins and their affections from which your soul has already been purged, you are beset by sundry inclinations and tendencies to venial sin; mind, I do not say you will find venial sins, but the inclination and tendency to them. Now, one is quite different from the other. We can never be altogether free from venial sin,—at least not until after a very long persistence in this purity; but we can be without any affection for venial sin. It is altogether one thing to have said something unimportant not strictly true, out of carelessness or liveliness, and quite a different matter to take pleasure in lying, and in the habitual practice thereof. But I tell you that you must purify your soul from all inclination to venial sin;—that is to say, you must not voluntarily retain any deliberate intention of permitting yourself to commit any venial sin whatever. It would be most unworthy consciously to admit anything so displeasing to God, as the will to offend Him in anywise. Venial sin, however small, is displeasing to God, although it be not so displeasing as the greater sins which involve eternal condemnation; and if venial sin is displeasing to Him, any clinging which we tolerate to mortal sin is nothing less than a resolution to offend His Divine Majesty. Is it really possible that a rightly disposed soul can not only offend God, but take pleasure therein?

These inclinations, my daughter, are in direct opposition to devotion, as inclinations to mortal sin are to love:—they weaken the mental power, hinder Divine consolations, and open the door to temptations;—and although they may not destroy the soul, at least they bring on very serious disease. "Dead flies cause the ointment to send forth a stinking savour," says the Wise Man.[17] He means that the flies which settle upon and taste of the ointment only damage it temporarily, leaving the mass intact, but if they fall into it, and die there, they spoil and corrupt it. Even so venial sins which pass over a devout soul without being harboured, do not permanently injure it, but if such sins are fostered and cherished, they destroy the sweet savour of that soul—that is to say, its devotion. The spider cannot kill bees, but it can spoil their honey, and so encumber their combs with its webs in course of time, as to hinder the bees materially. Just so, though venial sins may not lose the soul, they will spoil its devotion, and so cumber its faculties with bad habits and evil inclinations, as to deprive it of all that cheerful readiness which is the very essence of true devotion; that is to say, if they are harboured in the conscience by delight taken therein. A trifling inaccuracy, a little hastiness in word or action, some small excess in mirth, in dress, in gaiety, may not be very important, if these are forthwith heeded and swept out as spiritual cobwebs;—but if they are permitted to linger in the heart, or, worse still, if we take pleasure in them and indulge them, our honey will soon be spoilt, and the

---

[17] Eccles. x. 1.

hive of our conscience will be cumbered and damaged. But I ask again, how can a generous heart take delight in anything it knows to be displeasing to its God, or wish to do what offends Him?

Chapter XXIII: It is needful to put away all Inclination for Useless and Dangerous Things.

SPORTS, balls, plays, festivities, pomps, are not in themselves evil, but rather indifferent matters, capable of being used for good or ill; but nevertheless they are dangerous, and it is still more dangerous to take great delight in them. Therefore, my daughter, I say that although it is lawful to amuse yourself, to dance, dress, feast, and see seemly plays,—at the same time, if you are much addicted to these things, they will hinder your devotion, and become extremely hurtful and dangerous to you. The harm lies, not in doing them, but in the degree to which you care for them. It is a pity to sow the seed of vain and foolish tastes in the soil of your heart, taking up the place of better things, and hindering the soul from cultivating good dispositions. It was thus that the Nazarites of old abstained not merely from all intoxicating liquors, but from grapes fresh or dried, and from vinegar, not because these were intoxicating, but because they might excite the desire for fermented liquors. Just so, while I do not forbid the use of these dangerous pleasures, I say that you cannot take an excessive delight in them without their telling upon your devotion. When the stag has waxed fat he hides himself amid the thicket, conscious that his fleetness is impaired should he be in need to fly: and so the human heart which is cumbered with useless, superfluous, dangerous clingings becomes incapacitated for that earnest following after God which is the true life of devotion. No one blames children for running after butterflies, because they are children, but is it not ridiculous and pitiful to see full-grown men eager about such worthless trifles as the worldly amusements before named, which are likely to throw them off their balance and disturb their spiritual life? Therefore, dear child, I would have you cleanse your heart from all such tastes, remembering that while the acts themselves are not necessarily incompatible with a devout life, all delight in them must be harmful.

Chapter XXIV: All Evil Inclinations must be purged away.

FURTHERMORE, my daughter, we have certain natural inclinations, which are not strictly speaking either mortal or venial sins, but rather imperfections; and the acts in which they take shape, failings and deficiencies. Thus S. Jerome says that S. Paula had so strong a tendency to excessive sorrow, that when she lost her husband and children she nearly died of grief: that was not a sin, but an imperfection, since it did not depend upon her wish and will. Some people are naturally easy, some oppositions; some are indisposed to accept other men's opinions, some naturally disposed to be cross, some to be affectionate—in short, there is hardly any one in whom some such imperfections do not exist. Now, although they be natural and instinctive in each person, they may be remedied and corrected, or even eradicated, by cultivating the reverse disposition. And this, my child, must be done. Gardeners have found how to make the bitter almond tree bear sweet fruit, by grafting the juice of the latter upon it, why should we not purge out our perverse dispositions and infuse such as are good? There is no disposition so good but it may be made bad by dint of vicious habits, and neither is there any natural disposition so perverse but that it may be conquered and overcome by God's Grace primarily, and then by our earnest diligent endeavour. I shall therefore now proceed to give you counsels and suggest practices by which you may purify your soul from all dangerous affections and imperfections, and from all tendencies to venial sin, thereby strengthening yourself more and more against mortal sin. May God give you grace to use them.

Chapter I: The Necessity of Prayer.

1. PRAYER opens the understanding to the brightness of Divine Light, and the will to the warmth of Heavenly Love—nothing can so effectually purify the mind from its many ignorances, or the will from its perverse affections. It is as a healing water which causes the roots of our good desires to send forth fresh shoots, which washes away the soul's imperfections, and allays the thirst of passion.

2. But especially I commend earnest mental prayer to you, more particularly such as bears upon the Life and Passion of our Lord. If you contemplate Him frequently in meditation, your whole soul will be filled with Him, you will grow in His Likeness, and your actions will be moulded on His. He is the Light of the world; therefore in Him, by Him, and for Him we shall be enlightened and illuminated; He is the Tree of Life, beneath the shadow of which we must find rest;—He is the Living Fountain of Jacob's well, wherein we may wash away every stain. Children learn to speak by hearing their mother talk, and stammering forth their childish sounds in imitation; and so if we cleave to the Savior in meditation, listening to His words, watching His actions and intentions, we shall learn in time, through His Grace, to speak, act and will like Himself. Believe me, my daughter, there is no way to God save through this door. Just as the glass of a mirror would give no reflection save for the metal behind it, so neither could we here below contemplate the Godhead, were it not united to the Sacred Humanity of our Saviour, Whose Life and Death are the best, sweetest and most profitable subjects that we can possibly select for meditation. It is not without meaning that the Saviour calls Himself the Bread come down from Heaven;—just as we eat bread with all manner of other food, so we need to meditate and feed upon our Dear Lord in every prayer and action. His Life has been meditated and written about by various authors. I should specially commend to you the writings of S. Bonaventura, Bellintani, Bruno, Capilla, Grenada and Da Ponte.[1]

3. Give an hour every day to meditation before dinner;—if you can, let it be early in the morning, when your mind will be less cumbered, and fresh after the night's rest. Do not spend more than an hour thus, unless specially advised to do so by your spiritual father.

4. If you can make your meditation quietly in church, it will be well, and no one, father or mother, husband or wife, can object to an hour spent there, and very probably you could not secure a time so free from interruption at home.

5. Begin all prayer, whether mental or vocal, by an act of the Presence of God. If you observe this rule strictly, you will soon see how useful it is.

6. It may help you to say the Creed, Lord's Prayer, etc., in Latin, but you should also study them diligently in your own language, so as thoroughly to gather up the meaning of these holy words, which must be used fixing your thoughts steadily on their purport, not striving to say many words so much as seeking to say a few with your whole heart. One Our Father said devoutly is worth more than many prayers hurried over.

---

[1] S. Bonaventura, Louis of Grenada, and Da Ponte's works are still available and are admirable helps to meditation. Among more modern works might be suggested Isaac Williams on the Passion, Avrillon's Lent Guide, &c. &c.

7. The Rosary is a useful devotion when rightly used, and there are various little books to teach this. It is well, too, to say pious Litanies, and the other vocal prayers appointed for the Hours and found in Manuals of devotion,—but if you have a gift for mental prayer, let that always take the chief place, so that if, having made that, you are hindered by business or any other cause from saying your wonted vocal prayers, do not be disturbed, but rest satisfied with saying the Lord's Prayer, the Angelic Salutation, and the Creed after your meditation.

8. If, while saying vocal prayers, your heart feels drawn to mental prayer, do not resist it, but calmly let your mind fall into that channel, without troubling because you have not finished your appointed vocal prayers. The mental prayer you have substituted for them is more acceptable to God, and more profitable to your soul. I should make an exception of the Church's Offices, if you are bound to say those by your vocation—in such a case these are your duty.

9. If it should happen that your morning goes by without the usual meditation, either owing to a pressure of business, or from any other cause, (which interruptions you should try to prevent as far as possible,) try to repair the loss in the afternoon, but not immediately after a meal, or you will perhaps be drowsy, which is bad both for your meditation and your health. But if you are unable all day to make up for the omission, you must remedy it as far as may be by ejaculatory prayer, and by reading some spiritual book, together with an act of penitence for the neglect, together with a stedfast resolution to do better the next day.

Chapter II: A short Method of Meditation. And first, the Presence of God, the First Point of Preparation.

IT may be, my daughter, that you do not know how to practise mental prayer, for unfortunately it is a thing much neglected now-adays. I will therefore give you a short and easy method for using it, until such time as you may read sundry books written on the subject, and above all till practice teaches you how to use it more perfectly. And first of all, the Preparation, which consists of two points: first, placing yourself in the Presence of God; and second, asking His Aid. And in order to place your self in the Presence of God, I will suggest four chief considerations which you can use at first.

First, a lively earnest realisation that His Presence is universal; that is to say, that He is everywhere, and in all, and that there is no place, nothing in the world, devoid of His Most Holy Presence, so that, even as birds on the wing meet the air continually, we, let us go where we will, meet with that Presence always and everywhere. It is a truth which all are ready to grant, but all are not equally alive to its importance. A blind man when in the presence of his prince will preserve a reverential demeanour if told that the king is there, although unable to see him; but practically, what men do not see they easily forget, and so readily lapse into carelessness and irreverence. Just so, my child, we do not see our God, and although faith warns us that He is present, not beholding Him with our mortal eyes, we are too apt to forget Him, and act as though He were afar: for, while knowing perfectly that He is everywhere, if we do not think about it, it is much as though we knew it not. And therefore, before beginning to pray, it is needful always to rouse the soul to a stedfast remembrance and thought of the Presence of God. This is what David meant when he exclaimed, "If I climb up to Heaven, Thou art there, and if I go down to hell, Thou art there also!"[2] And in like manner Jacob, who, beholding the ladder which went up to Heaven, cried out, "Surely the Lord is in this place and I knew it not"[3] meaning thereby that he had not thought of it; for assuredly he could not fail to know that God was everywhere and in all things. Therefore, when you make ready to pray, you must say with your whole heart, "God is indeed here."

The second way of placing yourself in this Sacred Presence is to call to mind that God is not only present in the place where you are, but that He is very specially present in your heart and mind, which He kindles and inspires with His Holy Presence, abiding there as Heart of your heart, Spirit of your spirit. Just as the soul animates the whole body, and every member thereof, but abides especially in the heart, so God, while present everywhere, yet makes His special abode with our spirit. Therefore David calls Him "the Strength of my heart;"[4] and S. Paul said that in Him "we live and move and have our being."[5] Dwell upon this thought until you have kindled a great reverence within your heart for God Who is so closely present to you.

The third way is to dwell upon the thought of our Lord, Who in His Ascended Humanity looks down upon all men, but most particularly on all Christians, because they are His children; above all, on those who pray, over whose doings He keeps watch. Nor is this any mere imagination, it is very truth, and although we see Him not, He is looking down upon us. It was given to S. Stephen in the hour of martyrdom thus to behold Him, and we may well say with the Bride of the Canticles, "He looketh forth at the windows, shewing Himself through the lattice."[6]

The fourth way is simply to exercise your ordinary imagination, picturing the Saviour to yourself in His Sacred Humanity as if He were beside you just as we are wont to think of our friends, and fancy that we see or hear them at our side. But when the Blessed Sacrament of the Altar is there, then this Presence is no longer imaginary, but most real; and the sacred species are but as a veil from behind which the Present Saviour beholds and considers us, although we cannot see Him as He is.

Make use of one or other of these methods for placing yourself in the Presence of God before you begin to pray;—do not try to use them all at once, but take one at a time, and that briefly and simply.

Chapter III: Invocation, the Second Point of Preparation.

INVOCATION is made as follows: your soul, having realised God's Presence, will prostrate itself with the utmost reverence, acknowledging its unworthiness to abide before His Sovereign Majesty; and yet knowing that He of His Goodness would have you come to Him, you must ask of Him grace to serve and worship Him in this your meditation. You may use some such brief and earnest words as those of David: "Cast me not away from Thy Presence, and take not Thy Holy Spirit from me."[7] "Shew me Thy Ways, O Lord, and teach me Thy paths."[8] "Give me understanding, and I shall keep Thy Law: yea, I shall

---

[2] Ps. cxxxix. 7.
[3] Gen. xxviii. 16.
[4] Ps. lxxiii. 26.
[5] Acts xvii. 28.
[6] Cant. ii. 9.
[7] Ps. li. 11.
[8] Ps. xxv. 4.

keep it with my whole heart."[9] "I am Thy servant, O grant me understanding."[10] Dwell too upon the thought of your guardian Angel, and of the Saints connected with the special mystery you are considering, as the Blessed Virgin, S. John, the Magdalene, the good thief, etc., if you are meditating in the Passion, so that you may share in their devout feelings and intention,—and in the same way with other subjects.

Chapter IV: The Third Point of Preparation, representing the Mystery to be meditated to Your Imagination.

FOLLOWING upon these two ordinary points, there ere is a third, which is not necessary to all meditation, called by some the local representation, and by others the interior picture. It is simply kindling a vivid picture of the mystery to be meditated within your imagination, even as though you were actually beholding it. For instance, if you wish to meditate upon our Lord on His Cross, you will place yourself in imagination on Mount Calvary, as though you saw and heard all that occurred there during the Passion; or you can imagine to yourself all that the Evangelists describe as taking place where you are. In the same way, when you meditate upon death, bring the circumstances that will attend your own vividly to mind, and so of hell, or any subjects which involve visible, tangible circumstances. When it is a question of such mysteries as God's Greatness, His Attributes, the end of our creation, or other invisible things, you cannot make this use of your imagination. At most you may employ certain comparisons and similitudes, but these are not always opportune, and I would have you follow a very simple method, and not weary your mind with striving after new inventions. Still, often this use of the imagination tends to concentrate the mind on the mystery we wish to meditate, and to prevent our thoughts from wandering hither and thither, just as when you shut a bird within a cage, or fasten a hawk by its lures. Some people will tell you that it is better to confine yourself to mere abstract thought, and a simple mental and spiritual consideration of these mysteries, but this is too difficult for beginners; and until God calls you up higher, I would advise you, my daughter, to abide contentedly in the lowly valley I have pointed out.

Chapter V: Considerations, the Second Part of Meditation.

AFTER this exercise of the imagination, we come to that of the understanding: for meditations, properly so called, are certain considerations by which we raise the affections to God and heavenly things. Now meditation differs therein from study and ordinary methods of thought which have not the Love of God or growth in holiness for their object, but some other end, such as the acquisition of learning or power of argument. So, when you have, as I said, limited the efforts of your mind within due bounds,—whether by the imagination, if the subject be material, or by propositions, if it be a spiritual subject,—you will begin to form reflections or considerations after the pattern of the meditations I have already sketched for you. And if your mind finds sufficient matter, light and fruit wherein to rest in any one consideration, dwell upon it, even as the bee, which hovers over one flower so long as it affords honey. But if you do not find wherewith to feed your mind,

---

[9] Ps. cxix. 34.
[10] Ps. cxix. 125.

after a certain reasonable effort, then go on to another consideration,—only be quiet and simple, and do not be eager or hurried.

Chapter VI: The Third Part of Meditation, Affections and Resolutions.

MEDITATION excites good desires in the will, or sensitive part of the soul,—such as love of God and of our neighbour, a craving for the glory of Paradise, zeal for the salvation of others, imitation of our Lord's Example, compassion, thanksgiving, fear of God's wrath and of judgment, hatred of sin, trust in God's Goodness and Mercy, shame for our past life; and in all such affections you should pour out your soul as much as possible. If you want help in this, turn to some simple book of devotions, the Imitation of Christ, the Spiritual Combat, or whatever you find most helpful to your individual wants.

But, my daughter, you must not stop short in general affections, without turning them into special resolutions for your own correction and amendment. For instance, meditating on Our Dear Lord's First Word from the Cross, you will no doubt be roused to the desire of imitating Him in forgiving and loving your enemies. But that is not enough, unless you bring it to some practical resolution, such as, "I will not be angered any more by the annoying things said of me by such or such a neighbour, nor by the slights offered me by such an one; but rather I will do such and such things in order to soften and conciliate them." In this way, my daughter, you will soon correct your faults, whereas mere general resolutions would take but a slow and uncertain effect.

Chapter VII: The Conclusion and Spiritual Bouquet.

THE meditation should be concluded by three acts, made with the utmost humility. First, an act of thanksgiving;—thanking God for the affections and resolutions with which He has inspired you, and for the Mercy and Goodness He has made known to you in the mystery you have been meditating. Secondly, an act of oblation, by which you offer your affections and resolutions to God, in union with His Own Goodness and Mercy, and the Death and Merits of His Son. The third act is one of petition, in which you ask God to give you a share in the Merits of His Dear Son, and a blessing on your affections and resolutions, to the end that you may be able to put them in practice. You will further pray for the Church, and all her Ministers, your relations, friends, and all others, using the Our Father as the most comprehensive and necessary of prayers.

Besides all this, I bade you gather a little bouquet of devotion, and what I mean is this. When walking in a beautiful garden most people are wont to gather a few flowers as they go, which they keep, and enjoy their scent during the day. So, when the mind explores some mystery in meditation, it is well to pick out one or more points that have specially arrested the attention, and are most likely to be helpful to you through the day, and this should be done at once before quitting the subject of your meditation.

Chapter VIII: Some Useful Hints as to Meditation.

ABOVE all things, my daughter, strive when your meditation is ended to retain the thoughts and resolutions you have made as your earnest practice throughout the day. This is the real fruit of meditation, without which it is apt to be unprofitable, if not actually harmful—inasmuch as to dwell upon virtues without practising them lends to puff us up with unrealities, until we begin to fancy ourselves all that we have meditated upon and resolved to be; which is all very well if our resolutions are earnest and substantial, but on the contrary hollow and dangerous if they are not put in practice. You must then diligently endeavour to carry out your resolutions, and seek for all opportunities, great or small. For instance, if your resolution was to win over those who oppose you by gentleness, seek through the day any occasion of meeting such persons kindly, and if none offers, strive to speak well of them, and pray for them.

When you leave off this interior prayer, you must be careful to keep your heart in an even balance, lest the balm it has received in meditation be scattered. I mean, try to maintain silence for some brief space, and let your thoughts be transferred gradually from devotion to business, keeping alive the feelings and affections aroused in meditation as long as possible. Supposing some one to have received a precious porcelain vessel, filled with a most costly liquid, which he is going to carry home; how carefully he would go, not looking about, but watching stedfastly lest he trip or stumble, or lest he spill any of the contents of his vessel. Just so, after meditation, do not allow yourself forthwith to be distracted, but look straight before you. Of course, if you meet any one to whom you are bound to attend, you must act according to the circumstances in which you find yourself, but even thus give heed to your heart, so as to lose as little as possible of the precious fruits of your meditation. You should strive, too, to accustom yourself to go easily from prayer to all such occupations as your calling or position lawfully require of you, even although such occupations may seem uncongenial to the affections and thoughts just before forming part of your prayer. Thus the lawyer should be able to go from meditation to his pleading, the tradesman to his business, the mistress of a family to the cares of her household and her wifely duties, so calmly and gently as not to be in any way disturbed by so doing. In both you are fulfilling God's Will, and you should be able to turn from one to the other in a devout and humble spirit.

It may be that sometimes, immediately after your preparation, your affections will be wholly drawn to God, and then, my child, you must let go the reins, and not attempt to follow any given method; since, although as a general rule your considerations should precede your affections and resolutions, when the Holy Spirit gives you those affections at once, it is unnecessary to use the machinery which was intended to bring about the same result. In short, whenever such affections are kindled in your heart, accept them, and give them place in preference to all other considerations. The only object in placing the affections after the points of consideration in meditation, is to make the different parts of meditation clearer, for it is a general rule that when affections arise they are never to be checked, but always encouraged to flow freely. And this applies also to the acts of thanksgiving, of oblation and petition, which must not be restrained either, although it is well to repeat or renew them at the close of your meditation. But your resolutions must be made after the affections, and quite at the end of your meditation, and that all the more because in these you must enter upon ordinary familiar subjects and things which would be liable to cause distractions if they were intruded among your spiritual affections.

Amid your affections and resolutions it is well occasionally to make use of colloquies, and to speak sometimes to your Lord, sometimes to your guardian Angel, or to those persons who are concerned in the mystery you are meditating, to the Saints, to yourself, your own heart, to sinners, and even to the inanimate creation around, as David so often does in the Psalms, as well as other Saints in their meditations and prayers.

Chapter IX: Concerning Dryness in Meditation.

SHOULD it happen sometimes, my daughter, that you have no taste for or consolation in your meditation, I entreat you not to be troubled, but seek relief in vocal prayer, bemoan yourself to our Lord, confess your unworthiness, implore His Aid, kiss His Image, if it be beside you, and say in the words of Jacob, "I will not let Thee go, except Thou bless me;" or with the Canaanitish woman, "Yes, Lord, I am as a dog before Thee, but the dogs eat of the crumbs which fall from their master's table."

Or you can take a book, and read attentively till such time as your mind is calmed and quickened; or sometimes you may find help from external actions, such as prostrating yourself folding your hands upon your breast, kissing your Crucifix,—that is, supposing you are alone. But if, after all this, you are still unrelieved, do not be disturbed at your dryness, however great it be, but continue striving after a devout attitude in God's Sight. What numbers of courtiers appear a hundred times at court without any hope of a word from their king, but merely to pay their homage and be seen of him. Just so, my daughter, we ought to enter upon mental prayer purely to fulfil our duty and testify our loyalty. If it pleases God's Divine Majesty to speak to us, and discourse in our hearts by His Holy Inspirations and inward consolations, it is doubtless a great honour, and very sweet to our soul; but if He does not vouchsafe such favours, but makes as though He saw us not,—as though we were not in His Presence,—nevertheless we must not quit it, but on the contrary we must remain calmly and devoutly before Him, and He is certain to accept our patient waiting, and give heed to our assiduity and perseverance; so that another time He will impart to us His consolations, and let us taste all the sweetness of holy meditation. But even were it not so, let us, my child, be satisfied with the privilege of being in His Presence and seen of Him.

Chapter X: Morning Prayer.

BESIDES your systematic meditation and your other vocal prayers, there are five shorter kinds of prayer, which are as aids and assistants to the great devotion, and foremost among these is your morning prayer, as a general preparation for all the day's work. It should be made in this wise.

1. Thank God, and adore Him for His Grace which has kept you safely through the night, and if in anything you have offended against Him, ask forgiveness.

2. Call to mind that the day now beginning is given you in order that you may work for Eternity, and make a stedfast resolution to use this day for that end.

3. Consider beforehand what occupations, duties and occasions are likely this day to enable you to serve God; what temptations to offend Him, either by vanity, anger, etc., may arise; and make a fervent resolution to use all means of serving Him and confirming your own piety; as also to avoid and resist whatever might hinder your salvation and God's Glory. Nor is it enough to make such a resolution,—you must also prepare to carry it into effect. Thus, if you foresee having to meet some one who is hottempered and irritable, you must not merely resolve to guard your own temper, but you must consider by what gentle words to conciliate him. If you know you will see some sick person, consider how best to minister comfort to him, and so on.

4. Next, humble yourself before God, confessing that of yourself you could carry out nothing that you have planned, either in avoiding evil or seeking good. Then, so to say,

take your heart in your hands, and offer it and all your good intentions to God's Gracious Majesty, entreating Him to accept them, and strengthen you in His Service, which you may do in some such words as these: "Lord, I lay before Thee my weak heart, which Thou dost fill with good desires. Thou knowest that I am unable to bring the same to good effect, unless Thou dost bless and prosper them, and therefore, O Loving Father, I entreat of Thee to help me by the Merits and Passion of Thy Dear Son, to Whose Honour I would devote this day and my whole life."

All these acts should be made briefly and heartily, before you leave your room if possible, so that all the coming work of the day may be prospered with God's blessing; but anyhow, my daughter, I entreat you never to omit them.

Chapter XI: Evening Prayer and Examination of Conscience.

AS I have counselled you before your material dinner to make a spiritual repast in meditation, so before your evening meal you should make at least a devout spiritual collation. Make sure of some brief leisure before suppertime, and then prostrating yourself before God, and recollecting yourself in the Presence of Christ Crucified, setting Him before your mind with a stedfast inward glance, renew the warmth of your morning's meditation by some hearty aspirations and humble upliftings of your soul to your Blessed Saviour, either repeating those points of your meditation which helped you most, or kindling your heart with anything else you will.

As to the examination of conscience, which we all should make before going to bed, you know the rules:

1. Thank God for having preserved you through the day past.

2. Examine how you have conducted yourself through the day, in order to which recall where and with whom you have been, and what you have done.

3. If you have done anything good, offer thanks to God; if you have done amiss in thought, word, or deed, ask forgiveness of His Divine Majesty, resolving to confess the fault when opportunity offers, and to be diligent in doing better.

4. Then commend your body and soul, the Church, your relations and friends, to God. Ask that the Saints and Angels may keep watch over you, and with God's Blessing go to the rest He has appointed for you. Neither this practice nor that of the morning should ever be omitted; by your morning prayer you open your soul's windows to the sunshine of Righteousness, and by your evening devotions you close them against the shades of hell.

Chapter XII: On Spiritual Retirement.

THIS is a matter, dear daughter, to which I am very anxious to win your attention, for in it lies one of the surest means of spiritual progress. Strive as often as possible through the day to place yourself in God's Presence by some one of the methods already suggested. Consider what God does, and what you are doing;—you will see His Eyes ever fixed upon you in Love incomparable. "O my God," you will cry out, "why cannot I always be looking upon Thee, even as Thou lookest on me? why do I think so little about Thee? O my soul, thy only resting-place is God, and yet how often dost thou wander?" The birds have nests in lofty trees, and the stag his refuge in the thick coverts, where he can shelter from the sun's burning heat; and just so, my daughter, our hearts ought daily to choose some resting-place, either Mount Calvary, or the Sacred Wounds, or some other spot close to Christ, where they can retire at will to seek rest and refreshment amid toil, and to be as in a fortress, protected from temptation. Blessed indeed is the soul which can truly say, "Thou, Lord, art my Refuge, my Castle, my Stay, my Shelter in the storm and in the heat of the day."

Be sure then, my child, that while externally occupied with business and social duties, you frequently retire within the solitude of your own heart. That solitude need not be in any way hindered by the crowds which surround you—they surround your body, not your soul, and your heart remains alone in the Sole Presence of God. This is what David sought after amid his manifold labours;—the Psalms are full of such expressions as "Lord, I am ever with Thee. The Lord is always at my right hand. I lift up mine eyes to Thee, O Thou Who dwellest in the heavens. Mine eyes look unto God."

There are few social duties of sufficient importance to prevent an occasional retirement of the heart into this sacred solitude. When S. Catherine of Sienna was deprived by her parents of any place or time for prayer and meditation, Our Lord inspired her with the thought of making a little interior oratory in her mind, into which she could retire in heart, and so enjoy a holy solitude amid her outward duties. And henceforward, when the world assaulted her, she was able to be indifferent, because, so she said, she could retire within her secret oratory, and find comfort with her Heavenly Bridegroom. So she counselled her spiritual daughters to make a retirement within their heart, in which to dwell. Do you in like manner let your heart withdraw to such an inward retirement, where, apart from all men, you can lay it bare, and treat face to face with God, even as David says that he watched like a "pelican in the wilderness, or an owl in the desert, or a sparrow sitting alone upon the housetop."[11] These words have a sense beyond their literal meaning, or King David's habit of retirement for contemplation;—and we may find in them three excellent kinds of retreats in which to seek solitude after the Saviour's Example, Who is symbolised as He hung upon Mount Calvary by the pelican of the wilderness, feeding her young ones with her blood.[12] So again His Nativity in a lonely stable might find a foreshadowing in the owl of the desert, bemoaning and lamenting: and in His Ascension He was like the sparrow rising high above the dwellings of men. Thus in each of these ways we can make a retreat amid the daily cares of life and its business.

When the blessed Elzear, Count of Arian-en-Provence, had been long separated from his pious and beloved wife Delphine, she sent a messenger to inquire after him, and he returned answer, "I am well, dear wife, and if you would see me, seek me in the Wounded Side of our Dear Lord Jesus; that is my sure dwelling-place, and elsewhere you will seek me in vain." Surely he was a true Christian knight who spoke thus.

Chapter XIII: Aspirations, Ejaculatory Prayer and Holy Thoughts.

WE retire with God, because we aspire to Him, and we aspire in order to retire with Him; so that aspiration after God and spiritual retreat excite one another, while both spring from the one Source of all holy thoughts. Do you then, my daughter, aspire continually to

---

[11] Ps. cii. 6, 7.

[12] The Egyptians used the pelican as a symbol of parental devotion; and among the early Christians, as may be seen in the Catacombs, it was employed to shadow forth the deep mysteries of Christ's love. On many a monumental brass, church window, or chalice of old time, occurs this device, with the motto, "Sic Christus dilexit nos." "Thus hath Christ loved us." And so Saint Thomas in his Eucharistic Hymn "Adoro Te devote,"—"Pie Pelicane, Jesu Domine, Me immundum munda, Tuo sausguine!"

God, by brief, ardent upliftings of heart; praise His Excellence, invoke His Aid, cast yourself in spirit at the Foot of His Cross, adore His Goodness, offer your whole soul a thousand times a day to Him, fix your inward gaze upon Him, stretch out your hands to be led by Him, as a little child to its father, clasp Him to your breast as a fragrant nosegay, upraise Him in your soul as a standard. In short, kindle by every possible act your love for God, your tender, passionate desire for the Heavenly Bridegroom of souls. Such is ejaculatory prayer, as it was so earnestly inculcated by S. Augustine upon the devout Proba; and be sure, my daughter, that if you seek such nearness and intimacy with God your whole soul will imbibe the perfume of His Perfections. Neither is this a difficult practice,—it may be interwoven with all our duties and occupations, without hindering any; for neither the spiritual retreat of which I have spoken, nor these inward upliftings of the heart, cause more than a very brief distraction, which, so far from being any hindrance, will rather promote whatever you have in hand. When a pilgrim pauses an instant to take a draught of wine, which refreshes his lips and revives his heart, his onward journey is nowise hindered by the brief delay, but rather it is shortened and lightened, and he brings it all the sooner to a happy end, pausing but to advance the better.

Sundry collections of ejaculatory prayer have been put forth, which are doubtless very useful, but I should advise you not to tie yourself to any formal words, but rather to speak with heart or mouth whatever springs forth from the love within you, which is sure to supply you with all abundance. There are certain utterances which have special force, such as the ejaculatory prayers of which the Psalms are so full, and the numerous loving invocations of Jesus which we find in the Song of Songs. Many hymns too may be used with the like intention, provided they are sung attentively. In short, just as those who are full of some earthly, natural love are ever turning in thought to the beloved one, their hearts overflowing with tenderness, and their lips ever ready to praise that beloved object; comforting themselves in absence by letters, carving the treasured name on every tree;— so those who love God cannot cease thinking of Him, living for Him, longing after Him, speaking of Him, and fain would they grave the Holy Name of Jesus in the hearts of every living creature they behold. And to such an outpour of love all creation bids us—nothing that He has made but is filled with the praise of God, and, as says S. Augustine, everything in the world speaks silently but clearly to the lovers of God of their love, exciting them to holy desires, whence gush forth aspirations and loving cries to God. St. Gregory Nazianzen tells his flock, how, walking along the seashore, he watched the waves as they washed up shells and sea weeds, and all manner of small substances, which seemed, as it were, rejected by the sea, until a return wave would often wash part thereof back again; while the rocks remained firm and immoveable, let the waves beat against them never so fiercely. And then the Saint went on to reflect that feeble hearts let themselves be carried hither and thither by the varying waves of sorrow or consolation, as the case might be, like the shells upon the seashore, while those of a nobler mould abide firm and immoveable amid every storm;—whence he breaks out into David's cry, "Lord, save me, for the waters are gone over my soul; deliver me from the great deep, all Thy waves and storms are gone over me;" for he was himself then in trouble by reason of the ungodly usurpation of his See by Maximus.

When S. Fulgentius, Bishop of Ruspe, heard Theodoric, King of the Goths, harangue a general assembly of Roman nobles, and beheld their splendour, he exclaimed, "O God, how glorious must Thy Heavenly Jerusalem be, if even earthly Rome be thus!"[13] And if this world can afford so much gratification to mere earthly lovers of vanity, what must there be in store hereafter for those who love the truth?

> *"If thus Thy lower works are fair,—*
> *If thus Thy glories gild the span*
> *Of ruined earth and guilty man,—*
> *How glorious must the mansions be*
> *Where Thy redeemed dwell with Thee!"*

We are told that S. Anselm of Canterbury, (our mountains may glory in being his birthplace[14]) was much given to such thoughts. On one occasion a hunted hare took refuge from imminent death beneath the Bishop's horse, the hounds clamouring round, but not daring to drag it from its asylum, whereat his attendants began to laugh; but the great Anselm wept, saying, "You may laugh forsooth, but to the poor hunted beast it is no laughing matter; even so the soul which has been led astray in all manner of sin finds a host of enemies waiting at its last hour to devour it, and terrified, knows not where to seek a refuge, and if it can find none, its enemies laugh and rejoice." And so he went on his way, sighing.

Constantine the Great wrote with great respect to S. Anthony, at which his religious expressed their surprise. "Do you marvel," he said, "that a king should write to an ordinary man? Marvel rather that God should have written His Law for men, and yet more that He should have spoken with them Face to face through His Son." When S. Francis saw a solitary sheep amid a flock of goats; "See," said he to his companion, "how gentle the poor sheep is among the goats, even as was Our Lord among the Pharisees;" and seeing a boar devour a little lamb, "Poor little one," he exclaimed, weeping, "how vividly is my Saviour's Death set forth in thee!"

A great man of our own day, Francis Borgia, then Duke of Candia, was wont to indulge in many devout imaginations as he was hunting. "I used to ponder," he said, "how the falcon returns to one's wrist, and lets one hood its eyes or chain it to the perch, and yet men are so perverse in refusing to turn at God's call." St. Basil the Great says that the rose amid its thorns preaches a lesson to men. "All that is pleasant in this life" (so it tells us mortals) "is mingled with sadness—no joy is altogether pure—all enjoyment is liable to be marred by regrets, marriage is saddened by widowhood, children bring anxiety, glory often turns to shame, neglect follows upon honour, weariness on pleasure, sickness on health. Truly the rose is a lovely flower," the Saint goes on to say, "but it moves me to sadness, reminding me as it does that for my sin the earth was condemned to bring forth thorns."

Another devout soul, gazing upon a brook wherein the starlit sky of a calm summer's night was reflected, exclaims, "O my God, when Thou callest me to dwell in Thy heavenly tabernacles, these stars will be beneath my feet; and even as those stars are now reflected here below, so are we Thy creatures reflected above in the living waters of Thy Divine Love." So another cried out, beholding a rapid river as it flowed, "Even thus my soul will know no rest until it plunge into that Divine Sea whence it came forth!" S. Frances, as she knelt to pray beside the banks of a pleasant streamlet, cried out in ecstasy, "The Grace of

---

[13] Was it in imitation of this that the hymn was written?

[14] S. Anselm was born at Aosta in Piedmont, A.D. 1033.

my Dear Lord flows softly and sweetly even as these refreshing waters" And another saintly soul, looking upon the blooming orchards, cried out, "Why am I alone barren in the Church's garden!" So S. Francis of Assisi, beholding a hen gathering her chickens beneath her wings, exclaimed, "Keep me, O Lord, under the shadow of Thy Wings" And looking upon the sunflower, he ejaculated, "When, O Lord, will my soul follow the attractions of Thy Love?"[15] And gathering pansies in a garden which are fair to see, but scentless,[16] "Ah," he cried out, "even so are the thoughts of my heart, fair to behold, but without savour or fruit!"

Thus it is, my daughter, that good thoughts and holy aspirations may be drawn from all that surrounds us in our ordinary life. Woe to them that turn aside the creature from the Creator, and thrice blessed are they who turn all creation to their Creator's Glory, and make human vanities subservient to the truth. "Verily," says Saint Gregory Nazianzen, "I am wont to turn all things to my spiritual profit."

Read the pious epitaph written for S. Paula by S. Jerome; it is marvellous therein to see how she conceived spiritual thoughts and aspirations at every turn.

Now, in the practice of this spiritual retreat and of these ejaculatory prayers the great work of devotion lies: it can supply all other deficiencies, but there is hardly any means of making up where this is lacking. Without it no one can lead a true contemplative life, and the active life will be but imperfect where it is omitted: without it rest is but indolence, labour but weariness,—therefore I beseech you to adopt it heartily, and never let it go.

Chapter XIV: Of Holy Communion, and how to join in it.

1. SO far I have said nothing concerning the Sun of all spiritual exercises, even the most holy, sacred and Sovereign Sacrifice and Sacrament of the Eucharist,—the very centre point of our Christian religion, the heart of all devotion, the soul of piety;—that Ineffable Mystery which embraces the whole depth of Divine Love, by which God, giving Himself really to us, conveys all His Graces and favours to men with royal magnificence.

2. Prayer made in union with this Divine Sacrifice has untold power; through which, indeed, the soul overflows with heavenly grace, and leaning on her Beloved, becomes so filled with spiritual sweetness and perfume, that we may ask in the words of the Canticles: "Who is this that cometh out of the wilderness like pillars of smoke, perfumed with myrrh and frankincense, with all powders of the merchant?"[17]

3. Strive then to your utmost to be present every day at this holy Celebration, in order that with the priest you may offer the Sacrifice of your Redeemer on behalf of yourself and the whole Church to God the Father. Saint Chrysostom says that the Angels crowd

---

[15] Moore has preserved the graceful imagery of the sunflower, anciently called "tourne-soleil" (as by S. Francis here). "Oh the heart that once truly loved, never forgets, But as truly loves on to the close, As the sunflower turns to her God when he sets The same look which she turned when he rose."

[16] "Pensees." This play on words is common—as Ophelia says in Hamlet, Act iv. sc. 5: "There is pansies—that's for thoughts." But the name of this pretty viola is really derived from *panacea*, signifying *all-heal*, just as Tansy is derived from Athanasia, i.e. immortelle or everlasting. Its other name of heart's-ease also refers to the potent virtues ascribed to it of old. Cawdray, in his *Treasurie of Similies*, London, 1609, says: "As the herb *Panax* or *Panace* hath in it a remedy against all diseases, so is the Death of Christ against all sin sufficient and effectual." In the preface to our English Bible of 1611, the translators speak of "Panaces, the herb that is good for all diseases."

[17] Cant. iii. 6.

around it in adoration, and if we are found together with them, united in one intention, we cannot but be most favourably influenced by such society. Moreover, all the heavenly choirs of the Church triumphant, as well as those of the Church militant, are joined to our Dear Lord in this divine act, so that with Him, in Him, and by Him, they may win the favour of God the Father, and obtain His Mercy for us. How great the blessing to my soul to contribute its share towards the attainment of so gracious a gift!

4. If any imperative hindrance prevents your presence at this sovereign sacrifice of Christ's most true Presence, at least be sure to take part in it spiritually. If you cannot go to Church, choose some morning hour in which to unite your intention to that of the whole Christian world, and make the same interior acts of devotion wherever you are that you would make if you were really present at the Celebration of the Holy Eucharist in Church.

5. In order to join in this rightly, whether actually or mentally, you must give heed to several things: (1) In the beginning, and before the priest goes up to the Altar, make your preparation with his—placing yourself in God's Presence, confessing your unworthiness, and asking forgiveness. (2) Until the Gospel, dwell simply and generally upon the Coming and the Life of our Lord in this world. (3) From the Gospel to the end of the Creed, dwell upon our Dear Lord's teaching, and renew your resolution to live and die in the faith of the Holy Catholic Church. (4) From thence, fix your heart on the mysteries of the Word, and unite yourself to the Death and Passion of our Redeemer, now actually and essentially set forth in this holy Sacrifice, which, together with the priest and all the congregation, you offer to God the Father, to His Glory and your own salvation. (5) Up to the moment of communicating, offer all the longings and desires of your heart, above all desiring most earnestly to be united for ever to our Saviour by His Eternal Love. (6) From the time of Communion to the end, thank His Gracious Majesty for His Incarnation, His Life, Death, Passion, and the Love which He sets forth in this holy Sacrifice, intreating through it His favour for yourself, your relations and friends, and the whole Church; and humbling yourself sincerely, devoutly receive the blessing which our Dear Lord gives you through the channel of His minister. If, however, you wish to follow your daily course of meditation on special mysteries during the Sacrifice, it is not necessary that you should interrupt yourself by making these several acts but it will suffice that at the beginning you dispose your intention to worship and to offer the holy Sacrifice in your meditation and prayer; since every meditation includes all the abovenamed acts either explicitly or implicitly.

Chapter XV: Of the other Public Offices of the Church.

FURTHERMORE, my daughter, you should endeavour to assist at the Offices, Hours, Vespers, etc., as far as you are able, especially on Sundays and Festivals, days which are dedicated to God, wherein we ought to strive to do more for His Honour and Glory than on others. You will greatly increase the fervour of your devotion by so doing, even as did S. Augustine, who tells us in his Confessions, that in the early days of his conversion he was touched to the quick, and his heart overflowed in happy tears, when he took part in the Offices of the Church.[18] Moreover (let me say it here once for all), there

---

[18] "Nor was I sated in those days with the wondrous sweetness of considering the depth of Thy counsels concerning the salvation of mankind. How did I weep, in Thy hymns and canticles, touched to the quick by the voices of Thy sweet-attuned church The voices flowed into mine ears, and the truth distilled into my heart, whence the affections of my devotion overflowed, and tears ran down, and happy

is always more profit and more consolation in the public Offices of the Church than in private acts of devotion, God having willed to give the preference to communion in prayer over all individual action. Be ready to take part in any confraternities and associations you may find in the place where you are called to dwell, especially such as are most fruitful and edifying. This will be pleasing to God; for although confraternities are not ordained, they are recommended by the Church, which grants various privileges to those who are united thereby. And it is always a work of love to join with others and take part in their good works. And although it may be possible that you can use equally profitable devotions by yourself as in common with others,—perhaps even you may like doing so best,— nevertheless God is more glorified when we unite with our brethren and neighbours and join our offerings to theirs.

I say the same concerning all public services and prayers, in which, as far as possible, each one of us is bound to contribute the best example we can for our neighbour's edification, and our hearty desire for God's Glory and the general good of all men.

Chapter XVI: How the Saints are united to us.

INASMUCH as God continually sends us inspirations by means of His Angels, we may fitly send back our aspirations through the same channel. The souls of the holy dead, resting in Paradise, who are, as our Lord Himself has told us, "as the Angels in Heaven,"[19] are also united to us in their prayers. My child, let us gladly join our hearts with these heavenly blessed ones; for even as the newly-fledged nightingale learns to sing from the elder birds, so by our sacred communing with the Saints we shall learn better to pray and sing the praises of the Lord. David is continually uniting his prayers with those of all the Saints and Angels.

Honour, revere and respect the Blessed Virgin Mary with a very special love; she is the Mother of our Sovereign Lord, and so we are her children. Let us think of her with all the love and confidence of affectionate children; let us desire her love, and strive with true filial hearts to imitate her graces.

Seek to be familiar with the Angels; learn to realise that they are continually present, although invisible. Specially love and revere the Guardian Angel of the Diocese in which you live, those of the friends who surround you, and your own. Commune with them frequently, join in their songs of praise, and seek their protection and help in all you do, spiritual or temporal.

That pious man Peter Faber, the first companion of Saint Ignatius, and the first priest, first preacher and first theological teacher of the Company of the Jesuits, who was a native of our Diocese,[20] once passing through this country on his way from Germany, (where he had been labouring for God's Glory,) told how great comfort he had found as he went among places infested with heresy in communing with the guardian Angels thereof, whose help had often preserved him from danger, and softened hearts to receive the faith. He spoke with such earnestness, that a lady who, when quite young, heard him, was so impressed, that she repeated his words to me only four years ago, sixty years after their utterance, with the utmost feeling. I had the happiness only last year of consecrating an

was I therein."—conf. bk. ix. 14.
[19] S. Mark xii. 25.
[20] Faber was a Savoyard.

altar in the place where it pleased God to give that blessed man birth, the little village of Villaret, amid the wildest of our mountains.

You will do well to choose out for yourself some individual Saint, whose life specially to study and imitate, and whose prayers may be more particularly offered on your behalf. The Saint bearing your own baptismal name would seem to be naturally assigned to you.

Chapter XVII: How to Hear and Read God's Word.

CULTIVATE a special devotion to God's Word, whether studied privately or in public; always listen to it with attention and reverence, strive to profit by it, and do not let it fall to the ground, but receive it within your heart as a precious balm, thereby imitating the Blessed Virgin, who "kept all these sayings in her heart."[21] Remember that our Lord receives our words of prayer according to the way in which we receive His words in teaching.

You should always have some good devout book at hand, such as the writings of S. Bonaventura, Gerson, Denis the Carthusian, Blosius, Grenada, Stella, Arias, Pinella, Da Ponte, Avila, the Spiritual Combat, the Confessions of S. Augustine, S. Jerome's Epistles, or the like; and daily read some small portion attentively, as though you were reading letters sent by the Saints from Paradise to teach you the way thither, and encourage you to follow them. Read the Lives of the Saints too, which are as a mirror to you of Christian life, and try to imitate their actions according to your circumstances; for although many things which the Saints did may not be practicable for those who live in the world, they may be followed more or less. Thus, in our spiritual retreats we imitate the solitude of the first hermit, S. Paul; in the practice of poverty we imitate S. Francis, and so on. Of course some Lives throw much more light upon our daily course than others, such as the Life of Saint Theresa, which is most admirable, the first Jesuits, Saint Charles Borromeo, Archbishop of Milan, S. Louis, S. Bernard, S. Francis, and such like. Others are more the subjects of our admiring wonder than of imitation, such as S. Mary of Egypt, S. Simeon Stylites, S. Catherine of Genoa, and S. Catherine of Sienna, S. Angela, etc., although these should tend to kindle a great love of God in our hearts.

Chapter XVIII: How to receive Inspirations.

BY inspirations I mean all drawings, feelings, interior reproaches, lights and intuitions, with which God moves us, preventing our hearts by His Fatherly love and care, and awakening, exciting, urging, and attracting them to goodness, to Heavenly love, to good resolutions, in short, to whatever tends to our eternal welfare. This it is of which we read in the Canticles, when the Bridegroom knocks at the door, awakens His beloved, calls upon her, seeks her, bids her eat of His honey, gather the fruit and flowers of His garden, and let Him hear her voice, which is sweet to Him.[22]

Let me make use of an illustration of my meaning. In contracting a marriage, the bride must be a party to three separate acts: first, the bridegroom is proposed to her; secondly, she entertains the proposal; and thirdly, she gives her consent. Just so when God intends to perform some act of love in us, by us, and with us; He first suggests it by His inspiration;

---

[21] S. Luke ii. 51.
[22] Cant. v. vii. ii.

secondly, we receive that inspiration; and thirdly, we consent to it: for, like as we fall into sin by three steps, temptation, delectation, and consent, so there are three steps whereby we ascend to virtue; inspiration, as opposed to temptation; delectation in God's inspiration, as opposed to that of temptation; and consent to the one instead of to the other. Were God's inspirations to last all our lives, we should be nowise more acceptable to Him, unless we took pleasure therein; on the contrary, we should rather offend Him as did the Israelites, of whom He says that they "grieved Him for forty years long, refusing to hear His pleadings, so that at last" I "sware in My wrath that they should not enter into My rest."[23] And (to recur to my first illustration) one who has long been devoted to his lady-love, would feel greatly injured if, after all, she would not consent to the alliance he seeks.

The delight we take in God's inspirations is an important step gained towards His Glory, and we begin at once to please Him thereby; for although such delectation is not the same thing as a full consent, it shows a strong tendency thereto; and if it is a good and profitable sign when we take pleasure in hearing God's Word, which is, so to say, an external inspiration, still more is it good and acceptable in His Sight when we take delight in His interior inspirations. Such is the delight of which the Bride says, "My soul melted within me when my Beloved spake."[24] And so, too, the earthly lover is well satisfied when he sees that his lady-love finds pleasure in his attentions.

But, after all, consent only perfects the good action; for if we are inspired of God, and take pleasure in that inspiration, and yet, nevertheless, refuse our consent to His inspiration, we are acting a very contemptuous, offensive part towards Him. We read of the Bride, that although the voice of her Beloved touched her heart, she made trivial excuses, and delayed opening the door to Him, and so He withdrew Himself and "was gone."[25] And the earthly lover, who had long sought a lady, and seemed acceptable to her, would have the more ground for complaint if at last he was spurned and dismissed, than if he had never been favourably received.

Do you, my daughter, resolve to accept whatever inspirations God may vouchsafe you, heartily; and when they offer themselves, receive them as the ambassadors of your Heavenly King, seeking alliance with you. Hearken gently to their propositions, foster the love with which you are inspired, and cherish the holy Guest. Give your consent, and let it be a full, loving, stedfast consent to His holy inspirations; for, so doing, God will reckon your affection as a favour, although truly we can confer none upon Him. But, before consenting to inspirations which have respect to important or extraordinary things, guard against self-deception, by consulting your spiritual guide, and let him examine whether the inspiration be real or no; and that the rather, because when the enemy sees a soul ready to hearken to inspirations, he is wont to set false delusions in the way to deceive it,—a snare you will not fall into so long as you humbly obey your guide.

Consent once given, you must carefully seek to produce the intended results, and carry out the inspiration, the crown of true virtue; for to give consent, without producing the result thereof, were like planting a vine without meaning it to bear fruit. All this will be greatly promoted by careful attention to your morning exercises, and the spiritual

---

[23] Ps. xcv. 10, 11.

[24] In the English version this passage is, "My soul failed when he spake." (Cant. V. 6.) But in the Vulgate it is in the far more expressive form quoted by S. Francis de Sales, "Anima mea liquefacta est, ut locutus est."

[25] Cant. v. 6.

retirement already mentioned, because therein you learn to carry general principles to a special application.

Chapter XIX: On Confession.

OUR Saviour has bequeathed the Sacrament of Penitence and Confession to His Church,[26] in order that therein we may be cleansed from all our sins, however and whenever we may have been soiled thereby. Therefore, my child, never allow your heart to abide heavy with sin, seeing that there is so sure and safe a remedy at hand. If the lioness has been in the neighbourhood of other beasts she hastens to wash away their scent, lest it should be displeasing to her lord; and so the soul which has ever so little consented to sin, ought to abhor itself and make haste to seek purification, out of respect to His Divine Gaze Who beholds it always. Why should we die a spiritual death when there is a sovereign remedy available?

Make your confession humbly and devoutly every week, and always, if you can, before communicating, even although your conscience is not burdened with mortal sin; for in confession you do not only receive absolution for your venial sins, but you also receive great strength to help you in avoiding them henceforth, clearer light to discover your failings, and abundant grace to make up whatever loss you have incurred through those faults. You exercise the graces of humility, obedience, simplicity and love, and by this one act of confession you practise more virtue than in any other.

Be sure always to entertain a hearty sorrow for the sins you confess, however small they are; as also a stedfast resolution to correct them in future. Some people go on confessing venial sins out of mere habit, and conventionally, without making any effort to correct them, thereby losing a great deal of spiritual good. Supposing that you confess having said something untrue, although without evil consequences, or some careless words, or excessive amusement;—repent, and make a firm resolution of amendment: it is a mere abuse to confess any sin whatever, be it mortal or venial, without intending to put it altogether away, that being the express object of confession.

Beware of unmeaning self-accusations, made out of a mere routine, such as, "I have not loved God as much as I ought; I have not prayed with as much devotion as I ought; I have not loved my neighbour as I ought; I have not received the Sacraments with sufficient reverence;" and the like. Such things as these are altogether useless in setting the state of your conscience before your Confessor, inasmuch as all the Saints in Paradise and all men living would say the same. But examine closely what special reason you have for accusing yourself thus, and when you have discovered it, accuse yourself simply and plainly of your fault. For instance, when confessing that you have not loved your neighbour as you ought, it may be that what you mean is, that having seen some one in great want whom you could have succoured, you have failed to do so. Well then, accuse yourself of that special omission: say, "Having come across a person in need, I did not help him as I might have done," either through negligence, or hardness, or indifference, according as the case may be. So again, do not accuse yourself of not having prayed to God with sufficient devotion; but if you have given way to voluntary distractions, or if you have neglected the proper circumstances of devout prayer—whether place, time, or attitude—say so plainly, just as it is, and do not deal in generalities, which, so to say, blow neither hot nor cold.

---

[26] S. Matt. xvi. 19, xviii. 18; S. John xx. 23.

Again, do not be satisfied with mentioning the bare fact of your venial sins, but accuse yourself of the motive cause which led to them. For instance, do not be content with saying that you told an untruth which injured no one; but say whether it was out of vanity, in order to win praise or avoid blame, out of heedlessness, or from obstinacy. If you have exceeded in society, say whether it was from the love of talking, or gambling for the sake of money, and so on. Say whether you continued long to commit the fault in question, as the importance of a fault depends greatly upon its continuance: e.g., there is a wide difference between a passing act of vanity which is over in a quarter of an hour, and one which fills the heart for one or more days. So you must mention the fact, the motive and the duration of your faults. It is true that we are not bound to be so precise in confessing venial sins, or even, technically speaking, to confess them at all; but all who aim at purifying their souls in order to attain a really devout life, will be careful to show all their spiritual maladies, however slight, to their spiritual physician, in order to be healed.

Do not spare yourself in telling whatever is necessary to explain the nature of your fault, as, for instance, the reason why you lost your temper, or why you encouraged another in wrong-doing. Thus, some one whom I dislike says a chance word in joke, I take it ill, and put myself in a passion. If one I like had said a stronger thing I should not have taken it amiss; so in confession, I ought to say that I lost my temper with a person, not because of the words spoken so much as because I disliked the speaker; and if in order to explain yourself clearly it is necessary to particularize the words, it is well to do so; because accusing one's self thus simply one discovers not merely one's actual sins, but one's bad habits, inclinations and ways, and the other roots of sin, by which means one's spiritual Father acquires a fuller knowledge of the heart he is dealing with, and knows better what remedies to apply. But you must always avoid exposing any one who has borne any part in your sin as far as possible. Keep watch over a variety of sins, which are apt to spring up and flourish, often insensibly, in the conscience, so that you may confess them and put them away; and with this view read Chapters VI., XXVII., XXVIII., XXIX., XXXV. and XXXVI. of Part III., and Chapter VII. of Part IV., attentively.

Do not lightly change your Confessor, but having chosen him, be regular in giving account of your conscience to him at the appointed seasons, telling him your faults simply and frankly, and from time to time—say every month or every two months, show him the general state of your inclinations, although there be nothing wrong in them; as, for instance, whether you are depressed and anxious, or cheerful, desirous of advancement, or money, and the like.

Chapter XX: Of Frequent Communion.

IT is said that Mithridates, King of Pontus, who invented the poison called after him, mithridate, so thoroughly impregnated his system with it, that when eventually he tried to poison himself to avoid becoming the Romans' slave, he never could succeed. The Saviour instituted the most holy Sacrament of the Eucharist, really containing His Body and His Blood, in order that they who eat it might live for ever. And therefore whosoever receives it frequently and devoutly, so strengthens the health and life of his soul, that it is hardly possible for him to be poisoned by any evil desires. We cannot be fed by that Living Flesh and hold to the affections of death; and just as our first parents could not die in Paradise, because of the Tree of Life which God had placed therein, so this Sacrament of Life makes spiritual death impossible. The most fragile, easily spoilt fruits, such as cherries, apricots, and strawberries, can be kept all the year by being preserved in sugar or honey; so what wonder if our hearts, frail and weakly as they are, are kept from the corruption of sin when they are preserved in the sweetness ("sweeter than honey and the honeycomb") of the Incorruptible Body and Blood of the Son of God. O my daughter, those Christians who are lost will indeed have no answer to give when the Just Judge sets before them that they have voluntarily died the spiritual death, since it was so easy for them to have preserved life and health, by eating His Body which He gave them for that very end. "Miserable men!" He will say, "wherefore would ye die, with the Bread of Life itself in your hands?"

As to daily Communion, I neither commend nor condemn it; but with respect to communicating every Sunday, I counsel and exhort every one to do so, providing the mind has no attachment to sin. So says S. Augustine, and with him I neither find fault nor unconditionally commend daily Communion, leaving that matter to the discretion of every person's own spiritual Guide; as the requisite dispositions for such frequent Communion are too delicate for one to advise it indiscriminately. On the other hand, these very special dispositions may be found in sundry devout souls, and therefore it would not be well to discourage everybody. It is a subject which must be dealt with according to each individual mind; it were imprudent to advise such frequent Communion to all, while, on the other hand, it would be presumptuous to blame any one for it, especially if he therein follows the advice of some wise director. Saint Catherine of Sienna, when blamed for her frequent Communions, under the plea that Saint Augustine neither commended nor condemned daily Communion, replied gently, "Well, then, since Saint Augustine does not condemn it, neither, I pray you, do you condemn it, and I shall be content." But Saint Augustine earnestly exhorts all to communicate every Sunday. And as I presume, my daughter, that you have no attachment either to mortal or venial sins, you are in the condition which Saint Augustine requires; and if your spiritual Father approves, you may profitably communicate more frequently. Nevertheless, there are various hindrances which may arise, not so much from yourself, as from those among whom you live, which may lead a wise director to tell you not to communicate so often. For instance, if you are in a position of subjection, and those whom you are bound to obey should be so ignorant or so prejudiced, as to be uneasy at your frequent Communions, all things considered, it may be well to show consideration for their weakness, and to make your Communion fortnightly; only, of course, where there is no possible way of overcoming the difficulty otherwise. But one cannot give any general rule on such a point, each person must follow the advice of their own spiritual Guide; only this much I will say, that monthly Communions are the very fewest which any one seeking to serve God devoutly can make.

If you are discreet, neither father nor mother, husband nor wife, will ever hinder you from communicating frequently, and that because on the day of your Communion you will give good heed always to be more than usually gentle and amiable towards them, doing all you can to please them, so that they are not likely to prevent your doing a thing which in nowise inconveniences themselves, unless they were most particularly unreasonable and perverse, in which case, as I have said, your Director might advise you to yield. There is nothing in the married life to hinder frequent Communion. Most certainly the Christians of the Primitive Church communicated daily, whether married or single. Neither is any malady a necessary impediment, except, indeed, anything producing constant sickness.

Those who communicate weekly must be free from mortal sin, and also from any attachment to venial sin, and they should feel a great desire for Communion; but for daily Communion people should furthermore have conquered most of their inclinations to evil, and no one should practise it without the advice of their spiritual Guide.

Chapter XXI: How to Communicate.

BEGIN your preparation over-night, by sundry aspirations and loving ejaculations. Go to bed somewhat earlier than usual, so that you may get up earlier the next morning; and if you should wake during the night, fill your heart and lips at once with sacred words wherewith to make your soul ready to receive the Bridegroom, Who watches while you sleep, and Who intends to give you countless gifts and graces, if you on your part are prepared to accept them. In the morning rise with joyful expectation of the Blessing you hope for, and (having made your Confession) go with the fullest trust, but at the same time with the fullest humility, to receive that Heavenly Food which will sustain your immortal life. And after having said the sacred words, "Lord, I am not worthy," do not make any further movement whatever, either in prayer or otherwise, but gently opening your mouth, in the fulness of faith, hope, and love, receive Him in Whom, by Whom, and through Whom, you believe, hope, and love. O my child, bethink you that just as the bee, having gathered heaven's dew and earth's sweetest juices from amid the flowers, carries it to her hive; so the Priest, having taken the Saviour, God's Own Son, Who came down from Heaven, the Son of Mary, Who sprang up as earth's choicest flower, from the Altar, feeds you with that Bread of Sweetness and of all delight. When you have received it kindle your heart to adore the King of our Salvation, tell Him of all your own personal matters, and realise that He is within you, seeking your best happiness. In short, give Him the very best reception you possibly can, and act so that in all you do it may be evident that God is with you. When you cannot have the blessing of actual Communion, at least communicate in heart and mind, uniting yourself by ardent desire to the Life-giving Body of the Saviour.

Your main intention in Communion should be to grow, strengthen, and abound in the Love of God; for Love's Sake receive that which Love Alone gives you. Of a truth there is no more loving or tender aspect in which to gaze upon the Saviour than this act, in which He, so to say, annihilates Himself, and gives Himself to us as food, in order to fill our souls, and to unite Himself more closely to the heart and flesh of His faithful ones.

If men of the world ask why you communicate so often, tell them that it is that you may learn to love God; that you may be cleansed from imperfections, set free from trouble, comforted in affliction, strengthened in weakness. Tell them that there are two manner of men who need frequent Communion—those who are perfect, since being ready they were much to blame did they not come to the Source and Fountain of all perfection; and the imperfect, that they may learn how to become perfect; the strong, lest they become weak, and the weak, that they may become strong; the sick that they may be healed, and the sound lest they sicken. Tell them that you, imperfect, weak and ailing, need frequently to communicate with your Perfection, your Strength, your Physician. Tell them that those who are but little engaged in worldly affairs should communicate often, because they have leisure; and those who are heavily pressed with business, because they stand so much in need of help; and he who is hard worked needs frequent and substantial food. Tell them that you receive the Blessed Sacrament that you may learn to receive it better; one rarely does that well which one seldom does. Therefore, my child, communicate frequently,—

as often as you can, subject to the advice of your spiritual Father. Our mountain hares turn white in winter, because they live in, and feed upon, the snow, and by dint of adoring and feeding upon Beauty, Goodness, and Purity itself in this most Divine Sacrament you too will become lovely, holy, pure.

Chapter I: How to select that which we should chiefly Practise.

THE queen bee never takes wing without being surrounded by all her Subjects; even so Love never enters the heart but it is sure to bring all other virtues in its train; marshalling and employing them as a captain his soldiers; yet, nevertheless, Love does not set them all to work suddenly, or equally, at all times and everywhere. The righteous man is "like a tree planted by the water side, that will bring forth his fruit in due season;"[1] inasmuch as Love, watering and refreshing the soul, causes it to bring forth good works, each in season as required. There is an old proverb to the effect that the sweetest music is unwelcome at a time of mourning; and certain persons have made a great mistake when, seeking to cultivate some special virtue, they attempt to obtrude it on all occasions, like the ancient philosophers we read of, who were always laughing or weeping. Worse still if they take upon themselves to censure those who do not make a continual study of this their pet virtue. S. Paul tells us to "rejoice with them that do rejoice, and weep with them that weep;"[2] and Charity is patient, kind, liberal, prudent, indulgent.

At the same time, there are virtues of universal account, which must not only be called into occasional action, but ought to spread their influence over everything. We do not very often come across opportunities for exercising strength, magnanimity, or magnificence; but gentleness, temperance, modesty, and humility, are graces which ought to colour everything we do. There may be virtues of a more exalted mould, but at all events these are the most continually called for in daily life. Sugar is better than salt, but we use salt more generally and oftener. Consequently, it is well to have a good and ready stock in hand of those general virtues of which we stand in so perpetual a need.

In practising any virtue, it is well to choose that which is most according to our duty, rather than most according to our taste. It was Saint Paula's liking to practise bodily mortifications with a view to the keener enjoyment of spiritual sweetness, but obedience to her superiors was a higher duty; and therefore Saint Jerome acknowledges that she was wrong in practising excessive abstinence contrary to the advice of her Bishop. And the Apostles, whose mission it was to preach the Gospel, and feed souls with the Bread of Life, judged well that it was not right for them to hinder this holy work in order to minister to the material wants of the poor, weighty as that work was also.[3] Every calling stands in special need of some special virtue; those required of a prelate, a prince, or a soldier, are quite different; so are those beseeming a wife or a widow, and although all should possess every virtue, yet all are not called upon to exercise them equally, but each should cultivate chiefly those which are important to the manner of life to which he is called.

Among such virtues as have no special adaptation to our own calling, choose the most excellent, not the most showy. A comet generally looks larger than the stars, and fills the eye more; but all the while comets are not nearly so important as the stars, and only seem so large to us because they are nearer to us than stars, and are of a grosser kind. So there are certain virtues which touch us very sensibly and are very material, so to say, and

---

[1] Ps. i. 3.
[2] Rom. xii. 15.
[3] Acts vi. 2.

therefore ordinary people give them the preference. Thus the common run of men ordinarily value temporal almsgiving more than spiritual; and think more of fasting, exterior discipline and bodily mortification than of meekness, cheerfulness, modesty, and other interior mortifications, which nevertheless are far better. Do you then, my daughter, choose the best virtues, not those which are most highly esteemed; the most excellent, not the most visible; the truest, not the most conspicuous.

It is well for everybody to select some special virtue at which to aim, not as neglecting any others, but as an object and pursuit to the mind. Saint John, Bishop of Alexandria, saw a vision of a lovely maiden, brighter than the sun, in shining garments, and wearing an olive crown, who said to him, "I am the King's eldest daughter, and if thou wilt have me for thy friend, I will bring thee to see His Face." Then he knew that it was pity for the poor which God thus commended to him, and from that time he gave himself so heartily to practise it, that he is universally known as Saint John the Almoner. Eulogius Alexandrinus desired to devote himself wholly to God, but he had not courage either to adopt the solitary life, or to put himself under obedience, and therefore he took a miserable beggar, seething in dirt and leprosy, to live with him; and to do this more thoroughly, he vowed to honour and serve him as a servant does his lord and master. After a while, both feeling greatly tempted to part company, they referred to the great Saint Anthony, who said, "Beware of separating, my sons, for you are both near your end, and if the Angel find you not together, you will be in danger of losing your crowns."

Saint Louis counted it a privilege to visit the hospitals, where he used to tend the sick with his own royal hands. Saint Francis loved poverty above all things, and called her his lady-love. Saint Dominic gave himself up to preaching, whence his Order takes its name.[4] Saint Gregory the Great specially delighted to receive pilgrims after the manner of faithful Abraham, and like him entertained the King of Glory under a pilgrim's garb. Tobit devoted himself to the charitable work of burying the dead. Saint Elizabeth, albeit a mighty princess, loved above all things to humble herself. When Saint Catherine of Genoa became a widow, she gave herself up to work in an hospital. Cassian relates how a certain devout maiden once besought Saint Athanasius to help her in cultivating the grace of patience; and he gave her a poor widow as companion, who was cross, irritable, and altogether intolerable, and whose perpetual fretfulness gave the pious lady abundant opportunity of practising gentleness and patience. And so some of God's servants devote themselves to nursing the sick, helping the poor, teaching little children in the faith, reclaiming the fallen, building churches, and adorning the altar, making peace among men. Therein they resemble embroidresses who work all manner of silks, gold and silver on various grounds, so producing beautiful flowers. Just so the pious souls who undertake some special devout practice use it as the ground of their spiritual embroidery, and frame all manner of other graces upon it, ordering their actions and affections better by means of this their chief thread which runs through all.

"Upon Thy Right Hand did stand the Queen in a vesture of gold wrought about with divers colours."[5]

When we are beset by any particular vice, it is well as far as possible to make the opposite virtue our special aim, and turn everything to that account; so doing, we shall

---

[4] The Preaching Friars.
[5] Psalm 5. 13, 14. "En son beau vestement de drap d'or recame, Et d'ouvrages divers a l'aiguile seme."

overcome our enemy, and meanwhile make progress in all virtue. Thus, if I am beset with pride or anger, I must above all else strive to cultivate humility and gentleness, and I must turn all my religious exercises,—prayer, sacraments, prudence, constancy, moderation, to the same object. The wild boar sharpens its tusks by grinding them against its other teeth, which by the same process are sharpened and pointed; and so when a good man endeavours to perfect himself in some virtue which he is conscious of specially needing, he ought to give it edge and point by the aid of other virtues, which will themselves be confirmed and strengthened as he uses them with that object. It was so with Job, who, while specially exercising the virtue of patience amid the numberless temptations which beset him, was confirmed in all manner of holiness and godly virtues. And Saint Gregory Nazianzen says, that sometimes a person has attained the height of goodness by one single act of virtue, performed with the greatest perfection; instancing Rahab as an example, who, having practised the virtue of hospitality very excellently, reached a high point of glory.[6] Of course, any such action must needs be performed with a very exceeding degree of fervour and charity.

Chapter II: The same Subject continued.

SAINT AUGUSTINE says very admirably, that beginners in devotion are wont to commit certain faults which, while they are blameable according to the strict laws of perfection, are yet praiseworthy by reason of the promise they hold forth of a future excellent goodness, to which they actually tend. For instance, that common shrinking fear which gives rise to an excessive scrupulosity in the souls of some who are but just set free from a course of sin, is commendable at that early stage, and is the almost certain forerunner of future purity of conscience. But this same fear would be blameable in those who are farther advanced, because love should reign in their hearts, and love is sure to drive away all such servile fear by degrees.

In his early days, Saint Bernard was very severe and harsh towards those whom he directed, telling them, to begin with, that they must put aside the body, and come to him with their minds only. In confession, he treated all faults, however small, with extreme severity, and his poor apprentices in the study of perfection were so urged onwards, that by dint of pressing he kept them back, for they lost heart and breath when they found themselves thus driven up so steep and high an ascent. Therein, my daughter, you can see that, although it was his ardent zeal for the most perfect purity which led that great Saint so to act, and although such zeal is a great virtue, still it was a virtue which required checking. And so God Himself checked it in a vision, by which He filled S. Bernard with so gentle, tender, and loving a spirit, that he was altogether changed, blaming himself heavily for having been so strict and so severe, and becoming so kindly and indulgent, that he made himself all things to all men in order to win all.

S. Jerome tells us that his beloved daughter, S. Paula, was not only extreme, but obstinate in practising bodily mortifications, and refusing to yield to the advice given her upon that head by her Bishop, S. Epiphanius; and furthermore, she gave way so excessively to her grief at the death of those she loved as to peril her own life. Whereupon S. Jerome says: "It will be said that I am accusing this saintly woman rather than praising her, but I affirm before Jesus, Whom she served, and Whom I seek to serve, that I am not

---

[6] S. Francis evidently alludes here to the mention made of Rahab by S. Paul. Heb. xi. 31.

saying what is untrue on one side or the other, but simply describing her as one Christian another; that is to say, I am writing her history, not her panegyric, and her faults are the virtues of others." He means to say that the defects and faults of S. Paula would have been looked upon as virtues in a less perfect soul; and indeed there are actions which we must count as imperfections in the perfect, which yet would be highly esteemed in the imperfect. When at the end of a sickness the invalid's legs swell, it is a good sign, indicating that natural strength is returning, and throwing off foul humours; but it would be a bad sign in one not avowedly sick, as showing that nature was too feeble to disperse or absorb those humours.

So, my child, we must think well of those whom we see practising virtues, although imperfectly, since the Saints have done the like; but as to ourselves we must give heed to practise them, not only diligently, but discreetly, and to this end we shall do well strictly to follow the Wise Man's counsel,[7] and not trust in our own wisdom, but lean on those whom God has given as our guides. And here I must say a few words concerning certain things which some reckon as virtues, although they are nothing of the sort—I mean ecstasies, trances, rhapsodies, extraordinary transformations, and the like, which are dwelt on in some books, and which promise to raise the soul to a purely intellectual contemplation, an altogether supernatural mental altitude, and a life of pre-eminent excellence. But I would have you see, my child, that these perfections are not virtues, they are rather rewards which God gives to virtues, or perhaps, more correctly speaking, tokens of the joys of everlasting life, occasionally granted to men in order to kindle in them a desire for the fulness of joy which is only to be found in Paradise. But we must not aspire to such graces, which are in nowise necessary to us in order to love and serve God, our only lawful ambition. Indeed, for the most part, these graces are not to be acquired by labour or industry, and that because they are rather passions than actions, which we may receive, but cannot create. Moreover, our business only is to become good, devout people, pious men and women; and all our efforts must be to that end. If it should please God further to endow us with angelic perfection, we should then be prepared to become good angels; but meanwhile let us practise, in all simplicity, humility and devotion, those lowly virtues to the attainment of which our Lord has bidden us labour,—I mean patience, cheerfulness, self-mortification, humility, obedience, poverty, chastity, kindness to our neighbour, forbearance towards his failings, diligence, and a holy fervour. Let us willingly resign the higher eminences to lofty souls. We are not worthy to take so high a rank in God's service; let us be content to be as scullions, porters, insignificant attendants in His household, leaving it to Him if He should hereafter see fit to call us to His own council chamber. Of a truth, my child, the King of Glory does not reward His servants according to the dignity of their office, but according to the humility and love with which they have exercised it. While Saul was seeking his father's asses, he found the kingdom of Israel:[8] Rebecca watering Abraham's camels, became his son's wife:[9] Ruth gleaning after Boaz' reapers, and lying down at his feet, was raised up to become his bride.[10] Those who pretend to such great and extraordinary graces are very liable to delusions and mistakes, so that sometimes it turns out that people who aspire to be angels are not ordinarily good men, and that their goodness lies more in high-flown words than in heart and deed. But

[7] Ecclus. vi. 2, 32, 36.
[8] 1 Sam. ix.
[9] Gen. xxiv.
[10] Ruth ii. iii.

we must beware of despising or presumptuously condemning anything. Only, while thanking God for the pre-eminence of others, let us abide contentedly in our own lower but safer path,—a path of less distinction, but more suitable to our lowliness, resting satisfied that if we walk steadily and faithfully therein, God will lift us up to greater things.

Chapter III: On Patience.

"YE have need of patience, that, after ye have done the Will of God, ye might receive the promise," says Saint Paul;[11] and the Saviour said, "In your patience possess ye your souls."[12] The greatest happiness of any one is "to possess his soul;" and the more perfect our patience, the more fully we do so possess our souls. Call often to mind that our Saviour redeemed us by bearing and suffering, and in like manner we must seek our own salvation amid sufferings and afflictions; bearing insults, contradictions and troubles with all the gentleness we can possibly command. Do not limit your patience to this or that kind of trial, but extend it universally to whatever God may send, or allow to befall you. Some people will only bear patiently with trials which carry their own salve of dignity,—such as being wounded in battle, becoming a prisoner of war, being ill-used for the sake of their religion, being impoverished by some strife out of which they came triumphant. Now these persons do not love tribulation, but only the honour which attends it. A really patient servant of God is as ready to bear inglorious troubles as those which are honourable. A brave man can easily bear with contempt, slander and false accusation from an evil world; but to bear such injustice at the hands of good men, of friends and relations, is a great test of patience. I have a greater respect for the gentleness with which the great S. Charles Borromeo long endured the public reproaches which a celebrated preacher of a reformed Order used to pour out upon him, than for all the other attacks he bore with. For, just as the sting of a bee hurts far more than that of a fly, so the injuries or contradictions we endure from good people are much harder to bear than any others. But it is a thing which very often happens, and sometimes two worthy men, who are both highly well-intentioned after their own fashion, annoy and even persecute one another grievously.

Be patient, not only with respect to the main trials which beset you, but also under the accidental and accessory annoyances which arise out of them. We often find people who imagine themselves ready to accept a trial in itself who are impatient of its consequences. We hear one man say, "I should not mind poverty, were it not that I am unable to bring up my children and receive my friends as handsomely as I desire." And another says, "I should not mind, were it not that the world will suppose it is my own fault;" while another would patiently bear to be the subject of slander provided nobody believed it. Others, again, accept one side of a trouble but fret against the rest—as, for instance, believing themselves to be patient under sickness, only fretting against their inability to obtain the best advice, or at the inconvenience they are to their friends. But, dear child, be sure that we must patiently accept, not sickness only, but such sickness as God chooses to send, in the place, among the people, and subject to the circumstances which He ordains;—and so with all other troubles. If any trouble comes upon you, use the remedies with which God supplies you. Not to do this is to tempt Him; but having done so, wait whatever result He wills with perfect resignation. If He pleases to let the evil be remedied, thank Him humbly;

---

[11] Heb. x. 36.
[12] S. Luke xxi. 19.

but if it be His will that the evil grow greater than the remedies, patiently bless His Holy Name.

Follow Saint Gregory's advice: When you are justly blamed for some fault you have committed, humble yourself deeply, and confess that you deserve the blame. If the accusation be false, defend yourself quietly, denying the fact; this is but due respect for truth and your neighbour's edification. But if after you have made your true and legitimate defence you are still accused, do not be troubled, and do not try to press your defence—you have had due respect for truth, have the same now for humility. By acting thus you will not infringe either a due care for your good name, or the affection you are bound to entertain for peace, humility and gentleness of heart.

Complain as little as possible of your wrongs, for as a general rule you may be sure that complaining is sin;[13] the rather that self-love always magnifies our injuries: above all, do not complain to people who are easily angered and excited. If it is needful to complain to some one, either as seeking a remedy for your injury, or in order to soothe your mind, let it be to some calm, gentle spirit, greatly filled with the Love of God; for otherwise, instead of relieving your heart, your confidants will only provoke it to still greater disturbance; instead of taking out the thorn which pricks you, they will drive it further into your foot.

Some people when they are ill, or in trouble, or injured by any one, restrain their complaints, because they think (and that rightly) that to murmur betokens great weakness or a narrow mind; but nevertheless, they exceedingly desire and maneuvre to make others pity them, desiring to be considered as suffering with patience and courage. Now this is a kind of patience certainly, but it is a spurious patience, which in reality is neither more nor less than a very refined, very subtle form of ambition and vanity. To them we may apply the Apostle's words, "He hath whereof to glory, but not before God."[14] A really patient man neither complains nor seeks to be pitied; he will speak simply and truly of his trouble, without exaggerating its weight or bemoaning himself; if others pity him, he will accept their compassion patiently, unless they pity him for some ill he is not enduring, in which case he will say so with meekness, and abide in patience and truthfulness, combating his grief and not complaining of it.

As to the trials which you will encounter in devotion (and they are certain to arise), bear in mind our dear Lord's words: "A woman, when she is in travail, hath sorrow, because her hour is come; but as soon as she is delivered of the child, she remembereth no more the anguish, for joy that a child is born into the world."[15] You, too, have conceived in your soul the most gracious of children, even Jesus Christ, and before He can be brought forth you must inevitably travail with pain; but be of good cheer, for when these pangs are over, you will possess an abiding joy, having brought such a man into the world. And He will be really born for you, when He is perfected in your heart by love, and in your actions by imitating His life.

When you are sick, offer all your pains and weakness to our Dear Lord, and ask Him to unite them to the sufferings which He bore for you. Obey your physician, and take all medicines, remedies and nourishment, for the Love of God, remembering the vinegar and gall He tasted for love of us; desire your recovery that you may serve Him; do not shrink

---

[13] "Qui se plaint, peche."

[14] Rom. iv. 2.

[15] S. John xvi. 21.

from languor and weakness out of obedience to Him, and be ready to die if He wills it, to His Glory, and that you may enter into His Presence.

Bear in mind that the bee while making its honey lives upon a bitter food: and in like manner we can never make acts of gentleness and patience, or gather the honey of the truest virtues, better than while eating the bread of bitterness, and enduring hardness. And just as the best honey is that made from thyme, a small and bitter herb, so that virtue which is practised amid bitterness and lowly sorrow is the best of all virtues.

Gaze often inwardly upon Jesus Christ crucified, naked, blasphemed, falsely accused, forsaken, overwhelmed with every possible grief and sorrow, and remember that none of your sufferings can ever be compared to His, either in kind or degree, and that you can never suffer anything for Him worthy to be weighed against what He has borne for you.

Consider the pains which martyrs have endured, and think how even now many people are bearing afflictions beyond all measure greater than yours, and say, "Of a truth my trouble is comfort, my torments are but roses as compared to those whose life is a continual death, without solace, or aid or consolation, borne down with a weight of grief tenfold greater than mine."

Chapter IV: On Greater Humility.

ELISHA bade the poor widow "borrow vessels, even empty vessels not a few, and pour oil into all those vessels;"[16] and so in order to receive God's Grace in our hearts, they must be as empty vessels—not filled with self-esteem. The swallow with its sharp cry and keen glance has the power of frightening away birds of prey, and for that reason the dove prefers it to all other birds, and lives surely beside it;—even so humility drives Satan away, and cherishes the gifts and graces of the Holy Spirit within us, and for that reason all the Saints—and especially the King of Saints and His Blessed Mother—have always esteemed the grace of humility above all other virtues.

We call that vainglory which men take to themselves, either for what is not in them, or which being in them is not their own, or which being in them and their own yet is not worthy of their self-satisfaction. For instance, noble birth, favour of great men, popular applause, all these are things nowise belonging to ourselves, but coming from our forefathers, or the opinion of others. Some people are proud and conceited because they ride a fine horse, wear a feather in their hat, and are expensively dressed, but who can fail to see their folly, or that if any one has reason to be proud over such things, it would be the horse, the bird, and the tailor! Or what can be more contemptible than to found one's credit on a horse, a plume, or a ruff? Others again pride themselves upon their dainty moustaches, their well-trimmed beard or curled hair, their white hands, or their dancing, singing and the like: but is it not a petty vanity which can seek to be esteemed for any such trivial and frivolous matters? Then again, some look for the world's respect and honour because they have acquired some smatterings of science, expecting all their neighbours to listen and yield to them, and such men we call pedants. Others make great capital of their personal beauty, and imagine that every one is lost in admiration of it; but all this is utterly vain, foolish and impertinent, and the glory men take to themselves for such matters must be called vain, childish and frivolous.

---

[16] 2 Kings iv. 3, 4.

You may test real worth as we test balm, which is tried by being distilled in water, and if it is precipitated to the bottom, it is known to be pure and precious. So if you want to know whether a man is really wise, learned, generous or noble, see if his life is moulded by humility, modesty and submission. If so, his gifts are genuine; but if they are only surface and showy, you may be sure that in proportion to their demonstrativeness so is their unreality. Those pearls which are formed amid tempest and storm have only an outward shell, and are hollow within; and so when a man's good qualities are fed by pride, vanity and boasting, they will soon have nothing save empty show, without sap, marrow or substance.

Honour, rank and dignity are like the saffron, which never thrives so well as when trodden under foot. Beauty only attracts when it is free from any such aim. Self-conscious beauty loses its charm, and learning becomes a discredit and degenerates into pedantry, when we are puffed up by it.

Those who are punctilious about rank, title or precedence, both lay themselves open to criticism and degradation, and also throw contempt on all such things; because an honour which is valuable when freely paid, is worthless when sought for or exacted. When the peacock opens his showy tail, he exhibits the ugliness of his body beneath; and many flowers which are beautiful while growing, wither directly we gather them. And just as men who inhale mandragora from afar as they pass, find it sweet, while those who breathe it closely are made faint and ill by the same, so honour may be pleasant to those who merely taste it as they pass, without seeking or craving for it, but it will become very dangerous and hurtful to such as take delight in and feed upon it.

An active effort to acquire virtue is the first step towards goodness; but an active effort to acquire honour is the first step towards contempt and shame. A well-conditioned mind will not throw away its powers upon such sorry trifles as rank, position or outward forms—it has other things to do, and will leave all that to meaner minds. He who can find pearls will not stop to pick up shells; and so a man who aims at real goodness will not be keen about outward tokens of honour. Undoubtedly every one is justified in keeping his own place, and there is no want of humility in that so long as it is done simply and without contention. Just as our merchant-ships coming from Peru with gold and silver often bring apes and parrots likewise, because these cost but little and do not add to the weight of a cargo, so good men seeking to grow in grace can take their natural rank and position, so long as they are not engrossed by such things, and do not involve themselves in anxiety, contention or ill-will on their account. I am not speaking here of those whose position is public, or even of certain special private persons whose dignity may be important. In all such cases each man must move in his own sphere, with prudence and discretion, together with charity and courtesy.

Chapter V: On Interior Humility.

TO you however, my daughter, I would teach a deeper humility, for that of which I have been speaking is almost more truly to be called worldly wisdom than humility. There are some persons who dare not or will not think about the graces with which God has endowed them, fearing lest they should become self-complacent and vain-glorious; but they are quite wrong. For if, as the Angelic Doctor says, the real way of attaining to the Love of God is by a careful consideration of all His benefits given to us, then the better we realise these the more we shall love Him; and inasmuch as individual gifts are more acceptable than general gifts, so they ought to be more specially dwelt upon. Of a truth, nothing so tends to humble us before the Mercy of God as the multitude of His gifts to us; just as nothing so tends to humble us before His Justice as the multitude of our misdeeds. Let us consider what He has done for us, and what we have done contrary to His Will, and as we review our sins in detail, so let us review His Grace in the same. There is no fear that a perception of what He has given you will puff you up, so long as you keep steadily in mind that whatever is good in you is not of yourself. Do mules cease to be clumsy, stinking beasts because they are used to carry the dainty treasures and perfumes of a prince? "What hast thou that thou didst not receive? Now, if thou didst receive it, why dost thou glory as if thou hadst not received it?"[17] On the contrary, a lively appreciation of the grace given to you should make you humble, for appreciation begets gratitude. But if, when realising the gifts God has given you, any vanity should beset you, the infallible remedy is to turn to the thought of all our ingratitude, imperfection, and weakness. Any one who will calmly consider what he has done without God, cannot fail to realise that what he does with God is no merit of his own; and so we may rejoice in that which is good in us, and take pleasure in the fact, but we shall give all the glory to God Alone, Who Alone is its Author.

It was in this spirit that the Blessed Virgin confessed that God had done "great things" to her;[18] only that she might humble herself and exalt Him. "My soul doth magnify the Lord," she said, by reason of the gifts He had given her.

We are very apt to speak of ourselves as nought, as weakness itself, as the offscouring of the earth; but we should be very much vexed to be taken at our word and generally considered what we call ourselves. On the contrary, we often make-believe to run away and hide ourselves, merely to be followed and sought out; we pretend to take the lowest place, with the full intention of being honourably called to come up higher. But true humility does not affect to be humble, and is not given to make a display in lowly words. It seeks not only to conceal other virtues, but above all it seeks and desires to conceal itself; and if it were lawful to tell lies, or feign or give scandal, humility would perhaps sometimes affect a cloak of pride in order to hide itself utterly. Take my advice, my daughter, and either use no professions of humility, or else use them with a real mind corresponding to your outward expressions; never cast down your eyes without humbling your heart; and do not pretend to wish to be last and least, unless you really and sincerely mean it. I would make this so general a rule as to have no exception; only courtesy sometimes requires us to put forward those who obviously would not put themselves forward, but this is not deceitful or mock humility; and so with respect to certain expressions of regard which do not seem strictly true, but which are not dishonest, because the speaker really intends to give honour and respect to him to whom they are addressed; and even though the actual words may be somewhat excessive, there is no harm in them if they are the ordinary forms of society, though truly I wish that all our expressions were as nearly as possible regulated by real heart feeling in all truthfulness and simplicity. A really humble man would rather that some one else called him worthless and good-for-nothing, than say so of himself; at all events, if such things are said, he does not contradict them, but acquiesces contentedly, for it is his own opinion. We meet people who tell us that they leave mental prayer to those who are more perfect, not feeling themselves worthy

[17] 1 Cor. iv. 7.
[18] S. Luke i. 46-49.

of it; that they dare not communicate frequently, because they do not feel fit to do so; that they fear to bring discredit on religion if they profess it, through their weakness and frailty; while others decline to use their talents in the service of God and their neighbour, because, forsooth, they know their weakness, and are afraid of becoming proud if they do any good thing,—lest while helping others they might destroy themselves. But all this is unreal, and not merely a spurious but a vicious humility, which tacitly and secretly condemns God's gifts, and makes a pretext of lowliness while really exalting self-love, self-sufficiency, indolence, and evil tempers. "Ask thee a sign of the Lord thy God; ask it either in the depth or in the height above."[19] So spake the prophet to King Ahaz; but he answered, "I will not ask, neither will I tempt the Lord." Unhappy man! he affects to show exceeding reverence to God, and under a pretence of humility refuses to seek the grace offered by the Divine Goodness. Could he not see that when God wills to grant us a favour, it is mere pride to reject it, that God's gifts must needs be accepted, and that true humility lies in obedience and the most literal compliance with His Will! Well then, God's Will is that we should be perfect, uniting ourselves to Him, and imitating Him to the utmost of our powers. The proud man who trusts in himself may well undertake nothing, but the humble man is all the braver that he knows his own helplessness, and his courage waxes in proportion to his low opinion of himself, because all his trust is in God, Who delights to show forth His Power in our weakness, His Mercy in our misery. The safest course is humbly and piously to venture upon whatever may be considered profitable for us by those who undertake our spiritual guidance.

Nothing can be more foolish than to fancy we know that of which we are really ignorant; to affect knowledge while conscious that we are ignorant is intolerable vanity. For my part, I would rather not put forward that which I really do know, while on the other hand neither would I affect ignorance. When Charity requires it, you should readily and kindly impart to your neighbour not only that which is necessary for his instruction, but also what is profitable for his consolation. The same humility which conceals graces with a view to their preservation is ready to bring them forth at the bidding of Charity, with a view to their increase and perfection; therein reminding me of that tree in the Isles of Tylos,[20] which closes its beautiful carnation blossoms at night, only opening them to the rising sun, so that the natives say they go to sleep. Just so humility hides our earthly virtues and perfections, only expanding them at the call of Charity, which is not an earthly, but a heavenly, not a mere moral, but a divine virtue; the true sun of all virtues, which should all be ruled by it, so that any humility which controverts charity is unquestionably false.

I would not affect either folly or wisdom; for just as humility deters me from pretending to be wise, so simplicity and straightforwardness deter me from pretending to be foolish; and just as vanity is opposed to humility, so all affectation and pretence are opposed to honesty and simplicity. If certain eminent servants of God have feigned folly in order to be despised by the world, we may marvel, but not imitate them; for they had special and extraordinary reasons for doing extraordinary things, and cannot be used as a rule for such as we are. When David[21] danced more than was customary before the Ark of the Covenant, it was not with the intention of affecting folly, but simply as expressing the unbounded and extraordinary gladness of his heart. Michal his wife reproached him

---

[19] Isa. vii. 11, 12.
[20] Islands in the Persian Gulf.
[21] 2 Sam. vi. 14.

with his actions as folly, but he did not mind being "vile and base in his own sight," but declared himself willing to be despised for God's Sake. And so, if you should be despised for acts of genuine devotion, humility will enable you to rejoice in so blessed a contempt, the cause of which does not lie with you.

Chapter VI: Humility makes us rejoice in our own Abjection.

BUT, my daughter, I am going a step further, and I bid you everywhere and in everything to rejoice in your own abjection. Perhaps you will ask in reply what I mean by that. In Latin *abjection* means humility, and humility means abjection, so that when Our Lady says in the Magnificat that all generations shall call her blessed, because God hath regarded the low estate of His handmaiden,[22] she means that He has accepted her abjection and lowliness in order to fill her with graces and favours. Nevertheless, there is a difference between humility and abjection; for abjection is the poverty, vileness and littleness which exist in us, without our taking heed to them; but humility implies a real knowledge and voluntary recognition of that abjection. And the highest point of humility consists in not merely acknowledging one's abjection, but in taking pleasure therein, not from any want of breadth or courage, but to give the more glory to God's Divine Majesty, and to esteem one's neighbour more highly than one's self. This is what I would have you do; and to explain myself more clearly, let me tell you that the trials which afflict us are sometimes abject, sometimes honourable. NOW many people will accept the latter, but very few are willing to accept the former. Everybody respects and pities a pious hermit shivering in his worn-out garb; but let a poor gentleman or lady be in like case, and they are despised for it,—and so their poverty is abject. A religious receives a sharp rebuke from his superior meekly, or a child from his parent, and every one will call it obedience, mortification, wisdom; but let a knight or a lady accept the like from some one, albeit for the Love of God, and they will forthwith be accused of cowardice. This again is abject suffering. One person has a cancer in the arm, another in the face; the former only has the pain to bear, but the latter has also to endure all the disgust and repulsion caused by his disease; and this is abjection. And what I want to teach you is, that we should not merely rejoice in our trouble, which we do by means of patience, but we should also cherish the abjection, which is done by means of humility. Again, there are abject and honourable virtues; for the world generally despises patience, gentleness, simplicity, and even humility itself, while, on the contrary, it highly esteems prudence, valour, and liberality. Sometimes even there may be a like distinction drawn between acts of one and the same virtue—one being despised and the other respected. Thus almsgiving and forgiveness of injuries are both acts of charity, but while every one esteems the first, the world looks down upon the last. A young man or a girl who refuses to join in the excesses of dress, amusement, or gossip of their circle, is laughed at and criticised, and their self-restraint is called affectation or bigotry. Well, to rejoice in that is to rejoice in abjection. Or, to take another shape of the same thing. We are employed in visiting the sick—if I am sent to the most wretched cases, it is an abjection in the world's sight, and consequently I like it. If I am sent to those of a better class, it is an interior abjection, for there is less grace and merit in the work, and so I can accept that abjection. If one has a fall in the street, there is the ridiculous part of it to be borne, as well as the possible pain; and this is an abjection we

---

[22] S. Luke i. 48.

must accept. There are even some faults, in which there is no harm beyond their abjection, and although humility does not require us to commit them intentionally, it does require of us not to be disturbed at having committed them. I mean certain foolish acts, incivilities, and inadvertencies, which we ought to avoid as far as may be out of civility and decorum, but of which, if accidentally committed, we ought to accept the abjection heartily, out of humility. To go further still,—if in anger or excitement I have been led to use unseemly words, offending God and my neighbour thereby, I will repent heartily, and be very grieved for the offence, which I must try to repair to the utmost; but meanwhile I will accept the abjection and disgrace which will ensue, and were it possible to separate the two things, I ought earnestly to reject the sin, while I retained the abjection readily.

But while we rejoice in the abjection, we must nevertheless use all due and lawful means to remedy the evil whence it springs, especially when that evil is serious. Thus, if I have an abject disease in my face, I should endeavour to get it cured, although I do not wish to obliterate the abjection it has caused me. If I have done something awkward which hurts no one, I will not make excuses, because, although it was a failing, my own abjection is the only result; but if I have given offence or scandal through my carelessness or folly, I am bound to try and remedy it by a sincere apology. There are occasions when charity requires us not to acquiesce in abjection, but in such a case one ought the more to take it inwardly to heart for one's private edification.

Perhaps you will ask what are the most profitable forms of abjection. Unquestionably, those most helpful to our own souls, and most acceptable to God, are such as come accidentally, or in the natural course of events, because we have not chosen them ourselves, but simply accepted God's choice, which is always to be preferred to ours. But if we are constrained to choose, the greatest abjections are best; and the greatest is whatever is most contrary to one's individual inclination, so long as it is in conformity with one's vocation; for of a truth our self-will and self-pleasing mars many graces. Who can teach any of us truly to say with David, "I had rather be a doorkeeper in the house of my God, than to dwell in the tents of ungodliness"?[23] None, dear child, save He Who lived and died the scorn of men, and the outcast of the people, in order that we might be raised up. I have said things here which must seem very hard to contemplate, but, believe me, they will become sweet as honey when you try to put them in practice.

Chapter VII: How to combine due care for a Good Reputation with Humility.

PRAISE, honour, and glory are not bestowed on men for ordinary, but for extraordinary virtue. By praise we intend to lead men to appreciate the excellence of certain individuals; giving them honour is the expression of our own esteem for them; and I should say that glory is the combination of praise and honour from many persons. If praise and honour are like precious stones, glory is as an enamel thereof. Now, as humility forbids us to aim at excelling or being preferred to others, it likewise forbids us to aim at praise, honour, and glory; but it allows us to give heed, as the Wise Man says, to our good name, and that because a good name does not imply any one particular excellence, but a general straightforward integrity of purpose, which we may recognise in ourselves, and desire to be known as possessing, without any breach of humility. Humility might make

---

[23] Ps. lxxxiv. 10.

us indifferent even to a good reputation, were it not for charity's sake; but seeing that it is a groundwork of society, and without it we are not merely useless but positively harmful to the world, because of the scandal given by such a deficiency, therefore charity requires, and humility allows, us to desire and to maintain a good reputation with care.

Moreover, just as the leaves of a tree are valuable, not merely for beauty's sake, but also as a shelter to the tender fruit, so a good reputation, if not in itself very important, is still very useful, not only as an embellishment of life, but as a protection to our virtues, especially to those which are weakly. The necessity for acting up to our reputation, and being what we are thought to be, brings a strong though kindly motive power to bear upon a generous disposition. Let us foster all our virtues, my daughter, because they are pleasing to God, the Chief Aim of all we do. But just as when men preserve fruits, they do not only conserve them, but put them into suitable vessels, so while Divine Love is the main thing which keeps us in the ways of holiness, we may also find help from the effects of a good reputation. But it will not do to be over-eager or fanciful about it. Those who are so very sensitive about their reputation are like people who are perpetually physicking themselves for every carnal ailment; they mean to preserve their health, but practically they destroy it; and those who are so very fastidious over their good name are apt to lose it entirely, for they become fanciful, fretful, and disagreeable, provoking ill-natured remarks.

As a rule, indifference to insult and slander is a much more effectual remedy than resentment, wrath, and vengeance. Slander melts away beneath contempt, but indignation seems a sort of acknowledgment of its truth. Crocodiles never meddle with any but those who are afraid of them, and slander only persists in attacking people who are disturbed by it.

An excessive fear of losing reputation indicates mistrust as to its foundations, which are to be found in a good and true life. Those towns where the bridges are built of wood are very uneasy whenever a sign of flood appears, but they who possess stone bridges are not anxious unless some very unusual storm appears. And so a soul built up on solid Christian foundations can afford to despise the outpour of slanderous tongues, but those who know themselves to be weak are for ever disturbed and uneasy. Be sure, my daughter, that he who seeks to be well thought of by everybody will be esteemed by nobody, and those people deserve to be despised who are anxious to be highly esteemed by ungodly, unworthy men.

Reputation, after all, is but a signboard giving notice where virtue dwells, and virtue itself is always and everywhere preferable. Therefore, if it is said that you are a hypocrite because you are professedly devout, or if you are called a coward because you have forgiven an insult, despise all such accusations. Such judgments are the utterances of foolish men, and you must not give up what is right, even though your reputation suffer, for fruit is better than foliage, that is to say, an inward and spiritual gain is worth all external gains. We may take a jealous care of our reputation, but not idolise it; and while we desire not to displease good men, neither should we seek to please those that are evil. A man's natural adornment is his beard, and a woman's her hair; if either be torn out they may never grow again, but if only shaven or shorn, they will grow all the thicker; and in like manner, if our reputation be shorn or even shaven by slanderous tongues (of which David says, that "with lies they cut like a sharp razor"[24]), there is no need to be disturbed, it will soon spring again, if not brighter, at all events more substantial. But if it be lost

---

[24] Ps. lii. 2.

through our own vices or meanness or evil living, it will not be easily restored, because its roots are plucked up. And the root of a good name is to be found in virtue and honesty, which will always cause it to spring up afresh, however it may be assaulted. If your good name suffers from some empty pursuit, some useless habit, some unworthy friendship, they must be renounced, for a good name is worth more than any such idle indulgence; but if you are blamed or slandered for pious practices, earnestness in devotion, or whatever tends to win eternal life, then let your slanderers have their way, like dogs that bay at the moon! Be sure that, if they should succeed in rousing any evil impression against you (clipping the beard of your reputation, as it were), your good name will soon revive, and the razor of slander will strengthen your honour, just as the pruning-knife strengthens the vine and causes it to bring forth more abundant fruit. Let us keep Jesus Christ Crucified always before our eyes; let us go on trustfully and simply, but with discretion and wisdom, in His Service, and He will take care of our reputation; if He permits us to lose it, it will only be to give us better things, and to train us in a holy humility, one ounce of which is worth more than a thousand pounds of honour. If we are unjustly blamed, let us quietly meet calumny with truth; if calumny perseveres, let us persevere in humility; there is no surer shelter for our reputation or our soul than the Hand of God. Let us serve Him in good report or evil report alike, with S. Paul;[25] so that we may cry out with David, "For Thy Sake have I suffered reproof, shame hath covered my face."[26]

Of course certain crimes, so grievous that no one who can justify himself should remain silent, must be excepted; as, too, certain persons whose reputation closely affects the edification of others. In this case all theologians say that it is right quietly to seek reparation.

Chapter VIII: Gentleness towards others and Remedies against Anger.

THE holy Chrism, used by the Church according to apostolic tradition, is made of olive oil mingled with balm, which, among other things, are emblematic of two virtues very specially conspicuous in our Dear Lord Himself, and which He has specially commended to us, as though they, above all things, drew us to Him and taught us to imitate Him: "Take My yoke upon you, and learn of Me, for I am meek and lowly in heart."[27] Humility makes our lives acceptable to God, meekness makes us acceptable to men. Balm, as I said before, sinking to the bottom of all liquids, is a figure of humility; and oil, floating as it does to the top, is a figure of gentleness and cheerfulness, rising above all things, and excelling all things, the very flower of Love, which, so says S. Bernard, comes to perfection when it is not merely patient, but gentle and cheerful. Give heed, then, daughter, that you keep this mystic chrism of gentleness and humility in your heart, for it is a favourite device of the Enemy to make people content with a fair outside semblance of these graces, not examining their inner hearts, and so fancying themselves to be gentle and humble while they are far otherwise. And this is easily perceived, because, in spite of their ostentatious gentleness and humility, they are stirred up with pride and anger by the smallest wrong or contradiction. There is a popular belief that those who take the antidote commonly called "Saint Paul's gift,"[28] do not suffer from the viper's bite, provided, that

---

[25] 2 Cor. vi. 8.

[26] Ps. lxix. 7.

[27] S. Matt. xi. 29.

[28] "La grace de Saint Paul," in one old edition: in another, "la graisse de Saint Paul;" the latter

is, that the remedy be pure; and even so true gentleness and humility will avert the burning and swelling which contradiction is apt to excite in our hearts. If, when stung by slander or ill-nature, we wax proud and swell with anger, it is a proof that our gentleness and humility are unreal, and mere artificial show. When the Patriarch Joseph sent his brethren back from Egypt to his father's house, he only gave them one counsel, "See that ye fall not out by the way."[29] And so, my child, say I to you. This miserable life is but the road to a blessed life; do not let us fall out by the way one with another; let us go on with the company of our brethren gently, peacefully, and kindly. Most emphatically I say it, If possible, fall out with no one, and on no pretext whatever suffer your heart to admit anger and passion. S. James says, plainly and unreservedly, that "the wrath of man worketh not the righteousness of God."[30] Of course it is a duty to resist evil and to repress the faults of those for whom we are responsible, steadily and firmly, but gently and quietly. Nothing so stills the elephant when enraged as the sight of a lamb; nor does anything break the force of a cannon ball so well as wool. Correction given in anger, however tempered by reason, never has so much effect as that which is given altogether without anger; for the reasonable soul being naturally subject to reason, it is a mere tyranny which subjects it to passion, and whereinsoever reason is led by passion it becomes odious, and its just rule obnoxious. When a monarch visits a country peaceably the people are gratified and flattered; but if the king has to take his armies through the land, even on behalf of the public welfare, his visit is sure to be unwelcome and harmful, because, however strictly military discipline may be enforced, there will always be some mischief done to the people. Just so when reason prevails, and administers reproof, correction, and punishment in a calm spirit, although it be strict, every one approves and is content; but if reason be hindered by anger and vexation (which Saint Augustine calls her soldiers) there will be more fear than love, and reason itself will be despised and resisted. The same Saint Augustine, writing to Profuturus, says that it is better to refuse entrance to any even the least semblance of anger, however just; and that because once entered in, it is hard to be got rid of, and what was but a little mote soon waxes into a great beam. For if anger tarries till night, and the sun goes down upon our wrath (a thing expressly forbidden by the Apostle[31]), there is no longer any way of getting rid of it; it feeds upon endless false fancies; for no angry man ever yet but thought his anger just.

Depend upon it, it is better to learn how to live without being angry than to imagine one can moderate and control anger lawfully; and if through weakness and frailty one is overtaken by it, it is far better to put it away forcibly than to parley with it; for give anger ever so little way, and it will become master, like the serpent, who easily works in its body wherever it can once introduce its head. You will ask how to put away anger. My child, when you feel its first movements, collect yourself gently and seriously, not hastily or with impetuosity. Sometimes in a law court the officials who enforce quiet make more noise than those they affect to hush; and so, if you are impetuous in restraining your temper, you will throw your heart into worse confusion than before, and, amid the excitement, it will lose all self-control.

---

probably is the true reading, as there was a quack salve formerly in use for the bites of snakes, partly compounded of adders' fat. The name is obviously derived from S. Paul's adventure with the viper in the Island of Melita. (Acts xxviii.)

[29] Gen. xlv. 24.
[30] S. James i. 20.
[31] Eph. iv. 26.

Having thus gently exerted yourself, follow the advice which the aged S. Augustine gave to a younger Bishop, Auxilius. "Do," said he, "what a man should do." If you are like the Psalmist, ready to cry out, "Mine eye is consumed for very anger,"[32] go on to say, "Have mercy upon me, O Lord;" so that God may stretch forth His Right Hand and control your wrath. I mean, that when we feel stirred with anger, we ought to call upon God for help, like the Apostles, when they were tossed about with wind and storm, and He is sure to say, "Peace, be still." But even here I would again warn you, that your very prayers against the angry feelings which urge you should be gentle, calm, and without vehemence. Remember this rule in whatever remedies against anger you may seek. Further, directly you are conscious of an angry act, atone for the fault by some speedy act of meekness towards the person who excited your anger. It is a sovereign cure for untruthfulness to unsay what you have falsely said at once on detecting yourself in falsehood; and so, too, it is a good remedy for anger to make immediate amends by some opposite act of meekness. There is an old saying, that fresh wounds are soonest closed.

Moreover, when there is nothing to stir your wrath, lay up a store of meekness and kindliness, speaking and acting in things great and small as gently as possible. Remember that the Bride of the Canticles is described as not merely dropping honey, and milk also, from her lips, but as having it "under her tongue;"[33] that is to say, in her heart. So we must not only speak gently to our neighbour, but we must be filled, heart and soul, with gentleness; and we must not merely seek the sweetness of aromatic honey in courtesy and suavity with strangers, but also the sweetness of milk among those of our own household and our neighbours; a sweetness terribly lacking to some who are as angels abroad and devils at home!

Chapter IX: On Gentleness towards Ourselves.

ONE important direction in which to exercise gentleness, is with respect to ourselves, never growing irritated with one's self or one's imperfections; for although it is but reasonable that we should be displeased and grieved at our own faults, yet ought we to guard against a bitter, angry, or peevish feeling about them. Many people fall into the error of being angry because they have been angry, vexed because they have given way to vexation, thus keeping up a chronic state of irritation, which adds to the evil of what is past, and prepares the way for a fresh fall on the first occasion. Moreover, all this anger and irritation against one's self fosters pride, and springs entirely from self-love, which is disturbed and fretted by its own imperfection. What we want is a quiet, steady, firm displeasure at our own faults. A judge gives sentence more effectually speaking deliberately and calmly than if he be impetuous and passionate (for in the latter case he punishes not so much the actual faults before him, but what they appear to him to be); and so we can chasten ourselves far better by a quiet stedfast repentance, than by eager hasty ways of penitence, which, in fact, are proportioned not by the weight of our faults, but according to our feelings and inclinations. Thus one man who specially aims at purity will be intensely vexed with himself at some very trifling fault against it, while he looks upon some gross slander of which he has been guilty as a mere laughing matter. On the other hand, another will torment himself painfully over some slight exaggeration, while he

---

[32] In the English version it is, "Mine eye is consumed for very heaviness" (Ps. xxxi. 9), but in the Vulgate we find, "Conturbatus est in ira oculus meus." (Vulg. Ps. xxx. 10.)

[33] Cant. iv. 11.

altogether overlooks some serious offence against purity; and so on with other things. All this arises solely because men do not judge themselves by the light of reason, but under the influence of passion.

Believe me, my daughter, as a parent's tender affectionate remonstrance has far more weight with his child than anger and sternness, so, when we judge our own heart guilty, if we treat it gently, rather in a spirit of pity than anger, encouraging it to amendment, its repentance will be much deeper and more lasting than if stirred up in vehemence and wrath.

For instance:—Let me suppose that I am specially seeking to conquer vanity, and yet that I have fallen conspicuously into that sin;—instead of taking myself to task as abominable and wretched, for breaking so many resolutions, calling myself unfit to lift up my eyes to Heaven, as disloyal, faithless, and the like, I would deal pitifully and quietly with myself. "Poor heart! so soon fallen again into the snare! Well now, rise up again bravely and fall no more. Seek God's Mercy, hope in Him, ask Him to keep you from falling again, and begin to tread the pathway of humility afresh. We must be more on our guard henceforth." Such a course will be the surest way to making a stedfast substantial resolution against the special fault, to which should be added any external means suitable, and the advice of one's director. If any one does not find this gentle dealing sufficient, let him use sterner self-rebuke and admonition, provided only, that whatever indignation he may rouse against himself, he finally works it all up to a tender loving trust in God, treading in the footsteps of that great penitent who cried out to his troubled soul: "Why art thou so vexed, O my soul, and why art thou so disquieted within me? O put thy trust in God, for I will yet thank Him, Which is the help of my countenance, and my God."[34]

So then, when you have fallen, lift up your heart in quietness, humbling yourself deeply before God by reason of your frailty, without marvelling that you fell;—there is no cause to marvel because weakness is weak, or infirmity infirm. Heartily lament that you should have offended God, and begin anew to cultivate the lacking grace, with a very deep trust in His Mercy, and with a bold, brave heart.

Chapter X: We must attend to the Business of Life carefully, but without Eagerness or Over-anxiety.

THE care and diligence due to our ordinary business are very different from solicitude, anxiety and restlessness. The Angels care for our salvation and seek it diligently, but they are wholly free from anxiety and solicitude, for, whereas care and diligence naturally appertain to their love, anxiety would be wholly inconsistent with their happiness; for although care and diligence can go hand in hand with calmness and peace, those angelic properties could not unite with solicitude or anxiety, much less with over-eagerness.

Therefore, my daughter, be careful and diligent in all your affairs; God, Who commits them to you, wills you to give them your best attention; but strive not to be anxious and solicitous, that is to say, do not set about your work with restlessness and excitement, and do not give way to bustle and eagerness in what you do;—every form of excitement affects both judgment and reason, and hinders a right performance of the very thing which excites us.

[34] Ps. xlii. 11, 15.

Our Lord, rebuking Martha, said, "Thou art careful and troubled about many things."[35] If she had been simply careful, she would not have been troubled, but giving way to disquiet and anxiety, she grew eager and troubled, and for that our Lord reproved her. The rivers which flow gently through our plains bear barges of rich merchandise, and the gracious rains which fall softly on the land fertilise it to bear the fruits of the earth;— but when the rivers swell into torrents, they hinder commerce and devastate the country, and violent storms and tempests do the like. No work done with impetuosity and excitement was ever well done, and the old proverb, "Make haste slowly," is a good one,[36] Solomon says, "There is one that laboureth and taketh pains, and maketh haste, and is so much the more behind;"[37] we are always soon enough when we do well. The bumble bee makes far more noise and is more bustling than the honey bee, but it makes nought save wax—no honey; just so those who are restless and eager, or full of noisy solicitude, never do much or well. Flies harass us less by what they do than by reason of their multitude, and so great matters give us less disturbance than a multitude of small affairs. Accept the duties which come upon you quietly, and try to fulfil them methodically, one after another. If you attempt to do everything at once, or with confusion, you will only cumber yourself with your own exertions, and by dint of perplexing your mind you will probably be overwhelmed and accomplish nothing.

In all your affairs lean solely on God's Providence, by means of which alone your plans can succeed. Meanwhile, on your part work on in quiet co-operation with Him, and then rest satisfied that if you have trusted entirely to Him you will always obtain such a measure of success as is most profitable for you, whether it seems so or not to your own individual judgment.

Imitate a little child, whom one sees holding tight with one hand to its father, while with the other it gathers strawberries or blackberries from the wayside hedge. Even so, while you gather and use this world's goods with one hand, always let the other be fast in your Heavenly Father's Hand, and look round from time to time to make sure that He is satisfied with what you are doing, at home or abroad. Beware of letting go, under the idea of making or receiving more—if He forsakes you, you will fall to the ground at the first step. When your ordinary work or business is not specially engrossing, let your heart be fixed more on God than on it; and if the work be such as to require your undivided attention, then pause from time to time and look to God, even as navigators who make for the haven they would attain, by looking up at the heavens rather than down upon the deeps on which they sail. So doing, God will work with you, in you, and for you, and your work will be blessed.

Chapter XI: On Obedience.

LOVE alone leads to perfection, but the three chief means for acquiring it are obedience, chastity, and poverty. Obedience is a consecration of the heart, chastity of the body, and poverty of all worldly goods to the Love and Service of God. These are the three members of the Spiritual Cross, and all three must be raised upon the fourth, which is humility. I am not going here to speak of these three virtues as solemn vows, which only

---

[35] S. Luke x. 41.
[36] "Festina lente." "Il faut depescher tout bellement."
[37] Ecclus. xi. 11.

concern religious, nor even as ordinary vows, although when sought under the shelter of a vow all virtues receive an enhanced grace and merit; but it is not necessary for perfection that they should be undertaken as vows, so long as they are practised diligently. The three vows solemnly taken put a man into the state of perfection, whereas a diligent observance thereof brings him to perfection. For, observe, there is a great difference between the state of perfection and perfection itself, inasmuch as all prelates and religious are in the former, although unfortunately it is too obvious that by no means all attain to the latter. Let us then endeavour to practise these three virtues, according to our several vocations, for although we are not thereby called to a state of perfection, we may attain through them to perfection itself, and of a truth we are all bound to practise them, although not all after the same manner.

There are two kinds of obedience, one necessary, the other voluntary. The first includes a humble obedience to your ecclesiastical superiors, whether Pope, Bishop, Curate, or those commissioned by them. You are likewise bound to obey your civil superiors, king and magistrates; as also your domestic superiors, father, mother, master or mistress. Such obedience is called necessary, because no one can free himself from the duty of obeying these superiors, God having appointed them severally to bear rule over us. Therefore do you obey their commands as of right, but if you would be perfect, follow their counsels, and even their wishes as far as charity and prudence will allow: obey as to things acceptable; as when they bid you eat, or take recreation, for although there may be no great virtue in obedience in such a case, there is great harm in disobedience. Obey in things indifferent, as concerning questions of dress, coming and going, singing or keeping silence, for herein is a very laudable obedience. Obey in things hard, disagreeable and inconvenient, and therein lies a very perfect obedience. Moreover, obey quietly, without answering again, promptly, without delay, cheerfully, without reluctance; and, above all, render a loving obedience for His Sake Who became obedient even to the death of the Cross for our sake; Who, as Saint Bernard says, chose rather to resign His Life than His Obedience.

If you would acquire a ready obedience to superiors, accustom yourself to yield to your equals, giving way to their opinions where nothing wrong is involved, without arguing or peevishness; and adapt yourself easily to the wishes of your inferiors as far as you reasonably can, and forbear the exercise of stern authority so long as they do well.

It is a mistake for those who find it hard to pay a willing obedience to their natural superiors to suppose that if they were professed religious they would find it easy to obey.

Voluntary obedience is such as we undertake by our own choice, and which is not imposed by others. Persons do not choose their own King or Bishop, or parents—often not even their husband; but most people choose their confessor or director. And whether a person takes a vow of obedience to him (as Saint Theresa, beyond her formal vow to the Superior of her Order, bound herself by a simple vow to obey Father Gratian), or without any vow they resolve to obey their chosen spiritual guide, all such obedience is voluntary, because it depends upon our own will.

Obedience to lawful superiors is regulated by their official claims. Thus, in all public and legal matters, we are bound to obey our King; in ecclesiastical matters, our Bishop; in domestic matters, our father, master or husband; and in personal matters which concern the soul, our confessor or spiritual guide.

Seek to be directed in your religious exercises by your spiritual father, because thereby they will have double grace and virtue;—that which is inherent in that they are devout, and that which comes by reason of the spirit of obedience in which they are performed. Blessed indeed are the obedient, for God will never permit them to go astray.

Chapter XII: On Purity.

PURITY is the lily among virtues—by it men approach to the Angels. There is no beauty without purity, and human purity is chastity. We speak of the chaste as honest, and of the loss of purity as dishonour; purity is an intact thing, its converse is corruption. In a word, its special glory is in the spotless whiteness of soul and body.

No unlawful pleasures are compatible with chastity; the pure heart is like the mother of pearl which admits no drop of water save that which comes from Heaven,—it is closed to every attraction save such as are sanctified by holy matrimony. Close your heart to every questionable tenderness or delight, guard against all that is unprofitable though it may be lawful, and strive to avoid unduly fixing your heart even on that which in itself is right and good.

Every one has great need of this virtue: those living in widowhood need a brave chastity not only to forego present and future delights, but to resist the memories of the past, with which a happy married life naturally fills the imagination, softening and weakening the will. Saint Augustine lauds the purity of his beloved Alipius, who had altogether forgotten and despised the carnal pleasures in which his youth was passed. While fruits are whole, you may store them up securely, some in straw, some in sand or amid their own foliage, but once bruised there is no means of preserving them save with sugar or honey. Even so the purity which has never been tampered with may well be preserved to the end, but when once that has ceased to exist nothing can ensure its existence but the genuine devotion, which, as I have often said, is the very honey and sugar of the mind.

The unmarried need a very simple sensitive purity, which will drive away all over-curious thoughts, and teach them to despise all merely sensual satisfactions. The young are apt to imagine that of which they are ignorant to be wondrous sweet, and as the foolish moth hovers around a light, and, persisting in coming too near, perishes in its inquisitive folly, so they perish through their unwise approach to forbidden pleasures. And married people need a watchful purity whereby to keep God ever before them, and to seek all earthly happiness and delight through Him Alone, ever remembering that He has sanctified the state of holy matrimony by making it the type of His own union with the Church.

The Apostle says, "Follow peace with all men, and holiness, without which no man shall see the Lord:"[38] by which holiness he means purity. Of a truth, my daughter, without purity no one can ever see God;[39] nor can any hope to dwell in His tabernacle except he lead an uncorrupt life;[40] and our Blessed Lord Himself has promised the special blessing of beholding Him to those that are pure in heart.

---

[38] Heb. xii. 14.
[39] S. Matt. v. 8.
[40] Ps. xv. 2.

Chapter XIII: How to maintain Purity.

BE exceedingly quick in turning aside from the slightest thing leading to impurity, for it is an evil which approaches stealthily, and in which the very smallest beginnings are apt to grow rapidly. It is always easier to fly from such evils than to cure them.

Human bodies are like glasses, which cannot come into collision without risk of breaking; or to fruits, which, however fresh and ripe, are damaged by pressure. Never permit any one to take any manner of foolish liberty with you, since, although there may be no evil intention, the perfectness of purity is injured thereby.

Purity has its source in the heart, but it is in the body that its material results take shape, and therefore it may be forfeited both by the exterior senses and by the thoughts and desires of the heart. All lack of modesty in seeing, hearing, speaking, smelling, or touching, is impurity, especially when the heart takes pleasure therein. S. Paul says without any hesitation that impurity and uncleanness, or foolish and unseemly talking, are not to be "so much as named"[41] among Christians. The bee not only shuns all carrion, but abhors and flies far from the faintest smell proceeding therefrom. The Bride of the Canticles is represented with "hands dropping with myrrh."[42] a preservative against all corruption; her "lips are like a thread of scarlet," the type of modest words;[43] her eyes are "dove's eyes,"[44] clear and soft; her "nose is as the tower of Lebanon which looketh towards Damascus"[45] an incorruptible wood; her ears are hung with earrings of pure gold;[46] and even so the devout soul should be pure, honest and transparent in hand, lip, eye, ear, and the whole body.

Remember that there are things which blemish perfect purity, without being in themselves downright acts of impurity. Anything which tends to lessen its intense sensitiveness, or to cast the slightest shadow over it, is of this nature; and all evil thoughts or foolish acts of levity or heedlessness are as steps towards the most direct breaches of the law of chastity. Avoid the society of persons who are wanting in purity, especially if they are bold, as indeed impure people always are. If a foul animal licks the sweet almond tree its fruit becomes bitter; and so a corrupt pestilential man can scarcely hold communication with others, whether men or women, without damaging their perfect purity—their very glance is venomous, and their breath blighting like the basilisk. On the other hand, seek out good and pure men, read and ponder holy things; for the Word of God is pure, and it will make those pure who study it: wherefore David likens it to gold and precious stones.[47] Always abide close to Jesus Christ Crucified, both spiritually in meditation and actually in Holy Communion; for as all those who sleep upon the plant called Agnus castus become pure and chaste, so, if you rest your heart upon Our Dear Lord, the Very Lamb, Pure and Immaculate, you will find that soon both heart and soul will be purified of all spot or stain.

---

[41] Eph. v. 4.

[42] Cant. v. 5.

[43] iv. 3.

[44] i. 15.

[45] vii. 4.

[46] There is no mention of earrings in the Canticles, but S. Francis probably was writing from memory, and had in mind "Thy cheeks are comely with rows of jewels, thy neck with chains of gold." (i. 10.)

[47] Ps. cxix. 127.

Chapter XIV: On Poverty of Spirit amid Riches.

"BLESSED are the poor in spirit, for theirs is the Kingdom of God;"[48] and if so, woe be to the rich in spirit, for theirs must be the bitterness of hell. By rich in spirit I mean him whose riches engross his mind, or whose mind is buried in his riches. He is poor in spirit whose heart is not filled with the love of riches, whose mind is not set upon them. The halcyon builds its nest like a ball, and leaving but one little aperture in the upper part, launches it on the sea, so secure and impenetrable, that the waves carry it along without any water getting in, and it floats on the sea, superior, so to say, to the waves. And this, my child, is what your heart should be—open only to heaven, impenetrable to riches and earthly treasures. If you have them, keep your heart from attaching itself to them; let it maintain a higher level, and amidst riches be as though you had none,—superior to them. Do not let that mind which is the likeness of God cleave to mere earthly goods; let it always be raised above them, not sunk in them.

There is a wide difference between having poison and being poisoned. All apothecaries have poisons ready for special uses, but they are not consequently poisoned, because the poison is only in their shop, not in themselves; and so you may possess riches without being poisoned by them, so long as they are in your house or purse only, and not in your heart. It is the Christian's privilege to be rich in material things, and poor in attachment to them, thereby having the use of riches in this world and the merit of poverty in the next.

Of a truth, my daughter, no one will ever own themselves to be avaricious;—every one denies this contemptible vice:—men excuse themselves on the plea of providing for their children, or plead the duty of prudent forethought:—they never have too much, there is always some good reason for accumulating more; and even the most avaricious of men not only do not own to being such, but sincerely believe that they are not; and that because avarice is as a strong fever which is all the less felt as it rages most fiercely. Moses saw that sacred fire which burnt the bush without consuming it,[49] but the profane fire of avarice acts precisely the other way,—it consumes the miser, but without burning, for, amid its most intense heat, he believes himself to be deliciously cool, and imagines his insatiable thirst to be merely natural and right.

If you long earnestly, anxiously, and persistently after what you do not possess, it is all very well to say that you do not wish to get it unfairly, but you are all the time guilty of avarice. He who longs eagerly and anxiously to drink, though it may be water only, thereby indicates that he is feverish. I hardly think we can say that it is lawful to wish lawfully to possess that which is another's:—so doing we surely wish our own gain at the expense of that other? and he who possesses anything lawfully, surely has more right to possess it, than we to obtain it? Why should we desire that which is his? Even were the wish lawful, it is not charitable, for we should not like other men to desire what we possess, however lawfully. This was Ahab's sin when he sought to acquire Naboth's vineyard by lawful purchase, when Naboth lawfully desired to keep it himself;—he coveted it eagerly, continually, and anxiously, and so doing he displeased God.[50]

Do not allow yourself to wish for that which is your neighbour's until he wishes to part with it,—then his wish will altogether justify yours,—and I am quite willing that you

---

[48] S. Matt. v. 3.
[49] Exod. iii. 2.
[50] I Kings xxi.

should add to your means and possessions, provided it be not merely with strict justice, but kindly and charitably done. If you cleave closely to your possessions, and are cumbered with them, setting your heart and thoughts upon them, and restlessly anxious lest you should suffer loss, then, believe me, you are still somewhat feverish;—for fever patients drink the water we give them with an eagerness and satisfaction not common to those who are well.

It is not possible to take great pleasure in anything without becoming attached to it. If you lose property, and find yourself grievously afflicted at the loss, you may be sure that you were warmly attached to it;—there is no surer proof of affection for the thing lost than our sorrow at its loss.

Therefore, do not fix your longings on anything which you do not possess; do not let your heart rest in that which you have; do not grieve overmuch at the losses which may happen to you;—and then you may reasonably believe that although rich in fact, you are not so in affection, but that you are poor in spirit, and therefore blessed, for the Kingdom of Heaven is yours.

Chapter XV: How to exercise real Poverty, although actually Rich.

THE painter Parrhasius drew an ingenious and imaginative representation of the Athenians, ascribing sundry opposite qualities to them, calling them at once capricious, irascible, unjust, inconstant, courteous, merciful, compassionate, haughty, vain-glorious, humble, boastful, and cowardly;—and for my part, dear daughter, I would fain see united in your heart both riches and poverty, a great care and a great contempt for temporal things.

Do you take much greater pains than is the wont of worldly men to make your riches useful and fruitful? Are not the gardeners of a prince more diligent in cultivating and beautifying the royal gardens than if they were their own? Wherefore? Surely because these gardens are the king's, to whom his gardeners would fain render an acceptable service. My child, our possessions are not ours,—God has given them to us to cultivate, that we may make them fruitful and profitable in His Service, and so doing we shall please Him. And this we must do more earnestly than worldly men, for they look carefully after their property out of self-love, and we must work for the love of God. Now self-love is a restless, anxious, over-eager love, and so the work done on its behalf is troubled, vexatious, and unsatisfactory;—whereas the love of God is calm, peaceful, and tranquil, and so the work done for its sake, even in worldly things, is gentle, trustful, and quiet. Let us take such a quiet care to preserve, and even when practicable to increase, our temporal goods, according to the duties of our position,—this is acceptable to God for His Love's Sake.

But beware that you be not deceived by self-love, for sometimes it counterfeits the Love of God so cleverly that you may mistake one for the other. To avoid this, and to prevent a due care for your temporal interests from degenerating into avarice, it is needful often to practise a real poverty amid the riches with which God has endowed you.

To this end always dispose of a part of your means by giving them heartily to the poor; you impoverish yourself by whatever you give away. It is true that God will restore it to you, not only in the next world, but in this, for nothing brings so much temporal prosperity as free almsgiving, but meanwhile, you are sensibly poorer for what you give. Truly that is a holy and rich poverty which results from almsgiving.

Love the poor and poverty,—this love will make you truly poor, since, as Holy Scripture says, we become like to that we love.[51] Love makes lovers equal. "Who is weak and I am not weak?"[52] says St. Paul? He might have said, Who is poor and I am not poor? for it was love which made him like to those he loved; and so, if you love the poor, you will indeed share their poverty, and be poor like them.

And if you love the poor, seek them out, take pleasure in bringing them to your home, and in going to theirs, talk freely with them, and be ready to meet them, whether in Church or elsewhere. Let your tongue be poor with them in converse, but let your hands be rich to distribute out of your abundance. Are you prepared to go yet further, my child? not to stop at being poor like the poor, but even poorer still? The servant is not so great as his lord; do you be the servant of the poor, tend their sickbed with your own hands, be their cook, their needlewoman. O my daughter, such servitude is more glorious than royalty! How touchingly S. Louis, one of the greatest of kings, fulfilled this duty; serving the poor in their own houses, and daily causing three to eat at his own table, often himself eating the remains of their food in his loving humility. In his frequent visits to the hospitals he would select those afflicted with the most loathsome diseases, ulcers, cancer, and the like; and these he would tend, kneeling down and bare-headed, beholding the Saviour of the world in them, and cherishing them with all the tenderness of a mother's love. Saint Elizabeth of Hungary used to mix freely with the poor, and liked to dress in their homely garments amid her gay ladies. Surely these royal personages were poor amid their riches and rich in poverty.

Blessed are the poor in spirit, for theirs is the Kingdom of Heaven. In the Day of Judgment the King of prince and peasant will say to them, "I was an hungred, and ye gave Me meat, I was naked, and ye clothed Me; come, inherit the Kingdom prepared for you from the foundation of the world."[53]

Everybody finds themselves sometimes deficient in what they need, and put to inconvenience. A guest whom we would fain receive honorably arrives, and we cannot entertain him as we would; we want our costly apparel in one place, and it all happens to be somewhere else: all the wine in our cellar suddenly turns sour: we find ourselves accidentally in some country place where everything is wanting, room, bed, food, attendance: in short, the richest people may easily be without something they want, and that is practically to suffer poverty. Accept such occurrences cheerfully, rejoice in them, bear them willingly.

Again, if you are impoverished much or little by unforeseen events, such as storm, flood, fire, drought, theft, or lawsuit; then is the real time to practise poverty, accepting the loss quietly, and adapting yourself patiently to your altered circumstances. Esau and Jacob both came to their father with hairy hands,[54] but the hair on Jacob's hands did not grow from his skin, and could be torn off without pain; while that on Esau's hands being the natural growth of his skin, he would have cried out and resisted if any one had torn it off. So if our possessions are very close to our heart, and storm or thief tear them away, we shall break forth in impatient murmurs and lamentations. But if we only cleave to them with that solicitude which God wills us to have, and not with our whole heart, we shall see

---

[51] "Their abominations were according as they loved." Hosea ix. 10.

[52] 2 Cor. xi. 29.

[53] S. Matt. xxv. 34-36.

[54] Gen. xxvii.

them rent away without losing our sense of calmness. This is just the difference between the clothing of men and beasts; the beast's clothing grows on its flesh, and man's is only laid on so that it may be laid aside at will.

Chapter XVI: How to possess a rich Spirit amid real Poverty.

BUT if you are really poor, my daughter, for God's Sake be so in spirit; make a virtue of necessity, and turn that precious stone poverty to its true value. The brilliancy thereof is not perceived in this world, but nevertheless it is very great.

Patience then! you are in good company. Our Dear Lord, Our Lady, the Apostles, numberless Saints, both men and women, were poor, and although they might have been rich, disdained to be so. How many great ones of this world have gone through many difficulties to seek holy poverty amid hospitals and cloisters! What pains they took to find it, let S. Alexis, S. Paula, S. Paulinus, S. Angela, and many another witness; whereas to you, my child, it has come unasked—you have met poverty without seeking it—do you then embrace it as the beloved friend of Jesus Christ, Who was born, lived and died in poverty, and cherished it all His Life.

There are two great privileges connected with your poverty, through which you may acquire great merit. First, it is not your own choice, but God's Will alone, which has made you poor. Now, whatever we accept simply because it is God's Will is acceptable in His Sight, so long as we accept it heartily and out of love:—the less of self the more of God,—and a singlehearted acceptance of God's Will purifies any suffering very greatly.

The second privilege is, that this poverty is so very poor. There is a be-praised, caressed poverty, so petted and cared for, that it can hardly be called poor like the despised, contemned, neglected poverty which also exists. Now, most secular poverty is of this last kind, for those who are involuntarily poor, and cannot help themselves, are not much thought of, and for that very reason their poverty is poorer than that of religious, although religious poverty has a very special and excellent grace, through the intention and the vow by which it is accepted.

Do not complain then of your poverty, my daughter,—we only complain of that which is unwelcome, and if poverty is unwelcome to you, you are no longer poor in spirit. Do not fret under such assistance as is needful; therein lies one great grace of poverty. It were overambitious to aim at being poor without suffering any inconvenience, in other words, to have the credit of poverty and the convenience of riches.

Do not be ashamed of being poor, or of asking alms. Receive what is given you with humility, and accept a refusal meekly. Frequently call to mind Our Lady's journey into Egypt with her Holy Child, and of all the poverty, contempt and suffering they endured. If you follow their example you will indeed be rich amid your poverty.

Chapter XVII: On Friendship: Evil and Frivolous Friendship.

FOREMOST among the soul's affections is love. Love is the ruler of every motion of the heart; drawing all to itself, and making us like to that we love. Beware, then, my daughter, of harbouring any evil affection, or you too will become evil. And friendship is the most dangerous of all affections, because any other love may exist without much mental communication, but as friendship is founded thereon, it is hardly possible to be closely bound by its ties to any one without sharing in his qualities.

All love is not friendship, for one may love without any return, and friendship implies mutual love. Further, those who are bound by such affection must be conscious that it is reciprocal,—otherwise there may be love but not friendship; and moreover, there must be something communicated between the friends as a solid foundation of friendship.

Friendship varies according to these communications, and they vary according to that which people have to communicate. If men share false and vain things, their friendship will be false and vain; if that which is good and true, their friendship will be good and true, and the better that which is the staple of the bond, so much the better will the friendship be. That honey is best which is culled from the choicest flowers, and so friendship built upon the highest and purest intercommunion is the best. And just as a certain kind of honey brought from Pontus is poisonous, being made from aconite, so that those who eat it lose their senses, so the friendship which is based on unreal or evil grounds will itself be hollow and worthless.

Mere sensual intercourse is not worthy of the name of friendship; and were there nothing more in married love it would not deserve to bear the name; but inasmuch as that involves the participation of life, industry, possessions, affections, and an unalterable fidelity, marriage, when rightly understood, is a very real and holy friendship.

Whatever is founded on mere sensuality, vanity, or frivolity, is unworthy to be called friendship. I mean such attractions as are purely external; a sweet voice, personal beauty, and the cleverness or outward show which have great weight with some. You will often hear women and young people unhesitatingly decide that such an one is very delightful, very admirable, because he is good-looking, well-dressed, sings, or dances, or talks well. Even charlatans esteem the wittiest clown amongst them as their best man. But all these things are purely sensual, and the connections built on such foundation must be vain and frivolous, more fitly to be called trifling than friendship. They spring up chiefly among young people, who are easily fascinated by personal attractions, dress, and gossip—friendships in which the tailor and hairdresser have the chief part. How can such friendships be other than shortlived, melting away like snow wreaths in the sun!

Chapter XVIII: On Frivolous Attachments.

SUCH foolish attachments between man and woman without any matrimonial intentions as are called amourettes,—mere abortions, or rather phantoms of friendship,—must not, idle and empty as they are, profane the name of friendship or love. Yet such frivolous, contemptible attractions often snare the hearts of both men and women, and although they may end in downright sin, there is no such intention on the part of their victims, who consciously do but yield to foolish trifling and toying. Some such have no object beyond the actual indulgence of a passing inclination; others are excited by vanity, which takes pleasure in captivating hearts; some are stimulated by a combination of both these motives. But all such friendships are evil, hollow, and vain; evil, in that they often lead to sinful deeds, and draw the heart from God, and from the husband or wife who is its lawful owner; hollow, in that they are baseless and without root; vain, in that neither gain, honour, nor satisfaction can come from such. On the contrary, nothing comes of them but a loss of time and credit, and unreasoning excitement, mistrust, jealousy, and perturbation.

S. Gregory Nazianzen speaks very wisely on this subject, admonishing vain women, and his words are equally applicable to men:—"Your natural beauty will suffice your husband, but if it is exhibited to all, like a net spread before birds, what will be the end? You will be taken by whoever admires you, looks and glances will be exchanged, smiles and tender words, at first hesitatingly exchanged, but soon more boldly given and received. Far be it from me to describe the end, but this much I will say, nothing said or done by young men and women under such circumstances but is perilous. One act of levity leads to another, as the links in a chain." They who tamper with such things will fall into the trap. They fancy that they only mean to amuse themselves, but will not go too far. Little you know, forsooth! The tiny spark will burst into a flame, and, overpowering your heart, it will reduce your good resolutions to ashes, and your reputation to smoke. "Who will pity a charmer that is bitten with a serpent?" asks the Wise Man;[55] and with him I ask, Do you, in your folly, imagine that you can lightly handle love as you please? You think to trifle with it, but it will sting you cruelly, and then every one will mock you, and laugh at your foolish pretension to harbour a venomous serpent in your bosom, which has poisoned and lost alike your honour and your soul. What fatal blindness this to stake all that is most precious to man! Yes, I say it advisedly, for God desires to have us only for the sake of our soul, or the soul through our will, and our will for love's sake. Surely we have not by any means a sufficient store of love to offer God, and yet in our madness and folly we lavish and waste it on vain frivolous objects, as though we had enough and to spare. Our Dear Lord, Who demands nought save our love in return for our creation, preservation and redemption, will require a strict account of the senseless way in which we have frittered and wasted it. If He will call us to account for idle words, how will it be with respect to idle, foolish, pernicious friendships? Husbandmen know that the walnut tree is very harmful in a vineyard or field, because it absorbs the fatness of the land and draws it away from the other crops; its thick foliage overshadows and deprives them of sunshine; and, moreover, it attracts passers-by, who tread down and spoil all that is around while striving to gather its fruit. So with these foolish love affairs and the soul; they engross it, so that it is unable to bring forth good works; their superfluous foliage— flirtations, dallyings and idle talk—consume profitable time; and, moreover, they lead to so many temptations, distractions, suspicions, and the like, that the heart becomes altogether crushed and spoiled. Such follies not only banish Heavenly Love, they likewise drive out the fear of God, enervate the mind, and damage reputation. They may be the plaything of courts, but assuredly they are as a plague spot of the heart.[56]

Chapter XIX: Of Real Friendship.

DO you, my child, love every one with the pure love of charity, but have no friendship save with those whose intercourse is good and true, and the purer the bond which unites you so much higher will your friendship be. If your intercourse is based on science it is praiseworthy, still more if it arises from a participation in goodness, prudence, justice and the like; but if the bond of your mutual liking be charity, devotion and Christian perfection, God knows how very precious a friendship it is! Precious because it comes from God, because it tends to God, because God is the link that binds you, because it will last for ever in Him. Truly it is a blessed thing to love on earth as we hope to love in Heaven, and to begin that friendship here which is to endure for ever there. I am not now speaking of simple charity, a love due to all mankind, but of that spiritual friendship which binds souls

---

[55] Ecclus. xii. 13.
[56] "C'est en un mot le jouet des cours, mais la peste des coeurs."

together, leading them to share devotions and spiritual interests, so as to have but one mind between them. Such as these may well cry out, "Behold, how good and joyful a thing it is, brethren, to dwell together in unity!"[57] Even so, for the "precious ointment" of devotion trickles continually from one heart to the other, so that truly we may say that to such friendship the Lord promises His Blessing and life for evermore. To my mind all other friendship is but as a shadow with respect to this, its links mere fragile glass compared to the golden bond of true devotion. Do you form no other friendships. I say "form," because you have no right to cast aside or neglect the natural bonds which draw you to relations, connexions, benefactors or neighbours. My rules apply to those you deliberately choose to make. There are some who will tell you that you should avoid all special affection or friendship, as likely to engross the heart, distract the mind, excite jealousy, and what not. But they are confusing things. They have read in the works of saintly and devout writers that individual friendships and special intimacies are a great hindrance in the religious life, and therefore they suppose it to be the same with all the world, which is not at all the case. Whereas in a well-regulated community every one's aim is true devotion, there is no need for individual intercourse, which might exceed due limits;—in the world those who aim at a devout life require to be united one with another by a holy friendship, which excites, stimulates and encourages them in well-doing. Just as men traversing a plain have no need to hold one another up, as they have who are amid slippery mountain paths, so religious do not need the stay of individual friendships; but those who are living in the world require such for strength and comfort amid the difficulties which beset them. In the world all have not one aim, one mind, and therefore we must take to us congenial friends, nor is there any undue partiality in such attachments, which are but as the separation of good from evil, the sheep from the goats, the bee from the drone—a necessary separation.

No one can deny that our Dear Lord loved S. John, Lazarus, Martha, Magdalene, with a specially tender friendship, since we are told so in Holy Scripture; and we know that S. Paul dearly loved S. Mark, S. Petronilla, as S. Paul Timothy and Thecla.[58] S. Gregory Nazianzen boasts continually of his friendship with the great S. Basil, of which he says: "It seemed as though with two bodies we had but one soul, and if we may not believe those who say that all things are in all else, at least one must affirm that we were two in one, and one in two —the only object that both had being to grow in holiness, and to mould our present life to our future hopes, thereby forsaking this mortal world before our death." And S. Augustine says that S. Ambrose loved S. Monica by reason of her many virtues, and that she in return loved him as an Angel of God.

What need to affirm so unquestionable a fact! S. Jerome, S. Augustine, S. Gregory, S. Bernard, and all the most notable servants of God, have had special friendships, which in nowise hindered their perfection. S. Paul, in describing evil men, says that they were "without natural affection,"[59] i.e. without friendship. And S. Thomas, in common with

---

[57] Ps. cxxxiii. 1.

[58] S. Thecla (V.M.) was a native of Lycaonia, converted (so say S. Augustine, S. Ambrose, S. Epiphanius, and others of the Fathers) by S. Paul, who kindled so strong a love of virginity in her heart that she broke off her intended marriage, and devoted herself to Christ. She is said to have followed S. Paul in several of his journeys, and a very ancient Martyrology, which bears the name of S. Jerome, published by Florentinus, says that she was miraculously delivered unhurt from the persecutors' flames at Rome. It seems doubtful whether she died a natural or a martyr's death. The first Christian Emperors built a great Church at Seleucia, where she died.

[59] Rom. i. 31.

other philosophers, acknowledges that friendship is a virtue, and he certainly means individual friendships, because he says that we cannot bestow perfect friendship on many persons. So we see that the highest grace does not lie in being without friendships, but in having none which are not good, holy and true.

Chapter XX: Of the Difference between True and False Friendship.

TAKE notice, my child, that the honey of Heraclyum, which is so poisonous, altogether resembles that which is wholesome, and there is great danger of mistaking one for the other, or of mixing them, for the virtue of one would not counteract the harmfulness of the other. We must be on our guard not to be deceived in making friendships, especially between persons of the opposite sexes, for not unfrequently Satan deludes those who love one another. They may begin with a virtuous affection, but if discretion be lacking, frivolity will creep in, and then sensuality, till their love becomes carnal: even in spiritual love there is a danger if people are not on the watch, although it is not so easy to be deluded therein, inasmuch as the very purity and transparency of spiritual affection show Satan's stains more promptly. Consequently, when he seeks to interpose, he does it stealthily, and strives to insinuate impurity almost imperceptibly.

You may distinguish between worldly friendship and that which is good and holy, just as one distinguishes that poisonous honey from what is good—it is sweeter to the taste than ordinary honey, owing to the aconite infused;—and so worldly friendship is profuse in honeyed words, passionate endearments, commendations of beauty and sensual charms, while true friendship speaks a simple honest language, lauding nought save the Grace of God, its one only foundation. That strange honey causes giddiness; and so false friendship upsets the mind, makes its victim to totter in the ways of purity and devotion, inducing affected, mincing looks, sensual caresses, inordinate sighings, petty complaints of not being loved, slight but questionable familiarities, gallantries, embraces, and the like, which are sure precursors of evil; whereas true friendship is modest and straightforward in every glance, loving and pure in caresses, has no sighs save for Heaven, no complaints save that God is not loved sufficiently. That honey confuses the sight, and worldly friendship confuses the judgment, so that men think themselves right while doing evil, and assume their excuses and pretexts to be valid reasoning. They fear the light and love darkness; but true friendship is clear-sighted, and hides nothing—rather seeks to be seen of good men. Lastly, this poisonous honey leaves an exceeding bitter taste behind; and so false friendship turns to evil desires, upbraidings, slander, deceit, sorrow, confusion and jealousies, too often ending in downright sin; but pure friendship is always the same— modest, courteous and loving—knowing no change save an increasingly pure and perfect union, a type of the blessed friendships of Heaven.

When young people indulge in looks, words or actions which they would not like to be seen by their parents, husbands or confessors, it is a sure sign that they are damaging their conscience and their honour. Our Lady was troubled[60] when the Angel appeared to her in human form, because she was alone, and he spoke to her with flattering although heavenly words. O Saviour of the world, if purity itself fears an Angel in human shape, how much more need that our impurity should fear men, although they take the likeness of an Angel, if they speak words of earthliness and sensuality!

---

[60] S. Luke i. 29.

Chapter XXI: Remedies against Evil Friendships.

HOW are you to meet the swarm of foolish attachments, triflings, and undesirable inclinations which beset you? By turning sharply away, and thoroughly renouncing such vanities, flying to the Saviour's Cross, and clasping His Crown of thorns to your heart, so that these little foxes may not spoil your vines.[61] Beware of entering into any manner of treaty with the Enemy; do not delude yourself by listening to him while intending to reject him. For God's Sake, my daughter, be firm on all such occasions; the heart and ear are closely allied, and just as you would vainly seek to check the downward course of a mountain torrent, so difficult will you find it to keep the smooth words which enter in at the ear from finding their way down into the heart. Alcmeon says (what indeed Aristotle denies) that the goat breathes through its ears, not its nostrils. I know not whether this be so, but one thing I know, that our heart breathes through the ear, and that while it exhales its own thoughts through the mouth, it inhales those of others by the ear. Let us then carefully guard our ears against evil words which would speedily infect the heart. Never hearken to any indiscreet conversation whatsoever—never mind if you seem rude and uncourteous in rejecting all such. Always bear in mind that you have dedicated your heart to God, and offered your love to Him; so that it were sacrilege to deprive Him of one particle thereof. Do you rather renew the offering continually by fresh resolutions, entrenching yourself therein as in a fortress;—cry out to God, He will succour you, and His Love will shelter you, so that all your love may be kept for Him only.

If unhappily you are already entangled in the nets of any unreal affection, truly it is hard to set you free! But place yourself before His Divine Majesty, acknowledge the depth of your wretchedness, your weakness and vanity, and then with all the earnestness of purpose you can muster, arrest the budding evil, abjure your own empty promises, and renounce those you have received, and resolve with a firm, absolute will never again to indulge in any trifling or dallying with such matters.

If you can remove from the object of your unworthy affection, it is most desirable to do so. He who has been bitten by a viper cannot heal his wound in the presence of another suffering from the like injury, and so one bitten with a false fancy will not shake it off while near to his fellow-victim. Change of scene is very helpful in quieting the excitement and restlessness of sorrow or love. S. Ambrose tells a story in his Second Book on Penitence, of a young man, who coming home after a long journey quite cured of a foolish attachment, met the unworthy object of his former passion, who stopped him, saying, "Do you not know me, I am still myself?" "That may be," was the answer, "but I am not myself:"—so thoroughly and happily was he changed by absence. And S. Augustine tells us how, after the death of his dear friend, he soothed his grief by leaving Tagaste and going to Carthage.

But what is he to do, who cannot try this remedy? To such I would say, abstain from all private intercourse, all tender glances and smiles, and from every kind of communication which can feed the unholy flame. If it be necessary to speak at all, express clearly and tersely the eternal renunciation on which you have resolved. I say unhesitatingly to whosoever has become entangled in any such worthless love affairs, Cut it short, break it off—do not play with it, or pretend to untie the knot; cut it through, tear it asunder. There must be no dallying with an attachment which is incompatible with the Love of God.

---

[61] Cant. ii. 15.

But, you ask, after I have thus burst the chains of my unholy bondage, will no traces remain, and shall I not still carry the scars on my feet—that is, in my wounded affections? Not so, my child, if you have attained a due abhorrence of the evil; in that case all you will feel is an exceeding horror of your unworthy affection, and all appertaining thereto; no thought will linger in your breast concerning it save a true love of God. Or if, by reason of the imperfection of your repentance, any evil inclinations still hover round you, seek such a mental solitude as I have already described, retire into it as much as possible, and then by repeated efforts and ejaculations renounce your evil desires; abjure them heartily; read pious books more than is your wont; go more frequently to Confession and Communion; tell your director simply and humbly all that tempts and troubles you, if you can, or at all events take counsel with some faithful, wise friend. And never doubt but that God will set you free from all evil passions, if you are stedfast and devout on your part. Perhaps you will say that it is unkind, ungrateful, thus pitilessly to break off a friendship. Surely it were a happy unkindness which is acceptable to God; but of a truth, my child, you are committing no unkindness, rather conferring a great benefit on the person you love, for you break his chains as well as your own, and although at the moment he may not appreciate his gain, he will do so by and by, and will join you in thanksgiving, "Thou, Lord, hast broken my bonds in sunder. I will offer to Thee the sacrifice of thanksgiving, and will call upon the Name of the Lord."[62]

Chapter XXII: Further Advice concerning Intimacies.

FRIENDSHIP demands very close correspondence between those who love one another, otherwise it can never take root or continue. And together with the interchange of friendship, other things imperceptibly glide in, and a mutual giving and receiving of emotions and inclinations takes place; especially when we esteem the object of our love very highly, because then we so entirely open our heart to him, that his influence rules us altogether, whether for good or evil. The bees which make that oriental honey of which I spoke, seek to gather nought save honey, but with it they suck up the poisonous juices of the aconite on which they light. So here, my child, we must bear in mind what our Saviour said about putting out our money to the exchangers;[63] we must seek to make a good exchange, not receiving bad money and good alike, and learning to distinguish that which is valuable from what is worthless, since scarcely any one is free from some imperfection, nor is there any reason why we should adopt all our friend's faults as well as his friendship. Of course we should love him notwithstanding his faults, but without loving those faults; true friendship implies an interchange of what is good, not what is evil. As men who drag the river Tagus sift the gold from its sands and throw the latter back upon the shore, so true friends should sift the sand of imperfections and reject it. S. Gregory Nazianzen tells us how certain persons who loved and admired S. Basil were led to imitate even his external blemishes, his slow, abstracted manner of speaking, the cut of his beard, and his peculiar gait. And so we see husbands and wives, children, friends, who, by reason of their great affection for one another, acquire—either accidentally or designedly—many foolish little ways and tricks peculiar to each. This ought not to be; for every one has enough imperfections of their own without adding those of anybody else, and friendship requires no such thing; on the contrary, it rather constrains us to help one another in getting rid of

---

[62] Ps. cxvi. 14, 15.
[63] S. Matt. xxv. 27.

all sorts of imperfections. Of course we should bear with our friend's infirmities, but we should not encourage them, much less copy them.

Of course I am speaking of imperfections only, for, as to sins, we must neither imitate or tolerate these in our friends. That is but a sorry friendship which would see a friend perish, and not try to save him; would watch him dying of an abscess without daring to handle the knife of correction which would save him. True and living friendship cannot thrive amid sin. There is a tradition that the salamander extinguishes any fire into which it enters, and so sin destroys friendship. Friendship will banish a casual sin by brotherly correction, but if the sin be persistent, friendship dies out,—it can only live in a pure atmosphere. Much less can true friendship ever lead any one into sin; our friend becomes an enemy if he seeks to do so, and deserves to lose our friendship, and there is no surer proof of the hollowness of friendship than its profession between evil-doers. If we love a vicious person, our friendship will be vicious too; it will be like those to whom it is given.

Those who draw together for mere temporal profit, have no right to call their union friendship; it is not for love of one another that they unite, but for love of gain.

There are two sayings in Holy Scripture on which all Christian friendship should be built:—that of the Wise Man, "Whoso feareth the Lord shall direct his friendship aright;"[64] and that of S. James, "The friendship of the world is enmity with God."[65]

Chapter XXIII: On The Practice of Bodily Mortification.

IT has been said that if one writes a word on an almond, and then replace it carefully in its husk, and sow it, all the fruit borne by that tree will be marked by the word so inscribed. For my own part, I never could approve of beginning to reform any one by merely external things,—dress, the arrangement of hair, and outward show. On the contrary, it seems to me that one should begin from within. "Turn ye to Me with all your heart;"[66] "My son, give Me thine heart;"[67] for as the heart is the fount whence all our actions spring, they will be according to what it is. And the Heavenly Bridegroom, calling the soul, says, "Set Me as a seal upon thine heart, as a seal upon thine arm."[68] Yes verily, for whosoever has Jesus Christ in his heart will soon show it in all his external actions. Therefore, my daughter, above all things I would write that precious and Holy Name JESUS in your heart, certain that having done so, your life—like the almond tree in the fable—will bear the stamp of that Saving Name in every act; and if the Dear Lord dwells within your heart, He will live in your every action, and will be traced in every member and part of you, so that you will be able to say with S. Paul, "I live, yet not I, but Christ liveth in me."[69] In a word, whosoever gains the heart has won the whole man. But this heart needs to be trained in its external conduct, so that it may display not merely a true devotion, but also wisdom and discretion. To this end I would make one or two suggestions.

If you are able to fast, you will do well to observe some days beyond what are ordered by the Church, for besides the ordinary effect of fasting in raising the mind, subduing the

---

[64] Ecclus. vi. 17.
[65] S. James iv. 4.
[66] Joel ii. 12.
[67] Prov. xxiii. 26.
[68] Cant. viii. 6.
[69] Gal. ii. 20.

flesh, confirming goodness, and obtaining a heavenly reward, it is also a great matter to be able to control greediness, and to keep the sensual appetites and the whole body subject to the law of the Spirit; and although we may be able to do but little, the enemy nevertheless stands more in awe of those whom he knows can fast. The early Christians selected Wednesday, Friday and Saturday as days of abstinence. Do you follow therein according as your own devotion and your director's discretion may appoint.

I am prepared to say with S. Jerome (to the pious Leta) that I disapprove of long and immoderate fasting, especially for the young. I have learnt by experience that when the colt grows weary it turns aside, and so when young people become delicate by excessive fasting, they readily take to self-indulgence. The stag does not run with due speed either when over fat or too thin, and we are in peril of temptation both when the body is overfed or underfed; in the one case it grows indolent, in the other it sinks through depression, and if we cannot bear with it in the first case, neither can it bear with us in the last. A want of moderation in the use of fasting, discipline and austerity has made many a one useless in works of charity during the best years of his life, as happened to S. Bernard, who repented of his excessive austerity. Those who misuse the body at the outset will have to indulge it overmuch at last. Surely it were wiser to deal sensibly with it, and treat it according to the work and service required by each man's state of life.

Fasting and labour both exhaust and subdue the body. If your work is necessary or profitable to God's Glory, I would rather see you bear the exhaustion of work than of fasting. Such is the mind of the Church, who dispenses those who are called to work for God or their neighbour even from her prescribed fasts. One man finds it hard to fast, another finds it as hard to attend the sick, to visit prisons, to hear confessions, preach, minister to the afflicted, pray, and the like. And the last hardship is better than the other; for while it subdues the flesh equally, it brings forth better fruit. And as a general rule it is better to preserve more bodily strength than is absolutely necessary, than to damage it more than is necessary. Bodily strength can always be lowered if needful, but we cannot restore it at will. It seems to me that we ought to have in great reverence that which our Saviour and Redeemer Jesus Christ said to His disciples, "Eat such things as are set before you."[70] To my mind there is more virtue in eating whatever is offered you just as it comes, whether you like it or not, than in always choosing what is worst; for although the latter course may seem more ascetic, the former involves greater submission of will, because by it you give up not merely your taste, but your choice; and it is no slight austerity to hold up one's likings in one's hand, and subject them to all manner of accidents. Furthermore, this kind of mortification makes no show, inconveniences no one, and is admirably adapted to social life. To be always discarding one dish for another, examining everything, suspicious as to everything, making a fuss over every morsel—all this to my mind is contemptible, and implies too much thought of meats and platters. To my mind there was more austerity in S. Bernard's drinking oil by mistake for wine or water than if he had deliberately drunk wormwood, for it showed that he was not thinking of what he drank. And the real meaning of those sacred words, "Eat such things as are set before you," lies in such an indifference to what one eats and drinks. I should make an exception of any food which is unwholesome, or likely to be injurious to the mind's energies, such as certain hot, spiced, or stimulating dishes; as also on certain occasions when nature requires to be refreshed and invigorated in order to perform the work needful for God's Glory. At

---

[70] S. Luke x. 8.

all times a constant habitual moderation is better than occasional excessive abstinence, alternated with great indulgence. The discipline has a surprising effect in rousing the taste for devotion, if used moderately. The body is greatly subdued by the use of the hair shirt, but it is not fit for ordinary people, married persons, those who are delicate, or who have to bear considerable fatigue. On certain days of special penitence it may be used, subject to the counsel of a judicious confessor.

Every one must take so much of the night for sleep, as his constitution, and the profitable performance of his day's work, requires. Holy Scripture continually teaches us that the morning is the best and most profitable part of the day, and so do the examples of the Saints and our natural reason. Our Lord Himself is called the Sun, risinig upon the earth, and our Lady the Day-star; and so I think it is wise to go to sleep early at night in order to be ready to waken and rise early. Moreover, that is the pleasantest, the freshest, and the freest hour of the day,—the very birds stimulate us to rise and sing God's praises. Early rising promotes both health and holiness.

Balaam saddled his ass and went to meet Balak, but his heart was not right with God, and therefore the Angel of the Lord stood in the way, with a sword in his hand to kill him, had not the ass three times turned out of the way as though she were restive; whereat Balaam smote her with his staff, until at last she fell down beneath him, and her mouth being miraculously opened, she said unto him, "What have I done unto thee that thou hast smitten me these three times?" Then Balaam's eyes were opened, and he saw the Angel, who said to him, "Wherefore hast thou smitten thine ass? unless she had turned from me surely now I had slain thee, and saved her alive." Then Balaam said to the Angel of the Lord, "I have sinned, for I knew not that thou stoodest in the way against me."[71] Do you see, my daughter, it was Balaam who did wrong, but he beat the poor ass, who was not to blame. It is often so with us. A woman's husband or child is ill, and forthwith she has recourse to fasting, the discipline, and hair shirt, even as David did on a like occasion.[72] But, dear friend, you are smiting the ass! you afflict your body, which can do nothing when God stands before you with His sword unsheathed. Rather correct your heart, which idolises your husband, and has indulged your child, letting him give way to pride, vanity, and ambition. Or, again, a man falls often into fleshly sins, and the voice of conscience stands before him in the way, rousing him to a holy fear. Then recollecting himself, he begins to abuse his flesh for betraying him, he deals out strict fasts, severe discipline, and the like, to it, and meanwhile the poor flesh might cry out like Balaam's ass, Why smitest thou me? It is you yourself, O my soul, that are guilty. Wherefore do you force me into evil, using my eyes, and hands, and lips for unholy purposes, and tormenting me with evil imaginations? Do you entertain only good thoughts, and I shall feel no unholy impulses, frequent none save pious people, and I shall not be kindled with guilty fire. You cast me yourself into the flames, and bid me not to burn! you fill my eyes with smoke, and wonder that they are inflamed! But God bids you deal chiefly with your heart, for that is the chief offender. When a man suffers from the itch, there is less need to bathe him, and cleanse the surface, than to purify his blood; and so, in order to purge our vices, no doubt it is well to mortify the flesh, but above all it is necessary to purify the affections and renew the heart. Make it a rule then never to undertake any bodily austerities without the advice of your spiritual guide.

---

[71] Numb. xxii.
[72] 2 Sam. xii. 16.

Chapter XXIV: Of Society and Solitude.

EITHER to seek or to shun society is a fault in one striving to lead a devout life in the world, such as I am now speaking of. To shun society implies indifference and contempt for one's neighbours; and to seek it savours of idleness and uselessness. We are told to love one's neighbour as one's self. In token that we love him, we must not avoid being with him, and the test of loving one's self is to be happy when alone. "Think first on thyself," says S. Bernard, "and then on other men." So that, if nothing obliges you to mix in society either at home or abroad, retire within yourself, and hold converse with your own heart. But if friends come to you, or there is fitting cause for you to go forth into society, then, my daughter, by all means go, and meet your neighbour with a kindly glance and a kindly heart.

Bad society is all such intercourse with others as has an evil object, or when those with whom we mix are vicious, indiscreet, or profligate. From such as these turn away, like the bee from a dunghill. The breath and saliva of those who have been bitten by a mad dog is dangerous, especially to children or delicate people, and in like manner it is perilous to associate with vicious, reckless people, above all to those whose devotion is still weakly and unstable.

There is a kind of social intercourse which merely tends to refresh us after more serious labour, and although it would not be well to indulge in this to excess, there is no harm in enjoying it during your leisure hours.

Other social meetings are in compliance with courtesy, such as mutual visits, and certain assemblies with a view to pay respect to one another. As to these, without being a slave to them, it is well not to despise them altogether, but to bear one's own due part in them quietly, avoiding rudeness and frivolity. Lastly, there is a profitable society;—that of good devout people, and it will always be very good for you to meet with them. Vines grown amid olivetrees are wont to bear rich grapes, and he who frequents the society of good people will imbibe some of their goodness. The bumble bee makes no honey alone, but if it falls among bees it works with them. Our own devout life will be materially helped by intercourse with other devout souls.

Simplicity, gentleness and modesty are to be desired in all society;—there are some people who are so full of affectation in whatever they do that every one is annoyed by them. A man who could not move without counting his steps, or speak without singing, would be very tiresome to everybody, and just so any one who is artificial in all he does spoils the pleasure of society; and moreover such people are generally more or less self-conceited. A quiet cheerfulness should be your aim in society. S. Romuald and S. Anthony are greatly lauded because, notwithstanding their asceticism, their countenance and words were always courteous and cheerful. I would say to you with S. Paul, "Rejoice with them that do rejoice;"[73] and again, "Rejoice in the Lord alway: let your moderation be known unto all men."[74] And if you would rejoice in the Lord, the cause of your joy must not only be lawful, but worthy; and remember this, because there are lawful things which nevertheless are not good; and in order that your moderation may be known, you must avoid all that is impertinent and uncivil, which is sure to be wrong. Depreciating this person, slandering another, wounding a third, stimulating the folly of a fourth—all such things, however amusing, are foolish and impertinent.

---

[73] Rom. xii. 15.
[74] Phil. iv. 4, 5.

I have already spoken of that mental solitude into which you can retire when amid the greatest crowd, and furthermore you should learn to like a real material solitude. Not that I want you to fly to a desert like S. Mary of Egypt, S. Paul, S. Anthony, Arsenius, or the other hermits, but it is well for you to retire sometimes within your own chamber or garden, or wheresoever you can best recollect your mind, and refresh your soul with good and holy thoughts, and some spiritual reading, as the good Bishop of Nazianzum tells us was his custom. "I was walking alone," he says, "at sunset, on the seashore, a recreation I am wont to take in order somewhat to lay aside my daily worries." And S. Augustine says that he often used to go into S. Ambrose' room—his door was open to every one,—and after watching him absorbed in reading for a time, he would retire without speaking, fearing to interrupt the Bishop, who had so little time for refreshing his mind amid the burden of his heavy duties. And we read how when the disciples came to Jesus, and told Him all they had been doing and preaching, He said to them, "Come ye yourselves apart into a desert place, and rest awhile."[75]

Chapter XXV: On Modesty in Dress.

S. PAUL expresses his desire that all Christian women should wear "modest apparel, with shamefacedness and sobriety;"[76] —and for that matter he certainly meant that men should do so likewise. Now, modesty in dress and its appurtenances depends upon the quality, the fashion and the cleanliness thereof. As to cleanliness, that should be uniform, and we should never, if possible, let any part of our dress be soiled or stained. External seemliness is a sort of indication of inward good order, and God requires those who minister at His Altar, or minister in holy things, to be attentive in respect of personal cleanliness. As to the quality and fashion of clothes, modesty in these points must depend upon various circumstances, age, season, condition, the society we move in, and the special occasion. Most people dress better on a high festival than at other times; in Lent, or other penitential seasons, they lay aside all gay apparel; at a wedding they wear wedding garments, at a funeral, mourning garb; and at a king's court the dress which would be unsuitable at home is suitable. A wife may and should adorn herself according to her husband's wishes when he is present;—if she does as much in his absence one is disposed to ask in whose eyes she seeks to shine? We may grant somewhat greater latitude to maidens, who may lawfully desire to attract many, although only with the view of ultimately winning one in holy matrimony. Neither do I blame such widows as purpose to marry again for adorning themselves, provided they keep within such limits as are seemly for those who are at the head of a family, and who have gone through the sobering sorrows of widowhood. But for those who are widows indeed, in heart as well as outwardly, humility, modesty and devotion are the only suitable ornaments. If they seek to attract men's admiration they are not widows indeed, and if they have no such intention, why should they wear its tokens? Those who do not mean to entertain guests should take down their signboard. So, again, every one laughs at old women who affect youthful graces,—such things are only tolerable in the young.

Always be neat, do not ever permit any disorder or untidiness about you. There is a certain disrespect to those with whom you mix in slovenly dress; but at the same time

[75] S. Mark vi. 30, 31.
[76] 1 Tim. ii. 9.

avoid all vanity, peculiarity, and fancifulness. As far as may be, keep to what is simple and unpretending—such dress is the best adornment of beauty and the best excuse for ugliness. S. Peter bids women not to be over particular in dressing their hair. Every one despises a man as effeminate who lowers himself by such things, and we count a vain woman as wanting in modesty, or at all events what she has becomes smothered among her trinkets and furbelows. They say that they mean no harm, but I should reply that the devil will contrive to get some harm out of it all. For my own part I should like my devout man or woman to be the best dressed person in the company, but the least fine or splendid, and adorned, as S. Peter says, with "the ornament of a meek and quiet spirit."[77] S. Louis said that the right thing is for every one to dress according to his position, so that good and sensible people should not be able to say they are over-dressed, or younger gayer ones that they are under-dressed. But if these last are not satisfied with what is modest and seemly, they must be content with the approbation of the elders.

Chapter XXVI: Of Conversation; and, first, how to Speak of God.

PHYSICIANS judge to a great extent as to the health or disease of a man by the state of his tongue, and our words are a true test of the state of our soul. "By thy words thou shalt be justified, and by thy words thou shalt be condemned,"[78] the Saviour says. We are apt to apply the hand quickly to the place where we feel pain, and so too the tongue is quick to point out what we love.

If you love God heartily, my child, you will often speak of Him among your relations, household and familiar friends, and that because "the mouth of the righteous speaketh wisdom, and his tongue talketh of judgment."[79] Even as the bee touches nought save honey with his tongue, so should your lips be ever sweetened with your God, knowing nothing more pleasant than to praise and bless His Holy Name,—as we are told that when S. Francis uttered the Name of the Lord, he seemed to feel the sweetness lingering on his lips, and could not let it go. But always remember, when you speak of God, that He is God; and speak reverently and with devotion,—not affectedly or as if you were preaching, but with a spirit of meekness, love, and humility; dropping honey from your lips (like the Bride in the Canticles[80]) in devout and pious words, as you speak to one or another around, in your secret heart the while asking God to let this soft heavenly dew sink into their minds as they hearken. And remember very specially always to fulfil this angelic task meekly and lovingly, not as though you were reproving others, but rather winning them. It is wonderful how attractive a gentle, pleasant manner is, and how much it wins hearts.

Take care, then, never to speak of God, or those things which concern Him, in a merely formal, conventional manner; but with earnestness and devotion, avoiding the affected way in which some professedly religious people are perpetually interlarding their conversation with pious words and sayings, after a most unseasonable and unthinking manner. Too often they imagine that they really are themselves as pious as their words, which probably is not the case.

---

[77] 1 Pet. iii. 3.
[78] S. Matt. xii. 37.
[79] Ps. xxxvii. 30.
[80] Cant. iv. 11.

Chapter XXVII: Of Unseemly Words, and the Respect due to Others.

SAINT JAMES says, "If any man offend not in word, the same is, a perfect man."[81] Beware most watchfully against ever uttering any unseemly expression; even though you may have no evil intention, those who hear it may receive it with a different meaning. An impure word falling upon a weak mind spreads its infection like a drop of oil on a garment, and sometimes it will take such a hold of the heart, as to fill it with an infinitude of lascivious thoughts and temptations. The body is poisoned through the mouth, even so is the heart through the ear; and the tongue which does the deed is a murderer, even when the venom it has infused is counteracted by some antidote preoccupying the listener's heart. It was not the speaker's fault that he did not slay that soul. Nor let any one answer that he meant no harm. Our Lord, Who knoweth the hearts of men, has said, "Out of the abundance of the heart the mouth speaketh."[82] And even if we do mean no harm, the Evil One means a great deal, and he will use those idle words as a sharp weapon against some neighbour's heart. It is said that those who eat the plant called Angelica always have a sweet, pleasant breath; and those who cherish the angelic virtues of purity and modesty, will always speak simply, courteously, and modestly. As to unclean and light-minded talk, S. Paul says such things should not even be named[83] among us, for, as he elsewhere tells us, "Evil communications corrupt good manners."[84]

Those impure words which are spoken in disguise, and with an affectation of reserve, are the most harmful of all; for just as the sharper the point of a dart, so much deeper it will pierce the flesh, so the sharper an unholy word, the more it penetrates the heart. And as for those who think to show themselves knowing when they say such things, they do not even understand the first object of mutual intercourse among men, who ought rather to be like a hive of bees gathering to make honey by good and useful conversation, than like a wasps' nest, feeding on corruption. If any impertinent person addresses you in unseemly language, show that you are displeased by turning away, or by whatever other method your discretion may indicate.

One of the most evil dispositions possible is that which satirises and turns everything to ridicule. God abhors this vice, and has sometimes punished it in a marked manner. Nothing is so opposed to charity, much more to a devout spirit, as contempt and depreciation of one's neighbour, and where satire and ridicule exist contempt must be. Therefore contempt is a grievous sin, and our spiritual doctors have well said that ridicule is the greatest sin we can commit in word against our neighbour, inasmuch as when we offend him in any other way, there may still be some respect for him in our heart, but we are sure to despise those whom we ridicule.

There is a light-hearted talk, full of modest life and gaiety, which the Greeks called *Eutrapelia*, and which we should call good conversation, by which we may find an innocent and kindly amusement out of the trifling occurrences which human imperfections afford. Only beware of letting this seemly mirth go too far, till it becomes ridicule. Ridicule excites mirth at the expense of one's neighbour; seemly mirth and playful fun never lose sight of a trustful, kindly courtesy, which can wound no one. When the religious around him would fain have discussed serious matters with S. Louis at meal-

---

[81] S. James iii. 2.
[82] S. Matt. xii. 34.
[83] Eph. v. 3.
[84] 1 Cor. xv. 33.

times, he used to say, "This is not the time for grave discussion, but for general conversation and cheerful recreation,"—out of consideration for his courtiers. But, my daughter, let our recreation always be so spent, that we may win all eternity through devotion.

Chapter XXVIII: Of Hasty Judgments.

JUDGE not, and ye shall not be judged," said the Saviour of our souls; "condemn not, and ye shall not be condemned:"[85] and the Apostle S. Paul, "Judge nothing before the time, until the Lord come, Who both will bring to light the hidden things of darkness, and will make manifest the counsels of the hearts."[86] Of a truth, hasty judgments are most displeasing to God, and men's judgments are hasty, because we are not judges one of another, and by judging we usurp our Lord's own office. Man's judgment is hasty, because the chief malice of sin lies in the intention and counsel of the heart, which is shrouded in darkness to us. Moreover, man's judgments are hasty, because each one has enough to do in judging himself, without undertaking to judge his neighbour. If we would not be judged, it behoves us alike not to judge others, and to judge ourselves. Our Lord forbids the one, His Apostle enjoins the other, saying, "If we would judge ourselves, we should not be judged."[87] But alas! for the most part we precisely reverse these precepts, judging our neighbour, which is forbidden on all sides, while rarely judging ourselves, as we are told to do.

We must proceed to rectify rash judgments, according to their cause. Some hearts there are so bitter and harsh by nature, that everything turns bitter under their touch; men who, in the Prophet's words, "turn judgment to wormwood, and leave off righteousness in the earth."[88] Such as these greatly need to be dealt with by some wise spiritual physician, for this bitterness being natural to them, it is hard to conquer; and although it be rather an imperfection than a sin, still it is very dangerous, because it gives rise to and fosters rash judgments and slander within the heart. Others there are who are guilty of rash judgments less out of a bitter spirit than from pride, supposing to exalt their own credit by disparaging that of others. These are self-sufficient, presumptuous people, who stand so high in their own conceit that they despise all else as mean and worthless. It was the foolish Pharisee who said, "I am not as other men are."[89] Others, again, have not quite such overt pride, but rather a lurking little satisfaction in beholding what is wrong in others, in order to appreciate more fully what they believe to be their own superiority. This satisfaction is so well concealed, so nearly imperceptible, that it requires a clear sight to discover it, and those who experience it need that it be pointed out to them. Some there are who seek to excuse and justify themselves to their own conscience, by assuming readily that others are guilty of the same faults, or as great ones, vainly imagining that the sin becomes less culpable when shared by many. Others, again, give way to rash judgments merely because they take pleasure in a philosophic analysis and dissection of their neighbours' characters; and if by ill luck they chance now and then to be right, their presumption and love of criticism strengthens almost incurably.

---

[85] S. Luke vi. 37.
[86] 1 Cor. iv. 5.
[87] 1 Cor. xi. 31.
[88] Amos v. 7.
[89] S. Luke xviii. 11.

Then there are people whose judgment is solely formed by inclination; who always think well of those they like, and ill of those they dislike. To this, however, there is one rare exception, which nevertheless we do sometimes meet, when an excessive love provokes a false judgment concerning its object; the hideous result of a diseased, faulty, restless affection, which is in fact jealousy; an evil passion capable, as everybody knows, of condemning others of perfidy and adultery upon the most trivial and fanciful ground. In like manner, fear, ambition, and other moral infirmities often tend largely to produce suspicion and rash judgments.

What remedy can we apply? They who drink the juice of the Ethiopian herb *Ophiusa* imagine that they see serpents and horrors everywhere; and those who drink deep of pride, envy, ambition, hatred, will see harm and shame in every one they look upon. The first can only be cured by drinking palm wine, and so I say of these latter,—Drink freely of the sacred wine of love, and it will cure you of the evil tempers which lead you to these perverse judgments. So far from seeking out that which is evil, Love dreads meeting with it, and when such meeting is unavoidable, she shuts her eyes at the first symptom, and then in her holy simplicity she questions whether it were not merely a fantastic shadow which crossed her path rather than sin itself. Or if Love is forced to recognise the fact, she turns aside hastily, and strives to forget what she has seen. Of a truth, Love is the great healer of all ills, and of this above the rest. Everything looks yellow to a man that has the jaundice; and it is said that the only cure is through the soles of the feet. Most assuredly the sin of rash judgments is a spiritual jaundice, which makes everything look amiss to those who have it; and he who would be cured of this malady must not be content with applying remedies to his eyes or his intellect, he must attack it through the affections, which are as the soul's feet. If your affections are warm and tender, your judgment will not be harsh; if they are loving, your judgment will be the same. Holy Scripture offers us three striking illustrations. Isaac, when in the Land of Gerar, gave out that Rebecca was his sister, but when Abimelech saw their familiarity, he at once concluded that she was his wife.[90] A malicious mind would rather have supposed that there was some unlawful connection between them, but Abimelech took the most charitable view of the case that was possible. And so ought we always to judge our neighbour as charitably as may be; and if his actions are many-sided, we should accept the best. Again, when S. Joseph found that the Blessed Virgin was with child,[91] knowing her to be pure and holy, he could not believe that there was any sin in her, and he left all judgment to God, although there was strong presumptive evidence on which to condemn her. And the Holy Spirit speaks of S. Joseph as "a just man." When a just man cannot see any excuse for what is done by a person in whose general worth he believes, he still refrains from judging him, and leaves all to God's Judgment. Again, our Crucified Saviour, while He could not wholly ignore the sin of those who Crucified Him, yet made what excuse He might for them, pleading their ignorance.[92] And so when we cannot find any excuse for sin, let us at least claim what compassion we may for it, and impute it to the least damaging motives we can find, as ignorance or infirmity.

Are we never, then, to judge our neighbour? you ask. Never, my child. It is God Who judges criminals brought before a court of law. He uses magistrates to convey His sentence

---

[90] Gen. xxvi.
[91] S. Matt. i.
[92] S. Luke xxiii. 34.

to us; they are His interpreters, and have only to proclaim His law. If they go beyond this, and are led by their own passions, then they do themselves judge, and for so doing they will be judged. It is forbidden to all men alike, as men, to judge one another.

We do not necessarily judge because we see or are conscious of something wrong. Rash judgment always presupposes something that is not clear, in spite of which we condemn another. It is not wrong to have doubts concerning a neighbour, but we ought to be very watchful lest even our doubts or suspicions be rash and hasty. A malicious person seeing Jacob kiss Rachel at the well-side,[93] or Rebecca accepting jewels from Eleazer,[94] a stranger, might have suspected them of levity, though falsely and unreasonably. If an action is in itself indifferent, it is a rash suspicion to imagine that it means evil, unless there is strong circumstantial evidence to prove such to be the case. And it is a rash judgment when we draw condemnatory inferences from an action which may be blameless.

Those who keep careful watch over their conscience are not often liable to form rash judgments, for just as when the clouds lower the bees make for the shelter of their hive, so really good people shrink back into themselves, and refuse to be mixed up with the clouds and fogs of their neighbour's questionable doings, and rather than meddle with others, they consecrate their energies on their own improvement and good resolutions.

No surer sign of an unprofitable life than when people give way to censoriousness and inquisitiveness into the lives of other men. Of course exception must be made as to those who are responsible for others, whether in family or public life;—to all such it becomes a matter of conscience to watch over the conduct of their fellows. Let them fulfil their duty lovingly, and let them also give heed to restrain themselves within the bounds of that duty.

Chapter XXIX: On Slander.

FROM rash judgments proceed mistrust, contempt for others, pride, and self-sufficiency, and numberless other pernicious results, among which stands forth prominently the sin of slander, which is a veritable pest of society. Oh, wherefore can I not take a live coal from God's Altar, and touch the lips of men, so that their iniquity may be taken away and their sin purged, even as the Seraphim purged the lips of Isaiah.[95] He who could purge the world of slander would cleanse it from a great part of its sinfulness!

He who unjustly takes away his neighbour's good name is guilty of sin, and is bound to make reparation, according to the nature of his evil speaking; since no man can enter into Heaven cumbered with stolen goods, and of all worldly possessions the most precious is a good name. Slander is a kind of murder; for we all have three lives—a spiritual life, which depends upon the Grace of God; a bodily life, depending on the soul; and a civil life, consisting in a good reputation. Sin deprives us of the first, death of the second, and slander of the third. But the slanderer commits three several murders with his idle tongue: he destroys his own soul and that of him who hearkens, as well as causing civil death to the object of his slander; for, as S. Bernard says, the Devil has possession both of the slanderer and of those who listen to him, of the tongue of the one, the ear of the other. And David says of slanderers, "They have sharpened their tongues like a serpent; adders'

---

[93] Gen. xxix. 11.
[94] Gen. xxiv. 22.
[95] Isa. vi. 6, 7.

poison is under their lips."[96] Aristotle says that, like the forked, two-edged tongue of the serpent, so is that of the slanderer, who at one dart pricks and poisons the ear of those who hear him, and the reputation of him who is slandered.

My daughter, I entreat you never speak evil of any, either directly or indirectly; beware of ever unjustly imputing sins or faults to your neighbour, of needlessly disclosing his real faults, of exaggerating such as are overt, of attributing wrong motives to good actions, of denying the good that you know to exist in another, of maliciously concealing it, or depreciating it in conversation. In all and each of these ways you grievously offend God, although the worst is false accusation, or denying the truth to your neighbour's damage, since therein you combine his harm with falsehood.

Those who slander others with an affectation of good will, or with dishonest pretences of friendliness, are the most spiteful and evil of all. They will profess that they love their victim, and that in many ways he is an excellent man, but all the same, truth must be told, and he was very wrong in such a matter; or that such and such a woman is very virtuous generally, but and so on. Do you not see through the artifice? He who draws a bow draws the arrow as close as he can to himself, but it is only to let it fly more forcibly; and so such slanderers appear to be withholding their evil-speaking, but it is only to let it fly with surer aim and go deeper into the listeners' minds. Witty slander is the most mischievous of all; for just as some poisons are but feeble when taken alone, which become powerful when mixed with wine, so many a slander, which would go in at one ear and out at the other of itself, finds a resting-place in the listener's brain when it is accompanied with amusing, witty comments. "The poison of asps is under their lips." The asp's bite is scarcely perceptible, and its poison at first only causes an irritation which is scarcely disagreeable, so that the heart and nervous system dilate and receive that poison, against which later on there is no remedy.

Do not pronounce a man to be a drunkard although you may have seen him drunk, or an adulterer, because you know he has sinned; a single act does not stamp him for ever. The sun once stood still while Joshua and the children of Israel avenged themselves upon their enemies;[97] and another time it was darkened at mid-day when the Lord was crucified;[98] but no one would therefore say that it was stationary or dark. Noah was drunk once, and Lot, moreover, was guilty of incest, yet neither man could be spoken of as habitually given to such sins; neither would you call S. Paul a man of blood or a blasphemer, because he had blasphemed and shed blood before he became a Christian. Before a man deserves to be thus stigmatised, he must have formed a habit of the sin he is accused of, and it is unfair to call a man passionate or a thief, because you have once known him steal or fly into a passion. Even when a man may have persisted long in sin, you may say what is untrue in calling him vicious. Simon the leper called Magdalene a sinner, because she had once lived a life of sin; but he lied, for she was a sinner no longer, but rather a very saintly penitent, and so our Lord Himself undertook her defence.[99]

The Pharisee looked upon the publican as a great sinner,—probably as unjust, extortionate, adulterous;[100] but how mistaken he was, inasmuch as the condemned publican was even then justified! If God's Mercy is so great, that one single moment is

---

[96] Ps. cxl. 3.
[97] Josh. x. 13.
[98] S. Luke xxiii. 44.
[99] S. Luke vii. 37-39.
[100] S. Luke xviii. 11.

sufficient for it to justify and save a man, what assurance have we that he who yesterday was a sinner is the same to-day? Yesterday may not be the judge of today, nor to-day of yesterday: all will be really judged at the Last Great Day. In short, we can never affirm a man to be evil without running the risk of lying. If it be absolutely necessary to speak, we may say that he was guilty of such an act, that he led an evil life at such and such a time, or that he is doing certain wrong at the present day; but we have no right to draw deductions for to-day from yesterday, nor of yesterday from today; still less to speak with respect to the future.

But while extremely sensitive as to the slightest approach to slander, you must also guard against an extreme into which some people fall, who, in their desire to speak evil of no one, actually uphold and speak well of vice. If you have to do with one who is unquestionably a slanderer, do not excuse him under the expressions of frank and free-spoken; do not call one who is notoriously vain, liberal and elegant; do not call dangerous levities mere simplicity; do not screen disobedience under the name of zeal, or arrogance of frankness, or evil intimacy of friendship. No, my child, we must never, in our wish to shun slander, foster or flatter vice in others; but we must call evil evil, and sin sin, and so doing we shall serve God's Glory, always bearing in mind the following rules.

If you would be justified in condemning a neighbour's sin, you must be sure that it is needful either for his good or that of others to do so. For instance, if light, unseemly conduct is spoken of before young people in a way calculated to injure their purity, and you pass it over, or excuse it, they may be led to think lightly of evil, and to imitate it; and therefore you are bound to condemn all such things freely and at once, unless it is obvious that by reserving your charitable work of reprehension to a future time, you can do it more profitably.

Furthermore, on such occasions it is well to be sure that you are the most proper person among those present to express your opinion, and that your silence would seem in any way to condone the sin. If you are one of the least important persons present, it is probably not your place to censure; but supposing it to be your duty, be most carefully just in what you say,—let there not be a word too much or too little. For instance, you censure the intimacy of certain people, as dangerous and indiscreet. Well, but you must hold the scales with the most exact justice, and not exaggerate in the smallest item. If there be only a slight appearance of evil, say no more than that; if it be a question of some trifling imprudence, do not make it out to be more; if there be really neither imprudence nor positive appearance of evil, but only such as affords a pretext for malicious slander, either say simply so much, or, better still, say nothing at all. When you speak of your neighbour, look upon your tongue as a sharp razor in the surgeon's hand, about to cut nerves and tendons; it should be used so carefully, as to insure that no particle more or less than the truth be said. And finally, when you are called upon to blame sin, always strive as far as possible to spare the sinner.

Public, notorious sinners may be spoken of freely, provided always even then that a spirit of charity and compassion prevail, and that you do not speak of them with arrogance or presumption, or as though you took pleasure in the fall of others. To do this is the sure sign of a mean ungenerous mind. And, of course, you must speak freely in condemnation of the professed enemies of God and His Church, heretics and schismatics,—it is true charity to point out the wolf wheresoever he creeps in among the flock. Most people permit themselves absolute latitude in criticising and censuring rulers, and in calumniating nationalities, according to their own opinions and likings. But do you avoid this fault; it is displeasing to God, and is liable to lead you into disputes and quarrels. When you hear evil of any one, cast any doubt you fairly can upon the accusation; or if that is impossible, make any available excuse for the culprit; and where even that may not be, be yet pitiful and compassionate, and remind those with whom you are speaking that such as stand upright do so solely through God's Grace. Do your best kindly to check the scandal-bearer, and if you know anything favourable to the person criticised, take pains to mention it.

Chapter XXX: Further Counsels as to Conversation.

LET your words be kindly, frank, sincere, straightforward, simple and true; avoid all artifice, duplicity and pretence, remembering that, although it is not always well to publish abroad everything that may be true, yet it is never allowable to oppose the truth. Make it your rule never knowingly to say what is not strictly true, either accusing or excusing, always remembering that God is the God of Truth. If you have unintentionally said what is not true, and it is possible to correct yourself at once by means of explanation or reparation, do so. A straightforward excuse has far greater weight than any falsehood.

It may be lawful occasionally to conceal or disguise the truth, but this should never be done save in such special cases as make this reserve obviously a necessity for the service and glory of God. Otherwise all such artifice is dangerous; and we are told in Holy Scripture that God's Holy Spirit will not abide with the false or double-minded. Depend upon it there is no craft half so profitable and successful as simplicity. Worldly prudence and artifice belong to the children of this world; but the children of God go straight on with a single heart and in all confidence;—falsehood, deceit and duplicity are sure signs of a mean, weak mind.

In the Fourth Book of his Confessions, S. Augustine spoke in very strong terms of his passionate devotion to a friend, saying that they had but as one soul, and that after his friend's death his life was a horror to him, although he feared to die. But later on these expressions seemed unreal and affected to him, and he withdrew them in his Retractations.[101] You see how sensitive that great mind was to unreality or affectation. Assuredly straightforward honesty and sincerity in speech is a great beauty in the Christian life. "I said I will take heed to my ways, that I offend not in my tongue."[102] "Set a watch, O Lord, before my mouth, and keep the door of my lips."[103]

It was a saying of S. Louis, that one should contradict nobody, unless there was sin or harm in consenting; and that in order to avoid contention and dispute. At any rate, when it is necessary to contradict anybody, or to assert one's own opinion, it should be done gently and considerately, without irritation or vehemence. Indeed, we gain nothing by sharpness or petulance.

---

[101] "My dearest Nebridius . . . I wondered that others subject to death should live, since he whom I loved, as if he should never die, was dead; and I wondered yet more that myself, who was to him as a second self, could live, he being dead. . . . I felt that my soul and his soul were one soul in two bodies, and therefore my life was a horror to me, because I would not live halved, and therefore perchance I feared to die, lest he whom I had much loved should die wholly."—Confessions, Oxf. Trans. Bk. iv. p. 52.". . . which seems to me rather an empty declamation than a grave confession."—Retract., Bk. ii. c. 6.

[102] Ps. xxxix. 1.

[103] Ps. cxli. 3.

The silence, so much commended by wise men of old, does not refer so much to a literal use of few words, as to not using many useless words. On this score, we must look less to the quantity than the quality, and, as it seems to me, our aim should be to avoid both extremes. An excessive reserve and stiffness, which stands aloof from familiar friendly conversation, is untrusting, and implies a certain sort of contemptuous pride; while an incessant chatter and babble, leaving no opportunity for others to put in their word, is frivolous and troublesome.

S. Louis objected to private confidences and whisperings in society, especially at table, lest suspicion should be aroused that scandal was being repeated. "Those who have anything amusing or pleasant to say," he argued, "should let everybody share the entertainment, but if they want to speak of important matters, they should wait a more suitable time."

Chapter XXXI: Of Amusements and Recreations: what are allowable.

WE must needs occasionally relax the mind, and the body requires some recreation also. Cassian relates how S. John the Evangelist was found by a certain hunter amusing himself by caressing a partridge, which sat upon his wrist. The hunter asked how a man of his mental powers could find time for so trifling an occupation. In reply, S. John asked why he did not always carry his bow strung? The man answered, Because, if always bent, the bow would lose its spring when really wanted. "Do not marvel then," the Apostle replied, "if I slacken my mental efforts from time to time, and recreate myself, in order to return more vigorously to contemplation." It is a great mistake to be so strict as to grudge any recreation either to others or one's self.

Walking, harmless games, music, instrumental or vocal, field sports, etc., are such entirely lawful recreations that they need no rules beyond those of ordinary discretion, which keep every thing within due limits of time, place, and degree. So again games of skill, which exercise and strengthen body or mind, such as tennis, rackets, running at the ring, chess, and the like, are in themselves both lawful and good. Only one must avoid excess, either in the time given to them, or the amount of interest they absorb; for if too much time be given up to such things, they cease to be a recreation and become an occupation; and so far from resting and restoring mind or body, they have precisely the contrary effect. After five or six hours spent over chess, one's mind is spent and weary, and too long a time given to tennis results in physical exhaustion; or if people play for a high stake, they get anxious and discomposed, and such unimportant objects are unworthy of so much care and thought. But, above all, beware of setting your heart upon any of these things, for however lawful an amusement may be, it is wrong to give one's heart up to it. Not that I would not have you take pleasure in what you are doing,—it were no recreation else,—but I would not have you engrossed by it, or become eager or over fond of any of these things.

Chapter XXXII: Of Forbidden Amusements.

DICE, cards, and the like games of hazard, are not merely dangerous amusements, like dancing, but they are plainly bad and harmful, and therefore they are forbidden by the civil as by the ecclesiastical law. What harm is there in them? you ask. Such games are unreasonable:—the winner often has neither skill nor industry to boast of, which is contrary to reason. You reply that this is understood by those who play. But though that may prove that you are not wronging anybody, it does not prove that the game is in accordance with reason, as victory ought to be the reward of skill or labour, which it cannot be in mere games of chance. Moreover, though such games may be called a recreation, and are intended as such, they are practically an intense occupation. Is it not an occupation, when a man's mind is kept on the stretch of close attention, and disturbed by endless anxieties, fears and agitations? Who exercises a more dismal, painful attention than the gambler? No one must speak or laugh,—if you do but cough you will annoy him and his companions. The only pleasure in gambling is to win, and this cannot be a satisfactory pleasure, since it can only be enjoyed at the expense of your antagonist. Once, when he was very ill, S. Louis heard that his brother the Comte d'Anjou and Messire Gautier de Nemours were gambling, and in spite of his weakness the King tottered into the room where they were, and threw dice and money and everything out of the window, in great indignation. And the pure and pious Sara, in her appeal to God, declared that she had never had dealings with gamblers.[104]

Chapter XXXIII: Of Balls, and other Lawful but Dangerous Amusements.

DANCES and balls are things in themselves indifferent, but the circumstances ordinarily surrounding them have so generally an evil tendency, that they become full of temptation and danger. The time of night at which they take place is in itself conducive to harm, both as the season when people's nerves are most excited and open to evil impressions; and because, after being up the greater part of the night, they spend the mornings afterwards in sleep, and lose the best part of the day for God's Service. It is a senseless thing to turn day into night, light into darkness, and to exchange good works for mere trifling follies. Moreover, those who frequent balls almost inevitably foster their Vanity, and vanity is very conducive to unholy desires and dangerous attachments.

I am inclined to say about balls what doctors say of certain articles of food, such as mushrooms and the like—the best are not good for much; but if eat them you must, at least mind that they are properly cooked. So, if circumstances over which you have no control take you into such places, be watchful how you prepare to enter them. Let the dish be seasoned with moderation, dignity and good intentions. The doctors say (still referring to the mushrooms), eat sparingly of them, and that but seldom, for, however well dressed, an excess is harmful. So dance but little, and that rarely, my daughter, lest you run the risk of growing over fond of the amusement.

Pliny says that mushrooms, from their porous, spongy nature, easily imbibe meretricious matter, so that if they are near a serpent, they are infected by its poison. So balls and similar gatherings are wont to attract all that is bad and vicious; all the quarrels, envyings, slanders, and indiscreet tendencies of a place will be found collected in the ballroom. While people's bodily pores are opened by the exercise of dancing, the heart's pores will be also opened by excitement, and if any serpent be at hand to whisper foolish

[104] It is not very clear what S. Francis means by this. In the English version, Sara only says, "Thou knowest, Lord . . . that I never polluted my name, nor the name of my father" (Tobit iii. 15). In the Vulgate the words are "Numquam cum ludentibus miscui me; neque cum his, qui in levitate ambulant, participem me praebui" (iii. 17).

words of levity or impurity, to insinuate unworthy thoughts and desires, the ears which listen are more than prepared to receive the contagion.

Believe me, my daughter, these frivolous amusements are for the most part dangerous; they dissipate the spirit of devotion, enervate the mind, check true charity, and arouse a multitude of evil inclinations in the soul, and therefore I would have you very reticent in their use.

To return to the medical simile;—it is said that after eating mushrooms you should drink some good wine. So after frequenting balls you should frame pious thoughts which may counteract the dangerous impressions made by such empty pleasures on your heart. Bethink you, then—

1. That while you were dancing, souls were groaning in hell by reason of sins committed when similarly occupied, or in consequence thereof.

2. Remember how, at the selfsame time, many religious and other devout persons were kneeling before God, praying or praising Him. Was not their time better spent than yours?

3. Again, while you were dancing, many a soul has passed away amid sharp sufferings; thousands and tens of thousands were lying all the while on beds of anguish, some perhaps untended, unconsoled, in fevers, and all manner of painful diseases. Will you not rouse yourself to a sense of pity for them? At all events, remember that a day will come when you in your turn will lie on your bed of sickness, while others dance and make merry.

4. Bethink you that our Dear Lord, Our Lady, all the Angels and Saints, saw all that was passing. Did they not look on with sorrowful pity, while your heart, capable of better things, was engrossed with such mere follies?

5. And while you were dancing time passed by, and death drew nearer. Trifle as you may, the awful dance of death[105] must come, the real pastime of men, since therein they must, whether they will or no, pass from time to an eternity of good or evil. If you think of the matter quietly, and as in God's Sight, He will suggest many a like thought, which will steady and strengthen your heart.

Chapter XXXIV: When to use such Amusements rightly.

IF you would dance or play rightly, it must be done as a recreation, not as a pursuit, for a brief space of time, not so as make you unfit for other things, and even then but seldom. If it is a constant habit, recreation turns into occupation. You will ask when it is right to dance or play? The occasions on which it is right to play at questionable games are rare; ordinary games and dances may be indulged in more frequently. But let your rule be to do so chiefly when courteous consideration for others among whom you are thrown requires it, subject to prudence and discretion; for consideration towards others often sanctions things indifferent or dangerous, and turns them to good, taking away what is evil. Thus certain games of chance, bad in themselves, cease to be so to you, if you join in them merely out of a due courtesy. I have been much comforted by reading in the Life of

[105] S. Francis de Sales doubtless had in his thoughts the then common pictorial representations of the Dance of Death, with which (although to our own modern ideas there would be almost irreverence if reproduced) we are familiar through Holbein's celebrated Dance, and others. The old covered bridge at Lucerne is one of the most striking illustrations.

S. Carlo Borromeo, how he joined in certain things to please the Swiss, concerning which ordinarily he was very strict; as also how S. Ignatius Loyola, when asked to play, did so. As to S. Elizabeth of Hungary, she both played and danced occasionally, when in society, without thereby hindering her devotion, which was so firmly rooted that, like the rocks of a mountain lake, it stood unmoved amid the waves and storms of pomp and vanity which it encountered.

Great fires are fanned by the wind, but a little one is soon extinguished if left without shelter.

Chapter XXXV: We must be Faithful in Things Great and Small.

THE Bridegroom of the Canticles says that the Bride has ravished His heart with "one of her eyes, one lock of her hair."[106] In all the human body no part is nobler either in mechanism or activity than the eye, none more unimportant than the hair. And so the Divine Bridegroom makes us to know that He accepts not only the great works of devout people, but every poor and lowly offering too; and that they who would serve Him acceptably must give heed not only to lofty and important matters, but to things mean and little, since by both alike we may win His Heart and Love.

Be ready then, my child, to bear great afflictions for your Lord, even to martyrdom itself; resolve to give up to Him all that you hold most precious, if He should require it of you;—father, mother, husband, wife, or child; the light of your eyes; your very life; for all such offering your heart should be ready. But so long as God's Providence does not send you these great and heavy afflictions; so long as He does not ask your eyes, at least give Him your hair. I mean, take patiently the petty annoyances, the trifling discomforts, the unimportant losses which come upon all of us daily; for by means of these little matters, lovingly and freely accepted, you will give Him your whole heart, and win His. I mean the acts of daily forbearance, the headache, or toothache, or heavy cold; the tiresome peculiarities of husband or wife, the broken glass, the loss of a ring, a handkerchief, a glove; the sneer of a neighbour, the effort of going to bed early in order to rise early for prayer or Communion, the little shyness some people feel in openly performing religious duties; and be sure that all of these sufferings, small as they are, if accepted lovingly, are most pleasing to God's Goodness, Which has promised a whole ocean of happiness to His children in return for one cup of cold water. And, moreover, inasmuch as these occasions are for ever arising, they give us a fertile field for gathering in spiritual riches, if only we will use them rightly.

When I read in the Life of S. Catherine of Sienna of her ecstasies and visions, her wise sayings and teaching, I do not doubt but that she "ravished" her Bridegroom's heart with this eye of contemplation; but I must own that I behold her with no less delight in her father's kitchen, kindling the fire, turning the spit, baking the bread, cooking the dinner, and doing all the most menial offices in a loving spirit which looked through all things straight to God. Nor do I prize the lowly meditations she was wont to make while so humbly employed less than the ecstasies with which she was favoured at other times, probably as a reward for this very humility and lowliness. Her meditations would take the shape of imagining that all she prepared for her father was prepared for Our Lord, as by

---

[106] Cant. iv. 9. In the English version this passage stands as "one chain of her neck;" but in the Vulgate it is "uno crine colli tui."

Martha; her mother was a symbol to her of Our Lady, her brothers of the Apostles, and thus she mentally ministered to all the Heavenly Courts, fulfilling her humble ministrations with an exceeding sweetness, because she saw God's Will in each. Let this example, my daughter, teach you how important it is to dedicate all we do, however trifling, to His service. And to this end I earnestly counsel you to imitate that "virtuous woman" whom King Solomon lauds,[107] who "layeth her hands" to all that is good and noble, and yet at the same time to the spindle and distaff. Do you seek the higher things, such as prayer and meditation, the Sacraments leading souls to God and kindling good thoughts in them, in a word, by all manner of good works according to your vocation; but meanwhile do not neglect your spindle and distaff. I mean, cultivate those lowly virtues which spring like flowers round the foot of the Cross, such as ministering to the poor and sick, family cares, and the duties arising therefrom, and practical diligence and activity; and amid all these things cultivate such spiritual thoughts as S. Catherine intermingled with her work.

Great occasions for serving God come seldom, but little ones surround us daily; and our Lord Himself has told us that "he that is faithful in that which is least is faithful also in much."[108] If you do all in God's Name, all you do will be well done, whether you eat, drink or sleep, whether you amuse yourself or turn the spit, so long as you do all wisely, you will gain greatly as in God's Sight, doing all because He would have you do it.

Chapter XXXVI: Of a Well-Balanced, Reasonable Mind.

REASON is the special characteristic of man, and yet it is a rare thing to find really reasonable men, all the more that self-love hinders reason, and beguiles us insensibly into all manner of trifling, but yet dangerous acts of injustice and untruth, which, like the little foxes in the Canticles,[109] spoil our vines, while, just because they are trifling, people pay no attention to them, and because they are numerous, they do infinite harm. Let me give some instances of what I mean.

We find fault with our neighbour very readily for a small matter, while we pass over great things in ourselves. We strive to sell dear and buy cheap. We are eager to deal out strict justice to others, but to obtain indulgence for ourselves. We expect a good construction to be put on all we say, but we are sensitive and critical as to our neighbour's words. We expect him to let us have whatever we want for money, when it would be more reasonable to let him keep that which is his, if he desires to do so, and leave us to keep our gold. We are vexed with him because he will not accommodate us, while perhaps he has better reason to be vexed with us for wanting to disturb him. If we have a liking for any one particular thing, we despise all else, and reject whatever does not precisely suit our taste. If some inferior is unacceptable to us, or we have once caught him in error, he is sure to be wrong in our eyes whatever he may do, and we are for ever thwarting, or looking coldly on him, while, on the other hand, some one who happens to please us is sure to be right. Sometimes even parents show unfair preference for a child endowed with personal gifts over one afflicted with some physical imperfection. We put the rich before the poor,

---

[107] Prov. xxxi. Those who desire a helpful book will find one in Mgr. Landriot's "Femme Forte," a series of lectures on this chapter of Holy Scripture, which, as well as his "Femme Picuse" is largely imbued with the spirit of S. Francis de Sales, who is frequently quoted in both.

[108] S. Luke xvi. 10.

[109] Cant. ii. 15.

although they may have less claim, and be less worthy; we even give preference to well-dressed people. We are strict in exacting our own rights, but expect others to be yielding as to theirs;—we complain freely of our neighbours, but we do not like them to make any complaints of us. Whatever we do for them appears very great in our sight, but what they do for us counts as nothing. In a word, we are like the Paphlagonian partridge, which has two hearts; for we have a very tender, pitiful, easy heart towards ourselves, and one which is hard, harsh and strict towards our neighbour. We have two scales, one wherein to measure our own goods to the best advantage, and the other to weigh our neighbours' to the worst. Holy Scripture tells us that lying lips are an abomination unto the Lord,[110] and the double heart, with one measure whereby to receive, and another to give, is also abominable in His Sight.

Be just and fair in all you do. Always put yourself in your neighbour's place, and put him into yours, and then you will judge fairly. Sell as you would buy, and buy as you would sell, and your buying and selling will alike be honest. These little dishonesties seem unimportant, because we are not obliged to make restitution, and we have, after all, only taken that which we might demand according to the strict letter of the law; but, nevertheless, they are sins against right and charity, and are mere trickery, greatly needing correction—nor does any one ever lose by being generous, noble-hearted and courteous. Be sure then often to examine your dealings with your neighbour, whether your heart is right towards him, as you would have his towards you, were things reversed—this is the true test of reason. When Trajan was blamed by his confidential friends for making the Imperial presence too accessible, he replied, "Does it not behove me to strive to be such an emperor towards my subjects as I should wish to meet with were I a subject?"

Chapter XXXVII: Of Wishes.

EVERYBODY grants that we must guard against the desire for evil things, since evil desires make evil men. But I say yet further, my daughter, do not desire dangerous things, such as balls or pleasures, office or honour, visions or ecstacies. Do not long after things afar off; such, I mean, as cannot happen till a distant time, as some do who by this means wear themselves out and expend their energies uselessly, fostering a dangerous spirit of distraction. If a young man gives way to overweening longings for an employment he cannot obtain yet a while, what good will it do him? If a married woman sets her heart on becoming a religious, or if I crave to buy my neighbour's estate, he not being willing to sell it, is it not mere waste of time? If, when sick, I am restlessly anxious to preach or celebrate, to visit other sick people, or generally to do work befitting the strong, is it not an unprofitable desire, inasmuch as I have no power to fulfil it? and meanwhile these useless wishes take the place of such as I ought to have,—namely, to be patient, resigned, self-denying, obedient, gentle under suffering,—which are what God requires of me under the circumstances. We are too apt to be like a sickly woman, craving ripe cherries in autumn and grapes in spring. I can never think it well for one whose vocation is clear to waste time in wishing for some different manner of life than that which is adapted to his duty, or practices unsuitable to his present position—it is mere idling, and will make him slack in his needful work. If I long after a Carthusian solitude, I am losing my time, and such longing usurps the place of that which I ought to entertain—to fulfil my actual duties

---

[110] Prov. xii. 22.

rightly. No indeed, I would not even have people wish for more wit or better judgment, for such desires are frivolous, and take the place of the wish every one ought to possess of improving what he has. We ought not to desire ways of serving God which He does not open to us, but rather desire to use what we have rightly. Of course I mean by this, real earnest desires, not common superficial wishes, which do no harm if not too frequently indulged.

Do not desire crosses, unless you have borne those already laid upon you well—it is an abuse to long after martyrdom while unable to bear an insult patiently. The Enemy of souls often inspires men with ardent desires for unattainable things, in order to divert their attention from present duties, which would be profitable however trifling in themselves. We are apt to fight African monsters in imagination, while we let very petty foes vanquish us in reality for want of due heed.

Do not desire temptations, that is temerity, but prepare your heart to meet them bravely, and to resist them when they come.

Too great variety and quantity of food loads the stomach, and (especially when it is weakly) spoils the digestion. Do not overload your soul with innumerable longings, either worldly, for that were destruction,—or even spiritual, for these only cumber you. When the soul is purged of the evil humours of sin, it experiences a ravenous hunger for spiritual things, and sets to work as one famished at all manner of spiritual exercises;—mortification, penitence, humility, charity, prayer. Doubtless such an appetite is a good sign, but it behoves you to reflect whether you are able to digest all that you fain would eat. Make rather a selection from all these desires, under the guidance of your spiritual father, of such as you are able to perform, and then use them as perfectly as you are able. When you have done this, God will send you more, to be fulfilled in their turn, and so you will not waste time in unprofitable wishes. Not that I would have you lose any good desires, but rather treat them methodically, putting them aside in one corner of your heart till due time comes, while you carry out such as are ripe for action. And this counsel I give to worldly people as well as those who are spiritual, for without heeding it no one can avoid anxiety and over-eagerness.

Chapter XXXVIII: Counsels to Married People.

MARRIAGE is a great Sacrament both in Jesus Christ and His Church, and one to be honoured to all, by all and in all. To all, for even those who do not enter upon it should honour it in all humility. By all, for it is holy alike to poor as to rich. In all, for its origin, its end, its form and matter are holy. It is the nursery of Christianity, whence the earth is peopled with faithful, till the number of the elect in Heaven be perfected; so that respect for the marriage tie is exceedingly important to the commonwealth, of which it is the source and supply.

Would to God that His Dear Son were bidden to all weddings as to that of Cana! Truly then the wine of consolation and blessing would never be lacking; for if these are often so wanting, it is because too frequently now men summon Adonis instead of our Lord, and Venus rather than Our Lady. He who desires that the young of his flock should be like Jacob's, fair and ring-straked, must set fair objects before their eyes; and he who would find a blessing in his marriage, must ponder the holiness and dignity of this Sacrament, instead of which too often weddings become a season of mere feasting and disorder.

Above all, I would exhort all married people to seek that mutual love so commended to them by the Holy Spirit in the Bible. It is little to bid you love one another with a mutual love,—turtle-doves do that; or with human love,—the heathen cherished such love as that. But I say to you in the Apostle's words: "Husbands, love your wives, even as Christ also loved the Church. Wives, submit yourselves to your husbands as unto the Lord."[111] It was God Who brought Eve to our first father Adam, and gave her to him to wife; and even so, my friends, it is God's Invisible Hand Which binds you in the sacred bonds of marriage; it is He Who gives you one to the other, therefore cherish one another with a holy, sacred, heavenly love.

The first effect of this love is the indissoluble union of your hearts. If you glue together two pieces of deal, provided that the glue be strong, their union will be so close that the stick will break more easily in any other part than where it is joined. Now God unites husband and wife so closely in Himself, that it should be easier to sunder soul from body than husband from wife; nor is this union to be considered as mainly of the body, but yet more a union of the heart, its affections and love.

The second effect of this love should be an inviolable fidelity to one another. In olden times finger-rings were wont to be graven as seals. We read of it in Holy Scripture, and this explains the meaning of the marriage ceremony, when the Church, by the hand of her priest, blesses a ring, and gives it first to the man in token that she sets a seal on his heart by this Sacrament, so that no thought of any other woman may ever enter therein so long as she, who now is given to him, shall live. Then the bridegroom places the ring on the bride's hand, so that she in her turn may know that she must never conceive any affection in her heart for any other man so long as he shall live, who is now given to her by our Lord Himself.

The third end of marriage is the birth and bringing up of children. And herein, O ye married people! are you greatly honoured, in that God, willing to multiply souls to bless and praise Him to all Eternity, He associates you with Himself in this His work, by the production of bodies into which, like dew from Heaven, He infuses the souls He creates as well as the bodies into which they enter.

Therefore, husbands, do you preserve a tender, constant, hearty love for your wives. It was that the wife might be loved heartily and tenderly that woman was taken from the side nearest Adam's heart. No failings or infirmities, bodily or mental, in your wife should ever excite any kind of dislike in you, but rather a loving, tender compassion; and that because God has made her dependent on you, and bound to defer to and obey you; and that while she is meant to be your helpmeet, you are her superior and her head. And on your part, wives, do you love the husbands God has given you tenderly, heartily, but with a reverential, confiding love, for God has made the man to have the predominance, and to be the stronger; and He wills the woman to depend upon him,—bone of his bone, flesh of his flesh,—taking her from out the ribs of the man, to show that she must be subject to his guidance. All Holy Scripture enjoins this subjection, which nevertheless is not grievous; and the same Holy Scripture, while it bids you accept it lovingly, bids your husband to use his superiority with great tenderness, lovingkindness, and gentleness. "Husbands, dwell with your wives according to knowledge, giving honour unto the wife as unto the weaker vessel."[112]

[111] Eph. v. 25, 22.
[112] 1 Pet. iii. 7.

But while you seek diligently to foster this mutual love, give good heed that it do not turn to any manner of jealousy. Just as the worm is often hatched in the sweetest and ripest apple, so too often jealousy springs up in the most warm and loving hearts, defiling and ruining them, and if it is allowed to take root, it will produce dissension, quarrels, and separation. Of a truth, jealousy never arises where love is built up on true virtue, and therefore it is a sure sign of an earthly, sensual love, in which mistrust and inconstancy is soon infused. It is a sorry kind of friendship which seeks to strengthen itself by jealousy; for though jealousy may be a sign of strong, hot friendship, it is certainly no sign of a good, pure, perfect attachment; and that because perfect love implies absolute trust in the person loved, whereas jealousy implies uncertainty.

If you, husbands, would have your wives faithful, be it yours to set them the example. "How have you the face to exact purity from your wives," asks S. Gregory Nazianzen, "if you yourself live an impure life? or how can you require that which you do not give in return? If you would have them chaste, let your own conduct to them be chaste. S. Paul bids you possess your vessel in sanctification; but if, on the contrary, you teach them evil, no wonder that they dishonour you. And ye, O women! whose honour is inseparable from modesty and purity, preserve it jealously, and never allow the smallest speck to soil the whiteness of your reputation."

Shrink sensitively from the veriest trifles which can touch it; never permit any gallantries whatsoever. Suspect any who presume to flatter your beauty or grace, for when men praise wares they cannot purchase they are often tempted to steal; and if any one should dare to speak in disparagement of your husband, show that you are irrecoverably offended, for it is plain that he not only seeks your fall, but he counts you as half fallen, since the bargain with the new-comer is half made when one is disgusted with the first merchant.

Ladies both in ancient and modern times have worn pearls in their ears, for the sake (so says Pliny) of hearing them tinkle against each other. But remembering how that friend of God, Isaac, sent earrings as first pledges of his love to the chaste Rebecca, I look upon this mystic ornament as signifying that the first claim a husband has over his wife, and one which she ought most faithfully to keep for him, is her ear; so that no evil word or rumour enter therein, and nought be heard save the pleasant sound of true and pure words, which are represented by the choice pearls of the Gospel. Never forget that souls are poisoned through the ear as much as bodies through the mouth.

Love and faithfulness lead to familiarity and confidence, and Saints have abounded in tender caresses. Isaac and Rebecca, the type of chaste married life, indulged in such caresses, as to convince Abimelech that they must be husband and wife. The great S. Louis, strict as he was to himself, was so tender towards his wife, that some were ready to blame him for it; although in truth he rather deserved praise for subjecting his lofty, martial mind to the little details of conjugal love. Such minor matters will not suffice to knit hearts, but they tend to draw them closer, and promote mutual happiness.

Before giving birth to S. Augustine, S. Monica offered him repeatedly to God's Glory, as he himself tells us; and it is a good lesson for Christian women how to offer the fruit of their womb to God, Who accepts the free oblations of loving hearts, and promotes the desires of such faithful mothers: witness Samuel, S. Thomas Aquinas, S. Andrea di Fiesole, and others.[113] S. Bernard's mother, worthy of such a son, was wont to take her

---

[113] S. Francis de Sales himself is an instance, his mother having offered him up to God while yet

new-born babes in her arms to offer them to Jesus Christ, thenceforward loving them with a reverential love, as a sacred deposit from God; and so entirely was her offering accepted, that all her seven children became Saints.[114] And when children begin to use their reason, fathers and mothers should take great pains to fill their hearts with the fear of God. This the good Queen Blanche did most earnestly by S. Louis, her son: witness her oft-repeated words, "My son, I would sooner see you die than guilty of a mortal sin;" words which sank so deeply into the saintly monarch's heart, that he himself said there was no day on which they did not recur to his mind, and strengthen him in treading God's ways.

We call races and generations Houses; and the Hebrews were wont to speak of the birth of children as "the building up of the house;" as it is written of the Jewish midwives in Egypt, that the Lord "made them houses;"[115] whereby we learn that a good house is not reared so much by the accumulation of worldly goods, as by the bringing up of children in the ways of holiness and of God; and to this end no labour or trouble must be spared, for children are the crown of their parents.[116] Thus it was that S. Monica stedfastly withstood S. Augustine's evil propensities, and, following him across sea and land, he became more truly the child of her tears in the conversion of his soul, than the son of her body in his natural birth.

S. Paul assigns the charge of the household to the woman; and consequently some hold that the devotion of the family depends more upon the wife than the husband, who is more frequently absent, and has less influence in the house. Certainly King Solomon, in the Book of Proverbs, refers all household prosperity to the care and industry of that virtuous woman whom he describes.[117]

We read in Genesis that Isaac "entreated the Lord for his wife, because she was barren;"[118] or as the Hebrews read it, he prayed "over against" her,—on opposite sides of the place of prayer,—and his prayer was granted. That is the most fruitful union between husband and wife which is founded in devotion, to which they should mutually stimulate one another. There are certain fruits, like the quince, of so bitter a quality, that they are scarcely eatable, save when preserved; while others again, like cherries and apricots, are so delicate and soft, that they can only be kept by the same treatment. So the wife must seek that her husband be sweetened with the sugar of devotion, for man without religion is a rude, rough animal; and the husband will desire to see his wife devout, as without it her frailty and weakness are liable to tarnish and injury. S. Paul says that "the unbelieving husband is sanctified by the wife, and the unbelieving wife is sanctified by the husband;"[119] because in so close a tie one may easily draw the other to what is good. And how great is the blessing on those faithful husbands and wives who confirm one another continually in the Fear of the Lord!

Moreover, each should have such forbearance towards the other, that they never grow angry, or fall into discussion and argument. The bee will not dwell in a spot where there

unborn.

[114] Cf. Marie Jenna's lovely poem, "L'aimeras-tu?" "Je ne veux plus d'enfants, si ce ne sont des saints."

[115] Exod. i. 21.

[116] Prov. xvii. 6.

[117] Prov. xxxi.

[118] Gen. xxv. 21.

[119] 1 Cor. vii. 14.

is much loud noise or shouting, or echo; neither will God's Holy Spirit dwell in a household where altercation and tumult, arguing and quarrelling, disturb the peace.

S. Gregory Nazianzen says that in his time married people were wont to celebrate the anniversary of their wedding, and it is a custom I should greatly approve, provided it were not a merely secular celebration; but if husbands and wives would go on that day to Confession and Communion, and commend their married life specially to God, renewing their resolution to promote mutual good by increased love and faithfulness, and thus take breath, so to say, and gather new vigour from the Lord to go on stedfastly in their vocation.

Chapter XXXIX: The Sanctity of the Marriage Bed.

THE marriage bed should be undefiled, as the Apostle tells us,[120] i.e. pure, as it was when it was first instituted in the earthly Paradise, wherein no unruly desires or impure thought might enter. All that is merely earthly must be treated as means to fulfil the end God sets before His creatures. Thus we eat in order to preserve life, moderately, voluntarily, and without seeking an undue, unworthy satisfaction therefrom. "The time is short," says S. Paul; "it remaineth that both they that have wives be as though they had not, and they that use this world, as not abusing it."[121]

Let every one, then, use this world according to his vocation, but so as not to entangle himself with its love, that he may be as free and ready to serve God as though he used it not. S. Augustine says that it is the great fault of men to want to enjoy things which they are only meant to use, and to use those which they are only meant to enjoy. We ought to enjoy spiritual things, and only use those which are material; but when we turn the use of these latter into enjoyment, the reasonable soul becomes degraded to a mere brutish level.

Chapter XL: Counsels to Widows.

SAINT PAUL teaches us all in the person of S. Timothy when he says, "Honour widows that are widows indeed."[122] Now to be "a widow indeed" it is necessary:—

1. That the widow be one not in body only, but in heart also; that is to say, that she be fixed in an unalterable resolution to continue in her widowhood Those widows who are but waiting the opportunity of marrying again are only widowed in externals, while in will they have already laid aside their loneliness. If the "widow indeed" chooses to confirm her widowhood by offering herself by a vow to God, she will adorn that widowhood, and make her resolution doubly sure, for the remembrance that she cannot break her vow without danger of forfeiting Paradise, will make her so watchful over herself, that a great barrier will be raised against all kind of temptation that may assail her. S. Augustine strongly recommends Christian widows to take this vow, and the learned Origen goes yet further, for he advises married women to take a vow of chastity in the event of losing their husbands, so that amid the joys of married life they may yet have a share in the merits of a chaste widowhood. Vows render the actions performed under their shelter more acceptable to God, strengthen us to perform good works, and help us to devote to Him not merely those good works which are, so to say, the fruits of a holy will, but to consecrate

[120] Heb. xiii. 4.
[121] 1 Cor. vii. 30, 31.
[122] 1 Tim. v. 3.

that will itself; the source of all we do, to Him. By ordinary chastity we offer our body to God, retaining the power to return to sensual pleasure; but the vow of chastity is an absolute and irrevocable gift to Him, without any power to recall it, thereby making ourselves the happy slaves of Him Whose service is to be preferred to royal power. And as I greatly approve the counsels of the two venerable Fathers I have named, I would have such persons as are so favoured as to wish to embrace them, do so prudently, and in a holy, stedfast spirit, after careful examination of their own courage, having asked heavenly guidance, and taken the advice of some discreet and pious director, and then all will be profitably done.

2. Further, all such renunciation of second marriage must be done with a single heart, in order to fix the affections more entirely on God, and to seek a more complete union with Him. For if the widow retains her widowhood merely to enrich her children, or for any other worldly motive, she may receive the praise of men, but not that of God, inasmuch as nothing is worthy of His Approbation save that which is done for His Sake. Moreover, she who would be a widow indeed must be voluntarily cut off from all worldly delights. "She that liveth in pleasure is dead while she liveth," S. Paul says.[123] A widow who seeks to be admired and followed and flattered, who frequents balls and parties, who takes pleasure in dressing, perfuming and adorning herself, may be a widow in the body, but she is dead as to the soul. What does it matter, I pray you, whether the flag of Adonis and his profane love be made of white feathers or a net of crape? Nay, sometimes there is a conscious vanity in that black is the most becoming dress; and she who thereby endeavours to captivate men, and who lives in empty pleasure, is "dead while she liveth," and is a mere mockery of widowhood.

"The time of retrenchment is come, the voice of the turtle is heard in our land."[124] Retrenchment of worldly superfluity is required of whosoever would lead a devout life, but above all, it is needful for the widow indeed, who mourns the loss of her husband like a true turtle-dove. When Naomi returned from Moab to Bethlehem, those that had known her in her earlier and brighter days were moved, and said, "Is this Naomi? And she said unto them, Call me not Naomi (which means beautiful and agreeable), call me Mara, for the Almighty hath dealt very bitterly with me. I went out full, and the Lord hath brought me home again empty."[125] Even so the devout widow will not desire to be called or counted beautiful or agreeable, asking no more than to be that which God wills,—lowly and abject in His Eyes.

The lamp which is fed with aromatic oil sends forth a yet sweeter odour when it is extinguished; and so those women whose married love was true and pure, give out a stronger perfume of virtue and chastity when their light (that is, their husband) is extinguished by death. Love for a husband while living is a common matter enough among women, but to love him so deeply as to refuse to take another after his death, is a kind of love peculiar to her who is a widow indeed. Hope in God, while resting on a husband, is not so rare, but to hope in Him, when left alone and desolate, is a very gracious and worthy thing. And thus it is that widowhood becomes a test of the perfection of the virtues displayed by a woman in her married life.

[123] 1 Tim. v. 6.
[124] Cant. ii. 12. in the Vulgate, "Tempus putationis advenit; vox turturis audita est in terra nostra."
[125] Ruth i. 20, 21.

The widow who has children requiring her care and guidance, above all in what pertains to their souls and the shaping of their lives, cannot and ought not on any wise to forsake them. S. Paul teaches this emphatically, and says that those who "provide not for their own, and specially for those of their own house, are worse than an infidel;"[126] but if her children do not need her care, then the widow should gather together all her affections and thoughts, in order to devote them more wholly to making progress in the love of God. If there is no call obliging her in conscience to attend to external secular matters (legal or other), I should advise her to leave them all alone, and to manage her affairs as quietly and peacefully as may be, even if such a course does not seem the most profitable. The fruit of disputes and lawsuits must be very great indeed before it can be compared in worth to the blessing of holy peace; not to say that those legal entanglements and the like are essentially distracting, and often open the way for enemies who sully the purity of a heart which should be solely devoted to God.

Prayer should be the widow's chief occupation: she has no love left save for God,— she should scarce have ought to say to any save God; and as iron, which is restrained from yielding to the attraction of the magnet when a diamond is near, darts instantly towards it so soon as the diamond is removed, so the widow's heart, which could not rise up wholly to God, or simply follow the leadings of His Heavenly Love during her husband's life, finds itself set free, when he is dead, to give itself entirely to Him, and cries out, with the Bride in the Canticles, "Draw me, I will run after Thee."[127] I will be wholly Thine, and seek nothing save the "savour of Thy good ointments."

A devout widow should chiefly seek to cultivate the graces of perfect modesty, renouncing all honours, rank, title, society, and the like vanities; she should be diligent in ministering to the poor and sick, comforting the afflicted, leading the young to a life of devotion, studying herself to be a perfect model of virtue to younger women. Necessity and simplicity should be the adornment of her garb, humility and charity of her actions, simplicity and kindliness of her words, modesty and purity of her eyes,—Jesus Christ Crucified the only Love of her heart.

Briefly, the true widow abides in the Church as a little March violet,[128] shedding forth an exquisite sweetness through the perfume of her devotion, ever concealing herself beneath the ample leaves of her heart's lowliness, while her subdued colouring indicates her mortification. She dwells in waste, uncultivated places, because she shrinks from the world's intercourse, and seeks to shelter her heart from the glare with which earthly longings, whether of honours, wealth, or love itself, might dazzle her. "Blessed is she if she so abide," says the holy Apostle.[129]

Much more could I say on this subject, but suffice it to bid her who seeks to be a widow indeed, read S. Jerome's striking Letters to Salvia, and the other noble ladies who

---

[126] 1 Tim. v. 8.

[127] Cant. i. 3, 4.

[128] "Quarn gloriosa enirn Ecclesia, et quanta virtutum multitudine, quasi florum varietate! Habet hortus ille Dominicus non solum rosas martyrum, sed et lilia virginum, et conjugatorum hederas, violasque viduarum Prorsus, Dilectissimi, nullum genus hominum de sua vocatione desperet: pro omnibus passus est Christus."—S. Aug. Serm. ccciv., In Laurent. Mart. iii. cap. 1-3. "How glorious is the Church, how countless her graces, varied as the flowers of earth in beauty! This garden of the Lord bears not only the martyr's rose, but the virgin's lily, the ivy wreath of wedded love, and the violet of widowhood. Therefore, beloved, let none despair of his calling, since Christ suffered for all."

[129] 1 Cor. vii. 40. "Beatior autem erit si sic permanserit."—Vulgate.

rejoiced in being the spiritual children of such a Father. Nothing can be said more, unless it be to warn the widow indeed not to condemn or even censure those who do resume the married life, for there are cases in which God orders it thus to His Own greater Glory. We must ever bear in mind the ancient teaching, that in Heaven virgins, wives, and widows will know no difference, save that which their true hearts' humility assigns them.

Chapter XLI: One Word to Maidens.

O YE virgins, I have but a word to say to you. If you look to married life in this life, guard your first love jealously for your husband. It seems to me a miserable fraud to give a husband a worn-out heart, whose love has been frittered away and despoiled of its first bloom instead of a true, whole-hearted love. But if you are happily called to be the chaste and holy bride of spiritual nuptials, and purpose to live a life of virginity, then in Christ's Name I bid you keep all your purest, most sensitive love for your Heavenly Bridegroom, Who, being Very Purity Himself, has a special love for purity; Him to Whom the first-fruits of all good things are due, above all those of love.

S. Jerome's Epistles will supply you with the needful counsels; and inasmuch as your state of life requires obedience, seek out a guide under whose direction you may wholly dedicate yourself, body and soul, to His Divine Majesty.

Chapter I: We must not trifle with the Words of Worldly Wisdom.

DIRECTLY that your worldly friends perceive that you aim at leading a devout life, they will let loose endless shafts of mockery and misrepresentation upon you; the more malicious will attribute your change to hypocrisy, designing, or bigotry; they will affirm that the world having looked coldly upon you, failing its favour you turn to God; while your friends will make a series of what, from their point of view, are prudent and charitable remonstrances. They will tell you that you are growing morbid; that you will lose your worldly credit, and will make yourself unacceptable to the world; they will prognosticate your premature old age, the ruin of your material prosperity; they will tell you that in the world you must live as the world does; that you can be saved without all this fuss; and much more of the like nature.

My daughter, all this is vain and foolish talk: these people have no real regard either for your bodily health or your material prosperity. "If ye were of the world," the Saviour has said, "the world would love his own; but because ye are not of the world, but I have chosen you out of the world, therefore the world hateth you."[1]

We have all seen men, and women too, pass the whole night, even several in succession, playing at chess or cards; and what can be a more dismal, unwholesome thing than that? But the world has not a word to say against it, and their friends are nowise troubled. But give up an hour to meditation, or get up rather earlier than usual to prepare for Holy Communion, and they will send for the doctor to cure you of hypochondria or jaundice! People spend every night for a month dancing, and no one will complain of being the worse; but if they keep the one watch of Christmas Eve, we shall hear of endless colds and maladies the next day! Is it not as plain as possible that the world is an unjust judge; indulgent and kindly to its own children, harsh and uncharitable to the children of God? We cannot stand well with the world save by renouncing His approval. It is not possible to satisfy the world's unreasonable demands: "John the Baptist came neither eating bread nor drinking wine; and ye say he hath a devil. The Son of Man is come eating and drinking, and ye say, Behold a gluttonous man, and a winebibber, the friend of publicans and sinners."[2] Even so, my child, if we give in to the world, and laugh, dance, and play as it does, it will affect to be scandalized; if we refuse to do so, it will accuse us of being hypocritical or morbid. If we adorn ourselves after its fashion, it will put some evil construction on what we do; if we go in plain attire, it will accuse us of meanness; our cheerfulness will be called dissipation; our mortification dulness; and ever casting its evil eye upon us, nothing we can do will please it. It exaggerates our failings, and publishes them abroad as sins; it represents our venial sins as mortal, and our sins of infirmity as malicious. S. Paul says that charity is kind, but the world is unkind; charity thinks no evil, but the world thinks evil of every one, and if it cannot find fault with our actions, it is sure at least to impute bad motives to them,—whether the sheep be black or white, horned or no, the wolf will devour them if he can. Do what we will, the world must wage war upon us. If we spend any length of time in confession, it will speculate on what we have so

[1] S. John xv. 19.
[2] S. Luke vii. 33, 34.

much to say about! if we are brief, it will suggest that we are keeping back something! It spies out our every act, and at the most trifling angry word, sets us down as intolerable. Attention to business is avarice, meekness mere silliness; whereas the wrath of worldly people is to be reckoned as generosity, their avarice, economy, their mean deeds, honourable. There are always spiders at hand to spoil the honey-bee's comb.

Let us leave the blind world to make as much noise as it may,—like a bat molesting the songbirds of day; let us be firm in our ways, unchangeable in our resolutions, and perseverance will be the test of our self-surrender to God, and our deliberate choice of the devout life.

The planets and a wandering comet shine with much the same brightness, but the comet's is a passing blaze, which does not linger long, while the planets cease not to display their brightness. Even so hypocrisy and real goodness have much outward resemblance; but one is easily known from the other, inasmuch as hypocrisy is short-lived, and disperses like a mist, while real goodness is firm and abiding. There is no surer groundwork for the beginnings of a devout life than the endurance of misrepresentation and calumny, since thereby we escape the danger of vainglory and pride, which are like the midwives of Egypt, who were bidden by Pharaoh to kill the male children born to Israel directly after their birth. We are crucified to the world, and the world must be as crucified to us. It esteems us as fools, let us esteem it as mad.

Chapter II: The need of a Good Courage.

HOWEVER much we may admire and crave for light, it is apt to dazzle our eyes when they have been long accustomed to darkness; and on first visiting a foreign country, we are sure to feel strange among its inhabitants, however kindly or courteous they may be. Even so, my child, your changed life may be attended with some inward discomfort, and you may feel some reaction of discouragement and weariness after you have taken a final farewell of the world and its follies. Should it be so, I pray you take it patiently, for it will not last,—it is merely the disturbance caused by novelty; and when it is gone by, you will abound in consolations. At first you may suffer somewhat under the loss what you enjoyed among your vain, frivolous companions; but would you forfeit the eternal gifts of God for such things as these? The empty amusements which have engrossed you hitherto may rise up attractively before your imagination, and strive to win you back to rest in them; but are you bold enough to give up a blessed eternity for such deceitful snares? Believe me, if you will but persevere you will not fail to enjoy a sweetness so real and satisfying, that you will be constrained to confess that the world has only gall to give as compared with this honey, and that one single day of devotion is worth more than a thousand years of worldly life.

But you see before you the mountain of Christian perfection, which is very high, and you exclaim in fearfulness that you can never ascend it. Be of good cheer, my child. When the young bees first begin to live they are mere grubs, unable to hover over flowers, or to fly to the mountains, or even to the little hills where they might gather honey; but they are fed for a time with the honey laid up by their predecessors, and by degrees the grubs put forth their wings and grow strong, until they fly abroad and gather their harvest from all the country round. Now we are yet but as grubs in devotion, unable to fly at will, and attain the desired aim of Christian perfection; but if we begin to take shape through our desires and resolutions, our wings will gradually grow, and we may hope one day to become spiritual bees, able to fly. Meanwhile let us feed upon the honey left us in the teaching of so many holy men of old, praying God that He would grant us doves' wings, so that we may not only fly during this life, but find an abiding resting-place in Eternity.

Chapter III: Of Temptations, and the difference between experiencing them and consenting to them.

PICTURE to yourself a young princess beloved of her husband, to whom some evil wretch should send a messenger to tempt her to infidelity. First, the messenger would bring forth his propositions. Secondly, the princess would either accept or reject the overtures. Thirdly, she would consent to them or refuse them. Even so, when Satan, the world, and the flesh look upon a soul espoused to the Son of God, they set temptations and suggestions before that soul, whereby—1. Sin is proposed to it. 2. Which proposals are either pleasing or displeasing to the soul. 3. The soul either consents, or rejects them. In other words, the three downward steps of temptation, delectation, and consent. And although the three steps may not always be so clearly defined as in this illustration, they are to be plainly traced in all great and serious sins.

If we should undergo the temptation to every sin whatsoever during our whole life, that would not damage us in the Sight of God's Majesty, provided we took no pleasure in it, and did not consent to it; and that because in temptation we do not act, we only suffer, and inasmuch as we take no delight in it, we can be liable to no blame. S. Paul bore long time with temptations of the flesh, but so far from displeasing God thereby, He was glorified in them. The blessed Angela di Foligni underwent terrible carnal temptations, which move us to pity as we read of them. S. Francis and S. Benedict both experienced grievous temptations, so that the one cast himself amid thorns, the other into the snow, to quench them, but so far from losing anything of God's Grace thereby, they greatly increased it.

Be then very courageous amid temptation, and never imagine yourself conquered so long as it is displeasing to you, ever bearing in mind the difference between experiencing and consenting to temptation,[3]—that difference being, that whereas they may be experienced while most displeasing to us, we can never consent to them without taking pleasure in them, inasmuch as pleasure felt in a temptation is usually the first step towards consent. So let the enemies of our salvation spread as many snares and wiles in our way as they will, let them besiege the door of our heart perpetually, let them ply us with endless proposals to sin,—so long as we abide in our firm resolution to take no pleasure therein, we cannot offend God any more than the husband of the princess in my illustration could be displeased with her because of the overtures made to her, so long as she was in no way gratified by them. Of course, there is one great difference between my imaginary princess and the soul, namely, that the former has it in her power to drive away the messenger of evil and never hear him more, while the latter cannot always refuse to experience temptation, although it be always in its power to refuse consent. But how long soever the temptation may persist, it cannot harm us so long as it is unwelcome to us.

But again, as to the pleasure which may be taken in temptation (technically called delectation), inasmuch as our souls have two parts, one inferior, the other superior, and the inferior does not always choose to be led by the superior, but takes its own line,—it

---

[3] The English language does not contain the precise relative terms equivalent to "sentir et con-sentir."

not unfrequently happens that the inferior part takes pleasure in a temptation not only without consent from, but absolutely in contradiction to the superior will. It is this contest which S. Paul describes when he speaks of the "law in my members, warring against the law of my mind,"[4] and of the "flesh lusting against the spirit."[5]

Have you ever watched a great burning furnace heaped up with ashes? Look at it some ten or twelve hours afterwards, and there will scarce be any living fire there, or only a little smouldering in the very heart thereof. Nevertheless, if you can find that tiny lingering spark, it will suffice to rekindle the extinguished flames. So it is with love, which is the true spiritual life amid our greatest, most active temptations. Temptation, flinging its delectation into the inferior part of the soul, covers it wholly with ashes, and leaves but a little spark of God's Love, which can be found nowhere save hidden far down in the heart or mind, and even that is hard to find. But nevertheless it is there, since however troubled we may have been in body and mind, we firmly resolved not to consent to sin or the temptation thereto, and that delectation of the exterior man was rejected by the interior spirit. Thus though our will may have been thoroughly beset by the temptation, it was not conquered, and so we are certain that all such delectation was involuntary, and consequently not sinful.

Chapter IV: Two striking Illustrations of the same.

THIS distinction, which is very important, is well illustrated by the description S. Jerome gives of a young man bound to a voluptuous bed by the softest silken cords, and subjected to the wiles and lures of a treacherous tempter, with the express object of causing him to fall. Greatly as all his senses and imagination must inevitably have been possessed by so vehement an assault, he proved that his heart was free and his will unconquered, for, having physical control over no member save his tongue, he bit that off and spat it out at his foe, a foe more terrible than the tyrant's executioners.

S. Catherine of Sienna has left a somewhat similar record. The Evil One having obtained permission from God to assault that pious virgin with all his strength, so long as he laid no hand upon her, filled her heart with impure suggestions, and surrounded her with every conceivable temptation of sight and sound, which, penetrating into the Saint's heart, so filled it, that, as she herself has said, nothing remained free save her most acute superior will. This struggle endured long, until at length Our Lord appeared to her, and she exclaimed, "Where wert Thou, O most Dear Lord, when my heart was so overwhelmed with darkness and foulness?" Whereupon He answered, "I was within thy heart, My child." "How could that be, Lord," she asked, "when it was so full of evil? Canst Thou abide in a place so foul?" Then our Lord replied, "Tell Me, did these evil thoughts and imaginations give thee pain or pleasure? didst thou take delight, or didst thou grieve over them?" To which S. Catherine made answer, "They grieved me exceedingly." Then the Lord said, "Who, thinkest thou, was it that caused thee to be thus grieved, save I Myself, hidden within thy soul? Believe Me, My child, had I not been there, these evil thoughts which swarmed around thy soul, and which thou couldst not banish, would speedily have overpowered it, and entering in, thy free will would have accepted them, and so death had struck that soul; but inasmuch as I was there, I filled thy heart with

---

[4] Rom. vii. 23.
[5] Gal. v. 17.

reluctance and resistance, so that it set itself stedfastly against the temptation, and finding itself unable to contend as vigorously as it desired, it did but experience a yet more vehement abhorrence of sin and of itself. Thus these very troubles became a great merit again to thee, and a great accession of virtue and strength to thy soul."

Here, you see, were the embers covered over with ashes, while temptation and delectation had entered the heart and surrounded the will, which, aided only by the Saviour, resisted all evil inspirations with great disgust, and a persevering refusal to consent to sin. Verily the soul which loves God is sometimes in sore straits to know whether He abideth in it or no, and whether that Divine Love for which it fights is extinguished or burns yet. But it is the very essence of the perfection of that Heavenly Love to require its lovers to endure and fight for Love's sake, without knowing even whether they possess the very Love for which and in which they strive.

Chapter V: Encouragement for the Tempted Soul.

GOD never permits such grievous temptations and assaults to try any, save those souls whom He designs to lead on to His own living, highest love, but nevertheless it does not follow as a natural consequence that they are certain to attain thereto. Indeed, it has often happened that those who had been stedfast under violent assaults, failing to correspond faithfully to Divine Grace, have yielded under the pressure of very trifling temptations. I would warn you of this, my child, so that, should you ever be tried by great temptations, you may know that God is showing special favour to you, thereby proving that He means to exalt you in His Sight; but that at the same time you may ever be humble and full of holy fear, not overconfident in your power to resist lesser temptations because you have overcome those that were greater, unless by means of a most stedfast faithfulness to God.

Come what may in the shape of temptation, attended by whatsoever of delectation,— so long as your will refuses consent, not merely to the temptation itself, but also to the delectation, you need have no fear,—God is not offended. When any one has swooned away, and gives no sign of life, we put our hand to his heart, and if we find the slightest fluttering there, we conclude that he still lives, and that, with the help of stimulants and counter-irritants, we may restore consciousness and power. Even so, sometimes amid the violence of temptation the soul seems altogether to faint away, and to lose all spiritual life and action. But if you would be sure how it really is, put your hand on the heart. See whether heart and will yet have any spiritual motion; that is to say, whether they fulfil their own special duty in refusing consent to and acceptance of temptation and its gratification; for so long as the power to refuse exists within the soul, we may be sure that Love, the life of the soul, is there, and that Jesus Christ, our Lord and Saviour, is within, although, it may be, hidden; and that by means of stedfast perseverance in prayer, and the Sacraments, and confidence in God, strength will be restored, and the soul will live with a full and joyous life.

Chapter VI: When Temptation and Delectation are Sin.

THAT princess, whom we have already taken as an illustration, was not to blame in the unlawful pursuit we supposed to be made of her, because it was against her will; but if, on the contrary, she had in any way led to it, or sought to attract him who sought her, she were certainly guilty of the pursuit itself; and even if she withheld her consent, she would still deserve censure and punishment. Thus it sometimes happens that temptation in itself is sin to us, because we have ourselves brought it upon us. For instance, if I know that gaming leads me to passion and blasphemy, and that all play is a temptation to me, I sin each and every time that I play, and I am responsible for all the temptations which may come upon me at the gaming table. So again, if I know that certain society involves me in temptation to evil, and yet I voluntarily seek it, I am unquestionably responsible for all that I may encounter in the way of temptation therein.

When it is possible to avoid the delectation arising out of temptation, it is always a sin to accept it, in proportion to the pleasure we take, and the amount of consent given, whether that be great or small, brief or lasting. The princess of our illustration is to blame if she merely listens to the guilty propositions made to her but still more so if, after listening, she takes pleasure in them, and allows her heart to feed and rest thereupon; for although she has no intention of really doing that which is proposed, her heart gives a spiritual consent when she takes pleasure in it, and it must always be wrong to let either body or mind rest on anything unworthy,—and wrongdoing lies so entirely in the heart's co-operation, that without this no mere bodily action can be sin.

Therefore, when you are tempted to any sin, examine whether you voluntarily exposed yourself to the temptation, and if you find that you have done so by putting yourself into its way, or by not foreseeing the temptation, as you ought to have done, then it is sin; but if you have done nothing to bring about the temptation, it is not in anywise to be imputed to you as sin.

When the delectation which attends temptation might have been avoided, but has not been avoided, there is always a certain amount of sin according to the degree to which we have lingered over it, and the kind of pleasure we have taken in it. If a woman who has not wilfully attracted unlawful admiration, nevertheless takes pleasure in such admiration, she is doing wrong, always supposing that what pleases her is the admiration. But if the person who courts her plays exquisitely on the lute, and she took pleasure, not in the personal attentions paid to herself, but in the sweetness and harmony of the music, there would be no sin in that, although it would be wrong to give way to any extent to her pleasure, for fear of its leading on to pleasure in the pursuit of herself. So again, if some clever stratagem whereby to avenge me of an enemy is suggested, and I take no satisfaction and give no consent to the vengeance, but am only pleased at the cleverness of the invention, I am not sinning; although it were very inexpedient to dwell long upon it, lest little by little I should go on to take pleasure in the thought of revenge.

Sometimes we are taken by surprise by some sense of delectation following so closely upon the temptation, that we are off our guard. This can be but a very slight venial sin, which would become greater if, after once we perceive the danger, we allow ourselves to dally with it, or question as to admitting or rejecting it,—greater still if we carelessly neglect to resist it;—and if we deliberately allow ourselves to rest in any such pleasure, it becomes very great sin, especially if the thing attracting us be unquestionably evil. Thus it is a great sin in a woman to allow herself to dwell upon any unlawful affections, although she may have no intention of ever really yielding to them.

Chapter VII: Remedies for Great Occasions.

SO soon as you feel yourself anywise tempted, do as our little children when they see a wolf or a bear in the mountains. Forthwith they run to the protection of their father or mother, or at least cry out for help. Do you fly in like manner to God, claiming His compassion and succour,—it is the remedy taught us by our Lord Himself: "Pray that ye enter not into temptation"[6]

If, nevertheless, the temptation persists or increases, hasten in spirit to embrace the holy Cross, as though you beheld Jesus Christ Crucified actually Present. Make firm protests against consenting, and ask His Help thereto; and, so long as the temptation lasts, do you persist in making acts of non-consent. But while making these acts and these protests, do not fix your eyes on the temptation,—look solely on Our Lord, for if you dwell on the temptation, especially when it is strong, your courage may be shaken. Divert your mind with any right and healthy occupation, for if that takes possession and fills your thoughts, it will drive away temptation and evil imaginations.

One great remedy against all manner of temptation, great or small, is to open the heart and lay bare its suggestions, likings, and dislikings, to your director; for, as you may observe, the first condition which the Evil One makes with a soul, when he wants to seduce it, is silence. Even as a bad man, seeking to seduce a woman, enjoins silence concerning himself to her father or husband, whereas God would always have us make known all His inspirations to our superiors and guides.

If, after all, the temptation still troubles and persecutes us, there is nothing to be done on our side save to persist in protesting that we will not consent; for just as no maiden can be married while she persists in saying No, so no soul, however oppressed, can be guilty while it says the same.

Do not argue with your Enemy, and give but one answer,—that with which Our Lord confounded him, "Get thee hence, Satan, for it is written, Thou shalt worship the Lord thy God, and Him only shalt thou serve."[7] Just as the pure wife would make no reply, and cast no glance on the foul seducer who strove to lead her astray, but would straightway fly from him to her husband's side, not arguing, but cleaving to her lawful lord in renewed fidelity;—so the devout soul when assailed by temptation should never trifle with it by answer or argument, but simply fly to the Side of Jesus Christ, its Bridegroom; renewing its pledges of unchanging devotion and faithfulness to Him.

Chapter VIII: How to resist Minor Temptations.

WHILE it is right to resist great temptations with invincible courage, and all such victories will be most valuable, still there is perhaps more absolute profit to our souls in resisting little ones. For although the greater temptations exceed in power, there are so infinitely more in number of little temptations, that a victory over them is fully as important as over the greater but rarer ones. No one will question but that wolves and bears are more dangerous than flies, but they do not worry and annoy us, or try our patience as these do. While is not a hard thing to abstain from murder, but it is very difficult to avoid all passing fits of anger, which assail us at every moment. A man or woman can easily keep from adultery, but it is less easy to abstain from all words and glances which are disloyal. While is easy to keep from stealing another man's goods, but often difficult to resist coveting them; easy to avoid bearing false witness in direct judgment, difficult to be perfectly truthful in conversation; easy to refrain from getting drunk, difficult to be

---

[6] S. Luke xxii. 40.
[7] S. Matt. iv. 10.

absolutely sober; easy not to wish for a neighbour's death, difficult not to wish anything contrary to his interests; easy to keep from slander, difficult to avoid all contempt.

In short, all these minor temptations to anger, suspicion, jealousy, envy, levity, vanity, duplicity, affectation, foolish thoughts, and the like, are a perpetual trial even to those who are most devout and most resolute; and therefore, my daughter, we ought carefully and diligently to prepare for this warfare. Be assured that every victory won over these little foes is as a precious stone in the crown of glory which God prepares for us in Paradise. So, while awaiting and making ready for a stedfast and brave resistance to great temptations should they come, let us not fail diligently to fight against these meaner, weaker foes.

Chapter IX: How remedy Minor Temptations.

NOW as to all these trifling temptations of vanity, suspicion, vexation, jealousy, envy, and the like, which flit around one like flies or gnats, now settling on one's nose,—anon stinging one's cheek,—as it is wholly impossible altogether to free one's-self from their importunity; the best resistance one can make is not to be fretted by them. All these things may worry one, but they cannot really harm us, so long as our wills are firmly resolved to serve God.

Therefore despise all these trivial onslaughts, and do not even deign to think about them; but let them buzz about your ears as much as they please, and flit hither and thither just as you tolerate flies;—even if they sting you, and strive to light within your heart, do no more than simply remove them, not fighting with them, or arguing, but simply doing that which is precisely contrary to their suggestions, and specially making acts of the Love of God. If you will take my advice, you will not toil on obstinately in resisting them by exercising the contrary virtue, for that would become a sort of struggle with the foe;—but, after making an act of this directly contrary virtue (always supposing you have time to recognise what the definite temptation is), simply turn with your whole heart towards Jesus Christ Crucified, and lovingly kiss His Sacred Feet. This is the best way to conquer the Enemy, whether in small or great temptations; for inasmuch as the Love of God contains the perfection of every virtue, and that more excellently than the very virtues themselves; it is also the most sovereign remedy against all vice, and if you accustom your mind under all manner of temptation to have recourse to this safety-place, you will not be constrained to enter upon a worryingly minute investigation of your temptations, but, so soon as you are anywise troubled, your mind will turn naturally to its one sovereign remedy. Moreover, this way of dealing with temptation is so offensive to the Evil One, that, finding he does but provoke souls to an increased love of God by his assaults, he discontinues them.

In short, you may be sure that if you dally with your minor, oft-recurring temptations, and examine too closely into them in detail, you will simply stupefy yourself to no purpose.

Chapter X: How to strengthen the Heart against Temptation.

EXAMINE from time to time what are the dominant passions of your soul, and having ascertained this, mould your life, so that in thought, word and deed you may as far as possible counteract them. For instance, if you know that you are disposed to be vain, reflect often upon the emptiness of this earthly life, call to mind how burdensome all mere earthly vanities will be to the conscience at the hour of death, how unworthy of a generous heart, how puerile and childish, and the like. See that your words have no tendency to foster your vanity, and even though you may seem to be doing so but reluctantly, strive to despise it heartily, and to rank yourself in every way among its enemies. Indeed, by dint of steady opposition to anything, we teach ourselves to hate even that which we began by liking. Do as many lowly, humble deeds as lie in your power, even if you perform them unwillingly at first; for by this means you will form a habit of humility, and you will weaken your vanity, so that when temptation arises, you will be less predisposed to yield, and stronger to resist. Or if you are given to avarice, think often of the folly of this sin, which makes us the slave of what was made only to serve us; remember how when we die we must leave all we possess to those who come after us, who may squander it, ruin their own souls by misusing it, and so forth. Speak against covetousness, commend the abhorrence in which it is held by the world; and constrain yourself to abundant almsgiving, as also to not always using opportunities of accumulation. If you have a tendency to trifle with the affections, often call to mind what a dangerous amusement it is for yourself and others; how unworthy a thing it is to use the noblest feelings of the heart as a mere pastime; and how readily such trifling becomes mere levity. Let your conversation turn on purity and simplicity of heart, and strive to frame your actions accordingly, avoiding all that savours of affectation or flirting.

In a word, let your time of peace,—that is to say, the time when you are not beset by temptations to sin,—be used in cultivating the graces most opposed to your natural difficulties, and if opportunities for their exercise do not arise, go out of your way to seek them, and by so doing you will strengthen your heart against future temptations.

Chapter XI: Anxiety of Mind.

ANXIETY of mind is not so much an abstract temptation, as the source whence various temptations arise. Sadness, when defined, is the mental grief we feel because of our involuntary ailments;—whether the evil be exterior, such as poverty, sickness or contempt; or interior, such as ignorance, dryness, depression or temptation. Directly that the soul is conscious of some such trouble, it is downcast, and so trouble sets in. Then we at once begin to try to get rid of it, and find means to shake it off; and so far rightly enough, for it is natural to us all to desire good, and shun that which we hold to be evil.

If any one strives to be delivered from his troubles out of love of God, he will strive patiently, gently, humbly and calmly, looking for deliverance rather to God's Goodness and Providence than to his own industry or efforts; but if self-love is the prevailing object he will grow hot and eager in seeking relief, as though all depended more upon himself than upon God. I do not say that the person thinks so, but he acts eagerly as though he did think it. Then if he does not find what he wants at once, he becomes exceedingly impatient and troubled, which does not mend matters, but on the contrary makes them worse, and so he gets into an unreasonable state of anxiety and distress, till he begins to fancy that there is no cure for his trouble. Thus you see how a disturbance, which was right at the outset, begets anxiety, and anxiety goes on into an excessive distress, which is exceedingly dangerous.

This unresting anxiety is the greatest evil which can happen to the soul, sin only excepted. Just as internal commotions and seditions ruin a commonwealth, and make it incapable of resisting its foreign enemies, so if our heart be disturbed and anxious, it loses power to retain such graces as it has, as well as strength to resist the temptations of the Evil One, who is all the more ready to fish (according to an old proverb) in troubled waters.

Anxiety arises from an unregulated desire to be delivered from any pressing evil, or to obtain some hoped-for good. Nevertheless nothing tends so greatly to enchance the one or retard the other as over-eagerness and anxiety. Birds that are captured in nets and snares become inextricably entangled therein, because they flutter and struggle so much. Therefore, whensoever you urgently desire to be delivered from any evil, or to attain some good thing, strive above all else to keep a calm, restful spirit,—steady your judgment and will, and then go quietly and easily after your object, taking all fitting means to attain thereto. By easily I do not mean carelessly, but without eagerness, disquietude or anxiety; otherwise, so far from bringing about what you wish, you will hinder it, and add more and more to your perplexities. "My soul is alway in my hand, yet do I not forget Thy Law,"[8] David says. Examine yourself often, at least night and morning, as to whether your soul is "in your hand;" or whether it has been wrested thence by any passionate or anxious emotion. See whether your soul is fully under control, or whether it has not in anywise escaped from beneath your hand, to plunge into some unruly love, hate, envy, lust, fear, vexation or joy. And if it has so strayed, before all else seek it out, and quietly bring it back to the Presence of God, once more placing all your hopes and affections under the direction of His Holy Will. Just as one who fears to lose some precious possession holds it tight in his hand, so, like King David, we ought to be able to say, "My soul is alway in my hand, and therefore I have not forgotten Thy Law."

Do not allow any wishes to disturb your mind under the pretext of their being trifling and unimportant; for if they gain the day, greater and weightier matters will find your heart more accessible to disturbance. When you are conscious that you are growing anxious, commend yourself to God, and resolve stedfastly not to take any steps whatever to obtain the result you desire, until your disturbed state of mind is altogether quieted;—unless indeed it should be necessary to do something without delay, in which case you must restrain the rush of inclination, moderating it, as far as possible, so as to act rather from reason than impulse.

If you can lay your anxiety before your spiritual guide, or at least before some trusty and devout friend, you may be sure that you will find great solace. The heart finds relief in telling its troubles to another, just as the body when suffering from persistent fever finds relief from bleeding. It is the best of remedies, and therefore it was that S. Louis counselled his son, "If thou hast any uneasiness lying heavy on thy heart, tell it forthwith to thy confessor, or to some other pious person, and the comfort he will give will enable thee to bear it easily."

Chapter XII: Of Sadness and Sorrow.

S. PAUL says that "godly sorrow worketh repentance to salvation not to be repented of, but the sorrow of the world worketh death."[9] So we see that sorrow may be good or bad according to the several results it produces in us. And indeed there are more bad than good results arising from it, for the only good ones are mercy and repentance; whereas

---

[8] Ps. cxix. 109.
[9] 2 Cor. vii. 10.

there are six evil results, namely, anguish, sloth, indignation, jealousy, envy and impatience. The Wise Man says that "sorrow hath killed many, and there is no profit therein,"[10] and that because for the two good streams which flow from the spring of sadness, there are these six which are downright evil.

The Enemy makes use of sadness to try good men with his temptations:—just as he tries to make bad men merry in their sin, so he seeks to make the good sorrowful amid their works of piety; and while making sin attractive so as to draw men to it, he strives to turn them from holiness by making it disagreeable. The Evil One delights in sadness and melancholy, because they are his own characteristics. He will be in sadness and sorrow through all Eternity, and he would fain have all others the same.

The "sorrow of the world" disturbs the heart, plunges it into anxiety, stirs up unreasonable fears, disgusts it with prayer, overwhelms and stupefies the brain, deprives the soul of wisdom, judgment, resolution and courage, weakening all its powers; in a word, it is like a hard winter, blasting all the earth's beauty, and numbing all animal life; for it deprives the soul of sweetness and power in every faculty.

Should you, my daughter, ever be attacked by this evil spirit of sadness, make use of the following remedies. "Is any among you afflicted?" says S. James, "let him pray."[11] Prayer is a sovereign remedy, it lifts the mind to God, Who is our only Joy and Consolation. But when you pray let your words and affections, whether interior or exterior, all tend to love and trust in God. "O God of Mercy, most Loving Lord, Sweet Saviour, Lord of my heart, my Joy, my Hope, my Beloved, my Bridegroom."

Vigorously resist all tendencies to melancholy, and although all you do may seem to be done coldly, wearily and indifferently, do not give in. The Enemy strives to make us languid in doing good by depression, but when he sees that we do not cease our efforts to work, and that those efforts become all the more earnest by reason of their being made in resistance to him, he leaves off troubling us.

Make use of hymns and spiritual songs; they have often frustrated the Evil One in his operations, as was the case when the evil spirit which possessed Saul was driven forth by music and psalmody. It is well also to occupy yourself in external works, and that with as much variety as may lead us to divert the mind from the subject which oppresses it, and to cheer and kindle it, for depression generally makes us dry and cold. Use external acts of fervour, even though they are tasteless at the time; embrace your crucifix, clasp it to your breast, kiss the Feet and Hands of your Dear Lord, raise hands and eyes to Heaven, and cry out to God in loving, trustful ejaculations: "My Beloved is mine, and I am His.[12] A bundle of myrrh is my Well-beloved, He shall lie within my breast. Mine eyes long sore for Thy Word, O when wilt Thou comfort me![13] O Jesus, be Thou my Saviour, and my soul shall live. Who shall separate me from the Love of Christ?"[14] etc.

Moderate bodily discipline is useful in resisting depression, because it rouses the mind from dwelling on itself; and frequent Communion is specially valuable; the Bread of Life strengthens the heart and gladdens the spirits.

---

[10] "Multos enim occidit tristitia, et non est utilitas in illa." Ecclus. xxx. 25.
[11] S. James v. 13.
[12] Cant. ii. 16.
[13] Ps. cxix. 82.
[14] Rom. viii 35.

Lay bare all the feelings, thoughts and longings which are the result of your depression to your confessor or director, in all humility and faithfulness; seek the society of spiritually-minded people, and frequent such as far as possible while you are suffering. And, finally, resign yourself into God's Hands, endeavouring to bear this harassing depression patiently, as a just punishment for past idle mirth. Above all, never doubt but that, after He has tried you sufficiently, God will deliver you from the trial.

Chapter XIII: Of Spiritual and Sensible Consolations, and how to receive them.

THE order of God's Providence maintains a perpetual vicissitude in the material being of this world; day is continually turning to night, spring to summer, summer to autumn, autumn to winter, winter to spring; no two days are ever exactly alike. Some are foggy, rainy, some dry or windy; and this endless variety greatly enhances the beauty of the universe. And even so precisely is it with man (who, as ancient writers have said, is a miniature of the world), for he is never long in any one condition, and his life on earth flows by like the mighty waters, heaving and tossing with an endless variety of motion; one while raising him on high with hope, another plunging him low in fear; now turning him to the right with rejoicing, then driving him to the left with sorrows; and no single day, no, not even one hour, is entirely the same as any other of his life.

All this is a very weighty warning, and teaches us to aim at an abiding and unchangeable evenness of mind amid so great an uncertainty of events; and, while all around is changing, we must seek to remain immoveable, ever looking to, reaching after and desiring our God. Let the ship take what tack you will, let her course be eastward or westward, northern or southern, let any wind whatsoever fill her sails, but meanwhile her compass will never cease to point to its one unchanging lodestar. Let all around us be overthrown, nay more, all within us; I mean let our soul be sad or glad, in bitterness or joy, at peace or troubled, dry and parched, or soft and fruitful, let the sun scorch, or the dew refresh it; but all the while the magnet of our heart and mind, our superior will, which is our moral compass, must continually point to the Love of God our Creator, our Saviour, our only Sovereign Good. "Whether we live, we live unto the Lord, or whether we die, we die unto the Lord; whether we live therefore or die, we are the Lord's. Who shall separate us from the Love of Christ?"[15] Nay, verily, nothing can ever separate us from that Love;—neither tribulation nor distress, neither death nor life, neither present suffering nor fear of ills to come; neither the deceits of evil spirits nor the heights of satisfaction, nor the depths of sorrow; neither tenderness nor desolation, shall be able to separate us from that Holy Love, whose foundation is in Christ Jesus. Such a fixed resolution never to forsake God, or let go of His Precious Love, serves as ballast to our souls, and will keep them stedfast amid the endless changes and chances of this our natural life. For just as bees, when overtaken by a gust of wind, carry little pebbles to weight themselves,[16] in order that they may resist the storm, and not be driven at its will,—so the soul, which has firmly grasped the Unchanging Love of God, will abide unshaken amid the changes and

---

[15] Rom. xiv. 8, and viii. 35.

[16] This notion seems to have arisen from the habits of the solitary mason bee, which early writers did not distinguish from other bees.

vicissitudes of consolations and afflictions,—whether spiritual or temporal, external or internal.

But let us come to some special detail, beyond this general doctrine.

1. I would say, then, that devotion does not consist in conscious sweetness and tender consolations, which move one to sighs and tears, and bring about a kind of agreeable, acceptable sense of self-satisfaction. No, my child, this is not one and the same as devotion, for you will find many persons who do experience these consolations, yet who, nevertheless, are evilminded, and consequently are devoid of all true Love of God, still more of all true devotion. When Saul was in pursuit of David, who fled from him into the wilderness of En-gedi, he entered into a cave alone, wherein David and his followers were hidden; and David could easily have killed him, but he not only spared Saul's life, he would not even frighten him; but, letting him depart quietly, hastened after the King, to affirm his innocence, and tell him how he had been at the mercy of his injured servant. Thereupon Saul testified to the softening of his heart by tender words, calling David his son, and exalting his generosity; lifting up his voice, he wept, and, foretelling David's future greatness, besought him to deal kindly with Saul's "seed after him."[17] What more could Saul have done? Yet for all this he had not changed his real mind, and continued to persecute David as bitterly as before. Just so there are many people who, while contemplating the Goodness of God, or the Passion of His Dear Son, feel an emotion which leads to sighs, tears, and very lively prayers and thanksgivings, so that it might fairly be supposed that their hearts were kindled by a true devotion;—but when put to the test, all this proves but as the passing showers of a hot summer, which splash down in large drops, but do not penetrate the soil, or make it to bring forth anything better than mushrooms. In like manner these tears and emotions do not really touch an evil heart, but are altogether fruitless;—inasmuch as in spite of them all those poor people would not renounce one farthing of illgotten gain, or one unholy affection; they would not suffer the slightest worldly inconvenience for the Sake of the Saviour over Whom they wept. So that their pious emotions may fairly be likened to spiritual fungi,—as not merely falling short of real devotion, but often being so many snares of the Enemy, who beguiles souls with these trivial consolations, so as to make them stop short, and rest satisfied therewith, instead of seeking after true solid devotion, which consists in a firm, resolute, ready, active will, prepared to do whatsoever is acceptable to God. A little child, who sees the surgeon bleed his mother, will cry when he sees the lancet touch her; but let that mother for whom he weeps ask for his apple or a sugar-plum which he has in his hand, and he will on no account part with it; and too much of our seeming devotion is of this kind. We weep feelingly at the spear piercing the Crucified Saviour's Side, and we do well,—but why cannot we give Him the apple we hold, for which He asks, heartily? I mean our heart, the only love-apple which that Dear Saviour craves of us. Why cannot we resign the numberless trifling attachments, indulgences, and self-complacencies of which He fain would deprive us, only we will not let Him do so; because they are the sugar-plums, sweeter to our taste than His Heavenly Grace? Surely this is but as the fondness of children;—demonstrative, but weak, capricious, unpractical. Devotion does not consist in such exterior displays of a tenderness which may be purely the result of a naturally impressionable, plastic character; or which may be the seductive action of the Enemy, or an excitable imagination stirred up by him.

---

[17] 1 Sam. xxiv.

2. Nevertheless these tender warm emotions are sometimes good and useful, for they kindle the spiritual appetite, cheer the mind, and infuse a holy gladness into the devout life, which embellishes all we do even externally. It was such a taste for holy things that made David cry out, "O how sweet are Thy words unto my throat, yea, sweeter than honey unto my mouth."[18] And assuredly the tiniest little comfort received through devotion is worth far more than the most abundant delights of this world. The milk of the Heavenly Bridegroom, in other words His spiritual favours, are sweeter to the soul than the costliest wine of the pleasures of this world, and to those who have tasted thereof all else seems but as gall and wormwood. There is a certain herb which, if chewed, imparts so great a sweetness that they who keep it in their mouth cannot hunger or thirst; even so those to whom God gives His Heavenly manna of interior sweetness and consolation, cannot either desire or even accept worldly consolations with any real zest or satisfaction. It is as a little foretaste of eternal blessedness which God gives to those who seek it; it is as the sugar-plum with which He attracts His little ones; as a cordial offered to strengthen their heart; as the first-fruits of their future reward. The legend tells us that Alexander the Great discovered Arabia Felix by means of the perfumes carried by the winds across the ocean upon which he sailed, reviving his courage and that of his comrades. And so the blessings and sweetnesses, which are wafted to us as we sail across the stormy sea of this mortal life, are a foretaste of the bliss of that Ever-blessed Heavenly Home to which we look and long.

3. But, perhaps you will say, if there are sensible consolations which are undoubtedly good and come from God, and at the same time others which are unprofitable, perilous, even harmful, because they proceed from mere natural causes, or even from the Enemy himself, how am I to know one from the other, or distinguish what is most profitable even among those which are good? It is a general rule, with respect to the feelings and affections, that their test is in their fruits. Our hearts are as trees, of which the affections and passions are their branches, and deeds and acts their fruits. That is, a good heart, of which the affections are good, and those are good affections which result in good and holy actions. If our spiritual tenderness and sweetness and consolation make us more humble,—patient, forbearing, charitable and kindly towards our neighbours,—more earnest in mortifying our own evil inclinations and lusts, more diligent in our duties, more docile and submissive to those who have a claim to our obedience, more simple in our whole manner of life,—then doubtless, my daughter, they come from God. But if this sweetness and tenderness is sweet only to ourselves, if we are fanciful, bitter, punctilious, impatient, obstinate, proud, presumptuous, harsh towards our neighbour, while reckoning ourselves as half-made saints, indocile to correction or guidance, then we may be assured our consolations are spurious and hurtful. A good tree will bring forth none save good fruit.

4. If we are favoured with any such sweetness, we must humble ourselves deeply before God, and beware of being led to cry out "How good I am!" No indeed, such gifts do not make us any better, for, as I have already said, devotion does not consist in such things; rather let us say, "How good God is to those who hope in Him, and to the souls that seek Him!" If a man has sugar in his mouth, he cannot call his mouth sweet, but the sugar; and so although our spiritual sweetness is admirable, and God Who imparts it is all good, it by no means follows that he who receives it is good. Let us count ourselves but

[18] Ps. cxix. 103.

as little children, having need of milk, and believe that these sugar-plums are only given us because we are still feeble and delicate, needing bribes and wiles to lead us on to the Love of God. But, as a general rule, we shall do well to receive all such graces and favours humbly, making much of them, not for their own importance, but rather because it is God's Hand which fills our hearts with them, as a mother coaxes her child with one sugar-plum after another. If the child were wise, he would prize the loving caresses of his mother, more than the material sugar-plum, however sweet. So while it is a great thing to have spiritual sweetnesses, the sweetest of all is to know that it is the loving parental Hand of God which feeds us, heart, mind and soul, with them. And, having received them humbly, let us be diligent in using them according to the intention of the Giver. Why do you suppose God gives us such sweetness? To make us kinder one to another, and more loving towards Him. A mother gives her child a sweetmeat to win a kiss; be it ours reverently to kiss the Saviour Who gives us these good things. And by kissing Him, I mean obeying Him, keeping His Commandments, doing His Will, heeding His wishes, in a word, embracing Him tenderly, obediently, and faithfully. So the day on which we have enjoyed some special spiritual consolation should be marked by extra diligence and humility. And from time to time it is well to renounce all such, realising to ourselves that although we accept and cherish them humbly, because they come from God, and kindle His Love in our hearts, still they are not our main object, but God and His Holy Love;—that we seek less the consolation than the Consoler, less His tangible sweetness than our sweet Saviour, less external pleasure than Him Who is the Delight of Heaven and earth; and with such a mind we should resolve to abide stedfast in God's Holy Love, even if our whole life were to be utterly devoid of all sweetness; as ready to abide on Mount Calvary as on Mount Tabor; to cry out, "It is good for us to be here," whether with our Lord on the Cross or in glory.

Lastly, I advise you to take counsel with your director concerning any unusual flow of consolations or emotions, so that he may guide you in their wise usage; for it is written, "Hast thou found honey? eat so much as is sufficient for thee."[19]

Chapter XIV: Of Dryness and Spiritual Barrenness.

SO much for what is to be done in times of spiritual consolations. But these bright days will not last for ever, and sometimes you will be so devoid of all devout feelings, that it will seem to you that your soul is a desert land, fruitless, sterile, wherein you can find no path leading to God, no drop of the waters of Grace to soften the dryness which threatens to choke it entirely. Verily, at such a time the soul is greatly to be pitied, above all, when this trouble presses heavily, for then, like David, its meat are tears day and night, while the Enemy strives to drive it to despair, crying out, "Where is now thy God? how thinkest thou to find Him, or how wilt thou ever find again the joy of His Holy Grace?"

What will you do then, my child? Look well whence the trial comes, for we are often ourselves the cause of our own dryness and barrenness. A mother refuses sugar to her sickly child, and so God deprives us of consolations when they do but feed self-complacency or presumption. "It is good for me that I have been in trouble, for before I was troubled I went wrong."[20] So if we neglect to gather up and use the treasures of God's

[19] Prov. xxv. 16.
[20] Ps. cxix. 67, 71.

Love in due time, He withdraws them as a punishment of our sloth. The Israelite who neglected to gather his store of manna in the early morning, found none after sunrise, for it was all melted. Sometimes, too, we are like the Bride of the Canticles, slumbering on a bed of sensual satisfaction and perishable delight, so that when the Bridegroom knocks at the door of our heart, and calls us to our spiritual duties, we dally with Him, loath to quit our idle and delusive pleasures, and then He "withdraws Himself, and is gone," and "when I sought Him, I could not find Him; I called Him, but He gave me no answer."[21] Of a truth we deserved as much for having been so disloyal as to have rejected Him for the things of this world. If we are content with the fleshpots of Egypt we shall never receive heavenly manna. Bees abhor all artificial scents, and the sweetness of the Holy Spirit is incompatible with the world's artificial pleasures.

Again, any duplicity or unreality in confession or spiritual intercourse with your director tends to dryness and barrenness, for, if you lie to God's Holy Spirit, you can scarcely wonder that He refuses you His comfort. If you do not choose to be simple and honest as a little child, you will not win the child's sweetmeats.

Or you have satiated yourself with worldly delights; and so no wonder that spiritual pleasures are repulsive to you. "To the overfed dove even cherries are bitter," says an old proverb; and Our Lady in her song of praise says, "He has filled the hungry with good things, and the rich He hath sent empty away." They who abound in earthly pleasures are incapable of appreciating such as are spiritual.

If you have carefully stored up the fruits of past consolations, you will receive more; "to him that hath yet more shall be given," but from him who has not kept that which he had, who has lost it through carelessness, that which he hath shall be taken away, in other words, he will not receive the grace destined for him. Rain refreshes living plants, but it only brings rottenness and decay to those which are already dead. There are many such causes whereby we lose the consolations of religion, and fall into dryness and deadness of spirit, so that it is well to examine our conscience, and see if we can trace any of these or similar faults. But always remember that this examination must not be made anxiously, or in an over-exacting spirit. Thus if, after an honest investigation of our own conduct, we find the cause of our wrongdoing, we must thank God, for an evil is half cured when we have found out its cause. But if, on the contrary, you do not find any particular thing which has led to this dryness, do not trifle away your time in a further uneasy search, but, without more ado, and in all simplicity, do as follows:—

1. Humble yourself profoundly before God, acknowledging your nothingness and misery. Alas, what am I when left to myself! no better, Lord, than a parched ground, whose cracks and crevices on every side testify its need of the gracious rain of Heaven, while, nevertheless, the world's blasts wither it more and more to dust.

2. Call upon God, and ask for His Gladness. "O give me the comfort of Thy help again! My Father, if it be possible, let this cup pass from me." "Depart, O ye unfruitful wind, which parcheth up my soul, and come, O gracious south wind, blow upon my garden." Such loving desires will fill you with the perfume of holiness.

3. Go to your confessor, open your heart thoroughly, let him see every corner of your soul, and take all his advice with the utmost simplicity and humility, for God loves obedience, and He often makes the counsel we take, specially that of the guides of souls, to be more useful than would seem likely; just as He caused the waters of Jordan,

---

[21] Cant. v. 2-7.

commended by Elijah to Naaman, to cure his leprosy in spite of the improbability to human reason.

4. But, after all, nothing is so useful, so fruitful amid this dryness and barrenness, as not to yield to a passionate desire of being delivered from it. I do not say that one may not desire to be set free, but only that one ought not to desire it over-eagerly, but to leave all to the sole Mercy of God's special Providence, in order that, so long as He pleases, He may keep us amid these thorns and longings. Let us say to God at such seasons, "O my Father, if it be possible, let this cup pass from me;"—but let us add heartily, "Nevertheless, not my will, but Thine be done," and there let us abide as trustingly as we are able. When God sees us to be filled with such pious indifference, He will comfort us with His grace and favour, as when He beheld Abraham ready to offer up his son Isaac, and comforted him with His blessing. In every sort of affliction, then, whether bodily or spiritual, in every manner of distraction or loss of sensible devotion, let us say with our whole heart, and in the deepest submission, "The Lord gave me all my blessings, the Lord taketh them away, blessed be the Name of the Lord." If we persevere in this humility, He will restore to us His mercies as he did to Job, who ever spake thus amid all his troubles.

5. And lastly, my daughter, amid all our dryness let us never grow discouraged, but go steadily on, patiently waiting the return of better things; let us never be misled to give up any devout practices because of it, but rather if possible, let us increase our good works, and if we cannot offer liquid preserves to our Bridegroom, let us at least offer Him dried fruit—it is all one to Him, so long as the heart we offer be fully resolved to love Him. In fine weather bees make more honey and breed fewer grubs, because they spend so much time in gathering the sweet juices of the flowers that they neglect the multiplication of their race. But in a cold, cloudy spring they have a fuller hive and less honey. And so sometimes, my daughter, in the glowing springtide of spiritual consolations, the soul spends so much time in storing them up, that amid such abundance it performs fewer good works; while, on the contrary, when amid spiritual dryness and bitterness, and devoid of all that is attractive in devotion, it multiplies its substantial good works, and abounds in the hidden virtues of patience, humility, self-abnegation, resignation and unselfishness.

Some people, especially women, fall into the great mistake of imagining that when we offer a dry, distasteful service to God, devoid of all sentiment and emotion, it is unacceptable to His Divine Majesty; whereas, on the contrary, our actions are like roses, which, though they may be more beautiful when fresh, have a sweeter and stronger scent when they are dried. Good works, done with pleasurable interest, are pleasanter to us who think of nothing save our own satisfaction, but when they are done amid dryness and deadness they are more precious in God's Sight. Yes indeed, my daughter, for in seasons of dryness our will forcibly carries us on in God's Service, and so it is stronger and more vigorous than at a softer time. There is not much to boast of in serving our Prince in the comfort of a time of peace, but to serve Him amid the toils and hardness of war, amid trial and persecution, is a real proof of faithfulness and perseverance. The blessed Angela di Foligni said, that the most acceptable prayer to God is what is made forcibly and in spite of ourselves; that is to say, prayer made not to please ourselves or our own taste, but solely to please God;—carried on, as it were, in spite of inclination, the will triumphing over all our drynesses and repugnances. And so of all good works;—the more contradictions, exterior or interior, against which we contend in their fulfilment, the more precious they are in God's Sight; the less of self-pleasing in striving after any virtue, the more Divine Love shines forth in all its purity. A child is easily moved to fondle its mother when she gives it sweet things, but if he kisses her in return for wormwood or camomile it is a proof of very real affection on his part.

Chapter XV: An Illustration.

LET me illustrate what I have said by an anecdote of Saint Bernard.

It is common to most beginners in God's Service, being as yet inexperienced in the fluctuations of grace and in spiritual vicissitudes, that when they lose the glow of sensible devotion, and the first fascinating lights which led them in their first steps towards God, they lose heart, and fall into depression and discouragement. Those who are practised in the matter say that it is because our human nature cannot bear a prolonged deprivation of some kind of satisfaction, either celestial or earthly; and so as souls, which have been raised beyond their natural level by a taste of superior joys, readily renounce visible delights when the higher joys are taken away, as well as those more earthly pleasures, they, not being yet trained to a patient waiting for the true sunshine, fancy that there is no light either in heaven or earth, but that they are plunged in perpetual darkness. They are just like newly-weaned babes, who fret and languish for want of the breast, and are a weariness to every one, especially to themselves.

Just so it fell out with a certain Geoffroy de Peronne, a member of S. Bernard's community, newly dedicated to God's Service, during a journey which he and some others were making. He became suddenly dry, deprived of all consolations, and amid his interior darkness he began to think of the friends and relations he had parted from, and of his worldly pursuits and interests, until the temptation grew so urgent that his outward aspect betrayed it, and one of those most in his confidence perceiving that he was sorely troubled, accosted him tenderly, asking him secretly, "What means this, Geoffroy? and what makes thee, contrary to thy wont, so pensive and sad?" Whereupon Geoffroy, sighing heavily, made answer, "Woe is me, my brother, never again in my life shall I be glad!"

The other was moved to pity by these words, and in his fraternal love he hastened to tell it all to their common father S. Bernard, and he, realising the danger, went into the nearest church to pray for Geoffroy, who meanwhile cast himself down in despair, and, resting his head on a stone, fell asleep. After a while both rose up, the one full of grace won by prayer, the other from his sleep, with so peaceful and gladsome a countenance, that his friend, marvelling to see so great and unexpected a change, could not refrain from gently reproaching him for his recent words. Thereupon Geoffroy answered, "If just now I told thee that I should never more be glad, so now I promise thee I will never more be sad!" Such was the result of this devout man's temptation; but from this history I would have you observe:—

1. That God is wont to give some foretaste of His heavenly joys to beginners in His Service, the better to wean them from earthly pleasures, and to encourage them in seeking His Divine Love, even as a mother attracts her babe to suck by means of honey.

2. That nevertheless it is the same Good God Who sometimes in His Wisdom deprives us of the milk and honey of His consolations, in order that we may learn to eat the dry substantial bread of a vigorous devotion, trained by means of temptations and trials.

3. That sometimes very grievous temptations arise out of dryness and barrenness, and that at such times these temptations must be stedfastly resisted, inasmuch as they are not of God; but the dryness must be patiently endured, because He sends that to prove us.

4. That we must never grow discouraged amid our inward trials, nor say, like Geoffroy, "I shall never be glad;" but through the darkness we must look for light; and in like manner, in the brightest spiritual sunshine, we must not presume to say, "I shall never be sad." Rather we must remember the saying of the Wise Man, "In the day of prosperity remember the evil."[22] It behoves us to hope amid trials, and to fear in prosperity, and in both circumstances always to be humble.

5. That it is a sovereign remedy to open our grief to some spiritual friend able to assist us.

And, in conclusion, I would observe that here, as everywhere, our Gracious God and our great Enemy are in conflict, for by means of these trials God would bring us to great purity of heart, to an entire renunciation of self-interest in all concerning His Service, and a perfect casting aside of self-seeking; but the Evil One seeks to use our troubles to our discouragement, so as to turn us back to sensual pleasures, and to make us a weariness to ourselves and others, in order to injure true devotion. But if you will give heed to the above instructions you will advance greatly towards perfection amid such interior trials, concerning which I have yet one word to say. Sometimes revulsions and dryness and incapacity proceed from bodily indisposition, as when excessive watching, 1 fasting, or overwork produce weariness, lassitude, heaviness, and the like; which, while wholly caused by the body, interfere greatly with the soul, so intimately are they linked together. When this is the case, you must always remember to make marked acts of virtue with your higher will, for, although your whole soul may seem to be sunk in drowsy weariness, such mental efforts are acceptable to God. At such a time you may say with the Bride of the Canticles, "I sleep, but my heart waketh."[23] And, as I have already said, if there is less enjoyment in such efforts, there is more virtue and merit. But the best remedy under the last-named circumstances is to reinvigorate the body by some lawful recreation and solace.

S. Francis enjoined his religious to use such moderation in their labours as never to impair the fervour of their minds. And speaking of that great Saint, he was himself once attacked by such deep depression of mind that he could not conceal it; if he sought to associate with his religious he was unable to talk; if he kept apart he only grew worse; abstinence and maceration of the flesh overwhelmed him, and he found no comfort in prayer. For two years he continued in this state, as though altogether forsaken of God, but after humbly enduring the heavy storm, his Saviour restored him to a happy calm quite suddenly.

From this we should learn that God's greatest servants are liable to such trials, so that less worthy people should not be surprised if they experience the same.

---

[22] Ecclus. xi. 25, Vulgate: "In die bonorum ne immemor sis malorum." English version: "In the day of prosperity there is a forgetfulness of affliction."

[23] Cant. v. 2.

Chapter I: It is well yearly to renew Good Resolutions by means of the following Exercises.

THE first point in these exercises is to appreciate their importance. Our earthly nature easily falls away from its higher tone by reason of the frailty and evil tendency of the flesh, oppressing and dragging down the soul, unless it is constantly rising up by means of a vigorous resolution, just as a bird would speedily fall to the ground if it did not maintain its flight by repeated strokes of its wings. In order to this, my daughter, you need frequently to reiterate the good resolutions you have made to serve God, for fear that, failing to do so, you fall away, not only to your former condition, but lower still; since it is a characteristic of all spiritual falls that they invariably throw us lower than we were at the beginning. There is no clock, however good, but must be continually wound up; and moreover, during the course of each year it will need taking to pieces, to cleanse away the rust which clogs it, to straighten bent works, and renew such as are worn. Even so, any one who really cares for his heart's devotion will wind it up to God night and morning, and examine into its condition, correcting and improving it; and at least once a year he will take the works to pieces and examine them carefully;—I mean his affections and passions,—so as to repair whatever may be amiss. And just as the clockmaker applies a delicate oil to all the wheels and springs of a clock, so that it may work properly and be less liable to rust, so the devout soul, after thus taking the works of his heart to pieces, will lubricate them with the Sacraments of Confession and the Eucharist. These exercises will repair the waste caused by time, will kindle your heart, revive your good resolutions, and cause the graces of your mind to flourish anew.

The early Christians observed some such practice on the Anniversary of our Lord's Baptism, when, as S. Gregory, Bishop of Nazianzen, tells us, they renewed the profession and promises made in that Sacrament. It were well to do the like, my child, making due and earnest preparation, and setting very seriously to work.

Having then chosen a suitable time, according to the advice of your spiritual father, and having retired somewhat more than usual into a literal and spiritual solitude, make one, two, or three meditations on the following points, according to the method I set before you in Part II.

Chapter II: Meditation on the Benefit conferred on us by God in calling us to His Service.

1. CONSIDER the points on which you are about to renew your resolutions.

Firstly, that you have forsaken, rejected, detested and renounced all mortal sin for ever.

Secondly, that you have dedicated and consecrated your soul, heart and body, with everything appertaining thereto, to the Service and Love of God.

Thirdly, that if you should unhappily fall into any sin, you would forthwith rise up again, with the help of God's Grace.

Are not these worthy, right, noble resolutions? Consider well within your soul how holy, reasonable and desirable an act it is to renew them.

2. Consider to Whom you make these promises; for if a deliberate promise made to men is strictly binding, how much more those which we make to God. "My heart is inditing of a good matter. I will not forget Thee," David cried out.[1]

3. Consider before Whom you promised. It was before the whole Court of Heaven. The Blessed Virgin, S. Joseph, your Guardian Angel, S. Louis, the whole Company of the Blessed, were looking on with joy and approbation, beholding, with love unspeakable, your heart cast at your Saviour's Feet and dedicated to His Service. That act of yours called forth special delight in the Heavenly Jerusalem, and it will now be renewed if you on your part heartily renew your good resolutions.

4. Consider how you were led to make those resolutions. How good and gracious God was then to you! Did He not draw you by the tender wiles of His Holy Spirit? Were not the sails by which your little bark was wafted into the haven of safety those of love and charity? Did not God lure you on with His Heavenly Sweetness, by Sacraments, prayer, and pious books? Ah, my child, while you slept God watched over you with His boundless Love, and breathed thoughts of peace into your heart!

5. Consider when God led you to these important resolutions. It was in the flower of your life, and how great the blessing of learning early what we can never know soon enough. S. Augustine, who acquired that knowledge when he was thirty years old, exclaimed, "Oh, Thou Beauty of ancient days, yet ever new, too late I loved Thee! Thou wert within and I abroad: Thou wert with me, but I was not with Thee."[2] Even so you may say, "Oh, Blessedness of ancient days, wherefore did I not appreciate Thee sooner!" You were not yet worthy of it, and yet God gave you such grace in your youth;—therefore say with David, "Thou, O God, hast taught me from my youth up until now; therefore will I tell of Thy wondrous works."[3] Or if you who read should not have known Him till old age, bethink you how great His Grace in calling you after you had wasted so many years; how gracious the Mercy which drove you from your evil courses before the hour of death, which, had it found you unchanged, must have brought you eternal woe.

Consider the results of this call; you will surely find a change for the better, comparing what you are with what you were. Is it not a blessing to know how to talk with God in prayer, to desire to love Him, to have stilled and subdued sundry passions which disturbed you, to have conquered sundry sins and perplexities, and to have received so many more Communions than formerly, thereby being united to the Great Source of all eternal grace? Are not all these things exceeding blessings? Weigh them, my child, in the balances of the sanctuary, for it is God's Right Hand which has done all this: "The Right Hand of the Lord hath the pre-eminence, the Right Hand of the Lord bringeth mighty things to pass. I shall not die, but live, and declare the works of the Lord"[4] with heart, lips and deeds.

After dwelling upon all these considerations, which will kindle abundance of lively affections in you, you should conclude simply with an act of thanksgiving, and a hearty prayer that they may bring forth fruit, leaving off with great humility and trust in God, and

---

[1] Ps. xlv. 1.; xliv. 18.
[2] Conf., Oxf. Trans. bk. x. p. 203.
[3] Ps. lxxi. 15.
[4] Ps. cxviii. 16, 17.

reserving the final results of your resolution till after the second point of this spiritual exercise.

Chapter III: Examination of the Soul as to its Progress in the Devout Life.

THIS second point is somewhat lengthy, and I would begin by saying that there is no need for you to carry it out all at once. Divide it by taking your conduct towards God at one time, all that concerns yourself another time, all that concerns your neighbour, and fourthly, the examination of your passions. It is neither necessary nor expedient that you make it upon your knees, always excepting the beginning and the end, which includes the affections. The other points of self-examination you may make profitably when out walking, or better still, in bed, that is, if you can keep wide awake and free from drowsiness; but to do this you must read them over carefully beforehand. Anyhow, it is desirable to go through this second point in three days and two nights at the most, taking that season which you can best manage; for if you go through it at too distant intervals you will lose the depth of impression which ought to be made by this spiritual exercise. After each point of examination observe wherein you have failed, and what is lacking to you, and in what you have chiefly failed, so that you may be able to explain your troubles, get counsel and comfort, and make fresh resolutions. It is not necessary entirely to shun all society on the days you select for this work, but you must contrive a certain amount of retirement, especially in the evening, so as to get to bed somewhat earlier than usual, with a view to that rest, bodily and mental, which is so important for serious thought. And during the day make frequent aspirations to Our Lord, Our Lady, the Angels, and all the Heavenly Jerusalem. Everything must be done with a heart full of God's Love, and an earnest desire for spiritual perfection. To begin this examination,—

1. Place yourself in the Presence of God.

2. Invoke the Holy Spirit, and ask light of Him, so that you may know yourself, as S. Augustine did, crying out, "Lord, teach me to know Thee, and to know myself;" and S. Francis, who asked, "Who art Thou, Lord, and who am I?" Resolve not to note any progress with any self-satisfaction or self-glorification, but give the glory to God Alone, and thank Him duly for it.

Resolve, too, that if you should seem to yourself to have made but little progress, or even to have gone back, that you will not be discouraged thereby, nor grow cool or indolent in the matter; but that, on the contrary, you will take fresh pains to humble yourself and conquer your faults, with God's Help.

Then go on to examine quietly and patiently how you have conducted yourself towards God, your neighbour and yourself, up to the present time.

Chapter IV: Examination of the Soul's Condition as regards God.

1. WHAT is the aspect of your heart with respect to mortal sin? Are you firmly resolved never to commit it, let come what may? And have you kept that resolution from the time you first made it? Therein lies the foundation of the spiritual life.

2. What is your position with respect to the Commandments of God? Are they acceptable, light and easy to you? He who has a good digestion and healthy appetite likes good food, and turns away from that which is bad.

3. How do you stand as regards venial sins? No one can help committing some such occasionally; but are there none to which you have any special tendency, or worse still, any actual liking and clinging?

4. With respect to spiritual exercises—do you like and value them? or do they weary and vex you? To which do you feel most or least disposed, hearing or reading God's Word, meditating upon it, calling upon God, Confession, preparing for Communion and communicating, controlling your inclinations, etc.? What of all these is most repugnant to you? And if you find that your heart is not disposed to any of these things, examine into the cause, find out whence the disinclination comes.

5. With respect to God Himself—does your heart delight in thinking of God, does it crave after the sweetness thereof? "I remembered Thine everlasting judgments, O Lord, and received comfort," says David.[5] Do you feel a certain readiness to love Him, and a definite inclination to enjoy His Love? Do you take pleasure in dwelling upon the Immensity, the Goodness, the Tenderness of God? When you are immersed in the occupations and vanities of this world, does the thought of God come across you as a welcome thing? do you accept it gladly, and yield yourself up to it, and your heart turn with a sort of yearning to Him? There are souls that do so.

6. If a wife has been long separated from her husband, so soon as she sees him returning, and hears his voice, however cumbered she may be with business, or forcibly hindered by the pressure of circumstances, her heart knows no restraint, but turns at once from all else to think upon him she loves. So it is with souls which really love God, however engrossed they may be; when the thought of Him is brought before them, they forget all else for joy at feeling His Dear Presence nigh, and this is a very good sign.

7. With respect to Jesus Christ as God and Man—how does your heart draw to Him? Honey bees seek their delight in their honey, but wasps hover over stinking carrion. Even so pious souls draw all their joy from Jesus Christ, and love Him with an exceeding sweet Love, but those who are careless find their pleasure in worldly vanities.

8. With respect to Our Lady, the Saints, and your Guardian Angel—do you love them well? Do you rejoice in the sense of their guardianship? Do you take pleasure in their lives, their pictures, their memories?

9. As to your tongue—how do you speak of God? Do you take pleasure in speaking His Praise, and singing His Glory in psalms and hymns?

10. As to actions—have you God's visible glory at heart, and do you delight in doing whatever you can to honour Him? Those who love God will love to adorn and beautify His House. Are you conscious of having ever given up anything you liked, or of renouncing anything for God's Sake? for it is a good sign when we deprive ourselves of something we care for on behalf of those we love. What have you ever given up for the Love of God?

---

[5] Ps. cxix. 52.

Chapter V: Examination of your Condition as regards yourself.

1. HOW do you love yourself? Is it a love which concerns this life chiefly? If so, you will desire to abide here for ever, and you will diligently seek your worldly establishment,—but if the love you bear yourself has a heavenward tendency, you will long, or, at all events you will be ready to go hence whensoever it may please our Lord.

2. Is your love of yourself well regulated? for nothing is more ruinous than an inordinate love of self. A well-regulated love implies greater care for the soul than for the body; more eagerness in seeking after holiness than aught else; a greater value for heavenly glory than for any mean earthly honour. A well regulated heart much oftener asks itself, "What will the angels say if I follow this or that line of conduct?" than what will men say.

3. What manner of love do you bear to your own heart? Are you willing to minister to it in its maladies? for indeed you are bound to succour it, and seek help for it when harassed by passion, and to leave all else till that is done.

4. What do you imagine yourself worth in God's Sight? Nothing, doubtless, nor is there any great humility in the fly which confesses it is nought, as compared with a mountain, or a drop of water, which knows itself to be nothing compared with the sea, or a cornflower, or a spark, as compared with the sun. But humility consists in not esteeming ourselves above other men, and in not seeking to be esteemed above them. How is it with you in this respect?

5. In speech—do you never boast in any way? Do you never indulge in self-flattery when speaking of yourself?

6. In deed—do you indulge in anything prejudicial to your health,—I mean useless idle pleasures, unprofitable night-watches, and the like?

Chapter VI: Examination of the Soul's Condition as regards our Neighbour.

HUSBAND and wife are bound to love one another with a tender, abiding, restful love, and this tie stands foremost by God's order and Will. And I say the same with respect to children and all near relations, as also friends in their respective degrees. But, generally speaking, how is it with you as concerning your neighbour? Do you love him cordially, and for God's Sake? In order to answer this fairly, you must call to mind sundry disagreeable, annoying people, for it is in such cases that we really practise the Love of God with respect to our neighbours, and still more towards them that do us wrong, either by word or deed. Examine whether your heart is thoroughly clear as regards all such, and whether it costs you a great effort to love them. Are you quick to speak ill of your neighbours, especially of such as do not love you? Do you act unkindly in any way, directly or indirectly, towards them? A very little honest self-dealing will enable you to find this out.

Chapter VII: Examination as to the Affectations of the Soul.

I HAVE dwelt thus at length on these points, on a due examination of which all true knowledge of our spiritual progress rests; as to an examination of sins, that rather pertains to the confessions of those who are not eager to advance. But it is well to take ourselves to task soberly concerning these different matters, investigating how we have been going on since we made good resolutions concerning them, and what notable faults we have committed. But the summary of all is to examine into our passions; and if you are worried by so detailed an investigation as that already suggested, you may make a briefer inquiry as to what you have been, and how you have acted, in some such manner as this:—In your love of God, your neighbour, and yourself.

In hatred for the sin which is in yourself, for the sin which you find in others, since you ought to desire the extirpation of both; in your desires concerning riches, pleasure, and honour.

In fear of the perils of sin, and of the loss of this world's goods; we fear the one too much and the other too little.

In hope, fixed overmuch it may be on things of this world and the creature; too little on God and things eternal.

In sadness, whether it be excessive concerning unimportant matters.

In gladness, whether it be excessive concerning unworthy objects.

In short, examine what attachments hinder your spiritual life, what passions engross it, and what chiefly attracts you.

It is by testing the passions of the soul, one by one, that we ascertain our spiritual condition, just as one who plays the lute tries every string, touching those which are discordant, either raising or lowering them. Thus having tried our soul as to love, hate, desire, fear, hope, sadness and joy, if we find our strings out of tune for the melody we wish to raise, which is God's Glory, we must tune them afresh with the help of His Grace, and the counsel of our spiritual father.

Chapter VIII: The Affections to be excited after such Examination.

WHEN you have quietly gone through each point of this examination, and have ascertained your own position, you will excite certain feelings and affections in your heart. Thank God for such amendment, however slight, as you may have found in yourself, confessing that it is the work of His Mercy Alone in you.

Humble yourself deeply before God, confessing that if your progress has been but small, it is your own fault, for not having corresponded faithfully, bravely and continually to the inspirations and lights which He has given you in prayer or otherwise.

Promise to praise Him for ever for the graces He has granted to you, and because He has led you against your will to make even this small progress.

Ask forgiveness for the disloyalty and faithlessness with which you have answered Him.

Offer your whole heart to Him that He Alone may rule therein. Entreat Him to keep you faithful to Himself.

Ponder over the examples of the Saints, the Blessed Virgin, your guardian Angel and patron Saint, S. Joseph, etc.

Chapter IX: Reflections suitable to the renewal of Good Resolutions.

AFTER you have made this self-examination, and having conferred with some holy director as to your shortcomings and their remedies, you will do well to pursue the following considerations, taking one daily as a meditation, and giving to it the time usually so spent; always making the same preparation and kindling the same affections as you learnt to use before meditating in Part I. Above all, placing yourself in the Presence of God, and earnestly asking His Grace to confirm you and keep you stedfast in His Holy Love and Service.

Chapter X: First Consideration—of the Worth of Souls.

CONSIDER how noble and excellent a thing your soul is, endowed with understanding, capable of knowing, not merely this visible world around us, but Angels and Paradise, of knowing that there is an All-Mighty, All-Merciful, Ineffable God; of knowing that eternity lies before you, and of knowing what is necessary in order so to live in this visible world as to attain to fellowship with those Angels in Paradise, and the eternal fruition of God.

Yet more;——your soul is possessed of a noble will, capable of loving God, irresistibly drawn to that love; your heart is full of generous enthusiasm, and can no more find rest in any earthly creation, or in aught save God, than the bee can find honey on a dunghill, or in aught save flowers. Let your mind boldly review the wild earthly pleasures which once filled your heart, and see whether they did not abound in uneasiness and doubts, in painful thoughts and uncomfortable cares, amid which your troubled heart was miserable.

When the heart of man seeks the creature, it goes to work eagerly, expecting to satisfy its cravings; but directly it obtains what it sought, it finds a blank, and dissatisfied, begins to seek anew; for God will not suffer our hearts to find any rest, like the dove going forth from Noah's ark, until it returns to God, whence it came. Surely this is a most striking natural beauty in our heart;—why should we constrain it against its will to seek creature love?

In some such wise might you address your soul: "You are capable of realising a longing after God, why should you trifle with anything lower? you can live for eternity, why should you stop short in time? One of the sorrows of the prodigal son was, that, when he might have been living in plenty at his father's table, he had brought himself to share the swine's husks. My soul, you are made for God, woe be to you if you stop short in anything short of Him!" Lift up your soul with thoughts such as these, convince it that it is eternal, and worthy of eternity; fill it with courage in this pursuit.

Chapter XI: Second Consideration—on the Excellence of Virtue.

CONSIDER that nothing save holiness and devotion can satisfy your soul in this world: behold how gracious they are; draw a contrast between each virtue and its opposite vice; how gracious patience is compared with vengeance; gentleness compared with anger; humility with pride and arrogance; liberality with avarice; charity with envy; sobriety with unsteadiness. It is one charm of all virtues that they fill the soul with untold sweetness after being practised, whereas vice leaves it harassed and ill at ease. Who would not speedily set to work and obtain such sweetness?

In the matter of evil, he who has a little is not contented, and he who has much is discontented; but he who has a little virtue is gladsome, and his gladness is for ever greater as he goes on. O devout life! you are indeed lovely, sweet and pleasant; you can soften sorrows and sweeten consolations; without you good becomes evil, pleasure is marred by anxiety and distress: verily whoso knows what you are may well say with the woman of Samaria, "Lord, give me this water,"[6] an aspiration often uttered by Saint Theresa and Saint Catherine of Genoa.

Chapter XII: The Example of the Saints.

CONSIDER the example of the Saints on all sides, what have they not done in order to love God and lead a devout life? Call to mind the Martyrs in their invincible firmness, and the tortures they endured in order to maintain their resolutions; remember the matrons and maidens, whiter than lilies in their purity, ruddier than the rose in their love, who at every age, from childhood upward, bore all manner of martyrdom sooner than forsake their resolutions, not only such as concerned their profession of faith, but that of devotion; some dying rather than lose their virginity, others rather than cease their works of mercy to the sick and sorrowful. Truly the frail sex has set forth no small courage in such ways. Consider all the Saintly Confessors, how heartily they despised the world, and how they stood by their resolutions, taken unreservedly and kept inviolably. Remember what S. Augustine says of his mother Monica, of her determination to serve God in her married life and in her widowhood; and S. Jerome and his beloved daughter S. Paula amid so many changes and chances. What may we not achieve with such patterns before our eyes? They were but what we are, they wrought for the same God, seeking the same graces; why may not we do as much in our own state of life, and according to our several vocations, on behalf of our most cherished resolutions and holy profession of faith?

Chapter XIII: The Love which Jesus Christ bears to us.

CONSIDER the Love with which our Dear Lord Jesus Christ bore so much in this world, especially in the Garden of Olives and on Mount Calvary; that Love bore you in mind, and through all those pains and toils He obtained your good resolutions for you, as also all that is needful to maintain, foster, strengthen and consummate those resolutions. How precious must the resolutions be which are the fruits of our Lord's Passion! and how dear to my heart, since they were dear to that of Jesus! Saviour of my soul, Thou didst die to win them for me; grant me grace sooner to die than forget them. Be sure, my daughter, that the Heart of our most Dear Lord beheld you from the tree of the Cross and loved you, and by that Love He won for you all good things which you were ever to have, and amongst them your good resolutions. Of a truth we have all reason like Jeremiah to confess that the Lord knew us, and called us by our name or ever we were born,[7] the more that His Divine Goodness in its Love and Mercy made ready all things, general and individual, which could promote our salvation, and among them our resolutions. A woman with child makes ready for the babe she expects, prepares its cradle, its swaddling clothes and its nurse; even so our Lord, while hanging on His Cross, prepared all that you could need for your happiness, all the means, the graces, the leadings, by which He leads your soul onwards towards perfection.

Surely we ought ever to remember this, and ask fervently: Is it possible that I was loved, and loved so tenderly by my Saviour, that He should have thought of me

---

[6] S. John iv. 15.
[7] Jer. i. 5.

individually, and in all these details by which He has drawn me to Himself? With what love and gratitude ought I to use all He has given me? The Loving Heart of my God thought of my soul, loved it, and prepared endless means to promote its salvation, even as though there were no other soul on earth of which He thought; just as the sun shines on each spot of earth as brightly as though it shone nowhere else, but reserved all its brightness for that alone. So Our Dear Lord thought and cared for every one of His children as though none other existed. "Who loved me, and gave Himself for me,"[8] S. Paul says, as though he meant, "for me alone, as if there were none but me He cared for."

Let this be graven in your soul, my child, the better to cherish and foster your good resolutions, which are so precious to the Heart of Jesus.

Chapter XIV: The Eternal Love of God for us.

CONSIDER the Eternal Love God has borne you, in that, even before our Lord Jesus Christ became Man and suffered on the Cross for you, His Divine Majesty designed your existence and loved you. When did He begin to love you? When He began to be God, and that was never, for He ever was, without beginning and without end. Even so He always loved you from eternity, and therefore He made ready all the graces and gifts with which He has endowed you. He says by His prophet, "I have loved thee" (and it is YOU that He means) "with an everlasting love, therefore with lovingkindness have I drawn thee."[9] And amid these drawings of His Love He led you to make these resolutions to serve Him.

What must resolutions be which God has foreseen, pondered, dwelt upon from all eternity? how dear and precious to us! Surely we should be ready to suffer anything whatsoever rather than let go one particle of the same. The whole world is not worth one soul, and the soul is worth but little without its good resolutions.

Chapter XV: General Affections which should result from these Considerations, and Conclusion of the Exercise.

O PRECIOUS resolutions! ye are as the lovely tree of life planted by God's Own Hand in the midst of my heart, a tree which my Saviour has watered with His Blood. Rather would I die a thousand deaths than suffer any blast of wind to root you up—neither vanity, nor pleasure, nor wealth, nor sorrows shall ever overthrow my intentions.

Lord, Thou hast planted and nurtured this tree in Thy Bosom, but how many souls there are which have not been thus favoured, how can I ever sufficiently acknowledge Thy Mercy? Blessed and holy resolutions, if I do but keep you, you will keep me! if you live in my soul, my soul will live in you. Live ever, then, ye resolutions, which have an eternity of your own in God's Mercy, live ever in me, and may I never forsake you.

Next, you must particularise the necessary means for maintaining your good resolutions, determining to use them diligently,—such as frequency in prayer, in Sacraments, in good works; the amendment of the faults you have already discovered, cutting off occasions of sin, and following out carefully all the advice given you with this view. Then, take breath as it were in a renewed profession of your resolutions, and, as though you held your heart in your hands,—dedicate, consecrate, sacrifice, immolate it to

[8] Gal. ii. 20.
[9] Jer. xxxi. 3.

God, vowing never to recall it, but leave it for ever in His Right Hand of Majesty, prepared everywhere and in all things to obey His Commands. Ask God to renew your will, to bless your renewed resolutions and to strengthen them. While your heart is thus roused and excited, hasten to your spiritual father, accuse yourself of any faults which you have discovered since you made your general confession, and receive absolution as you did at the first. Make your protest and sign it in his presence, and then lose no time in uniting your renewed heart to its Creator and Saviour, in the most holy Sacrament of the Eucharist.

Chapter XVI: The Impressions which should remain after this Exercise.

ON the day you make this renewal of your resolutions, and on those immediately following, you should often repeat with heart and voice the earnest words of S. Paul, S. Augustine, S. Catherine of Genoa, and others like-minded, "I am not mine own, whether I live or whether I die, I am the Lord's. There is no longer any me or mine, my 'me' is Jesus, my 'mine' is to be His. Thou world, wilt ever be thyself, and hitherto I have been myself, but henceforth I will be so no more." We shall indeed not be ourselves any more, for our heart will be changed, and the world which has so often deceived us will in its turn be deceived in us; our change will be so gradual that the world will still suppose us to be Esau, while really we are Jacob.

All our devout exercises must sink into the heart, and when we come forth from our meditation and retirement it behoves us to tread warily in business or society, lest the wine of our good resolutions be heedlessly spilt; rather let it soak in and penetrate every faculty of the soul, but quietly, and without bodily or mental excitement.

Chapter XVII: An Answer to Two Objections which may be made to this Book.

THE world will tell you, my child, that all these counsels and practices are so numerous, that anybody who tries to heed them can pay no attention to anything else. Verily, my dear daughter, if we did nothing else we should not be far wrong, since we should be doing all that we ought to do in this world. But you see the fallacy? If all these exercises were to be performed every day they would undoubtedly fill up all our time, but it is only necessary to use them according to time and place as they are wanted. What a quantity of laws there are in our civil codes and digests! But they are only called into use from time to time, as circumstances arise, not every day. Besides, for that matter, David, king as he was, and involved in a multiplicity of complicated affairs, fulfilled more religious duties than those which I have suggested; and S. Louis, a monarch unrivalled in time of peace or war, who was most diligent in the administration of justice and in ruling his country, nevertheless was wont to hear two masses daily, to say vespers and compline with his chaplain, and to make his meditation daily. He used to visit the hospitals every Friday, was regular at confession, took the discipline, often attended sermons and spiritual conferences, and withal he never lost any opportunity of promoting the public welfare, and his court was more flourishing and notable than that of any of his predecessors. Be bold and resolute then in performing the spiritual exercises I have set before you, and God will give you time and strength for all other duties, yea, even if He were to cause the sun to stand still, as He did in Joshua's time.[10] We are sure always to do enough when God works with us.

Moreover, the world will say that I take it for granted that those I address have the gift of mental prayer, which nevertheless every one does not possess, and that consequently this book will not be of use to all. Doubtless it is true that I have assumed this, and it is also true that every one has not the gift of mental prayer, but it is a gift which almost every one can obtain, even the most ignorant, provided they are under a good director, and will take as much pains as the thing deserves to acquire it. And if there are any altogether devoid of this gift (which I believe will very rarely be the case), a wise spiritual father will easily teach them how to supply the deficiency, by reading or listening to the meditations and considerations supplied in this book or elsewhere.

Chapter XVIII: Three Important and Final Counsels.

ON the first day of every month renew the resolution given in Part I. after meditation, and make continual protestation of your intention to keep it, saying with David, "I will never forget Thy Commandments, for with them Thou hast quickened me."[11] And whenever you feel any deterioration in your spiritual condition, take out your protest, and prostrating yourself in a humble spirit, renew it heartily, and you will assuredly find great relief.

Make open profession of your desire to be devout; I will not say to be devout, but to desire it; and do not be ashamed of the ordinary, needful actions which lead us on in the Love of God. Acknowledge boldly that you try to meditate, that you would rather die than commit a mortal sin; that you frequent the Sacraments, and follow the advice of your director (although for various reasons it may not be necessary to mention his name). This open confession that you intend to serve God, and that you have devoted yourself deliberately and heartily to His Holy Love, is very acceptable to His Divine Majesty, for He would not have any of us ashamed of Him or of His Cross. Moreover, it cuts at the root of many a hindrance which the world tries to throw in our way, and so to say, commits us to the pursuit of holiness. The philosophers of old used to give themselves out as such, in order to be left unmolested in their philosophic life; and we ought to let it be known that we aim at devotion in order that we may be suffered to live devoutly. And if any one affirms that you can live a devout life without following all these practices and counsels, do not deny it, but answer meekly that your infirmity is great, and needs more help and support than many others may require.

Finally, my beloved child, I intreat you by all that is sacred in heaven and in earth, by your own Baptism, by the breast which Jesus sucked, by the tender Heart with which He loves you, and by the bowels of compassion in which you hope—be stedfast and persevere in this most blessed undertaking to live a devout life. Our days pass away, death is at hand. "The trumpet sounds a recall," says S. Gregory Nazianzen, "in order that every one may make ready, for Judgment is near." When S. Symphorian was led to his martyrdom, his mother cried out to him, "My son, my son, remember life eternal, look to Heaven, behold Him Who reigns there; for the brief course of this life will soon be ended." Even so would I say to you: Look to Heaven, and do not lose it for earth; look at Hell, and do not plunge

---

[10] Josh. x. 12, 13.
[11] Ps. cxix. 93.

therein for the sake of this passing life; look at Jesus Christ, and do not deny Him for the world's sake; amid if the devout life sometimes seems hard and dull, join in Saint Francis' song,[12] —

> *"So vast the joys that I await,*
> *No earthly travail seemeth great."*

Glory be to Jesus, to Whom, with the Father and the Holy Ghost, be honour and glory, now and ever, and to all Eternity. Amen.

---

[12] "Tanto e il bene ch' io aspetto Ch' ogni pena m' e diletto." These are the words of Saint Francis d'Assisi, which S. Francis de Sales renders— "A cause des biens que j'attends, Les travaux me sont passe-temps."

The Pursuit of God

~ ※ ~

By *A. W. Tozer*

"Then shall we know, if we follow on to know the Lord: his going forth is prepared as the morning." —Hosea 6:3

The 1948 Edition

~ ※ ~

Introduction

Here is a masterly study of the inner life by a heart thirsting after God, eager to grasp at least the outskirts of His ways, the abyss of His love for sinners, and the height of His unapproachable majesty—and it was written by a busy pastor in Chicago!

Who could imagine David writing the twenty-third Psalm on South Halsted Street, or a medieval mystic finding inspiration in a small study on the second floor of a frame house on that vast, flat checker-board of endless streets

Where cross the crowded ways of life

Where sound the cries of race and clan,

In haunts of wretchedness and need,

On shadowed threshold dark with fears,

And paths where hide the lures of greed…

But even as Dr. Frank Mason North, of New York, says in his immortal poem, so Mr. Tozer says in this book:

Above the noise of selfish strife

We hear Thy voice, O Son of Man.

My acquaintance with the author is limited to brief visits and loving fellowship in his church. There I discovered a self-made scholar, an omnivorous reader with a remarkable library of theological and devotional books, and one who seemed to burn the midnight oil in pursuit of God. His book is the result of long meditation and much prayer. It is not a collection of sermons. It does not deal with the pulpit and the pew but with the soul athirst for God. The chapters could be summarized in Moses' prayer, "Show me thy glory," or Paul's exclamation, "O the depth of the riches both of the wisdom and knowledge of God!" It is theology not of the head but of the heart.

There is deep insight, sobriety of style, and a catholicity of outlook that is refreshing. The author has few quotations but he knows the saints and mystics of the centuries—Augustine, Nicholas of Cusa, Thomas à Kempis, von Hügel, Finney, Wesley and many more. The ten chapters are heart searching and the prayers at the close of each are for closet, not pulpit. *I felt the nearness of God while reading them.*

Here is a book for every pastor, missionary, and devout Christian. It deals with the deep things of God and the riches of His grace. Above all, it has the keynote of sincerity and humility.

Dr. Samuel M. Zwemer

New York City

Preface

In this hour of all-but-universal darkness one cheering gleam appears: within the fold of conservative Christianity there are to be found increasing numbers of persons whose religious lives are marked by a growing hunger after God Himself. They are eager for spiritual realities and will not be put off with words, nor will they be content with correct "interpretations" of truth. They are athirst for God, and they will not be satisfied till they have drunk deep at the Fountain of Living Water.

This is the only real harbinger of revival which I have been able to detect anywhere on the religious horizon. It may be the cloud the size of a man's hand for which a few saints here and there have been looking. It can result in a resurrection of life for many souls and a recapture of that radiant wonder which should accompany faith in Christ, that wonder which has all but fled the Church of God in our day.

But this hunger must be recognized by our religious leaders. Current evangelicalism has (to change the figure) laid the altar and divided the sacrifice into parts, but now seems satisfied to count the stones and rearrange the pieces with never a care that there is not a sign of fire upon the top of lofty Carmel. But God be thanked that there are a few who care. They are those who, while they love the altar and delight in the sacrifice, are yet unable to reconcile themselves to the continued absence of fire. They desire God above all. They are athirst to taste for themselves the "piercing sweetness" of the love of Christ about Whom all the holy prophets did write and the psalmists did sing.

There is today no lack of Bible teachers to set forth correctly the principles of the doctrines of Christ, but too many of these seem satisfied to teach the fundamentals of the faith year after year, strangely unaware that there is in their ministry no manifest Presence, nor anything unusual in their personal lives. They minister constantly to believers who feel within their breasts a longing which their teaching simply does not satisfy.

I trust I speak in charity, but the lack in our pulpits is real. Milton's terrible sentence applies to our day as accurately as it did to his: "The hungry sheep look up, and are not fed." It is a solemn thing, and no small scandal in the Kingdom, to see God's children starving while actually seated at the Father's table. The truth of Wesley's words is established before our eyes: "Orthodoxy, or right opinion, is, at best, a very slender part of religion. Though right tempers cannot subsist without right opinions, yet right opinions may subsist without right tempers. There may be a right opinion of God without either love or one right temper toward Him. Satan is a proof of this."

Thanks to our splendid Bible societies and to other effective agencies for the dissemination of the Word, there are today many millions of people who hold "right opinions," probably more than ever before in the history of the Church. Yet I wonder if there was ever a time when true spiritual worship was at a lower ebb. To great sections of the Church the art of worship has been lost entirely, and in its place has come that strange and foreign thing called the "program." This word has been borrowed from the stage and applied with sad wisdom to the type of public service which now passes for worship among us.

Sound Bible exposition is an imperative *must* in the Church of the Living God. Without it no church can be a New Testament church in any strict meaning of that term. But exposition may be carried on in such way as to leave the hearers devoid of any true spiritual nourishment whatever. For it is not mere words that nourish the soul, but God Himself, and unless and until the hearers find God in personal experience they are not the better for having heard the truth. The Bible is not an end in itself, but a means to bring men to an intimate and satisfying knowledge of God, that they may enter into Him, that they may delight in His Presence, may taste and know the inner sweetness of the very God Himself in the core and center of their hearts.

This book is a modest attempt to aid God's hungry children so to find Him. Nothing here is new except in the sense that it is a discovery which my own heart has made of spiritual realities most delightful and wonderful to me. Others before me have gone much farther into these holy mysteries than I have done, but if my fire is not large it is yet real, and there may be those who can light their candle at its flame.

A. W. Tozer

Chicago, Ill.

June 16, 1948

I: Following Hard after God

My soul followeth hard after thee: thy right hand upholdeth me.
— Psa. 63:8

Christian theology teaches the doctrine of prevenient grace, which briefly stated means this, that before a man can seek God, God must first have sought the man.

Before a sinful man can think a right thought of God, there must have been a work of enlightenment done within him; imperfect it may be, but a true work nonetheless, and the secret cause of all desiring and seeking and praying which may follow.

We pursue God because, and only because, He has first put an urge within us that spurs us to the pursuit. "No man can come to me," said our Lord, "except the Father which hath sent me draw him," and it is by this very prevenient *drawing* that God takes from us every vestige of credit for the act of coming. The impulse to pursue God originates with God, but the outworking of that impulse is our following hard after Him; and all the time we are pursuing Him we are already in His hand: "Thy right hand upholdeth me."

In this divine "upholding" and human "following" there is no contradiction. All is of God, for as von Hügel teaches, *God is always previous.* In practice, however, (that is, where God's previous working meets man's present response) man must pursue God. On our part there must be positive reciprocation if this secret drawing of God is to eventuate in identifiable experience of the Divine. In the warm language of personal feeling this is stated in the Forty-second Psalm: "As the hart panteth after the water brooks, so panteth my soul after thee, O God. My soul thirsteth for God, for the living God: when shall I come and appear before God?" This is deep calling unto deep, and the longing heart will understand it.

The doctrine of justification by faith—a Biblical truth, and a blessed relief from sterile legalism and unavailing self-effort—has in our time fallen into evil company and been interpreted by many in such manner as actually to bar men from the knowledge of God. The whole transaction of religious conversion has been made mechanical and spiritless. Faith may now be exercised without a jar to the moral life and without embarrassment to the Adamic ego. Christ may be "received" without creating any special love for Him in the soul of the receiver. The man is "saved," but he is not hungry nor thirsty after God. In fact he is specifically taught to be satisfied and encouraged to be content with little.

The modern scientist has lost God amid the wonders of His world; we Christians are in real danger of losing God amid the wonders of His Word. We have almost forgotten that God is a Person and, as such, can be cultivated as any person can. It is inherent in personality to be able to know other personalities, but full knowledge of one personality by another cannot be achieved in one encounter. It is only after long and loving mental intercourse that the full possibilities of both can be explored.

All social intercourse between human beings is a response of personality to personality, grading upward from the most casual brush between man and man to the fullest, most intimate communion of which the human soul is capable. Religion, so far as it is genuine, is in essence the response of created personalities to the Creating Personality, God. "This is life eternal, that they might know thee the only true God, and Jesus Christ, whom thou hast sent."

God is a Person, and in the deep of His mighty nature He thinks, wills, enjoys, feels, loves, desires and suffers as any other person may. In making Himself known to us He stays by the familiar pattern of personality. He communicates with us through the avenues of our minds, our wills and our emotions. The continuous and unembarrassed interchange of love and thought between God and the soul of the redeemed man is the throbbing heart of New Testament religion.

This intercourse between God and the soul is known to us in conscious personal awareness. It is personal: that is, it does not come through the body of believers, as such, but is known to the individual, and to the body through the individuals which compose it. And it is conscious: that is, it does not stay below the threshold of consciousness and work there unknown to the soul (as, for instance, infant baptism is thought by some to do), but comes within the field of awareness where the man can "know" it as he knows any other fact of experience.

You and I are in little (our sins excepted) what God is in large. Being made in His image we have within us the capacity to know Him. In our sins we lack only the power. The moment the Spirit has quickened us to life in regeneration our whole being senses its kinship to God and leaps up in joyous recognition. That is the heavenly birth without which we cannot see the Kingdom of God. It is, however, not an end but an inception, for now begins the glorious pursuit, the heart's happy exploration of the infinite riches of the Godhead. That is where we begin, I say, but where we stop no man has yet discovered, for there is in the awful and mysterious depths of the Triune God neither limit nor end.

Shoreless Ocean, who can sound Thee?

Thine own eternity is round Thee,

Majesty divine!

To have found God and still to pursue Him is the soul's paradox of love, scorned indeed by the too-easily-satisfied religionist, but justified in happy experience by the children of the burning heart. St. Bernard stated this holy paradox in a musical quatrain that will be instantly understood by every worshipping soul:

We taste Thee, O Thou Living Bread,

And long to feast upon Thee still:

We drink of Thee, the Fountainhead

And thirst our souls from Thee to fill.

Come near to the holy men and women of the past and you will soon feel the heat of their desire after God. They mourned for Him, they prayed and wrestled and sought for Him day and night, in season and out, and when they had found Him the finding was all the sweeter for the long seeking. Moses used the fact that he knew God as an argument for knowing Him better. "Now, therefore, I pray thee, if I have found grace in thy sight, show me now thy way, that I may know thee, that I may find grace in thy sight"; and from there he rose to make the daring request, "I beseech thee, show me thy glory." God was frankly pleased by this display of ardor, and the next day called Moses into the mount, and there in solemn procession made all His glory pass before him.

David's life was a torrent of spiritual desire, and his psalms ring with the cry of the seeker and the glad shout of the finder. Paul confessed the mainspring of his life to be his burning desire after Christ. "That I may know Him," was the goal of his heart, and to this he sacrificed everything. "Yea doubtless, and I count all things but loss for the excellency of the knowledge of Christ Jesus my Lord: for whom I have suffered the loss of all things, and do count them but refuse, that I may win Christ."

Hymnody is sweet with the longing after God, the God whom, while the singer seeks, he knows he has already found. "His track I see and I'll pursue," sang our fathers only a short generation ago, but that song is heard no more in the great congregation. How tragic that we in this dark day have had our seeking done for us by our teachers. Everything is made to center upon the initial act of "accepting" Christ (a term, incidentally, which is not found in the Bible) and we are not expected thereafter to crave any further revelation of God to our souls. We have been snared in the coils of a spurious logic which insists that if we have found Him we need no more seek Him. This is set before us as the last word in orthodoxy, and it is taken for granted that no Bible-taught Christian ever believed otherwise. Thus the whole testimony of the worshipping, seeking, singing Church on that subject is crisply set aside. The experiential heart-theology of a grand army of fragrant saints is rejected in favor of a smug interpretation of Scripture which would certainly have sounded strange to an Augustine, a Rutherford or a Brainerd.

In the midst of this great chill there are some, I rejoice to acknowledge, who will not be content with shallow logic. They will admit the force of the argument, and then turn away with tears to hunt some lonely place and pray, "O God, show me thy glory." They want to taste, to touch with their hearts, to see with their inner eyes the wonder that is God.

I want deliberately to encourage this mighty longing after God. The lack of it has brought us to our present low estate. The stiff and wooden quality about our religious lives is a result of our lack of holy desire. Complacency is a deadly foe of all spiritual growth. Acute desire must be present or there will be no manifestation of Christ to His people. He waits to be wanted. Too bad that with many of us He waits so long, so very long, in vain.

Every age has its own characteristics. Right now we are in an age of religious complexity. The simplicity which is in Christ is rarely found among us. In its stead are programs, methods, organizations and a world of nervous activities which occupy time and attention but can never satisfy the longing of the heart. The shallowness of our inner experience, the hollowness of our worship, and that servile imitation of the world which marks our promotional methods all testify that we, in this day, know God only imperfectly, and the peace of God scarcely at all.

If we would find God amid all the religious externals we must first determine to find Him, and then proceed in the way of simplicity. Now as always God discovers Himself to "babes" and hides Himself in thick darkness from the wise and the prudent. We must simplify our approach to Him. We must strip down to essentials (and they will be found to be blessedly few). We must put away all effort to impress, and come with the guileless candor of childhood. If we do this, without doubt God will quickly respond.

When religion has said its last word, there is little that we need other than God Himself. The evil habit of seeking *God-and* effectively prevents us from finding God in full revelation. In the "and" lies our great woe. If we omit the "and" we shall soon find God, and in Him we shall find that for which we have all our lives been secretly longing.

We need not fear that in seeking God only we may narrow our lives or restrict the motions of our expanding hearts. The opposite is true. We can well afford to make God our All, to concentrate, to sacrifice the many for the One.

The author of the quaint old English classic, *The Cloud of Unknowing*, teaches us how to do this. "Lift up thine heart unto God with a meek stirring of love; and mean Himself, and none of His goods. And thereto, look thee loath to think on aught but God Himself. So that nought work in thy wit, nor in thy will, but only God Himself. This is the work of the soul that most pleaseth God."

Again, he recommends that in prayer we practice a further stripping down of everything, even of our theology. "For it sufficeth enough, a naked intent direct unto God without any other cause than Himself." Yet underneath all his thinking lay the broad foundation of New Testament truth, for he explains that by "Himself" he means "God that made thee, and bought thee, and that graciously called thee to thy degree." And he is all for simplicity: If we would have religion "lapped and folden in one word, for that thou shouldst have better hold thereupon, take thee but a little word of one syllable: for so it is better than of two, for even the shorter it is the better it accordeth with the work of the Spirit. And such a word is this word GOD or this word LOVE."

When the Lord divided Canaan among the tribes of Israel Levi received no share of the land. God said to him simply, "I am thy part and thine inheritance," and by those words made him richer than all his brethren, richer than all the kings and rajas who have ever lived in the world. And there is a spiritual principle here, a principle still valid for every priest of the Most High God.

The man who has God for his treasure has all things in One. Many ordinary treasures may be denied him, or if he is allowed to have them, the enjoyment of them will be so tempered that they will never be necessary to his happiness. Or if he must see them go, one after one, he will scarcely feel a sense of loss, for having the Source of all things he has in One all satisfaction, all pleasure, all delight. Whatever he may lose he has actually lost nothing, for he now has it all in One, and he has it purely, legitimately and forever.

O God, I have tasted Thy goodness, and it has both satisfied me and made me thirsty for more. I am painfully conscious of my need of further grace. I am ashamed of my lack of desire. O God, the Triune God, I want to want Thee; I long to be filled with longing; I thirst to be made more thirsty still. Show me Thy glory, I pray Thee, that so I may know Thee indeed. Begin in mercy a new work of love within me. Say to my soul, "Rise up, my love, my fair one, and come away." Then give me grace to rise and follow Thee up from this misty lowland where I have wandered so long. In Jesus' Name, Amen.

II: The Blessedness of Possessing Nothing

Blessed are the poor in spirit: for theirs is the kingdom of heaven.
— Matt. 5:3

Before the Lord God made man upon the earth He first prepared for him by creating a world of useful and pleasant things for his sustenance and delight. In the Genesis account of the creation these are called simply "things." They were made for man's uses, but they were meant always to be external to the man and subservient to him. In the deep heart of the man was a shrine where none but God was worthy to come. Within him was God; without, a thousand gifts which God had showered upon him.

But sin has introduced complications and has made those very gifts of God a potential source of ruin to the soul.

Our woes began when God was forced out of His central shrine and "things" were allowed to enter. Within the human heart "things" have taken over. Men have now by nature no peace within their hearts, for God is crowned there no longer, but there in the moral dusk stubborn and aggressive usurpers fight among themselves for first place on the throne.

This is not a mere metaphor, but an accurate analysis of our real spiritual trouble. There is within the human heart a tough fibrous root of fallen life whose nature is to possess, always to possess. It covets "things" with a deep and fierce passion. The pronouns "my" and "mine" look innocent enough in print, but their constant and universal use is significant. They express the real nature of the old Adamic man better than a thousand volumes of theology could do. They are verbal symptoms of our deep disease. The roots of our hearts have grown down into *things*, and we dare not pull up one rootlet lest we die. Things have become necessary to us, a development never originally intended. God's gifts now take the place of God, and the whole course of nature is upset by the monstrous substitution.

Our Lord referred to this tyranny of *things* when He said to His disciples, "If any man will come after me, let him deny himself, and take up his cross, and follow me. For whosoever will save his life shall lose it: and whosoever shall lose his life for my sake shall find it."

Breaking this truth into fragments for our better understanding, it would seem that there is within each of us an enemy which we tolerate at our peril. Jesus called it "life" and "self," or as we would say, the *self-life*. Its chief characteristic is its possessiveness: the words "gain" and "profit" suggest this. To allow this enemy to live is in the end to lose everything. To repudiate it and give up all for Christ's sake is to lose nothing at last, but to preserve everything unto life eternal. And possibly also a hint is given here as to the only effective way to destroy this foe: it is by the Cross. "Let him take up his cross and follow me."

The way to deeper knowledge of God is through the lonely valleys of soul poverty and abnegation of all things. The blessed ones who possess the Kingdom are they who have repudiated every external thing and have rooted from their hearts all sense of possessing. These are the "poor in spirit." They have reached an inward state paralleling the outward circumstances of the common beggar in the streets of Jerusalem; that is what the word "poor" as Christ used it actually means. These blessed poor are no longer slaves to the tyranny of *things*. They have broken the yoke of the oppressor; and this they have done not by fighting but by surrendering. Though free from all sense of possessing, they yet possess all things. "Theirs is the kingdom of heaven."

Let me exhort you to take this seriously. It is not to be understood as mere Bible teaching to be stored away in the mind along with an inert mass of other doctrines. It is a marker on the road to greener pastures, a path chiseled against the steep sides of the mount of God. We dare not try to by-pass it if we would follow on in this holy pursuit. We must ascend a step at a time. If we refuse one step we bring our progress to an end.

As is frequently true, this New Testament principle of spiritual life finds its best illustration in the Old Testament. In the story of Abraham and Isaac we have a dramatic picture of the surrendered life as well as an excellent commentary on the first Beatitude.

Abraham was old when Isaac was born, old enough indeed to have been his grandfather, and the child became at once the delight and idol of his heart. From that moment when he first stooped to take the tiny form awkwardly in his arms he was an eager love slave of his son. God went out of His way to comment on the strength of this affection. And it is not hard to understand. The baby represented everything sacred to his father's heart: the promises of God, the covenants, the hopes of the years and the long messianic dream. As he watched him grow from babyhood to young manhood the heart of the old man was knit closer and closer with the life of his son, till at last the relationship bordered upon the perilous. It was then that God stepped in to save both father and son from the consequences of an uncleansed love.

"Take now thy son," said God to Abraham, "thine only son Isaac, whom thou lovest, and get thee into the land of Moriah; and offer him there for a burnt-offering upon one of the mountains which I will tell thee of." The sacred writer spares us a close-up of the agony that night on the slopes near Beersheba when the aged man had it out with his God, but respectful imagination may view in awe the bent form and convulsive wrestling alone under the stars. Possibly not again until a Greater than Abraham wrestled in the Garden of Gethsemane did such mortal pain visit a human soul. If only the man himself might have been allowed to die. That would have been easier a thousand times, for he was old now, and to die would have been no great ordeal for one who had walked so long with God. Besides, it would have been a last sweet pleasure to let his dimming vision rest upon the figure of his stalwart son who would live to carry on the Abrahamic line and fulfill in himself the promises of God made long before in Ur of the Chaldees.

How should he slay the lad! Even if he could get the consent of his wounded and protesting heart, how could he reconcile the act with the promise, "In Isaac shall thy seed be called"? This was Abraham's trial by fire, and he did not fail in the crucible. While the stars still shone like sharp white points above the tent where the sleeping Isaac lay, and long before the gray dawn had begun to lighten the east, the old saint had made up his mind. He would offer his son as God had directed him to do, and *then trust God to raise him from the dead*. This, says the writer to the Hebrews, was the solution his aching heart found sometime in the dark night, and he rose "early in the morning" to carry out the plan. It is beautiful to see that, while he erred as to God's method, he had correctly sensed the secret of His great heart. And the solution accords well with the New Testament Scripture, "Whosoever will lose for my sake shall find."

God let the suffering old man go through with it up to the point where He knew there would be no retreat, and then forbade him to lay a hand upon the boy. To the wondering patriarch He now says in effect, "It's all right, Abraham. I never intended that you should actually slay the lad. I only wanted to remove him from the temple of your heart that I might reign unchallenged there. I wanted to correct the perversion that existed in your love. Now you may have the boy, sound and well. Take him and go back to your tent. Now I know that thou fearest God, seeing that thou hast not withheld thy son, thine only son, from me."

Then heaven opened and a voice was heard saying to him, "By myself have I sworn, saith the Lord, for because thou hast done this thing, and hast not withheld thy son, thine only son: that in blessing I will bless thee, and in multiplying I will multiply thy seed as the stars of the heaven, and as the sand which is upon the sea shore; and thy seed shall possess the gate of his enemies; and in thy seed shall all the nations of the earth be blessed; because thou hast obeyed my voice."

The old man of God lifted his head to respond to the Voice, and stood there on the mount strong and pure and grand, a man marked out by the Lord for special treatment, a friend and favorite of the Most High. Now he was a man wholly surrendered, a man utterly obedient, a man who possessed nothing. He had concentrated his all in the person of his dear son, and God had taken it from him. God could have begun out on the margin of Abraham's life and worked inward to the center; He chose rather to cut quickly to the heart and have it over in one sharp act of separation. In dealing thus He practiced an economy of means and time. It hurt cruelly, but it was effective.

I have said that Abraham possessed nothing. Yet was not this poor man rich? Everything he had owned before was his still to enjoy: sheep, camels, herds, and goods of every sort. He had also his wife and his friends, and best of all he had his son Isaac safe by his side. He had everything, but *he possessed nothing*. There is the spiritual secret. There is the sweet theology of the heart which can be learned only in the school of renunciation. The books on systematic theology overlook this, but the wise will understand.

After that bitter and blessed experience I think the words "my" and "mine" never had again the same meaning for Abraham. The sense of possession which they connote was gone from his heart. *Things* had been cast out forever. They had now become external to the man. His inner heart was free from them. The world said, "Abraham is rich," but the aged patriarch only smiled. He could not explain it to them, but he knew that he owned nothing, that his real treasures were inward and eternal.

There can be no doubt that this possessive clinging to things is one of the most harmful habits in the life. Because it is so natural it is rarely recognized for the evil that it is; but its outworkings are tragic.

We are often hindered from giving up our treasures to the Lord out of fear for their safety; this is especially true when those treasures are loved relatives and friends. But we need have no such fears. Our Lord came not to destroy but to save. Everything is safe which we commit to Him, and nothing is really safe which is not so committed.

Our gifts and talents should also be turned over to Him. They should be recognized for what they are, God's loan to us, and should never be considered in any sense our own. We have no more right to claim credit for special abilities than for blue eyes or strong muscles. "For who maketh thee to differ from another? and what hast thou that thou didst not receive?"

The Christian who is alive enough to know himself even slightly will recognize the symptoms of this possession malady, and will grieve to find them in his own heart. If the longing after God is strong enough within him he will want to do something about the matter. Now, what should he do?

First of all he should put away all defense and make no attempt to excuse himself either in his own eyes or before the Lord. Whoever defends himself will have himself for his defense, and he will have no other; but let him come defenseless before the Lord and he will have for his defender no less than God Himself. Let the inquiring Christian trample under foot every slippery trick of his deceitful heart and insist upon frank and open relations with the Lord.

Then he should remember that this is holy business. No careless or casual dealings will suffice. Let him come to God in full determination to be heard. Let him insist that God accept his all, that He take *things* out of his heart and Himself reign there in power. It may be he will need to become specific, to name things and people by their names one by one. If he will become drastic enough he can shorten the time of his travail from years to minutes and enter the good land long before his slower brethren who coddle their feelings and insist upon caution in their dealings with God.

Let us never forget that such a truth as this cannot be learned by rote as one would learn the facts of physical science. They must be *experienced* before we can really know them. We must in our hearts live through Abraham's harsh and bitter experiences if we would know the blessedness which follows them. The ancient curse will not go out painlessly; the tough old miser within us will not lie down and die obedient to our command. He must be torn out of our heart like a plant from the soil; he must be extracted in agony and blood like a tooth from the jaw. He must be expelled from our soul by violence as Christ expelled the money changers from the temple. And we shall need to steel ourselves against his piteous begging, and to recognize it as springing out of self-pity, one of the most reprehensible sins of the human heart.

If we would indeed know God in growing intimacy we must go this way of renunciation. And if we are set upon the pursuit of God He will sooner or later bring us to this test. Abraham's testing was, at the time, not known to him as such, yet if he had taken some course other than the one he did, the whole history of the Old Testament would have been different. God would have found His man, no doubt, but the loss to Abraham would have been tragic beyond the telling. So we will be brought one by one to the testing place, and we may never know when we are there. At that testing place there will be no dozen possible choices for us; just one and an alternative, but our whole future will be conditioned by the choice we make.

Father, I want to know Thee, but my coward heart fears to give up its toys. I cannot part with them without inward bleeding, and I do not try to hide from Thee the terror of the parting. I come trembling, but I do come. Please root from my heart all those things which I have cherished so long and which have become a very part of my living self, so that Thou mayest enter and dwell there without a rival. Then shalt Thou make the place of Thy feet glorious. Then shall my heart have no need of the sun to shine in it, for Thyself wilt be the light of it, and there shall be no night there. In Jesus' Name, Amen.

III: Removing the Veil

Having therefore, brethren, boldness to enter into the holiest by the blood of Jesus. —Heb. 10:19

Among the famous sayings of the Church fathers none is better known than Augustine's, "Thou hast formed us for Thyself, and our hearts are restless till they find rest in Thee."

The great saint states here in few words the origin and interior history of the human race. God made us for Himself: that is the only explanation that satisfies the *heart* of a thinking man, whatever his wild reason may say. Should faulty education and perverse reasoning lead a man to conclude otherwise, there is little that any Christian can do for him. For such a man I have no message. My appeal is addressed to those who have been previously taught in secret by the wisdom of God; I speak to thirsty hearts whose longings have been wakened by the touch of God within them, and such as they need no reasoned proof. Their restless hearts furnish all the proof they need.

God formed us for Himself. The *Shorter Catechism*, "Agreed upon by the Reverend Assembly of Divines at Westminster," as the old *New-England Primer* has it, asks the ancient questions *what* and *why* and answers them in one short sentence hardly matched in any uninspired work. "*Question*: What is the chief End of Man? *Answer:* Man's chief End is to glorify God and enjoy Him forever." With this agree the four and twenty elders who fall on their faces to worship Him that liveth for ever and ever, saying, "Thou art worthy, O Lord, to receive glory and honour and power: for thou hast created all things, and for thy pleasure they are and were created."

God formed us for His pleasure, and so formed us that we as well as He can in divine communion enjoy the sweet and mysterious mingling of kindred personalities. He meant us to see Him and live with Him and draw our life from His smile. But we have been guilty of that "foul revolt" of which Milton speaks when describing the rebellion of Satan and his hosts. We have broken with God. We have ceased to obey Him or love Him and in guilt and fear have fled as far as possible from His Presence.

Yet who can flee from His Presence when the heaven and the heaven of heavens cannot contain Him? when as the wisdom of Solomon testifies, "the Spirit of the Lord filleth the world?" The omnipresence of the Lord is one thing, and is a solemn fact necessary to His perfection; the *manifest* Presence is another thing altogether, and from that Presence we have fled, like Adam, to hide among the trees of the garden, or like Peter to shrink away crying, "Depart from me, for I am a sinful man, O Lord."

So the life of man upon the earth is a life away from the Presence, wrenched loose from that "blissful center" which is our right and proper dwelling place, our first estate which we kept not, the loss of which is the cause of our unceasing restlessness.

The whole work of God in redemption is to undo the tragic effects of that foul revolt, and to bring us back again into right and eternal relationship with Himself. This required that our sins be disposed of satisfactorily, that a full reconciliation be effected and the way opened for us to return again into conscious communion with God and to live again in the Presence as before. Then by His prevenient working within us He moves us to return. This first comes to our notice when our restless hearts feel a yearning for the Presence of God and we say within ourselves, "I will arise and go to my Father." That is the first step, and as the Chinese sage Lao-tze has said, "The journey of a thousand miles begins with a first step."

The interior journey of the soul from the wilds of sin into the enjoyed Presence of God is beautifully illustrated in the Old Testament tabernacle. The returning sinner first entered the outer court where he offered a blood sacrifice on the brazen altar and washed himself in the laver that stood near it. Then through a veil he passed into the holy place where no natural light could come, but the golden candlestick which spoke of Jesus the Light of the World threw its soft glow over all. There also was the shewbread to tell of Jesus, the Bread of Life, and the altar of incense, a figure of unceasing prayer.

Though the worshipper had enjoyed so much, still he had not yet entered the Presence of God. Another veil separated from the Holy of Holies where above the mercy seat dwelt the very God Himself in awful and glorious manifestation. While the tabernacle stood, only the high priest could enter there, and that but once a year, with blood which he offered for his sins and the sins of the people. It was this last veil which was rent when our Lord gave up the ghost on Calvary, and the sacred writer explains that this rending of the veil opened the way for every worshipper in the world to come by the new and living way straight into the divine Presence.

Everything in the New Testament accords with this Old Testament picture. Ransomed men need no longer pause in fear to enter the Holy of Holies. *God wills that we should push on into His Presence and live our whole life there.* This is to be known to us in conscious experience. It is more than a doctrine to be held, it is a life to be enjoyed every moment of every day.

This Flame of the Presence was the beating heart of the Levitical order. Without it all the appointments of the tabernacle were characters of some unknown language; they had no meaning for Israel or for us. The greatest fact of the tabernacle was that *Jehovah was there*; a Presence was waiting within the veil. Similarly the Presence of God is the central fact of Christianity. At the heart of the Christian message is God Himself waiting for His redeemed children to push in to conscious awareness of His Presence. That type of Christianity which happens now to be the vogue knows this Presence only in theory. It fails to stress the Christian's privilege of present realization. According to its teachings we are in the Presence of God positionally, and nothing is said about the need to experience that Presence actually. The fiery urge that drove men like McCheyne is wholly missing. And the present generation of Christians measures itself by this imperfect rule. Ignoble contentment takes the place of burning zeal. We are satisfied to rest in our *judicial* possessions and for the most part we bother ourselves very little about the absence of personal experience.

Who is this within the veil who dwells in fiery manifestations? It is none other than God Himself, "One God the Father Almighty, Maker of heaven and earth, and of all things visible and invisible," and "One Lord Jesus Christ, the only begotten Son of God; begotten of His Father before all worlds, God of God, Light of Light, Very God of Very God; begotten, not made; being of one substance with the Father," and "the Holy Ghost, the Lord and Giver of life, Who proceedeth from the Father and the Son, Who with the Father and the Son together is worshipped and glorified." Yet this holy Trinity is One God, for "we worship one God in Trinity, and Trinity in Unity; neither confounding the Persons, nor dividing the Substance. For there is one Person of the Father, another of the Son, and another of the Holy Ghost. But the Godhead of the Father, of the Son, and of the Holy Ghost, is all one: the glory equal and the majesty co-eternal." So in part run the ancient creeds, and so the inspired Word declares.

Behind the veil is God, that God after Whom the world, with strange inconsistency, has felt, "if haply they might find Him." He has discovered Himself to some extent in nature, but more perfectly in the Incarnation; now He waits to show Himself in ravishing fulness to the humble of soul and the pure in heart.

The world is perishing for lack of the knowledge of God and the Church is famishing for want of His Presence. The instant cure of most of our religious ills would be to enter the Presence in spiritual experience, to become suddenly aware that we are in God and that God is in us. This would lift us out of our pitiful narrowness and cause our hearts to be enlarged. This would burn away the impurities from our lives as the bugs and fungi were burned away by the fire that dwelt in the bush.

What a broad world to roam in, what a sea to swim in is this God and Father of our Lord Jesus Christ. He is *eternal*, which means that He antedates time and is wholly independent of it. Time began in Him and will end in Him. To it He pays no tribute and from it He suffers no change. He is *immutable*, which means that He has never changed and can never change in any smallest measure. To change He would need to go from better to worse or from worse to better. He cannot do either, for being perfect He cannot become more perfect, and if He were to become less perfect He would be less than God. He is *omniscient*, which means that He knows in one free and effortless act all matter, all spirit, all relationships, all events. He has no past and He has no future. He *is*, and none of the limiting and qualifying terms used of creatures can apply to Him. *Love* and *mercy* and *righteousness* are His, and *holiness* so ineffable that no comparisons or figures will avail to express it. Only fire can give even a remote conception of it. In fire He appeared at the burning bush; in the pillar of fire He dwelt through all the long wilderness journey. The fire that glowed between the wings of the cherubim in the holy place was called the "shekinah," the Presence, through the years of Israel's glory, and when the Old had given place to the New, He came at Pentecost as a fiery flame and rested upon each disciple.

Spinoza wrote of the intellectual love of God, and he had a measure of truth there; but the highest love of God is not intellectual, it is spiritual. God is spirit and only the spirit of man can know Him really. In the deep spirit of a man the fire must glow or his love is not the true love of God. The great of the Kingdom have been those who loved God more than others did. We all know who they have been and gladly pay tribute to the depths and sincerity of their devotion. We have but to pause for a moment and their names come trooping past us smelling of myrrh and aloes and cassia out of the ivory palaces.

Frederick Faber was one whose soul panted after God as the roe pants after the water brook, and the measure in which God revealed Himself to his seeking heart set the good man's whole life afire with a burning adoration rivaling that of the seraphim before the throne. His love for God extended to the three Persons of the Godhead equally, yet he seemed to feel for each One a special kind of love reserved for Him alone. Of God the Father he sings:

Only to sit and think of God,

Oh what a joy it is!

To think the thought, to breathe the Name;

Earth has no higher bliss.

Father of Jesus, love's reward!

What rapture will it be,

Prostrate before Thy throne to lie,

And gaze and gaze on Thee!

His love for the Person of Christ was so intense that it threatened to consume him; it burned within him as a sweet and holy madness and flowed from his lips like molten gold. In one of his sermons he says, "Wherever we turn in the church of God, there is Jesus. He is the beginning, middle and end of everything to us…. There is nothing good, nothing holy, nothing beautiful, nothing joyous which He is not to His servants. No one need be poor, because, if he chooses, he can have Jesus for his own property and possession. No one need be downcast, for Jesus is the joy of heaven, and it is His joy to enter into sorrowful hearts. We can exaggerate about many things; but we can never exaggerate our obligation to Jesus, or the compassionate abundance of the love of Jesus to us. All our lives long we might talk of Jesus, and yet we should never come to an end of the sweet things that might be said of Him. Eternity will not be long enough to learn all He is, or to praise Him for all He has done, but then, that matters not; for we shall be always with Him, and we desire nothing more." And addressing our Lord directly he says to Him:

I love Thee so, I know not how

My transports to control;

Thy love is like a burning fire

Within my very soul.

Faber's blazing love extended also to the Holy Spirit. Not only in his theology did he acknowledge His deity and full equality with the Father and the Son, but he celebrated it constantly in his songs and in his prayers. He literally pressed his forehead to the ground in his eager fervid worship of the Third Person of the Godhead. In one of his great hymns to the Holy Spirit he sums up his burning devotion thus:

O Spirit, beautiful and dread!

My heart is fit to break

With love of all Thy tenderness

For us poor sinners' sake.

I have risked the tedium of quotation that I might show by pointed example what I have set out to say, viz., that God is so vastly wonderful, so utterly and completely delightful that He can, without anything other than Himself, meet and overflow the deepest demands of our total nature, mysterious and deep as that nature is. Such worship as Faber knew (and he is but one of a great company which no man can number) can never come from a mere doctrinal knowledge of God. Hearts that are "fit to break" with love for the Godhead are those who have been in the Presence and have looked with opened eye upon the majesty of Deity. Men of the breaking hearts had a quality about them not known to or understood by common men. They habitually spoke with spiritual authority. They had been in the Presence of God and they reported what they saw there. They were prophets, not scribes, for the scribe tells us what he has read, and the prophet tells what he has seen.

The distinction is not an imaginary one. Between the scribe who has read and the prophet who has seen there is a difference as wide as the sea. We are today overrun with orthodox scribes, but the prophets, where are they? The hard voice of the scribe sounds over evangelicalism, but the Church waits for the tender voice of the saint who has penetrated the veil and has gazed with inward eye upon the Wonder that is God. And yet, thus to penetrate, to push in sensitive living experience into the holy Presence, is a privilege open to every child of God.

With the veil removed by the rending of Jesus' flesh, with nothing on God's side to prevent us from entering, why do we tarry without? Why do we consent to abide all our days just outside the Holy of Holies and never enter at all to look upon God? We hear the Bridegroom say, "Let me see thy countenance, let me hear thy voice; for sweet is thy voice and thy countenance is comely." We sense that the call is for us, but still we fail to draw near, and the years pass and we grow old and tired in the outer courts of the tabernacle. What doth hinder us?

The answer usually given, simply that we are "cold," will not explain all the facts. There is something more serious than coldness of heart, something that may be back of that coldness and be the cause of its existence. What is it? What but the presence of *a veil in our hearts*? a veil not taken away as the first veil was, but which remains there still shutting out the light and hiding the face of God from us. It is the veil of our fleshly fallen nature living on, unjudged within us, uncrucified and unrepudiated. It is the close-woven veil of the self-life which we have never truly acknowledged, of which we have been secretly ashamed, and which for these reasons we have never brought to the judgment of the cross. It is not too mysterious, this opaque veil, nor is it hard to identify. We have but to look in our own hearts and we shall see it there, sewn and patched and repaired it may be, but there nevertheless, an enemy to our lives and an effective block to our spiritual progress.

This veil is not a beautiful thing and it is not a thing about which we commonly care to talk, but I am addressing the thirsting souls who are determined to follow God, and I know they will not turn back because the way leads temporarily through the blackened hills. The urge of God within them will assure their continuing the pursuit. They will face the facts however unpleasant and endure the cross for the joy set before them. So I am bold to name the threads out of which this inner veil is woven.

It is woven of the fine threads of the self-life, the hyphenated sins of the human spirit. They are not something we do, they are something we *are*, and therein lies both their subtlety and their power.

To be specific, the self-sins are these: self-righteousness, self-pity, self-confidence, self-sufficiency, self-admiration, self-love and a host of others like them. They dwell too deep within us and are too much a part of our natures to come to our attention till the light of God is focused upon them. The grosser manifestations of these sins, egotism, exhibitionism, self-promotion, are strangely tolerated in Christian leaders even in circles of impeccable orthodoxy. They are so much in evidence as actually, for many people, to become identified with the gospel. I trust it is not a cynical observation to say that they appear these days to be a requisite for popularity in some sections of the Church visible. Promoting self under the guise of promoting Christ is currently so common as to excite little notice.

One should suppose that proper instruction in the doctrines of man's depravity and the necessity for justification through the righteousness of Christ alone would deliver us from the power of the self-sins; but it does not work out that way. Self can live unrebuked at the very altar. It can watch the bleeding Victim die and not be in the least affected by what it sees. It can fight for the faith of the Reformers and preach eloquently the creed of salvation by grace, and gain strength by its efforts. To tell all the truth, it seems actually to feed upon orthodoxy and is more at home in a Bible Conference than in a tavern. Our very state of longing after God may afford it an excellent condition under which to thrive and grow.

Self is the opaque veil that hides the Face of God from us. It can be removed only in spiritual experience, never by mere instruction. As well try to instruct leprosy out of our system. There must be a work of God in destruction before we are free. We must invite the cross to do its deadly work within us. We must bring our self-sins to the cross for judgment. We must prepare ourselves for an ordeal of suffering in some measure like that through which our Savior passed when He suffered under Pontius Pilate.

Let us remember: when we talk of the rending of the veil we are speaking in a figure, and the thought of it is poetical, almost pleasant; but in actuality there is nothing pleasant about it. In human experience that veil is made of living spiritual tissue; it is composed of the sentient, quivering stuff of which our whole beings consist, and to touch it is to touch us where we feel pain. To tear it away is to injure us, to hurt us and make us bleed. To say otherwise is to make the cross no cross and death no death at all. It is never fun to die. To rip through the dear and tender stuff of which life is made can never be anything but deeply painful. Yet that is what the cross did to Jesus and it is what the cross would do to every man to set him free.

Let us beware of tinkering with our inner life in hope ourselves to rend the veil. God must do everything for us. Our part is to yield and trust. We must confess, forsake, repudiate the self-life, and then reckon it crucified. But we must be careful to distinguish lazy "acceptance" from the real work of God. We must insist upon the work being done. We dare not rest content with a neat doctrine of self-crucifixion. That is to imitate Saul and spare the best of the sheep and the oxen.

Insist that the work be done in very truth and it will be done. The cross is rough, and it is deadly, but it is effective. It does not keep its victim hanging there forever. There comes a moment when its work is finished and the suffering victim dies. After that is resurrection glory and power, and the pain is forgotten for joy that the veil is taken away and we have entered in actual spiritual experience the Presence of the living God.

Lord, how excellent are Thy ways, and how devious and dark are the ways of man. Show us how to die, that we may rise again to newness of life. Rend the veil of our self-life from the top down as Thou didst rend the veil of the Temple. We would draw near in full assurance of faith. We would dwell with Thee in daily experience here on this earth so that we may be accustomed to the glory when we enter Thy heaven to dwell with Thee there. In Jesus' name, Amen.

IV: Apprehending God

O taste and see. —Psa. 34:8

It was Canon Holmes, of India, who more than twenty-five years ago called attention to the inferential character of the average man's faith in God. To most people God is an inference, not a reality. He is a deduction from evidence which they consider adequate; but He remains personally unknown to the individual. "He *must* be," they say, "therefore we believe He is." Others do not go even so far as this; they know of Him only by hearsay. They have never bothered to think the matter out for themselves, but have heard about Him from others, and have put belief in Him into the back of their minds along with the various odds and ends that make up their total creed. To many others God is but an ideal, another name for goodness, or beauty, or truth; or He is law, or life, or the creative impulse back of the phenomena of existence.

These notions about God are many and varied, but they who hold them have one thing in common: they do not know God in personal experience. The possibility of intimate acquaintance with Him has not entered their minds. While admitting His existence they do not think of Him as knowable in the sense that we know things or people.

Christians, to be sure, go further than this, at least in theory. Their creed requires them to believe in the personality of God, and they have been taught to pray, "Our Father, which art in heaven." Now personality and fatherhood carry with them the idea of the possibility of personal acquaintance. This is admitted, I say, in theory, but for millions of Christians, nevertheless, God is no more real than He is to the non-Christian. They go through life trying to love an ideal and be loyal to a mere principle.

Over against all this cloudy vagueness stands the clear scriptural doctrine that God can be known in personal experience. A loving Personality dominates the Bible, walking among the trees of the garden and breathing fragrance over every scene. Always a living Person is present, speaking, pleading, loving, working, and manifesting Himself whenever and wherever His people have the receptivity necessary to receive the manifestation.

The Bible assumes as a self-evident fact that men can know God with at least the same degree of immediacy as they know any other person or thing that comes within the field of their experience. The same terms are used to express the knowledge of God as are used to express knowledge of physical things. "O *taste* and see that the Lord is good." "All thy garments *smell* of myrrh, and aloes, and cassia, out of the ivory palaces." "My sheep *hear* my voice." "Blessed are the pure in heart, for they shall *see* God." These are but four of countless such passages from the Word of God. And more important than any proof text is the fact that the whole import of the Scripture is toward this belief.

What can all this mean except that we have in our hearts organs by means of which we can know God as certainly as we know material things through our familiar five senses? We apprehend the physical world by exercising the faculties given us for the purpose, and we possess spiritual faculties by means of which we can know God and the spiritual world if we will obey the Spirit's urge and begin to use them.

That a saving work must first be done in the heart is taken for granted here. The spiritual faculties of the unregenerate man lie asleep in his nature, unused and for every purpose dead; that is the stroke which has fallen upon us by sin. They may be quickened to active life again by the operation of the Holy Spirit in regeneration; that is one of the immeasurable benefits which come to us through Christ's atoning work on the cross.

But the very ransomed children of God themselves: why do they know so little of that habitual conscious communion with God which the Scriptures seem to offer? The answer is our chronic unbelief. Faith enables our spiritual sense to function. Where faith is defective the result will be inward insensibility and numbness toward spiritual things. This is the condition of vast numbers of Christians today. No proof is necessary to support that statement. We have but to converse with the first Christian we meet or enter the first church we find open to acquire all the proof we need.

A spiritual kingdom lies all about us, enclosing us, embracing us, altogether within reach of our inner selves, waiting for us to recognize it. God Himself is here waiting our response to His Presence. This eternal world will come alive to us the moment we begin to reckon upon its reality.

I have just now used two words which demand definition; or if definition is impossible, I must at least make clear what I mean when I use them. They are "reckon" and "reality."

What do I mean by *reality*? I mean that which has existence apart from any idea any mind may have of it, and which would exist if there were no mind anywhere to entertain a thought of it. That which is real has being in itself. It does not depend upon the observer for its validity.

I am aware that there are those who love to poke fun at the plain man's idea of reality. They are the idealists who spin endless proofs that nothing is real outside of the mind. They are the relativists who like to show that there are no fixed points in the universe from which we can measure anything. They smile down upon us from their lofty intellectual peaks and settle us to their own satisfaction by fastening upon us the reproachful term "absolutist." The Christian is not put out of countenance by this show of contempt. He can smile right back at them, for he knows that there is only One who is Absolute, that is God. But he knows also that the Absolute One has made this world for man's uses, and, while there is nothing fixed or real in the last meaning of the words (the meaning as applied to God) *for every purpose of human life we are permitted to act as if there were*. And every man does act thus except the mentally sick. These unfortunates also have trouble with reality, but they are consistent; they insist upon living in accordance with their ideas of things. They are honest, and it is their very honesty that constitutes them a social problem.

The idealists and relativists are not mentally sick. They prove their soundness by living their lives according to the very notions of reality which they in theory repudiate and by counting upon the very fixed points which they prove are not there. They could earn a lot more respect for their notions if they were willing to live by them; but this they are careful not to do. Their ideas are brain-deep, not life-deep. Wherever life touches them they repudiate their theories and live like other men.

The Christian is too sincere to play with ideas for their own sake. He takes no pleasure in the mere spinning of gossamer webs for display. All his beliefs are practical. They are geared into his life. By them he lives or dies, stands or falls for this world and for all time to come. From the insincere man he turns away.

The sincere plain man knows that the world is real. He finds it here when he wakes to consciousness, and he knows that he did not think it into being. It was here waiting for him when he came, and he knows that when he prepares to leave this earthly scene it will be here still to bid him good-bye as he departs. By the deep wisdom of life he is wiser than a thousand men who doubt. He stands upon the earth and feels the wind and rain in his face and he knows that they are real. He sees the sun by day and the stars by night. He sees the hot lightning play out of the dark thundercloud. He hears the sounds of nature and the cries of human joy and pain. These he knows are real. He lies down on the cool earth at night and has no fear that it will prove illusory or fail him while he sleeps. In the morning the firm ground will be under him, the blue sky above him and the rocks and trees around him as when he closed his eyes the night before. So he lives and rejoices in a world of reality.

With his five senses he engages this real world. All things necessary to his physical existence he apprehends by the faculties with which he has been equipped by the God who created him and placed him in such a world as this.

Now, by our definition also God is real. He is real in the absolute and final sense that nothing else is. All other reality is contingent upon His. The great Reality is God who is the Author of that lower and dependent reality which makes up the sum of created things, including ourselves. God has objective existence independent of and apart from any notions which we may have concerning Him. The worshipping heart does not create its Object. It finds Him here when it wakes from its moral slumber in the morning of its regeneration.

Another word that must be cleared up is the word *reckon*. This does not mean to visualize or imagine. Imagination is not faith. The two are not only different from, but stand in sharp opposition to, each other. Imagination projects unreal images out of the mind and seeks to attach reality to them. Faith creates nothing; it simply reckons upon that which is already *there*.

God and the spiritual world are real. We can reckon upon them with as much assurance as we reckon upon the familiar world around us. Spiritual things are there (or rather we should say *here*) inviting our attention and challenging our trust.

Our trouble is that we have established bad thought habits. We habitually think of the visible world as real and doubt the reality of any other. We do not deny the existence of the spiritual world but we doubt that it is real in the accepted meaning of the word.

The world of sense intrudes upon our attention day and night for the whole of our lifetime. It is clamorous, insistent and self-demonstrating. It does not appeal to our faith; it is here, assaulting our five senses, demanding to be accepted as real and final. But sin has so clouded the lenses of our hearts that we cannot see that other reality, the City of God, shining around us. The world of sense triumphs. The visible becomes the enemy of the invisible; the temporal, of the eternal. That is the curse inherited by every member of Adam's tragic race.

At the root of the Christian life lies belief in the invisible. The object of the Christian's faith is unseen reality.

Our uncorrected thinking, influenced by the blindness of our natural hearts and the intrusive ubiquity of visible things, tends to draw a contrast between the spiritual and the real; but actually no such contrast exists. The antithesis lies elsewhere: between the real and the imaginary, between the spiritual and the material, between the temporal and the eternal; but between the spiritual and the real, never. The spiritual *is* real.

If we would rise into that region of light and power plainly beckoning us through the Scriptures of truth we must break the evil habit of ignoring the spiritual. We must shift our interest from the seen to the unseen. For the great unseen Reality is God. "He that cometh to God must believe that he is, and that he is a rewarder of them that diligently seek him." This is basic in the life of faith. From there we can rise to unlimited heights. "Ye believe in God," said our Lord Jesus Christ, "believe also in me." Without the first there can be no second.

If we truly want to follow God we must seek to be other-worldly. This I say knowing well that that word has been used with scorn by the sons of this world and applied to the Christian as a badge of reproach. So be it. Every man must choose his world. If we who follow Christ, with all the facts before us and knowing what we are about, deliberately choose the Kingdom of God as our sphere of interest I see no reason why anyone should object. If we lose by it, the loss is our own; if we gain, we rob no one by so doing. The "other world," which is the object of this world's disdain and the subject of the drunkard's mocking song, is our carefully chosen goal and the object of our holiest longing.

But we must avoid the common fault of pushing the "other world" into the future. It is not future, but present. It parallels our familiar physical world, and the doors between the two worlds are open. "Ye are come," says the writer to the Hebrews (and the tense is plainly present), "unto Mount Zion, and unto the city of the living God, the heavenly Jerusalem, and to an innumerable company of angels, to the general assembly and church of the firstborn, which are written in heaven, and to God the Judge of all, and to the spirits of just men made perfect, and to Jesus the mediator of the new covenant, and to the blood of sprinkling, that speaketh better things than that of Abel." All these things are contrasted with "the mount that might be touched" and "the sound of a trumpet and the voice of words" that might be heard. May we not safely conclude that, as the realities of Mount Sinai were apprehended by the senses, so the realities of Mount Zion are to be grasped by the soul? And this not by any trick of the imagination, but in downright actuality. The soul has eyes with which to see and ears with which to hear. Feeble they may be from long disuse, but by the life-giving touch of Christ alive now and capable of sharpest sight and most sensitive hearing.

As we begin to focus upon God the things of the spirit will take shape before our inner eyes. Obedience to the word of Christ will bring an inward revelation of the Godhead (John 14:21-23). It will give acute perception enabling us to see God even as is promised to the pure in heart. A new God consciousness will seize upon us and we shall begin to taste and hear and inwardly feel the God who is our life and our all. There will be seen the constant shining of the light that lighteth every man that cometh into the world. More and more, as our faculties grow sharper and more sure, God will become to us the great All, and His Presence the glory and wonder of our lives.

O God, quicken to life every power within me, that I may lay hold on eternal things. Open my eyes that I may see; give me acute spiritual perception; enable me to taste Thee and know that Thou art good. Make heaven more real to me than any earthly thing has ever been. Amen.

V: The Universal Presence

Whither shall I go from thy spirit? or whither shall I flee from thy presence? —Psa. 139:7

In all Christian teaching certain basic truths are found, hidden at times, and rather assumed than asserted, but necessary to all truth as the primary colors are found in and necessary to the finished painting. Such a truth is the divine immanence.

God dwells in His creation and is everywhere indivisibly present in all His works. This is boldly taught by prophet and apostle and is accepted by Christian theology generally. That is, it appears in the books, but for some reason it has not sunk into the average Christian's heart so as to become a part of his believing self. Christian teachers shy away from its full implications, and, if they mention it at all, mute it down till it has little meaning. I would guess the reason for this to be the fear of being charged with pantheism; but the doctrine of the divine Presence is definitely not pantheism.

Pantheism's error is too palpable to deceive anyone. It is that God is the sum of all created things. Nature and God are one, so that whoever touches a leaf or a stone touches God. That is of course to degrade the glory of the incorruptible Deity and, in an effort to make all things divine, banish all divinity from the world entirely.

The truth is that while God dwells in His world He is separated from it by a gulf forever impassable. However closely He may be identified with the work of His hands *they* are and must eternally be *other than He*, and He is and must be antecedent to and independent of them. He is transcendent above all His works even while He is immanent within them.

What now does the divine immanence mean in direct Christian experience? It means simply that *God is here*. Wherever we are, God is here. There is no place, there can be no place, where He is not. Ten million intelligences standing at as many points in space and separated by incomprehensible distances can each one say with equal truth, God is here. No point is nearer to God than any other point. It is exactly as near to God from any place as it is from any other place. No one is in mere distance any further from or any nearer to God than any other person is.

These are truths believed by every instructed Christian. It remains for us to think on them and pray over them until they begin to glow within us.

"In the beginning God." Not *matter*, for matter is not self-causing. It requires an antecedent cause, and God is that Cause. Not *law*, for law is but a name for the course which all creation follows. That course had to be planned, and the Planner is God. Not *mind*, for mind also is a created thing and must have a Creator back of it. In the beginning God, the uncaused Cause of matter, mind and law. There we must begin.

Adam sinned and, in his panic, frantically tried to do the impossible: he tried to hide from the Presence of God. David also must have had wild thoughts of trying to escape from the Presence, for he wrote, "Whither shall I go from thy spirit? or whither shall I flee from thy presence?" Then he proceeded through one of his most beautiful psalms to celebrate the glory of the divine immanence. "If I ascend up into heaven, thou art there: if I make my bed in hell, behold, thou art there. If I take the wings of the morning, and dwell in the uttermost parts of the sea; even there shall thy hand lead me, and thy right hand shall hold me." And he knew that God's *being* and God's *seeing* are the same, that the seeing Presence had been with him even before he was born, watching the mystery of unfolding life. Solomon exclaimed, "But will God indeed dwell on the earth? behold the heaven and the heaven of heavens cannot contain thee: how much less this house which I have builded." Paul assured the Athenians that "God is not far from any one of us: for in him we live, and move, and have our being."

If God is present at every point in space, if we cannot go where He is not, cannot even conceive of a place where He is not, why then has not that Presence become the one universally celebrated fact of the world? The patriarch Jacob, "in the waste howling wilderness," gave the answer to that question. He saw a vision of God and cried out in wonder, "Surely the Lord is in this place; and I knew it not." Jacob had never been for one small division of a moment outside the circle of that all-pervading Presence. But he knew it not. That was his trouble, and it is ours. Men do not know that God is here. What a difference it would make if they knew.

The Presence and the manifestation of the Presence are not the same. There can be the one without the other. God is here when we are wholly unaware of it. He is *manifest* only when and as we are aware of His Presence. On our part there must be surrender to the Spirit of God, for His work it is to show us the Father and the Son. If we co-operate with Him in loving obedience God will manifest Himself to us, and that manifestation will be the difference between a nominal Christian life and a life radiant with the light of His face.

Always, everywhere God is present, and always He seeks to discover Himself. To each one he would reveal not only that He is, but *what* He is as well. He did not have to be persuaded to discover Himself to Moses. "And the Lord descended in the cloud, and stood with him there, and proclaimed the name of the Lord." He not only made a verbal proclamation of His nature but He revealed His very Self to Moses so that the skin of Moses' face shone with the supernatural light. It will be a great moment for some of us when we begin to believe that God's promise of self-revelation is literally true: that He promised much, but promised no more than He intends to fulfill.

Our pursuit of God is successful just because He is forever seeking to manifest Himself to us. The revelation of God to any man is not God coming from a distance upon a time to pay a brief and momentous visit to the man's soul. Thus to think of it is to misunderstand it all. The approach of God to the soul or of the soul to God is not to be thought of in spatial terms at all. There is no idea of physical distance involved in the concept. It is not a matter of miles but of experience.

To speak of being near to or far from God is to use language in a sense always understood when applied to our ordinary human relationships. A man may say, "I feel that my son is coming nearer to me as he gets older," and yet that son has lived by his father's side since he was born and has never been away from home more than a day or so in his entire life. What then can the father mean? Obviously he is speaking of *experience*. He means that the boy is coming to know him more intimately and with deeper understanding, that the barriers of thought and feeling between the two are disappearing, that father and son are becoming more closely united in mind and heart.

So when we sing, "Draw me nearer, nearer, blessed Lord," we are not thinking of the nearness of place, but of the nearness of relationship. It is for increasing degrees of awareness that we pray, for a more perfect consciousness of the divine Presence. We need never shout across the spaces to an absent God. He is nearer than our own soul, closer than our most secret thoughts.

Why do some persons "find" God in a way that others do not? Why does God manifest His Presence to some and let multitudes of others struggle along in the half-light of imperfect Christian experience? Of course the will of God is the same for all. He has no favorites within His household. All He has ever done for any of His children He will do for all of His children. The difference lies not with God but with us.

Pick at random a score of great saints whose lives and testimonies are widely known. Let them be Bible characters or well known Christians of post-Biblical times. You will be struck instantly with the fact that the saints were not alike. Sometimes the unlikenesses were so great as to be positively glaring. How different for example was Moses from Isaiah; how different was Elijah from David; how unlike each other were John and Paul, St. Francis and Luther, Finney and Thomas à Kempis. The differences are as wide as human life itself: differences of race, nationality, education, temperament, habit and personal qualities. Yet they all walked, each in his day, upon a high road of spiritual living far above the common way.

Their differences must have been incidental and in the eyes of God of no significance. In some vital quality they must have been alike. What was it?

I venture to suggest that the one vital quality which they had in common was *spiritual receptivity*. Something in them was open to heaven, something which urged them Godward. Without attempting anything like a profound analysis I shall say simply that they had spiritual awareness and that they went on to cultivate it until it became the biggest thing in their lives. They differed from the average person in that when they felt the inward longing they *did something about it*. They acquired the lifelong habit of spiritual response.

They were not disobedient to the heavenly vision. As David put it neatly, "When thou said, Seek ye my face; my heart said unto thee, Thy face, Lord, will I seek.[1]"

As with everything good in human life, back of this receptivity is God. The sovereignty of God is here, and is felt even by those who have not placed particular stress upon it theologically. The pious Michael Angelo confessed this in a sonnet:

My unassisted heart is barren clay,

That of its native self can nothing feed:

Of good and pious works Thou art the seed,

That quickens only where Thou sayest it may:

Unless Thou show to us Thine own true way

No man can find it: Father! Thou must lead.

These words will repay study as the deep and serious testimony of a great Christian.

Important as it is that we recognize God working in us, I would yet warn against a too-great preoccupation with the thought. It is a sure road to sterile passivity. God will not hold us responsible to understand the mysteries of election, predestination and the divine sovereignty. The best and safest way to deal with these truths is to raise our eyes to God and in deepest reverence say, "O Lord, Thou knowest." Those things belong to the deep and mysterious Profound of God's omniscience. Prying into them may make theologians, but it will never make saints.

Receptivity is not a single thing; it is a compound rather, a blending of several elements within the soul. It is an affinity for, a bent toward, a sympathetic response to, a desire to have. From this it may be gathered that it can be present in degrees, that we may have little or more or less, depending upon the individual. It may be increased by exercise or destroyed by neglect. It is not a sovereign and irresistible force which comes upon us as a seizure from above. It is a gift of God, indeed, but one which must be recognized and cultivated as any other gift if it is to realize the purpose for which it was given.

Failure to see this is the cause of a very serious breakdown in modern evangelicalism. The idea of cultivation and exercise, so dear to the saints of old, has now no place in our total religious picture. It is too slow, too common. We now demand glamour and fast flowing dramatic action. A generation of Christians reared among push buttons and automatic machines is impatient of slower and less direct methods of reaching their goals. We have been trying to apply machine-age methods to our relations with God. We read our chapter, have our short devotions and rush away, hoping to make up for our deep inward bankruptcy by attending another gospel meeting or listening to another thrilling story told by a religious adventurer lately returned from afar.

The tragic results of this spirit are all about us. Shallow lives, hollow religious philosophies, the preponderance of the element of fun in gospel meetings, the glorification of men, trust in religious externalities, quasi-religious fellowships, salesmanship methods, the mistaking of dynamic personality for the power of the Spirit: these and such as these are the symptoms of an evil disease, a deep and serious malady of the soul.

---

[1] Psalm 27:8

For this great sickness that is upon us no one person is responsible, and no Christian is wholly free from blame. We have all contributed, directly or indirectly, to this sad state of affairs. We have been too blind to see, or too timid to speak out, or too self-satisfied to desire anything better than the poor average diet with which others appear satisfied. To put it differently, we have accepted one another's notions, copied one another's lives and made one another's experiences the model for our own. And for a generation the trend has been downward. Now we have reached a low place of sand and burnt wire grass and, worst of all, we have made the Word of Truth conform to our experience and accepted this low plane as the very pasture of the blessed.

It will require a determined heart and more than a little courage to wrench ourselves loose from the grip of our times and return to Biblical ways. But it can be done. Every now and then in the past Christians have had to do it. History has recorded several large-scale returns led by such men as St. Francis, Martin Luther and George Fox. Unfortunately there seems to be no Luther or Fox on the horizon at present. Whether or not another such return may be expected before the coming of Christ is a question upon which Christians are not fully agreed, but that is not of too great importance to us now.

What God in His sovereignty may yet do on a world-scale I do not claim to know: but what He will do for the plain man or woman who seeks His face I believe I do know and can tell others. Let any man turn to God in earnest, let him begin to exercise himself unto godliness, let him seek to develop his powers of spiritual receptivity by trust and obedience and humility, and the results will exceed anything he may have hoped in his leaner and weaker days.

Any man who by repentance and a sincere return to God will break himself out of the mold in which he has been held, and will go to the Bible itself for his spiritual standards, will be delighted with what he finds there.

Let us say it again: The Universal Presence is a fact. God is here. The whole universe is alive with His life. And He is no strange or foreign God, but the familiar Father of our Lord Jesus Christ whose love has for these thousands of years enfolded the sinful race of men. And always He is trying to get our attention, to reveal Himself to us, to communicate with us. We have within us the ability to know Him if we will but respond to His overtures. (And this we call pursuing God!) We will know Him in increasing degree as our receptivity becomes more perfect by faith and love and practice.

O God and Father, I repent of my sinful preoccupation with visible things. The world has been too much with me. Thou hast been here and I knew it not. I have been blind to Thy Presence. Open my eyes that I may behold Thee in and around me. For Christ's sake, Amen.

VI: The Speaking Voice

*In the beginning was the Word, and the Word was with God,
and the Word was God. —John 1:1*

An intelligent plain man, untaught in the truths of Christianity, coming upon this text, would likely conclude that John meant to teach that it is the nature of God to speak, to communicate His thoughts to others. And he would be right. A word is a medium by which thoughts are expressed, and the application of term to the Eternal Son leads us to believe that self-expression is inherent in the Godhead, that God is forever seeking to speak Himself out to His creation. The whole Bible supports the idea. God is speaking. Not God spoke, but *God is speaking*. He is by His nature continuously articulate. He fills the world with His speaking Voice.

One of the great realities with which we have to deal is the Voice of God in His world. The briefest and only satisfying cosmogony is this: "He spake and it was done." The *why* of natural law is the living Voice of God immanent in His creation. And this word of God which brought all worlds into being cannot be understood to mean the Bible, for it is not a written or printed word at all, but the expression of the will of God spoken into the structure of all things. This word of God is the breath of God filling the world with living potentiality. The Voice of God is the most powerful force in nature, indeed the only force in nature, for all energy is here only because the power-filled Word is being spoken.

The Bible is the written word of God, and because it is written it is confined and limited by the necessities of ink and paper and leather. The Voice of God, however, is alive and free as the sovereign God is free. "The words that I speak unto you, they are spirit, and they are life." The life is in the speaking words. God's word in the Bible can have power only because it corresponds to God's word in the universe. It is the present Voice which makes the written Word all-powerful. Otherwise it would lie locked in slumber within the covers of a book.

We take a low and primitive view of things when we conceive of God at the creation coming into physical contact with things, shaping and fitting and building like a carpenter. The Bible teaches otherwise: "By the word of the Lord were the heavens made; and all the host of them by the breath of his mouth…. For he spake, and it was done; he commanded, and it stood fast." "Through faith we understand that the worlds were framed by the word of God." Again we must remember that God is referring here not to His written Word, but to His speaking Voice. His world-filling Voice is meant, that Voice which antedates the Bible by uncounted centuries, that Voice which has not been silent since the dawn of creation, but is sounding still throughout the full far reaches of the universe.

The Word of God is quick and powerful. In the beginning He spoke to nothing, and it became *something*. Chaos heard it and became order, darkness heard it and became light. "And God said—and it was so." These twin phrases, as cause and effect, occur throughout the Genesis story of the creation. The *said* accounts for the *so*. The *so* is the *said* put into the continuous present.

That God is here and that He is speaking—these truths are back of all other Bible truths; without them there could be no revelation at all. God did not write a book and send it by messenger to be read at a distance by unaided minds. He spoke a Book and lives in His spoken words, constantly speaking His words and causing the power of them to persist across the years. God breathed on clay and it became a man; He breathes on men and they become clay. "Return ye children of men" was the word spoken at the Fall by which God decreed the death of every man, and no added word has He needed to speak. The sad procession of mankind across the face of the earth from birth to the grave is proof that His original Word was enough.

We have not given sufficient attention to that deep utterance in the Book of John, "That was the true Light, which lighteth every man that cometh into the world." Shift the punctuation around as we will and the truth is still there: the Word of God affects the hearts of all men as light in the soul. In the hearts of all men the light shines, the Word sounds, and there is no escaping them. Something like this would of necessity be so if God is alive and in His world. And John says that it is so. Even those persons who have never heard of the Bible have still been preached to with sufficient clarity to remove every excuse from their hearts forever. "Which show the work of the law written in their hearts, their conscience also bearing witness, and their thoughts the mean while either accusing or else excusing one another." "For the invisible things of him from the creation of the world are clearly seen, being understood by the things that are made, even his eternal power and Godhead; so that they are without excuse."

This universal Voice of God was by the ancient Hebrews often called Wisdom, and was said to be everywhere sounding and searching throughout the earth, seeking some response from the sons of men. The eighth chapter of the Book of Proverbs begins, "Doth not wisdom cry? and understanding put forth her voice?" The writer then pictures wisdom as a beautiful woman standing "in the top of the high places, by the way in the places of the paths." She sounds her voice from every quarter so that no one may miss hearing it. "Unto you, O men, I call; and my voice is to the sons of men." Then she pleads for the simple and the foolish to give ear to her words. It is spiritual response for which this Wisdom of God is pleading, a response which she has always sought and is but rarely able to secure. The tragedy is that our eternal welfare depends upon our hearing, and we have trained our ears not to hear.

This universal Voice has ever sounded, and it has often troubled men even when they did not understand the source of their fears. Could it be that this Voice distilling like a living mist upon the hearts of men has been the undiscovered cause of the troubled conscience and the longing for immortality confessed by millions since the dawn of recorded history? We need not fear to face up to this. The speaking Voice is a fact. How men have reacted to it is for any observer to note.

When God spoke out of heaven to our Lord, self-centered men who heard it explained it by natural causes: they said, "It thundered." This habit of explaining the Voice by appeals to natural law is at the very root of modern science. In the living breathing cosmos there is a mysterious Something, too wonderful, too awful for any mind to understand. The believing man does not claim to understand. He falls to his knees and whispers, "God." The man of earth kneels also, but not to worship. He kneels to examine, to search, to find the cause and the how of things. Just now we happen to be living in a secular age. Our thought habits are those of the scientist, not those of the worshipper. We are more likely to explain than to adore. "It thundered," we exclaim, and go our earthly way. But still the Voice sounds and searches. The order and life of the world depend upon that Voice, but men are mostly too busy or too stubborn to give attention.

Everyone of us has had experiences which we have not been able to explain: a sudden sense of loneliness, or a feeling of wonder or awe in the face of the universal vastness. Or we have had a fleeting visitation of light like an illumination from some other sun, giving us in a quick flash an assurance that we are from another world, that our origins are divine. What we saw there, or felt, or heard, may have been contrary to all that we had been taught in the schools and at wide variance with all our former beliefs and opinions. We were forced to suspend our acquired doubts while, for a moment, the clouds were rolled back and we saw and heard for ourselves. Explain such things as we will, I think we have not been fair to the facts until we allow at least the possibility that such experiences may arise from the Presence of God in the world and His persistent effort to communicate with mankind. Let us not dismiss such an hypothesis too flippantly.

It is my own belief (and here I shall not feel bad if no one follows me) that every good and beautiful thing which man has produced in the world has been the result of his faulty and sin-blocked response to the creative Voice sounding over the earth. The moral philosophers who dreamed their high dreams of virtue, the religious thinkers who speculated about God and immortality, the poets and artists who created out of common stuff pure and lasting beauty: how can we explain them? It is not enough to say simply, "It was genius." What then is genius? Could it be that a genius is a man haunted by the speaking Voice, laboring and striving like one possessed to achieve ends which he only vaguely understands? That the great man may have missed God in his labors, that he may even have spoken or written against God does not destroy the idea I am advancing. God's redemptive revelation in the Holy Scriptures is necessary to saving faith and peace with God. Faith in a risen Savior is necessary if the vague stirrings toward immortality are to bring us to restful and satisfying communion with God. To me this is a plausible explanation of all that is best out of Christ. But you can be a good Christian and not accept my thesis.

The Voice of God is a friendly Voice. No one need fear to listen to it unless he has already made up his mind to resist it. The blood of Jesus has covered not only the human race but all creation as well. "And having made peace through the blood of his cross, by him to reconcile all things unto himself; by him, I say, whether they be things in earth, or things in heaven." We may safely preach a friendly Heaven. The heavens as well as the earth are filled with the good will of Him that dwelt in the bush. The perfect blood of atonement secures this forever.

Whoever will listen will hear the speaking Heaven. This is definitely not the hour when men take kindly to an exhortation to *listen*, for listening is not today a part of popular religion. We are at the opposite end of the pole from there. Religion has accepted the monstrous heresy that noise, size, activity and bluster make a man dear to God. But we may take heart. To a people caught in the tempest of the last great conflict God says, "Be still, and know that I am God," and still He says it, as if He means to tell us that our strength and safety lie not in noise but in silence.

It is important that we get still to wait on God. And it is best that we get alone, preferably with our Bible outspread before us. Then if we will we may draw near to God and begin to hear Him speak to us in our hearts. I think for the average person the progression will be something like this: First a sound as of a Presence walking in the garden. Then a voice, more intelligible, but still far from clear. Then the happy moment when the Spirit begins to illuminate the Scriptures, and that which had been only a sound, or at best a voice, now becomes an intelligible word, warm and intimate and clear as the word of a dear friend. Then will come life and light, and best of all, ability to see and rest in and embrace Jesus Christ as Savior and Lord and All.

The Bible will never be a living Book to us until we are convinced that God is articulate in His universe. To jump from a dead, impersonal world to a dogmatic Bible is too much for most people. They may admit that they *should* accept the Bible as the Word of God, and they may try to think of it as such, but they find it impossible to believe that the words there on the page are actually for them. A man may *say*, "These words are addressed to me," and yet in his heart not feel and know that they are. He is the victim of a divided psychology. He tries to think of God as mute everywhere else and vocal only in a book.

I believe that much of our religious unbelief is due to a wrong conception of and a wrong feeling for the Scriptures of Truth. A silent God suddenly began to speak in a book and when the book was finished lapsed back into silence again forever. Now we read the book as the record of what God said when He was for a brief time in a speaking mood. With notions like that in our heads how can we believe? The facts are that God is not silent, has never been silent. It is the nature of God to speak. The second Person of the Holy Trinity is called the *Word*. The Bible is the inevitable outcome of God's continuous speech. It is the infallible declaration of His mind for us put into our familiar human words.

I think a new world will arise out of the religious mists when we approach our Bible with the idea that it is not only a book which was once spoken, but a book which is *now speaking*. The prophets habitually said, "Thus *saith* the Lord." They meant their hearers to understand that God's speaking is in the continuous present. We may use the past tense properly to indicate that at a certain time a certain word of God was spoken, but a word of God once spoken continues to be spoken, as a child once born continues to be alive, or a world once created continues to exist. And those are but imperfect illustrations, for children die and worlds burn out, but the Word of our God endureth forever.

If you would follow on to know the Lord, come at once to the open Bible expecting it to speak to you. Do not come with the notion that it is a *thing* which you may push around at your convenience. It is more than a thing, it is a voice, a word, the very Word of the living God.

Lord, teach me to listen. The times are noisy and my ears are weary with the thousand raucous sounds which continuously assault them. Give me the spirit of the boy Samuel when he said to Thee, "Speak, for thy servant heareth." Let me hear Thee speaking in my heart. Let me get used to the sound of Thy Voice, that its tones may be familiar when the sounds of earth die away and the only sound will be the music of Thy speaking Voice. Amen.

VII: The Gaze of the Soul

Looking unto Jesus the author and finisher of our faith. —Heb. 12:2

Let us think of our intelligent plain man mentioned in chapter six coming for the first time to the reading of the Scriptures. He approaches the Bible without any previous knowledge of what it contains. He is wholly without prejudice; he has nothing to prove and nothing to defend.

Such a man will not have read long until his mind begins to observe certain truths standing out from the page. They are the spiritual principles behind the record of God's dealings with men, and woven into the writings of holy men as they "were moved by the Holy Ghost." As he reads on he might want to number these truths as they become clear to him and make a brief summary under each number. These summaries will be the tenets of his Biblical creed. Further reading will not affect these points except to enlarge and strengthen them. Our man is finding out what the Bible actually teaches.

High up on the list of things which the Bible teaches will be the doctrine of *faith*. The place of weighty importance which the Bible gives to faith will be too plain for him to miss. He will very likely conclude: Faith is all-important in the life of the soul. Without faith it is impossible to please God. Faith will get me anything, take me anywhere in the

Kingdom of God, but without faith there can be no approach to God, no forgiveness, no deliverance, no salvation, no communion, no spiritual life at all.

By the time our friend has reached the eleventh chapter of Hebrews the eloquent encomium which is there pronounced upon faith will not seem strange to him. He will have read Paul's powerful defense of faith in his Roman and Galatian epistles. Later if he goes on to study church history he will understand the amazing power in the teachings of the Reformers as they showed the central place of faith in the Christian religion.

Now if faith is so vitally important, if it is an indispensable *must* in our pursuit of God, it is perfectly natural that we should be deeply concerned over whether or not we possess this most precious gift. And our minds being what they are, it is inevitable that sooner or later we should get around to inquiring after the nature of faith. What *is* faith? would lie close to the question, Do I *have* faith? and would demand an answer if it were anywhere to be found.

Almost all who preach or write on the subject of faith have much the same things to say concerning it. They tell us that it is believing a promise, that it is taking God at His word, that it is reckoning the Bible to be true and stepping out upon it. The rest of the book or sermon is usually taken up with stories of persons who have had their prayers answered as a result of their faith. These answers are mostly direct gifts of a practical and temporal nature such as health, money, physical protection or success in business. Or if the teacher is of a philosophic turn of mind he may take another course and lose us in a welter of metaphysics or snow us under with psychological jargon as he defines and re-defines, paring the slender hair of faith thinner and thinner till it disappears in gossamer shavings at last. When he is finished we get up disappointed and go out "by that same door where in we went." Surely there must be something better than this.

In the Scriptures there is practically no effort made to define faith. Outside of a brief fourteen-word definition in Hebrews 11:1, I know of no Biblical definition, and even there faith is defined functionally, not philosophically; that is, it is a statement of what faith is *in operation*, *not* what it is *in essence*. It assumes the presence of faith and shows what it results in, rather than what it is. We will be wise to go just that far and attempt to go no further. We are told from whence it comes and by what means: "Faith is a gift of God," and "Faith cometh by hearing, and hearing by the word of God." This much is clear, and, to paraphrase Thomas à Kempis, "I had rather exercise faith than know the definition thereof."

From here on, when the words "faith is" or their equivalent occur in this chapter I ask that they be understood to refer to what faith is in operation as exercised by a believing man. Right here we drop the notion of definition and think about faith as it may be experienced in action. The complexion of our thoughts will be practical, not theoretical.

In a dramatic story in the Book of Numbers faith is seen in action. Israel became discouraged and spoke against God, and the Lord sent fiery serpents among them. "And they bit the people; and much people of Israel died." Then Moses sought the Lord for them and He heard and gave them a remedy against the bite of the serpents. He commanded Moses to make a serpent of brass and put it upon a pole in sight of all the people, "and it shall come to pass, that everyone that is bitten, when he looketh upon it, shall live." Moses obeyed, "and it came to pass, that if a serpent had bitten any man, when he beheld the serpent of brass, he lived" (Num. 21:4-9).

In the New Testament this important bit of history is interpreted for us by no less an authority than our Lord Jesus Christ Himself. He is explaining to His hearers how they may be saved. He tells them that it is by believing. Then to make it clear He refers to this incident in the Book of Numbers. "As Moses lifted up the serpent in the wilderness, even so must the Son of man be lifted up: that whosoever believeth in him should not perish, but have eternal life" (John 3:14-15).

Our plain man in reading this would make an important discovery. He would notice that "look" and "believe" were synonymous terms. "Looking" on the Old Testament serpent is identical with "believing" on the New Testament Christ. That is, the *looking* and the *believing* are the same thing. And he would understand that while Israel looked with their external eyes, believing is done with the heart. I think he would conclude that *faith is the gaze of a soul upon a saving God.*

When he had seen this he would remember passages he had read before, and their meaning would come flooding over him. "They looked unto him, and were lightened: and their faces were not ashamed" (Psa. 34:5). "Unto thee lift I up mine eyes, O thou that dwellest in the heavens. Behold, as the eyes of servants look unto the hand of their masters, and as the eyes of a maiden unto the hand of her mistress; so our eyes wait upon the Lord our God, until that he have mercy upon us" (Psa. 123:1-2). Here the man seeking mercy looks straight at the God of mercy and never takes his eyes away from Him till mercy is granted. And our Lord Himself looked always at God. "Looking up to heaven, he blessed, and brake, and gave the bread to his disciples" (Matt. 14:19). Indeed Jesus taught that He wrought His works by always keeping His inward eyes upon His Father. His power lay in His continuous look at God (John 5:19-21).

In full accord with the few texts we have quoted is the whole tenor of the inspired Word. It is summed up for us in the Hebrew epistle when we are instructed to run life's race "looking unto Jesus the author and finisher of our faith." From all this we learn that faith is not a once-done act, but a continuous gaze of the heart at the Triune God.

Believing, then, is directing the heart's attention to Jesus. It is lifting the mind to "behold the Lamb of God," and never ceasing that beholding for the rest of our lives. At first this may be difficult, but it becomes easier as we look steadily at His wondrous Person, quietly and without strain. Distractions may hinder, but once the heart is committed to Him, after each brief excursion away from Him the attention will return again and rest upon Him like a wandering bird coming back to its window.

I would emphasize this one committal, this one great volitional act which establishes the heart's intention to gaze forever upon Jesus. God takes this intention for our choice and makes what allowances He must for the thousand distractions which beset us in this evil world. He knows that we have set the direction of our hearts toward Jesus, and we can know it too, and comfort ourselves with the knowledge that a habit of soul is forming which will become after a while a sort of spiritual reflex requiring no more conscious effort on our part.

Faith is the least self-regarding of the virtues. It is by its very nature scarcely conscious of its own existence. Like the eye which sees everything in front of it and never sees itself, faith is occupied with the Object upon which it rests and pays no attention to itself at all. While we are looking at God we do not see ourselves—blessed riddance. The man who has struggled to purify himself and has had nothing but repeated failures will experience real relief when he stops tinkering with his soul and looks away to the perfect One. While he looks at Christ the very things he has so long been trying to do will be getting done within him. It will be God working in him to will and to do.

Faith is not in itself a meritorious act; the merit is in the One toward Whom it is directed. Faith is a redirecting of our sight, a getting out of the focus of our own vision and getting God into focus. Sin has twisted our vision inward and made it self-regarding. Unbelief has put self where God should be, and is perilously close to the sin of Lucifer who said, "I will set my throne above the throne of God." Faith looks *out* instead of *in* and the whole life falls into line.

All this may seem too simple. But we have no apology to make. To those who would seek to climb into heaven after help or descend into hell God says, "The word is nigh thee, even the word of faith." The word induces us to lift up our eyes unto the Lord and the blessed work of faith begins.

When we lift our inward eyes to gaze upon God we are sure to meet friendly eyes gazing back at us, for it is written that the eyes of the Lord run to and fro throughout all the earth. The sweet language of experience is "Thou God seest me." When the eyes of the soul looking out meet the eyes of God looking in, heaven has begun right here on this earth.

"When all my endeavor is turned toward Thee because all Thy endeavor is turned toward me; when I look unto Thee alone with all my attention, nor ever turn aside the eyes of my mind, because Thou dost enfold me with Thy constant regard; when I direct my love toward Thee alone because Thou, who art Love's self hast turned Thee toward me alone. And what, Lord, is my life, save that embrace wherein Thy delightsome sweetness doth so lovingly enfold me?"[2] So wrote Nicholas of Cusa four hundred years ago.

I should like to say more about this old man of God. He is not much known today anywhere among Christian believers, and among current Fundamentalists he is known not at all. I feel that we could gain much from a little acquaintance with men of his spiritual flavor and the school of Christian thought which they represent. Christian literature, to be accepted and approved by the evangelical leaders of our times, must follow very closely the same train of thought, a kind of "party line" from which it is scarcely safe to depart. A half-century of this in America has made us smug and content. We imitate each other with slavish devotion and our most strenuous efforts are put forth to try to say the same thing that everyone around us is saying—and yet to find an excuse for saying it, some little safe variation on the approved theme or, if no more, at least a new illustration.

Nicholas was a true follower of Christ, a lover of the Lord, radiant and shining in his devotion to the Person of Jesus. His theology was orthodox, but fragrant and sweet as everything about Jesus might properly be expected to be. His conception of eternal life, for instance, is beautiful in itself and, if I mistake not, is nearer in spirit to John 17:3 than that which is current among us today. Life eternal, says Nicholas, is "naught other than that blessed regard wherewith Thou never ceasest to behold me, yea, even the secret places of my soul. With Thee, to behold is to give life; 'tis unceasingly to impart sweetest love of Thee; 'tis to inflame me to love of Thee by love's imparting, and to feed me by inflaming, and by feeding to kindle my yearning, and by kindling to make me drink of the dew of gladness, and by drinking to infuse in me a fountain of life, and by infusing to make it increase and endure."[3]

[2] Nicholas of Cusa, *The Vision of God*, E. P. Dutton & Co., Inc., New York, 1928.
[3] *The Vision of God*

Now, if faith is the gaze of the heart at God, and if this gaze is but the raising of the inward eyes to meet the all-seeing eyes of God, then it follows that it is one of the easiest things possible to do. It would be like God to make the most vital thing easy and place it within the range of possibility for the weakest and poorest of us.

Several conclusions may fairly be drawn from all this. The simplicity of it, for instance. Since believing is looking, it can be done without special equipment or religious paraphernalia. God has seen to it that the one life-and-death essential can never be subject to the caprice of accident. Equipment can break down or get lost, water can leak away, records can be destroyed by fire, the minister can be delayed or the church burn down. All these are external to the soul and are subject to accident or mechanical failure: but *looking* is of the heart and can be done successfully by any man standing up or kneeling down or lying in his last agony a thousand miles from any church.

Since believing is looking it can be done *any time*. No season is superior to another season for this sweetest of all acts. God never made salvation depend upon new moons nor holy days or sabbaths. A man is not nearer to Christ on Easter Sunday than he is, say, on Saturday, August 3, or Monday, October 4. As long as Christ sits on the mediatorial throne every day is a good day and all days are days of salvation.

Neither does *place* matter in this blessed work of believing God. Lift your heart and let it rest upon Jesus and you are instantly in a sanctuary though it be a Pullman berth or a factory or a kitchen. You can see God from anywhere if your mind is set to love and obey Him.

Now, someone may ask, "Is not this of which you speak for special persons such as monks or ministers who have by the nature of their calling more time to devote to quiet meditation? I am a busy worker and have little time to spend alone." I am happy to say that the life I describe is for everyone of God's children regardless of calling. It is, in fact, happily practiced every day by many hard working persons and is beyond the reach of none.

Many have found the secret of which I speak and, without giving much thought to what is going on within them, constantly practice this habit of inwardly gazing upon God. They know that something inside their hearts sees God. Even when they are compelled to withdraw their conscious attention in order to engage in earthly affairs there is within them a secret communion always going on. Let their attention but be released for a moment from necessary business and it flies at once to God again. This has been the testimony of many Christians, so many that even as I state it thus I have a feeling that I am quoting, though from whom or from how many I cannot possibly know.

I do not want to leave the impression that the ordinary means of grace have no value. They most assuredly have. Private prayer should be practiced by every Christian. Long periods of Bible meditation will purify our gaze and direct it; church attendance will enlarge our outlook and increase our love for others. Service and work and activity; all are good and should be engaged in by every Christian. But at the bottom of all these things, giving meaning to them, will be the inward habit of beholding God. A new set of eyes (so to speak) will develop within us enabling us to be looking at God while our outward eyes are seeing the scenes of this passing world.

Someone may fear that we are magnifying private religion out of all proportion, that the "us" of the New Testament is being displaced by a selfish "I." Has it ever occurred to you that one hundred pianos all tuned to the same fork are automatically tuned to each other? They are of one accord by being tuned, not to each other, but to another standard to which each one must individually bow. So one hundred worshippers met together, each one looking away to Christ, are in heart nearer to each other than they could possibly be were they to become "unity" conscious and turn their eyes away from God to strive for closer fellowship. Social religion is perfected when private religion is purified. The body becomes stronger as its members become healthier. The whole Church of God gains when the members that compose it begin to seek a better and a higher life.

All the foregoing presupposes true repentance and a full committal of the life to God. It is hardly necessary to mention this, for only persons who have made such a committal will have read this far.

When the habit of inwardly gazing Godward becomes fixed within us we shall be ushered onto a new level of spiritual life more in keeping with the promises of God and the mood of the New Testament. The Triune God will be our dwelling place even while our feet walk the low road of simple duty here among men. We will have found life's *summum bonum* indeed. "There is the source of all delights that can be desired; not only can naught better be thought out by men and angels, but naught better can exist in mode of being! For it is the absolute maximum of every rational desire, than which a greater cannot be."[4]

O Lord, I have heard a good word inviting me to look away to Thee and be satisfied. My heart longs to respond, but sin has clouded my vision till I see Thee but dimly. Be pleased to cleanse me in Thine own precious blood, and make me inwardly pure, so that I may with unveiled eyes gaze upon Thee all the days of my earthly pilgrimage. Then shall I be prepared to behold Thee in full splendor in the day when Thou shalt appear to be glorified in Thy saints and admired in all them that believe. Amen.

VIII: Restoring the Creator-creature Relation

Be thou exalted, O God, above the heavens;
let thy glory be above all the earth. —Psa. 57:5

It is a truism to say that order in nature depends upon right relationships; to achieve harmony each thing must be in its proper position relative to each other thing. In human life it is not otherwise.

I have hinted before in these chapters that the cause of all our human miseries is a radical moral dislocation, an upset in our relation to God and to each other. For whatever else the Fall may have been, it was most certainly a sharp change in man's relation to his Creator. He adopted toward God an altered attitude, and by so doing destroyed the proper Creator-creature relation in which, unknown to him, his true happiness lay. Essentially salvation is the restoration of a right relation between man and his Creator, a bringing back to normal of the Creator-creature relation.

A satisfactory spiritual life will begin with a complete change in relation between God and the sinner; not a judicial change merely, but a conscious and experienced change affecting the sinner's whole nature. The atonement in Jesus' blood makes such a change judicially possible and the working of the Holy Spirit makes it emotionally satisfying. The

---

[4] *The Vision of God*

story of the prodigal son perfectly illustrates this latter phase. He had brought a world of trouble upon himself by forsaking the position which he had properly held as son of his father. At bottom his restoration was nothing more than a re-establishing of the father-son relation which had existed from his birth and had been altered temporarily by his act of sinful rebellion. This story overlooks the legal aspects of redemption, but it makes beautifully clear the experiential aspects of salvation.

In determining relationships we must begin somewhere. There must be somewhere a fixed center against which everything else is measured, where the law of relativity does not enter and we can say "IS" and make no allowances. Such a center is God. When God would make His Name known to mankind He could find no better word than "I AM." When He speaks in the first person He says, "I AM"; when we speak of Him we say, "He is"; when we speak to Him we say, "Thou art." Everyone and everything else measures from that fixed point. "I am that I am," says God, "I change not."

As the sailor locates his position on the sea by "shooting" the sun, so we may get our moral bearings by looking at God. We must begin with God. We are right when and only when we stand in a right position relative to God, and we are wrong so far and so long as we stand in any other position.

Much of our difficulty as seeking Christians stems from our unwillingness to take God as He is and adjust our lives accordingly. We insist upon trying to modify Him and to bring Him nearer to our own image. The flesh whimpers against the rigor of God's inexorable sentence and begs like Agag for a little mercy, a little indulgence of its carnal ways. It is no use. We can get a right start only by accepting God as He is and learning to love Him for what He is. As we go on to know Him better we shall find it a source of unspeakable joy that God is just what He is. Some of the most rapturous moments we know will be those we spend in reverent admiration of the Godhead. In those holy moments the very thought of change in Him will be too painful to endure.

So let us begin with God. Back of all, above all, before all is God; first in sequential order, above in rank and station, exalted in dignity and honor. As the self-existent One He gave being to all things, and all things exist out of Him and for Him. "Thou art worthy, O Lord, to receive glory and honour and power: for thou hast created all things, and for thy pleasure they are and were created."

Every soul belongs to God and exists by His pleasure. God being Who and What He is, and we being who and what we are, the only thinkable relation between us is one of full lordship on His part and complete submission on ours. We owe Him every honor that it is in our power to give Him. Our everlasting grief lies in giving Him anything less.

The pursuit of God will embrace the labor of bringing our total personality into conformity to His. And this not judicially, but actually. I do not here refer to the act of justification by faith in Christ. I speak of a voluntary exalting of God to His proper station over us and a willing surrender of our whole being to the place of worshipful submission which the Creator-creature circumstance makes proper.

The moment we make up our minds that we are going on with this determination to exalt God over all we step out of the world's parade. We shall find ourselves out of adjustment to the ways of the world, and increasingly so as we make progress in the holy way. We shall acquire a new viewpoint; a new and different psychology will be formed within us; a new power will begin to surprise us by its upsurgings and its outgoings.

Our break with the world will be the direct outcome of our changed relation to God. For the world of fallen men does not honor God. Millions call themselves by His Name, it is true, and pay some token respect to Him, but a simple test will show how little He is really honored among them. Let the average man be put to the proof on the question of who is *above*, and his true position will be exposed. Let him be forced into making a choice between God and money, between God and men, between God and personal ambition, God and self, God and human love, and God will take second place every time. Those other things will be exalted above. However the man may protest, the proof is in the choices he makes day after day throughout his life.

"Be thou exalted" is the language of victorious spiritual experience. It is a little key to unlock the door to great treasures of grace. It is central in the life of God in the soul. Let the seeking man reach a place where life and lips join to say continually "Be thou exalted," and a thousand minor problems will be solved at once. His Christian life ceases to be the complicated thing it had been before and becomes the very essence of simplicity. By the exercise of his will he has set his course, and on that course he will stay as if guided by an automatic pilot. If blown off course for a moment by some adverse wind he will surely return again as by a secret bent of the soul. The hidden motions of the Spirit are working in his favor, and "the stars in their courses" fight for him. He has met his life problem at its center, and everything else must follow along.

Let no one imagine that he will lose anything of human dignity by this voluntary sell-out of his all to his God. He does not by this degrade himself as a man; rather he finds his right place of high honor as one made in the image of his Creator. His deep disgrace lay in his moral derangement, his unnatural usurpation of the place of God. His honor will be proved by restoring again that stolen throne. In exalting God over all he finds his own highest honor upheld.

Anyone who might feel reluctant to surrender his will to the will of another should remember Jesus' words, "Whosoever committeth sin is the servant of sin." We must of necessity be servant to someone, either to God or to sin. The sinner prides himself on his independence, completely overlooking the fact that he is the weak slave of the sins that rule his members. The man who surrenders to Christ exchanges a cruel slave driver for a kind and gentle Master whose yoke is easy and whose burden is light.

Made as we were in the image of God we scarcely find it strange to take again our God as our All. God was our original habitat and our hearts cannot but feel at home when they enter again that ancient and beautiful abode.

I hope it is clear that there is a logic behind God's claim to pre-eminence. That place is His by every right in earth or heaven. While we take to ourselves the place that is His the whole course of our lives is out of joint. Nothing will or can restore order till our hearts make the great decision: God shall be exalted above.

"Them that honour me I will honour," said God once to a priest of Israel, and that ancient law of the Kingdom stands today unchanged by the passing of time or the changes of dispensation. The whole Bible and every page of history proclaim the perpetuation of that law. "If any man serve me, him will my Father honour," said our Lord Jesus, tying in the old with the new and revealing the essential unity of His ways with men.

Sometimes the best way to see a thing is to look at its opposite. Eli and his sons are placed in the priesthood with the stipulation that they honor God in their lives and ministrations. This they fail to do, and God sends Samuel to announce the consequences.

Unknown to Eli this law of reciprocal honor has been all the while secretly working, and now the time has come for judgment to fall. Hophni and Phineas, the degenerate priests, fall in battle, the wife of Hophni dies in childbirth, Israel flees before her enemies, the ark of God is captured by the Philistines and the old man Eli falls backward and dies of a broken neck. Thus stark utter tragedy followed upon Eli's failure to honor God.

Now set over against this almost any Bible character who honestly tried to glorify God in his earthly walk. See how God winked at weaknesses and overlooked failures as He poured upon His servants grace and blessing untold. Let it be Abraham, Jacob, David, Daniel, Elijah or whom you will; honor followed honor as harvest the seed. The man of God set his heart to exalt God above all; God accepted his intention as fact and acted accordingly. Not perfection, but holy intention made the difference.

In our Lord Jesus Christ this law was seen in simple perfection. In His lowly manhood He humbled Himself and gladly gave all glory to His Father in heaven. He sought not His own honor, but the honor of God who sent Him. "If I honour myself," He said on one occasion, "my honour is nothing; it is my Father that honoureth me." So far had the proud Pharisees departed from this law that they could not understand one who honored God at his own expense. "I honour my Father," said Jesus to them, "and ye do dishonour me."

Another saying of Jesus, and a most disturbing one, was put in the form of a question, "How can ye believe, which receive honour one of another, and seek not the honour that cometh from God alone?" If I understand this correctly Christ taught here the alarming doctrine that the desire for honor among men made belief impossible. Is this sin at the root of religious unbelief? Could it be that those "intellectual difficulties" which men blame for their inability to believe are but smoke screens to conceal the real cause that lies behind them? Was it this greedy desire for honor from man that made men into Pharisees and Pharisees into Deicides? Is this the secret back of religious self-righteousness and empty worship? I believe it may be. The whole course of the life is upset by failure to put God where He belongs. We exalt ourselves instead of God and the curse follows.

In our desire after God let us keep always in mind that God also hath desire, and His desire is toward the sons of men, and more particularly toward those sons of men who will make the once-for-all decision to exalt Him over all. Such as these are precious to God above all treasures of earth or sea. In them God finds a theater where He can display His exceeding kindness toward us in Christ Jesus. With them God can walk unhindered, toward them He can act like the God He is.

In speaking thus I have one fear; it is that I may convince the mind before God can win the heart. For this God-above-all position is one not easy to take. The mind may approve it while not having the consent of the will to put it into effect. While the imagination races ahead to honor God, the will may lag behind and the man never guess how divided his heart is. The whole man must make the decision before the heart can know any real satisfaction. God wants us all, and He will not rest till He gets us all. No part of the man will do.

Let us pray over this in detail, throwing ourselves at God's feet and meaning everything we say. No one who prays thus in sincerity need wait long for tokens of divine acceptance. God will unveil His glory before His servant's eyes, and He will place all His treasures at the disposal of such a one, for He knows that His honor is safe in such consecrated hands.

O God, be Thou exalted over my possessions. Nothing of earth's treasures shall seem dear unto me if only Thou art glorified in my life. Be Thou exalted over my friendships. I am determined that Thou shalt be above all, though I must stand deserted and alone in the midst of the earth. Be Thou exalted above my comforts. Though it mean the loss of bodily comforts and the carrying of heavy crosses I shall keep my vow made this day before Thee. Be Thou exalted over my reputation. Make me ambitious to please Thee even if as a result I must sink into obscurity and my name be forgotten as a dream. Rise, O Lord, into Thy proper place of honor, above my ambitions, above my likes and dislikes, above my family, my health and even my life itself. Let me decrease that Thou mayest increase, let me sink that Thou mayest rise above. Ride forth upon me as Thou didst ride into Jerusalem mounted upon the humble little beast, a colt, the foal of an ass, and let me hear the children cry to Thee, "Hosanna in the highest."

IX: Meekness and Rest

Blessed are the meek: for they shall inherit the earth. —Matt. 5:5

A fairly accurate description of the human race might be furnished one unacquainted with it by taking the Beatitudes, turning them wrong side out and saying, "Here is your human race." For the exact opposite of the virtues in the Beatitudes are the very qualities which distinguish human life and conduct.

In the world of men we find nothing approaching the virtues of which Jesus spoke in the opening words of the famous Sermon on the Mount. Instead of poverty of spirit we find the rankest kind of pride; instead of mourners we find pleasure seekers; instead of meekness, arrogance; instead of hunger after righteousness we hear men saying, "I am rich and increased with goods and have need of nothing"; instead of mercy we find cruelty; instead of purity of heart, corrupt imaginings; instead of peacemakers we find men quarrelsome and resentful; instead of rejoicing in mistreatment we find them fighting back with every weapon at their command.

Of this kind of moral stuff civilized society is composed. The atmosphere is charged with it; we breathe it with every breath and drink it with our mother's milk. Culture and education refine these things slightly but leave them basically untouched. A whole world of literature has been created to justify this kind of life as the only normal one. And this is the more to be wondered at seeing that these are the evils which make life the bitter struggle it is for all of us. All our heartaches and a great many of our physical ills spring directly out of our sins. Pride, arrogance, resentfulness, evil imaginings, malice, greed: these are the sources of more human pain than all the diseases that ever afflicted mortal flesh.

Into a world like this the sound of Jesus' words comes wonderful and strange, a visitation from above. It is well that He spoke, for no one else could have done it as well; and it is good that we listen. His words are the essence of truth. He is not offering an opinion; Jesus never uttered opinions. He never guessed; He knew, and He knows. His words are not as Solomon's were, the sum of sound wisdom or the results of keen observation. He spoke out of the fulness of His Godhead, and His words are very Truth itself. He is the only one who could say "blessed" with complete authority, for He is the Blessed One come from the world above to confer blessedness upon mankind. And His words were supported by deeds mightier than any performed on this earth by any other man. It is wisdom for us to listen.

As was often so with Jesus, He used this word "meek" in a brief crisp sentence, and not till some time later did He go on to explain it. In the same book of Matthew He tells us more about it and applies it to our lives. "Come unto me, all ye that labor and are heavy laden, and I will give you rest. Take my yoke upon you, and learn of me; for I am meek and lowly in heart: and ye shall find rest unto your souls. For my yoke is easy, and my burden is light." Here we have two things standing in contrast to each other, a burden and a rest. The burden is not a local one, peculiar to those first hearers, but one which is borne by the whole human race. It consists not of political oppression or poverty or hard work. It is far deeper than that. It is felt by the rich as well as the poor for it is something from which wealth and idleness can never deliver us.

The burden borne by mankind is a heavy and a crushing thing. The word Jesus used means a load carried or toil borne to the point of exhaustion. Rest is simply release from that burden. It is not something we do, it is what comes to us when we cease to do. His own meekness, that is the rest.

Let us examine our burden. It is altogether an interior one. It attacks the heart and the mind and reaches the body only from within. First, there is the burden of *pride*. The labor of self-love is a heavy one indeed. Think for yourself whether much of your sorrow has not arisen from someone speaking slightingly of you. As long as you set yourself up as a little god to which you must be loyal there will be those who will delight to offer affront to your idol. How then can you hope to have inward peace? The heart's fierce effort to protect itself from every slight, to shield its touchy honor from the bad opinion of friend and enemy, will never let the mind have rest. Continue this fight through the years and the burden will become intolerable. Yet the sons of earth are carrying this burden continually, challenging every word spoken against them, cringing under every criticism, smarting under each fancied slight, tossing sleepless if another is preferred before them.

Such a burden as this is not necessary to bear. Jesus calls us to His rest, and meekness is His method. The meek man cares not at all who is greater than he, for he has long ago decided that the esteem of the world is not worth the effort. He develops toward himself a kindly sense of humor and learns to say, "Oh, so you have been overlooked? They have placed someone else before you? They have whispered that you are pretty small stuff after all? And now you feel hurt because the world is saying about you the very things you have been saying about yourself? Only yesterday you were telling God that you were nothing, a mere worm of the dust. Where is your consistency? Come on, humble yourself, and cease to care what men think."

The meek man is not a human mouse afflicted with a sense of his own inferiority. Rather he may be in his moral life as bold as a lion and as strong as Samson; but he has stopped being fooled about himself. He has accepted God's estimate of his own life. He knows he is as weak and helpless as God has declared him to be, but paradoxically, he knows at the same time that he is in the sight of God of more importance than angels. In himself, nothing; in God, everything. That is his motto. He knows well that the world will never see him as God sees him and he has stopped caring. He rests perfectly content to allow God to place His own values. He will be patient to wait for the day when everything will get its own price tag and real worth will come into its own. Then the righteous shall shine forth in the Kingdom of their Father. He is willing to wait for that day.

In the meantime he will have attained a place of soul rest. As he walks on in meekness he will be happy to let God defend him. The old struggle to defend himself is over. He has found the peace which meekness brings.

Then also he will get deliverance from the burden of *pretense.* By this I mean not hypocrisy, but the common human desire to put the best foot forward and hide from the world our real inward poverty. For sin has played many evil tricks upon us, and one has been the infusing into us a false sense of shame. There is hardly a man or woman who dares to be just what he or she is without doctoring up the impression. The fear of being found out gnaws like rodents within their hearts. The man of culture is haunted by the fear that he will some day come upon a man more cultured than himself. The learned man fears to meet a man more learned than he. The rich man sweats under the fear that his clothes or his car or his house will sometime be made to look cheap by comparison with those of another rich man. So-called "society" runs by a motivation not higher than this, and the poorer classes on their level are little better.

Let no one smile this off. These burdens are real, and little by little they kill the victims of this evil and unnatural way of life. And the psychology created by years of this kind of thing makes true meekness seem as unreal as a dream, as aloof as a star. To all the victims of the gnawing disease Jesus says, "Ye must become as little children." For little children do not compare; they receive direct enjoyment from what they have without relating it to something else or someone else. Only as they get older and sin begins to stir within their hearts do jealousy and envy appear. Then they are unable to enjoy what they have if someone else has something larger or better. At that early age does the galling burden come down upon their tender souls, and it never leaves them till Jesus sets them free.

Another source of burden is *artificiality.* I am sure that most people live in secret fear that some day they will be careless and by chance an enemy or friend will be allowed to peep into their poor empty souls. So they are never relaxed. Bright people are tense and alert in fear that they may be trapped into saying something common or stupid. Traveled people are afraid that they may meet some Marco Polo who is able to describe some remote place where they have never been.

This unnatural condition is part of our sad heritage of sin, but in our day it is aggravated by our whole way of life. Advertising is largely based upon this habit of pretense. "Courses" are offered in this or that field of human learning frankly appealing to the victim's desire to shine at a party. Books are sold, clothes and cosmetics are peddled, by playing continually upon this desire to appear what we are not. Artificiality is one curse that will drop away the moment we kneel at Jesus' feet and surrender ourselves to His meekness. Then we will not care what people think of us so long as God is pleased. Then *what we are* will be everything; what we appear will take its place far down the scale of interest for us. Apart from sin we have nothing of which to be ashamed. Only an evil desire to shine makes us want to appear other than we are.

The heart of the world is breaking under this load of pride and pretense. There is no release from our burden apart from the meekness of Christ. Good keen reasoning may help slightly, but so strong is this vice that if we push it down one place it will come up somewhere else. To men and women everywhere Jesus says, "Come unto me, and I will give you rest." The rest He offers is the rest of meekness, the blessed relief which comes when we accept ourselves for what we are and cease to pretend. It will take some courage at first, but the needed grace will come as we learn that we are sharing this new and easy yoke with the strong Son of God Himself. He calls it "my yoke," and He walks at one end while we walk at the other.

Lord, make me childlike. Deliver me from the urge to compete with another for place or prestige or position. I would be simple and artless as a little child. Deliver me from pose and pretense. Forgive me for thinking of myself. Help me to forget myself and find my true peace in beholding Thee. That Thou mayest answer this prayer I humble myself before Thee. Lay upon me Thy easy yoke of self-forgetfulness that through it I may find rest. Amen.

X: The Sacrament of Living

Whether therefore ye eat, or drink, or whatsoever ye do, do all to the glory of God. —I Cor. 10:31

One of the greatest hindrances to internal peace which the Christian encounters is the common habit of dividing our lives into two areas, the sacred and the secular. As these areas are conceived to exist apart from each other and to be morally and spiritually incompatible, and as we are compelled by the necessities of living to be always crossing back and forth from the one to the other, our inner lives tend to break up so that we live a divided instead of a unified life.

Our trouble springs from the fact that we who follow Christ inhabit at once two worlds, the spiritual and the natural. As children of Adam we live our lives on earth subject to the limitations of the flesh and the weaknesses and ills to which human nature is heir. Merely to live among men requires of us years of hard toil and much care and attention to the things of this world. In sharp contrast to this is our life in the Spirit. There we enjoy another and higher kind of life; we are children of God; we possess heavenly status and enjoy intimate fellowship with Christ.

This tends to divide our total life into two departments. We come unconsciously to recognize two sets of actions. The first are performed with a feeling of satisfaction and a firm assurance that they are pleasing to God. These are the sacred acts and they are usually thought to be prayer, Bible reading, hymn singing, church attendance and such other acts as spring directly from faith. They may be known by the fact that they have no direct relation to this world, and would have no meaning whatever except as faith shows us another world, "an house not made with hands, eternal in the heavens."

Over against these sacred acts are the secular ones. They include all of the ordinary activities of life which we share with the sons and daughters of Adam: eating, sleeping, working, looking after the needs of the body and performing our dull and prosaic duties here on earth. These we often do reluctantly and with many misgivings, often apologizing to God for what we consider a waste of time and strength. The upshot of this is that we are uneasy most of the time. We go about our common tasks with a feeling of deep frustration, telling ourselves pensively that there's a better day coming when we shall slough off this earthly shell and be bothered no more with the affairs of this world.

This is the old sacred-secular antithesis. Most Christians are caught in its trap. They cannot get a satisfactory adjustment between the claims of the two worlds. They try to walk the tight rope between two kingdoms and they find no peace in either. Their strength is reduced, their outlook confused and their joy taken from them.

I believe this state of affairs to be wholly unnecessary. We have gotten ourselves on the horns of a dilemma, true enough, but the dilemma is not real. It is a creature of misunderstanding. The sacred-secular antithesis has no foundation in the New Testament. Without doubt a more perfect understanding of Christian truth will deliver us from it.

The Lord Jesus Christ Himself is our perfect example, and He knew no divided life. In the Presence of His Father He lived on earth without strain from babyhood to His death on the cross. God accepted the offering of His total life, and made no distinction between act and act. "I do always the things that please him," was His brief summary of His own life as it related to the Father. As He moved among men He was poised and restful. What pressure and suffering He endured grew out of His position as the world's sin bearer; they were never the result of moral uncertainty or spiritual maladjustment.

Paul's exhortation to "do all to the glory of God" is more than pious idealism. It is an integral part of the sacred revelation and is to be accepted as the very Word of Truth. It opens before us the possibility of making every act of our lives contribute to the glory of God. Lest we should be too timid to include everything, Paul mentions specifically eating and drinking. This humble privilege we share with the beasts that perish. If these lowly animal acts can be so performed as to honor God, then it becomes difficult to conceive of one that cannot.

That monkish hatred of the body which figures so prominently in the works of certain early devotional writers is wholly without support in the Word of God. Common modesty is found in the Sacred Scriptures, it is true, but never prudery or a false sense of shame. The New Testament accepts as a matter of course that in His incarnation our Lord took upon Him a real human body, and no effort is made to steer around the downright implications of such a fact. He lived in that body here among men and never once performed a non-sacred act. His presence in human flesh sweeps away forever the evil notion that there is about the human body something innately offensive to the Deity. God created our bodies, and we do not offend Him by placing the responsibility where it belongs. He is not ashamed of the work of His own hands.

Perversion, misuse and abuse of our human powers should give us cause enough to be ashamed. Bodily acts done in sin and contrary to nature can never honor God. Wherever the human will introduces moral evil we have no longer our innocent and harmless powers as God made them; we have instead an abused and twisted thing which can never bring glory to its Creator.

Let us, however, assume that perversion and abuse are not present. Let us think of a Christian believer in whose life the twin wonders of repentance and the new birth have been wrought. He is now living according to the will of God as he understands it from the written Word. Of such a one it may be said that every act of his life is or can be as truly sacred as prayer or baptism or the Lord's Supper. To say this is not to bring all acts down to one dead level; it is rather to lift every act up into a living kingdom and turn the whole life into a sacrament.

If a sacrament is an external expression of an inward grace than we need not hesitate to accept the above thesis. By one act of consecration of our total selves to God we can make every subsequent act express that consecration. We need no more be ashamed of our body—the fleshly servant that carries us through life—than Jesus was of the humble beast upon which He rode into Jerusalem. "The Lord hath need of him" may well apply to our mortal bodies. If Christ dwells in us we may bear about the Lord of glory as the little beast did of old and give occasion to the multitudes to cry, "Hosanna in the highest."

That we *see* this truth is not enough. If we would escape from the toils of the sacred-secular dilemma the truth must "run in our blood" and condition the complexion of our thoughts. We must practice living to the glory of God, actually and determinedly. By meditation upon this truth, by talking it over with God often in our prayers, by recalling it to our minds frequently as we move about among men, a *sense* of its wondrous meaning will begin to take hold of us. The old painful duality will go down before a restful unity of life. The knowledge that we are all God's, that He has received all and rejected nothing, will unify our inner lives and make everything sacred to us.

This is not quite all. Long-held habits do not die easily. It will take intelligent thought and a great deal of reverent prayer to escape completely from the sacred-secular psychology. For instance it may be difficult for the average Christian to get hold of the idea that his daily labors can be performed as acts of worship acceptable to God by Jesus Christ. The old antithesis will crop up in the back of his head sometimes to disturb his peace of mind. Nor will that old serpent the devil take all this lying down. He will be there in the cab or at the desk or in the field to remind the Christian that he is giving the better part of his day to the things of this world and allotting to his religious duties only a trifling portion of his time. And unless great care is taken this will create confusion and bring discouragement and heaviness of heart.

We can meet this successfully only by the exercise of an aggressive faith. We must offer all our acts to God and believe that He accepts them. Then hold firmly to that position and keep insisting that every act of every hour of the day and night be included in the transaction. Keep reminding God in our times of private prayer that we mean every act for His glory; then supplement those times by a thousand thought-prayers as we go about the job of living. Let us practice the fine art of making every work a priestly ministration. Let us believe that God is in all our simple deeds and learn to find Him there.

A concomitant of the error which we have been discussing is the sacred-secular antithesis as applied to places. It is little short of astonishing that we can read the New Testament and still believe in the inherent sacredness of places as distinguished from other places. This error is so widespread that one feels all alone when he tries to combat it. It has acted as a kind of dye to color the thinking of religious persons and has colored the eyes as well so that it is all but impossible to detect its fallacy. In the face of every New Testament teaching to the contrary it has been said and sung throughout the centuries and accepted as a part of the Christian message, the which it most surely is not. Only the Quakers, so far as my knowledge goes, have had the perception to see the error and the courage to expose it.

Here are the facts as I see them. For four hundred years Israel had dwelt in Egypt, surrounded by the crassest idolatry. By the hand of Moses they were brought out at last and started toward the land of promise. The very idea of holiness had been lost to them. To correct this, God began at the bottom. He localized Himself in the cloud and fire and later when the tabernacle had been built He dwelt in fiery manifestation in the Holy of Holies. By innumerable distinctions God taught Israel the difference between holy and unholy. There were holy days, holy vessels, holy garments. There were washings, sacrifices, offerings of many kinds. By these means Israel learned that *God is holy*. It was this that He was teaching them. Not the holiness of things or places, but the holiness of Jehovah was the lesson they must learn.

Then came the great day when Christ appeared. Immediately He began to say, "Ye have heard that it was said by them of old time—but *I* say unto you." The Old Testament schooling was over. When Christ died on the cross the veil of the temple was rent from top to bottom. The Holy of Holies was opened to everyone who would enter in faith. Christ's words were remembered, "The hour cometh, when ye shall neither in this mountain, nor yet at Jerusalem, worship the Father.... But the hour cometh, and now is, when the true worshippers shall worship the Father in spirit and in truth: for the Father seeketh such to worship Him. God is Spirit, and they that worship him must worship him in spirit and in truth."

Shortly after, Paul took up the cry of liberty and declared all meats clean, every day holy, all places sacred and every act acceptable to God. The sacredness of times and places, a half-light necessary to the education of the race, passed away before the full sun of spiritual worship.

The essential spirituality of worship remained the possession of the Church until it was slowly lost with the passing of the years. Then the natural *legality* of the fallen hearts of men began to introduce the old distinctions. The Church came to observe again days and seasons and times. Certain places were chosen and marked out as holy in a special sense. Differences were observed between one and another day or place or person, "The sacraments" were first two, then three, then four until with the triumph of Romanism they were fixed at seven.

In all charity, and with no desire to reflect unkindly upon any Christian, however misled, I would point out that the Roman Catholic church represents today the sacred-secular heresy carried to its logical conclusion. Its deadliest effect is the complete cleavage it introduces between religion and life. Its teachers attempt to avoid this snare by many footnotes and multitudinous explanations, but the mind's instinct for logic is too strong. In practical living the cleavage is a fact.

From this bondage reformers and puritans and mystics have labored to free us. Today the trend in conservative circles is back toward that bondage again. It is said that a horse after it has been led out of a burning building will sometimes by a strange obstinacy break loose from its rescuer and dash back into the building again to perish in the flame. By some such stubborn tendency toward error Fundamentalism in our day is moving back toward spiritual slavery. The observation of days and times is becoming more and more prominent among us. "Lent" and "holy week" and "good" Friday are words heard more and more frequently upon the lips of gospel Christians. We do not know when we are well off.

In order that I may be understood and not be misunderstood I would throw into relief the practical implications of the teaching for which I have been arguing, i.e., the sacramental quality of every day living. Over against its positive meanings I should like to point out a few things it does not mean.

It does not mean, for instance, that everything we do is of equal importance with everything else we do or may do. One act of a good man's life may differ widely from another in importance. Paul's sewing of tents was not equal to his writing of an Epistle to the Romans, but both were accepted of God and both were true acts of worship. Certainly it is more important to lead a soul to Christ than to plant a garden, but the planting of the garden *can* be as holy an act as the winning of a soul.

Again, it does not mean that every man is as useful as every other man. Gifts differ in the body of Christ. A Billy Bray is not to be compared with a Luther or a Wesley for sheer usefulness to the Church and to the world; but the service of the less gifted brother is as pure as that of the more gifted, and God accepts both with equal pleasure.

The "layman" need never think of his humbler task as being inferior to that of his minister. Let every man abide in the calling wherein he is called and his work will be as sacred as the work of the ministry. It is not what a man does that determines whether his work is sacred or secular, it is *why* he does it. The motive is everything. Let a man sanctify the Lord God in his heart and he can thereafter do no common act. All he does is good and acceptable to God through Jesus Christ. For such a man, living itself will be sacramental and the whole world a sanctuary. His entire life will be a priestly ministration. As he performs his never so simple task he will hear the voice of the seraphim saying, "Holy, Holy, Holy, is the Lord of hosts: the whole earth is full of his glory."

Lord, I would trust Thee completely; I would be altogether Thine; I would exalt Thee above all. I desire that I may feel no sense of possessing anything outside of Thee. I want constantly to be aware of Thy overshadowing Presence and to hear Thy speaking Voice. I long to live in restful sincerity of heart. I want to live so fully in the Spirit that all my thought may be as sweet incense ascending to Thee and every act of my life may be an act of worship. Therefore I pray in the words of Thy great servant of old, "I beseech Thee so for to cleanse the intent of mine heart with the unspeakable gift of Thy grace, that I may perfectly love Thee and worthily praise Thee." And all this I confidently believe Thou wilt grant me through the merits of Jesus Christ Thy Son. Amen.

Humility

~ ※ ~

By *Andrew Murray*

Lord Jesus! may our Holiness be perfect Humility!

Let Thy perfect Humility be our Holiness!

The 1884 Edition

~ ※ ~

Preface

There are three great motives that urge us to humility. It becomes me as a creature, as a sinner, as a saint. The first we see in the heavenly hosts, in unfallen man, in Jesus as Son of Man. The second appeals to us in our fallen state, and points out the only way through which we can return to our right place as creatures. In the third we have the mystery of grace, which teaches us that, as we lose ourselves in the overwhelming greatness of redeeming love, humility becomes to us the consummation of everlasting blessedness and adoration.

In our ordinary religious teaching, the second aspect has been too exclusively put in the foreground, so that some have even gone to the extreme of saying that we must keep sinning if we are indeed to keep humble. Others again have thought that the strength of self-condemnation is the secret of humility. And the Christian life has suffered loss, where believers have not been distinctly guided to see that, even in our relation as creatures, nothing is more natural and beautiful and blessed than to be nothing, that God may be all; or where it has not been made clear that it is not sin that humbles most, but grace, and that it is the soul, led through its sinfulness to be occupied with God in His wonderful glory as God, as Creator and Redeemer, that will truly take the lowest place before Him.

In these meditations I have, for more than one reason, almost exclusively directed attention to the humility that becomes us as creatures. It is not only that the connection between humility and sin is so abundantly set forth in all our religious teaching, but because I believe that for the fullness of the Christian life it is indispensable that prominence be given to the other aspect. If Jesus is indeed to be our example in His lowliness, we need to understand the principles in which it was rooted, and in which we find the common ground on which we stand with Him, and in which our likeness to Him is to be attained. If we are indeed to be humble, not only before God but towards men, if humility is to be our joy, we must see that it is not only the mark of shame, because of sin, but, apart from all sin, a being clothed upon with the very beauty and blessedness of heaven and of Jesus. We shall see that just as Jesus found His glory in taking the form of a servant, so when He said to us, 'Whosoever would be first among you, shall be your servant,' He simply taught us the blessed truth that there is nothing so divine and heavenly as being the servant and helper of all. The faithful servant, who recognizes his position, finds a real pleasure in supplying the wants of the master or his guests. When we see that humility is something infinitely deeper than contrition, and accept it as our participation in the life of Jesus, we shall begin to learn that it is our true nobility, and that to prove it in being servants of all is the highest fulfilment of our destiny, as men created in the image of God.

When I look back upon my own religious experience, or round upon the Church of Christ in the world, I stand amazed at the thought of how little humility is sought after as the distinguishing feature of the discipleship of Jesus. In preaching and living, in the daily intercourse of the home and social life, in the more special fellowship with Christians, in the direction and performance of work for Christ, —alas! how much proof there is that humility is not esteemed the cardinal virtue, the only root from which the graces can grow, the one indispensable condition of true fellowship with Jesus. That it should have been possible for men to say of those who claim to be seeking the higher holiness, that the profession has not been accompanied with increasing humility, is a loud call to all earnest Christians, however much or little truth there be in the charge, to prove that meekness and lowliness of heart are the chief mark by which they who follow the meek and lowly Lamb of God are to be known.

Humility: The Beauty of Holiness

Humility: The Glory of the Creature

'They shall cast their crowns before the throne, saying: Worthy art Thou, our Lord and our God, to receive the glory, and the honor and the power: for Thou didst create all things, and because of Thy will they were, and were created.'
— REV. iv. 11.

WHEN God created the universe, it was with the one object of making the creature partaker of His perfection and blessedness, and so showing forth in it the glory of His love and wisdom and power. God wished to reveal Himself in and through created beings by communicating to them as much of His own goodness and glory as they were capable of receiving. But this communication was not a giving to the creature something which it could possess in itself, a certain life or goodness, of which it had the charge and disposal. By no means. But as God is the ever-living, ever-present, ever-acting One, who upholdeth all things by the word of His power, and in whom all things exist, the relation of the creature to God could only be one of unceasing, absolute, universal dependence. As truly as God by His power once created, so truly by that same power must God every moment maintain. The creature has not only to look back to the origin and first beginning of existence, and acknowledge that it there owes everything to God; its chief care, its highest virtue, its only happiness, now and through all eternity, is to present itself an empty vessel, in which God can dwell and manifest His power and goodness.

The life God bestows is imparted not once for all, but each moment continuously, by the unceasing operation of His mighty power. Humility, the place of entire dependence on God, is, from the very nature of things, the first duty and the highest virtue of the creature, and the root of every virtue.

And so pride, or the loss of this humility, is the root of every sin and evil. It was when the now fallen angels began to look upon themselves with self-complacency that they were led to disobedience, and were cast down from the light of heaven into outer darkness. Even so it was, when the serpent breathed the poison of his pride, the desire to be as God, into the hearts of our first parents, that they too fell from their high estate into all the wretchedness in which man is now sunk. In heaven and earth, pride, self-exaltation, is the gate and the birth, and the curse, of hell.[1]

---

[1] 'All this is to make it known the region of eternity that pride can degrade the highest angels into devils, and humility raise fallen flesh and blood to the thrones of angels. Thus, this is the great end of God raising a new creation out of a fallen kingdom of angels: for this end it stands in its state of war betwixt the fire and pride of fallen angels, and the humility of the Lamb of God, that the last trumpet may sound the great truth through the depths of eternity, that evil can have no beginning but from pride, and no end but from humility. The truth is this: Pride may die in you, or nothing of heaven can live in you. Under the banner of the truth, give yourself up to the meek and humble spirit of the holy Jesus. Humility must sow seed, or there can be no reaping in Heaven. Look not at pride only as an unbecoming temper, nor at humility only

Hence it follows that nothing can be our redemption, but the restoration of the lost humility, the original and only true relation of the creature to its God. And so Jesus came to bring humility back to earth, to make us partakers of it, and by it to save us. In heaven He humbled Himself to become man. The humility we see in Him possessed Him in heaven; it brought Him, He brought it, from there. Here on earth 'He humbled Himself, and became obedient unto death'; His humility gave His death its value, and so became our redemption. And now the salvation He imparts is nothing less and nothing else than a communication of His own life and death, His own disposition and spirit, His own humility, as the ground and root of His relation to God and His redeeming work. Jesus Christ took the place and fulfilled the destiny of man, as a creature, by His life of perfect humility. His humility is our salvation. His salvation is our humility.

And so the life of the saved ones, of the saints, must needs bear this stamp of deliverance from sin, and full restoration to their original state; their whole relation to God and man marked by an all-pervading humility. Without this there can be no true abiding in God's presence, or experience of His favor and the power of His Spirit; without this no abiding faith, or love or joy or strength. Humility is the only soil in which the graces root; the lack of humility is the sufficient explanation of every defect and failure. Humility is not so much a grace or virtue along with others; it is the root of all, because it alone takes the right attitude before God, and allows Him as God to do all.

God has so constituted us as reasonable beings, that the truer the insight into the real nature or the absolute need of a command, the readier and fuller will be our obedience to it. The call to humility has been too little regarded in the Church because its true nature and importance has been too little apprehended. It is not a something which we bring to God, or He bestows; it is simply *the sense of entire nothingness, which comes when we see how truly God is all, and in which we make way for God to be all.* When the creature realizes that this is the true nobility, and consents to be with his will, his mind, and his affections, the form, the vessel in which the life and glory of God are to work and manifest themselves, he sees that humility is simply acknowledging the truth of his position as creature, and yielding to God His place.

In the life of earnest Christians, of those who pursue and profess holiness, humility ought to be the chief mark of their uprightness. It is often said that it is not so. May not one reason be that in the teaching and example of the Church, it has never had that place of supreme importance which belongs to it? And that this, again, is owing to the neglect of this truth, that strong as sin is as a motive to humility, there is one of still wider and mightier influence, that which makes the angels, that which made Jesus, that which makes the holiest of saints in heaven, so humble; that the first and chief mark of the relation of the creature, the secret of his blessedness, is the humility and nothingness which leaves God free to be all?

---

as a decent virtue: for the one is death, and the other is life; the one is all hell, the other is all heaven. So much as you have of pride within you, you have of the fallen angels alive in you; so much as you have of true humility, so much you have of the Lamb of God within you. Could you see what every stirring of pride does to your soul, you would beg of everything you meet to tear the viper from you, though with the loss of a hand or an eye. Could you see what a sweet, divine, transforming power there is in humility, how it expels the poison of your nature, and makes room for the Spirit of God to live in you, you would rather wish to be the footstool of all the world than want the smallest degree of it.' —Spirit of Prayer, Pt. II. p. 73, Edition of Moreton, Canterbury, 1893.

I am sure there are many Christians who will confess that their experience has been very much like my own in this, that we had long known the Lord without realizing that meekness and lowliness of heart are to be the distinguishing feature of the disciple as they were of the Master. And further, that this humility is not a thing that will come of itself, but that it must be made the object of special desire and prayer and faith and practice. As we study the word, we shall see what very distinct and oft-repeated instructions Jesus gave His disciples on this point, and how slow they were in understanding Him. Let us, at the very commencement of our meditations, admit that there is nothing so natural to man, nothing so insidious and hidden from our sight, nothing so difficult and dangerous, as pride. Let us feel that nothing but a very determined and persevering waiting on God and Christ will discover how lacking we are in the grace of humility, and how impotent to obtain what we seek. Let us study the character of Christ until our souls are filled with the love and admiration of His lowliness. And let us believe that, when we are broken down under a sense of our pride, and our impotence to cast it out, Jesus Christ Himself will come in to impart this grace too, as a part of His wondrous life within us.

Humility: The Secret of Redemption

'Have this mind in you which was also in Christ Jesus: who emptied Himself; taking the form of a servant; and humbled Himself; becoming obedient even unto death. Wherefore God also highly exalted Him.' —PHIL. ii. 5-7.

NO tree can grow except on the root from which it sprang. Through all its existence it can only live with the life that was in the seed that gave it being. The full apprehension of this truth in its application to the first and the Second Adam cannot but help us greatly to understand both the need and the nature of the redemption there is in Jesus.

The Need. — When the Old Serpent, he who had been cast out from heaven for his pride, whose whole nature as devil was pride, spoke his words of temptation into the ear of Eve, these words carried with them the very poison of hell. And when she listened, and yielded her desire and her will to the prospect of being as God, knowing good and evil, the poison entered into her soul and blood and life, destroying forever that blessed humility and dependence upon God which would have been our everlasting happiness. And instead of this, her life and the life of the race that sprang from her became corrupted to its very root with that most terrible of all sins and all curses, the poison of Satan's own pride. All the wretchedness of which this world has been the scene, all its wars and bloodshed among the nations, all its selfishness and suffering, all its ambitions and jealousies, all its broken hearts and embittered lives, with all its daily unhappiness, have their origin in what this cursed, hellish pride, either our own, or that of others, has brought us. It is pride that made redemption needful; it is from our pride we need above everything to be redeemed. And our insight into the need of redemption will largely depend upon our knowledge of the terrible nature of the power that has entered our being.

No tree can grow except on the root from which it sprang. The power that Satan brought from hell, and cast into man's life, is working daily, hourly, with mighty power throughout the world. Men suffer from it; they fear and fight and flee it; and yet they know not whence it comes, whence it has its terrible supremacy. No wonder they do not know where or how it is to be overcome. Pride has its root and strength in a terrible spiritual power, outside of us as well as within us; as needful as it is that we confess and deplore it as our very own, is to know it in its Satanic origin. If this leads us to utter despair of ever conquering or casting it out, it will lead us all the sooner to that supernatural power in which alone our deliverance is to be found—the redemption of the Lamb of God. The hopeless struggle against the workings of self and pride within us may indeed become still more hopeless as we think of the power of darkness behind it all; the utter despair will fit us the better for realizing and accepting a power and a life outside of ourselves too, even the humility of heaven as brought down and brought nigh by the Lamb of God, to cast out Satan and his pride.

No tree can grow except on the root from which it sprang. Even as we need to look to the first Adam and his fall to know the power of the sin within us, we need to know well the Second Adam and His power to give within us a life of humility as real and abiding and overmastering as has been that of pride. We have our life from and in Christ, as truly, yea more truly, than from and in Adam. We are to walk 'rooted in Him,' 'holding fast the Head from whom the whole body increaseth with the increase of God.' The life of God which in the incarnation entered human nature, is the root in which we are to stand and grow; it is the same almighty power that worked there, and thence onward to the resurrection, which works daily in us. Our one need is to study and know and trust the life that has been revealed in Christ as the life that is now ours, and waits for our consent to gain possession and mastery of our whole being.

In this view it is of inconceivable importance that we should have right thoughts of what Christ is, of what really constitutes Him the Christ, and specially of what may be counted His chief characteristic, the root and essence of all His character as our Redeemer. There can be but one answer: it is His humility. What is the incarnation but His heavenly humility, His emptying Himself and becoming man? What is His life on earth but humility; His taking the form of a servant? And what is His atonement but humility? 'He humbled Himself and became obedient unto death.' And what is His ascension and His glory, but humility exalted to the throne and crowned with glory? 'He humbled Himself, therefore God highly exalted Him.' In heaven, where He was with the Father, in His birth, in His life, in His death, in His sitting on the throne, it is all, it is nothing but humility. Christ is the humility of God embodied in human nature; the Eternal Love humbling itself, clothing itself in the garb of meekness and gentleness, to win and serve and save us. As the love and condescension of God makes Him the benefactor and helper and servant of all, so Jesus of necessity was the Incarnate Humility. And so He is still in the midst of the throne, the meek and lowly Lamb of God.

If this be the root of the tree, its nature must be seen in every branch and leaf and fruit. If humility be the first, the all-including grace of the life of Jesus, —if humility be the secret of His atonement, —then the health and strength of our spiritual life will entirely depend upon our putting this grace first too, and making humility the chief thing we admire in Him, the chief thing we ask of Him, the one thing for which we sacrifice all else.[2]

---

[2] 'We need to know two things: 1. That our salvation consists wholly in being saved from ourselves, or that which we are by nature; 2. That in the whole nature of things nothing could be this salvation or savior to us but such a humility of God as is beyond all expression. Hence the first unalterable term of the Savior to fallen man: Except a man denies himself, he cannot be My disciple. Self is the whole evil of fallen nature; self-denial is our capacity of being saved; humility is our savior.... Self is the root, the branches, the tree, of all the evil of our fallen state. All the evils of fallen angels and men have their birth in the pride of self. On the other hand, all the virtues of the heavenly life are the virtues of humility. It is humility alone that makes

Is it any wonder that the Christian life is so often feeble and fruitless, when the very root of the Christ life is neglected, is unknown? Is it any wonder that the joy of salvation is so little felt, when that in which Christ found it and brings it, is so little sought? Until a humility which will rest in nothing less than the end and death of self; which gives up all the honor of men as Jesus did, to seek the honor that comes from God alone; which absolutely makes and counts itself nothing, that God may be all, that the Lord alone may be exalted, —until such a humility be what we seek in Christ above our chief joy, and welcome at any price, there is very little hope of a religion that will conquer the world.

I cannot too earnestly plead with my reader, if possibly his attention has never yet been specially directed to the want there is of humility within him or around him, to pause and ask whether he sees much of the spirit of the meek and lowly Lamb of God in those who are called by His name. Let him consider how all want of love, all indifference to the needs, the feelings, the weakness of others; all sharp and hasty judgments and utterances, so often excused under the plea of being outright and honest; all manifestations of temper and touchiness and irritation; all feelings of bitterness and estrangement, have their root in nothing but pride, that ever seeks itself, and his eyes will be opened to see how a dark, shall I not say a devilish pride, creeps in almost everywhere, the assemblies of the saints not excepted. Let him begin to ask what would be the effect, if in himself and around him, if towards fellow-saints and the world, believers were really permanently guided by the humility of Jesus; and let him say if the cry of our whole heart, night and day, ought not to be, Oh for the humility of Jesus in myself and all around me! Let him honestly fix his heart on his own lack of the humility which has been revealed in the likeness of Christ's life, and in the whole character of His redemption, and he will begin to feel as if he had never yet really known what Christ and His salvation is.

Believer! *study the humility of Jesus.* This is the secret, the hidden root of thy redemption. Sink down into it deeper day by day. Believe with thy whole heart that this Christ, whom God has given thee, even as His divine humility wrought the work for thee, will enter in to dwell and work within thee too, and make thee what the Father would have thee be.

Humility in the Life of Jesus

'I am in the midst of you as he that serveth.' —LUKE xxii. 26.

IN the Gospel of John we have the inner life of our Lord laid open to us. Jesus speaks frequently of His relation to the Father, of the motives by which He is guided, of His consciousness of the power and spirit in which He acts. Though the word humble does not occur, we shall nowhere in Scripture see so clearly wherein His humility consisted. We have already said that this grace is in truth nothing but that simple consent of the creature to let God be all, in virtue of which it surrenders itself to His working alone. In

the unpassable gulf between heaven and hell. What is then, or in what lies, the great struggle for eternal life? It all lies in the strife between pride and humility: pride and humility are the two master powers, the two kingdoms in strife for the eternal possession of man. There never was, nor ever will be, but one humility, and that is the one humility of Christ. Pride and self have the all of man, till man has his all from Christ. He therefore only fights the good fight whose strife is that the self-idolatrous nature which he hath from Adam may be brought to death by the supernatural humility of Christ brought to life in him.' —W. Law, Address to the Clergy, p. 52.

Jesus we shall see how both as the Son of God in heaven, and as man upon earth, He took the place of entire subordination, and gave God the honor and the glory which is due to Him. And what He taught so often was made true to Himself: 'He that humbleth him: shall be exalted.' As it is written, 'He humbled Himself, therefore God highly exalted Him.'

Listen to the words in which our Lord speaks of His relation to the Father, and how unceasingly He uses the words *not*, and *nothing*, of Himself. The *not I*, in which Paul expresses his relation to Christ, is the very spirit of what Christ says of His relation the Father.

'The Son can do *nothing* of Himself' (John v. 19).

'I can of My own self do *nothing*; My judgment is just, because I seek *not* Mine own will' (John v 30).

'I receive *not* glory from men' (John v. 41).

'I am come *not* to do Mine own will' (John vi. 38).

'My teaching is *not* Mine' (John vii. 16).

'I am *not* come of Myself' (John vii. 28).

'I do *nothing* of Myself' (John vii. 28).

'I have *not* come of Myself, but He sent Me' (John viii. 42).

'I seek *not* Mine own glory' (John viii. 50).

'The words that I say, I speak *not* from Myself' (John xiv. 10).

'The word which ye hear is *not* Mine' (John xiv. 24).

These words open to us the deepest roots of Christ's life and work. They tell us how it was that the Almighty God was able to work His mighty redemptive work through Him. They show what Christ counted the state of heart which became Him as the Son of the Father. They teach us what the essential nature and life is of that redemption which Christ accomplished and now communicates. It is this: He was nothing, that God might be all. He resigned Himself with His will and His powers entirely for the Father to work in Him. Of His own power, His own will, and His own glory, of His whole mission with all His works and His teaching, —of all this He said, It is not I; I am nothing; I have given Myself to the Father to work; I am nothing, the Father is all.

This life of entire self-abnegation, of absolute submission and dependence upon the Father's will, Christ found to be one of perfect peace and joy. He lost nothing by giving all to God. God honored His trust, and did all for Him, and then exalted Him to His own right hand in glory. And because Christ had thus humbled Himself before God, and God was ever before Him, He found it possible to humble Himself before men too, and to be the Servant of all. His humility was simply the surrender of Himself to God, to allow Him to do in Him what He pleased, whatever men around might say of Him, or do to Him.

It is in this state of mind, in this spirit and disposition, that the redemption of Christ has its virtue and efficacy. It is to bring us to this disposition that we are made partakers of Christ. This is the true self-denial to which our Savior calls us, the acknowledgment that self has nothing good in it, except as an empty vessel which God must fill, and that its claim to be or do anything may not for a moment be allowed. It is in this, above and before everything, in which the conformity to Jesus consists, the being and doing nothing of ourselves, that God may be all.

Here we have the root and nature of true humility. It is because this is not understood or sought after, that our humility is so superficial and so feeble. We must learn of Jesus, how He is meek and lowly of heart. He teaches us where true humility takes its rise and finds its strength—in the knowledge that it is God who worketh all in all, that our place is to yield to Him in perfect resignation and dependence, in full consent to be and to do nothing of ourselves. This is the life Christ came to reveal and to impart—a life to God that came through death to sin and self. If we feel that this life is too high for us and beyond our reach, it must but the more urge us to seek it in Him; it is the indwelling Christ who will live in us this life, meek and lowly. If we long for this, let us, meantime, above everything, seek the holy secret of the knowledge of the nature of God, as He every moment works all in all; the secret, of which all nature and every creature, and above all, every child of God, is to be the witness, —that it is nothing but a vessel, a channel, through which the living God can manifest the riches of His wisdom, power, and goodness. The root of all virtue and grace, of all faith and acceptable worship, is that we know that we have nothing but what we receive, and bow in deepest humility to wait upon God for it.

It was because this humility was not only a temporary sentiment, wakened up and brought into exercise when He thought of God, but the very spirit of His whole life, that Jesus was just as humble in His intercourse with men as with God. He felt Himself the Servant of God for the men whom God made and loved; as a natural consequence, He counted Himself the Servant of men, that through Him God might do His work of love. He never for a moment thought of seeking His honor, or asserting His power to vindicate Himself. His whole spirit was that of a life yielded to God to work in. It is not until Christians study the humility of Jesus as the very essence of His redemption, as the very blessedness of the life of the Son of God, as the only true relation to the Father, and therefore as that which Jesus must give us if we are to have any part with Him, that the terrible lack of actual, heavenly, manifest humility will become a burden and a sorrow, and our ordinary religion be set aside to secure this, the first and the chief of the marks of the Christ within us.

Brother, are you clothed with humility? Ask your daily life. Ask Jesus. Ask your friends. Ask the world. And begin to praise God that there is opened up to you in Jesus a heavenly humility of which you have hardly known, and through which a heavenly blessedness you possibly have never yet tasted can come in to you.

Humility in the Teaching of Jesus

'Learn of Me, for I am meek and lowly of heart.' —MATT. xi. 29. 'Whosoever will be chief among you, let him be your servant, even as the Son of Man came to serve.' —MATT. xx. 27.

WE have seen humility in the life of Christ, as He laid open His heart to us: let us listen to His teaching. There we shall hear how He speaks of it, and how far He expects men, and specially His disciples, to be humble as He was. Let us carefully study the passages, which I can scarce do more than quote, to receive the full impression of how often and how earnestly He taught it: it may help us to realize what He asks of us.

1. Look at the commencement of His ministry. In the Beatitudes with which the Sermon on the Mount opens, He speaks: *'Blessed are the poor in spirit; for theirs is the kingdom of heaven. Blessed are the meek; for they shall inherit the earth.'* The very first

words of His proclamation of the kingdom of heaven reveal the open gate through which alone we enter. The poor, who have nothing in themselves, to them the kingdom comes. The meek, who seek nothing in themselves, theirs the earth shall be. The blessings of heaven and earth are for the lowly. For the heavenly and the earthly life, humility is the secret of blessing.

2. *'Learn of Me; for I am meek and lowly of heart, and ye shall find rest for your souls.'* Jesus offers Himself as Teacher. He tells what the spirit both is, which we shall find Him as Teacher, and which we can learn and receive from Him. Meekness and lowliness the one thing He offers us; in it we shall find perfect rest of soul. Humility is to be a salvation.

3. The disciples had been disputing who would be the greatest in the kingdom, and had agreed to ask the Master (Luke 9:46; Matt. 18:3). He set a child in their midst and said, *'Whosoever shall humble himself as this little child, shall be exalted.'* 'Who the greatest in the kingdom of heaven?' The question is indeed a far-reaching one. What will be the chief distinction in the heavenly kingdom? The answer, none but Jesus would have given. The chief glory of heaven, the true heavenly-mindedness, the chief of the graces, is humility. *'He that is least among you, the same shall be great.'*

4. The sons of Zebedee had asked Jesus to sit on His right and left, the highest place in the kingdom. Jesus said it was not His to give, but the Father's, who would give it to those for whom it was prepared. They must not look or ask for it. Their thought must be of the cup and the baptism of humiliation. And then He added, *'Whosoever will be chief among you, let him be your servant. Even as the Son of Man came to serve.'* Humility, as it is the mark of Christ the heavenly, will be the one standard of glory in heaven: the lowliest is the nearest to God. The primacy in the Church is promised to the humblest.

5. Speaking to the multitude and the disciples, of the Pharisees and their love of the chief seats, Christ said once again (Matt. xxxiii. 11), *'He that is greatest among you shall be your servant.'* Humiliation is the only ladder to honor in God's kingdom.

6. On another occasion, in the house of a Pharisee, He spoke the parable of the guest who would be invited to come up higher (Luke xiv. 1-11), and added, *'For whosoever exalteth himself shall be abased; and he that humbleth himself shall be exalted.'* The demand is inexorable; there is no other way. Self-abasement alone will be exalted.

7. After the parable of the Pharisee and the Publican, Christ spake again (Luke xviii. 14), *'Everyone that exalteth himself shall be abased; and he that humbleth himself shall be exalted.'* In the temple and presence and worship of God, everything is worthless that is not pervaded by deep, true humility towards God and men.

8. After washing the disciples' feet, Jesus said (John xiii. 14), *'If I then, the Lord and Master, have washed your feet, ye also ought to wash one another's feet.'* The authority of command, and example, every thought, either of obedience or conformity, make humility the first and most essential element of discipleship.

9. At the Holy Supper table, the disciples still disputed who should be greatest (Luke xxii. 26). Jesus said, *'He that is greatest among you, let him be as the younger; and he that is chief, as he that doth serve. I am among you as he that serveth.'* The path in which Jesus walked, and which He opened up for us, the power and spirit in which He wrought out salvation, and to which He saves us, is ever the humility that makes me the servant of all.

How little this is preached. How little it is practiced. How little the lack of it is felt or confessed. I do not say, how few attain to it, some recognizable measure of likeness to Jesus in His humility. But how few ever think, of making it a distinct object of continual desire or prayer. How little the world has seen it. How little has it been seen even in the inner circle of the Church.

'Whosoever will be chief among you, let him be your servant.' Would God that it might be given us to believe that Jesus means this! We all know what the character of a faithful servant or slave implies. Devotion to the master's interests, thoughtful study and care to please him, delight in his prosperity and honor and happiness. There are servants on earth in whom these dispositions have been seen, and to whom the name of servant has never been anything but a glory. To how many of us has it not been a new joy in the Christian life to know that we may yield ourselves as servants, as slaves to God, and to find that His service is our highest liberty, —the liberty from sin and self? We need now to learn another lesson, —that Jesus calls us to be servants of one another, and that, as we accept it heartily, this service too will be a most blessed one, a new and fuller liberty too from sin and self. At first it may appear hard; this is only because of the pride which still counts itself something. If once we learn that to be nothing before God is the glory of the creature, the spirit of Jesus, the joy of heaven, we shall welcome with our whole heart the discipline we may have in serving even those who try to vex us. When our own heart is set upon this, the true sanctification, we shall study each word of Jesus on self-abasement with new zest, and no place will be too low, and no stooping too deep, and no service too mean or too long continued, if we may but share and prove the fellowship with Him who spake, 'I am among you as he that serveth.'

Brethren, here is the path to the higher life. Down, lower down! This was what Jesus ever said to the disciples who were thinking of being great in the kingdom, and of sitting on His right hand and His left. Seek not, ask not for exaltation; that is God's work. Look to it that you abase and humble yourselves, and take no place before God or man but that of servant; that is your work; let that be your one purpose and prayer. God is faithful. Just as water ever seeks and fills the lowest place, so the moment God finds the creature abased and empty, His glory and power flow in to exalt and to bless. He that humbleth himself— that must be our one care—shall be exalted; that is God's care; by His mighty power and in His great love He will do it.

Men sometimes speak as if humility and meekness would rob us of what is noble and bold and manlike. Oh that all would believe that this is the nobility of the kingdom of heaven, that this is the royal spirit that the King of heaven displayed, that this is Godlike, to humble oneself, to become the servant of all! This is the path to the gladness and the glory of Christ's presence ever in us, His power ever resting on us.

Jesus, the meek and lowly One, calls us to learn of Him the path to God. Let us study the words we have been reading, until our heart is filled with the thought: My one need is humility. And let us believe that what He shows, He gives; what He is, He imparts. As the meek and lowly One, He will come in and dwell in the longing heart.

Humility in the Disciples of Jesus

'Let him that is chief among you be as he that doth serve.' —LUKE xxii. 26

WE have studied humility in the person and teaching of Jesus; let us now look for it in the circle of His chosen companions—the twelve apostles. If, in the lack of it we find in them, the contrast between Christ and men is brought out more clearly, it will help us to appreciate the mighty change which Pentecost wrought in them, and prove how real our participation can be in the perfect triumph of Christ's humility over the pride Satan had breathed into man.

In the texts quoted from the teaching of Jesus, we have already seen what the occasions were on which the disciples had proved how entirely wanting they were in the grace of humility. Once, they had been disputing the way which of them should be the greatest Another time, the sons of Zebedee with their mother had asked for the first places—the seat on the right hand and the left. And, later on, at the Supper table on the last night, there was again a contention which should be accounted the greatest. Not that there were not moments when they indeed humbled themselves before their Lord. So it was with Peter when he cried out, 'Depart from me, Lord, for I am a sinful man.' So, too, with the disciples when they fell down and worshipped Him who had stilled the storm. But such occasional expressions of humility only bring out into stronger relief what was the habitual tone of their mind, as shown in the natural and spontaneous revelation given at other times of the place and the power of self. The study of the meaning of all this will teach us most important lessons.

First, *How much there may be of earnest and active, religion while humility is still sadly wanting.* —See it in the disciples. There was in them fervent attachment to Jesus. They had forsaken all for Him. The Father had revealed to them that He was the Christ of God. They believed in Him, they loved Him, they obeyed His commandments. They had forsaken all to follow Him. When others went back, they clave to Him. They were ready to die with Him. But deeper down than all this there was a dark power, of the existence and the hideousness of which they were hardly conscious, which had to be slain and cast out, ere they could be the witnesses of the power of Jesus to save. It is even so still. We may find professors and ministers, evangelists and workers, missionaries and teachers, in whom the gifts of the Spirit are many and manifest, and who are the channels of blessing to multitudes, but of whom, when the testing time comes, or closer intercourse gives fuller knowledge, it is only too painfully manifest that the grace of humility, as an abiding characteristic, is scarce to be seen. All tends to confirm the lesson that humility is one of the chief and the highest graces; one of the most difficult of attainment; one to which our first and chiefest efforts ought to be directed; one that only comes in power, when the fullness of the Spirit makes us partakers of the indwelling Christ, and He lives within us.

Second, *How impotent all external teaching and all personal effort is, to conquer pride or give the meek and lowly heart.* —For three years the disciples had been in the training school of Jesus. He had told them what the chief lesson was He wished to teach them: 'Learn of Me, for I am meek and lowly in heart.' Time after time He had spoken to them, to the Pharisees, to the multitude, of humility as the only path to the glory of God. He had not only lived before them as the Lamb of God in His divine humility, He had more than once unfolded to them the inmost secret of His life: 'The Son of Man came not to be served, but to serve'; 'I am among you as one that serveth.' He had washed their feet, and told them they were to follow His example. And yet all had availed but little. At the Holy Supper there was still the contention as to who should be greatest. They had doubtless often tried to learn His lessons, and firmly resolved not again to grieve Him. But all in vain. To teach them and us the much needed lesson, that no outward instruction, not even of Christ Himself; no argument however convincing; no sense of the beauty of humility, however deep; no personal resolve or effort, however sincere and earnest, —can cast out the devil of pride. When Satan casts out Satan, it is only to enter afresh in a mightier, though more hidden power. Nothing can avail but this, that the new nature in its divine humility be revealed in power to take the place of the old, to become as truly our very nature as that ever was.

Third, *It is only by the indwelling of Christ in His divine humility that we become truly humble.* —We have our pride from another, from Adam; we must have our humility from Another too. Pride is ours, and rules in us with such terrible power, because it is ourself, our very nature. Humility must be ours in the same way; it must be our very self, our very nature. As natural and easy as it has been to be proud, it must be, it will be, to be humble. The promise is, 'Where,' even in the heart, 'sin abounded, grace did abound more exceedingly.' All Christ's teaching of His disciples, and all their vain efforts, were the needful preparation for His entering into them in divine power, to give and be in them what He had taught them to desire. In His death He destroyed the power of the devil, He put away sin, and effected an everlasting redemption. In His resurrection He received from the Father an entirely new life, the life of man in the power of God, capable of being communicated to men, and entering and renewing and filling their lives with His divine power. In His ascension He received the Spirit of the Father, through whom He might do what He could not do while upon earth, make Himself one with those He loved, actually live their life for them, so that they could live before the Father in a humility like His, because it was Himself who lived and breathed in them. And on Pentecost He came and took possession. The work of preparation and conviction, the awakening of desire and hope which His teaching had effected, was perfected by the mighty change that Pentecost wrought. And the lives and the epistles of James and Peter and John bear witness that all was changed, and that the spirit of the meek and suffering Jesus had indeed possession of them.

What shall we say to these things? Among my readers I am sure there is more than one class. There may be some who have never yet thought very specially of the matter, and cannot at once realize its immense importance as a life question for the Church and its every member. There are others who have felt condemned for their shortcomings, and have put forth very earnest efforts, only to fail and be discouraged. Others, again, may be able to give joyful testimony of spiritual blessing and power, and yet there has never been the needed conviction of what those around them still see as wanting. And still others may be able to witness that in regard to this grace too the Lord has given deliverance and victory, while He has taught them how much they still need and may expect out of the fullness of Jesus. To whichever class we belong, may I urge the pressing need there is for our all seeking a still deeper conviction of the unique place that humility holds in the religion of Christ, and the utter impossibility of the Church or the believer being what Christ would have them be, as long as *His humility is not recognized as His chief glory, His first command, and our highest blessedness.* Let us consider deeply how far the disciples were advanced while this grace was still so terribly lacking, and let us pray to God that other gifts may not so satisfy us, that we never grasp the fact that the absence of this grace is the secret cause why the power of God cannot do its mighty work. It is only where we, like the Son, truly know and show that we can do nothing of ourselves, that God will do all.

It is when the truth of an indwelling Christ takes the place it claims in the experience of believers, that the Church will put on her beautiful garments and humility be seen in her teachers and members as the beauty of holiness.

Humility in Daily Life

'He that loveth not his brother whom he hath seen, how can he love God whom he hath not seen?' —1 JOHN iv. 20.

WHAT a solemn thought, that our love to God will be measured by our everyday intercourse with men and the love it displays; and that our love to God will be found to be a delusion, except was its truth is proved in standing the test of daily life with our fellowmen. It is even so with our humility. It is easy to think we humble ourselves before God: humility towards men will be the only sufficient proof that our humility before God is real; that humility has taken up its abode in us; and become our very nature; that we actually, like Christ, have made ourselves of no reputation. When in the presence of God lowliness of heart has become, not a posture we pray to Him, but the very spirit of our life, it will manifest itself in all our bearing towards our brethren. The lesson is one of deep import: the only humility that is really ours is not that which we try to show before God in prayer, but that which we carry with us, and carry out, in our ordinary conduct; the insignificances of daily life are the importances and the tests of eternity, because they prove what really is the spirit that possesses us. It is in our most unguarded moments that we really show and see what we are. To know the humble man, to know how the humble man behaves, you must follow him in the common course of daily life.

Is not this what Jesus taught? It was when the disciples disputed who should be greatest; when He saw how the Pharisees loved the chief place at feasts and the chief seats in the synagogues; when He had given them the example of washing their feet, —that He taught His lessons of humility. Humility before God is nothing if not proved in humility before men.

It is even so in the teaching of Paul. To the Romans He writes: 'In honor preferring one *another*'; 'Set not your mind on high things, but condescend to *those that are lowly*.' 'Be not wise in your own conceit.' To the Corinthians: 'Love,' and there is no love without humility as its root, 'vaunteth not itself, is not puffed up, seeketh not its own, is not provoked.' To the Galatians: 'Through love be servants *one of another*. Let us not be desirous of vainglory, provoking *one another*, envying *one another*.' To the Ephesians, immediately after the three wonderful chapters on the heavenly life: 'Therefore, walk with all lowliness and meekness, with long-suffering, forbearing *one another* in love'; 'Giving thanks always, subjecting yourselves *one to another* in the fear of Christ.' To the Philippians: 'Doing nothing through faction or vainglory, but in lowliness of mind, each counting *other* better than himself. Have the mind in you which was also in Christ Jesus, who emptied Himself, taking the form of a servant, and humbled Himself.' And to the Colossians: 'Put on a heart of compassion, kindness, humility, meekness, long-suffering, forbearing *one another*, and forgiving *each other*, even as the Lord forgave you.' It is in our relation to one another, in our treatment of one another, that the true lowliness of mind and the heart of humility are to be seen. Our humility before God has no value, but as it prepares us to reveal the humility of Jesus to our fellow-men. Let us study humility in daily life in the light of these words.

The humble man seeks at all times to act up to the rule, *'In honor preferring one another; Servants one of another; Each counting others better than himself; Subjecting yourselves one to another.'* The question is often asked, how we can count others better than ourselves, when we see that they are far below us in wisdom and in holiness, in natural gifts, or in grace received. The question proves at once how little we understand what real lowliness of mind is. True humility comes when, in the light of God, we have seen ourselves to be nothing, have consented to part with and cast away self, to let God be all. The soul that has done this, and can say, So have I lost myself in finding Thee, no longer compares itself with others. It has given up forever every thought of self in God's presence; it meets its fellow-men as one who is nothing, and seeks nothing for itself; who is a servant of God, and for His sake a servant of all. A faithful servant may be wiser than the master, and yet retain the true spirit and posture of the servant. The humble man looks upon every, the feeblest and unworthiest, child of God, and honors him and prefers him in honor as the son of a King. The spirit of Him who washed the disciples' feet, makes it a joy to us to be indeed the least, to be servants one of another.

The humble man feels no jealousy or envy. He can praise God when others are preferred and blessed before him. He can bear to hear others praised and himself forgotten, because in God's presence he has learnt to say with Paul, 'I am nothing.' He has received the spirit of Jesus, who pleased not Himself, and sought not His own honor, as the spirit of his life.

Amid what are considered the temptations to impatience and touchiness, to hard thoughts and sharp words, which come from the failings and sins of fellow-Christians, the humble man carries the oft-repeated injunction in his heart, and shows it in his life, *'Forbearing one another, and forgiving one another, even as the Lord forgave you.'* He has learnt that in putting on the Lord Jesus he *has put on the heart of compassion, kindness, humility, meekness, and long-suffering.* Jesus has taken the place of self, and it is not an impossibility to forgive as Jesus forgave. His humility does not consist merely in thoughts or words of self-depreciation, but, as Paul puts it, in 'a heart of humility,' encompassed by compassion and kindness, meekness and long-suffering, —the sweet and lowly gentleness recognized as the mark of the Lamb of God.

In striving after the higher experiences of the Christian life, the believer is often in danger of aiming at and rejoicing in what one might call the more human, the manly, virtues, such as boldness, joy, contempt of the world, zeal, self-sacrifice, —even the old Stoics taught and practiced these, —while the deeper and gentler, the diviner and more heavenly graces, those which Jesus first taught upon earth, because He brought them from heaven; those which are more distinctly connected with His cross and the death of self, — poverty of spirit, meekness, humility, lowliness, —are scarcely thought of or valued. Therefore, let us put on a heart of compassion, kindness, humility, meekness, long-suffering; and let us prove our Christlikeness, not only in our zeal for saving the lost, but before all in our intercourse with the brethren, forbearing and forgiving one another, *even as the Lord forgave us.*

Fellow-Christians, do let us study the Bible portrait of the humble man. And let us ask our brethren, and ask the world, whether they recognize in us the likeness to the original. Let us be content with nothing less than taking each of these texts as the promise of what God will work in us, as the revelation in words of what the Spirit of Jesus will give as a birth within us. And let each failure and shortcoming simply urge us to turn humbly and meekly to the meek and lowly Lamb of God, in the assurance that where He is enthroned in the heart, His humility and gentleness will be one of the streams of living water that flow from within us.[3]

Once again I repeat what I have said before. I feel deeply that we have very little conception of what the Church suffers from the lack of this divine humility, —the nothingness that makes room for God to prove His power. It is not long since a Christian, of an humble, loving spirit, acquainted with not a few mission stations of various societies, expressed his deep sorrow that in some cases the spirit of love and forbearance was sadly lacking. Men and women, who in Europe could each choose their own circle of friends, brought close together with others of uncongenial minds, find it hard to bear, and to love, and to keep the unity of the Spirit in the bond of peace. And those who should have been fellow-helpers of each other's joy, became a hindrance and a weariness. And all for the one reason, the lack of the humility which counts itself nothing, which rejoices in becoming and being counted the least, and only seeks, like Jesus, to be the servant, the helper and comforter of others, even the lowest and unworthiest.

And whence comes it that men who have joyfully given up themselves for Christ, find it so hard to give up themselves for their brethren? Is not the blame with the Church? It has so little taught its sons that the humility of Christ is the first of the virtues, the best of all the graces and powers of the Spirit. It has so little proved that a Christlike humility is what it, like Christ, places and preaches first, as what is in very deed needed, and possible too. But let us not be discouraged. Let the discovery of the lack of this grace stir us to larger expectation from God. Let us look upon every brother who tries or vexes us, as God's means of grace, God's instrument for our purification, for our exercise of the humility Jesus our Life breathes within us. And let us have such faith in the All of God, and the nothing of self, that, as nothing in our own eyes, we may, in God's power, only seek to serve one another in love.

Humility and Holiness

'Which say, Stand by thyself; for I am holier than thou.' —ISAIAH lxv. 5.

WE speak of the Holiness movement in our times, and praise God for it. We hear a great deal of seekers after holiness and professors of holiness, of holiness teaching and holiness meetings. The blessed truths of holiness in Christ, and holiness by faith, are being emphasized as never before. The great test of whether the holiness we profess to seek or to attain, is truth and life, will be *whether it be manifest in the increasing humility it produces.* In the creature, humility is the one thing needed to allow God's holiness to dwell in him and shine through him. In Jesus, the Holy One of God who makes us holy, a divine humility was the secret of His life and His death and His exaltation; the one infallible test of our holiness will be the humility before God and men which marks us. Humility is the bloom and the beauty of holiness.

The chief mark of counterfeit holiness is its lack of humility. Every seeker after holiness needs to be on his guard, lest unconsciously what was begun in the spirit be perfected in the flesh, and pride creep in where its presence is least expected. Two men

---

[3] 'I knew Jesus, and He was very precious to my soul: but I found something in me that would not keep sweet and patient and kind. I did what I could to keep it down, but it was there. I besought Jesus to do something for me, and when I gave Him my will, He came to my heart, and took out all that would not be sweet, all that would not be kind, all that would not be patient, and then He shut the door.' —George Foxe

went up into the temple to pray: the one a Pharisee, the other a publican. There is no place or position so sacred but the Pharisee can enter there. Pride can lift its head in the very temple of God, and make His worship the scene of its self exaltation. Since the time Christ so exposed his pride, the Pharisee has put on the garb of the publican, and the confessor of deep sinfulness equally with the professor of the highest holiness, must be on the watch. Just when We are most anxious to have our heart the temple of God, we shall find the two men coming up to pray. And the publican will find that his danger is not from the Pharisee beside him, who despises him, but the Pharisee within who commends and exalts. In God's temple, when we think we are in the holiest of all, in the presence of His holiness, let us beware of pride. 'Now there was a day when the sons of God came to present themselves before the Lord, and Satan came also among them.'

'God, I thank thee, I am not as the rest of men, or even as this publican.' It is in that which is just cause for thanksgiving, it is in the very thanksgiving which we render to God, it may be in the very confession that God has done it all, that self finds its cause of complacency. Yes, even when in the temple the language of penitence and trust in God's mercy alone is heard, the Pharisee may take up the note of praise, and in thanking God be congratulating himself. Pride can clothe itself in the garments of praise or of penitence. Even though the words, 'I am not as the rest of men' are rejected and condemned, their spirit may too often be found in our feelings and language towards our fellow-worshippers and fellow-men. Would you know if this really is so, just listen to the way in which Churches and Christians often speak of one another. How little of the meekness and gentleness of Jesus is to be seen. It is so little remembered that deep humility must be the keynote of what the servants of Jesus say of themselves or each other. Is there not many a Church or assembly of the saints, many a mission or convention, many a society or committee, even many a mission away in heathendom, where the harmony has been disturbed and the work of God hindered, because men who are counted saints have proved in touchiness and haste and impatience, in self-defense and self-assertion, in sharp judgments and unkind words, that they did not each reckon others better than themselves, and that their holiness has but little in it of the meekness of the saints?[4] In their spiritual history men may have had times of great humbling and brokenness, but what a different thing this is from being clothed with humility, from having an humble spirit, from having that lowliness of mind in which each counts himself the servant of others, and so shows forth the very mind which was also in Jesus Christ.

'Stand by; for I am holier than thou!' What a parody on holiness! Jesus the Holy One is the humble One: the holiest will ever be the humblest. There is none holy but God: we have as much of holiness as we have of God. And according to what we have of God will be our real humility, because humility is nothing but the disappearance of self in the vision that God is all. The holiest will be the humblest. Alas! though the barefaced boasting Jew of the days of Isaiah is not often to be found, —even our manners have taught us not to speak thus, how often his spirit is still seen, whether in the treatment of fellow-saints or of the children of the world. In the spirit in which opinions are given, and work is undertaken,

---

[4] ME is a most exacting personage, requiring the best seat and the highest place for itself, and feeling grievously wounded if its claim is not recognized. Most of the quarrels among Christian workers arise from the clamoring of this gigantic ME. How few of us understand the true secret of taking our seats in the lowest rooms. —Mrs. Smith, Everyday Religion.

and faults are exposed, how often, though the garb be that of the publican, the voice is still that of the Pharisee: 'Oh God, I thank Thee that I am not as other men.'

And is there, then, such humility to be found, that men shall indeed still count themselves 'less than the least of all saints,' the servants of all? There is. 'Love vaunteth not itself, is not puffed up, seeketh not its own.' Where the spirit of love is shed abroad in the heart, where the divine nature comes to a full birth where Christ the meek and lowly Lamb of God is truly formed within, there is given the power of a perfect love that forgets itself and finds its blessedness in blessing others, in bearing with them and honoring them, however feeble they be. Where this love enters, there God enters. And where God has entered in His power, and reveals Himself as All, there the creature becomes nothing. And where the creature becomes nothing before God; it cannot be anything but humble towards the fellow-creature. The presence of God becomes not a thing of times and seasons, but the covering under which the soul ever dwells, and its deep abasement before God becomes the holy place of His presence whence all its words and works proceed.

May God teach us that our thoughts and words and feelings concerning our fellowmen are His test of our humility towards Him, and that our humility before Him is the only power that can enable us to be always humble with our fellow-men. Our humility must be the life of Christ, the Lamb of God, within us.

Let all teachers of holiness, whether in the pulpit or on the platform, and all seekers after holiness, whether in the closet or the convention, take warning. There is no pride so dangerous, because none so subtle and insidious, as the pride of holiness. It is not that a man ever says, or even thinks, 'Stand by; I am holier than thou.' No, indeed, the thought would be regarded with abhorrence. But there grows up, all unconsciously, a hidden habit of soul, which feels complacency its attainments, and cannot help seeing how far it is in advance of others. It can be recognized, not always in any special self-assertion or self-laudation, but simply in the absence of that deep self-abasement which cannot but be the mark of the soul that has seen the glory of God (Job xlii. 5, 6; Isa. vi. 5). It reveals itself, not only in words or thoughts, but in a tone, a way of speaking of others, in which those who have the gift of spiritual discernment cannot but recognize the power of self. Even the world with its keen eyes notices it, and points to it as a proof that the profession of a heavenly life does not bear any specially heavenly fruits. O brethren! let us beware. Unless we make, with each advance in what we think holiness, the increase of humility our study, we may find that we have been delighting in beautiful thoughts and feelings, in solemn acts of consecration and faith, while the only sure mark of the presence of God, the disappearance of self, was all the time wanting. Come and let us flee to Jesus, and hide ourselves in Him until we be clothed upon with His humility. That alone is our holiness.

Humility and Sin

'Sinners, of whom I am chief.' —1 TIM. i. 15

HUMILITY is often identified with penitence and contrition. As a consequence, there appears to be no way of fostering humility but by keeping the soul occupied with its sin. We have learned, I think, that humility is something else and something more. We have seen in the teaching of our Lord Jesus and the Epistles how often the virtue is inculcated without any reference to sin. In the very nature of things, in the whole relation of the creature to the Creator, in the life of Jesus as He lived it and imparts it to us, humility is the very essence of holiness as of blessedness. It is the displacement of self by the enthronement of God. Where God is all, self is nothing.

But though it is this aspect of the truth I have felt it specially needful to press, I need scarce say what new depth and intensity man's sin and God's grace give to the humility of the saints. We have only to look at a man like the Apostle Paul, to see how, through his life as a ransomed and a holy man, the deep consciousness of having been a sinner lives inextinguishably. We all know the passages in which he refers to his life as a persecutor and blasphemer. 'I am *the least of the apostles*, that am *not worthy to be called an apostle*, because I persecuted the Church of God…. I labored more abundantly than they all; yet not I, but the grace of God which was with me' (1 Cor. xv. 9,10). 'Unto me, who am *less than the least of all saints,* was this grace given, to preach to the heathen' (Eph. iii. 8). 'I was before a *blasphemer, and a persecutor, and injurious;* howbeit I obtained mercy, because I did it ignorantly in unbelief…. Christ Jesus came into the world to save *sinners, of whom I am chief'* (1 Tim. i. 13, 15). God's grace had saved him; God remembered his sins no more for ever; but never, never could he forget how terribly he had sinned. The more he rejoiced in God's salvation, and the more his experience of God's grace filled him with joy unspeakable, the clearer was his consciousness that he was a saved sinner, and that salvation had no meaning or sweetness except as the sense of his being a sinner made it precious and real to him. Never for a moment could he forget that it was a sinner God had taken up in His arms and crowned with His love.

The texts we have just quoted are often appealed to as Paul's confession of daily sinning. One has only to read them carefully in their connection, to see how little this is the case. They have a far deeper meaning, they refer to that which lasts throughout eternity, and which will give its deep undertone of amazement and adoration to the humility with which the ransomed bow before the throne, as those who have been washed from their sins in the blood of the Lamb. Never, never, even in, glory, can they be other than ransomed sinners; never for a moment in this life can God's child live in the full light of His love, but as he feels that the sin, out of which he has been saved, is his one only right and title to all that grace has promised to do. The humility with which first he came as a sinner, acquires a new meaning when he learns how it becomes him as a creature. And then ever again, the humility, in which he was born as a creature, has its deepest, richest tones of adoration, in the memory of what it is to be a monument of God's wondrous redeeming love.

The true import of what these expressions of St. Paul teach us comes out all the more strongly when we notice the remarkable fact that, through his whole Christian course, we never find from his pen, even in those epistles in which we have the most intensely personal unbosomings, anything like confession of sin. Nowhere is there any mention of shortcoming or defect, nowhere any suggestion to his readers that he has failed in duty, or sinned against the law of perfect love. On the contrary, there are passages not a few in which he vindicates himself in language that means nothing if it does not appeal to a faultless life before God and men. 'Ye are witnesses, and God also, how holily, and righteously, and unblameably we behaved ourselves toward you' (1 Thess. ii. 10). 'Our glorying is this, the testimony of our conscience, that in holiness and sincerity of God we behaved ourselves in the world, and more abundantly to you ward' (2 Cor. i. 12). This is not an ideal or an aspiration; it is an appeal to what his actual life had been. However we may account for this absence of confession of sin, all will admit that it must point to a life in the power of the Holy Ghost, such as is but seldom realized or expected in these our days.

The point which I wish to emphasize is this—that the very fact of the absence of such confession of sinning only gives the more force to the truth that it is not in daily sinning that the secret of the deeper humility will be found, but in the habitual, never for a moment to be forgotten position, which just the more abundant grace will keep more distinctly alive, that our only place, the only place of blessing, our one abiding position before God, must be that of those whose highest joy it is to confess that they are sinners saved by grace.

With Paul's deep remembrance of having sinned so terribly in the past, ere grace had met him, and the consciousness of being kept from present sinning, there was ever coupled the abiding remembrance of the dark hidden power of sin ever ready to come in, and only kept out by the presence and power of the indwelling Christ. 'In me, that is, in my flesh, dwelleth no good thing;' —these words of Rom. vii. describe the flesh as it is to the end. The glorious deliverance of Rom. viii. —'The law of the Spirit of life in Christ Jesus hath now made me free from the law of sin, which once led me captive' —is neither the annihilation nor the sanctification of the flesh, but a continuous victory given by the Spirit as He mortifies the deeds of the body. As health expels disease, and light swallows up darkness, and life conquers death, the indwelling of Christ through the Spirit is the health and light and life of the soul. But with this, the conviction of helplessness and danger ever tempers the faith in the momentary and unbroken action of the Holy Spirit into that chastened sense of dependence which makes the highest faith and joy the handmaids of a humility that only lives by the grace of God.

The three passages above quoted all show that it was the wonderful grace bestowed upon Paul, and of which he felt the need every moment, that humbled him so deeply. The grace of God that was with him, and enabled him to labor more abundantly than they all; the grace to preach to the heathen the unsearchable riches of Christ; the grace that was exceeding abundant with faith and love which is in Christ Jesus, —it was this grace of which it is the very nature and glory that it is for sinners, that kept the consciousness of his having once sinned, and being liable to sin, so intensely alive. 'Where sin abounded, grace did abound more exceedingly.' This reveals how the very essence of grace is to deal with and take away sin, and how it must ever be the more abundant the experience of grace, the more intense the consciousness of being a sinner. It is not sin, but God's grace showing a man and ever reminding him what a sinner he was, that, will keep him truly humble. It is not sin, but grace, that will make me indeed know myself a sinner, and make the sinner's place of deepest self-abasement the place I never leave.

I fear that there are not a few who, by strong expressions of self-condemnation and self-denunciation, have sought to humble themselves, and have to confess with sorrow that a humble spirit, a 'heart of humility,' with its accompaniments of kindness and compassion, of meekness and forbearance, is still as far off as ever. Being occupied with self, even amid the deepest self-abhorrence, can never free us from self. It is the revelation of God, not only by the law condemning sin but by His grace delivering from it, that will make us humble. The law may break the heart with fear; it is only grace that works that sweet humility which becomes a joy to the soul as its second nature. It was the revelation of God in His holiness, drawing nigh to make Himself known in His grace, that made Abraham and Jacob, Job and Isaiah, bow so low. It is the soul in which God the Creator, as the All of the creature in its nothingness, God the Redeemer in His grace, as the All of the sinner in his sinfulness, is waited for and trusted and worshipped, that will find itself so filled with His presence, that there will be no place for self. So alone can the promise be fulfilled: 'The haughtiness of man shall be brought low, and the Lord alone be exalted in that day.'

It is the sinner dwelling in the full light of God's holy, redeeming love, in the experience of that full indwelling of divine love, which comes through Christ and the Holy Spirit, who cannot but be humble. Not to be occupied with thy sin, but to be occupied with God, brings deliverance from self.

Humility and Faith

'How can ye believe, which receive glory from one another, and the glory that cometh from the only God ye seek not?' JOHN v. 44.

In an address I lately heard, the speaker said that the blessings of the higher Christian life were often like the objects exposed in a shop window, —one could see them clearly and yet could not reach them. If told to stretch out his hand and take, a man would answer, I cannot; there is a thick pane of plate-glass between me and them. And even so Christians may see clearly the blessed promises of perfect peace and rest, of overflowing love and joy, of abiding communion and fruitfulness, and yet feel that there was something between hindering the true possession. And what might that be? *Nothing but pride.* The promises made to faith are so free and sure; the invitations and encouragements so strong; the mighty power of God on which it may count is so near and free, —that it can only be something that hinders faith that hinders the blessing being ours. In our text Jesus discovers to us that it is indeed pride that makes faith impossible. 'How can ye believe, which receive glory from one another?' As we see how in their very nature pride and faith are irreconcilably at variance, we shall learn that faith and humility are at root one, and that we never can have more of true faith than we have of true humility; we shall see that we may indeed have strong intellectual conviction and assurance of the truth while pride is kept in the heart, but that it makes the living faith, which has power with God, an impossibility.

We need only think for a moment what faith is. Is it not the confession of nothingness and helplessness, the surrender and the waiting to let God work? Is it not in itself the most humbling thing there can be, —the acceptance of our place as dependents, who can claim or get or do nothing but what grace bestows? Humility is 'simply the disposition which prepares the soul for living on trust. And every, even the most secret breathing of pride, in self-seeking, self-will, self-confidence, or self-exaltation, is just the strengthening of that self which cannot enter the kingdom, or possess the things of the kingdom, because it refuses to allow God to be what He is and must be there—the All in All.

Faith is the organ or sense for the perception and apprehension of the heavenly world and its blessings. Faith seeks the glory that comes from God, that only comes where God is All. As long as we take glory from one another, as long as ever we seek and love and jealously guard the glory of this life, the honor and reputation that comes from men, we do not seek, and cannot receive the glory that comes from God. Pride renders faith impossible. Salvation comes through a cross and a crucified Christ. Salvation is the fellowship with the crucified Christ in the Spirit of His cross. Salvation is union with and delight in, salvation is participation in, the humility of Jesus. Is it wonder that our faith is so feeble when pride still reigns so much, and we have scarce learnt even to long or pray for humility as the most needful and blessed part of salvation?

Humility and faith are more nearly allied in Scripture than many know. See it in the life of Christ. There are two cases in which He spoke of a great faith. Had not the centurion, at whose faith He marveled, saying, 'I have not found so great faith, no, not in Israel!' spoken, *'I am not worthy* that Thou shouldst come under my roof'? And had not the mother to whom He spoke, 'O woman, great is thy faith!' accepted the name of dog, and said, *'Yea, Lord, yet the dogs eat of the crumbs'*? It is the humility that brings a soul to be nothing before God, that also removes every hindrance to faith, and makes it only fear lest it should dishonor Him by not trusting Him wholly.

Brother, have we not here the cause of failure in the pursuit of holiness? Is it not this, though we knew it not, that made our consecration and our faith so superficial and so short-lived? We had no idea to what an extent pride and self were still secretly working within us, and how alone God by His incoming and His mighty power could cast them out. We understood not how nothing but the new and divine nature, taking entirely the place of the old self, could make us really humble. We knew not that absolute, unceasing, universal humility must be the root-disposition of every prayer and every approach to God as well as of every dealing with man; and that we might as well attempt to see without eyes, or live without breath, as believe or draw nigh to God or dwell in His love, without an all-pervading humility and lowliness of heart.

Brother, have we not been making a mistake in taking so much trouble to believe, while all the time there was the old self in its pride seeking to possess itself of God's blessing and riches? No wonder we could not believe. Let us change our course. Let us seek first of all to humble ourselves under the mighty hand of God: *He will exalt us.* The cross, and the death, and the grave, into which Jesus humbled Himself, were His path to the glory of God. And they are our path. Let our one desire and our fervent prayer be, to be humbled with Him and like Him; let us accept gladly whatever can humble us before God or men; —this alone is the path to the glory of God.

You perhaps feel inclined to ask a question. I have spoken of some who have blessed experiences, or are the means of bringing blessing to others, and yet are lacking in humility. You ask whether these do not prove that they have true, even strong faith, though they show too clearly that they still seek too much the honor that cometh from men. There is more than one answer can be given. But the principal answer in our present connection is this: They indeed have a measure of faith, in proportion to which, with the special gifts bestowed upon them, is the blessing they bring to others. But in that very blessing the work of their faith is hindered, through the lack of humility. The blessing is often superficial or transitory, just because they are not the nothing that opens the way for God to be all. A deeper humility would without doubt bring a deeper and fuller blessing. The Holy Spirit not only working in them as a Spirit of power, but dwelling in them in the fullness of His grace, and specially that of humility, would through them communicate Himself to these converts for a life of power and holiness and steadfastness now all too little seen.

'How can ye believe, which receive glory from one another?' Brother! nothing can cure you of the desire of receiving glory from men, or of the sensitiveness and pain and anger which come when it is not given, but giving yourself to seek only the glory that comes from God. Let the glory of the All-glorious God be everything to you. You will be freed from the glory of men and of self, and be content and glad to be nothing. Out of this nothingness you will grow strong in faith, giving glory to God, and you will find that the deeper you sink in humility before Him, the nearer He is to fulfil the every desire of your faith.

Humility and Death to Self

'He humbled Himself and became obedient unto death.' —PHIL. ii. 8.

HUMILITY is the path to death, because in death it gives the highest proof of its perfection. Humility is the blossom of which death to self is the perfect fruit. Jesus humbled Himself unto death, and opened the path in which we too must walk. As there was no way for Him to prove His surrender to God to the very uttermost, or to give up and rise out of our human nature to the glory of the Father but through death, so with us too. Humility must lead us to die to self: so we prove how wholly we have given ourselves up to it and to God; so alone we are freed from fallen nature, and find the path that leads to life in God, to that full birth of the new nature, of which humility is the breath and the joy.

We have spoken of what Jesus did for His disciples when He communicated His resurrection life to them, when in the descent of the Holy Spirit He, the glorified and enthroned Meekness, actually came from heaven Himself to dwell in them. He won the power to do this through death: in its inmost nature the life He imparted was a life out of death, a life that had been surrendered to death, and been won through death. He who came to dwell in them was Himself One who had been dead and now lives for evermore. His life, His person, His presence, bears the marks of death, of being a life begotten out of death. That life in His disciples ever bears the death-marks too; it is only as the Spirit of the death, of the dying One, dwells and works in the soul, that the power of His life can be known. The first and chief of the marks of the dying of the Lord Jesus, of the death-marks that show the true follower of Jesus, is humility. For these two reasons: Only humility leads to perfect death; Only death perfects humility. Humility and death are in their very nature one: humility is the bud; in death the fruit is ripened to perfection.

Humility leads to perfect death. —Humility means the giving up of self and the taking of the place of perfect nothingness before God. Jesus humbled Himself, and became obedient unto death. In death He gave the highest, the perfect proof of having given up His will to the will of God. In death He gave up His self, with its natural reluctance to drink the cup; He gave up the life He had in union with our human nature; He died to self, and the sin that tempted Him; so, as man, He entered into the perfect life of God. If it had not been for His boundless humility, counting Himself as nothing except as a servant to do and suffer the will of God, He never would have died.

This gives us the answer to the question so often asked, and of which the meaning is so seldom clearly apprehended: How can I die to self? The death to self is not your work, it is God's work. In Christ *you are dead* to sin the life there is in you has gone through the process of death and resurrection; you may be sure you are indeed dead to sin. But the full manifestation of the power of this death in your disposition and conduct, depends upon the measure in which the Holy Spirit imparts the power of the death of Christ And here it is that the teaching is needed: if you would enter into full fellowship with Christ in His death, and know the full deliverance from self, humble yourself. This is your one duty. Place yourself before God in your utter helplessness; consent heartily to the fact of your impotence to slay or make alive yourself; sink down into your own nothingness, in the spirit of meek and patient and trustful surrender to God. Accept every humiliation, look upon every fellow-man who tries or vexes you, as a means of grace to humble you. Use every opportunity of humbling yourself before your fellow-men as a help to abide humble before God. God will accept such humbling of yourself as the proof that your whole heart desires it, as the very best prayer for it, as your preparation for His mighty work of grace, when, by the mighty strengthening of His Holy Spirit, He reveals Christ fully in you, so that He, in His form of a servant, is truly formed in you, and dwells in your heart. It is the path of humility which leads to perfect death, the full and perfect experience that we are dead in Christ.

Then follows: *Only this death leads to perfect humility.* Oh, beware of the mistake so many make, who would fain be humble, but are afraid to be too humble. They have so many qualifications and limitations, so many reasonings and questionings, as to what true humility is to be and to do, that they never unreservedly yield themselves to it. Beware of this. Humble yourself unto the death. It is in the death to self that humility is perfected. Be sure that at the root of all real experience of more grace, of all true advance in consecration, of all actually increasing conformity to the likeness of Jesus, there must be a deadness to self that proves itself to God and men in our dispositions and habits. It is sadly possible to speak of the death-life and the Spirit-walk, while even the tenderest love cannot but see how much there is of self. The death to self has no surer death-mark than a humility which makes itself of no reputation, which empties out itself, and takes the form of a servant. It is possible to speak much and honestly of fellowship with a despised and rejected Jesus, and of bearing His cross, while the meek and lowly, the kind and gentle humility of the Lamb of God is not seen, is scarcely sought. The Lamb of God means to two things—meekness and death. Let us seek to receive Him in both forms. In Him they are inseparable: they must be in us too.

What a hopeless task if we had to do the work! Nature never can overcome nature, not even with the help of grace. Self can never cast out self, even in the regenerate man. Praise God! the work has been done, and finished and perfected for ever. The death of Jesus, once and forever, is our death to self. And the ascension of Jesus, His entering once and for ever into the Holiest, has given us the Holy Spirit to communicate to us in power, and make our very own, the power of the death-life. As the soul, in the pursuit and practice of humility, follows in the steps of Jesus, its consciousness of the need of something more is awakened, its desire and hope is quickened, its faith is strengthened, and it learns to look up and claim and receive that true fullness of the Spirit of Jesus, which can daily maintain His death to self and sin in its full power, and make humility the all pervading spirit of our life.[5]

---

[5] 'To die to self, or come from under its power, is not, cannot be done, by any active resistance we can make to it by the powers of nature. The one true way of dying to self is the way of patience, meekness, humility, and resignation to God. This is the truth and perfection of dying to self.... For if I ask you what the Lamb of God means, must you not tell me that it is and means the perfection of patience, meekness, humility, and resignation to God? Must you not therefore say that a desire and faith of these virtues is an application to Christ, is a giving up yourself to Him and the perfection of faith in Him? And then, because this inclination of your heart to sink down in patience, meekness, humility, and resignation to God, is truly giving up all that you are and all that you have from fallen Adam, it is perfectly leaving all you have to follow Christ; it is your highest act of faith in Him. Christ is nowhere but in these virtues; when they are there, He is in His own kingdom. Let this be the Christ you follow.

'The Spirit of divine love can have no birth in any fallen creature, till it wills and chooses to be dead to

'Are ye ignorant that all we who were baptized into Jesus Christ were *baptized into His death?* Reckon yourselves to be *dead unto sin,* but alive unto God in Christ Jesus. Present yourself unto God, as *alive from the dead.'* The whole self consciousness of the Christian is to be imbued and characterized by the spirit that animated the death of Christ. He has ever to present himself to God as one who has died in Christ, and in Christ is alive from the dead, bearing about in his body the dying of the Lord Jesus. His life ever bears the two-fold mark: its roots striking in true humility deep into the grave of Jesus, the death to sin and self; its head lifted up in resurrection power to the heaven where Jesus is.

Believer, claim in faith the death and the life of Jesus as thine. Enter in His grave into the rest from self and its work—the rest of God. With Christ, who committed His spirit into the Father's hands, humble thyself and descend each day into that perfect, helpless dependence upon God. God will raise thee up and exalt thee. Sink every morning in deep, deep nothingness into the grave of Jesus; every day the life of Jesus will be manifest in thee, Let a willing, loving, restful, happy humility be the mark that thou hast indeed claimed thy birthright—the baptism into the death of Christ. 'By one offering He has perfected for ever them that are sanctified.' The souls that enter into *His* humiliation will find *in Him* the power to see and count self dead, and, as those who have learned and received of Him, to walk with all lowliness and meekness, forbearing one another in love. The death-life is seen in a meekness and lowliness like that of Christ.

Humility and Happiness

'Most gladly therefore will I rather glory in my weaknesses, that the strength of Christ may rest upon me. Wherefore I take pleasure in weakness: for when I am weak then am I strong.' —2 COR. xii. 9. 10.

LEST Paul should exalt himself, by reason of the exceeding greatness of the revelations, a thorn in the flesh was sent him to keep him humble. Paul's first desire was to have it removed, and he besought the Lord thrice that it might depart. The answer came that the trial was a blessing; that, in the weakness and humiliation it brought, the grace and

---

all self, in a patient, humble resignation to the power and mercy of God.

'I seek for all my salvation through the merits and mediation of the meek, humble, patient, suffering Lamb of God, who alone hath power to bring forth the blessed birth of these heavenly virtues in my soul. There is no possibility of salvation but in and by the birth of the meek, humble, patient, resigned Lamb of God in our souls. When the Lamb of God hath brought forth a real birth of His own meekness, humility, and full resignation to God in our souls, then it is the birthday of the Spirit of love in our souls, which, whenever we attain, will feast our souls with such peace and joy in God as will blot out the remembrance of everything that we called peace or joy before.

'This way to God is infallible. This infallibility is grounded in the twofold character of our Savior: 1. As He is the Lamb of God, a principle of all meekness and humility in the soul; 2. As He is the Light of heaven, and blesses eternal nature, and turns it into a kingdom of heaven, —when we are willing to get rest to our souls in meek, humble resignation to God, then it is that He, as the Light of God and heaven, joyfully breaks in upon us, turns our darkness into light, and begins that kingdom of God and of love within us, which will never have an end.' —See Wholly For God, pp 84-102. (The whole passage deserves careful study, showing most remarkably how the continual sinking down in humility before God is, from man's side, the only way to die to self. The whole dialogue has been published separately under the title Dying to Self: A Golden Dialogue. By William Law. With Notes by A.M., Nisbet & Co. Everyone who would study and practice humility will find in this golden dialogue what it is that hinders our humility, how we are to be delivered from it, and what the blessing of the Spirit of Love is that comes to the humble from Christ, the meek and lowly Lamb of God.

strength of the Lord could be the better manifested. Paul at once entered upon a new stage in his relation to the trial: instead of simply enduring it, *he most gladly gloried* in it; instead of asking for deliverance, *he took pleasure* in it. He had learned that the place of humiliation is the place of blessing, of power, of joy.

Every Christian virtually passes through these two stages in his pursuit of humility. In the first he fears and flees and seeks deliverance from all that can humble him. He has not yet learnt to seek humility at any cost. He has accepted the command to be humble, and seeks to obey it, though only to find how utterly he fails. He prays for humility, at times very earnestly; but in his secret heart he prays more, if not in word, then in wish, to be kept from the very things that will make him humble. He is not yet so in love with humility as the beauty of the Lamb of God, and the joy of heaven, that he would sell all to procure it. In his pursuit of it, and his prayer for it, there is still somewhat of a sense of burden and of bondage; to humble himself has not yet become the spontaneous expression of a life and a nature that is essentially humble. It has not yet become his joy and only pleasure. He cannot yet say, 'Most gladly do I glory in weakness, I take pleasure in whatever humbles me.'

But can we hope to reach the stage in which this will be the case? Undoubtedly. And what will it be that brings us there? *That* which brought Paul there—*a new revelation of the Lord Jesus.* Nothing but the presence of God can reveal and expel self. A clearer insight was to be given to Paul into the deep truth that the presence of Jesus will banish every desire to seek anything in ourselves, and will make us delight in every humiliation that prepares us for His fuller manifestation. Our humiliations lead us, in the experience of the presence and power of Jesus, to choose humility as our highest blessing. Let us try to learn the lessons the story of Paul teaches us.

We may have advanced believers, eminent teachers, men of heavenly experiences, who have not yet fully learnt the lesson of perfect humility, gladly glorying in weakness. We see this in Paul. The danger of exalting himself was coming very near. He knew not yet perfectly what it was to be nothing; to die, that Christ alone might live in him; to take pleasure in all that brought him low. It appears as if this were the highest lesson that he had to learn, full conformity to his Lord in that self-emptying where he gloried in weakness that God might be all.

The highest lesson a believer has to learn is humility. Oh that every Christian who seek to advance in holiness may remember this well! There may be intense consecration, and fervent zeal and heavenly experience, and yet, if it is not prevented by very special dealings of the Lord, there may be an unconscious self-exaltation with it all. Let us learn the lesson, —the highest holiness is the deepest humility; and let us remember that comes not of itself, but only as it is made matter of special dealing on the part of our faithful Lord and His faithful servant.

Let us look at our lives in the light of this experience, and see whether we gladly glory in weakness, whether we take pleasure, as Paul did, in injuries, in necessities, in distresses. Yes, let us ask whether we have learnt to regard a reproof, just or unjust, a reproach from friend or enemy, an injury, or trouble, or difficulty into which others bring us, as above all an opportunity of proving Jesus is all to us, how our own pleasure or honor are nothing, and how humiliation is in very truth what we take pleasure in. It is indeed blessed, the deep happiness of heaven, to be so free from self that whatever is said of us or done to us is lost and swallowed up, in the thought that Jesus is all.

Let us trust Him who took charge of Paul to take charge of us too. Paul needed special discipline, and with it special instruction, to learn, what was more precious than even the unutterable things he had heard in heaven—what it is to glory in weakness and lowliness. We need it, too, oh so much. He who cared for him will care for us too. He watches over us with a jealous, loving care, 'lest we exalt ourselves'. When we are doing so, He seeks to discover to us the evil, and deliver us from it. In trial and weakness and trouble He seeks to bring us low, until we so learn that His grace is all, as to take pleasure in the very thing that brings us and keeps us low. His strength made perfect in our weakness, His presence filling and satisfying our emptiness, becomes the secret of a humility that need never fail. It can, as Paul, in full sight of what God works in us, and through us, ever say, 'In nothing was I behind the chiefest apostles, *though I am nothing.'* His humiliations had led him to true humility, with its wonderful gladness and glorying and pleasure in all that humbles.

'Most gladly will I glory in my weaknesses, that the power of Christ may rest upon me; wherefore I take pleasure in weaknesses. 'The humble man has learnt the secret of abiding gladness. The weaker he feels, the lower he sinks; the greater his humiliations appear, the more the power and the presence of Christ are his portion, until, as he says, 'I am nothing,' the word of his Lord brings ever deeper joy: 'My grace is sufficient for thee.'

I feel as if I must once again gather up all in the two lessons: the danger of pride is greater and nearer than we think, and the grace for humility too.

The danger of pride is greater and nearer than we think, and that especially at the time of our highest experiences. The preacher of spiritual truth with an admiring congregation hanging on his lips, the gifted speaker on a Holiness platform expounding the secrets of the heavenly life, the Christian giving testimony to a blessed experience, the evangelist moving on as in triumph, and made a blessing to rejoicing multitudes, —no man knows the hidden, the unconscious danger to which these are exposed. Paul was in danger without knowing it; what Jesus did for him is written for our admonition, that we may know our danger and know our only safety. If ever it has been said of a teacher or professor of holiness, —he is so full of self; or, he does not practice what he preaches; or, his blessing has not made him humbler or gentler, —let it be said no more. Jesus, in whom we trust, can make us humble.

Yes, the grace for humility is greater and nearer, too, than we think. The humility of Jesus is our salvation: Jesus Himself is our humility. Our humility is His care and His work. His grace is sufficient for us, to meet the temptation of pride too. His strength will be perfected in our weakness. Let us choose to be weak, to be low, to be nothing. Let humility be to us joy and gladness. Let us gladly glory and take pleasure in weakness, in all that can humble us and keep us low; the power of Christ will rest upon us. Christ humbled Himself, therefore God exalted Him. Christ will humble us, and keep us humble; let us heartily consent, let us trustfully and joyfully accept all that humbles; the power of Christ will rest upon us. We shall find that the deepest humility is the secret of the truest happiness, of a joy that nothing can destroy.

Humility and Exaltation

'He that humbleth himself shall be exalted.' —LUKE xiv. 11, xviii. 13.

'God giveth grace to the humble. Humble yourself in the sight of the Lord, and He shall exalt you.' —JAS. iv. 10.

'Humble yourselves therefore under the mighty hand of God, that He may exalt you in due time.' —1 PET. v. 6.

JUST yesterday I was asked the question, How am I to conquer this pride? The answer; was simple. Two things are needed. Do what; God says is your work: humble yourself. Trust Him to do what He says is His work: He will exalt you.

The command is clear: humble yourself. That does not mean that it is your work to conquer and cast out the pride of your nature, and to form within yourself the lowliness of the holy Jesus. No, this is God's work; the very essence of that exaltation, wherein He lifts you up into the real likeness of the beloved Son. What the command does mean is this: take every opportunity of humbling yourself before God and man. In the faith of the grace that is already working in you; in the assurance of the more grace for victory that is coming; up to the light that conscience each time flashes upon the pride of the heart and its workings; notwithstanding all there may be of failure and falling, stand persistently as under the unchanging command: humble yourself. Accept with gratitude everything that God allows from within or without, from friend or enemy, in nature or in grace, to remind you of your need of humbling, and to help you to it. Reckon humility to be indeed the mother-virtue, your very first duty before God, the one perpetual safeguard of the soul, and set your heart upon it as the source of all blessing. The promise is divine and sure: He that humbleth himself shall be exalted. See that you do the one thing God asks: humble yourself. God will see that does the one thing He has promised. He will give more grace; He will exalt you in due time.

All God's dealings with man are characterized by two stages. There is the time of preparation, when command and promise, with the mingled experience of effort and impotence, of failure and partial success, with the holy expectancy of something better which these waken, train and discipline men for a higher stage. Then comes the time of fulfilment, when faith inherits the promise, and enjoys what it had so often struggled for in vain. This law holds good in every part of the Christian life, and in the pursuit of every separate virtue. And that because it is grounded in the very nature of things. In all that concerns our redemption, God must needs take the initiative. When that has been done, man's turn comes. In the effort after obedience and attainment, he must learn to know his impotence, in self-despair to die to himself, and so be fitted voluntarily and intelligently to receive from God the end, the completion of that of which he had accepted the beginning in ignorance. So, God who had been the Beginning, ere man rightly knew Him, or fully understood what His purpose was, is longed for and welcomed as the End, as the All in All.

It is even thus, too, in the pursuit of humility. To every Christian the command comes from the throne of God Himself: humble yourself. The earnest attempt to listen and obey will be rewarded—yes, rewarded—with the painful discovery of two things. The one, what depth of pride, that is of unwillingness to count oneself and to be counted nothing, to submit absolutely to God, there was, that one never knew. The other, what utter impotence there is in all our efforts, and in all our prayers too for God's help, to destroy the hideous monster. Blessed the man who now learns to put his hope in God, and to persevere, notwithstanding all the power of pride within him, in acts of humiliation before God and Men. We know the law of human nature: acts produce habits, habits breed dispositions, dispositions form the will, and the rightly-formed will is character. It is no otherwise in the work of grace. As acts, persistently repeated, beget habits and dispositions, and these strengthened the will, He who works both to will and to do comes with His mighty power and Spirit; and the humbling of the proud heart with which the' penitent saint cast himself so often before God, is rewarded with the 'more grace' of the humble heart, in which the Spirit of Jesus has conquered, and brought the new nature to its maturity, and He the meek and lowly One now dwells for ever.

Humble yourselves in the sight of the Lord, and He will exalt you. And wherein does the exaltation consist? The highest glory of the creature is in being only a vessel, to receive and enjoy and show forth the glory of God. It can do this only as it is willing to be nothing in itself, that God may be all. Water always fills first the lowest places. The lower, the emptier a man lies before God, the speedier and the fuller will be the inflow of the divine glory. The exaltation God promises is not, cannot be, any external thing apart from Himself: all that He has to give or can give is only more of Himself, Himself to take more complete possession. The exaltation is not, like an earthly prize, something arbitrary, in no necessary connection with the conduct to be rewarded. No, but it is in its very nature the effect and result of the humbling of ourselves. It is nothing but the gift of such a divine indwelling humility, such a conformity to and possession of the humility of the Lamb of God, as fits us for receiving fully the indwelling of God.

He that humbleth himself shall be exalted. Of the truth of these words Jesus Himself is the proof; of the certainty of their fulfilment to us He is the pledge. Let us take His yoke upon us and learn of Him, for He is meek and lowly of heart. If we are but willing to stoop to Him, as He has stooped to us, He will yet stoop to each one of us again, and we shall find ourselves not unequally yoked with Him. As we enter deeper into the fellowship of His humiliation, and either humble ourselves or bear the humbling of men, we can count upon it that the Spirit of His exaltation, 'the Spirit of God and of glory,' will rest upon us. The presence and the power of the glorified Christ will come to them that are of an humble spirit. When God can again have His rightful place in us, He will lift us up. Make His glory thy care in humbling thyself; He will make thy glory His care in perfecting thy humility, and breathing into thee, as thy abiding life, the very Spirit of His Son. As the all-pervading life of God possesses thee, there will be nothing so natural, and nothing so sweet, as to be nothing, with not a thought or wish for self, because all is occupied with Him who filleth all. 'Most gladly will I glory in my weakness, that the strength of Christ may rest upon me.'

Brother, have we not here the reason that our consecration and our faith have availed so little in the pursuit of holiness? It was by self and its strength that the work was done under the name of faith; it was for self and its happiness that God was called in; it was, unconsciously, but still truly, in self and its holiness that the soul rejoiced. We never knew that humility, absolute, abiding, Christlike humility and self-effacement, pervading and marking our whole life with God and man, was the most essential element of the life of the holiness we sought for.

It is only in the possession of God that I lose myself. As it is in the height and breadth and glory of the sunshine that the littleness of the mote playing in its beams is seen, even so humility is the taking our place in God's presence to be nothing but a mote dwelling in the sunlight of His love.

> 'How great is God! how small am I!
> Lost, swallowed up in Love's immensity!
> God only there, not I.'

May God teach us to believe that to be humble, to be nothing in His presence, is the highest attainment, and the fullest blessing of the Christian life. He speaks to us: 'I dwell in the high and holy place, and with him the is of a contrite and humble spirit.' Be this our portion!

> '*Oh, to be emptier, lowlier,*
> *Mean, unnoticed, and unknown,*
> *And to God a vessel holier,*
> *Filled with Christ, and Christ alone!*'

Endnote

A Secret of Secrets: Humility the Soul of True Prayer. —Till the spirit of the heart be renewed, till it is emptied of all earthly desires, and stands in an habitual hunger and thirst after God, which is the true spirit of prayer; till then, all our prayer will be, more or less, but too much like lessons given to scholars; and we shall mostly say them, only because we dare not neglect them. But be not discouraged; take the following advice, and then you may go to church without any danger of mere lip-labor or hypocrisy, although there should be a hymn or a prayer, whose language is higher than that of your heart. Do this: go to the church as the publican went to the temple; stand inwardly in the spirit of your mind in that form which he outwardly expressed, when he cast down his eyes, and could only say, 'God be merciful to me, a sinner.' Stand unchangeably, at least in your desire, in this form or state of heart; it will sanctify every petition that comes out of your mouth; and when anything is read or sung or prayed, that is more exalted than your heart is, if you make this an occasion of further sinking down in the spirit of the publican, you will then be helped, and highly blessed, by those prayers and praises which seem only to belong to a heart better than yours.

This, my friend, is a secret of secrets; it will help you to reap where you have not sown, and be a continual source of grace in your soul; for everything that inwardly stirs in you, or outwardly happens to you, becomes a real good to you, if it finds or excites in you this humble state of mind. For nothing is in vain, or without profit to the humble soul; it stands always in a state of divine growth; everything that falls upon it is like a dew of heaven to it. Shut up yourself, therefore, in this form of Humility; all good is enclosed in it; it is a water of heaven, that turns the fire of the fallen soul into the meekness of the divine life, and creates that oil, out of which the love to God and man gets its flame. Be enclosed, therefore, always in it; let it be as a garment wherewith you are always covered, and a girdle with which you are girt; breathe nothing but in and from its spirit; see nothing but with its eyes; hear nothing but with its ears. And then, whether you are in the church or out of the church, hearing the praises of God or receiving wrongs from men and the world, all will be edification, and everything will help forward your growth in the life of God. —*The Spirit of Prayer,* Pt. II. p. 121.

A Prayer for Humility

I will here give you an infallible touchstone, that will try all to the truth. It is this: retire from the world and all conversation, only for one month; neither write, nor read, nor debate anything with yourself; stop all the former workings of your heart and mind: and, with all the strength of your heart, stand all this month, as continually as you can, in the following form of prayer to God. Offer it frequently on your knees; but whether sitting, walking, or standing, be always inwardly longing, and earnestly praying this one prayer to God: 'That of His great goodness He would make known to you, and take from your heart, *every kind and form and degree of Pride,* whether it be from evil spirits, or your own corrupt nature; and that He would awaken in you the *deepest depth and truth of that Humility,* which can make you capable of His light and Holy Spirit.' Reject every thought, but that of waiting and praying in this matter from the bottom of your heart, with such truth and earnestness, as people in torment wish to pray and be delivered from it…. If you can and will give yourself up in truth and sincerity to this spirit of prayer, I will venture to affirm that, if you had twice as many evil spirits in you as Mary Magdalene had, they will all be cast out of you, and you will be forced with her to weep tears of love at the feet of the holy Jesus. —*The Spirit of Prayer,* Pt. II. p. 124.

Calvin's Book on the
Christian Life

~ ※ ~

By *John Calvin*

Translated by Henry Beveridge

From the 1845 Edition

~ ※ ~

About This Edition

John Calvin (10 July 1509 – 27 May 1564) was an early theologian on Christian living and worship. His main work, "Institutes of the Christian Religion", runs over 1,000 pages in a modern printed format and describes his view of biblical teaching as he felt it to be practiced.

This book is a portion of his main work, specifically Book 3, chapters 6 through 10 (renumbered in this edition as I through V). People have read and reread just this section since it applies specifically to personal life and action.

Introduction

This and the four following chapters treat of the Life of the Christian, and are so arranged as to admit of being classed under two principal heads.

First, it must be held to be an universally acknowledged point, that no man is a Christian who does not feel some special love for righteousness, Chapter I.

Secondly, in regard to the standard by which every man ought to regulate his life, although it seems to be considered in Chapter II only, yet the three following chapters also refer to it. For it shows that the Christian has two duties to perform. First, the observance being so arduous, he needs the greatest patience. Hence Chapter III treats professedly of the utility of the cross, and Chapter IV invites to meditation on the future life.

Lastly, Chapter V clearly shows, as in no small degree conducive to this end, how we are to use this life and its comforts without abusing them.

CHAPTER I.

LIFE OF A CHRISTIAN MAN. SCRIPTURAL ARGUMENTS EXHORTING TO IT.

This first chapter consists of two parts,—I. Connection between this treatise on the Christian Life and the doctrine of Regeneration and Repentance. Arrangement of the treatise, sec. 1–3. II. Extremes to be avoided; 1. False Christians denying Christ by their works condemned, sec. 4. 2. Christians should not despair, though they have not attained perfection, provided they make daily progress in piety and righteousness.

1. WE have said that the object of regeneration is to bring the life of believers into concord and harmony with the righteousness of God, and so confirm the adoption by which they have been received as sons. But although the law comprehends within it that new life by which the image of God is restored in us, yet, as our sluggishness stands greatly in need both of helps and incentives it will be useful to collect out of Scripture a true account of this reformations lest any who have a heartfelt desire of repentance should in their zeal go astray. Moreover, I am not unaware that, in undertaking to describe the life of the Christian, I am entering on a large and extensive subject, one which, when fully considered in all its parts, is sufficient to fill a large volume. We see the length to which the Fathers in treating of individual virtues extend their exhortations. This they do, not from mere loquaciousness; for whatever be the virtue which you undertake to recommend,

your pen is spontaneously led by the copiousness of the matter so to amplify, that you seem not to have discussed it properly if you have not done it at length. My intention, however, in the plan of life which I now propose to give, is not to extend it so far as to treat of each virtue specially, and expatiate in exhortation. This must be sought in the writings of others, and particularly in the Homilies of the Fathers.[1] For me it will be sufficient to point out the method by which a pious man may be taught how to frame his life aright, and briefly lay down some universal rule by which he may not improperly regulate his conduct. I shall one day possibly find time for more ample discourse, (or leave others to perform an office for which I am not so fit. I have a natural love of brevity, and, perhaps, any attempt of mine at copiousness would not succeed. Even if I could gain the highest applause by being more prolix, I would scarcely be disposed to attempt it,[2]) while the nature of my present work requires me to glance at simple doctrine with as much brevity as possible. As philosophers have certain definitions of rectitude and honesty, from which they derive particular duties and the whole train of virtues; so in this respect Scripture is not without order, but presents a most beautiful arrangement, one too which is every way much more certain than that of philosophers. The only difference is, that they, under the influence of ambition, constantly affect an exquisite perspicuity of arrangement, which may serve to display their genius, whereas the Spirit of God, teaching without affectation, is not so perpetually observant of exact method, and yet by observing it at times sufficiently intimates that it is not to be neglected.

2. The Scripture system of which we speak aims chiefly at two objects. The former is, that the love of righteousness, to which we are by no means naturally inclined, may be instilled and implanted into our minds. The latter is, (see chap. ii.) to prescribe a rule which will prevent us while in the pursuit of righteousness from going astray. It has numerous admirable methods of recommending righteousness.[3] Many have been already pointed out in different parts of this work; but we shall here also briefly advert to some of them. With what better foundation can it begin than by reminding us that we must be holy, because "God is holy?" (Lev. xix. 1; 1 Pet. i. 16.) For when we were scattered abroad like lost sheep, wandering through the labyrinth of this world, he brought us back again to his own fold. When mention is made of our union with God, let us remember that holiness must be the bond; not that by the merit of holiness we come into communion with him, (we ought rather first to cleave to him, in order that, pervaded with his holiness, we may follow whither he calls,) but because it greatly concerns his glory not to have any fellowship with wickedness and impurity. Wherefore he tells us that this is the end of our calling, the end to which we ought ever to have respect, if we would answer the call of God. For to what end were we rescued from the iniquity and pollution of the world into which we were plunged, if we allow ourselves, during our whole lives, to wallow in them? Besides, we are at the same time admonished, that if we would be regarded as the Lord's people, we must inhabit the holy city Jerusalem, (Isaiah rev. 8, *et alibi*;) which, as he hath consecrated it to himself, it were impious for its inhabitants to profane by impurity. Hence the expressions, "Who shall abide in thy tabernacle? who shall dwell in thy holy hill? He that walketh uprightly, and worketh righteousness," (Ps. xv. 1, 2; xxiv. 3, 4) for the sanctuary in which he dwells certainly ought not to be like an unclean stall.

---

[1] The French adds, "C'est a dire, sermons populaires:"—that is to say, popular sermons.

[2] The passage in brackets is omitted in the French.

[3] The French begins the sentence thus, "Quant est du premier poinct;—As to the former point.

3. The better to arouse us, it exhibits God the Father, who, as he hath reconciled us to himself in his Anointed, has impressed his image upon us, to which he would have us to be conformed, (Rom. v. 4.) Come, then, and let them show me a more excellent system among philosophers, who think that they only have a moral philosophy duly and orderly arranged. They, when they would give excellent exhortations to virtue, can only tell us to live agreeably to nature. Scripture derives its exhortations from the true source,[4] when it not only enjoins us to regulate our lives with a view to God its author to whom it belongs; but after showing us that we have degenerated from our true origin, viz., the law of our Creator, adds, that Christ, through whom we have returned to favour with God, is set before us as a model, the image of which our lives should express. What do you require more effectual than this? Nay, what do you require beyond this? If the Lord adopts us for his sons on the condition that our life be a representation of Christ, the bond of our adoption,—then, unless we dedicate and devote ourselves to righteousness, we not only, with the utmost perfidy, revolt from our Creator, but also abjure the Saviour himself. Then, from an enumeration of all the blessings of God, and each part of our salvation, it finds materials for exhortation. Ever since God exhibited himself to us as a Father, we must be convicted of extreme ingratitude if we do not in turn exhibit ourselves as his sons. Ever since Christ purified us by the laver of his blood, and communicated this purification by baptism, it would ill become us to be defiled with new pollution. Ever since he ingrafted us into his body, we, who are his members, should anxiously beware of contracting any stain or taint. Ever since he who is our head ascended to heaven, it is befitting in us to withdraw our affections from the earth, and with our whole soul aspire to heaven. Ever since the Holy Spirit dedicated us as temples to the Lord, we should make it our endeavour to show forth the glory of God, and guard against being profaned by the defilement of sin. Ever since our soul and body were destined to heavenly incorruptibility and an unfading crown, we should earnestly strive to keep them pure and uncorrupted against the day of the Lord. These, I say, are the surest foundations of a well-regulated life, and you will search in vain for any thing resembling them among philosophers, who, in their commendation of virtue, never rise higher than the natural dignity of man.

4. This is the place to address those who, having nothing of Christ but the name and sign, would yet be called Christians. How dare they boast of this sacred name? None have intercourse with Christ but those who have acquired the true knowledge of him from the Gospel. The Apostle denies that any man truly has learned Christ who has not learned to put off "the old man, which is corrupt according to the deceitful lusts, and put on Christ," (Eph. iv. 22.) They are convicted, therefore, of falsely and unjustly pretending a knowledge of Christ, whatever be the volubility and eloquence with which they can talk of the Gospel. Doctrine is not an affair of the tongue, but of the life; is not apprehended by the intellect and memory merely, like other branches of learning; but is received only when it possesses the whole soul, and finds its seat and habitation in the inmost recesses of the heart. Let them, therefore, either cease to insult God, by boasting that they are what they are not, or let them show themselves not unworthy disciples of their divine Master. To doctrine in which our religion is contained we have given the first place, since by it our salvation commences; but it must be transfused into the breast, and pass into the conduct, and so transform us into itself, as not to prove unfruitful. If philosophers are justly

---

[4] Mal. i. 6; Eph. v. 1; 1 John iii. 1, 3; Eph. v. 26; Rom. vi. 1–4; 1 Cor. vi. 11; 1 Pet. i. 15, 19; 1 Cor. vi. 15; John xv. 3; Eph. v. 2, 3; Col. iii. 1, 2; 1 Cor. iii. 16; vi. 17; 2 Cor. vi. 16; 1 Thess. v. 23.

offended, and banish from their company with disgrace those who, while professing an art which ought to be the mistress of their conduct, convert it into mere loquacious sophistry, with how much better reason shall we detest those flimsy sophists who are contented to let the Gospel play upon their lips, when, from its efficacy, it ought to penetrate the inmost affections of the heart, fix its seat in the soul, and pervade the whole man a hundred times more than the frigid discourses of philosophers?

5. I insist not that the life of the Christian shall breathe nothing but the perfect Gospel, though this is to be desired, and ought to be attempted. I insist not so strictly on evangelical perfection, as to refuse to acknowledge as a Christian any man who has not attained it. In this way all would be excluded from the Church, since there is no man who is not far removed from this perfection, while many, who have made but little progress, would be undeservedly rejected. What then? Let us set this before our eye as the end at which we ought constantly to aim. Let it be regarded as the goal towards which we are to run. For you cannot divide the matter with God, undertaking part of what his word enjoins, and omitting part at pleasure. For, in the first place, God uniformly recommends integrity as the principal part of his worship, meaning by integrity real singleness of mind, devoid of gloss and fiction, and to this is opposed a double mind; as if it had been said, that the spiritual commencement of a good life is when the internal affections are sincerely devoted to God, in the cultivation of holiness and justice. But seeing that, in this earthly prison of the body, no man is supplied with strength sufficient to hasten in his course with due alacrity, while the greater number are so oppressed with weakness, that hesitating, and halting, and even crawling on the ground, they make little progress, let every one of us go as far as his humble ability enables him, and prosecute the journey once begun. No one will travel so badly as not daily to make some degree of progress. This, therefore, let us never cease to do, that we may daily advance in the way of the Lord; and let us not despair because of the slender measure of success. How little soever the success may correspond with our wish, our labour is not lost when to-day is better than yesterday, provided with true singleness of mind we keep our aim, and aspire to the goal, not speaking flattering things to ourselves, nor indulging our vices, but making it our constant endeavour to become better, until we attain to goodness itself. If during the whole course of our life we seek and follow, we shall at length attain it, when relieved from the infirmity of flesh we are admitted to full fellowship with God.

CHAPTER II.

A SUMMARY OF THE CHRISTIAN LIFE. OF SELF-DENIAL.[5]

The divisions of the chapter are,—I. The rule which permits us not to go astray in the study of righteousness, requires two things, viz., that man, abandoning his own will, devote himself entirely to the service of God; whence it follows, that we must seek not our own things, but the things of God, sec. 1, 2. II. A description of this renovation or Christian life taken from the Epistle to Titus, and accurately explained under certain special heads, sec. 3 to end.

---

[5] On this and the three following chapters, which contain the second part of the Treatise on the Christian Life, see Augustine, De Moribus Ecclesiae Catholicae, and Calvin de Scandalis.

1. ALTHOUGH the Law of God contains a perfect rule of conduct admirably arranged, it has seemed proper to our divine Master to train his people by a more accurate method, to the rule which is enjoined in the Law; and the leading principle in the method is, that it is the duty of believers to present their "bodies a living sacrifice, holy and acceptable unto God, which is their reasonable service," (Rom. xii. 1.) Hence he draws the exhortation: "Be not conformed to this world: but be ye transformed by the renewing of your mind, that ye may prove what is that good, and acceptable, and perfect will of God." The great point, then, is, that we are consecrated and dedicated to God, and, therefore, should not henceforth think, speak, design, or act, without a view to his glory. What he hath made sacred cannot, without signal insult to him, be applied to profane use. But if we are not our own, but the Lord's, it is plain both what error is to be shunned, and to what end the actions of our lives ought to be directed. We are not our own; therefore, neither is our own reason or will to rule our acts and counsels. We are not our own; therefore, let us not make it our end to seek what may be agreeable to our carnal nature. We are not our own; therefore, as far as possible, let us forget ourselves and the things that are ours. On the other hand, we are God's; let us, therefore, live and die to him (Rom. xiv. 8.) We are God's; therefore, let his wisdom and will preside over all our actions. We are God's; to him, then, as the only legitimate end, let every part of our life be directed. O how great the proficiency of him who, taught that he is not his own, has withdrawn the dominion and government of himself from his own reason that he may give them to God! For as the surest source of destruction to men is to obey themselves, so the only haven of safety is to have no other will, no other wisdom, than to follow the Lord wherever he leads. Let this, then be the first step, to abandon ourselves, and devote the whole energy of our minds to the service of God. By service, I mean not only that which consists in verbal obedience, but that by which the mind, divested of its own carnal feelings, implicitly obeys the call of the Spirit of God. This transformation, (which Paul calls *the renewing of the mind*, Rom. xii. 2; Eph. iv. 23.) though it is the first entrance to life, was unknown to all the philosophers. They give the government of man to reason alone, thinking that she alone is to be listened to; in short, they assign to her the sole direction of the conduct. But Christian philosophy bids her give place, and yield complete submission to the Holy Spirit, so that the man himself no longer lives, but Christ lives and reigns in him, (Gal. ii. 20.)

2. Hence follows the other principle, that we are not to seek our own, but the Lord's will, and act with a view to promote his glory. Great is our proficiency, when, almost forgetting ourselves, certainly postponing our own reason, we faithfully make it our study to obey God and his commandments. For when Scripture enjoins us to lay aside private regard to ourselves, it not only divests our minds of an excessive longing for wealth, or power, or human favour, but eradicates all ambition and thirst for worldly glory, and other more secret pests. The Christian ought, indeed, to be so trained and disposed as to consider, that during his whole life he has to do with God. For this reason, as he will bring all things to the disposal and estimate of God, so he will religiously direct his whole mind to him. For he who has learned to look to God in everything he does, is at the same time diverted from all vain thoughts. This is that self-denial which Christ so strongly enforces on his disciples from the very outset, (Matth. xvi. 24,) which, as soon as it takes hold of the mind, leaves no place either, first, for pride, show, and ostentation; or, secondly, for avarice, lust, luxury, effeminacy, or other vices which are engendered by self love. On the contrary, wherever it reigns not, the foulest vices are indulged in without shame; or, if

there is some appearance of virtue, it is vitiated by a depraved longing for applause. Show me, if you can, an individual who, unless he has renounced himself in obedience to the Lord's command, is disposed to do good for its own sake. Those who have not so renounced themselves have followed virtue at least for the sake of praise. The philosophers who have contended most strongly that virtue is to be desired on her own account, were so inflated with arrogance as to make it apparent that they sought virtue for no other reason than as a ground for indulging in pride. So far, therefore, is God from being delighted with these hunters after popular applause with their swollen breasts, that he declares they have received their reward in this world, (Matth. vi. 2,) and that harlots and publicans are nearer the kingdom of heaven than they, (Matth. xxi. 31.) We have not yet sufficiently explained how great and numerous are the obstacles by which a man is impeded in the pursuit of rectitude, so long as he has not renounced himself. The old saying is true, There is a world of iniquity treasured up in the human soul. Nor can you find any other remedy for this than to deny yourself, renounce your own reason, and direct your whole mind to the pursuit of those things which the Lord requires of you, and which you are to seek only because they are pleasing to Him.

3. In another passage, Paul gives a brief, indeed, but more distinct account of each of the parts of a well-ordered life: "The grace of God that bringeth salvation hath appeared to all men, teaching us that, denying ungodliness and worldly lusts, we should live soberly, righteously, and godly, in this present world; looking for that blessed hope, and the glorious appearance of the great God and our Saviour Jesus Christ; who gave himself for us, that he might redeem us from all iniquity, and purify to himself a peculiar people, zealous of good works," (Tit. ii. 11–14.) After holding forth the grace of God to animate us, and pave the way for His true worship, he removes the two greatest obstacles which stand in the way, viz., ungodliness, to which we are by nature too prone, and worldly lusts, which are of still greater extent. Under *ungodliness,* he includes not merely superstition, but everything at variance with the true fear of God. *Worldly lusts* are equivalent to the lusts of the flesh. Thus he enjoins us, in regard to both tables of the Law, to lay aside our own mind, and renounce whatever our own reason and will dictate. Then he reduces all the actions of our lives to three branches, sobriety, righteousness, and godliness. *Sobriety* undoubtedly denotes as well chastity and temperance as the pure and frugal use of temporal goods, and patient endurance of want. *Righteousness* comprehends all the duties of equity, in every one his due. Next follows *godliness*, which separates us from the pollutions of the world, and connects us with God in true holiness. These, when connected together by an indissoluble chain, constitute complete perfection. But as nothing is more difficult than to bid adieu to the will of the flesh, subdue, nay, abjure our lusts, devote ourselves to God and our brethren, and lead an angelic life amid the pollutions of the world, Paul, to set our minds free from all entanglements, recalls us to the hope of a blessed immortality, justly urging us to contend, because as Christ has once appeared as our Redeemer, so on his final advent he will give full effect to the salvation obtained by him. And in this way he dispels all the allurements which becloud our path, and prevent us from aspiring as we ought to heavenly glory; nay, he tells us that we must be pilgrims in the world, that we may not fail of obtaining the heavenly inheritance.

4. Moreover, we see by these words that self-denial has respect partly to men and partly (more especially) to God, (sec. 8–10.) For when Scripture enjoins us, in regard to our fellow men, to prefer them in honour to ourselves, and sincerely labour to promote their advantages (Rom. xii. 10; Phil. ii. 3,) he gives us commands which our mind is utterly

incapable of obeying until its natural feelings are suppressed. For so blindly do we all rush in the direction of self-love, that every one thinks he has a good reason for exalting himself and despising all others in comparison. If God has bestowed on us something not to be repented of, trusting to it, we immediately become elated, and not only swell, but almost burst with pride. The vices with which we abound we both carefully conceal from others, and flatteringly represent to ourselves as minute and trivial, nay, sometimes hug them as virtues. When the same qualities which we admire in ourselves are seen in others, even though they should be superior, we, in order that we may not be forced to yield to them, maliciously lower and carp at them; in like manner, in the case of vices, not contented with severe and keen animadversion, we studiously exaggerate them. Hence the insolence with which each, as if exempted from the common lot, seeks to exalt himself above his neighbour, confidently and proudly despising others, or at least looking down upon them as his inferiors. The poor man yields to the rich, the plebeian to the noble, the servant to the master, the unlearned to the learned, and yet every one inwardly cherishes some idea of his own superiority. Thus each flattering himself, sets up a kind of kingdom in his breast; the arrogant, to satisfy themselves, pass censure on the minds and manners of other men, and when contention arises, the full venom is displayed. Many bear about with them some measure of mildness so long as all things go smoothly and lovingly with them, but how few are there who, when stung and irritated, preserve the same tenor of moderation? For this there is no other remedy than to pluck up by the roots those most noxious pests, self-love and love of victory. This the doctrine of Scripture does. For it teaches us to remember, that the endowments which God has bestowed upon us are not our own, but His free gifts, and that those who plume themselves upon them betray their ingratitude. "Who maketh thee to differ," saith Paul, "and what hast thou that thou didst not receive? now if thou didst receive it, why dost thou glory, as if thou hadst not received it?" (1 Cor. iv. 7.) Then by a diligent examination of our faults let us keep ourselves humble. Thus while nothing will remain to swell our pride, there will be much to subdue it. Again, we are enjoined, whenever we behold the gifts of God in others, so to reverence and respect the gifts, as also to honour those in whom they reside. God having been pleased to bestow honour upon them, it would ill become us to deprive them of it. Then we are told to overlook their faults, not, indeed, to encourage by flattering them, but not because of them to insult those whom we ought to regard with honour and good will.[6] In this way, with regard to all with whom we have intercourse, our behaviour will be not only moderate and modest, but courteous and friendly. The only way by which you can ever attain to true meekness, is to have your heart imbued with a humble opinion of yourself and respect for others.

5. How difficult it is to perform the duty of seeking the good of our neighbour! Unless you leave off all thought of yourself and in a manner cease to be yourself, you will never accomplish it. How can you exhibit those works of charity which Paul describes unless you renounce yourself, and become wholly devoted to others? "Charity (says he, 1 Cor. xiii. 4) suffereth long, and is kind; charity envieth not; charity vaunteth not itself, is not puffed up, doth not behave itself unseemly, seeketh not her own, is not easily provoked &c. Were it the only thing required of us to seek not our own, nature would not have the least power to comply: she so inclines us to love ourselves only, that she will not easily allow us carelessly to pass by ourselves and our own interests that we may watch over the

---

[6] Calvin. de Sacerdotiis Eccles. Papal. in fine.

interests of others, nay, spontaneously to yield our own rights and resign it to another. But Scripture, to conduct us to this, reminds us, that whatever we obtain from the Lord is granted on the condition of our employing it for the common good of the Church, and that, therefore, the legitimate use of all our gifts is a kind and liberal communication of them with others. There cannot be a surer rule, nor a stronger exhortation to the observance of it, than when we are taught that all the endowments which we possess are divine deposits entrusted to us for the very purpose of being distributed for the good of our neighbour. But Scripture proceeds still farther when it likens these endowments to the different members of the body, (1 Cor. xii. 12.) No member has its function for itself, or applies it for its own private use, but transfers it to its fellow-members; nor does it derive any other advantage from it than that which it receives in common with the whole body. Thus, whatever the pious man can do, he is bound to do for his brethren, not consulting his own interest in any other way than by striving earnestly for the common edification of the Church. Let this, then, be our method of showing good-will and kindness, considering that, in regard to everything which God has bestowed upon us, and by which we can aid our neighbour, we are his stewards, and are bound to give account of our stewardship; moreover, that the only right mode of administration is that which is regulated by love. In this way, we shall not only unite the study of our neighbour's advantage with a regard to our own, but make the latter subordinate to the former. And lest we should have omitted to perceive that this is the law for duly administering every gift which we receive from God, he of old applied that law to the minutest expressions of his own kindness. He commanded the first-fruits to be offered to him as an attestation by the people that it was impious to reap any advantage from goods not previously consecrated to him, (Exod. xxii. 29; xxiii. 19.) But if the gifts of God are not sanctified to us until we have with our own hand dedicated them to the Giver, it must be a gross abuse that does not give signs of such dedication. It is in vain to contend that you cannot enrich the Lord by your offerings. Though, as the Psalmist says "Thou art my Lord: my goodness extendeth not unto thee," yet you can extend it "to the saints that are in the earth," (Ps. xvi. 2, 3;) and therefore a comparison is drawn between sacred oblations and alms as now corresponding to the offerings under the Law.[7]

6. Moreover, that we may not weary in well-doing, (as would otherwise forthwith and infallibly be the case,) we must add the other quality in the Apostle's enumeration, "Charity suffereth long, and is kind, is not easily provoked," (1 Cor. xiii. 4.) The Lord enjoins us to do good to all without exception, though the greater part, if estimated by their own merit, are most unworthy of it. But Scripture subjoins a most excellent reason, when it tells us that we are not to look to what men in themselves deserve, but to attend to the image of God, which exists in all, and to which we owe all honour and love. But in those who are of the household of faith, the same rule is to be more carefully observed, inasmuch as that image is renewed and restored in them by the Spirit of Christ. Therefore, whoever be the man that is presented to you as needing your assistance, you have no ground for declining to give it to him. Say he is a stranger. The Lord has given him a mark which ought to be familiar to you: for which reason he forbids you to despise your own flesh, (Gal. vi. 10.) Say he is mean and of no consideration. The Lord points him out as one whom he has distinguished by the lustre of his own image, (Isaiah lviii. 7.) Say that you are bound to him by no ties of duty. The Lord has substituted him as it were into his own

---

[7] Heb. xiii. 16; 2 Cor. ix. 12.

place, that in him you may recognize the many great obligations under which the Lord has laid you to himself. Say that he is unworthy of your least exertion on his account; but the image of God, by which he is recommended to you, is worthy of yourself and all your exertions. But if he not only merits no good, but has provoked you by injury and mischief, still this is no good reason why you should not embrace him in love, and visit him with offices of love. He has deserved very differently from me, you will say. But what has the Lord deserved?[8] Whatever injury he has done you, when he enjoins you to forgive him, he certainly means that it should be imputed to himself. In this way only we attain to what is not to say difficult but altogether against nature,[9] to love those that hate us, render good for evil, and blessing for cursing, remembering that we are not to reflect on the wickedness of men, but look to the image of God in them, an image which, covering and obliterating their faults, should by its beauty and dignity allure us to love and embrace them.

7. We shall thus succeed in mortifying ourselves if we fulfil all the duties of charity. Those duties, however, are not fulfilled by the mere discharge of them, though none be omitted, unless it is done from a pure feeling of love. For it may happen that one may perform every one of these offices, in so far as the external act is concerned, and be far from performing them aright. For you see some who would be thought very liberal, and yet accompany every thing they give with insult, by the haughtiness of their looks, or the violence of their words. And to such a calamitous condition have we come in this unhappy age, that the greater part of men never almost give alms without contumely. Such conduct ought not to have been tolerated even among the heathen; but from Christians something more is required than to carry cheerfulness in their looks, and give attractiveness to the discharge of their duties by courteous language. First, they should put themselves in the place of him whom they see in need of their assistance, and pity his misfortune as if they felt and bore it, so that a feeling of pity and humanity should incline them to assist him just as they would themselves. He who is thus minded will go and give assistance to his brethren, and not only not taint his acts with arrogance or upbraiding but will neither look down upon the brother to whom he does a kindness, as one who needed his help, or keep him in subjection as under obligation to him, just as we do not insult a diseased member when the rest of the body labours for its recovery, nor think it under special obligation to the other members, because it has required more exertion than it has returned. A communication of offices between members is not regarded as at all gratuitous, but rather as the payment of that which being due by the law of nature it were monstrous to deny. For this reason, he who has performed one kind of duty will not think himself thereby discharged, as is usually the case when a rich man, after contributing somewhat of his substance, delegates remaining burdens to others as if he had nothing to do with them. Every one should rather consider, that however great he is, he owes himself to his neighbours, and that the only limit to his beneficence is the failure of his means. The extent of these should regulate that of his charity.

8. The principal part of self-denial, that which as we have said has reference to God, let us again consider more fully. Many things have already been said with regard to it which it were superfluous to repeat; and, therefore, it will be sufficient to view it as forming us to equanimity and endurance. First, then, in seeking the convenience or

---

[8] French, "Car si nous disons qu'il n'a merité que mal de nous; Dieu nous pourra demander quel mal il nous a fait, lui dont nous tenons tout notre bien;'—For if we say that he has deserved nothing of us but evil, God may ask us what evil he has done us, he of whom we hold our every blessing.

[9] Matth. v. 44; vi. 14; xviii. 35; Luke xvii. 3.

tranquility of the present life, Scripture calls us to resign ourselves, and all we have, to the disposal of the Lord, to give him up the affections of our heart, that he may tame and subdue them. We have a frenzied desire, an infinite eagerness, to pursue wealth and honour, intrigue for power, accumulate riches, and collect all those frivolities which seem conducive to luxury and splendour. On the other hand, we have a remarkable dread, a remarkable hatred of poverty, mean birth, and a humble condition, and feel the strongest desire to guard against them. Hence, in regard to those who frame their life after their own counsel, we see how restless they are in mind, how many plans they try, to what fatigues they submit, in order that they may gain what avarice or ambition desires, or, on the other hand, escape poverty and meanness. To avoid similar entanglements, the course which Christian men must follow is this: first, they must not long for, or hope for, or think of any kind of prosperity apart from the blessing of God; on it they must cast themselves, and there safely and confidently recline. For, however much the carnal mind may seem sufficient for itself when in the pursuit of honour or wealth, it depends on its own industry and zeal, or is aided by the favour of men, it is certain that all this is nothing, and that neither intellect nor labour will be of the least avail, except in so far as the Lord prospers both. On the contrary, his blessing alone makes a way through all obstacles, and brings every thing to a joyful and favourable issue. Secondly, though without this blessing we may be able to acquire some degree of fame and opulence, (as we daily see wicked men loaded with honours and riches,) yet since those on whom the curse of God lies do not enjoy the least particle of true happiness, whatever we obtain without his blessing must turn out ill. But surely men ought not to desire what adds to their misery.

9. Therefore, if we believe that all prosperous and desirable success depends entirely on the blessing of God, and that when it is wanting all kinds of misery and calamity await us, it follows that we should not eagerly contend for riches and honours, trusting to our own dexterity and assiduity, or leaning on the favour of men, or confiding in any empty imagination of fortune; but should always have respect to the Lord, that under his auspices we may be conducted to whatever lot he has provided for us. First, the result will be, that instead of rushing on regardless of right and wrong, by wiles and wicked arts, and with injury to our neighbours, to catch at wealth and seize upon honours, we will only follow such fortune as we may enjoy with innocence. Who can hope for the aid of the divine blessing amid fraud, rapine, and other iniquitous arts? As this blessing attends him only who thinks purely and acts uprightly, so it calls off all who long for it from sinister designs and evil actions. Secondly, a curb will be laid upon us, restraining a too eager desire of becoming rich, or an ambitious striving after honour. How can any one have the effrontery to expect that God will aid him in accomplishing desires at variance with his word? What God with his own lips pronounces cursed, never can be prosecuted with his blessing. Lastly, if our success is not equal to our wish and hope, we shall, however, be kept from impatience and detestation of our condition, whatever it be, knowing that so to feel were to murmur against God, at whose pleasure riches and poverty, contempt and honours, are dispensed. In shorts he who leans on the divine blessing in the way which has been described, will not, in the pursuit of those things which men are wont most eagerly to desire, employ wicked arts which he knows would avail him nothing; nor when any thing prosperous befalls him will he impute it to himself and his own diligence, or industry, or fortune, instead of ascribing it to God as its author. If, while the affairs of others flourish, his make little progress, or even retrograde, he will bear his humble lot with greater equanimity and moderation than any irreligious man does the moderate success which

only falls short of what he wished; for he has a solace in which he can rest more tranquilly than at the very summit of wealth or power, because he considers that his affairs are ordered by the Lord in the manner most conducive to his salvation. This, we see, is the way in which David was affected, who, while he follows God and gives up himself to his guidance, declares, "Neither do I exercise myself in great matters, or in things too high for me. Surely I have behaved and quieted myself as a child that is weaned of his mother," (Ps. cxxxi. 1, 2.)

10. Nor is it in this respect only that pious minds ought to manifest this tranquility and endurance; it must be extended to all the accidents to which this present life is liable. He alone, therefore, has properly denied himself, who has resigned himself entirely to the Lord, placing all the course of his life entirely at his disposal. Happen what may, he whose mind is thus composed will neither deem himself wretched nor murmur against God because of his lot. How necessary this disposition is will appear, if you consider the many accidents to which we are liable. Various diseases ever and anon attack us: at one time pestilence rages; at another we are involved in all the calamities of war. Frost and hail, destroying the promise of the year, cause sterility, which reduces us to penury; wife, parents, children, relatives, are carried off by death; our house is destroyed by fire. These are the events which make men curse their life, detest the day of their birth, execrate the light of heaven, even censure God, and (as they are eloquent in blasphemy) charge him with cruelty and injustice. The believer must in these things also contemplate the mercy and truly paternal indulgence of God. Accordingly, should he see his house by the removal of kindred reduced to solitude even then he will not cease to bless the Lord; his thought will be, Still the grace of the Lord, which dwells within my house, will not leave it desolate. If his crops are blasted, mildewed, or cut off by frost, or struck down by hail,[10] and he sees famine before him, he will not however despond or murmur against God, but maintain his confidence in him; "We thy people, and sheep of thy pasture, will give thee thanks for ever," (Ps. lxxix. 13;) he will supply me with food, even in the extreme of sterility. If he is afflicted with disease, the sharpness of the pain will not so overcome him, as to make him break out with impatience, and expostulate with God; but, recognizing justice and lenity in the rod, will patiently endure. In short, whatever happens, knowing that it is ordered by the Lord, he will receive it with a placid and grateful mind, and will not contumaciously resist the government of him, at whose disposal he has placed himself and all that he has. Especially let the Christian breast eschew that foolish and most miserable consolation of the heathen, who, to strengthen their mind against adversity, imputed it to fortune, at which they deemed it absurd to feel indignant, as she was aimless and rash, and blindly wounded the good equally with the bad. On the contrary, the rule of piety is, that the hand of God is the ruler and arbiter of the fortunes of all, and, instead of rushing on with thoughtless violence, dispenses good and evil with perfect regularity.

---

[10] The French is, "Soit que ses bleds et vignes soyent gastées et destruites par gelée, gresle, ou autre tempeste;"—whether his corn and vines are hurt and destroyed by frost, hail, or other tempest.

CHAPTER III.

OF BEARING THE CROSS—ONE BRANCH OF SELF-DENIAL.

The four divisions of this chapter are,—I. The nature of the cross, its necessity and dignity, sec. 1, 2. II. The manifold advantages of the cross described, sec. 3–6. III. The form of the cross the most excellent of all, and yet it by no means removes all sense of pain, sec. 7, 8. IV. A description of warfare under the cross, and of true patience, (not that of philosophers,) after the example of Christ, sec. 9–11.

1. THE pious mind must ascend still higher, namely, whither Christ calls his disciples when he says, that every one of them must "take up his cross," (Matth. xvi. 24.) Those whom the Lord has chosen and honoured with his intercourse must prepare for a hard, laborious, troubled life, a life full of many and various kinds of evils; it being the will of our heavenly Father to exercise his people in this way while putting them to the proof. Having begun this course with Christ the first-born, he continues it towards all his children. For though that Son was dear to him above others, the Son in whom he was "well pleased," yet we see, that far from being treated gently and indulgently, we may say, that not only was he subjected to a perpetual cross while he dwelt on earth, but his whole life was nothing else than a kind of perpetual cross. The Apostle assigns the reason, "Though he was a Son, yet learned he obedience by the things which he suffered," (Heb. v. 8.) Why then should we exempt ourselves from that condition to which Christ our Head behoved to submit; especially since he submitted on our account, that he might in his own person exhibit a model of patience? Wherefore, the Apostle declares, that all the children of God are destined to be conformed to him. Hence it affords us great consolation in hard and difficult circumstances, which men deem evil and adverse, to think that we are holding fellowship with the sufferings of Christ; that as he passed to celestial glory through a labyrinth of many woes, so we too are conducted thither through various tribulations. For, in another passage, Paul himself thus speaks, "we must through much tribulation enter the kingdom of God," (Acts xiv. 22;) and again, "that I may know him, and the power of his resurrection, and the fellowship of his sufferings, being made conformable unto his death," (Rom viii. 29.) How powerfully should it soften the bitterness of the cross, to think that the more we are afflicted with adversity, the surer we are made of our fellowship with Christ; by communion with whom our sufferings are not only blessed to us, but tend greatly to the furtherance of our salvation.

2. We may add, that the only thing which made it necessary for our Lord to undertake to bear the cross, was to testify and prove his obedience to the Father; whereas there are many reasons which make it necessary for us to live constantly under the cross. Feeble as we are by nature, and prone to ascribe all perfection to our flesh, unless we receive as it were ocular demonstration of our weakness, we readily estimate our virtue above its proper worth, and doubt not that, whatever happens, it will stand unimpaired and invincible against all difficulties. Hence we indulge a stupid and empty confidence in the flesh, and then trusting to it wax proud against the Lord himself; as if our own faculties were sufficient without his grace. This arrogance cannot be better repressed than when He proves to us by experience, not only how great our weakness, but also our frailty is. Therefore, he visits us with disgrace, or poverty, or bereavement, or disease, or other afflictions. Feeling altogether unable to support them, we forthwith, in so far as regards

ourselves, give way, and thus humbled learn to invoke his strength, which alone can enable us to bear up under a weight of affliction. Nay, even the holiest of men, however well aware that they stand not in their own strength, but by the grace of God, would feel too secure in their own fortitude and constancy, were they not brought to a more thorough knowledge of themselves by the trial of the cross. This feeling gained even upon David, "In my prosperity I Said, I shall never be moved. Lord, by thy favour thou hast made my mountain to stand strong: thou didst hide thy face, and I was troubled," (Ps. xxx. 6, 7.) He confesses that in prosperity his feelings were dulled and blunted, so that, neglecting the grace of God, on which alone he ought to have depended, he leant to himself, and promised himself perpetuity. If it so happened to this great prophet, who of us should not fear and study caution? Though in tranquility they flatter themselves with the idea of greater constancy and patience, yet, humbled by adversity, they learn the deception. Believers, I say, warned by such proofs of their diseases, make progress in humility, and, divesting themselves of a depraved confidence in the flesh, betake themselves to the grace of God, and, when they have so betaken themselves, experience the presence of the divine power, in which is ample protection.

3. This Paul teaches when he says that tribulation worketh patience, and patience experience. God having promised that he will be with believers in tribulation, they feel the truth of the promise; while supported by his hand, they endure patiently. This they could never do by their own strength. Patience, therefore, gives the saints an experimental proof that God in reality furnishes the aid which he has promised whenever there is need. Hence also their faith is confirmed, for it were very ungrateful not to expect that in future the truth of God will be, as they have already found it, firm and constant. We now see how many advantages are at once produced by the cross. Overturning the overweening opinion we form of our own virtue, and detecting the hypocrisy in which we delight, it removes our pernicious carnal confidence, teaching us, when thus humbled, to recline on God alone, so that we neither are oppressed nor despond. Then victory is followed by hope, inasmuch as the Lord, by performing what he has promised, establishes his truth in regard to the future. Were these the only reasons, it is surely plain how necessary it is for us to bear the cross. It is of no little importance to be rid of your self-love, and made fully conscious of your weakness; so impressed with a sense of your weakness as to learn to distrust yourself—to distrust yourself so as to transfer your confidence to God, reclining on him with such heartfelt confidence as to trust in his aid, and continue invincible to the end, standing by his grace so as to perceive that he is true to his promises, and so assured of the certainty of his promises as to be strong in hope.

4. Another end which the Lord has in afflicting his people is to try their patience, and train them to obedience—not that they can yield obedience to him except in so far as he enables them; but he is pleased thus to attest and display striking proofs of the graces which he has conferred upon his saints, lest they should remain within unseen and unemployed. Accordingly, by bringing forward openly the strength and constancy of endurance with which he has provided his servants, he is said to try their patience. Hence the expressions that God tempted Abraham, (Gen. xxi. 1, 12,) and made proof of his piety by not declining to sacrifice his only son. Hence, too, Peter tells us that our faith is proved by tribulation, just as gold is tried in a furnace of fire. But who will say it is not expedient that the most excellent gift of patience which the believer has received from his God should be applied to uses by being made sure and manifest? Otherwise men would never value it according to its worth. But if God himself, to prevent the virtues which he has

conferred upon believers from lurking in obscurity, nay, lying useless and perishing, does aright in supplying materials for calling them forth, there is the best reason for the afflictions of the saints, since without them their patience could not exist. I say, that by the cross they are also trained to obedience, because they are thus taught to live not according to their own wish, but at the disposal of God. Indeed, did all things proceed as they wish, they would not know what it is to follow God. Seneca mentions (De Vit. Beata, cap. xv.) that there was an old proverb when any one was exhorted to endure adversity, "Follow God;" thereby intimating, that men truly submitted to the yoke of God only when they gave their back and hand to his rod. But if it is most right that we should in all things prove our obedience to our heavenly Father, certainly we ought not to decline any method by which he trains us to obedience.

5. Still, however, we see not how necessary that obedience is, unless we at the same time consider how prone our carnal nature is to shake off the yoke of God whenever it has been treated with some degree of gentleness and indulgence. It just happens to it as with refractory horses, which, if kept idle for a few days at hack and manger, become ungovernable, and no longer recognize the rider, whose command before they implicitly obeyed. And we invariably become what God complains of in the people of Israel— waxing gross and fat, we kick against him who reared and nursed us, (Deut. xxxii. 15.) The kindness of God should allure us to ponder and love his goodness; but since such is our malignity, that we are invariably corrupted by his indulgence, it is more than necessary for us to be restrained by discipline from breaking forth into such petulance. Thus, lest we become emboldened by an over-abundance of wealth; lest elated with honour, we grow proud; lest inflated with other advantages of body, or mind, or fortune, we grow insolent, the Lord himself interferes as he sees to be expedient by means of the cross, subduing and curbing the arrogance of our flesh, and that in various ways, as the advantage of each requires. For as we do not all equally labour under the same disease, so we do not all need the same difficult cure. Hence we see that all are not exercised with the same kind of cross. While the heavenly Physician treats some more gently, in the case of others he employs harsher remedies, his purpose being to provide a cure for all. Still none is left free and untouched, because he knows that all, without a single exception, are diseased.

6. We may add, that our most merciful Father requires not only to prevent our weakness, but often to correct our past faults, that he may keep us in due obedience. Therefore, whenever we are afflicted we ought immediately to call to mind our past life. In this way we will find that the faults which we have committed are deserving of such castigation. And yet the exhortation to patience is not to be founded chiefly on the acknowledgment of sin. For Scripture supplies a far better consideration when it says, that in adversity "we are chastened of the Lord, that we should not be condemned with the world," (1 Cor. xi. 32.) Therefore, in the very bitterness of tribulation we ought to recognise the kindness and mercy of our Father, since even then he ceases not to further our salvation. For he afflicts, not that he may ruin or destroy but rather that he may deliver us from the condemnation of the world. Let this thought lead us to what Scripture elsewhere teaches: "My son, despise not the chastening of the Lord; neither be weary of his correction: For whom the Lord loveth he correcteth; even as a father the son in whom he delighteth," (Prov. iii. 11, 12.) When we perceive our Father's rod, is it not our part to behave as obedient docile sons rather than rebelliously imitate desperate men, who are hardened in wickedness? God dooms us to destruction, if he does not, by correction, call us back when we have fallen off from him, so that it is truly said, "If ye be without

chastisement," "then are ye bastards, and not sons," (Heb. xii. 8.) We are most perverse then if we cannot bear him while he is manifesting his good-will to us, and the care which he takes of our salvation. Scripture states the difference between believers and unbelievers to be, that the latter, as the slaves of inveterate and deep-seated iniquity, only become worse and more obstinate under the lash; whereas the former, like free-born sons turn to repentance. Now, therefore, choose your class. But as I have already spoken of this subject, it is sufficient to have here briefly adverted to it.

7. There is singular consolation, moreover, when we are persecuted for righteousness' sake. For our thought should then be, How high the honour which God bestows upon us in distinguishing us by the special badge of his soldiers. By suffering persecution for righteousness' sake, I mean not only striving for the defence of the Gospel, but for the defence of righteousness in any way. Whether, therefore, in maintaining the truth of God against the lies of Satan, or defending the good and innocent against the injuries of the bad, we are obliged to incur the offence and hatred of the world, so as to endanger life, fortune, or honour, let us not grieve or decline so far to spend ourselves for God; let us not think ourselves wretched in those things in which he with his own lips has pronounced us blessed, (Matth. v. 10.) Poverty, indeed considered in itself, is misery; so are exile, contempt, imprisonment, ignominy: in fine, death itself is the last of all calamities. But when the favour of God breathes upon is, there is none of these things which may not turn out to our happiness. Let us then be contented with the testimony of Christ rather than with the false estimate of the flesh, and then, after the example of the Apostles, we will rejoice in being "counted worthy to suffer shame for his name," (Acts v. 41.) For why? If, while conscious of our innocence, we are deprived of our substance by the wickedness of man, we are, no doubt, humanly speaking, reduced to poverty; but in truth our riches in heaven are increased: if driven from our homes we have a more welcome reception into the family of God; if vexed and despised, we are more firmly rooted in Christ; if stigmatised by disgrace and ignominy, we have a higher place in the kingdom of God; and if we are slain, entrance is thereby given us to eternal life. The Lord having set such a price upon us, let us be ashamed to estimate ourselves at less than the shadowy and evanescent allurements of the present life.

8. Since by these, and similar considerations, Scripture abundantly solaces us for the ignominy or calamities which we endure in defence of righteousness, we are very ungrateful if we do not willingly and cheerfully receive them at the hand of the Lord, especially since this form of the cross is the most appropriate to believers, being that by which Christ desires to be glorified in us, as Peter also declares, (1 Pet. iv. 11, 14.) But as to ingenuous natures, it is more bitter to suffer disgrace than a hundred deaths, Paul expressly reminds us that not only persecution, but also disgrace awaits us, "because we trust in the living God," (1 Tim. iv. 10.) So in another passage he bids us, after his example, walk "by evil report and good report," (2 Cor. vi. 8.) The cheerfulness required, however, does not imply a total insensibility to pain. The saints could show no patience under the cross if they were not both tortured with pain and grievously molested. Were there no hardship in poverty, no pain in disease, no sting in ignominy, no fear in death, where would be the fortitude and moderation in enduring them? But while every one of these, by its inherent bitterness, naturally vexes the mind, the believer in this displays his fortitude, that though fully sensible of the bitterness and labouring grievously, he still withstands and struggles boldly; in this displays his patience, that though sharply stung, he is however curbed by the fear of God from breaking forth into any excess; in this

displays his alacrity, that though pressed with sorrow and sadness, he rests satisfied with spiritual consolation from God.

9. This conflict which believers maintain against the natural feeling of pain, while they study moderation and patience, Paul elegantly describes in these words: "We are troubled on every side, yet not distressed; we are perplexed, but not in despair; persecuted, but not forsaken; cast down, but not destroyed," (2 Cor. iv. 8, 9.) You see that to bear the cross patiently is not to have your feelings altogether blunted, and to be absolutely insensible to pain, according to the absurd description which the Stoics of old gave of their hero as one who, divested of humanity, was affected in the same way by adversity and prosperity, grief and joy; or rather, like a stone, was not affected by anything. And what did they gain by that sublime wisdom? they exhibited a shadow of patience, which never did, and never can, exist among men. Nay, rather by aiming at a too exact and rigid patience, they banished it altogether from human life. Now also we have among Christians a new kind of Stoics, who hold it vicious not only to groan and weep, but even to be sad and anxious. These paradoxes are usually started by indolent men who, employing themselves more in speculation than in action, can do nothing else for us than beget such paradoxes. But we have nothing to do with that iron philosophy which our Lord and Master condemned—not only in word, but also by his own example. For he both grieved and shed tears for his own and others' woes. Nor did he teach his disciples differently: "Ye shall weep and lament, but the world shall rejoice," (John xvi. 20.) And lest any one should regard this as vicious, he expressly declares, "Blessed are they that mourn," (Matth. v. 4.) And no wonder. If all tears are condemned, what shall we think of our Lord himself, whose "sweat was as it were great drops of blood falling down to the ground?" (Luke xxii. 44; Matth. xxvi. 38.) If every kind of fear is a mark of unbelief, what place shall we assign to the dread which, it is said, in no slight degree amazed him; if all sadness is condemned, how shall we justify him when he confesses, "My soul is exceeding sorrowful, even unto death?"

10. I wished to make these observations to keep pious minds from despair, lest, from feeling it impossible to divest themselves of the natural feeling of grief, they might altogether abandon the study of patience. This must necessarily be the result with those who convert patience into stupor, and a brave and firm man into a block. Scripture gives saints the praise of endurance when, though afflicted by the hardships they endure, they are not crushed; though they feel bitterly, they are at the same time filled with spiritual joy; though pressed with anxiety, breathe exhilarated by the consolation of God. Still there is a certain degree of repugnance in their hearts, because natural sense shuns and dreads what is adverse to it, while pious affection, even through these difficulties, tries to obey the divine will. This repugnance the Lord expressed when he thus addressed Peter: "Verily, verily, I say unto thee, When thou wast young, thou girdedst thyself and walkedst whither thou wouldst; but when thou shalt be old, thou shalt stretch forth thy hands, and another shall gird thee; and carry thee whither thou wouldest not," (John xxi. 18.) It is not probable, indeed, that when it became necessary to glorify God by death he was driven to it unwilling and resisting; had it been so, little praise would have been due to his martyrdom. But though he obeyed the divine ordination with the greatest alacrity of heart, yet, as he had not divested himself of humanity, he was distracted by a double will. When he thought of the bloody death which he was to die, struck with horror, he would willingly have avoided it: on the other hand, when he considered that it was God who called him to it, his fear was vanquished and suppressed, and he met death cheerfully. It must therefore

be our study, if we would be disciples of Christ, to imbue our minds with such reverence and obedience to God as may tame and subjugate all affections contrary to his appointment. In this way, whatever be the kind of cross to which we are subjected, we shall in the greatest straits firmly maintain our patience. Adversity will have its bitterness, and sting us. When afflicted with disease, we shall groan and be disquieted, and long for health; pressed with poverty, we shall feel the stings of anxiety and sadness, feel the pain of ignominy, contempt, and injury, and pay the tears due to nature at the death of our friends: but our conclusion will always be, The Lord so willed it, therefore let us follow his will. Nay, amid the pungency of grief, among groans and tears this thought will necessarily suggest itself and incline us cheerfully to endure the things for which we are so afflicted.

11. But since the chief reason for enduring the cross has been derived from a consideration of the divine will, we must in few words explain wherein lies the difference between philosophical and Christian patience. Indeed, very few of the philosophers advanced so far as to perceive that the hand of God tries us by means of affliction, and that we ought in this matter to obey God. The only reason which they adduce is, that so it must be. But is not this just to say, that we must yield to God, because it is in vain to contend against him? For if we obey God only because it is necessary, provided we can escape, we shall cease to obey him. But what Scripture calls us to consider in the will of God is very different, namely, first justice and equity, and then a regard to our own salvation. Hence Christian exhortations to patience are of this nature, Whether poverty, or exile, or imprisonment, or contumely, or disease, or bereavement, or any such evil affects us, we must think that none of them happens except by the will and providence of God; moreover, that every thing he does is in the most perfect order. What! do not our numberless daily faults deserve to be chastised, more severely, and with a heavier rod than his mercy lays upon us? Is it not most right that our flesh should be subdued, and be, as it were, accustomed to the yoke, so as not to rage and wanton as it lists? Are not the justice and the truth of God worthy of our suffering on their account?[11] But if the equity of God is undoubtedly displayed in affliction, we cannot murmur or struggle against them without iniquity. We no longer hear the frigid cant, Yield, because it is necessary; but a living and energetic precept, Obey, because it is unlawful to resist; bear patiently, because impatience is rebellion against the justice of God. Then as that only seems to us attractive which we perceive to be for our own safety and advantage, here also our heavenly Father consoles us, by the assurance, that in the very cross with which he afflicts us he provides for our salvation. But if it is clear that tribulations are salutary to us, why should we not receive them with calm and grateful minds? In bearing them patiently we are not submitting to necessity but resting satisfied with our own good. The effect of these thoughts is, that to whatever extent our minds are contracted by the bitterness which we naturally feel under the cross, to the same extent will they be expanded with spiritual joy. Hence arises thanksgiving, which cannot exist unless joy be felt. But if the praise of the Lord and thanksgiving can emanate only from a cheerful and gladdened breasts and there is nothing which ought to interrupt these feelings in us, it is clear how necessary it is to temper the bitterness of the cross with spiritual joy.

---

[11] See end of sec. 4, and sec. 5, 7, 8.

CHAPTER IV.

OF MEDITATING ON THE FUTURE LIFE.

The three divisions of this chapter,—I. The principal use of the cross is, that it in various ways accustoms us to despise the present, and excites us to aspire to the future life, sec. 1, 2. II. In withdrawing from the present life we must neither shun it nor feel hatred for it; but desiring the future life, gladly quit the present at the command of our sovereign Master, see. 3, 4. III. Our infirmity in dreading death described. The correction and safe remedy, sec. 6.

1. WHATEVER be the kind of tribulation with which we are afflicted, we should always consider the end of it to be, that we may be trained to despise the present, and thereby stimulated to aspire to the future life. For since God well knows how strongly we are inclined by nature to a slavish love of this world, in order to prevent us from clinging too strongly to it, he employs the fittest reason for calling us back, and shaking off our lethargy. Every one of us, indeed, would be thought to aspire and aim at heavenly immortality during the whole course of his life. For we would be ashamed in no respect to excel the lower animals; whose condition would not be at all inferior to ours, had we not a hope of immortality beyond the grave. But when you attend to the plans, wishes, and actions of each, you see nothing in them but the earth. Hence our stupidity; our minds being dazzled with the glare of wealth, power, and honours, that they can see no farther. The heart also, engrossed with avarice, ambition, and lust, is weighed down and cannot rise above them. In short, the whole soul, ensnared by the allurements of the flesh, seeks its happiness on the earth. To meet this disease, the Lord makes his people sensible of the vanity of the present life, by a constant proof of its miseries. Thus, that they may not promise themselves deep and lasting peace in it, he often allows them to be assailed by war, tumult, or rapine, or to be disturbed by other injuries. That they may not long with too much eagerness after fleeting and fading riches, or rest in those which they already possess, he reduces them to want, or, at least, restricts them to a moderate allowance, at one time by exile, at another by sterility, at another by fire, or by other means. That they may not indulge too complacently in the advantages of married life, he either vexes them by the misconduct of their partners, or humbles them by the wickedness of their children, or afflicts them by bereavement. But if in all these he is indulgent to them, lest they should either swell with vain-glory, or be elated with confidence, by diseases and dangers he sets palpably before them how unstable and evanescent are all the advantages competent to mortals. We duly profit by the discipline of the cross, when we learn that this life, estimated in itself, is restless, troubled, in numberless ways wretched, and plainly in no respect happy; that what are estimated its blessings are uncertain, fleeting, vain, and vitiated by a great admixture of evil. From this we conclude, that all we have to seek or hope for here is contest; that when we think of the crown we must raise our eyes to heaven. For we must hold, that our mind never rises seriously to desire and aspire after the future, until it has learned to despise the present life.

2. For there is no medium between the two things: the earth must either be worthless in our estimation, or keep us enslaved by an intemperate love of it. Therefore, if we have any regard to eternity, we must carefully strive to disencumber ourselves of these fetters. Moreover, since the present life has many enticements to allure us, and great semblance of delight, grace, and sweetness to soothe us, it is of great consequence to us to be now

and then called off from its fascinations.[12] For what, pray, would happen, if we here enjoyed an uninterrupted course of honour and felicity, when even the constant stimulus of affliction cannot arouse us to a due sense of our misery? That human life is like smoke or a shadow, is not only known to the learned; there is not a more trite proverb among the vulgar. Considering it a fact most useful to be known, they have recommended it in many well-known expressions. Still there is no fact which we ponder less carefully, or less frequently remember. For we form all our plans just as if we had fixed our immortality on the earth. If we see a funeral, or walk among graves, as the image of death is then present to the eye, I admit we philosophise admirably on the vanity of life. We do not indeed always do so, for those things often have no effect upon us at all. But, at the best, our philosophy is momentary. It vanishes as soon as we turn our back, and leaves not the vestige of remembrance behind; in short, it passes away, just like the applause of a theatre at some pleasant spectacle. Forgetful not only of death, but also of mortality itself, as if no rumour of it had ever reached us, we indulge in supine security as expecting a terrestrial immortality. Meanwhile, if any one breaks in with the proverb, that man is the creature of a day,[13] we indeed acknowledge its truth, but, so far from giving heed to it, the thought of perpetuity still keeps hold of our minds. Who then can deny that it is of the highest importance to us all, I say not, to be admonished by words, but convinced by all possible experience of the miserable condition of our earthly life; since even when convinced we scarcely cease to gaze upon it with vicious, stupid admiration, as if it contained within itself the sum of all that is good? But if God finds it necessary so to train us, it must be our duty to listen to him when he calls, and shakes us from our torpor, that we may hasten to despise the world, and aspire with our whole heart to the future life.

3. Still the contempt which believers should train themselves to feel for the present life, must not be of a kind to beget hatred of it or ingratitude to God. This life, though abounding in all kinds of wretchedness, is justly classed among divine blessings which are not to be despised. Wherefore, if we do not recognize the kindness of God in it, we are chargeable with no little ingratitude towards him. To believers, especially, it ought to be a proof of divine benevolence, since it is wholly destined to promote their salvation. Before openly exhibiting the inheritance of eternal glory, God is pleased to manifest himself to us as a Father by minor proofs, viz., the blessings which he daily bestows upon us. Therefore, while this life serves to acquaint us with the goodness of God, shall we disdain it as if it did not contain one particle of good? We ought, therefore, to feel and be affected towards it in such a manner as to place it among those gifts of the divine benignity which are by no means to be despised. Were there no proofs in Scripture, (they are most numerous and clear,) yet nature herself exhorts us to return thanks to God for having brought us forth into light, granted us the use of it, and bestowed upon us all the means necessary for its preservation. And there is a much higher reason when we reflect that here we are in a manner prepared for the glory of the heavenly kingdom. For the Lord hath ordained, that those who are ultimately to be crowned in heaven must maintain a previous

---

[12] French, "Or pource que la vie presente a tousiours force de delices pour nous attraire, et a grande apparence d'amenité, de grace et de douceur pour nous amieller, il nous est bien mestier d'estre retiré d'heure en d'heure, à ce que nous ne soyons point abusez, et comme ensorcelez de telles flatteries;" — Now because the present life has always a host of delights to attract us, and has great appearance of amenity, grace, and sweetness to entice us, it is of great importance to us to be hourly withdrawn, in order that we may not be deceived, and, as it were, bewitched with such flattery.

[13] Latin, "Animal esse;"—is an ephemereal animal.

warfare on the earth, that they may not triumph before they have overcome the difficulties of war, and obtained the victory. Another reason is, that we here begin to experience in various ways a foretaste of the divine benignity, in order that our hope and desire may be whetted for its full manifestation. When once we have concluded that our earthly life is a gift of the divine mercy, of which, agreeably to our obligation, it behoves us to have a grateful remembrance, we shall then properly descend to consider its most wretched condition, and thus escape from that excessive fondness for it, to which, as I have said, we are naturally prone.

4. In proportion as this improper love diminishes, our desire of a better life should increase. I confess, indeed, that a most accurate opinion was formed by those who thought, that the best thing was not to be born, the next best to die early. For, being destitute of the light of God and of true religion, what could they see in it that was not of dire and evil omen? Nor was it unreasonable for those[14] who felt sorrow and shed tears at the birth of their kindred, to keep holiday at their deaths. But this they did without profit; because, devoid of the true doctrine of faith, they saw not how that which in itself is neither happy nor desirable turns to the advantage of the righteous: and hence their opinion issued in despair. Let believers, then, in forming an estimate of this mortal life, and perceiving that in itself it is nothing but misery, make it their aim to exert themselves with greater alacrity, and less hinderance, in aspiring to the future and eternal life. When we contrast the two, the former may not only be securely neglected, but, in comparison of the latter, be disdained and contemned. If heaven is our country, what can the earth be but a place of exile? If departure from the world is entrance into life, what is the world but a sepulchre, and what is residence in it but immersion in death? If to be freed from the body is to gain full possession of freedom, what is the body but a prison? If it is the very summit of happiness to enjoy the presence of God, is it not miserable to want it? But "whilst we are at home in the body, we are absent from the Lord," (2 Cor. v. 6.) Thus when the earthly is compared with the heavenly life, it may undoubtedly be despised and trampled under foot. We ought never, indeed, to regard it with hatred, except in so far as it keeps us subject to sin; and even this hatred ought not to be directed against life itself. At all events, we must stand so affected towards it in regard to weariness or hatred as, while longing for its termination, to be ready at the Lord's will to continue in it, keeping far from everything like murmuring and impatience. For it is as if the Lord had assigned us a post, which we must maintain till he recalls us. Paul, indeed, laments his condition, in being still bound with the fetters of the body, and sighs earnestly for redemption, (Rom. vii. 24;) nevertheless, he declared that, in obedience to the command of Gods he was prepared for both courses, because he acknowledges it as his duty to God to glorify his name whether by life or by death, while it belongs to God to determine what is most conducive to His glory, (Phil. i. 20–24.) Wherefore, if it becomes us to live and die to the Lord, let us leave the period of our life and death at his disposal. Still let us ardently long for death, and constantly meditate upon it, and in comparison with future immortality, let us despise life, and, on account of the bondage of sin, long to renounce it whenever it shall so please the Lord.

5. But, most strange to say, many who boast of being Christians, instead of thus longing for death, are so afraid of it that they tremble at the very mention of it as a thing ominous and dreadful. We cannot wonder, indeed, that our natural feelings should be

---

[14] French, "Le peuple des Scythes;"—the Scythians.

somewhat shocked at the mention of our dissolution. But it is altogether intolerable that the light of piety should not be so powerful in a Christian breast as with greater consolation to overcome and suppress that fear. For if we reflect that this our tabernacle, unstable, defective, corruptible, fading, pining, and putrid, is dissolved, in order that it may forthwith be renewed in sure, perfect, incorruptible, in fine, in heavenly glory, will not faith compel us eagerly to desire what nature dreads? If we reflect that by death we are recalled from exile to inhabit our native country, a heavenly country, shall this give us no comfort? But everything longs for permanent existence. I admit this, and therefore contend that we ought to look to future immortality, where we may obtain that fixed condition which nowhere appears on the earth. For Paul admirably enjoins believers to hasten cheerfully to death, not because they a would be unclothed, but clothed upon," (2 Cor. v. 2.) Shall the lower animals, and inanimate creatures themselves even wood and stone, as conscious of their present vanity, long for the final resurrection, that they may with the sons of God be delivered from vanity, (Rom. viii. 19;) and shall we, endued with the light of intellect, and more than intellect, enlightened by the Spirit of God, when our essence is in question, rise no higher than the corruption of this earth? But it is not my purpose, nor is this the place, to plead against this great perverseness. At the outset, I declared that I had no wish to engage in a diffuse discussion of common-places. My advice to those whose minds are thus timid is to read the short treatise of Cyprian De Mortalitate, unless it be more accordant with their deserts to send them to the philosophers, that by inspecting what they say on the contempt of death, they may begin to blush. This, however let us hold as fixed, that no man has made much progress in the school of Christ who does not look forward with joy to the day of death and final resurrection, (2 Tim. iv. 18; Tit. ii. 13:) for Paul distinguishes all believers by this mark; and the usual course of Scripture is to direct us thither whenever it would furnish us with an argument for substantial joy. "Look up," says our Lord, "and lift up your heads: for your redemption draweth nigh," (Luke xxi. 28.) Is it reasonable, I ask, that what he intended to have a powerful effect in stirring us up to alacrity and exultation should produce nothing but sadness and consternation? If it is so, why do we still glory in him as our Master? Therefore, let us come to a sounder mind, and how repugnant so ever the blind and stupid longing of the flesh may be, let us doubt not to desire the advent of the Lord not in wish only, but with earnest sighs, as the most propitious of all events. He will come as a Redeemer to deliver us from an immense abyss of evil and misery, and lead us to the blessed inheritance of his life and glory.

6. Thus, indeed, it is; the whole body of the faithful, so long as they live on the earth, must be like sheep for the slaughter, in order that they may be conformed to Christ their head, (Rom. viii. 36.) Most deplorable, therefore, would their situation be did they not, by raising their mind to heaven, become superior to all that is in the world, and rise above the present aspect of affairs, (1 Cor. xv. 19.) On the other hand, when once they have raised their head above all earthly objects, though they see the wicked flourishing in wealth and honour, and enjoying profound peace, indulging in luxury and splendour, and revelling in all kinds of delights, though they should moreover be wickedly assailed by them, suffer insult from their pride, be robbed by their avarice, or assailed by any other passion, they will have no difficulty in bearing up under these evils. They will turn their eye to that day, (Isaiah xxv. 8; Rev. vii. 17,) on which the Lord will receive his faithful servants, wipe away all tears from their eyes, clothe them in a robe of glory and joy, feed them with the ineffable sweetness of his pleasures, exalt them to share with him in his greatness; in fine,

admit them to a participation in his happiness. But the wicked who may have flourished on the earth, he will cast forth in extreme ignominy, will change their delights into torments, their laughter and joy into wailing and gnashing of teeth, their peace into the gnawing of conscience, and punish their luxury with unquenchable fire. He will also place their necks under the feet of the godly, whose patience they abused. For, as Paul declares, "it is a righteous thing with God to recompense tribulation to them that trouble you; and to you who are troubled rest with us, when the Lord Jesus shall be revealed from heaven," (2 Thess. i. 6, 7.) This, indeed, is our only consolation; deprived of it, we must either give way to despondency, or resort to our destruction to the vain solace of the world. The Psalmist confesses, "My feet were almost gone: my steps had well nigh slipt: for I was envious at the foolish when I saw the prosperity of the wicked," (Psalm lxxiii. 3, 4;) and he found no resting-place until he entered the sanctuary, and considered the latter end of the righteous and the wicked. To conclude in one word, the cross of Christ then only triumphs in the breasts of believers over the devil and the flesh, sin and sinners, when their eyes are directed to the power of his resurrection.

CHAPTER V.

HOW TO USE THE PRESENT LIFE, AND THE COMFORTS OF IT.

The divisions of this chapter are,—I. The necessity and usefulness of this doctrine. Extremes to be avoided, if we would rightly use the present life and its comforts, sec. 1, 2. II. One of these extremes, viz, the intemperance of the flesh, to be carefully avoided. Four methods of doing so described in order, sec. 3–6.

1. BY such rudiments we are at the same time well instructed by Scripture in the proper use of earthly blessings, a subject which, in forming a scheme of life, is by no mean to be neglected. For if we are to live, we must use the necessary supports of life; nor can we even shun those things which seem more subservient to delight than to necessity. We must therefore observe a mean, that we may use them with a pure conscience, whether for necessity or for pleasure. This the Lord prescribes by his word, when he tells us that to his people the present life is a kind of pilgrimage by which they hasten to the heavenly kingdom. If we are only to pass through the earth, there can be no doubt that we are to use its blessings only in so far as they assist our progress, rather than retard it. Accordingly, Paul, not without cause, admonishes us to use this world without abusing it, and to buy possessions as if we were selling them, (1 Cor. vii. 30, 31.) But as this is a slippery place, and there is great danger of falling on either side, let us fix our feet where we can stand safely. There have been some good and holy men who, when they saw intemperance and luxury perpetually carried to excess, if not strictly curbed, and were desirous to correct so pernicious an evil, imagined that there was no other method than to allow man to use corporeal goods only in so far as they were necessaries: a counsel pious indeed, but unnecessarily austere; for it does the very dangerous thing of binding consciences in closer fetters than those in which they are bound by the word of God. Moreover, necessity, according to them,[15] was abstinence from every thing which could be wanted, so that they held it scarcely lawful to make any addition to bread and water. Others were still more

---

[15] See Chrysost. ad Heb. Hi. As to Cratetes the Theban, see Plutarch, Lib. de Vitand. aere alien. and Philostratus in Vita Apollonii.

austere, as is related of Cratetes the Theban, who threw his riches into the sea, because he thought, that unless he destroyed them they would destroy him. Many also in the present day, while they seek a pretext for carnal intemperance in the use of external things, and at the same time would pave the way for licentiousness, assume for granted, what I by no means concede, that this liberty is not to be restrained by any modification, but that it is to be left to every man's conscience to use them as far as he thinks lawful. I indeed confess that here consciences neither can nor ought to be bound by fixed and definite laws; but that Scripture having laid down general rules for the legitimate uses we should keep within the limits which they prescribe.

2. Let this be our principle, that we err not in the use of the gifts of Providence when we refer them to the end for which their author made and destined them, since he created them for our good, and not for our destruction. No man will keep the true path better than he who shall have this end carefully in view. Now then, if we consider for what end he created food, we shall find that he consulted not only for our necessity, but also for our enjoyment and delight. Thus, in clothing, the end was, in addition to necessity, comeliness and honour; and in herbs, fruits, and trees, besides their various uses, gracefulness of appearance and sweetness of smell. Were it not so, the Prophet would not enumerate among the mercies of God "wine that maketh glad the heart of man, and oil to make his face to shine," (Ps. civ. 15.) The Scriptures would not everywhere mention, in commendation of his benignity, that he had given such things to men. The natural qualities of things themselves demonstrate to what end, and how far, they may be lawfully enjoyed. Has the Lord adorned flowers with all the beauty which spontaneously presents itself to the eye, and the sweet odour which delights the sense of smell, and shall it be unlawful for us to enjoy that beauty and this odour? What? Has he not so distinguished colours as to make some more agreeable than others? Has he not given qualities to gold and silver, ivory and marble, thereby rendering them precious above other metals or stones? In short, has he not given many things a value without having any necessary use?

3. Have done, then, with that inhuman philosophy which, in allowing no use of the creatures but for necessity, not only maliciously deprives us of the lawful fruit of the divine beneficence, but cannot be realised without depriving man of all his senses, and reducing him to a block. But, on the other hand, let us with no less care guard against the lusts of the flesh, which, if not kept in order, break through all bounds, and are, as I have said, advocated by those who, under pretence of liberty, allow themselves every sort of license. First one restraint is imposed when we hold that the object of creating all things was to teach us to know their author, and feel grateful for his indulgence. Where is the gratitude if you so gorge or stupify yourself with feasting and wine as to be unfit for offices of piety, or the duties of your calling? Where the recognition of God, if the flesh, boiling forth in lust through excessive indulgences infects the mind with its impurity, so as to lose the discernment of honour and rectitude? Where thankfulness to God for clothing, if on account of sumptuous raiment we both admire ourselves and disdain others? if, from a love of show and splendour, we pave the way for immodesty? Where our recognition of God, if the glare of these things captivates our minds? For many are so devoted to luxury in all their senses that their mind lies buried: many are so delighted with marble, gold, and pictures, that they become marble-hearted—are changed as it were into metal, and made like painted figures. The kitchen, with its savoury smells, so engrosses them that they have no spiritual savour. The same thing may be seen in other matters. Wherefore, it is plain that there is here great necessity for curbing licentious abuse, and conforming to the rule

of Paul, "make not provision for the flesh to fulfil the lusts thereof," (Rom. xiii. 14.) Where too much liberty is given to them, they break forth without measure or restraint.

4. There is no surer or quicker way of accomplishing this than by despising the present life and aspiring to celestial immortality. For hence two rules arise: First, "it remaineth, that both they that have wives be as though they had none;" "and they that use this world, as not abusing it," (1 Cor. vii. 29, 31.) Secondly, we must learn to be no less placid and patient in enduring penury, than moderate in enjoying abundance. He who makes it his rule to use this world as if he used it not, not only cuts off all gluttony in regard to meat and drink, and all effeminacy, ambition, pride, excessive shows and austerity, in regard to his table, his house, and his clothes, but removes every care and affection which might withdraw or hinder him from aspiring to the heavenly life, and cultivating the interest of his soul.[16] It was well said by Cato: Luxury causes great care, and produces great carelessness as to virtue; and it is an old proverb,—Those who are much occupied with the care of the body, usually give little care to the soul. Therefore while the liberty of the Christian in external matters is not to be tied down to a strict rule, it is, however, subject to this law—he must indulge as little as possible; on the other hand, it must be his constant aims not only to curb luxury, but to cut off all show of superfluous abundance, and carefully beware of converting a help into an hinderance.

5. Another rule is, that those in narrow and slender circumstances should learn to bear their wants patiently, that they may not become immoderately desirous of things, the moderate use of which implies no small progress in the school of Christ. For in addition to the many other vices which accompany a longing for earthly good, he who is impatient under poverty almost always betrays the contrary disease in abundance. By this I mean, that he who is ashamed of a sordid garment will be vain-glorious of a splendid one; he who not contented with a slender, feels annoyed at the want of a more luxurious supper, will intemperately abuse his luxury if he obtains it; he who has a difficulty, and is dissatisfied in submitting to a private and humble condition, will be unable to refrain from pride if he attain to honour. Let it be the aim of all who have any unfeigned desire for piety to learn, after the example of the Apostle, "both to be full and to be hungry, both to abound and to suffer need," (Philip. iv. 12.) Scripture, moreover, has a third rule for modifying the use of earthly blessings. We have already adverted to it when considering the offices of charity. For it declares that they have all been given us by the kindness of God, and appointed for our use under the condition of being regarded as trusts, of which we must one day give account. We must, therefore, administer them as if we constantly heard the words sounding in our ears, "Give an account of your stewardship." At the same time, let us remember by whom the account is to be taken, viz., by him who, while he so highly commends abstinence, sobriety, frugality, and moderation, abominates luxury, pride, ostentation, and vanity; who approves of no administration but that which is combined with charity, who with his own lips has already condemned all those pleasures which withdraw the heart from chastity and purity, or darken the intellect.

6. The last thing to be observed is, that the Lord enjoins every one of us, in all the actions of life, to have respect to our own calling. He knows the boiling restlessness of the human mind, the fickleness with which it is borne hither and thither, its eagerness to hold opposites at one time in its grasp, its ambition. Therefore, lest all things should be thrown into confusion by our folly and rashness, he has assigned distinct duties to each in the

---

[16] French, "Parer notre ame de ses vrais ornemens;"—deck our soul with its true ornaments.

different modes of life. And that no one may presume to overstep his proper limits, he has distinguished the different modes of life by the name of callings. Every man's mode of life, therefore, is a kind of station assigned him by the Lord, that he may not be always driven about at random. So necessary is this distinction, that all our actions are thereby estimated in his sight, and often in a very different way from that in which human reason or philosophy would estimate them. There is no more illustrious deed even among philosophers than to free one's country from tyranny, and yet the private individual who stabs the tyrant is openly condemned by the voice of the heavenly Judge. But I am unwilling to dwell on particular examples; it is enough to know that in every thing the call of the Lord is the foundation and beginning of right action. He who does not act with reference to it will never, in the discharge of duty, keep the right path. He will sometimes be able, perhaps, to give the semblance of something laudable, but whatever it may be in the sight of man, it will be rejected before the throne of God; and besides, there will be no harmony in the different parts of his life. Hence, he only who directs his life to this end will have it properly framed; because free from the impulse of rashness, he will not attempt more than his calling justifies, knowing that it is unlawful to overleap the prescribed bounds. He who is obscure will not decline to cultivate a private life, that he may not desert the post at which God has placed him. Again, in all our cares, toils, annoyances, and other burdens, it will be no small alleviation to know that all these are under the superintendence of God. The magistrate will more willingly perform his office, and the father of a family confine himself to his proper sphere. Every one in his particular mode of life will, without repining, suffer its inconveniences, cares, uneasiness, and anxiety, persuaded that God has laid on the burden. This, too, will afford admirable consolation, that in following your proper calling, no work will be so mean and sordid as not to have a splendour and value in the eye of God.

The
God of All Comfort
And the Secret of His Comforting

~ ※ ~

By *Hannah Whitall Smith*
The 1906 Edition

~ ※ ~

Chapter 1: Why This Book Has Been Written

"My heart is inditing a good matter; I speak of the things which I have made touching the King."

I was once talking on the subject of religion with an intelligent agnostic, whom I very much wished to influence, and after listening to me politely for a little while, he said, "Well, madam, all I have to say is this. If you Christians want to make us agnostics inclined to look into your religion, you must try to be more comfortable in the possession of it yourselves. The Christians I meet seem to me to be the very most uncomfortable people anywhere around. They seem to carry their religion as a man carries a headache. He does not want to get rid of his head, but at the same time it is very uncomfortable to have it. And I for one do not care to have that sort of religion."

This was a lesson I have never forgotten, and it is the primary cause of my writing this book.

I was very young in the Christian life at the time of this conversation, and was still in the first joy of my entrance into it, so I could not believe that any of God's children could be as uncomfortable in their religious lives as my agnostic friend had asserted. But when the early glow of my conversion had passed, and I had come down to the dullness of everyday duties and responsibilities, I soon found from my own experience, and also from the similar experiences of most of the Christians around me, that there was far too much truth in his assertion, and that the religious life of most of us was full of discomfort and unrest. In fact, it seemed, as one of my Christian friends said to me one day when we were comparing our experiences, "as if we had just enough religion to make us miserable."

I confess that this was very disappointing, for I had expected something altogether different. It seemed to me exceedingly incongruous that a religion, whose fruits were declared in the Bible to be love, and joy, and peace should so often work out practically in an exactly opposite direction, and should develop the fruits of doubt, and fear, and unrest, and conflict, and discomforts of every kind; and I resolved if possible to find out what was the matter. Why, I asked myself, should the children of God lead such utterly uncomfortable religious lives when He has led us to believe that His yoke would be easy and His burden light? Why are we tormented with so many spiritual doubts, and such heavy spiritual anxieties? Why do we find it so hard to be sure that God really loves us, and why is it that we never seem able to believe long at a time in His kindness and His care? How is it that we can let ourselves suspect Him of forgetting us and forsaking us in times of need? We can trust our earthly friends, and can be comfortable in their companionship, and why is it then that we cannot trust our heavenly Friend, and that we seem unable to be comfortable in His service?

I believe I have found the answer to these questions, and I should like to state frankly that my object in writing this book is to try to bring into some troubled Christian lives around me a little real and genuine comfort. My own idea of the religion of the Lord Jesus Christ is that it was meant to be full of comfort. I feel sure any unprejudiced reader of the New Testament would say the same; and I believe that every newly converted soul, in the first joy of its conversion, fully expects it. And yet, as I have said, it seems as if, with a large proportion of Christians, their religious lives are the most uncomfortable part of their existence. Does the fault of this state of things lie with the Lord? Has He promised more than He is able to supply?

A writer has said, "We know what overadvertisement is. It is a twentieth-century disease from which we all suffer. There are posters on every billboard, exaggerations on every blank wall, representations and misrepresentations without number. What visions we have seen of impossible fruits and flowers grown from Mr. So-and-So's seeds. Everything is overadvertised. Is it the same with the kingdom of God? Do the fruits which we raise from the good seed of the kingdom verify the description given by Him from whom we obtained that good seed? Has He played us false? There is a feeling abroad that Christ has offered in His Gospel more than He has to give. People think that they have not exactly realized what was predicted as the portion of the children of God. But why is this so? Has the kingdom of God been overadvertised, or is it only that it has been underbelieved; has the Lord Jesus Christ been overestimated, or has He only been undertrusted?"

What I want to do in this book is to show, in my small measure, what I firmly believe, that the kingdom of God could not possibly be overadvertised, nor the Lord Jesus Christ overestimated, for eye hath not seen, nor ear heard, neither have entered into the heart of man, the things which God hath prepared for them that love Him; and that all the difficulty arises from the fact that we have underbelieved and undertrusted.

I want, therefore, to show as best I can the grounds there are in the religion of the Lord Jesus Christ for that deep and lasting peace and comfort of soul, which nothing earthly can disturb, and which is declared to be the portion of those who embrace it. And I want further to tell, if this is indeed our rightful portion, how we are to avail ourselves of it, and what are the things that hinder. There is God's part in the matter, and there is man's part, and we must look carefully at both.

A wild young fellow, who was brought to the Lord at a mission meeting, and who became a rejoicing Christian and lived an exemplary life afterward, was asked by someone what he did to get converted. "Oh," he said, "I did my part, and the Lord did His."

"But what was your part," asked the inquirer, "and what was the Lord's part?"

"My part," was the prompt reply, "was to run away, and the Lord's part was to run after me until He caught me." A most significant answer; but how few can understand it!

God's part is always to run after us. Christ came to seek and to save that which is lost. "What man of you," He says, "having a hundred sheep, if he lose one of them, doth not leave the ninety and nine in the wilderness, and go after that which is lost until he find it? And when he hath found it, he layeth it on his shoulders rejoicing." This is always the divine part; but in our foolishness we do not understand it, but think that the Lord is the one who is lost, and that our part is to seek and find Him. The very expressions we use show this. We urge sinners to "seek the Lord," and we talk about having "found" Him. "Have you found the Savior?" asked a too zealous mission worker of a happy, trusting little girl.

With a look of amazement, she replied in a tone of wonder, "Why, I did not know the Savior was lost!"

It is our ignorance of God that does it all. Because we do not know Him, we naturally get all sorts of wrong ideas about Him. We think He is an angry Judge who is on the watch for our slightest faults, or a harsh Taskmaster determined to exact from us the uttermost service, or a self-absorbed Deity demanding His full measure of honor and glory, or a far-off Sovereign concerned only with His own affairs and indifferent to our welfare. Who can wonder that such a God can neither be loved nor trusted? And who could expect

Christians, with such ideas concerning Him, to be anything but full of discomfort and misery?

But I can assert boldly, and without fear of contradiction, that it is impossible for anyone who really knows God to have such uncomfortable thoughts about Him. Plenty of outward discomforts there may be, and many earthly sorrows and trials, but through them all the soul that knows God cannot but dwell inwardly in a fortress of perfect peace. "Who so hearkeneth unto me," He says, "shall dwell safely; and shall be quiet from fear of evil." And this is a statement that no one dare question. If we would really hearken unto God, which means not only hearing Him, but believing what we hear, we could not fail to know that, just because He is God, He cannot do other than care for us as He cares for the apple of His eye; and that all that tender love and divine wisdom can do for our welfare, must be and will be unfailingly done. Not a single loophole for worry or fear is left to the soul that knows God.

"Ah, yes," you say, "but how am I to get to know Him. Other people seem to have some kind of inward revelation that makes them know Him, but I never do; and no matter how much I pray, everything seems dark to me. I want to know God, but I do not see how to manage it."

Your trouble is that you have got a wrong idea of what knowing God is, or at least the kind of knowing I mean. For I do not mean any mystical interior revelations of any kind. Such revelations are delightful when you can have them, but they are not always at your command, and they are often variable and uncertain. The kind of knowing I mean is just the plain matter-of-fact knowledge of God's nature and character that comes to us by believing what is revealed to us in the Bible concerning Him. The Apostle John at the close of his Gospel says, regarding the things he had been recording: "And many other signs truly did Jesus in the presence of His disciples which are not written in this book: but these are written that ye might believe that Jesus is the Christ, the Son of God; and that, believing, ye might have life through his name." It is believing the thing that is written, not the thing that is inwardly revealed, that is to give life; and the kind of knowing I mean is the knowing that comes from believing the things that are written.

I mean, to be practical, that when I read in the Bible that God is love, I am to believe it, just because "it is written," and not because I have had any inward revelation that is true; and when the Bible says that He cares for us as He cares for the lilies of the field and the birds of the air, and that the very hairs of our head are all numbered, I am to believe it, just because it is written, no matter whether I have any inward revelation of it or not.

It is of vital importance for us to understand that the Bible is a statement, not of theories, but of actual facts; and that things are not true because they are in the Bible, but they are only in the Bible because they are true. A little boy, who had been studying at school about the discovery of America, said to his father one day, "Father, if I had been Columbus I would not have taken all that trouble to discover America."

"Why, what would you have done?" asked the father.

"Oh," replied the little boy, "I would have just gone to the map and found it." This little boy did not understand that maps are only pictures of already known places, and that America did not exist because it was on the map, but it could not be on the map until it was already known to exist. And similarly with the Bible. It is, like the map, a simple statement of facts; so that when it tells us that God loves us, it is only telling us something that is a fact, and that would not be in the Bible if it had not been already known to be a fact.

It was a great discovery to me when I grasped this idea. It seemed to take all uncertainty and all speculation out of the revelation given us in the Bible of the salvation of the Lord Jesus Christ, and to make all that is written concerning Him to be simply a statement of incontrovertible facts. And facts we can believe, and what is more, we do believe them as soon as we see that they are facts. Inward revelations we cannot manage, but anyone in his senses can believe the thing that is written. And although this may seem very dry and bare to start with, it will, if steadfastly persevered in, result in very blessed inward revelations, and will sooner or later lead us out into such a knowledge of God as will transform our lives. This kind of knowing brings us convictions; and to my mind convictions are far superior to any inward revelations, delightful as these last are. An inward revelation may be upset by the state of one's health, or by many other upsetting things, but a conviction is permanent. Once convince a man that two and two make four, and no amount of dyspepsia, or liver complaint, or east winds, or anything else, but actual lunacy, can upset his conviction. He knows it just as well when he has an attack of dyspepsia as he does when his digestion is in good working order. Convictions come from knowledge, and no amount of good feelings or bad feelings, of good health or ill health, can alter knowledge.

It is to try to help my readers to come to a knowledge of God in the plain matter-of-fact sort of way of which I have spoken, and to the convictions which result from this knowledge, that this book is written. I shall first try to show what God is, not theologically, nor doctrinally, but simply what He is in actual, practical reality, as the God and Father of each one of us. And I shall also point out some of the things that seem to me the principal hindrances to becoming really acquainted with Him.

I am so absolutely certain that coming to know Him as He really is will bring unfailing comfort and peace to every troubled heart that I long unspeakably to help everyone within my reach to this knowledge. One of Job's friends said, in his arguments against Job's bitter complaints, "Acquaint now thyself with God, and be at peace"; and our Lord in His last recorded prayer said: "This is life eternal, that they might know thee, the only true God, and Jesus Christ whom thou has sent." It is not a question of acquaintance with ourselves, or of knowing what we are, or what we do, or what we feel; it is simply and only a question of becoming acquainted with God, and getting to know what He is, and what He does, and what He feels. Comfort and peace never come from anything we know about ourselves, but only and always from what we know about Him.

We may spend our days in what we call our religious duties, and we may fill our devotions with fervor, and still may be miserable. Nothing can set our hearts at rest but a real acquaintance with God; for, after all, everything in our salvation must depend upon Him in the last instance; and, according as He is worthy or not of our confidence, so must necessarily be our comfort. If we were planning to take a dangerous voyage, our first question would be as to the sort of captain we were to have. Our common sense would tell us that if the captain were untrustworthy, no amount of trustworthiness on our part would make the voyage safe; and it would be his character and not our own that would be the thing of paramount importance to us.

If I can only say this often enough and in enough different ways to bring conviction to some troubled hearts, and lift them out of their sad and uncomfortable religious lives into the kingdom of love, and joy, and peace, which is their undisputed inheritance, I shall feel that my object in writing this book has been accomplished. And I shall be able to say, Lord, now lettest Thou Thy servant depart in peace, for mine eyes have seen Thy salvation; and my pen has tried to tell it.

It must, however, be clearly understood that my book does not propose to touch on the critical or the theological aspects of our religion. It does not undertake to deal with any questions concerning the authenticity of the Bible. Other and far abler minds can deal with these matters. My book is written for people, who, like myself, profess to believe in the Lord Jesus Christ, and who accept the Bible simply as the revelation of Him.

Putting aside all critical questions, therefore, I seek only to tell such believers of what seems to me the necessary result of their belief, and how they can personally realize this result.

Mistakes in the telling there may be, and for these I ask the charity of my readers. But the thing I want to say, and to say in such a way that no one can fail to understand it, is not a mistake; and that thing is this, that our religious lives ought to be full of joy, and peace, and comfort, and that, if we become better acquainted with God, they will be.

Chapter 2: What is His Name?

"And Moses said unto God, Behold, when I come unto the children of Israel, and shall say unto them, The God of your fathers hath sent me unto you; and they shall say to me, What is his name? What shall I say unto them?"

The vital question of all ages and of every human heart is here expressed, "What is His Name?"

The whole fate of humanity hangs on the answer to this question.

As we know, the condition of a country depends upon the character of its rulers. The state of an army depends upon the officers who command it. And the more absolute the government, the more is this necessarily the case.

We can see how it must be, therefore, that everything in a universe will depend upon the sort of creator and ruler who has brought that universe into existence, and that the whole welfare of the human beings who have been placed there is of necessity bound up with the character of their Creator. If the God who created us is a good God, then everything must of necessity be all right for us, since a good God cannot ordain any but good things. But if He is a bad God, or a careless God, or an unkind God, then we cannot be sure that anything is right, and can have no peace or comfort anywhere.

The true ground for peace and comfort is only to be found in the sort of God we have. Therefore, we need first of all to find out what is His name, or, in other words, what is His character—in short, what sort of a God He is.

In Bible language *name* always means character. Names are not given arbitrarily there, as with us, but are always given with reference to the character or work of the person named. Cruden in his Concordance says that the names of God signify that which He really is, and are used throughout the Bible to express His attributes, and His purposes, His glory, His grace, His mercy, and His love, His wisdom, and power, and goodness. A careful study of His names will make this plain.

When, therefore, the children of Israel asked, "What is his name?" they meant, "Who and what is this God of whom you speak? What is His character; what are His attributes; what does He do? In short, what sort of a being is He?"

The Psalmist says, "They that know thy name will put their trust in thee: for thou, Lord, hast not forsaken them that seek thee." And again he says, "The name of the Lord is a strong tower, the righteous runneth into it and is safe." "They that know thy name will put their trust in thee." They cannot do anything else, because in knowing His name they know His character and His nature, that He is a God whom it is safe to trust to the uttermost. And there can be no doubt that a large part of the unrest and discomfort in so many Christian hearts comes simply from the fact that they do not yet know His name.

"Some trust in chariots and some in horses: but we will remember the name of the Lord our God. They are brought down and are fallen, but we are risen and stand upright." In all that we read concerning Israel of old we find this constant refrain, that all they were and all they had depended upon the fact that their God was the Lord. "Blessed is the nation whose God is the Lord; and the people whom he hath chosen for his own inheritance." "O Lord, there is none like thee, neither is there any God beside thee, according to all that we have heard with our ears. And what one nation in the earth is like thy people: to make thee a name of greatness and terribleness, by driving out nations from before thy people, whom thou hast redeemed out of Egypt? For thy people Israel didst thou make thine own people forever, and thou, Lord, becamest their God." "Happy is that people that is in the Lord."

Blessed is that nation, happy is that people whose God is the Lord! All the blessing and happiness of Israel arose from the fact that their God was the Lord. Nothing else was of sufficient importance to be mentioned in the recapitulation of their advantages. The fact that their God was the Lord Jehovah was enough to account for every good thing they possessed.

The question of all questions for each one of us, therefore, is this one, "What is his name?" To the Israelites God Himself answered this question. And God said unto Moses, "I am that I am"; and He said, "Thus shalt thou say unto the children of Israel, *I Am* hath sent me unto you." And God said, moreover, unto Moses: "Thus shalt thou say unto the children of Israel, the Lord God of your fathers, the God of Abraham, the God of Isaac, and the God of Jacob hath sent me unto you; this is my name forever, and this is my memorial unto all generations."

In the Gospel of John Christ adopts this name of "I am" as His own. When the Jews were questioning Him as to His authority, He said unto them: "Verily, verily, I say unto you, before Abraham was I am." And in the Book of Revelation He again declares: "I am Alpha and Omega, the beginning and the ending, saith the Lord, which is, and which was, and which is to come, the Almighty."

These simple words, *I am*, express therefore eternity and unchangeableness of existence, which is the very first element necessary in a God who is to be depended upon. No dependence could be placed by any one of us upon a changeable God. He must be the same yesterday, today, and forever, if we are to have any peace or comfort.

But is this all His name implies, simply "I am"? I am what?—we ask. What does this "I am" include?

I believe it includes everything the human heart longs for and needs. This unfinished name of God seems to me like a blank check signed by a rich friend given to us to be filled in with whatever sum we may desire. The whole Bible tells us what it means.

Every attribute of God, every revelation of His character, every proof of His undying love, every declaration of His watchful care, every assertion of His purposes of tender mercy, every manifestation of His loving kindness—all are the filling out of this unfinished "I am."

God tells us through all the pages of His Book what He is. "I am," He says, "all that my people need": "I am their strength"; "I am their wisdom"; "I am their righteousness"; "I am their peace"; "I am their salvation"; "I am their life"; "I am their all in all."

This apparently unfinished name, therefore, is the most comforting name the heart of man could devise, because it allows us to add to it, without any limitation, whatever we feel the need of, and even "exceeding abundantly" beyond all that we can ask or think.

But if our hearts are full of our own wretched "I ams" we will have no ears to hear His glorious, soul-satisfying "I am." We say, "Alas, I am such a poor weak creature," or "I am so foolish," or "I am so good-for-nothing," or "I am so helpless"; and we give these pitiful "I ams" of ours as the reason of the wretchedness and discomfort of our religious lives, and even feel that we are very much to be pitied that things are so hard for us. While all the time we entirely ignore the blank check of God's magnificent "I am," which authorizes us to draw upon Him for an abundant supply for every need.

If you are an uncomfortable Christian, then the only thing to give you a thoroughly comfortable religious life is to know God. The Psalmist says that they that know God's name will put their trust in Him, and it is, I am convinced, impossible for anyone really to know Him and not to trust Him. A trustworthy person commands trust; not in the sense of ordering people to trust him, but by irresistibly winning their trust by his trustworthiness.

What our Lord declares is eternally true, "I, if I be lifted up, will draw all men unto me." When once you know Him, Christ is absolutely irresistible. You can no more help trusting Him than you can help breathing. And could the whole world but know Him as He is, the whole world, sinners and all, would fall at His feet in adoring worship. They simply could not help it. His surpassing loveliness would carry all before it.

How then can we become acquainted with God?

There are two things necessary: first, God must reveal Himself; and second, we must accept His revelation and believe what He reveals.

The Apostle John tells us that "no man hath seen God at any time," but "the only begotten Son which is in the bosom of the Father, he hath declared him." Christ, then, is the revelation of God. We have none of us seen God, and we never can see Him in this present stage of our existence, for we have not the faculties that would make it possible. But He has incarnated Himself in Christ, and we can see Christ, since He was a man like one of us.

A man, who should want to talk with ants, might stand over an anthill and harangue for a whole day, and not one word would reach the ears of the ants. They would run to and fro utterly unconscious of his presence. As far as we know, ants have no faculties by which they can receive human communications. But if a man could incarnate himself in the body of an ant, and could go about among them, living an ant's life and speaking the ants' language, he would make himself intelligible to them at once. Incarnation is always necessary when a higher form of life would communicate with a lower.

Christ revealed God by what He was, by what He did, and by what He said. From the cradle to the grave, every moment of His life was a revelation of God. We must go to Him then for our knowledge of God, and we must refuse to believe anything concerning God that is not revealed to us in Christ. All other revelations are partial, and therefore not wholly true. Only in Christ do we see God as He is; for Christ is declared to be the "express image" of God.

Just what God would have said and done under the circumstances, that Christ said and did. "I do nothing of myself," was His continual assertion. "I say nothing of myself; the Father that dwelleth in me he doeth the works"; "I and my Father are one"; "He that seeth me seeth my Father".

Words could not tell us more plainly than the Bible tells us that in order to know God we have only to look at Christ; we have only to "receive the testimony" of Christ.

Over and over we are assured that God and Christ are one. When the Jews came to Christ, as He was walking in the porch of Solomon's Temple, and asked Him to tell them plainly who He was, He answered, "I and my Father are one." And to His disciples, at His last supper with them, He said, in answer to their questions: "If ye had known me, ye should have known my Father also, and from henceforth ye know him and have seen him." But Philip could not understand this, and said, "Lord, show us the Father, and it sufficeth us." And then Jesus repeated His former statement even more strongly: "Have I been so long time with you, and yet hast thou not known me Philip? He that hath seen me hath seen the Father; and how sayest thou then, Show us the Father?"

Nothing is more emphatically stated in the New Testament than this fact, that we are to behold the "light of the knowledge of the glory of God in the face of Jesus Christ," and that we can behold it fully nowhere else.

If we would know then the length, and breadth, and height, and depth of what God meant when He gave to Moses that apparently unfinished name of "I am," we shall find it revealed in Christ. He and He alone is the translation of God. He and He alone is the image of the invisible God.

It is evident, therefore, that we must never accept any conception of God that is contrary to what we see in Christ, and must utterly reject any view of His character or of His acts, or any statement of His relations with us as human beings, no matter how strongly upheld, which is at variance with what Christ has revealed.

We are all aware that the Old Testament revelation of God seems sometimes to contradict the revelation in Christ, and the question arises as to which we are to receive as the truest. In view of the fact that God Himself tells us that in these last days He has spoken to us by His Son, who is the "brightness of his glory and the express image of his person," we may not dare reject Christ's testimony, but must look upon the Old Testament revelation, where it differs from the revelation in Christ, as partial and imperfect; and must accept as a true setting forth of God only that which we find in Christ. Christ alone tells us the true and genuine name of God. In His last wonderful prayer He says: "I have manifested thy name unto the men whom thou gavest me out of the world, and they have known that all things whatsoever thou hast given me are of thee, for I have given unto them the words which thou gavest me; and they have received them, and have known surely that I came out from thee, and they have believed that thou didst send me."

Could we ask for greater authority than this?

In the whole life of Christ nothing is plainer or more emphatic than the fact that He claimed continually to be a full and complete manifestation of God. "The words that I speak unto you," He says, "I speak not of myself; but the Father that dwelleth in me, he doeth the works." Over and over He asserts that He says only what the Father tells Him to say. "I speak to the world those things which I have heard of him." "I do nothing of myself, but as my Father hath taught me I speak these things."

The Apostle declares most emphatically that it "pleased the Father" that in Christ should "dwell all the fullness of the Godhead bodily." And although we may not understand all that this means theologically, we at least cannot fail to see that if we want to know God, we need only to become acquainted with Christ's ways and Christ's character in order to become acquainted with God's ways and God's character. "He that hath seen me," He says, "hath seen the Father." And again He declares that "neither knoweth any man the Father save the son, and he to whomsoever the Son will reveal him." This settles it beyond the possibility of cavil. We may, and we do, have all sorts of thoughts of God, we may conjecture this or imagine that, but we are wasting our energies in it all. We simply cannot know, no man can, except through the revelation of Christ.

We may know a good many things about Him, but that is very different from knowing Him Himself, as He really is in nature and character. Other witnesses have told us of His visible acts, but from these we get often very wrong impressions of His true character. No other witness but Christ can tell us of the real secrets of God's bosom, for of none other can it be said, as it is of Him, that "the only begotten Son who is in the bosom of the Father, he hath declared him." It will make all the difference between comfort and discomfort in our Christian lives, whether or not we believe this to be a fact. If we do believe it to be a fact, then the stern Judge and hard Taskmaster whom we have feared, even while we tried to follow Him, and whose service we have found so irksome and so full of discomfort, will disappear; and His place will be taken by the God of love who is revealed to us in "the face of Jesus Christ," the God who cares for us as He cares for the sparrows, and for the flowers of the field, and who tells us that He numbers even the hairs of our head.

No human being could be afraid of a God like this.

If we have been accustomed, therefore, to approach God with any mistrust of the kindness of His feelings toward us; if our religious life has been poisoned by fear; if unworthy thoughts of His character and will have filled our hearts with suspicions of His goodness; if we have pictured Him as an unjust deposit of a self-seeking tyrant; if, in short, we have imagined Him in any way other than that which has been revealed to us in "the face of Jesus Christ," we must go back in all simplicity of heart to the records of that lovely life, lived in human guise among men, and must bring our conceptions of God into perfect accord with the character and ways of Him who declares that He came to manifest the name of God to men.

In reply then to the question, "What is His name?" I have only this one thing to say, Ask Christ. We are told He was "God manifest in the flesh," and that whoever sees Him sees the God who sent Him; therefore it is perfectly plain that, if we want to know the name, we have only to read the manifestation. And this means simply that we must study the life, and words, and ways of Christ, and must say to ourselves, he that seeth Christ seeth God, and what Christ was on earth that God is in Heaven. All the darkness that enshrouds the character of God will vanish if we will but accept the light Christ has shed on the matter, and believe the "manifestation of His name" that Christ has given us, and will utterly refuse to believe anything else.

When Nicodemus came to Jesus by night to ask Him how the things He was saying could possibly be true, Jesus told him that, whether he understood them or not, they still were true, and said with greatest emphasis: "Verily, verily, I say unto thee, we speak that we do know, and testify that we have seen." No one who believes in Christ at all can doubt that He knew God; and no one can question whether or not we ought to receive His testimony. He has assured us over and over again that He knew what He was talking about, and that what He said was to be received as the absolute truth, because He had come down from Heaven, and therefore knew about heavenly things.

We none of us would dare openly to question the truth of this; and yet practically a great many of God's children utterly ignore Christ's testimony and choose instead to listen to the testimony of their own doubting hearts, which tells them it is impossible that God could be as loving in His care for us, or as tender toward our weakness and foolishness, or as ready to forgive our sins, as Christ has revealed Him to be. And yet I must repeat again and again, at the risk of being accused of useless repetition, what so few people seem to realize, that if there is one thing taught in the Bible more plainly than any other, it is that the name, or, in other words, the character of His Father which Christ gave, must be His real name and character. He declares of Himself over and over that He was a living manifestation of the Father; and in all He said and did He assures us that He was simply saying and doing that which the Father would have said and done had he acted directly out of Heaven, and from off His heavenly throne.

In the face of such unqualified assertions as these out of the lips of our Lord Himself, it becomes, not only our privilege, but our bounded duty to cast out of our conception of God every element that could in any way conflict with the blessed life and character and teaching of Christ. If we would know the real name of God, we must accept the name Christ has revealed to us, and must listen to no other.

Whatever characteristics then we see in Christ, these are the filling out of the "I am" of God. As we look at the life of Christ and listen to His words, we can hear God saying, "I am rest for the weary; I am peace for the storm-tossed; I am strength for the strengthless; I am wisdom for the foolish; I am righteousness for the sinful; I am all that the neediest soul on earth can want; I am exceeding abundantly, beyond all you can ask or think, or blessing, and help, and care."

But here the doubter may say, "Ah yes, this is no doubt all true, but how can I get hold of it? I am such a poor, unworthy creature that I dare not believe such a fullness of grace can belong to me."

How can you get hold of it, you ask. You cannot get hold of it at all, but you can let it get hold of you. It is a piece of magnificent good news declared to you in the Bible; and you only need do with it exactly what you do when any earthly good news is told you by a reliable earthly source. If the speaker is trustworthy, you believe what he says, and act in accordance. And you must do the same here. If Christ is trustworthy when He tells you that He is the manifestation of God, you must believe what He says, and act accordingly.

You must take your stand on His trustworthiness. You must say to yourself, and to your friends if need be, "I am going to believe what Christ says about God. No matter what the seemings may be, nor what my own thoughts and feelings are, nor what anybody else may say, I know that what Christ says about God must be true, for He knew, and nobody else does, and I am going to believe Him right straight through, come what may. He says that He was one with God, so all that He was God is, and I will never be frightened of God any more. I will never again let myself think of Him as a stern Lawgiver who is angry with me because of my sins, nor as a hard Taskmaster who demands from me impossible tasks, nor as a far-off unapproachable Deity, who is wrapped up in His own glory, and is indifferent to my sorrows and my fears. All such ideas of God have become impossible, now that I know that Christ was the true manifestation of God."

If we will take our stand on this one fact, that Christ and God are one, with an intelligent comprehension of what it involves, and will refuse definitely and unwaveringly to cherish any thought of God that is at variance with what Christ has revealed, life will be transformed for us.

We may often have to set our faces like a flint to hold steadfastly here; for our old doubts and fears will be sure to come back and demand admittance; but we must turn our backs on them resolutely, and must declare that now at last we know the name, or in other words, the character of our God, and know that such things would be impossible to Him; and that therefore we simply refuse point-blank to listen for a moment to any such libels on His character or His ways.

It is unthinkable to suppose that when God told Moses His name was "I am," He could have meant to say, "I am a stern Lawgiver," or "I am a hard Taskmaster," or "I am a God who is wrapped up in my own glory, and am indifferent to the sorrows or the fears of my people." If we should try to fill in the blank of His "I am" with such things as these, all the Christians the world over would be horrified. But do not the doubts and fears of some of these very Christians say exactly these things in secret every day of their lives?

May God grant that what we shall learn in our consideration of the names of God may make all such doubts and fears impossible to us from this time forth and forevermore.

> *Jesus is God! Oh, could I now*
> *But compass land and sea,*
> *To teach and tell this single truth,*
> *How happy I should be!*
> *Oh, had I but an angel's voice,*
> *I would proclaim so loud—*
> *Jesus, the good, the beautiful,*
> *Is the image of our God!*

Chapter 3: The God Of All Comfort

"Blessed be God, even the Father of our Lord Jesus Christ, the
Father of mercies and the God of all comfort; who comforteth us in
all our tribulations, that we may be able to comfort them which are in
any trouble, by the comfort wherewith we ourselves
are comforted of God."

Among all the names that reveal God, this, the "God of all comfort," seems to me one of the loveliest and the most absolutely comforting. The words *all comfort* admit of no limitation and no deductions; and one would suppose that, however full of discomforts the outward life of the followers of such a God might be, their inward religious life must necessarily be always and under all circumstances a comfortable life. But, as a fact, it often seems as if exactly the opposite were the case, and the religious lives of large numbers of the children of God are full, not of comfort, but of the utmost discomfort. This discomfort arises from anxiety as to their relationship to God, and doubts as to His love. They torment themselves with the thought that they are too good-for-nothing to be worthy of His care, and they suspect Him of being indifferent to their trials and of forsaking them in times of need. They are anxious and troubled about everything in their religious life, about their disposition and feelings, their indifference to the Bible, their want of fervency in prayer, their coldness of heart. They are tormented with unavailing regrets over their past, and with devouring anxieties for their future. They feel unworthy to enter God's presence, and dare not believe that they belong to Him. They can be happy and comfortable with their earthly friends, but they cannot be happy or comfortable with God. And although He declares Himself to be the God of all comfort, they continually complain that they cannot find comfort anywhere; and their sorrowful looks and the doleful tones of their voice show that they are speaking the truth.

Such Christians, although they profess to be the followers of the God of all comfort, spread gloom and discomfort around them wherever they go; and it is out of the question for them to hope that they can induce anyone else to believe that this beautiful name, by which He has announced Himself, is anything more than a pious phrase, which in reality means nothing at all. And the manifestly uncomfortable religious lives of so many Christians is, I am very much afraid, responsible for a large part of the unbelief of the world.

The Apostle says that we are to be living epistles known and read of all men; and the question as to what men read in us is of far more vital importance to the spread of Christ's kingdom than we half the time realize. It is not what we say that tells, but what we are. It is easy enough to say a great many beautiful things about God being the God of all comfort; but unless we know what it is to be really and truly comforted ourselves, we might as well talk to the winds. People must read in our lives what they hear in our words, or all our preaching is worse than useless. It would be well for us to ask ourselves what they are reading in us. Is it comfort or discomfort that voices itself in our daily walk and life?

But at this point I may be asked what I mean by the comfort God gives. Is it a sort of pious grace, that may perhaps fit us for Heaven, but that is somehow unfit to bear the brunt of our everyday life with its trials and its pains? Or is it an honest and genuine comfort, as we understand comfort, that enfolds life's trials and pains in an all embracing peace?

With all my heart I believe it is the latter.

Comfort, whether human or divine, is pure and simple comfort, and is nothing else. We none of us care for pious phrases, we want realities; and the reality of being comforted and comfortable seems to me almost more delightful than any other thing in life. We all know what it is. When as little children we have cuddled up into our mother's lap after a fall or a misfortune, and have felt her dear arms around us, and her soft kisses on our hair, we have had comfort. When, as grown-up people, after a hard day's work, we have put on our slippers and seated ourselves by the fire, in an easy chair with a book, we have had comfort. When, after a painful illness, we have begun to recover, and have been able to stretch our limbs and open our eyes without pain, we have had comfort. When someone whom we dearly love has been ill almost unto death, and has been restored to us in health again, we have had comfort. A thousand times in our lives probably, have we said, with a sigh of relief, as a toil over or burdens laid down, "Well, this *is* comfortable," and in that word comfortable there has been comprised more a rest, and relief, and satisfaction, and pleasure, than any other word in the English language could possibly be made to express. We cannot fail, therefore, to understand the meaning of this name of God, the "God of all comfort."

But alas, we have failed to believe it. It has seemed to us too good to be true. The joy and delight of it, if it were really a fact, have been more than our poor suspicious natures could take in. We may venture to hope sometimes that little scraps of comfort may be vouchsafed to us; but we have run away frightened at the thought of the "all comfort" that is ours in the salvation of the Lord Jesus Christ.

And yet what more could He have said about it than He has said: "As one whom his mother comforteth, so will I comfort you; and ye shall be comforted." Notice the "as" and "so" in this passage: "As one whom his mother comforteth, so will I comfort you." It is real comforting that is meant here; the sort of comforting that a child feels when it is "dandled on its mother's knees, and borne on her sides"; and yet how many of us have really believed that God's comforting is actually as tender and true as a mother's comforting, or even half or quarter so real. Instead of thinking of ourselves as being "dandled" on His knees, and hugged to His heart, as mothers hug, have we not rather been inclined to look upon Him as a stern, unbending Judge, holding us at a distance, and demanding our respectful homage, and critical of our slightest faults? Is it any wonder that our religion, instead of making us comfortable, has made us thoroughly uncomfortable? Who could help being uncomfortable in the presence of such a Judge?

But I rejoice to say that that stern Judge is not there. He does not exist. The God who does exist is a God who is like a mother, a God who says to us as plainly as words can say it, "As one whom his mother comforteth, so will I comfort you."

Over and over again He declares this. "I, even I, am he that comforteth you," He says to the poor, frightened children of Israel. And then He reproaches them with not being comforted. "Why," He says, "should you let anything make you afraid when here is the Lord, your Maker, ready and longing to comfort you. You have feared continually every day the 'fury of the oppressor,' and have forgotten me who have stretched forth the heavens and laid the foundations of the earth? Where is the fury of the oppressor when I am by?"

The God who exists is the God and the Father of our Lord Jesus Christ, the God who so loved the world that He sent His Son, not to judge the world, but to save it. He is the God who "anointed" the Lord Jesus Christ to bind up the brokenhearted, and to proclaim liberty to the captives, and the opening of the prison to them that are bound, and to comfort all that mourn. Please notice that *all*. Not a few select ones only, but all. Every captive of sin, every prisoner in infirmity, every mourning heart throughout the whole world must be included in this "all." It would not be "all" if there should be a single one left out, no matter how insignificant, or unworthy, or even how feeble-minded that one might be. I have always been thankful that the feeble-minded are especially mentioned by Paul in his exhortations to the Thessalonian Christians, when he is urging them to comfort one another. In effect he says, Do not scold the feeble-minded, but comfort them. The very ones who need comfort most are the ones that our God, who is like a mother, wants to comfort—not the strong-minded ones, but the feeble-minded.

For this is the glory of a religion of love. And this is the glory of the religion of the Lord Jesus Christ. He was anointed to comfort "all that mourn." The "God of all comfort" sent His Son to be the comforter of a mourning world. And all through His life on earth He fulfilled His divine mission. When His disciples asked Him to call down fire from Heaven to consume some people who refused to receive Him, He turned and rebuked them, and said: "Ye know not what manner of spirit ye are of. For the Son of man is not come to destroy men's lives but to save them." He received sinners and ate with them. He welcomed Mary Magdalene when all men turned from her. He refused even to condemn the woman who was taken in the very act of sin, but said to the Scribes and Pharisees who had brought her before Him, "He that is without sin among you, let him first cast a stone at her"; and when, convicted by their own consciences, they all went out one by one without condemning her, He said to her, "Neither do I condemn thee: go, and sin no more." Always and everywhere He was on the side of sinners. That was what He was for. He came to save sinners. He had no other mission.

Two little girls were talking about God, and one said, "I know God does not love me. He could not care for such a teeny, tiny little girl as I am."

"Dear me, sis," said the other little girl, "don't you know that that is just what God is for—to take care of teeny, tiny little girls who can't take care of themselves, just like us?"

"Is He?" said the first little girl. "I did not know that. Then I don't need to worry any more, do I?"

If any troubled doubting heart, any heart that is fearing continually every day some form or other of evil should read these lines, let me tell you again in trumpet tones that this is just what the Lord Jesus Christ is for—to care for and comfort all who mourn. "All," remember, every single one, even you yourself, for it would not be "all" if you were left out. You may be so cast down that you can hardly lift up your head, but the Apostle tells us that He is the "God that comforteth those that are cast down"; the comforting of Christ. All who mourn, all who are cast down—I love to think of such a mission of comfort in a world of mourning like ours; and I long to see every cast down and sorrowing heart comforted with this comforting of God.

And our Comforter is not far off in Heaven where we cannot find Him. He is close at hand. He abides with us. When Christ was going away from this earth, He told His disciples that He would not leave them comfortless, but would send "another Comforter" who would abide with them forever. This Comforter, He said, would teach them all things, and would bring all things to their remembrance. And then He declared, as though it were the necessary result of the coming of this divine Comforter: "Peace I leave with you, my peace I give unto you; not as the world giveth, give I unto you. Let not your heart [therefore] be troubled, neither let it be afraid." Oh, how can we, in the face of these tender and loving words, go about with troubled and frightened hearts.

"Comforter"—what a word of bliss, if we only could realize it. Let us repeat it over and over to ourselves, until its meaning sinks into the very depths of our being. And an "abiding" Comforter, too, not one who comes and goes, and is never on hand when most needed, but one who is always present, and always ready to give us "joy for mourning, and the garment of praise for the spirit of heaviness."

The very words *abiding Comforter* are an amazing revelation. Try to comprehend them. If we can have a human comforter to stay with us for only a few days when we are in trouble, we think ourselves fortunate; but here is a divine Comforter who is always staying with us, and whose power to comfort is infinite. Never, never ought we for a single minute to be without comfort; never for a single minute ought we to be uncomfortable.

I have often wondered whether those early disciples realized at all what this glorious legacy of a Comforter meant. I am very sure the majority of the disciples of Christ now do not. If they did, there could not possibly be so many uncomfortable Christians about.

But you may ask whether this divine Comforter does not sometimes reprove us for our sins, and whether we can get any comfort out of this. In my opinion this is exactly one of the places where the comfort comes in. For what sort of creatures should we be if we had no divine Teacher always at hand to show us our faults and awaken in us a desire to get rid of them?

If I am walking along the street with a very disfiguring hole in the back of my dress, of which I am in ignorance, it is certainly a very great comfort to me to have a kind friend who will tell me of it. And similarly it is indeed a comfort to know that there is always abiding with me a divine, all-seeing Comforter, who will reprove me for all my faults, and will not let me go on in a fatal unconsciousness of them. Emerson says it is far more to a man's interest that he should see his own faults than that anyone else should see them, and a moment's thought will convince us that this is true, and will make us thankful for the Comforter who reveals them to us.

I remember vividly the comfort it used to be to me, when I was young, to have a sister who always knew what was the right and proper thing to do, and who, when we went out together, always kept me in order. I never felt any anxiety or responsibility about myself if she was by, for I knew she would keep a strict watch over me, and nudge me or whisper to me if I was making any mistakes. I was always made comfortable, and not uncomfortable, by her presence. But when it chanced that I went anywhere alone, then I would indeed feel uncomfortable, for then there was no one near to keep me straight.

The declaration is that He "comforts all our waste places"; and He does this by revealing them to us, and at the same time showing us how He can make our "wildernesses like Eden," and our "deserts like the garden of the Lord."

You may object, perhaps, because you are not worthy of His comforts. I do not suppose you are. No one ever is. But you need His comforting, and because you are not worthy you need it all the more. Christ came into the world to save sinners, not good people, and your unworthiness is your greatest claim for His salvation.

In the same passage in Isaiah in which He tells us that He has seen our ways and was "wroth" with us, He assures us that He will heal us and restore comforts to us. It is just because He is wroth with us (wroth in the sense in which love is always wroth with any fault in those it loves), that therefore He "restores comforts" to us. And He does it by revealing our sin and healing it.

The avenue to the comfortings of the divine Comforter lies through the need of comfort. And this explains to me better than anything else the reason why the Lord so often allows sorrow and trial to be our portion. "Therefore, behold, I will allure her, and bring her into the wilderness, and speak comfortably unto her." We find ourselves, it may be, in a "wilderness" of disappointment and of suffering, and we wonder why the God who loves us should have allowed it. But he knows that it is only in that very wilderness that we can hear and receive the "comfortable words" He has to pour out upon us. We must feel the need of comfort before we can listen to the words of comfort. And God knows that it is infinitely better and happier for us to need His comforts and receive them, than ever it could be not to need them and so be without them. The consolations of God mean the substituting of a far higher and better thing for what we lose to get them. The things we lose are earthly things, those He substitutes are heavenly. And who of us but would thankfully be "allured" by our God into any earthly wilderness, if only there we might find the unspeakable joys of union with Himself. Paul could say he "counted all things but loss" if he might but "win Christ"; and, if we have even the faintest glimpse of what winning Christ means, we will say so too.

But strangely enough, while it is easy for us when we are happy and do not need comforting, to believe that our God is the "God of all comfort," but as soon as we are in trouble and need it, it seems impossible to believe that there can be any comfort for us anywhere. It would almost seem as if, in our reading of the Bible, we had reversed its meaning, and made it say, not "Blessed are they that mourn, for they shall be comforted," but "Blessed are they that rejoice, for they, and they only, shall be comforted." It is very strange how often in our secret hearts we almost unconsciously alter the Bible words a little, and so make the meaning exactly opposite to what it actually is; or else we put in so many "ifs" and "buts" as to take the whole point out of what is said. Take for instance, those beautiful words, "God that comforteth those that are cast down," and ask ourselves whether we have never been tempted to make it read in our secret hearts, "God who forsaketh those who are cast down," or, "God who overlooks those who are cast down," or, "God who will comfort those who are cast down if they show themselves worthy of comfort"; and whether, consequently, instead of being comforted, we have not been plunged into misery and despair.

The Psalmist tells us that God will "comfort us on every side," and what an all-embracing bit of comfort this is. "On every side," no aching spot to be left uncomforted. And yet, in times of special trial, how many Christians secretly read this as though it said, "God will comfort us on every side except just the side where our trials lie; on that side there is no comfort anywhere." But God says every side, and it is only unbelief on our part that leads us to make an exception of our special side.

It is with too many, alas, just as it was with Israel of old. On one side God said to Zion: "Sing, O heavens, and be joyful, O earth, and break forth into singing, O mountains; for the Lord hath comforted his people, and will have mercy upon his afflicted"; and on the other side Zion said, "The Lord hath forsaken me, and my Lord hath forgotten me." And then God's answer came in those wonderful words, full forever of comfort enough to meet the needs of all the sorrows of all humanity: "Forget thee! Can a mother forget? Yea, perhaps a mother may forget, but I cannot. I have even graven thee upon the palms of my hands, so that it is impossible for me to forget thee! Be comforted, then, and sing for you."

But you may ask how you are to get hold of this divine comfort. My answer is that you must take it. God's comfort is being continually and abundantly given, but unless you will accept it you cannot have it.

Divine comfort does not come to us in any mysterious or arbitrary way. It comes as the result of a divine method. The indwelling Comforter "brings to our remembrance" comforting things concerning our Lord, and, if we believe them, we are comforted by them. A text is brought to our remembrance, perhaps, or the verse of a hymn, or some thought concerning the love of Christ and His tender care for us. If we receive the suggestion in simple faith, we cannot help being comforted. But if we refuse to listen to the voice of our Comforter, and insist instead on listening to the voice of discouragement or despair, no comfort can by any possibility reach our souls.

It is very possible for even a mother to lavish in vain all her stores of motherly comfort on a weeping child. The child sits up stiff and sullen, and "refuses to be comforted." All her comforting words fall on unbelieving ears. For to be comforted by comforting words it is absolutely necessary for us to believe these words. God has spoken "comforting words" enough, one would think, to comfort a whole universe, and yet we see all around us unhappy Christians, and worried Christians, and gloomy Christians, into whose comfortless hearts not one of these comforting words seems to be allowed to enter. In fact, a great many Christians actually think it is wrong to be comforted. They feel too unworthy. And if any rays of comfort steal into their hearts, they sternly shut them out; and like Rachel and Jacob, and the Psalmist, their souls "refuse to be comforted."

The Apostle tells us that whatsoever things are written in the Scriptures are for our learning, in order that we "through patience and comfort of the Scriptures may have hope." But if we are to be comforted by the Scriptures, we must first believe them. Nothing that God has said can possibly comfort a person who does not believe it to be really true. When the captain of a vessel tells us that his vessel is safe, we must first believe him to be telling the truth, before we can feel comfortable on board that vessel. When the conductor on a railway tells us we are on the right train, before we can settle down comfortably in our seats, we must trust his word. This is all so self-evident that it might seem folly to call attention to it. But in religious matters it often happens that the self-evident truths are the very ones most easily overlooked; and I have actually known people who insisted on realizing God's comfort while still doubting His words of comfort; and who even thought they could not believe His comforting words at all, until they had first felt the comfort in their own souls! As well might the passenger on the railway insist on having a feeling of comfortable assurance that he is on the right train, before he could make up his mind to believe the word of the conductor. Always and in everything comfort must follow faith, and can never precede it.

In this matter of comfort it is exactly as it is in every other experience in the religious life. God says, "Believe, and then you can feel." We say, "Feel, and then we can believe." God's order is not arbitrary, it exists in the very nature of things; and in all earthly matters we recognize this, and are never so foolish as to expect to feel we have anything until we first believe that it is in our possession. I could not possibly feel glad that I had a fortune in the bank, unless I knew that it was really there. But in spiritual things we reverse God's order (which is the order of nature as well), and refuse to believe that we possess anything until we first feel as if we had it.

Let me illustrate. We are, let us suppose, overwhelmed with cares and anxieties. It often happens in this world. To comfort us in these circumstances the Lord assures us that we need not be anxious about anything, but may commit all our cares to Him, for He careth for us. We are all familiar with the passages where He tells us to "behold the fowls of the air," and to "consider the lilies of the field" and assures us that we are of much more value than they, and that, if He cares for them, He will much more care for us. One would think there was comfort enough here for every care or sorrow all the wide world over. To have God assume our cares and our burdens, and carry them for us; the Almighty God, the Creator of Heaven and earth, who can control everything, and foresee everything, and consequently can manage everything in the very best possible way, to have Him declare that He will undertake for us; what could possibly be a greater comfort? And yet how few people are really comforted by it. Why is this? Simply and only because they do not believe it. They are waiting to have an inward feeling that His words are true, before they will believe them. They look upon them as beautiful things for Him to say, and they wish they could believe them, but they do not think they can be true in their own special case, unless they can have an inward feeling that they are; and if they should speak out honestly, they would confess that, since they have no such inward feeling, they do not believe His words apply to them; and as a consequence they do not in the least expect Him actually to care for their affairs at all. "Oh, if I could only feel it was all true," we say; and God says, "Oh, if you would only believe it is all true!"

It is pure and simple unbelief that is at the bottom of all our lack of comfort, and absolutely nothing else. God comforts us on every side, but we simply do not believe His words of comfort.

The remedy for this is plain. If we want to be comforted, we must make up our minds to believe every single solitary word of comfort God has ever spoken; and we must refuse utterly to listen to any words of discomfort spoken by our own hearts, or by our circumstances. We must set our faces like a flint to believe, under each and every sorrow and trial, in the divine Comforter, and to accept and rejoice in His all-embracing comfort. I say, "set our faces like a flint," because, when everything around us seems out of sorts, it is not always easy to believe God's words of comfort. We must put our wills into this matter of being comforted, just as we have to put our wills into all other matters in our spiritual life. We must choose to be comforted.

It may seem impossible, when things look all wrong and uncared for, to believe that God really can be caring for us as a mother cares for her children; and, although we know perfectly well that He says He does care for us in just this tender and loving way, yet we say, "Oh, if I could only believe that, of course I should be comforted." Now here is just where our wills must come in. We *must* believe it. We must say to ourselves, "God says it, and it is true, and I am going to believe it, no matter how it looks." And then we must never suffer ourselves to doubt or question it again.

I do not hesitate to say that whoever will adopt this plan will come, sooner or later, into a state of abounding comfort.

The Psalmist says, "In the multitude of my thoughts within me thy comforts delight my soul." But I am afraid that among the multitude of our thoughts within us there are far too often many more thoughts of our own discomforts than of God's comforts. We must think of His comforts if we are to be comforted by them. It might be a good exercise of soul for some of us to analyze our thoughts for a few days, and see how many thoughts we actually do give to God's comforts, compared with the number we give to our own discomforts. I think the result would amaze us!

One word I must add in conclusion. If any of my readers are preachers of the Gospel of our Lord Jesus Christ, I would like to ask them what they are commissioned to preach.

The true commission in my opinion is to be found in Isaiah 40:1,2: "Comfort ye, comfort ye my people, saith your God. Speak ye comfortably to Jerusalem, and cry unto her, that her warfare is accomplished, that her iniquity is pardoned; for she hath received of the Lord's hand double for all her sins." "Comfort ye my people" is the divine command; do not scold them. If it is the Gospel you feel called to preach, then see to it that you do really preach Christ's Gospel and not man's. Christ comforts, man scolds. Christ's Gospel is always good news, and never bad news. Man's gospel is generally a mixture of a little good news and a great deal of bad news; and even where it tries to be good news, it is so hampered with "ifs" and "buts," and with all sorts of man-made conditions, that it utterly fails to bring any lasting joy or comfort.

The only Gospel that, to my thinking, can rightly be called the Gospel is that one proclaimed by the angel to the frightened shepherds, who were in the field keeping watch over their flocks by night: "Fear not," said the angel, "for behold I bring you good tidings of great joy, which shall be to all people. For unto you is born this day in the city of David, a Savior which is Christ the Lord."

Never were more comfortable words preached to any congregation. And if only all the preachers in all the pulpits would speak the same comfortable words to the people; and if all the congregations, who hear these words, would believe them, and would take the comfort of them, there would be no more uncomfortable Christians left anywhere. And over the whole land would be fulfilled the Apostle's prayer for the Thessalonians: "Now our Lord Jesus Christ himself, and God, even our Father, which hath loved us and hath given us everlasting consolation and good hope through grace, comfort your hearts, and stablish you in every good word and work."

Chapter 4: The Lord Our Shepherd

"The Lord is my shepherd, I shall not want."

Perhaps no aspect in which the Lord reveals Himself to us is fuller of genuine comfort than the aspect set forth in the Twenty-third Psalm, and in its corresponding passage in the tenth chapter of John.

The Psalmist tells me that the Lord is my Shepherd, and the Lord Himself declares that He is the *good* Shepherd. Can we conceive of anything more comforting?

It is a very wonderful thing that the highest and grandest truths of the religion of the Lord Jesus Christ are so often shut up in the simplest and commonest texts in the Bible. Those texts with which we have been familiar from our childhood, which we learned in the nursery at our mother's knee, which were used by those who loved us to explain in the simplest possible way the love of our heavenly Father, and the reasons for our trusting Him—these very texts, I have discovered, contain in their simple statements the whole story.

I feel, therefore, that what we all need is just to get back into the nursery again, and take up our childish verses once more, and, while reading them with the intelligence of our grown-up years, to believe them with all our old childish faith.

Let me carry you back then with me, my dear reader, to the children's psalm, that one which is so universally taught to the little ones in the nursery and in the infant school. Do we not each one of us remember the Twenty-third Psalm, as long as we can remember anything, and can we not recall even now something of the joy and pride of our childish hearts when first we were able to repeat it without mistake? Since then we have always known it, and at this moment its words, perhaps, sound so old and familiar to some of you, that you cannot see what meaning they can convey.

But in truth they tell us the whole story of our religion in words of such wondrous depth of meaning that I very much doubt whether it has ever yet entered into the heart of any mortal man to conceive of the things they reveal.

Repeat these familiar words over to yourselves afresh: "The Lord is my shepherd, I shall not want."

Who is it that is your shepherd?

The Lord! Oh, my friends, what a wonderful announcement! The Lord God of Heaven and earth, the Almighty Creator of all things, He who holds the universe in His hand as though it were a very little thing, He is your Shepherd, and has charged Himself with the care and keeping of you, as a shepherd is charged with the care and keeping of his sheep.

If your hearts will only take in this thought, I can promise you that your religion will from henceforth be full of the profoundest comfort, and all your old uncomfortable religion will drop off forever, as the mist disappears in the blaze of the summer sun.

I had a vivid experience of this at one time in my Christian life. The Twenty-third Psalm had, of course, always been familiar to me from my nursery days, but it had never seemed to have any special meaning. Then came a critical moment in my life when I was sadly in need of comfort, but could see none anywhere. I could not at the moment lay my hands on my Bible, and I cast about in my mind for some passage of Scripture that would help me. Immediately there flashed into my mind the words, "The Lord is my shepherd, I shall not want." At first I turned from it almost with scorn. "Such a common text as that," I said to myself, "is not likely to do me any good"; and I tried hard to think of a more *recherché[1]* one, but none would come; and at last it almost seemed as if there were no other text in the whole Bible. And finally I was reduced to saying "Well, if I cannot think of any other text, I must try to get what little good I can out of this one," and I began to repeat to myself over and over, "The Lord is my shepherd, I shall not want." Suddenly, as I did so, the words were divinely illuminated, and there poured out upon me such floods of comfort that I felt as if I could never have a trouble again.

The moment I could get hold of a Bible I turned over its leaves with eagerness to see whether it could possibly be true that such untold treasures of comfort were really and actually mine, and whether I might dare to let out my heart into the full enjoyment of them. And I did what I have often found great profit in doing, I built up a pyramid of declarations and promises concerning the Lord being our Shepherd that, once built, presented an immovable and indestructible front to all the winds and storms of doubt or trial that could assail it. And I became convinced, beyond a shadow of doubt, that the Lord really was my Shepherd, and that in giving Himself this name He assumed the duties belonging to the name, and really would be, what He declares Himself to be, a "good shepherd who giveth his life for his sheep."

He Himself draws the contrast between a good shepherd and a bad shepherd, when He follows up His announcement "I am the good shepherd," with the words, "But he that is an hireling and not the shepherd, whose own the sheep are not, seeth the wolf coming and leaveth the sheep and fleeth; and the wolf catcheth them and scattereth the sheep." And through the mouth of His prophets the Lord pours down a scathing condemnation upon all such faithless shepherds. "And the Lord saith unto me," says the prophet Zechariah, "take unto thee yet the instruments of a foolish shepherd....Woe to the idle shepherd that leaveth the flock! The sword shall be upon his arm, and upon his right eye; his arm shall be clean dried up, and his right eye shall be utterly darkened."

Again the prophet Ezekiel says: "Thus saith the Lord God unto the shepherds: Woe be to the shepherds of Israel that do feed themselves! Should not the shepherds feed the flocks?... The diseased have ye not strengthened, neither have ye healed that which was sick, neither have ye bound up that which was broken, neither have ye brought back that which was driven away, neither have ye sought that which was lost; but with force and with cruelty have ye ruled them... Therefore, O ye shepherds, hear the word of the Lord:

[1] Rare.

Thus saith the Lord God, Behold I am against the shepherds, and I will require my flock at their hand, and cause them to cease from feeding the flock."

Surely one would think that no Christian could ever accuse our divine Shepherd of being as faithless and unkind as those He thus condemns. And yet, if the secrets of some Christian hearts should be revealed, I fear that it would be found that, although they do not put it into words, and perhaps hardly know themselves that such are their feelings about Him, yet at the bottom they do really look upon Him as a faithless Shepherd.

What else can it mean when Christians complain that the Lord has forsaken them; that they cry to Him for spiritual food and He does not hear; that they are beset by enemies on every side and He does not deliver them; that when their souls find themselves in dark places He does not come to their rescue; that when they are weak He does not strengthen them; and when they are spiritually sick He does not heal them?

What are all these doubts and discouragements but secret accusations against our good Shepherds of the very things which He Himself so scathingly condemns?

A dear Christian, who had just discovered what it meant to have known that that was what He was called, but it meant nothing to me; and I believe I read the Twenty-third Psalm as though it was written, 'The Lord is the sheep, and I am the shepherd, and, if I do not keep a tight hold on Him, He will run away.' When dark days came I never for a moment thought that He would stick by me, and when my soul was starving and cried out for food, I never dreamed He would feed me. I see now that I never looked upon Him as a faithful Shepherd at all. But now all is different. I myself am not one bit better or stronger, but I have discovered that I have a good Shepherd, and that is all I need. I see now that it really is true that the Lord is my Shepherd, and that I shall not want."

Dear fellow Christian, I pray you to look this matter fairly in the face. Are you like the Christian I have quoted above? You have said, I know, hundreds of times, "The Lord is my shepherd," but have you ever really believed it to be an actual fact? Have you felt safe and happy and free from care, as a sheep must feel when under the care of a good shepherd, or have you felt yourself to be like a poor forlorn sheep without a shepherd, or with an unfaithful, inefficient shepherd, who does not supply your needs, and who leaves you in times of danger and darkness?

I beg of you to answer this question honestly in your own soul. Have you had a comfortable religious life or an uncomfortable one? If the latter has been your condition, how can you reconcile it with the statement that the Lord is your Shepherd, and therefore you shall not want? You say He is your Shepherd, and yet you complain that you do want. Who has made the mistake? You or the Lord?

But here, perhaps, you will meet me with the words, "Oh, no, I do not blame the Lord, but I am so weak and so foolish, and so ignorant, that I am not worthy of His care." But do you not know that sheep are always weak, and helpless, and silly; and that the very reason they are compelled to have a shepherd to care for them is just because they are so unable to take care of themselves? Their welfare and their safety, therefore, do not in the least depend upon their own strength, nor upon their own wisdom, nor upon anything in themselves, but wholly and entirely upon the care of their shepherd. And, if you are a sheep, your self also must depend altogether upon your Shepherd, and not at all upon yourself.

Let us imagine two flocks of sheep meeting at the end of the winter to compare their experiences—one flock fat and strong and in good condition, and the other poor and lean and diseased. Will the healthy flock boast of themselves, and say, "See what splendid care we have taken of ourselves, what good, strong, wise sheep we must be?" Surely not. Their boasting would all be about their shepherd. "See what a good shepherd we have had," they would say, "and how he has cared for us. Through all the storms of the winter he has protected us, and has defended us from every wild beast, and has always provided us with the best of food."

Or, on the other hand, would the poor, wretched, diseased sheep blame themselves and say, "Alas, what wicked sheep we must be, to be in such a poor condition!" No, they too would speak only of their shepherd, but how different would be their story! "Alas," they would say, "our shepherd was very different from yours! He fed himself, but he did not feed us. He did not strengthen us when we were weak, nor heal us when we were sick, nor bind us up when we were broken nor look for us when we were lost. It is true he stayed by us in clear and pleasant weather, when no enemies were nigh, but in times of danger or of storm, he forsook us and fled. Oh, that we had had a good shepherd like yours!"

We all understand this responsibility of the shepherd in the case of sheep; but the moment we transfer the figure to our religion, we at once shift all the responsibility off the Shepherd's shoulders, and lay it upon the sheep; and demand of the poor human sheep the wisdom, and care, and power to provide, that can only belong to the divine Shepherd and be met by Him; and of course the poor human sheep fail, and their religious lives become thoroughly uncomfortable, and even sometimes most miserable.

I freely confess there is a difference between sheep and ourselves in this, that they have neither the intelligence nor the power to withdraw themselves from the care of their shepherd, while we have. We cannot imagine one of them saying, "Oh, yes, we have a good shepherd who says he will take care of us, but then we do not feel worthy of his care, and therefore we are afraid to trust him. He says he has provided for us green pastures and a safe and comfortable fold; but we are such poor good-for-nothing creatures that we have not dared to enter his fold, nor feed in this pastures. We have felt it would be presumption; and, in our humility, we have been trying to do the best we could for ourselves. The strong, healthy sheep may trust themselves to the shepherd's care, but not such miserable half-starved sheep as we are. It is true we have had a very hard time of it, and are in a sad and forlorn condition; but then we are such poor unworthy creatures that we must expect this, and must try to be resigned to it."

Silly as sheep are, we know well no sheep could be so silly as to talk in this way. And here comes the difference. We are so much wiser than sheep, in our own estimation, that we think the sort of trust sheep exercise will not do for us; and, in our superior intelligence, we presume to take matters into our own hands, and so shut ourselves out from the Shepherd's care.

Now the fact is simply this, if any sheep in the flock of Christ find themselves in a poor condition, there are only two explanations possible. Either the Lord is not a good Shepherd and does not care for His sheep, or else, His sheep have not believed in His care, and have been afraid or ashamed to trust themselves to it. I know not one of you will dare to say, or even to think, that the Lord can be anything but a good Shepherd, if He is a Shepherd at all. The fault, therefore, must lie just here; either you have not believed He was your Shepherd at all, or else, believing it, you have refused to let Him take care of you.

I entreat you to face this matter boldly, and give yourselves a definite answer. For not only your own welfare and comfort are dependent upon your right apprehension of this blessed relationship, but also the glory of your Shepherd is at stake. Have you ever thought of the grief and dishonor this sad condition of yours brings upon Him? The credit of a shepherd depends upon the condition of his flock. He might make a great boast of his qualifications as a shepherd, but it would all go for nothing if the flocks he had charge of were in a diseased condition, with many missing, and many with lean ribs and broken bones.

If an owner of sheep is thinking of employing a shepherd, he requires a reference from the shepherd's last employer, that he may learn from him how his flock fared under this shepherd's care. Now, the Lord makes statements about Himself as a good Shepherd. He is telling the universe, the world, and the Church, "I am the good shepherd"; and if they ask, "Where are Thy sheep, what condition are they in?" can He point to us as being a credit to His care? And is it not grievous if any of us refuse to let the Shepherd take care of us, and so bring discredit upon His name by our forlorn condition? The universe is looking on to see what the Lord Jesus Christ is able to make of us, and what kind of sheep we are, whether we are well fed, and healthy, and happy. Their verdict concerning Him will largely depend upon what they see in us.

When Paul was writing to the Ephesians that he had been called to preach to the Gentiles the unsearchable riches of Christ, and to make all men see what was the fellowship of the mystery which had been hid in God from the beginning of the world, he added the significant words that the object of it all was "to the intent that now unto principalities and powers in heavenly places might be known by the church the manifold wisdom of God, according to the eternal purpose which he purposed in Christ Jesus our Lord."

Well may we be lost in amazement at the thought that God has purposed such a glorious destiny for His sheep as to make known to the universe His "manifold wisdom" by means of what He has done for us! Surely this should make us eager to abandon ourselves to Him in the most generous trust for salvation to the very uttermost, that He may get great glory in the universe, and the whole world may be won to trust Him.

But if we will not let Him save us, if we reject His care, and refuse to feed in His pastures, or to lie down in His fold, then we shall be a starved and shivering flock, sick, and wretched, and full of complaints, bringing dishonor upon Him, and, by our forlorn condition, hindering the world from coming to Him.

I do not wonder that unbelievers are not drawn into the church, when I contemplate the condition of believers. I do not wonder that in some churches there are no conversions from one end of the year to the other. If I were a poor sheep, wandering in the wilderness, and I were to see some poor, wretched, sick-looking sheep peeping out of a fold, and calling me to come in, and I were to look into the fold, and should see it hard, bare, and uncomfortable, I do not think I would be much tempted to go into such a fold.

Somebody said once that some churches were too much like well-ordered graveyards: people were brought in and buried, and that was the end of it. Of course you cannot expect living people to want to take up their abodes in graveyards. We must have a fold that shows sheep in good condition if we expect outsiders to come into that fold; and if we want to attract others to the salvation of the Lord Jesus Christ, we must ourselves be able to show them that it is a satisfying and comfortable salvation. No one wants to add to their earthy discomforts by getting an uncomfortable religion, and it is useless to expect to win outsiders by the sight of our wretchedness.

Surely, if you do not care for yourselves, you cannot fail to care for the dishonor you bring upon your divine Shepherd by your poor and wretched condition. You long to serve Him, and to bring Him glory; and you can do it if you will but show to all the world that He is a Shepherd whom it is safe to trust.

Let me help you to do this. First face the fact of what a Shepherd must necessarily be and do in order to be a good Shepherd, and then face the fact that the Lord is really, and in the very highest sense of the term, a good Shepherd. Then say the words over to yourself with all the will power you can muster, "The Lord is my Shepherd. He is. He is. No matter what I feel, He says He is, and He is. I am going to believe it, come what may." Then repeat the words with a different emphasis each time:

The *Lord* is my Shepherd.

The Lord *is* my Shepherd.

The Lord is *my* Shepherd.

The Lord is my *Shepherd.*

Realize to yourself what your ideal Shepherd would be, all that you would require from anyone filling such a position of trust and of responsibility, and then know that an ideal far beyond yours, and a conception of the duties of such a position higher than any you ever dreamed of, were in the mind of our Lord when He said, "I am the good shepherd." He, better than any other, knew the sheep He had undertaken to save, and He knew the Shepherd's duties. He knew that the Shepherd is responsible for His flock, and that He is bound, at any loss of comfort, or of health, or even of life itself, to care for them and to bring them all home safely to the Master's fold. Therefore, He said: "And this is the Father's will which hath sent me that of all which he hath given me I should lose nothing, but should raise it up again at the last day." And again He said, "The good shepherd giveth his life for the sheep." And still again: "My sheep hear my voice, and I know them and they follow me, and I give unto them eternal life; and they shall never perish, neither shall any man pluck them out of my hand."

Centuries before Jesus came to be the Shepherd, the Father said: "Therefore I will save my flock. And I will set up one shepherd over them, and he shall feed them, even my servant David; he shall feed them, and he shall be their shepherd." And it seems to me, I catch a glimpse of the Father's yearning love as I read these words; and I feel sure He laid help upon One who is mighty; and that none, therefore, who are in this flock need fear any evil.

He has undertaken His duties, knowing perfectly well what the responsibilities are. He knows that He has to do with very silly sheep, who have no strength to protect themselves, no wisdom to guide themselves, and nothing to recommend them but their utter helplessness and weakness. But none of these things baffle Him. His strength and His skill are sufficient to meet every emergency that can possibly arise.

There is absolutely only one thing that can hinder Him, and that is, if the sheep will not trust Him and refuse to let Him take care of them. If they stand off at a distance, and look at the food He has provided, and long for it, and cry for it, but refuse to eat it, He cannot satisfy their hunger. If they linger outside the shelter He has made, and are afraid to go in and enjoy it because they feel too distrustful or too unworthy, He cannot protect them. No sheep is so silly as to act in this way, but we human beings, who are so much wiser than sheep, do it continually. No sheep, could it talk, would say to the shepherd: "I long for the food you have provided, and for the shelter and peace of your fold, and I wish

I might dare to enjoy them; but, alas! I feel too unworthy. I am too weak and foolish; I do not feel grateful enough; I am afraid I do not feel quite hungry enough, or enough in earnest about wanting it. I dare not presume to think you mean all these good things for me." One can imagine how grieved and wounded a good shepherd would be at such a speech as this. And surely our Lord has given us a glimpse into His tender sorrow over those who would not trust Him, when He beheld Jerusalem and wept over it, saying: "If thou hadst known, even thou, at least in this thy day, the things which belong unto thy peace! But now they are hid from thine eyes." Ah, dear Christians, have you not sometimes grieved and wounded your divine Shepherd by just such speeches? If you have, let me entreat of you to get over for a few moments on the Shepherd's side of the question, and try to think how He feels, and what His mind concerning you is. If He is your Shepherd, then He wants to care for you in the very best possible way; for He is a good Shepherd, and cares for His sheep. It is no matter what you think about it, or how you feel. You are not the Shepherd, you are only the sheep, and the great point is what He thinks and how He feels. Lose sight of yourself for a moment, and try to put yourself in the Shepherd's place. Consider your condition as He considers it. See Him coming out to seek you in your far-off wandering. See His tender, yearning love, His unutterable longing to save you. Believe His own description of Himself, and take Him at His own sweet word.

> If our faith were but more simple,
>   We would take Him at His word;
> And our lives would be all gladness
>   In the sunshine of our Lord.

Ah, yes, this is the trouble. Our faith is not simple enough to take Him at His word, but we must needs add all sorts of "buts" and "ifs" of our own; and obscure the sunshine of His love with clouds of our own imagining. If we but only knew the things which belong to our peace, how quickly we would throw aside every "if" and "but" of unbelief, and how rapturously we would plunge ourselves headlong into an unquestioning faith in all that He has told us of His almighty and never-failing love and care! But you may ask me, if all this is true of the Shepherd, what is the part of the sheep?

The part of the sheep is very simple. It is only to trust and to follow. The Shepherd does all the rest. He leads the sheep by a right way. He chooses their paths for them, and sees that those paths are paths where the sheep can walk in safety. When He putteth forth His sheep, He goeth before them. The sheep have none of the planning to do, none of the decisions to make, none of the forethought or wisdom to exercise; they have absolutely nothing to do but to trust themselves entirely to the care of the good Shepherd, and to follow Him whithersoever He leads. It is very simple. There is nothing complicated in trusting, when the one we are called upon to trust is absolutely trustworthy; and nothing complicated in obedience, when we have perfect confidence in the power we are obeying.

Let me entreat you, then, to begin to trust and to follow your Shepherd now and here. Abandon yourself to His care and guidance, as a sheep in the care of a shepherd, and trust Him utterly.

You need not be afraid to follow Him whithersoever He leads, for He always leads His sheep into green pastures and beside still waters. No matter though you may seem to yourself to be in the very midst of a desert, with nothing green about you inwardly or outwardly and you may think you will have to make a long journey before you can get into any green pastures, the good Shepherd will turn the very place where you are into green pastures; for He has power to make the desert rejoice and blossom as the rose; and He has promised that "instead of the thorn shall come up the fir-tree, and instead of the briar shall come up the myrtle-tree"; and "in the wilderness shall waters break out, and streams in the desert."

Or perhaps you may say, "My life is all a tempest of sorrow or of temptation, and it will be a long while before I can walk beside any still waters." But has not your Shepherd before this said to the raging seas, "Peace! be still. And there was a great calm"? And can He not do it again?

Thousands of the flock of Christ can testify that when they have put themselves absolutely into His hands, He has quieted the raging tempest, and has turned their deserts into blossoming gardens. I do not mean that there will be no more outward trouble, or care, or suffering; but these very places will become green pastures and still waters inwardly to the soul. The Shepherd knows what pastures are best for His sheep, and they must not question or doubt, but must trustingly follow Him. Perhaps He sees that the best pastures for some of us are to be found in the midst of opposition or of earthly trials. If He leads you there, you may be sure they are green pastures for you, and that you will grow to be made strong by feeding in them.

But words fail to tell the half of what the good Shepherd does for the flock that trusts him. He does indeed, according to His promise, make with them a covenant of peace, and causes the evil beasts to cease out of the land; and they shall dwell safely in the wilderness, and sleep in the woods. And He makes them and the places round about them a blessing; and He causes the shower to come down in its season; and there are showers of blessing. And the tree of the field yields her fruit, and the earth yields her increase; and they are safe in their land, and are no more a prey to the heathen, and none can make them afraid.

And now you will probably ask me how you can get the Lord to be your Shepherd. My answer is that you do not need to get Him to be your Shepherd at all, for He already *is* your Shepherd. All that is needed is for you to recognize that He is, and yield yourself to His control.

When the announcement is made in a family to the children who have been longing for a little sister, that one has just been born to them, they do not go on saying, "Oh, how we wish we had a little sister!" or, "what can we do to get a little sister?" But they begin at once to shout for joy, and to dance about calling out to everybody, "Hurrah! Hurrah! We have a little sister now."

And since likewise the announcement has been made to all of us by the angel of the Lord: "Fear not, for behold I bring you good tidings of great joy, which shall be to all people. For unto you is born this day in the city of David, a Savior which is Christ the Lord," we have no need and no right to go on crying out, "Oh, if I only had a Savior!" or, "What shall I do to make Christ my Savior?" He is already *born* our Savior, and we must begin at once to rejoice that He is, and must give ourselves into His care. There is nothing complicated about it. It is simply to believe it, and act as if it were true. And every soul that will begin from today believing in the good Shepherd and trusting itself to His care will sooner or later find itself feeding in His green pastures, and walking beside His still waters.

What else can the Lord, who is our Shepherd, do with His sheep, but just this? He has no folds that are not good folds, no pastures that are not green pastures, and no waters but still waters. They may not look so outwardly; but we who have tried them can testify that, let the outward seeming be what it may, His fold and His pastures are always places of peace and comfort to the inward life of the soul.

If you seem to have difficulties in understanding all this, and if the life of full trust looks complicated and mysterious, I would advise you not to try to understand it, but simply to begin to live it. Just take our nursery psalm and say, "this is my psalm, and I am going to believe it. I have always known it by heart, but it has never meant much to me. But now I have made up my mind to believe that the Lord really is my Shepherd and that He will care for me as a shepherd cares for his sheep. I will not doubt nor question it again." And then just abandon yourself to His care, as the sheep abandon themselves to the care of their shepherd, trusting Him fully, and following whithersoever He leads.

But we must not forget that while sheep trust unconsciously and by instinct, we shall need to trust intelligently and of purpose for our instincts, alas, are all against trusting. We shall have to make an effort to trust. We shall have to choose to do it. But we can do this, however weak and ignorant we may be. We may not understand all it means to be a sheep of such a Shepherd, but He knows. And if our faith will but claim Him in this blessed and wondrous relationship, He will care for us according to His love, and His wisdom, and His power, and not according to our poor comprehension of it.

It really seems to me as if we did not need any other passage out of the whole Bible besides this nursery psalm to make our religious lives full of comfort. I confess I do not see where there is any room left for the believer to worry, who actually believes this psalm. With the Lord for our Shepherd, how is it possible for anything to go wrong? With Him for our Shepherd, all that this psalm promises must be ours; and when we have learned thus to know Him, we will be able to say with a triumph of trust: "Surely goodness and mercy shall follow me [pursue, overtake] all the days of my life, and I shall dwell in the house of the Lord forever." Even the future will lose all its terrors for us, and our confidence in our Shepherd will deliver us from all fear of evil tidings.

And I can only say, in conclusion, that if each one of you will just enter into this relationship with Christ, and really be a helpless, docile, trusting sheep, and will believe Him to be your Shepherd, caring for you with all the love, and care, and tenderness that that name involves, and will follow Him whithersoever He leads, you will soon lose all your old spiritual discomfort, and will know the peace of God that passeth all understanding to keep your hearts and minds in Christ Jesus.

Chapter 5: He Spake To Them Of The Father

"They understood not that he spake to them of the Father."

One of the most illuminating names of God is the one especially revealed by our Lord Jesus Christ, the name of Father. I say especially revealed by Christ, because, while God had been called throughout the ages by many other names, expressing other aspects of His character, Christ alone has revealed Him to us under the all-inclusive name of Father—a name that holds within itself all other names of wisdom and power, and above all of love and goodness, a name that embodies for us a perfect supply for all our needs. Christ, who was the only begotten Son in the bosom of the Father, was the only one who could reveal this name, for He alone knew the Father. "As the Father knoweth me," He said, "even so know I the Father" "Not that any man hath seen the Father save he which is of God, he hath seen the Father."

In the Old Testament God was not revealed as the Father so much as a great warrior fighting for His people, or as a mighty king ruling over them and caring for them. The name of Father is only given to Him a very few times there, six or seven times at the most; while in the New Testament it is given about two or three hundred times. Christ, who knew Him, was the only one who could reveal Him. "no man," He said, "knoweth who the Father is, but the Son, and he to whom the Son will reveal him."

The vital question then that confronts each one of us is whether we individually understand that Christ speaks to us of the Father. We know He uses the word Father continually, but do we in the least understand what the word means? Have we even so much as an inkling of what the Father is?

All the discomfort and unrest of the religious life of so many of God's children come, I feel sure, from this very thing, that they do not understand that God is actually and truly their Father. They think of Him as a stern Judge, or a severe Taskmaster, or at the best as an unapproachable dignitary, seated on a far-off throne, dispensing exacting laws for a frightened and trembling world; and in their terror lest they should fail to meet His requirements they hardly know which way to turn. But of a God who is a Father, tender, and loving, and full of compassion, a God who, like a father, will be on their side against the whole universe they have no conception.

I am not afraid to say that discomfort and unrest are impossible to the souls that come to know that God is their real and actual Father.

But before I go any farther I must make it plain that it is a Father, such as our highest instincts tell us a good father ought to be, of whom I am speaking. Sometimes earthly fathers are unkind, or tyrannical, or selfish, or even cruel, or they are merely indifferent and neglectful; but none of these can by any stretch of charity be called good fathers. But God, who is good, must be a good father or not a father at all. We must all of us have known good fathers in this world, or at least can imagine them. I knew one, and he filled my childhood with sunshine by his most lovely fatherhood. I can remember vividly with what confidence and triumph I walked through my days, absolutely secure in the knowledge that I had a father. And I am very sure that I have learned to know a little about the perfect fatherhood of God, because of my experience with this lovely earthly father.

But God is not only a father, He is a mother as well, and we have all of us known mothers whose love and tenderness have been without bound or limit. And it is very certain that the God who created them both, and who is Himself father and mother in one, could never have created earthly fathers and mothers who were more tender and more loving than He is Himself. Therefore if we want to know what sort of a Father He is, we must heap together all the best of all the fathers and mothers we have ever known or can imagine, and we must tell ourselves that this is only a faint image of God, our Father in Heaven.

When our Lord was teaching His disciples how to pray, the only name by which He taught them to address God was, "Our Father which art in heaven." And this surely meant that we were to think of Him only in this light. Millions upon millions of times during all the centuries since then has this name been uttered by the children of God everywhere; and yet how much has it been understood? Had all who used the name known what it meant, it would have been impossible for the misrepresentations of His character, and the doubts of His love and care, that have so desolated the souls of His children throughout all the ages, to have crept in. Tyranny, unkindness, and neglect might perhaps be attributed to a God whose name was only a king, or a judge, or a lawgiver; but of a God, who is before all else a father, and, of necessity, since He is God, a good father, no such things could possibly be believed. Moreover, since He is an "everlasting Father," He must in the very nature of things act, always and under all circumstances, as a good father ought to act, and never in any other way. It is inconceivable that a good father could forget, or neglect, or be unfair to his children. A savage father might, or a wicked father; but a good father never! And in calling our God by the blessed name of Father, we ought to know that, if He is a father at all, He must be the very best of fathers, and His fatherhood must be the highest ideal of fatherhood of which we can conceive. It is, as I have said, a fatherhood that combines both father and mother in one, in our highest ideals of both, and comprises all the love, and all the tenderness, and all the compassion, and all the yearning, and all the self-sacrifice, that we cannot but recognize to be the inmost soul of parentage, even though we may not always see it carried out by all earthly parents.

But you may say what about the other names of God, do they not convey other and more terrifying ideas? They only do so because this blessed name of Father is not added to them. This name must underlie every other name by which He has ever been known. Has He been called a Judge? Yes, but He is a Father Judge, one who judges as a loving father would. Is He a King? Yes, but He is a King who is at the same time the Father of His subjects, and who rules them with a father's tenderness. Is He a Lawgiver? Yes, but He is a Lawgiver who gives laws as a father would, remembering the weakness and ignorance of his helpless children. "Like as a father pitieth his children, so the Lord pitieth them that fear him. For He knoweth our frame; He remembereth that we are dust." It is not "as a judge judges, so the Lord judges"; not "as a taskmaster controls, so the Lord controls"; not "as a lawgiver imposes laws, so the Lord imposes laws"; but, "as a father pitieth, so the Lord pitieth."

Never, never must we think of God in any other way than as "our Father." All other attributes with which we endow Him in our conceptions must be based upon and limited by this one of "our Father." What a good father could not do, God, who is our Father, cannot do either; and what a good father ought to do, God, who is our Father, is absolutely sure to do.

In our Lord's last prayer in John 17, He says that He has declared to us the name of the Father in order that we may discover the wonderful fact that the Father loves us *as* He loved His Son. Now, which one of us really believes this? We have read this chapter over, I suppose, oftener than almost any other chapter in the Bible, and yet do we any of us believe that it is an actual, tangible fact, that God loves us as much as He loved Christ? If we believed this to be actually the case, could we, by any possibility, ever have an anxious or rebellious thought again? Would we not be absolutely and utterly sure always under every conceivable circumstance that the divine Father, who loves us just as much as He loved His only begotten Son, our Lord Jesus Christ, would of course care for us in the best possible way, and could not tell us so emphatically not to be anxious or troubled about anything, for He knew His Father and knew that it was safe to trust Him utterly.

It is very striking that He so often said, "Your heavenly Father, not mine only, but yours just as much. Your heavenly Father," He says, "cares for the sparrows and the lilies, and of course, therefore, he will care for you who are of so much more value than many sparrows." How supremely foolish it is then for us to be worried and anxious about things, when Christ has said that our heavenly Father knows that we have need of all these things! For of course, being a good father, He must in the very nature of the case, when He knows our need, supply it.

What can be the matter with us that we do not understand this?

Again, our Lord draws the comparison between earthly fathers and our heavenly Father, in order to show us, not how much less good and tender and willing to bless is our heavenly Father, but how much more. "if ye, being evil," He says, "know how to give good gifts unto your children, how much more shall your Father which is in heaven give good things to them that ask him." Can we conceive of a good earthly father giving a stone or a serpent to a hungry child instead of bread or fish? Would not our whole souls revolt from a father who could do such things? And yet, I fear, there are a great many of God's children who actually think that their heavenly Father does this sort of thing to them, and gives them stones when they ask for bread, or curses when they ask for blessings. And perhaps these very people may belong to the Society for the Prevention of Cruelty to Children, a society which is the nation's protest against such behavior on the part of earthly fathers; and yet they never have thought of the dreadful wickedness of charging their heavenly Father with things which they are banded together to punish in earthly fathers!

But it is not only that our heavenly Father is willing to give us good things. He is far more than willing. Our Lord says, "Fear not, little flock, it is your Father's good pleasure to give you the kingdom." There is no grudging in His giving, it is His "good pleasure" to give; He likes to do it. He wants to give you the kingdom far more than you want to have it. Those of us who are parents know how eager we are to give good things to our children, often far more eager than our children are to have them; and this may help us to understand how it is that it is God's "good pleasure" to give us the kingdom. Why, then, should we ask Him in such fear and trembling, and why should we torment ourselves with anxiety lest He should fail to grant what we need?

There can be only one answer to these questions, and that is, that we do not know the Father.

We are told that we are of the "household of God." Now the principle is announced in the Bible that if any man provides not for his own household, he has "denied the faith and is worse than an infidel." Since then we are of the "household of God," this principle applies to Him, and if He should fail to provide for us, His own words would condemn Him. I say this reverently, but I want to say it emphatically, for so few people seem to have realized it.

It was in my own case a distinct era of immense importance when I first discovered this fact of the responsibility of my Father in Heaven. As it were, in a single moment, the burden of life was lifted off my shoulders and laid on His, and all my fears, and anxieties, and questionings dropped into the abyss of His loving care. I saw that the instinct of humanity, which demands that the parents who bring a child into the world are bound by every law, both human and divine, to care for and protect that child according to their best ability, is a divinely implanted instinct; and that it is meant to teach us the magnificent fact that the Creator, who has made human parents responsible toward their children, is Himself equally responsible toward His children. I could have shouted for joy! And from that glad hour my troubles were over. For when this insight comes to a soul, that soul must, in the very nature of things, enter into rest.

With such a God, who is at the same time a Father, there is no room for anything but rest. And when, ever since that glad day, temptations to doubt or anxiety or fear have come to me, I have not dared in the fact of what I then learned to listen to them, because I have seen that to do so would be to cast a doubt on the trustworthiness of my Father in Heaven.

We may have been accustomed to think that our doubts and fears were because of our own unworthiness and arose from humility; and we may even have taken them as a sign of especial piety, and have thought they were in some way pleasing to God. But if, in their relations with their earthly parents, children should let in doubts of their love, and fears lest their care should fail, would these doubts and fears be evidences of filial piety on the children's part, and would they be at all pleasing to their parents?

If God is our Father, the only thing we can do with doubts, and fears, and anxious thoughts is to cast them behind our backs forever, and have nothing more to do with them ever again. We *can* do this. We can give up our doubts just as we would urge a drunkard to give up his drink. We can pledge against doubting. And if once we see that our doubts are an actual sin against God, and imply a question of His trustworthiness, we will be eager to do it. We may have cherished our doubts heretofore because perhaps we have thought they were a part of our religion, and a becoming attitude of soul in one so unworthy; but if we now see that God is in very truth our Father, we will reject every doubt with horror, as being a libel on our Father's love and our Father's care.

What more can any soul want than to have a God whose name is "our Father," and whose character and ways must name? As Philip said, so we find it to be, "Show us the Father and it sufficeth us." It does indeed suffice, beyond what words can express!

A friend of mine went one day to see a poor negro woman living in one of the poorest parts of Philadelphia, whose case had been reported to her as being one of great need. She found things even worse than she had feared. The poor woman was old, crippled with rheumatism, and lived alone in a poor little room with only the help of a kind neighbor now and then to do things for her; and yet she was bright and cheerful, and full of thanksgiving for her many mercies. My friend marveled that cheerfulness or thankfulness could be possible under such circumstances, and said, "But do you never get frightened at the thought of what may happen to you, all alone here, and so lame as you are?"

The old negro saint looked at her with surprise, and said in a tone of the utmost amazement, "Frightened! Why, honey, doesn't you know I have got a Father, and doesn't you know He takes care of me the whole endurin' time?" And then, as my friend looked perplexed, she added in a tone of wondering reproof, "Why, honey, sholy my Father is your Father too, and you knows about Him, and you knows He always takes care of His chilluns." It was a lesson my friend never forgot.

"Behold," says the Apostle John, "what manner of love the Father hath bestowed upon us, that we should be called the sons of God." The "manner of love" bestowed upon us is the love of a father for his son, a tender protecting love, that knows our weakness and our need, and cares for us accordingly. He treats us as sons, and all He asks in return is that we shall treat Him as a Father, whom we can trust without anxiety. We must take the son's place of dependence and trust, and must let Him keep the father's place of care and responsibility. Because we are the children and He is the Father, we must let Him do the father's part. Too often we take upon our own shoulders the father's part, and try to take care of and provide for ourselves. But no good earthy father would want his children to take upon their young shoulders the burden of his duties, and surely much less would our heavenly Father want to lay upon us the burden of His.

No wonder we are told to cast all our care upon Him, for He careth for us. He careth for us; of course He does. It is His business, as a Father, to do so. He would not be a good Father if He did not. All He asks of us is to let Him know when we need anything, and then leave the supplying of that need to Him; and He assures us that if we do this the "peace of God that passeth all understanding shall keep our hearts and minds." The children of a good, human father are at peace because they trust in their father's care; but the children of the heavenly Father too often have no peace because they are afraid to trust in His care. They make their requests known to Him perhaps, but that is all they do. It is a sort of religious form they feel it necessary to go through. But as to supposing that He really will care for them, no such idea seems to cross their minds; and they go on carrying their cares and burdens on their own shoulders, exactly as if they had no Father in Heaven, and had never asked him to care for them.

What utter folly it all is! For if ever an earthly father was worthy of the confidence of his children, surely much more is our heavenly Father worthy of our confidence. And why it is that so few of His children trust Him can only be because they have not yet found out that He is really their Father; or else that, calling Him Father every day in their prayers, they still have never seen that He is the sort of Father a good and true human father is, a Father who is loving, and tender, pitiful, and full of kindness toward the helpless beings whom He has brought into existence, and whom He is therefore bound to protect. This sort of Father no one could help trusting; but the strange and far-off Creator, whose fatherhood stops at our creation, and has no care for our fate after once we are launched into the universe, no one could be expected to trust.

The remedy, therefore, for your discomfort and unrest is to be found in becoming acquainted with the Father.

"For," says the Apostle, "ye have not received the spirit of bondage again to fear; but ye have received the spirit of adoption, whereby we cry, Abba, Father." Is it this "spirit of adoption" that reigns in your hearts, my readers, or is it the "spirit of bondage"? Your whole comfort in the religious life depends upon which spirit it is; and no amount of wrestling or agonizing, no prayers, and no efforts will be able to bring you comfort, while the "spirit of adoption" is lacking in your heart.

But you may ask how you are to get this "spirit of adoption." I can only say that it is not a thing to be gotten. It comes; and it comes as the necessary result of the discovery that God is in very truth a real Father. When we have made this discovery, we cannot help feeling and acting like a child; and this is what the "spirit of adoption" means. It is nothing mystical nor mysterious; it is the simple natural result of having found a Father where you thought there was only a Judge.

The great need for every soul, therefore, is to make this supreme discovery. And to do this we have only to see what Christ tells us about the Father, and then believe it. "Verily, verily," He declares, "I say unto thee, We speak that we do know, and testify that we have seen," but, He adds sadly, "ye receive not our witness." In order to come to the knowledge of the Father, we must receive the testimony of Christ, who declares: "The words that I speak unto you I speak not of myself; but the Father that dwelleth in me, he doeth the works." Over and over He repeated this, and in John, after grieving over the fact that so few received his testimony, He adds these memorable words: "He that hath received his testimony hath set to his seal that God is true."

The whole authority of Christ stands or falls with this. If we receive His testimony, we set to our seal that God is true. If we reject that testimony, we make Him a liar.

"If ye had known me," says Christ, "ye should have known my Father also; and from henceforth ye know him, and have seen him." The thing for us to do then is to make up our minds that from henceforth we will receive His testimony, and will "know the Father."

Let other people worship whatever sort of a God they may, for us there must be henceforth "but one God, even the Father."

"For though there be that are called gods, whether in heaven or in earth (as there be gods many, and lords many), but to us there is but one God, the Father, of whom are all things, and we in him; and one Lord Jesus Christ, by whom are all things, and we by him."

Chapter 6: Jehovah

"That men may know that Thou, whose name alone is JEHOVAH,
art the Most High over all the earth."

Among all the names of God perhaps the most comprehensive is the name Jehovah. Cruden describes this name as the incommunicable name of God. The word Jehovah means the Self-Existing One, the "I am"; and it is generally used as a direct revelation of what God is. In several places an explanatory word is added, revealing some one of His special characteristics; and it is to these that I want particularly to call attention. They are as follows:

Jehovah-jireh, *i.e.*, The Lord will see, or the Lord will provide.

Jehovah-nissi, *i.e.*, The Lord my Banner.

Jehovah-shalom, *i.e.*, The Lord our Peace.

Jehovah-tsidkenu, *i.e.*, The Lord our Righteousness.

Jehovah-shammah, *i.e.*, The Lord is there.

These names were discovered by God's people in times of sore need; that is, the characteristics they describe were discovered, and the names were the natural expression of these characteristics.

When Abraham was about to sacrifice his son, and saw no way of escape, the Lord provided a lamb for the sacrifice and delivered Isaac; and Abraham made the grand discovery that it was one of the characteristics of Jehovah to see and provide for the needs of His people. Therefore he called Him Jehovah-jireh—the Lord will see, or the Lord will provide.

The counterparts to this in the New Testament are very numerous. Over and over our Lord urges us to take no care, because God careth for us. "Your heavenly Father knoweth," He says, "that ye have need of all these things." If the Lord sees and knows our need, it will be a matter of course with Him to provide for it. Being our Father, He could not do anything else. As soon as a good mother sees that her child needs anything, at once she sets about supplying that need. She does not even wait for the child to ask, the sight of the need is asking enough. Being a good mother, she could not do otherwise.

When God, therefore, says to us, "I am he that seeth thy need," He in reality says also, "I am he that provideth," for He cannot see, and fail to provide.

"Why do I not have everything I want, then?" you may ask. Only because God sees that what you want is not really the thing you need, but probably exactly the opposite. Often, in order to give us what we need, the Lord is obliged to keep from us what we want. Your heavenly Father knoweth what things ye have need of, you do not know; and were all your wants gratified, it might well be that all your needs would be left unsupplied. It surely ought to suffice us that our God is indeed Jehovah-jireh, the Lord who will see, and who will therefore provide.

But I am afraid a great many Christians of the present day have never made Abraham's discovery, and do not know that the Lord is really Jehovah-jirah. *They* are trusting Him, it may be, to save their souls in the future, but they never dream He wants to carry their cares for them now and here. They are like a man I have heard of, with a heavy load on his back, who was given a lift by a friend, and who thankfully availed himself of it. Climbing into the conveyance, but still keeping his burden on his back, he sat there bowed down under the weight of it. "Why do you not put your burden down on the bottom of the carriage?" asked his friend.

"Oh," replied the man, "it is a great deal to ask you to carry me myself, and I could not ask you to carry my burden also." You wonder that anyone could be so foolish, and yet are you not doing the same? Are you not trusting the Lord to take care of yourself, but are still going on carrying your burdens on your own shoulders? Which is the silliest—that man or you?

Jehovah-nissi, i.e., "The Lord my banner," was a discovery made by Moses when Amalek came to fight with Israel in Rephidim, and the Lord gave the Israelites a glorious victory. Moses realized that the Lord was fighting for them, and he built an altar to Jehovah-nissi, "The Lord my banner." The Bible is full of developments of this name. "The Lord is a man of war"; "The Lord your God, he it is that fighteth for you"; "The Lord shall fight for you, and ye shall hold your peace"; "Be not afraid nor dismayed, by reason of this great multitude, for the battle is not yours, but God's"; "God himself is with us for our captain."

Nothing is more abundantly proved in the Bible than this, that the Lord will fight for us if we will but let Him. He knows that we have no strength nor might against our spiritual enemies; and, like a tender mother when her helpless children are attacked by an enemy, He fights for us; and all He asks of us is to be still and let Him. This is the only sort of spiritual conflict that is ever successful. But we are very slow to learn this, and when temptations come, instead of handing the battle over to the Lord, we summon all our forces to fight them ourselves. We believe, perhaps, that the Lord is somewhere near, and, if the worst comes to the worst, will step in to help us; but for the most part we feel that we ourselves, and we only, must do all the fighting. Our method of fighting consists generally in a series of repentings, and making resolutions and promises, and weary struggles for victory, and then failing again; and again repentance, and resolutions, and promises, and renewed struggles, and all this over, and over, and over again, each time telling ourselves that now at last we certainly will have the victory, and each time failing even worse than before. And this may go on for weeks, or months, or even years, and no real or permanent deliverance ever comes.

But you may ask, "Are we not to do any fighting ourselves?" Of course we are to fight, but not in this fashion. We are to fight the "good fight of faith," as Paul exhorted Timothy; and the fight of faith is not a fight of effort or of struggle, but it is a fight of trusting. It is the kind of fight that Hezekiah fought when he and his army marched out to meet their enemy, singing songs of victory as they went, and finding their enemy all dead men. Our part in this fight is to hand the battle over to the Lord, and to trust Him for the victory.

And we are to put on His armor, not our own. The Apostle tells us what it is. It is the girdle of truth, and the breastplate of righteousness, and the preparation of the gospel of peace on our feet, and the helmet of salvation, and the sword of the Spirit which is the

Word of God; but above all, he says, we are to take the shield of faith wherewith we shall be able to quench all the fiery darts of the wicked.

There is nothing here about promises or resolutions; nothing about hours and days of agonizing struggles, and of bitter remorse. "Above all things taking the shield of faith." Above all things faith. Faith is the one essential thing, without which all else is useless. And it means that we must not only hand the battle over to the Lord, but we must leave it with Him, and must have absolute faith that He will conquer. It is here where the fight comes in. It seems so unsafe to sit still, and do nothing but trust the Lord; and the temptation to take the battle back into our own hands is often tremendous. To keep hands off in spiritual matters is as hard for us as it is for the drowning man to keep hands off the one who is trying to rescue him. We all know how impossible it is to rescue a drowning man who tries to help his rescuer, and it is equally impossible for the Lord to fight our battles for us when we insist upon trying to fight them ourselves. It is not that He will not, but He cannot. Our interference hinders His working. Spiritual forces cannot work while earthly forces are active.

Our Lord tells us that without Him we can do nothing, and we have read and repeated His words hundreds of times; but does anyone really believe they are actually true? If we should drag out into the light our secret thoughts on the subject, should we not find them to be something like this: "When Christ said those words He meant of course to say that we cannot of ourselves do much, or at any rate no great things. But nothing; ah, no, that is impossible. We are not babies, and we are certainly meant to use all the strength we have in fighting our enemies; and, when our own strength gives out, we can then call upon the Lord to help us." In spite of all our failures, we cannot help thinking that, if only we should try harder and be more persistent, we should be equal to any encounter. But we entirely overlook the vital fact that our natural powers are of no avail in spiritual regions or with spiritual enemies. The grub of the dragonfly, that lives at the bottom of the pond, may be a finely developed and vigorous grub; but, when it becomes a dragonfly, the powers of its grub life, that availed for creeping about in the mud, would be useless for winging its flight in the free air.

And just as our skill in walking on the earth would avail us nothing if we had to fly in the air, so our natural powers are of no avail in spiritual warfare. They are, in fact, if we try to depend on them, real hindrances, just as trying to walk would hinder us, if we sought to float or to fly. We can easily see, therefore, that the result of trusting in ourselves, when dealing with our spiritual enemies, must inevitable be very serious. It not only causes failure, but in the end it causes rebellion; and a great deal of what is called "spiritual conflict" might far better be named "spiritual rebellion." God has told us to cease from our own efforts, and to hand our battles over to Him, and we point blank refuse to obey Him. We fight, it is true, but it is not a fight of faith, but a fight of unbelief. Our spiritual "wrestling," of which we are often so proud, is really a wrestling, not for God against His enemies, but against Him on the side of His enemies. We allow ourselves to indulge in doubts and fears, and as a consequence we are plunged into darkness, and turmoil, and wrestlings of spirit. And then we call this "spiritual conflict," and look upon ourselves as an interesting and "peculiar case." The single word that explains our "peculiar case" is the word *unbelief*, and the simple remedy is to be found in the word *faith*.

But you may ask, what about "wrestling Jacob"? Did he not gain his victory by wrestling? To this I reply, that on the contrary he gained his victory by being made so weak that he could not wrestle any longer. It was not Jacob who wrestled with the angel, but the angel who wrestled with Jacob. Jacob was the one to be overcome; and when the angel found that Jacob's resistance was so great that he could not "prevail against him," he was obliged to make him lame by putting his thigh out of joint; and then the victory was won. As soon as Jacob was too weak to resist any longer, he prevailed with God. He gained power when he lost it. He conquered when he could no longer fight.

Jacob's experience is ours. The Lord wrestles with us in order to bring us to a place of entire dependence on Him. We resist as long as we have any strength; until at last He is forced to bring us to a place of helplessness, where we are obliged to yield; and then we conquer by this very yielding. Our victory is always the victory of weakness. Paul knew this victory when he said: "And the Lord said unto me, My grace is sufficient for thee; for my strength is made perfect in weakness. Most gladly therefore will I rather glory in my infirmities, that the power of Christ may rest upon me. Therefore I take pleasure in infirmities, in reproaches, in necessities, in persecutions, in distresses for Christ's sake; for when I am weak, then am I strong."

Who would ask for a more magnificent victory than this!

And this victory will be ours, if we take the Lord to be our Banner, and commit all our battles to Him.

The name of Jehovah-shalom, or "The Lord our peace," was discovered by Gideon when the Lord had called him to a work for which he felt himself to be utterly unfitted. "Oh, my Lord," he had said, "wherewith shall I save Israel? Behold, my family is poor in Manasseh, and I am the least of my father's house." And the Lord answered him, saying: "Surely I will be with thee, and thou shalt smite the Midianites as one man… And the Lord said unto him, Peace be unto thee: fear not; for thou shalt not die." Then Gideon believed the Lord; and, although the battle had not yet been fought, and no victories had been won, with the eye of faith he saw peace already secured and he built an altar unto the Lord, and called it Jehovah-shalom, i.e., "The Lord our peace."

Of all the needs of the human heart none is greater than the need for peace; and none is more abundantly promised in the Gospel. "Peace I leave with you," says our Lord, "my peace I give unto you. Let not your heart be troubled, neither let it be afraid." And again He says: "These things have I spoken unto you, that in me ye might have peace. In the world ye shall have tribulation: but be of good cheer, I have overcome the world."

Our idea of peace is that it must be outward before it can be inward, that all enemies must be driven away, and all troubles cease. But the Lord's idea was of an interior peace that could exist in the midst of turmoil, and could be triumphant over it. And the ground of this sort of peace is found in the fact, not that we have overcome the world, or that we ever can, but that Christ has overcome it. Only the conqueror can proclaim peace, and the people, whose battles He has fought, can do nothing but enter into it. They can neither make nor unmake it. But, if they choose, they can refuse to believe in it, and so can fail to let it reign in their hearts. You may be afraid to believe that Christ has made peace for you, and so may live on in a weary state of warfare; but nevertheless, He has done it, and all your continued warfare is worse than useless.

The Bible tells us that Christ is our peace, and consequently, whether I feel as if I had peace or not, peace is really mine in Christ, and I must take possession of it by faith. Faith is simply to believe and assert the thing that God says. If He says there is peace, faith asserts that there is, and enters into the enjoyment of it. If He has proclaimed peace in the Bible, I must proclaim it in my own heart, let the seemings be what they may. "The kingdom of God is righteousness, peace, and joy, in the Holy Ghost," and the soul that has not taken possession of peace has not yet fully entered into this kingdom.

Practically I believe we can always enter into peace by a simple obedience to Philippians 4:6,7: "Be careful for nothing; but in everything by prayer and supplication with thanksgiving let your requests be made known unto God. And the peace of God, which passeth all understanding, shall keep your hearts and minds through Christ Jesus." The steps here are very plain, and they are only two. First, give up all anxiety; and second, hand over your cares to God; and then stand steadfastly here; peace must come. It simply must, for there is no room for anything else.

The name Jehovah-tsidkenu, "The Lord our righteousness," was revealed by the Lord Himself through the mouth of the prophet Jeremiah, when he was announcing the coming of Christ. "Behold, the day is come, saith the Lord, that I will raise unto David a righteous Branch, and a King shall reign and prosper, and shall execute judgment and justice in the earth. In his days Judah shall be saved, and Israel shall dwell safely, and this is the name whereby he shall be called, Jehovah-tsidkenu, The Lord our righteousness."

Greater than any other need is our need for righteousness. Most of the struggles and conflicts of our Christian life come from our fights with sin, and our efforts after righteousness. And I need not say how great are our failures. As long as we try to conquer sin or attain to righteousness by our own efforts, we are bound to fail. But if we discover that the Lord is our righteousness, we shall have the secret of victory. In the Lord Jesus Christ we have a fuller revelation of this wonderful name of God. The Apostle Paul in his character as the "ambassador for Christ" declares that God hath made Christ to be sin for us, that we might be made the righteousness of God in Him. And again he says that Christ is made unto us wisdom, and righteousness, and sanctification, and redemption. I am afraid that very few Christians really understand what this means. We repeat the words as belonging to our religious vocabulary, and in a vague sort of way think of them as being somehow a part of the salvation of Christ, but what part or of what practical use we have very little real idea.

To me this name of God, the Lord our righteousness, *seems* of such tremendously practical use that I want if possible to make it plain to others. But it is difficult; and I cannot possibly explain it theologically. But experimentally it seems to me like this: We are not to try to have a stock of righteousness laid up in ourselves, from which to draw a supply when needed, but we are to draw continual fresh supplies as we need them from the righteousness that is laid up for us in Christ. I mean, that if we need righteousness of any sort, such as patience, or humility, or love, it is useless for us to look within, hoping to find a supply there, for we never will find it; but we must simply take it by faith, as a possession that is stored up for us in Christ, who is our righteousness. If I cannot tell theologically how this is done, I know experimentally that it can be done, and that the results are triumphant. I have seen sweetness and gentleness poured like a flood of sunshine into dark and bitter spirits, when the hand of faith has been reached out to grasp them as a present possession, stored up for all who need in Christ. I have seen sharp tongues made tender, anxious hearts made calm, and fretful spirits made quiet by the simple step of taking by faith the righteousness that is ours in Christ.

The Apostle, after proving to us in the third chapter of Romans the absolute impossibility of any satisfying righteousness coming to us by the law (that is, by our own efforts) goes on to say: "But now the righteousness of God without the law is manifested, being witnessed by the law and the prophets, even the righteousness of God which is by faith of Jesus Christ unto all and upon all them that believe; for there is no difference."

It is faith and faith only that can appropriate this righteousness that is ours in Christ. Just as we appropriate by faith the forgiveness that is ours in Christ, so must we appropriate by faith the patience that is ours in Him, or the gentleness, or the meekness, or the long-suffering, or any other virtue we may need. Our own efforts will not procure righteousness for us, any more than they will procure forgiveness. And yet how many Christians try! Paul describes them when he says: "For I bear them record that they have a zeal of God, but not according to knowledge. For they being ignorant of God's righteousness, and going about to establish their own righteousness, have not submitted themselves unto the righteousness of God. For Christ is the end of the law for righteousness to every one that believeth."

Would that all such zealous souls could discover this wonderful name of God, "The Lord our righteousness," and would give up at once and forever seeking to establish their own righteousness, and would submit themselves to the righteousness of God. The prophet tells us that our own righteousness, even if we could attain to any, is nothing but filthy rags; and Paul prays that he may be found in Christ, not having his own righteousness, which is of the law, but that which is through the faith of Christ, the righteousness which is of God by faith.

Do we at all comprehend the meaning of this prayer? And are we prepared to join in it with our whole hearts? If so, our struggle after righteousness will be over. Jehovah-tsidkenu will supply all our needs.

The name Jehovah-shammah, or "the Lord is there," was revealed to the prophet Ezekiel when he was shown by a vision, the twenty-fifth year of their captivity, what was to be the future home of the children of Israel. He described the land and the city of Jerusalem, and ended his description by saying: "And the name of that city shall be called Jehovah-shammah, or the Lord is there."

To me this name includes all the others. Wherever the Lord is, all must go right for His children. Where the good mother is, all goes right, up to the measure of her ability, for her children. And how much more God. His presence is enough. We can all remember how the simple presence is enough. We can all remember how the simple presence of our mothers was enough for us when we were children. All that we needed of comfort, rest, and deliverance was insured to us by the mere fact of our mother, as she sat in her accustomed chair with her work, or her book, or her writing, and we had burst in upon her with our doleful budget of childish woes. If we could but see that the presence of God is the same assurance of comfort, and rest, and deliverance, only infinitely more so, a well-spring of joy would be opened up in our religious lives that would drive out every vestige of discomfort and distress.

All through the Old Testament the Lord's one universal answer to all the fears and anxieties of the children of Israel was the simple words, "I will be with thee." He did not need to say anything more. His presence was to them a perfect guarantee that all their needs would be supplied; and the moment they were assured of it, they were no longer afraid to face the fiercest foe.

You may say, "Ah, yes, if the Lord would only say the same thing to me, I should not be afraid either." Well, He has said it, and has said it in unmistakable terms. When the "angel of the Lord" announced to Joseph the coming birth of Christ, he said: "They shall call his name Emmanuel; which being interpreted is, God with us." In this short sentence is revealed to us the grandest fact the world can ever know—that God, the Almighty God, the Creator of Heaven and earth, is not a far-off God, dwelling in a Heaven of unapproachable glory, but has come down in Christ to dwell with us right here in this world, in the midst of our poor, ignorant, helpless lives, as close to us as we are to ourselves. If we believe in Christ at all, we are shut up to believing this, for this is His name, "God with us."

Both these names then, Jehovah-shammah and Emmanuel, mean the same thing. They mean that God is everywhere present in His universe, surrounding everything, and sustaining everything, and holding all of us in His safe and blessed keeping. They mean that we can find no place in all His universe of which it cannot be said, "The Lord is there." The Psalmist says: "Whither shall I go from thy spirit? And whither shall I flee from thy presence? If I ascend up into heaven, thou art there; if I make my bed in hell, behold, thou art there. If I take the wings of the morning, and dwell in the uttermost parts of the sea, even there shall thy hand lead me, and thy right hand shall hold me."

We cannot drift from the love and care of an ever-present God. And those Christians who think He has forsaken them, and who cry out for His presence, are crying out in ignorance of the fact that He is always and everywhere present with them. In truth they cannot get out of His presence, even should they try. Oh, that they knew this wonderful and satisfying name of God!

> *Speak to Him, thou, for He hears; and spirit with spirit may meet;*
> *Closer is He than breathing, and nearer than hands and feet.*

Let us sum up, once more, the teaching of these five names of God. What is it they say to us?

Jehovah-jireh, *i.e.,* "I am He who sees thy need, and therefore provides for it."

Jehovah-nissi, *i.e.,* "I am the Captain, and thy Banner, and he who will fight thy battles for thee."

Jehovah-shalom, *i.e.,* "I am thy peace. I have made peace for thee, and My peace I give unto thee."

Jehovah-tsidkenu, *i.e.,* "I am thy righteousness. In Me thou wilt find all thou needest of wisdom, and righteousness, and sanctification, and redemption."

Jehovah-shammah, i.e., "I am with thee. I am thy ever-present, all-environing God and Savior. I will never leave thee nor forsake thee. Wherever thou goest, there I am, and there shall my hand hold thee, and my right hand lead thee."

All this is true, whether we know it and recognize it or not. We may never have dreamed that God was such a God as this, and we may have gone through our lives thus far starved, and weary, and wretched. But all the time we have been starving in the midst of plenty. The fullness of God's salvation has awaited our faith; and "abundance of grace and of the gift of righteousness" have awaited our receiving.

Would that I could believe that for some of my readers all this was ended, and that henceforth they would see that these all-embracing names of God leave no tiny corner of their need unsupplied. Then would they be able to testify with the prophet to all around them: "Behold, God is my salvation: for the Lord Jehovah is my strength and my song; he also is become my salvation. Therefore with joy shall we draw water out of the wells of salvation."

Chapter 7: "The Lord Is Good"

"O taste and see that the Lord is good; blessed is the man that trusteth in him."

Have you ever asked yourself what you honestly think of God down at the bottom of your heart whether you believe Him to be a good God or a bad God? I dare say the question will shock you, and you will be horrified at the suggestion that you could by any possibility think that God is a bad God. But before you have finished this chapter, I suspect some of you will be forced to acknowledge that, unconsciously perhaps, but nonetheless truly, you have, by your doubts and your upbraiding, attributed to Him a character that you would be horrified to have attributed to yourself.

I shall never forget the hour when I first discovered that God was really good. I had, of course, always known that the Bible said He was good, but I had thought it only meant He was religiously good; and it had never dawned on me that it meant He was actually and practically good, with the same kind of goodness He has commanded us to have. The expression, "The goodness of God," had seemed to me nothing more than a sort of heavenly statement, which I could not be expected to understand. And then one day I came in my reading of the Bible across the words, "O taste and see that the Lord is good," and suddenly they meant something. The Lord is good, I repeated to myself. What does it mean to be good? What but this, the living up to the best and highest that one knows. To be good is exactly the opposite of being bad. To be bad is to know the right and not to do it, but to be good is to do the best we know. And I saw that, since God is omniscient, He must know what is the best and highest good of all, and that therefore His goodness must necessarily be beyond question. I can never express what this meant to me. I had such a view of the real actual goodness of God that I saw nothing could possibly go wrong under His care, and it seemed to me that no one could ever be anxious again. And over and over, when appearance have been against Him, and when I have been tempted to question whether He had not been unkind, or neglectful, or indifferent, I have been brought up short by the words, "The Lord is good"; and I have seen that it was simply unthinkable that a God who was good could have done the bad things I had imagined.

You shrink with horror, perhaps, from the suggestion that you could under any circumstances, even in the secret depths of your heart, attribute to God what was bad. And yet you do not hesitate to accuse Him of doing things, which if one of your friends should do them, you would look upon as most dishonorable and unkind. For instance, Christians get into trouble; all looks dark, and they have no sense of the Lord's presence. They begin to question whether the Lord has not forsaken them, and sometimes even accuse Him of indifference and neglect. And they never realize that these accusations are tantamount to saying that the Lord does not keep His promises, and does not treat them as kindly and honorable as they expect all their human friends to treat them. If one of our human friends should forsake us because we were in trouble, we would consider such a friend as very far from being good. How is it, then, that we can even for one moment accuse our Lord of such actions? No, dear friend, if the Lord is good, not pious only, but really good, it must be because He always under every circumstance acts up to the highest ideal of that which He Himself has taught us is goodness. Goodness in Him must mean, just as it does with us, the living up to the best and highest He knows.

Practically, then, it means that He will not neglect any of His duties toward us, and that He will always treat us in the best possible way. This may sound like a platitude, and you may exclaim, "Why tell us this, for it is what we all believe?" But do you? If you did, would it be possible for you ever to think He was neglectful, or indifferent, or unkind, or self-absorbed, or inconsiderate? Do not put on a righteous air, and say, "Oh, but I never do accuse Him of any such things. I would not dare to." Do you not? Have you never laid to His charge things you would scorn to do yourselves? How was it when that last grievous disappointment came? Did you not feel as if the Lord had been unkind in permitting such a thing to come upon you, when you were trying so hard to serve Him? Do you never look upon His will as a tyrannical and arbitrary will, that must be submitted to, of course, but that could not by any possibility be loved? Does it never seem to you a hard thing to say, "Thy will be done"? But could it seem hard if you really believed that the Lord is good, and that He always does that which is good?

The Lord Jesus took great care to tell us that He was a good Shepherd, because He knew how often appearances would be against Him, and how tempted we should be to question His goodness. "I am a good Shepherd," He says in effect, "not a bad one. Bad shepherds neglect and forsake their sheep, but I am a good Shepherd, and never neglect nor forsake My sheep. I give My life for the sheep." His ideal of goodness in a shepherd was that the shepherd must protect the sheep entrusted to his care, even at the cost of his own life; and He came up to His own ideal. Now, can we not see that if we really believe that He is good, not in some mysterious, religious way, but in this common-sense, human way, we shall be brought out into a large place of peace and comfort at once. If I am a sheep, and the Lord is a good Shepherd, in the ordinary common-sense definition of *good,* how utterly secure I am! How sure I may be of the best of care in every respect! How safe I am for time and for eternity!

Let us be honest with ourselves. Have we never in our secret hearts accused the Lord of the characteristics that He has told us in Ezekiel are the marks of a bad shepherd. Have we not thought that He cared for His own comfort or glory more than He cared for ours? Have we not complained that He has not strengthened us when we were weak, or bound up our broken hearts, or sought for us when we were lost? Have we not even actually looked upon our diseased, and helpless, and lost condition, as a reason why He would not any longer have anything to do with us? In what does this differ from if we should say out plump and plain, the Lord is a bad shepherd, and does not fulfill His duties to His sheep. You shrink in horror, perhaps, at this translation of your inward murmurings and complainings, but what else, I ask you, can they in all honesty mean? It is of vital importance now and then to drag out our secret thoughts and feelings about the Lord into the full light of the Holy Spirit, that we may see what our attitude about Him really is. It is fatally easy to get into a habit of wrong thoughts about God, thoughts which will insensibly separate us from Him by a wide gulf of doubt and unbelief. More than anything else, more even than sin, wrong thoughts about God sap the foundations of our spiritual life, and grieve His heart of love. We can understand this from ourselves. Nothing grieves us so much as to have our friends misjudge and misunderstand us, and attribute to us motives we scorn. And nothing, I believe, so grieves the Lord. It is, in fact, idolatry. For what is idolatry but creating and worshipping a false God, and what are we doing but this very thing, when we allow ourselves to misjudge Him, and attribute to Him actions and feelings that are unkind and untrustworthy.

It is called in the Bible a speaking against God. "Yea, they spake against God; they said, Can God furnish a table in the wilderness?" This seemed a very innocent question to ask. But God had promised to supply all their needs in the wilderness; and to ask this question implied a secret want of confidence in His ability to do as He had promised; and it was therefore, in spite of its innocent appearance, a real "speaking against" Him. A good God could not have led His people into the wilderness, and then have failed to "furnish a table" for them; and to question whether He was able to do it was to imply that He was not good. In the same way we are sometimes sorely tempted to ask a similar question. Circumstances often seem to make it so impossible for God to supply our needs, that we find ourselves tempted over and over to "speak against" Him by asking if He can. Often as He has done it before, we seem unable to believe He can do it again, and in our hearts we "limit" Him, because we do not believe His Word or trust in His goodness.

If our faith were what it ought to be, no circumstances, however untoward, could make us "limit" the power of God to supply our needs. The God who can make circumstances can surely control circumstances, and can, even in the wilderness, "furnish a table" for all who trust in Him.

There are many similar questions to be found in the Bible, each one throwing doubts upon the goodness of God, and each one, I am afraid, is a duplicate of questions asked by God's children now.

"Is God among us or not?"

"Hath God forgotten to be gracious?"

"Is God's mercy clean gone forever?"

"Hath God in anger shut up his tender mercies?"

"Do God's promises fail forevermore?"

"O God, why hast thou cast us off forever?"

"Why hast thou made me thus?"

Let us consider these questions for a little, and see whether we can find any counterparts to them in our own secret questionings.

"Is God among us or not?"

He has declared to us in unmistakable terms, as He did to the children of Israel, that He is always with us, and will never forsake us; and yet when trouble comes, we begin, as they did, to doubt His Word and to question whether He really can be there. Moses called this, when the Israelites did it, "tempting the Lord," and it deserves the same condemnation when we do it. No one can ask such a question without casting a doubt upon the truthfulness and trustworthiness of the Lord; and to ask it is, if we only knew it, to insult Him, and to libel His character. I know that it is, alas! a common question even among God's own children, and I know also that many of them think it is only true humility to ask it, and that, for such unworthy creatures as they feel themselves to be, it would be the height of presumption to be sure of His presence with them. But what about His own Word in the matter? He has declared to us in every possible way that He is with us, and will never leave us nor forsake us, and dare we "make him a liar" by questioning the truth of His Word? A good God cannot lie, and we must give up forever asking such a question as this. The Lord is with us as truly as we are with ourselves, and we have simply just got to believe that He is, no matter what the seemings may be.

"Hath God forgotten to be gracious?"

To ask this question is to "speak against" Him as grievously as it would be to ask a good mother if she had forgotten her child. And yet the Lord Himself says: "Can a woman forget her sucking child? Yea, they may forget, yet will I not forget thee." Those of us who are mothers know very well how grieved and insulted we should feel if anyone should suggest the possibility of our forgetting our children; and we mothers at least, if no one else does, should be able to understand how such questioning must grieve the Lord.

"Is God's mercy clean gone forever?" "Hath God in anger shut up his tender mercies?"

To ask these two questions of a good God is to insult Him. It would be as impossible for His tender mercies to be shut up toward us, or for His mercy to go from us forever, as it would be for the tender mercies of a mother come to an end. The Psalmist says: "The Lord is good to all, and his tender mercies are over all his works." In the very nature of things this must be, because He is a good God, and cannot do otherwise.

"Do God's promises fail forevermore?"

There come times in every Christian's life when we are tempted to ask this question. Everything seems to be going wrong, and all God's promises seem to have failed. But if we remember that the Lord is good, we shall see that He would cease to be good if such a thing could be. A man who breaks his promises is looked upon as a dishonorable and untrustworthy man; and a God who could break His, if one could imagine such a thing, would be dishonorable and untrustworthy also. And to ask such a question is to cast a stigma on His goodness, that may well be characterized as "speaking against God." No matter how affairs may look, we may be sure of this, that because God is good no promise of His has ever failed, or can ever fail. Heaven and earth may pass away, but His Word never.

"O God, why hast thou cast us off forever?"

It will be impossible for a good God to cast us off as it would be for a good mother to cast off her child. We may be in trouble and darkness, and may feel as if we were cast off and forsaken, but our feelings have nothing to do with the facts, and the fact is that God is good, and could not do it. The good Shepherd does not cast off the sheep that is lost, and take no further care of it, but He goes out to seek for it, and He seeks until He finds it. To suspect Him of casting us off forever is to wound and grieve His faithful love, just as it would wound a good mother's heart is she should be supposed capable of casting off her child, let that child have wandered as far as it may. The thing is impossible in either case, but far more impossible in the case of God than even in the case of the best mother that ever lived.

"Why hast thou made me thus?"

This is a question we are very apt to ask. There is, I imagine, hardly one of us who has not been tempted at one time or another to "reply against God" in reference to the matter of our own personal make-up. We do not like our peculiar temperaments or our especial characteristics, and we long to be like someone else who has, we think, greater gifts of appearance or of talent. We are discontented with our make-up, both inward and outward, and we feel sure that all our failures are because of our unfortunate temperaments; and we are inclined to blame our Creator for having "made us thus."

I remember vividly a time in my life when I was tempted to be very rebellious about my own make-up. I was a plain-spoken, energetic sort of an individual, trying to be a good Christian, but with no especial air of piety about me. But I had a sister who was so saintly in her looks, and had such a pious manner, that she seemed to be the embodiment of piety; and I felt sure I could be a great deal better Christian if only I could get her saintly looks and manner. But all my struggles to get them were useless. My natural temperament was far too energetic and outspoken for any appearance of saintliness, and many a time I said upbraidingly in my heart to God, "Why hast thou made me thus?" But one day I came across a sentence in an old mystic book that seemed to open my eyes. It was as follows: "Be content to be what thy God has made thee"; and it flashed on me that it really was a fact that God had made me, and that He must know the sort of creature He wanted me to be; and that if He had made me a potato vine, I must be satisfied to grow potatoes, and must not want to be a rosebush and grow roses; and if He had fashioned me for humble tasks, I must be content to let others do the grander work. We are "God's workmanship," and God is good, therefore His workmanship must be good also; and we may securely trust that before He is done with us, He will make out of us something that will be to His glory, no matter how unlike this we may as yet feel ourselves to be.

The Psalmist seemed to delight in repeating over and over again this blessed refrain, "for the Lord is good." It would be worth while for you to take your concordances and see how often he says it. And he exhorted everyone to join him in saying it. "Let the redeemed of the Lord say so," was his earnest cry. We must join our voices to his—The Lord is good—The Lord is good. But we must not say it with our lips only, and then by our actions give the lie to our words. We must "say" it with our whole being, with thought, word, and action, so that people will see we really mean it, and will be convinced that it is a tremendous fact.

A great many things in God's divine providences do not look like goodness to the eye of sense, and in reading the Psalms we wonder perhaps how the Psalmist could say, after some of the things he records, "for his mercy endureth forever." But faith sits down before mysteries such as these, and says, "The Lord is good, therefore all that He does must be good, no matter how it looks, and I can wait for His explanations."

A housekeeping illustration has often helped me here. If I have a friend whom I know to be a good housekeeper, I do not trouble over the fact that at housecleaning time things in her house may seem to be more or less upset, carpets up, and furniture shrouded in coverings, and even perhaps painting and decorating making some rooms uninhabitable. I say to myself, "My friend is a good housekeeper, and although things look so uncomfortable now, all this upset is only because she means in the end to make it far more comfortable than ever it was before." This world is God's housekeeping; and although things at present look grievously upset, yet, since we know that He is good, and therefore must be a good Housekeeper, we may be perfectly sure that all this present upset is only to bring about in the end a far better state of things than could have been without it. I dare say we have all felt at times as though we could have done God's housekeeping better than He does it Himself, but, when we realize that God is good, we can feel this no longer. And it comforts me enormously, when the world seems to me to be going all wrong, just to say to myself, "It is not my housekeeping, but it is the Lord's; and the Lord is good, therefore His housekeeping must be good too; and it is foolish for me to trouble."

A deeply taught Christian was asked by a despairing child of God, "Does not the world look to you like a wreck?

"Yes," was the reply, in a tone of cheerful confidence; "yes, like the wreck of a bursting seed." Any of us who have watched the first sproutings of an oak tree from the heart of a decaying acorn will understand what this means. Before the acorn can bring forth the oak, it must become itself a wreck. No plant ever came from any but a wrecked seed.

Our Lord uses this fact to teach us the meaning of His processes with us. "Verily, verily, I say unto you, Except a corn of wheat fall into the ground and die, it abideth alone: but, if it die, it bringeth forth much fruit."

The whole explanation of the apparent wreckage of the world at large, or of our own personal lives in particular, is here set forth. And, looked at in this light, we can understand how it is that the Lord can be good, and yet can permit the existence of sorrow and wrong in the world He has created, and in the lives of the human beings He loves.

It is His very goodness that compels Him to permit it. For He knows that, only through such apparent wreckage, can the fruition of His glorious purposes for us be brought to pass. And we whose hearts also long for that fruition will, if we understand His ways, be able to praise Him for all His goodness, even when things seem hardest and most mysterious.

The Apostle tells us that the will of God is "good and acceptable, and perfect." The will of a good God cannot help being "good"—in fact, it must be perfect'; and, when we come to know this, we always find it "acceptable"; that is we come to love it. I am convinced that all trouble about submitting to the will of God would disappear, if once we could see clearly that His will is good. We struggle and struggle in vain to submit to a will that we do not believe to be good, but when we see that it is really good, we submit to it with delight. We want it to be accomplished. Our hearts spring out to meet it.

> I worship thee, sweet Will of God!
>   And all thy ways adore;
> And, every day I live, I seem
>   To love thee more and more.
> I love to kiss each print where thou
>   Hast set thine unseen feet:
> I cannot fear thee, blessed Will!
>   Thine empire is so sweet.

Space fails me to tell all that I might of the infinite goodness of the Lord. Each one must "taste and see" for himself. And if he will but do it honestly and faithfully, the words of the Psalmist will become true of him: "They shall abundantly utter the memory of Thy great goodness, and shall sing of Thy righteousness."

Chapter 8: The Lord Our Dwelling Place

"Lord, thou hast been our dwelling place in all generations."

The comfort or discomfort of our outward lives depends more largely upon the dwelling place of our bodies than upon almost any other material thing; and the comfort or discomfort of our inward life depends similarly upon the dwelling place of our souls.

Our dwelling place is the place where we live, and not the place we merely visit. It is our home. All the interests of our earthly lives are bound up in our home; and we do all we can to make them attractive and comfortable. But our souls need a comfortable dwelling place even more than our bodies; inward comfort, as we all know, is of far greater importance than outward; and, where the soul is full of peace and joy, outward surroundings are of comparatively little account.

It is of vital importance, then, that we should find out definitely where our souls are living. The Lord declares that He has been our dwelling place in all generations, but the question is, Are we living in our dwelling place? The Psalmist says of the children of Israel that "they wandered in the wilderness, in a solitary way; they found no city to dwell in. Hungry and thirsty, their soul fainted in them." And I am afraid there are many wandering souls in the Church of Christ, whom this description of the wandering Israelites would exactly fit. All their Christian lives they have been wandering in a spiritual wilderness, and have found no city to dwell in, and, hungry and thirsty, their souls have fainted in them. And yet all the while the dwelling place of God has been standing wide open, inviting them to come in and take up their abode there forever. Out Lord Himself urges this invitation upon us. "Abide in me," He says, "and I in you"; and He goes on to tell us what are the blessed results of this abiding, and what are the sad consequences of not abiding.

The truth is, our souls are made for God. He is our natural home, and we can never be at rest anywhere else. "My soul longeth, yea, even fainteth for the courts of the Lord; my heart and my flesh crieth out for the living God." We always shall hunger and faint for the courts of the Lord, as long as we fail to take up our abode there.

> *God only is the creature's home;*
> *Though rough and straight the road,*
> *Yet nothing else can satisfy*
> *The soul that longs for God.*

How shall we describe this Divine dwelling place? David describes it when he says: "The Lord is my rock, and my fortress, and my deliverer; the God of my rock; in him will I trust; he is my shield, and the horn of my salvation, my high tower, and my refuge, my Savior; thou savest me from violence."

So we see that our dwelling place is also our fortress, and our high tower, and our rock, and our refuge. We all know what a fortress is. It is a place of safety, where everything that is weak and helpless can be hidden from the enemy and kept in security. And when we are told that God, who is our dwelling place, is also our fortress, it can mean only one thing, and that is, that if we will but live in our dwelling place, we shall be perfectly safe and secure from every assault of every possible enemy that can attack us. "For in the time of trouble he shall hide me in his pavilion; in the secret of his tabernacle shall he hide me; he shall set me up upon a rock." "He that dwelleth in the secret place of the most High, shall abide under the shadow of the Almighty." "Thou shalt hide them in the secret of thy presence from the pride of man; thou shalt keep them secretly in a pavilion from the strife of tongues."

In the "secret of God's tabernacle" no enemy can find us, and no troubles can reach us. The "pride of man" and the "strife of tongues" find no entrance into the "pavilion" of God. The "secret of his presence" is a more secure refuge than a thousand Gibraltars. I do not mean that no trials come. They may come in abundance, but they cannot penetrate into the sanctuary of the soul, and we may dwell in perfect peace even in the midst of life's fiercest storms.

But alas! how few of us know this. We use David's language, it may be, but to us it is only a figure of speech that has no reality in it. We say the things he said, in the conventional, pious tone that is considered proper when speaking of religious matters. "Oh, yes, the Lord is my dwelling place I know, and I have committed myself and all my interests to His keeping, as of course every Christian ought to do. But"—and here one's natural tones are resumed—"but then I cannot forget that I am a poor good-for-nothing sort of person, and have no strength to conquer my temptations; and I can hardly expect that I can be kept in the perfect security David speaks of." And here will follow a story of all sorts of fears, and anxieties, exactly as if the dwelling place of God had never been heard of, and as if the soul was wandering alone and unprotected in a world of trouble and danger.

There is a psalm that I call the "Dwelling Place of God." It is the Ninety-first Psalm, and it gives us a wonderful description of what this dwelling place is. "He that dwelleth in the secret place of the Most High shall abide under the shadow of the Almighty. I will say of the Lord, he is my refuge and my fortress; my God; in him will I trust." Our idea of a fortress is generally of a hard, granite building, where one would be safe, perhaps, but also at the same time sadly uncomfortable. But there are other sorts of fortresses that are soft, and tender, and full of comfort; and this psalm describes them. "He shall cover thee with his feathers," just as the mother hen covers her little helpless chickens in the fortress of her warm, brooking wings. The fortress of a mother's heart, whether it be of a human mother, or a hen mother, or a tiger mother, is the most impregnable fortress the world knows, and yet the tenderest. And it is this sort of a fortress that the Lord is. "Under his wings shalt thou trust": "He shall carry them in his bosom"; "underneath are the everlasting arms."

Wings, bosom, arms! What blessed fortresses are these! And how safe is everything enfolded by them. Nature is full of such fortresses. Listen to what a late writer says of the tiger mother. "When her children are born, some power teaches the tiger to be gentle. A spirit she cannot resist, for it is the spirit of her Creator, enters her savage heart. It is a tiger's impulse to resent an injury. Pluck her by the hair, smite her on the flank, she will leap upon and rend you. But to resent an injury is not her strongest impulse. Watch those impotent kitten creatures playing with her. They are so weak, a careless movement of her giant paw will destroy them; but she makes no careless movement. They have caused her a hundredfold the pain your blow produced; yet she does not render evil for evil. These puny mites of helpless impotence she strokes with love's light in her eyes; she licks the shapeless forms of her tormentors, and, as they plunge at her, love transforms each groan of her anguish into a whinny of delight. She moves her massive head in a way which shows that He who bade you turn the other cheek created her. When strong enough to rise, the terrible creature goes forth to sacrifice herself for her own. She will starve that they may thrive. She is terrible for her little ones, as God is terrible for His."

We have all seen these mother fortresses hundreds of times, and have called them Godlike. And one would think that the sight would have made us fly to our refuge in the dwelling place of God, and leave outside all fear! But the trouble is, we point-blank refuse to believe that the Bible means any such good news. Not in words, perhaps, but in effect, we say, "The Lord's arms are not so dependable as the strong, loving arms of the weakest earthly mother; the Lord's bosom is not as tender as the tiger's bosom; the Lord's wings are not as brooding as the wings of the little mother hen. We know that all these beautiful earthly fortresses are made and fashioned by Him, but we cannot believe that He Himself is equal to them. To have Him for our fortress does not really mean to us anything half so safe or half so tender as to have a mother for our fortress." And so mothers are trusted, and God is not!

And yet how safe the Psalmist declares this Divine dwelling place to be! Notice how he says, that we who are in this dwelling place shall be afraid of nothing; not for the terror by night, nor the arrow by day, nor for the pestilence that walketh in darkness, nor for the destruction that wasteth at noonday; thousands shall fall beside us and around us, but no evil shall befall the soul that is hidden in this Divine dwelling place; no plague shall come nigh those who have made God their "habitation."

All the terrors and all the plagues that have made our religious lives so uncomfortable, an even so wretched, are provided for here, and from all of them we shall be delivered, if we make the Lord our habitation. This does not mean that we shall have no outward trials. Plagues in abundance may attack your body and your goods, but your body and your goods are not yourself; and nothing can come nigh you, the real interior you, while you are dwelling in God.

A large part of the pain of life comes from the haunting "fear of evil" which so often besets us. Our lives are full of supposes. Suppose this should happen, or suppose that should happen; what could we do; how could we bear it? But, if we are living in the "high tower" of the dwelling place of God, all these supposes will drop out of our lives. We shall be "quiet from the fear of evil," for no threatenings of evil can penetrate into the "high tower" of God. Even when walking through the valley of the shadow of death, the Psalmist could say, "I will fear no evil"; and, if we are dwelling in God, we can say so too.

But you may ask here how you are to get into this Divine dwelling place. To this I answer that you must simply move in. If a house should be taken for us by a friend, and we were told it was ready, and that the lease and all the necessary papers were duly attested and signed, we should not ask how we could get into it—we should just pack up and move in. And we must do the same here. God says that He is our dwelling place, and the Bible contains all the necessary papers, duly attested and signed. And our Lord invites us, nay more, commands us to enter in and abide there. In effect He says, "God is your dwelling place, and you must see to it that you take up your abode there. You must move in."

But how, you ask, how can I move in? You must do it by faith. God has said that He is your dwelling place, and now you must say it too. "I will say of the Lord, he is my refuge and my fortress: my God; in him will I trust." Faith takes up the Word of God, and asserts it to be true. Christ says, "Abide," and we must say, "I will abide." Thus we "make him our habitation" by faith. He is our habitation already, as to His side of it; but we must make Him so, as to our side of it, by believing that He is, and by continually asserting it. Coleridge says:

> *Faith is an affirmation and an act,*
> *That bids eternal truth be present fact.*

And we must make the eternal truth that the Lord is our dwelling place become present fact by the affirmation of our faith, and by putting on the thoughts and actions that would naturally result from having moved into the tabernacle of God.

And one of the first things we would have to do would be to give up forever all worry and anxiety. It is unthinkable that worry and anxiety could enter into the dwelling place of God; and when we enter there, we must leave them behind.

We talk about obeying the commands of the Lord, and make a great point of outward observances and outward duties, and all the while neglect and ignore the commands as to the inward life, which are a thousandfold more important. "Let not your heart be troubled, neither let it be afraid," is one of our Lord's commands that is almost universally disobeyed; and yet I question whether our disobedience of any other command is so grievous to His heart. I am very sure for myself, that I would be far more grieved if my child should mistrust me, and should feel her interests were unsafe in my care, than if in a moment of temptation she should disobey me. And I am convinced that none of us have appreciated how deeply it wounds the loving heart of our Lord, when He finds that His people do not feel safe in His care.

We can know this by ourselves. Suppose one of our friends should commit something to our keeping, receiving from us every assurance that we would keep it safe, and then should go away and worry over it, as we worry over the things we commit to God, and should express to others the anxieties about it that we allow ourselves to express about the things we have put into God's care. How, I would like to know, would we feel about it? Would we not be deeply hurt and wounded; and would we not finally be inclined to hand the thing back into our friend's own care, and to say, "Since it is very plain that you do not trust me, had you not better take care of your things yourself?" It is amazing that God's own children can dare to be anxious, after once they have committed a matter to Him; it is such a libel on His trustworthiness. And of course outsiders judge it in this way, and think to themselves that to have the Lord for your dwelling place does not evidently amount to much after all, or those who profess to be living there could not be so troubled.

He who cares for the sparrows, and numbers the hairs of our head, cannot possibly fail us. He is an impregnable fortress into which no evil can enter and no enemy penetrate. I hold it, therefore, as a self-evident truth that the moment I have really committed anything into this Divine dwelling place, that moment all fear and anxiety should cease. While I keep anything in my own care, I may well fear and tremble, for it is indeed to the last degree unsafe; but in God's care, no security could be more absolute.

The Psalmist says: "The name of the Lord is a strong tower: the righteous runneth into it, and is safe." The only point, therefore, is to "run into" this strong tower and stay there forever. It would be the height of folly, when the enemy was surrounding us on every side to stand outside of a fortress and cry out for safety. If I want to be safe, I must go in.

"O Jerusalem, Jerusalem!" said our Lord, "thou that killest the prophets, and stonest them which are sent unto thee, how often would I have gathered thy children together, even as a hen gathereth her chickens under her wings, and ye would not." If the little children wants to be safe, it must "run into" the fortress of its mother's wings. A great many people stay outside of God's dwelling place, because they feel themselves too unworthy and too weak to dare to go in. What would we think of the little chicken that would see the hawk coming, would hear the mother calling, and see her outspread wings, but would stand outside, trembling with fright, saying, "Oh, I am such a poor, weak, foolish, helpless little chicken that I am afraid I am not worthy to go under my mother's wings"? If the mother hen could speak, I am sure she would say, "You poor, foolish little thing, it is just because you are weak, and helpless, and good for nothing, that I want you under my wings. If you were a great, big, strong rooster, able to take care of yourself, I would not want you at all." Need I make the application?

But we must not only "run into" our dwelling place. The Psalmist says: "I will abide in thy tabernacle forever: I will trust in the covert of thy wings"; and we must do the same. This "abiding in his tabernacle forever" is, I am free to confess, sometimes very hard. It is comparatively easy to take a step of faith, but it is a far more difficult thing to abide steadfastly in the place into which we have stepped. A great many people "run into" God's fortress on Sunday, and come out of it again as soon as Monday morning dawns. Some even run into it when they kneel down to say their prayers at night, and come out of it five minutes afterward when they get into bed. Of course, this is the height of folly. One cannot imagine any sensible refugee running into a fortress one day, and the next day running out among the enemy again. We should think such a person had suddenly lost all his senses. But is it not even more foolish when it comes to the soul? Are our enemies any less active on Mondays than they are on Sundays, or are we any better able to cope with them when we are in bed than when we were kneeling at our prayers?

The question is, Do we want to pay visits only to the dwelling place of God, or do we want to live there? Do we want to "trust in the covert of his wings" today, and tomorrow be exposed to the buffetings of our enemies outside? No one would deliberately choose the latter, but far too many drift into it. Our abiding in Christ is altogether a matter of faith, but we fail to realize this. We think our earnest wrestlings or our strenuous efforts are a large part of the matter; and, when these slacken, our faith weakens. But if there is one thing more certain than another, it is that the whole Christian life is to be lived by faith. Without faith it is impossible to please God; and it is perfect folly to fancy that any amount of fervency or earnestness or anything whatever of our own doing can take its place; and it is manifestly useless to waste our time and energy over things that amount to nothing.

What we must do is to put all our will power and all our energy into faith. We must "set our faces like a flint" to move into the dwelling place of God, and to abide there steadfastly, let the temptations to doubt or discouragement be what they may.

"He that dwelleth in the secret place of the Most High shall abide under the shadow of the Almighty. *Abiding* and *trusting* are synonymous words, and mean exactly the same thing. While I trust the Lord, I am abiding in Him. If I trust Him steadfastly, I am abiding in Him steadfastly; if I trust Him intermittently, I am running into Him and running out again. I used to think there was some mystery about abiding in Christ, but I see now that it only means trusting Him fully. When once you understand this, it becomes really the simplest matter in the world. We sometimes say, speaking of two human beings, that they "live in each other's hearts," and we simply mean that perfect love and confidence exists between them, and that doubts of one another are impossible. If my trust in the fortress of the Lord is absolute, I am abiding in that fortress; and this is the whole story.

The practical thing to do, therefore, in face of the fact that God is declared to be our Fortress and our High Tower, is, by a definite act of surrender and faith, to put ourselves and all our interests of every kind into this Divine dwelling place, and then dismiss all care or anxiety about them from our minds. Since the Lord is our dwelling place, nothing can possibly come to any harm that is committed to His care. As long as we believe this, our affairs remain in His care; the moment we begin to doubt, we take our affairs into our own hands, and they are no longer in the divine fortress. Things cannot be in two places at once. If they are in our own care, they cannot be in God's care; and if they are in God's care, they cannot be in our own. This is as clear as daylight, and yet, for the want of a little common sense, people often get mixed up over it. They put their affairs into God's fortress, and at the same time put them into their own fortress as well, and then wonder why they are not taken care of. This is all folly. Either trust the Lord out and out, or else trust yourself out and out; but do not try to mix the two trusts, for they will not mix.

It will help you practically if you will put your trust into words. Say definitely, "God is my dwelling place, and I am going to abide in Him forever. It is all settled; I am in this divine habitation, and I am safe here, and I am not going to move out again." You must meet all assaults of doubt and discouragement with the simple assertion that you are there, and that you know you will not be confounded; let other people do as they may, but you must declare that you at any rate are going to abide in your Divine dwelling place forever. And then, having taken this stand, you must utterly refuse to reconsider the matter. It is all settled; and there is nothing more to be said about it.

In all this I do not, of course, mean that we are to lie in bed and let things go. I am talking about the inward aspect of our affairs, not the outward. Outwardly we may have to be full of active carefulness, but it must all be from the inward basis of a soul that has hidden itself and all its interests in the dwelling place of God, and that is therefore "careful for nothing" in the beautiful Bible sense of having no anxious thoughts. To be thus without care inwardly is the surest foundation for successful outward care; and the soul that is hidden in the dwelling place of God is the soul that will be able to bear triumphantly earth's greatest trials, and to conquer its strongest foes.

There is one point I must not fail to mention. When we move into a new house, we not only move in ourselves, but we take with us all our belongings of every sort or description, and above all we take our family. No one would be so foolish as to leave anything he cared for or anyone he loved outside. But I am afraid there are some of God's children, who move into the dwelling place of God themselves, but who, by their lack of faith, leave outside those they love best; and more often than not it is their children who are so abandoned. We would be horrified at a father who, in a time of danger, should flee into a fortress for safety, but should leave his children outside; and yet hundreds of Christians do this very thing. Every anxious thought in which we indulge about our children proves that we have not really taken them with us into the dwelling place of God.

What I mean is this, that if we trust for ourselves, we must trust for our loved ones also, and especially for our children. God is more their Father than their earthly fathers are and if they are dear to us, they are far dearer to Him. We cannot, therefore, do anything better for them than to trust them to His care, and hardly anything worse than to try to keep them in our own. I knew a Christian mother who trusted peacefully for her own salvation, but was racked with anxiety about her sons, who seemed entirely indifferent to all religious subjects. One evening she heard about the possibility of putting those we love into the fortress of God by faith and leaving them there; and, like a flash of heavenly light, she saw the inconsistency of hiding herself in God's fortress and leaving her beloved sons outside. At once her faith took them into the fortress with her, and she abandoned them to the care of God. So fully and completely did she do this that all her anxiety vanished, and perfect peace dawned upon her soul. She told me she felt somehow that her sons were God's sons now—no longer hers—and that He loved them far better than she could, and would care for them far more wisely and effectually. She held herself in readiness to do for them whatever the Lord might suggest; but she felt that He was the One who would know what was best, and she was content to leave the matter in His hands.

She went home from that meeting and called her sons into her room, telling them what had happened; she said, "You know, my dear boys, how anxious and troubled I have been about you, and how continually I have preached to you, and I am afraid have often worried you. But now I have learned to trust, and I have put you by faith into the fortress of God, and have left you in His care. I am sure that He will care for you far better than your poor mother ever could, and will save you in His own way. My anxieties are over."

I did not see her again for a year, but when I did, she came up to me with a beaming face; and with tears of joy filling her eyes, she said, "Rejoice with me, dear friend, that I learned how to put my boys into the fortress of God. They have been safe there ever since, and all of them are good Christian boys today."

The conclusion of the whole matter, then, is simply this, that we must make up our minds to move into our dwelling place in God and to take there with us all our possessions, above all, those we love. We must hide ourselves in Him away from ourselves, away from all others, and we must lose sight of everything that is outside of Him except as we see it through His eyes. God's eyes are the windows of God's house, and the only windows there are; and seen through His eyes, all things will put on a new aspect. We shall see our trials as blessings, and our enemies as disguised friends. We shall be calm and at rest in the face of all the frets and worries of life, untouched by any of them. "For he that dwelleth in God dwelleth in a peaceable habitation and in a quiet resting place."

Chapter 9: Much More Versus Much Less

"But where sin abounded grace did much more abound."

In our preceding chapters we have been trying to learn something about the Lord and His great salvation; and now the vital point is, what view do we take of it all? A very great deal of the comfort or discomfort of our religious lives depends on the view we take of things. I do not mean of course that our view of things affects their reality in any way, but what I do mean is that our view makes all the difference in our apprehension of this reality; and while our safety comes from what things really are, our comfort comes from what we suppose them to be.

There is an expression used over and over again in the Bible to describe the salvation of the Lord Jesus Christ, which gives a view of that salvation, so amazing and so perfectly satisfying, that I cannot help wondering whether any of us have ever yet grasped its full meaning. One thing is certain, that no one who grasps it could ever be uncomfortable or miserable again. It is the expression, "much more," and it is used to tell us, if only we would believe it, that there is no need which any human being can ever know that cannot be much more than met by the glorious salvation that is provided. But we are continually tempted to think that *much less* would be a truer term; and that, so far from this salvation being much more than our needs, it turns out in actual experience to be much less. And this "much less" view, if I may so express it, is in danger of making our whole spiritual lives a misery to us.

If all we have been learning in our preceding chapters of the fullness of God's salvation is indeed true, it would seem as if nothing but the language of "much more" could ever be used by any child of God. But since there are some Christians, who seem by their thoughts and their actions to declare that they consider the language of "much less" to be the only prudent language for poor sinners, I want us carefully to consider the matter in the light of what the Bible tells us, and discover whether we are really justified in saying much more.

It is, I believe, a far more vital question for each one of us than may appear at first sight. For if God declares that the salvation He has provided is much more than enough to meet our needs, and if we insist on declaring in our secret thoughts that it is much less, we are casting discredit on His trustworthiness, and are storing up for ourselves untold discomfort and misery.

"Much less" is the language of the seen thing, "much more" is the language of the unseen thing. "Much less" seems on the surface to be far more reasonable than "much more," because every seen thing confirms it. Our weakness and foolishness are visible; God's strength and wisdom are invisible. Our need is patent before our very eyes; God's supply is hidden in the secret of His presence, and can only be realized by faith.

It seems a paradox to tell us that we must see unseen things. How can it be possible? But there are other things to see than those which appear on surfaces, and other eyes to look through than those we generally use. An ox and a scientist may both *look* at the same field, but they will *see* very different things there. To see unseen things requires us to have that interior eye opened in our souls which is able to see below surfaces, and which can pierce through the outer appearance of things into their inner realities. This interior eye looks not at the seen things, which are temporal, but at the things that are not seen, which are eternal; and the vital question for each one of us is, whether that interior eye has been opened in us yet, and whether we can see the things that are eternal, or whether our vision is limited to the things that are temporal only.

Can and do we say of the salvation of the Lord Jesus Christ that it is much more than our need, or that it is much less?

There is a wonderful instance in the history of the children of Israel, when they saw the unseen things with such clearness of vision, that the "much less" of their enemy, and of the seen things around them, was powerless to disturb them. The story is told in II Chronicles 32:1-15. An enemy had come up against Judah, and had threatened to overwhelm them. This enemy had been so universally successful hitherto in all his wars with the nations round about that he had no doubt he would be able to conquer the Israelites also. But Hezekiah, the king of Israel, looked not at the seen enemy, but at the unseen God, and he saw that God was the strongest; and he spake comfortable to the people, and said: "Be strong and courageous, be not afraid nor dismayed for the king of Assyria, nor for all the multitude that is with him; for there be more with us than with him. With him is an arm of flesh; but with us is the Lord our God, to help us, and to fight our battles." What a tremendous contrast: on one side an arm of flesh; on the other, the Lord our God! No wonder the people "rested themselves" upon a declaration such as this.

And yet, I cannot help questioning whether if we had been there, we would have had faith enough to have so rested ourselves?

When Sennacherib saw their faith, he was enraged, and upbraided them with this folly in being persuaded by Hezekiah to expose themselves to the risk of death by thirst and famine in the vain hope that the Lord would deliver them. And then comes the taunt of the "much less": "Know you not," he said, "what I and my father have done unto all the people of other lands? Were the gods of the nations of those lands in any way able to deliver their lands out of mine hand? Who was there among all the gods of those nations that could deliver his people out of mine hand, that your God shall be able to deliver you out mine hand? Now therefore let not Hezekiah deceive you, nor persuade you on this manner, neither yet believe him; for no god of any nation or kingdom was able to deliver his people out of mine hand, how much less shall your God deliver you out of mine hand."

"How much less"—what a temptation to unbelief was contained in those words! All the seen things were on that side; and it did look impossible, in the face of the fact that all the nations round about had been defeated, that the nation of Israel, no stronger, and no better equipped than the others, should find deliverance. But Hezekiah kept his eyes and the eyes of the people fixed on the unseen things, and their faith stood firm; and the Lord in whom they trusted did not fail them, but sent them a grand deliverance. The "much less" of the enemy was turned for the Israelites into a "much more" of victory. The man who had promised them defeat and death was himself defeated; he was obliged to return to his own land with "shame of face," and was there slain by his disappointed relatives.

Is there nothing analogous to this story in our own personal history? Have we never been taunted with the discouraging thought that God is "much less" able to deliver us than His promises would lead us to expect? And when we have looked at the formidable *seen* things of our need has it not sometimes seemed to us as if it would be equivalent to giving ourselves over to "die by famine and thirst," if we were brought to the point of having absolutely nothing else to trust to but the Lord alone? I remember hearing of a Christian who was in great trouble, and who had tried every way for deliverance, but in vain, who said finally to another in a tone of the utmost despair, "Well, there is nothing left for me now but to trust the Lord."

"Alas!" exclaimed the friend in the greatest consternation, "is it possible it has come to *that*?"

We may shrink with horror from the thought of using such an expression, but, if we are honest with ourselves, I believe we shall be obliged to confess that sometimes, in the very bottom of our hearts, we have indulged in just this feeling. To come to the point of having nothing left to trust in but the Lord has, I am afraid, seemed to us at times a desperate condition of things. And yet, if our Lord is to be believed, His "much more's" of grace are abundantly equal to the worst emergency that can befall us. The Apostle tells us that God is able to do "exceeding abundantly above all that we can ask or think"; and this describes what His "much more's" mean. We can think of very wonderful things in the way of salvation—spiritual blessing that would transform life for us, and make the whole universe resplendent with joy and triumph—and we can ask for them. But do we really believe that God is able and willing to do for us "exceeding abundantly" above all that we can ask or think? Is the language of our hearts "much more" or "much less"?

In another place we are told that "eye hath not seen, nor ear heard, neither have entered into the heart of man, the things which God hath prepared for them that love him." If God has prepared more for us than it has ever entered into our hearts to conceive, surely we can have no question about obtaining that which has entered into our hearts, and "much more" beside. What can it be then but downright unbelief that leads any of us to harbor a thought of God's salvation being "much less" than the things it has entered into our hearts to long for.

Let us settle it then that the language of our souls must henceforth be not the "much less" of unbelief, but the "much more" of faith. And I feel sure we shall find that God's "much more's" will be enough to cover the whole range of our needs, both temporal and spiritual.

"For if through the offense of one many be dead, much more the grace of God and the gift by grace which is by one man, Jesus Christ, hath abounded unto man." This is a "much more" that really reaches, if only we could understand it, into the deepest depth of human need. There is no question in our minds as to the fact that "many be dead," but how is it with the "much more" of grace that is to abound unto many? Are we sure of the grace that is to abound unto many? Are we as sure of the grace as we are of the death? Do we really believe that the remedy is "much more" than the disease? Does the salvation seem to us "much more" than the need? Or do we believe in our hearts that it is "much less"? Which does God declare?

One of the deepest needs of our souls is the need for being saved. Is there a "much more" to meet this need? What does the Apostle say? "But God commendeth his love toward us, in that, while we were yet sinners, Christ died for us. Much more then, being now justified by his blood, we shall be saved from wrath through him. For if, when we were enemies, we were reconciled to God by the death of his Son, much more, being reconciled, we shall be saved by his life." The question of salvation seems to me to be absolutely settled by these "much more's." Since Christ has died for us, and has thereby reconciled us to God (not God to us, He did not need reconciling), of course "much more," if only we will let Him, will He now save us. There can be no question as to whether He will save us. There can be no question as to whether He will or will not, for the greater must necessarily include the lesser, and, having done the greater, "much more" will He do the lesser. We none of us doubt that He did the greater, and, in the face of these "much more's," we dare not doubt He will do the lesser.

Now the practical point for us in all this is, Do we really believe it? Have we got rid of all doubts as to our salvation? Can we speak with assurance of forgiveness and of eternal life? Do we say with the timidity of unbelief, "I *hope* I am a child of God"; or do we lift up our heads, with joyous confidence in God as our Father, and say with John, "Now *are* we the sons of God"? Is it in this respect "much more" with us, or "much less"?

We long and pray for the gift of the Holy Spirit, but it seems all in vain. We feel that our prayers are not answered. But our Lord gives faith a wonderful "much more" to lay hold of for this. "If ye then, being evil, know how to give good gifts unto your children, how much more shall your heavenly Father give the Holy Spirit to them that ask him?" There is not one of us who does not know how thankful and eager good parents are to give good gifts to their children—how they thrust them on the children often before the child is ready to receive, or even knows that it has a need. And yet, who of us really believes that God is actually "much more" eager to give the Holy Spirit to them that ask Him? Is it not rather that many feel secretly that He is "much less" willing, and that we will have to beg, and entreat, and wrestle, and wait, for this sorely needed gift? If we could only believe this "much more," how full of faith our asking would be in regard to it. We should then truly be able to believe that we actually did receive that for which we had asked, and should find that we were in actual possession of the Holy Spirit as our present and personal Comforter and Guide; and all our weary struggles and agonizing prayers for this promised gift would be over.

Sorer, perhaps, than any other need is our need of victory over sin and over circumstances. Like Juggernaut cars they roll over us with irresistible power, and crush us into the dust. And the language of "much less" seems the only language that our souls dare utter. But God has given us for this a most triumphant "much more." "For, if by one man's offense, death reigned by one, much more they which receive abundance of grace, and of the gift of righteousness, shall reign in life by one, Jesus Christ."

We have known the reigning of that spiritual death which comes by sin, and have groaned under its power. But how much do we know of that "much more" reigning in life by Jesus Christ of which the Apostle speaks? That is, have we now greater victories than we used to have defeats? Do we reign over things "much more" than they once reigned over us?

I mean this, that in the Gospel it is promised that we shall be "more than conquerors" over the very things that once conquered us, and the question is whether we really are. We have been reigned over by thousands of things, by the fear of man, by our peculiar temperaments, by our outward circumstances, by our irritable tempers, even by bad weather, by our environment of every kind. We have been slaves where we ought to have been kings. We have found our reigning to be "much less" rather than "much more." Why is this? Simply because we have not "received" enough of the abundance of grace that is ours in Christ. We have let unbelief cheat us out of our rightful possessions. We are called to be kings and are "made to have dominion," but here God declares that it shall be "much more" of a dominion than it was formerly a bondage; have we so found it? If not, why not? The lack cannot possibly be on God's side. He has not failed to provide the "much more" of victory. It must be that we have in some way failed to avail ourselves of it. And I cannot but believe that our failure arises from the fact that we have substituted our "much less" for God's "much more"; and in our heart of hearts have not believed there really is a sufficiency in the gift of righteousness in Christ to enable us to reign. We have failed through our unbelief to "receive the abundance of grace" that is necessary for reigning.

What then is our remedy? Only this—to abandon forever our "much less" of unbelief, and to accept as true God's declaration of "much more," and to claim at once the promised victory. And according to our faith it must and will be unto us.

But these assurances of the "much more's" of God's salvation are not for our spiritual needs only, but for our temporal needs as well. Do not be anxious, He says, about earthly things, for "if God so clothe the grass of the field, which today is, and tomorrow is cast into the oven, shall he not much more clothe you, O ye of little faith?"

I know that to many Christians this passage and others like it are so familiar that they have almost lost all meaning. But they do mean something, and something almost too wonderful for belief. They tell us that God cares for us human beings "much more" than He cares for the universe around us, and that He will watch over and provide for us much more than He will even for it.

Incredible, yet true! How often we have marveled at the orderly working of the universe, and have admired the great creative Power that made it and now controls it! But none of us, I suppose, has ever felt it necessary to take the burden of the universe upon our own shoulders. We have trusted the Creator to manage it all without our help. Although I must confess, from the way some people find fault with the Creator's management of things, and the advice they seem to feel it necessary to give Him in their prayers, one would think the whole burden was resting upon them!

But even where we have fully recognized that the universe is altogether in God's care, we have failed to see that we also are there, and have never dreamed that it could be true that "much more" than He cares for the universe will He care for us. We have looked at the seen things of our circumstances and our surroundings, and at the greatness of our need and our own helplessness, and have been anxious and afraid. We have burdened ourselves with the care of ourselves, feeling in our unbelief that, instead of being of "much more" value than the fowls of the air, or the lilies of the field, we are in reality of infinitely "much less"; and it seems to us that the God who cares for them is not at all likely to care for us. We say with the Psalmist: "When I consider thy heavens, the work of thy fingers, the moon and the stars, which thou hast ordained; what is man, that thou art mindful of him? and the son of man that thou visited him?" Man so puny, so insignificant, of so little account when compared with the great, wide universe, what is he, we ask, that God should care for him? And yet God declares that He does care for him, and that He even cares for him much more than He cares for the universe. Much more, remember, not much less. So that every thought of anxiety about ourselves must be immediately crushed with the common-sense reflection that, since we are not so foolish as to be anxious about the universe, we must not be so much more foolish as to be anxious about ourselves.

In the Sermon on the Mount, our Lord gives us the crowning "much more" of all. "Or what man is there of you, whom if his son ask bread, will he give him a stone? Or if he ask a fish, will he give him a serpent? If ye then, being evil, know how to give good gifts unto your children, how much more shall your Father which is in heaven gives good things to them that ask him?"

In this "much more" we have a warrant for the supply of every need. Whatever our Father sees to be good for us is here abundantly promised. And the illustration used to convince us is one of universal application. In all ranks and condition of life, among all nations, and even in the hearts of birds and beasts the mother instinct never fails to provide for its offspring the best it can compass. Under no conditions of life will a mother, unless she is wicked beyond compare, give a stone when asked for bread, or a serpent when asked for fish. And could our God, who created the mother heart, be worse than a mother? No, no, a thousand times no! What He will do is "much more," oh, so much more than even the tenderest mother could do. And if mothers "know how," as surely they do, to give good things to their children, "how much more" does He. But do we really believe this "much more"? Our hours of anxious tossing on our beds must answer. If God is actually much more willing and able to give good things to us than parents are to give good things to their children, then all possibility of doubt or anxiety as to our prayers being answered must vanish forever. All "good things" must be given to us when we ask, as inevitably as the mother who is able feeds her child when it asks her for bread. As inevitably, do I say? Ah, dear friends, far more inevitably. For it is "how much more" shall your Father which is in Heaven. Which of us has fathomed the meaning of this "how much more"? But at least this it must mean, that all human readiness to hear and answer the cry of need can only be a faint picture of God's readiness, and that, therefore, we can never dare to doubt again. And if parents would not give a stone for bread, neither would He; so that when we ask, we must be absolutely sure that we do receive the "good thing" for which we asked, whether what we receive looks like it or not.

The mother of St. Augustine, in her longing for the conversion of her son, prayed that he might not go to Rome, as she feared its dissipations. God answered her by sending him to Rome to be converted there. Things we call good are often God's evil things, and our evil is His good. But, however things may look, we always know that God must give the best because He is God and could do no other.

"He that spared not his own Son, but delivered him up for us all, how shall he not with him also freely give us all things." Since He has done the supreme thing of having given us Christ, "much more" will He do the less by giving us all things with Him. And yet we continually hear God's own children lamenting their spiritual poverty, and their state of spiritual starvation, and even, it seems sometimes, thinking it rather a pious thing to do and a mark of true humility. But what is this but glorying in the "much less" of their unbelief, instead of in the "much more" of God.

"Oh, I am such a poor creature," I heard a child of God say once with actual complacency when urged to some victory of faith; "I am such a poor creature that I cannot expect to attain to the heights you grand Christians reach." "Poor creature," indeed; of course you are, and so are we all! But God is not poor, and it is His part to supply your needs, not your part to supply His. He is able, no matter what unbelief may say, to "make all grace abound toward you, that ye always having all sufficiency in all things may abound to every good work." "All," "always," "every"—what all-embracing words these are! They include our needs to their utmost limit, and leave us no room for any question. How can we, how dare we, in the face of such declarations, ever doubt or question again?

We have only touched upon the wonders of grace hidden in these "much more's" of God. We can never exhaust their meaning in this life. But let us at least resolve henceforth to lay aside every "much less" of unbelief on all the lines of salvation, and out of the depths of our utter weakness, sinfulness, and need assert with a conquering faith always and everywhere the mighty "much more" of the grace of God!

Chapter 10: Self-Examination

"Examine yourselves, whether ye be in the faith."

Probably no subject connected with the religious life has been the cause of more discomfort and suffering to tender consciences than has this subject of self-examination; and none has led more frequently to the language of "much less," which we found in our last chapter to be so great an obstacle to all spiritual growth. And yet it has been so constantly impressed upon us that it is our duty to examine ourselves, that the eyes of most of us are continually turned inward, and our gaze is fixed on our own interior states and feelings to such an extent that self, and not Christ, has come at last to fill the whole horizon.

By *self* I mean here all that centers around this great big "Me" of ours. Its vocabulary rings out the changes on "I," "me," "my." It is a vocabulary with which we are all very familiar. The questions we ask ourselves in our times of self-examination are proof of this. Am I earnest enough? Have I repented enough? Have I the right sort of feelings? Do I realize religious truth as I ought? Are my prayers fervent enough? Is my interest in religious things as great as it ought to be? Do I love God with enough fervor? Is the Bible as much of a delight to me as it is to others? All these, and a hundred more questions about ourselves and our experiences fill up all our thoughts, and sometimes our little self-examination books as well; and day and night we ring the changes on the person pronoun "I," "me," "my," to the utter exclusion of any thought concerning Christ, or any word concerning "He," "His," "Him."

The misery of this, many of us know only too well. But the idea that the Bible is full of commands to self-examination is so prevalent that it seems one of the most truly pious things we can do; and, miserable as it makes us, we still feel it is our duty to go on with it in spite of an ever-increasing sense of hopelessness and despair.

In view of this idea many will be surprised to find that there are only two texts in the whole Bible that speak of self-examination, and that neither of these can at all be made to countenance the morbid self-analysis that results from what we call self-examination.

One of these passages I have quoted at the head of this chapter: "Examine yourselves, whether ye be in the faith." This is simply an exhortation to the Corinthians, who were in a sadly backsliding condition, to settle definitely whether they were still believers or not. "Examine yourselves, whether ye be in the *faith*." It does not say examine whether you are sufficiently earnest, or whether you have the right feelings, or whether your motives are pure, but simply and only, whether you are "in the faith." In short, do you believe in Christ or do you not? A simple question that required only a simple, straightforward answer, Yes or No. This is what it meant for the Corinthians then, and it is what it means for us now.

The other passage reads: "Wherefore, whosoever shall eat this bread and drink this cup of the Lord unworthily, shall be guilty of the body and blood of the Lord. But let a man examine himself, and so let him eat of that bread and drink of that cup." Paul was here writing of the abuses of greediness and drunkenness which had crept in at the celebration of the Lord's Supper; and, in this exhortation to examine themselves, he was simply urging them to see to it that they did none of these things, but partook of this religious feast in a decent and orderly manner.

In neither of these passages is there any hint of that morbid searching out of one's emotions and experiences that is called self-examination in the present day. And it is amazing that out of two such simple passages should have been evolved a teaching fraught with so much misery to earnest, conscientious souls.

The truth is there is no Scripture authority whatever for this disease of modern times; and those who are afflicted with it are the victims of mistaken ideas of God's ways with His children.

Some of my readers, however, are probably asking themselves whether I have not overlooked a large class of passages that tell us to "watch"; and whether these passages do not mean watching ourselves, or, in other words, self-examination. I will quote one of these passages as a sample, that we may see what their meaning really is. "But of that day and that hour knoweth no man, no not the angels which are in heaven, neither the Son, but the Father. Take ye heed, watch and pray; for ye know not when the time is. For the Son of man is as a man taking a far journey, who left his home, and gave authority to his servants, and to every man his work, and commanded the porter to watch. Watch ye therefore, for ye know not when the master of the house cometh, at even, or at midnight, or at the cock-crowing, or in the morning: lest coming suddenly he find you sleeping. And what I say unto you, I say unto all, Watch."

I think if we carefully examine this passage and others like it, we shall see that instead of teaching self-examination, they teach something that is exactly the opposite. They tell us to "watch," it is true, but they do not tell us to watch ourselves. They are plainly commands to forget ourselves in watching for Another. The return of the Lord is the thing we are to watch for. His coming footsteps, and not our own past footsteps, are to be the object of our gazing. We are to watch as a porter watches for the return of the master of the house, and are to be ready as a good watchman should be to receive and welcome Him at any moment that He may appear.

"Blessed are those servants whom the Lord when he cometh shall find watching." Watching what? Themselves? No, watching for Him, of course. If we can imagine a porter, instead of watching for the return of his master, spending his time morbidly analyzing his own past conduct, trying to discover whether he had been faithful enough, and becoming so absorbed in self-examination as to let the master's call go unheeded and the master's return unnoted, we shall have a picture of what goes on in the experience of the soul that is given up to the mistaken habit of watching and looking at self instead of watching and looking for Christ.

These passages, therefore, instead of teaching self-examination, teach exactly the opposite. God says, "Look unto me, and ye shall be saved"; but the self-analyzing soul says, "I must look unto myself, if I am to have any hope of being saved. It must be by getting myself right that salvation is to come." And yet the phrase, "Looking unto Jesus," is generally acknowledged to be one of the watchwords of the Christian religion; and all Christians everywhere will unhesitatingly declare that, of course, this is the one thing we all ought to do. But, after saying this, they will go on in their old way of self-introspection, trying to find some salvation in their own inward feelings, or in their own works of righteousness, and being continually plunged into despair because they never find it.

It is a fact that we see what we look at, and cannot see what we look away from; and we cannot look unto Jesus while we are looking at ourselves. The power for victory and the power for endurance are to come from looking unto Jesus and considering Him, not from looking unto or considering ourselves, or our circumstances, or our sins, or our temptations. Looking at ourselves causes weakness and defeat. The reason for this is that when we look at ourselves, we see nothing but ourselves, and our own weakness, and poverty, and sin; we do not and cannot see the remedy and the supply for these, and as a matter of course we are defeated. The remedy and the supply are there all the time, but they are not to be found in the place where we are looking, for they are not in self but in Christ; and we cannot be looking at ourselves and looking at Christ at the same time. Again I repeat that it is in the inexorable nature of things that what we look at that we shall see, and that, if we want to see the Lord, we must look at the Lord and not at self. It is a simple question of choice for us, whether it shall be I or Christ; whether we shall turn our backs on Christ and look at ourselves, or whether we shall turn our backs on self and look at Christ.

I was very much helped many years ago by the following sentence in a book by Adelaide Proctor: "For one look at self take ten looks at Christ." It was entirely contrary to all I had previously thought right; but it carried conviction to my soul, and delivered me from a habit of morbid self-examination and introspection that had made my life miserable for years. It was an unspeakable deliverance. And my experience since leads me to believe that even a better motto would be, "Take no look at self at all, but look only and always at Christ."

The Bible law in regard to the self-life is not that the self-life must be watched and made better, but that it must be "put off." The Apostle, when urging the Ephesian Christians to walk worthy of the vocation wherewith they had been called, tells them that they must "put off" the old man which is corrupt according to the deceitful lusts. The "old man" is, of course, the self-life, and this self-life (which we know only too well is indeed corrupt according to deceitful lusts) is not to be improved, but to be "put off." It is to be crucified. Paul says that our old man is crucified, put to death, with Christ; and he declares of the Colossians that they could no longer lie, seeing that they had "put of the old man with his deeds." Some people's idea of crucifying the "old man" is to set him up on a pinnacle, and then walk around him and stick nagging pins into him to make him miserable, but keeping him alive all the time. But, if I understand language, crucifixion means death, not making miserable; and to crucify the old man means to kill him outright, and to put him off as a snake puts off its dead and useless skin.

It is of no use, then, for us to examine self and to tinker with it in the hope of improving it, for the thing the Lord wants us to do with it is to get rid of it. Fenelon, in his *Spiritual Letters,* says that the only way to treat self is to refuse to have anything to do with it. He says we must turn our backs on this great big "I" of ours, and to say to it, "I do not know you, and am not interested in you, and I refuse to pay any attention to you whatever." But self is always determined to secure attention, and would rather be thought badly of than not to be thought of at all. And self-examination with all its miseries often gives a sort of morbid satisfaction to the self-life in us, and even deludes self into thinking it a very humble and pious sort of self after all.

The only safe and scriptural way is to have nothing to do with self at all, either with good self or with bad self, but simply to ignore self altogether; and to fix our eyes, and our thoughts, and our expectations on the Lord and on Him alone. We must substitute for the personal pronouns "I," "me," "my," the pronoun "He," "Him," "His"; and must ask ourselves, not "am I good?" but "is He good?"

The Psalmist says: "Mine eyes are ever toward the Lord, for he shall pluck my feet out of the net." As long as our eyes are toward our own feet, and toward the net in which they are entangled, we only get into worse tangles. But when we keep our eyes toward the Lord, He plucks our feet out of the net. This is a point in practical experience that I have tested hundreds of times, and I know it is a fact. No matter what sort of a snarl I may have been in, whether inward or outward, I have always found that while I kept my eyes on the snarl and tried to unravel it, it grew worse and worse; but when I turned my eyes away from the snarl and kept them fixed on the Lord, He always sooner or later unraveled it and delivered me.

Have you ever watched a farmer plowing a field? If you have, you will have noticed that in order to make straight furrows he is obliged to fix his eyes on a tree, or a post in the fence, or some object at the farther end of the field, and to guide his plow unwaveringly toward that object. If he begins to look back at the furrow behind him in order to see whether he has made a straight furrow, his plow begins to jerk from side to side, and the furrow he is making becomes a zigzag. If we would make straight paths for our feet we must do what the Apostle says he did. We must forget the things that are behind, and, reaching forth to those which are before, we must press toward the mark for the prize of the high calling of God in Christ Jesus.

To forget the things that are behind is an essential part of the pressing forward toward the prize of our high calling; and I am convinced this prize can never be reached unless we will consent to this forgetting. When we do consent to it, we come near to putting an end to all our self-examination; for, if we may not look back over our past misdoings, we shall find but little food for self-reflective acts.

We complain of spiritual hunger, and torment ourselves to know why our hunger is not satisfied. The Psalmist says: "The eyes of all wait upon thee, and thou givest them their meat in due season." Having our eyes upon ourselves and on our own hunger will never bring a supply of spiritual meat. When a man's larder is empty and he is starving, his eyes are not occupied with looking at the emptiness of his larder, but are turned toward the source from which he hopes or expects to get a supply of food. To examine self is to be like a man who should spend his time in examing his empty larder instead of going to the market for a supply to fill it. No wonder such Christians seem to be starving to death in the midst of all the fullness there is for them in Christ. They never see that fullness, for they never look at it; and again I repeat that the thing we look at is the thing we see.

I feel as if I could not repeat this evident truism too often, for somehow people seem to lay aside their common sense when they come to the subject of religion, and seem to expect to see things upon which they have deliberately kept their backs turned. They cry out, "O Lord, reveal thyself"; but instead of looking at Him they look at themselves, and keep their gaze steadily fixed on their own inward feelings, and then wonder at the "mysterious dealings" of God in hiding His face from their fervent prayers. But how can they see what they do not look at?

It is never God who hides His face from us, but it is always we who hide our face from Him, by "turning to him the back and not the face." The prophet reproaches the children of Israel with this, and adds that they "set up their abominations in the house which is called by God's name." When Christians spend their time examining their own condition, raking up all their sins, and bemoaning their shortcomings, what is this but to set up the "abomination" of their own sinful self upon the chief pedestal in their hearts, and to make it the center of their whole religious life, and of all their care and efforts. They gaze at this great, big, miserable self until it fills their whole horizon, and they "turn their back" on the Lord, until He is lost sight of altogether.

I will venture to say that there are many Christians who, for one look at the Lord, will give a thousand looks at self, and who, for one hour spent in rejoicing in Him, will spend hundreds of hours bemoaning themselves.

We are never anywhere commanded to behold our emotions, nor our experiences, nor even our sins, but we are commanded to turn our backs upon all these, and to behold the Lamb of God who taketh away our sins. One look at Christ is worth more for salvation than a million looks at self. Yet so mistaken are our ideas, we seem unable to avoid thinking that the mortification which results from self-examination must have in it some saving power, because it makes us so miserable. For we have to travel a long way on our heavenly journey before we fully learn that there is no saving power in misery, and that a cheerful, confident faith is the only successful attitude for the aspiring soul.

In Isaiah we see God's people complaining because they fasted, and He did not see; afflicted their souls, and He took no knowledge; and God gave them this significant answer: "Is it such a fast that I have chosen, a day for a man to afflict his soul? Is it to bow down his head as a bulrush, and to spread sackcloth and ashes under him? Wilt thou call this a fast, and an acceptable day to the Lord?" Whoever else is pleased with the miseries of our self-examination, it is very certain that God is not. He does not want us to bow down our heads as a bulrush, any more than He wanted His people of old to do it; and He calls upon us, as He did upon them, to forget our own miserable selves, and to go to work to lessen the miseries of others. "Is not this the fast that I have chosen," He says, "to loose the bands of wickedness, to undo the heavy burdens, and to let the oppressed go free, and that ye break every yoke? Is it not to deal thy bread to the hungry, and that thou bring the poor that are cast out to thy house; when thou seest the naked, that thou cover him?"

This service for others is of infinitely greater value to the Lord than the longest seasons of self-examination and self-abasement. And I am convinced that He has shown us here what is the surest way of deliverance out of the slough of misery into which our habits of self-examination have plunged us. He declares emphatically that if we will only keep the sort of "fast" He approves of, by giving up our own "fast" of afflicting our souls and bowing down our heads as a bulrush, and will instead "draw out our souls to the hungry," and will try to bear the burdens and relieve the miseries of others, then shall our light rise in obscurity, and our darkness be as the noonday; and the Lord shall guide us continually, satisfying our souls in drought, and making fat our bones; we shall be like a watered garden, and like a spring of water whose waters fail not.

All this is exactly what we have been striving for, but our strivings have been in our own way, not in God's. The "fast" we have chosen has been to afflict our souls, to bow down our heads as bulrushes, and to sit in sackcloth and ashes; and, as a consequence, instead of our bones being made fat, and our souls refreshed like a watered garden, we have found only leanness, and thirst, and misery. Our own "fasts," no matter how fervently they may be carried on, nor how many groans and tears may accompany them can never bring us anything else.

Now let us try God's "fast." Let us lay aside all care for ourselves, and care instead for our needy brothers and sisters. Let us stop trying to do something for our own poor miserable self-life, and begin to try to do something to help the spiritual lives of others. Let us give up our hopeless efforts to find something in ourselves to delight in, and delight ourselves only in the Lord and in His service. And if we will but do this, all the days of our misery will be ended.

But some may ask whether it is not necessary to examine ourselves in order to find out what is wrong and what needs mending. This would, of course, be necessary if we were our own workmanship, but since we are God's workmanship and not our own, He is the One to examine us, for He is the only One who can tell what is wrong. The man who makes watches is the one to examine a watch when it is out of order, and to set it straight. We have too much good sense to meddle with our watches; why is it that we have not enough good sense to give up meddling with ourselves? Surely we must see that the examining of the Lord is the only kind of examination that is of any use. His examination is like that of a physician who examines in order to cure; while our self-examination is like that of the patient who only becomes more of a hypochondriac the more he examines the symptoms of his disease.

But the question may be asked whether, when there has been actual sin, there ought not to be self-examination and self-reproach at least for a time. This is a fallacy which deceives a great many. It seems too much to believe that we can be forgiven without first going through a season of self-reproach. But what is the Bible teaching? John tells us that if we confess our sins (not bewail them, nor yet try to excuse them), but simply confess them, He is faithful and just to forgive us our sins, and to cleanse us from all unrighteousness. All that God wants is that we should turn to Him at once, acknowledge our sin, and believe in His forgiveness; and every minute that we delay doing this, in order to spend the time in self-examination and self-reproach, is only adding further sin to that which we have already committed. If ever we need to look away from self, and to have our eyes turned to the Lord, it is just when we become conscious of having sinned against Him. The greater the multitude of our enemies, the greater and more immediate our need of God.

All through the Bible we are taught this lesson of death to self and life in Christ alone. "Not I, but Christ," was not intended to be a unique experience of Paul's, but was simply a declaration of what ought to be the experience of every Christian. We sing sometimes, "Thou O Christ, art all I want," but as a fact, we really want a great many other things. We want good feelings, we want fervor and earnestness, we want realizations, we want satisfying experiences; and we continually examine ourselves to try to find out why we do not have these things. We think if we could only discover our points of failure, we should be able to set them straight. But there is no healing or transforming power in gazing at our failures. The only road to Christlikeness is to behold, not our own hatefulness, but His goodness and beauty. We grow like what we look at, and if we spend our lives looking at our hateful selves, we shall become more and more hateful. Do we not find as a fact that self-examination, instead of making us better, always seems to make us worse? Beholding self, we are more and more changed into the image of self. While on the contrary if we spend our time beholding the glory of the Lord, that is, letting our minds dwell upon His goodness and His love, and trying to drink in His spirit, the inevitable result will be that we shall be, slowly perhaps, but surely, changed into the image of the Lord upon whom we are gazing.

Fenelon says that we should never indulge in any self-reflective acts, either of mortification at our failures, or of congratulation at our successes; but that we should continually consign self and all self's doings to oblivion, and should keep our interior eyes upon the Lord only. It is very hard in self-examination not to try to find excuses for our faults; and our self-reflective acts are often in danger of being turned into self-glorying ones. The only way is to ignore self altogether and to forget there is any such being in existence.

No one who does not understand this can possibly appreciate the comfort and relief it is to be done with self and all self-reflective acts. I have known Christian workers whose lives have been one long torment because of these self-reflective acts; and I am convinced that the "Blue Mondays," of which so many clergymen complain, are nothing but the result of an indulgence in self-reflective acts concerning their services in the church the day before.

The only way to treat all forms of self-reflective acts, of whatever kind, is simply to give them up. They always do harm and never good. They are bound to result in one of two things: either they fill us full of self-praise and self-satisfaction, or they plunge us into the depths of discouragement and despair; and whichever it may be, the soul is in this way inevitably shut out from any sight of God and of His salvation.

One of the most effectual ways of conquering the habit is to make a rule that, whenever we are tempted to examine ourselves, we will always at once begin to examine the Lord instead, and will let thoughts of His love and His all-sufficiency sweep out all thoughts of our own unworthiness or our own helplessness.

I have been trying in this book to set the Lord before our eyes in all the beauty of His character and His ways in the hope that the sight will be so ravishing as to take our eyes off everything else. But no revelation of God will be of any use if we will not look at it, but will persist in turning our backs on what has been revealed, and in gazing instead at our own inward experiences. For again I must repeat that we cannot see self and see the Lord at the same time, and that while we are examining self we cannot be looking at Him.

Fenelon says concerning self-examination: "There is something very hidden and very deceptive in the suffering it causes; for while you seem to yourself to be wholly occupied with the glory of God, in your inmost soul it is self alone that occasions all your trouble. You are indeed desirous that God should be glorified, but you wish it should take place by means of your perfection, and you thus cherish the sentiments of self-love. It is simply a refined pretext for dwelling in self… It is a sort of infidelity to simple faith when we desire to be continually assured that we are doing well. It is, in fact, a desire to know what we are doing, which we shall never know, and of which it is the will of God we should be ignorant. It is trifling by the way, in order to reason about the way. The safest and shortest course is to renounce, forget, and abandon self, and, through faithfulness to God, to think no more of it. This is the whole of religion—to get out of self and self-love in order to get into God."

What we must do, therefore, is to shut the door definitely and resolutely at once and forever upon self, and all of self's experiences, whether they be good or bad; and to say with the Psalmist: "I have set the Lord (not self) always before me; because he is at my right hand, I shall not be moved. Therefore my heart is glad, and my glory rejoiceth: my flesh also shall rest in hope."

Chapter 11: Things That Cannot Be Shaken

"And this word, Yet once more, signifies the removing of those things that are shaken, as of things that are made, that those things which cannot be shaken may remain."

After all we have been considering of the unfathomable love and care of God, it might seem to those, who do not understand the deepest ways of love, that no trials or hardness could ever come into the lives of His children. But if we look deeply into the matter, we shall see that often love itself must needs bring the hardness. "Whom the Lord loveth he chasteneth, and scourgeth every son whom he receiveth. If ye endure chastening, God dealeth with you as with sons; for what son is he whom the father chasteneth not? But if ye be without chastisement, whereof all are partakers, then are ye bastards, and not sons."

If love sees those it loves going wrong, it must, because of its very love, do what it can to save them; and the love that fails to do this is only selfishness. Therefore, just because of His unfathomable love, the God of love, when He sees His children resting their souls on things that can be shaken, must necessarily remove those things from their lives in order that they may be driven to rest only on the things that cannot be shaken; and this process of removing is sometimes very hard.

We will all acknowledge, I think, that if our souls are to rest in peace and comfort, it can only be on unshakable foundations. It is no more possible for the soul to be comfortable when it is trying to rest on "things that can be shaken," than it is for the body. No one can rest comfortably in a shaking bed, or sit in comfort on a rickety chair.

Foundations to be reliable must always be unshakable. The house of the foolish man, which is built on the sand, may present a very fine appearance in clear and sunshiny weather; but when storms arise, and the winds blow, and floods come that house will fall, and great will be the fall of it. The wise man's house, on the contrary, which is built on the rock, is able to withstand all the stress of the storm, and remains unshaken through winds and floods, for it is "founded on the rock."

It is very possible in the Christian life to build one's spiritual house on such insecure foundations, that when storms beat upon it, the ruin of that house is great. Many a religious experience that has seemed fair enough when all was going well in life has tottered and fallen when trials have come, because its foundations have been insecure. It is therefore of vital importance to each one of us to see to it that our religious life is built upon "things that cannot be shaken."

Of course the immediate thought that will come to every mind is that it must be "built upon the rock Christ Jesus." This is true; but the great point is what is meant by that expression. It is one of those religious phrases that is often used conventionally with no definite or real meaning attached to it. Conventionally we believe that Christ is the only Rock upon which to build, but practically, though perhaps unconsciously, we believe that in order to have a rock upon which it will be really safe to build, many other things must be added to Christ. We think, for instance, that the right frames and feelings must be added, or the right doctrines or dogmas, or whatever else may seem to each one of us to constitute the necessary degree of security. And if we were only perfectly honest with ourselves, I suspect we should often find that our dependence was almost wholly upon these additions of our own; and that Christ Himself, as our rock of dependence, was of altogether secondary importance.

What we ought to mean when we talk of building upon the Rock Christ Jesus is what I am trying all through this book to make plain, and that is that the Lord is enough for our salvation, just the Lord only without any additions of our own, the Lord Himself, as He is in His own intrinsic character, our Creator and Redeemer, and our all-sufficient portion.

The "foundation of God standeth sure," and it is the only foundation that does. Therefore, we need to be "shaken" from off every other foundation in order that we may be forced to rest on the foundation of God alone. And this explains the necessity for those "shakings" through which so many Christians seem called to pass. The Lord sees that they are building their spiritual houses on flimsy foundations, which will not be able to withstand the "vehement beating" of the storms of life; and not in anger but in tenderest love, He shakes our earth and our heaven until all that "can be shaken" is removed, and only those "things which cannot be shaken" are left behind.

The Apostle tells us that the things that are shaken are the "things that are made"; that is, the things that are manufactured by our own efforts, feelings that we get up, doctrines that we elaborate, good works that we perform. It is not that these things are bad things in themselves. It is only when the soul begins to rest on them instead of upon the Lord that He is compelled to "shake" us from off them. And this shaking applies, we are told, "not to the earth only, but also to Heaven." This means, I am sure, that it is possible to have "things that are made" even in religious matters.

How much of the so-called religiousness of many Christians consists of these "things that are made," I cannot say; but I sometimes think the great overturnings and tossings in matters of faith, which so distress Christians in these times, may be only the necessary shaking of the "things that are made," in order that only that which "cannot be shaken" may remain.

There are times, it may be, in our religious lives, when our experience seems to us as settled and immovable as the roots of the everlasting mountains. But there comes an upheaval, and all our foundations are shaken and thrown down, and we are ready to despair and to question whether we can be Christians at all. Sometimes it is an upheaval in our outward circumstances, and sometimes it is in our inward experience. If people have rested on their good words and their faithful service, the Lord is often obliged to take away all power for work or else all opportunity in order that the soul may be driven from its false resting place and forced to rest in the Lord alone. Sometimes the dependence is upon good feelings or pious emotions, and the soul has to be deprived of these before it can learn to depend only upon God. Sometimes it is upon "sound doctrine" that the dependence is placed, and the man feels himself to be occupying an invulnerable position, because his views are so correct, and his doctrines are so orthodox; and then the Lord is obliged to shake his doctrines, and to plunge him, it may be, into confusion and darkness as to his views.

It was at just such a moment as this that my own soul caught its first real sight of God; and what had seemed certain spiritual ruin and defeat was turned into the most triumphant victory.

Or it may be that the upheaval comes in our outward circumstances. Everything has seemed so firmly established in prosperity that no dream of disaster disturbs us. Our reputation is assured, our work has prospered, our efforts have all been successful beyond our hopes, and our soul is at ease; and the need for God is in danger of becoming far off and vague. And then the Lord is obliged to put an end to it all, and our prosperity crumbles around us like a house built on sands, and we are tempted to think He is angry with us.

But in very truth it is not anger, but tenderest love. His very love it is that compels Him to take away the outward prosperity that is keeping our souls from entering into the interior spiritual kingdom for which we long. When the fig tree ceases to blossom, and there is not fruit in the vines; when the labor of the olive shall fail, and the fields shall yield no meat; when the flock shall be cut off from the fold, and there shall be no herd in the stalls, then, and often not until then, will our souls learn to rejoice in the Lord only, and to joy in the God of our salvation.

Paul declared that he counted all things but loss that he might win Christ; and when we learn to say the same, the peace and joy that the Gospel promises become our permanent possession.

"What iniquity," asks the Lord of the children of Israel, "have your fathers found in Me that they are gone far from Me and have walked after vanity? For My people have committed two evils; they have forsaken Me, the fountain of living waters, and hewed them out cisterns, broken cisterns that can hold no water." Like the Israelites, we too forsake the fountain of living waters, and try to hew out for ourselves cisterns of our own devising. We seek to slake our thirst with our own experiences or our own activities, and then wonder that we still thirst. And it is to save us from perishing for want of water that the Lord finds it necessary to destroy our broken cisterns; since only so can we be forced to drink from the fountain of living waters.

We are told that if we "trust in vanity," vanity shall be our recompense; and many a time have we found this to be true. Have you ever crossed a dangerous swamp abounding in quicksands, where every step was a risk, and where firm-looking hillocks continually deceived you into a false dependence, causing you to sink in the mire and water concealed beneath their deceptive appearances? If you have, you will be able to understand what it means to "trust in vanity," and you will appreciate the blessedness of any dispensation that shall discover to you the rottenness of your false dependencies, and shall drive you to trust in that which is safe and permanent. When our feet are walking on "miry clay," we can have nothing but welcome for the Divine Guide who shall bring us out from the clay, and shall "set our feet upon a rock," and "establish our goings," even though the ways in which He calls us to walk may seem narrow and hard.

The prophet Jeremiah, when lamenting the sins of his people, says: "We have made lies our refuge, and under falsehoods have we hid ourselves," and he adds that the Lord had declared He would sweep away the refuge of lies, and would cause the waters to overflow the hiding place. It might look, as far as the outward seeming goes, as though it was God's wrath that did this, and many a frightened Christian thinks it is; but His wrath is only against the refuges of lies, not against us, and love could do no less than destroy these refuges in order that we may be delivered.

A dear old friend of mine, who was very much interested in my spiritual welfare, gave me a little book called, *The Seventeen False Rests of the Soul,* evidently feeling that I was in danger of settling down upon one or another of these false rests. The book set forth in quaint old language the idea that the soul was continually tempted to sit down upon some falsity, as though it were a final resting place, and that God was continually obliged to "unbottom" all such false resting places, as though one should unbottom a chair and let the sitter fall through. All these seventeen false rests were described, and it was shown how the soul, being "unbottomed" off each one successively, settled down at last upon the only true rest in God. This "unbottoming" is only another word for the "shakings" and "emptyings" of which I have been writing. It is always a painful process, and often a most discouraging one. Everything seems unstable, and rest seems utterly unattainable. No sooner do we find an experience or a doctrine in which we think we may surely rest, than a great "shaking" comes, and we are forced out again. And this process must continue until all that can be shaken is removed, and only "those things which cannot be shaken" remain.

Often the answer to our most fervent prayers for deliverance comes in such a form that it seems as if the "very foundations of the hills moved and were shaken"; and we do not always see at first that it is by means of this very shaking that the deliverance for which we have prayed is to be accomplished, and we are to be brought forth into the "large place" for which we long.

The old mystics used to teach what they called "detachment"; meaning the cutting loose of the soul from all that could hold it back from God. This need for "detachment" is the secret of many of our "shakings." We cannot follow the Lord fully so long as we are tied fast to anything else, any more than a boat can sail out into the boundless ocean so long as it is tied fast to the shore.

If we could reach the "city which hath sure and steadfast foundations," we must go out like Abraham from all other cities, and must be detached from every earthly tie. Everything in Abraham's life that could be shaken was shaken. He was, as it were, emptied from vessel to vessel, here today and gone tomorrow; all his resting places were disturbed, and no settlement or comfort anywhere. We, like Abraham, are looking for a city which hath foundations, whose builder and maker is God, and therefore we too shall need to be emptied from vessel to vessel. But we do not realize this, and when the overturnings and shakings come, we are in despair and think we shall never reach the city that hath foundations at all. But it is these very shakings that make it possible for us to reach it. The Psalmist had learned this, and after all the shakings and emptying of his eventful life, he cried: "My soul, wait thou only upon God; for my expectation is from him. He only is my rock and my salvation: he is my defense; I shall not be moved. In God is my salvation and my glory: the rock of my strength and my refuge is in God."

At last God was everything to him; and then he found that God was enough.

And it is the same with us. When everything in our lives and experience is shaken that can be shaken, and only that which cannot be shaken remains, we are brought to see that God only is our rock and our foundation, and we learn to have our expectation from Him alone.

"Therefore will not we fear though the earth be removed, and though the mountains be carried into the midst of the sea; though the waters thereof roar and be troubled, though the mountains shake with the swelling thereof... God is in the midst of her, she shall not be moved. God shall help her, and that right early." "Shall not be moved"—what an inspiring declaration! Can it be possible that we, who are so easily moved by the things of earth, can arrive at a place where nothing can upset our temper or disturb our calm? Yes, it is possible; and the Apostle Paul knew it. When he was on his way to Jerusalem, where he foresaw that "bonds and afflictions" awaited him, he could say triumphantly, "But none of these things move me." Everything in Paul's life and experience that could be shaken had been shaken, and he no longer counted his life, or any of life's possessions, dear unto him. And we, if we will but let God have His way with us, may come to the same place so that neither the fret and fear of the little things of life, nor its great and heavy trials, can have power to move us from the peace that passeth all understanding, which is declared to be the portion of those who have learned to rest only on God.

In that wonderful Revelation made to John in the "Isle that is called Patmos," where the Spirit tells to the churches what awaits those who overcome, we have a statement that expresses in striking terms just what I mean. "Him that overcometh will I make a pillar in the temple of my God; and he shall go no more out." To be as immovable as a pillar in the house of our God is an end for which one would gladly endure all the "shakings" and "unbottomings" that may be necessary to bring us there!

"Wherefore we receiving a kingdom that cannot be moved, let us have grace whereby we may serve God acceptably with reverence and godly fear; for our God is a consuming fire." A great many people are afraid of the consuming fire of God, but that is only because they do not understand what it is. It is the fire of God's love, that must in the very nature of things consume everything that can harm His people; and if our hearts are set on being what the love of God would have us be, His fire is something we shall not be afraid of, but shall warmly welcome.

> Implacable is love.
> Foes may be bought or teased
>   From their malign intent;
> But he goes unappeased,
>   Who is on kindness bent.

Let us thank God, then, that He is "on kindness bent" toward us, and that the consuming fire of His love will not cease to burn until it has refined us as silver is refined. For the promise is that He shall sit as a refiner and purifier of silver, and He shall purge us as gold and silver are purged in order that we may offer unto Him an offering in righteousness; and He gives us this inspiring assurance, that if we will but submit to this purifying process, we shall become "pleasant unto the Lord," and all nations shall call us blessed, "for ye shall be a delightsome land, saith the Lord of Hosts."

To be "pleasant" and delightsome" to the Lord may seem to us impossible, when we look at our shortcomings and our unworthiness. But when we think of this lovely, consuming fire of God's love, we can be of good heart and take courage, for He will not fail nor be discouraged until all our dross and reprobate silver is burned up, and we ourselves come forth in His likeness and are conformed to His image.

Our souls long for the "kingdom which cannot be moved," and He "who is on kindness bent," will, if we will let Him, shake everything in our lives that can be shaken, and will unbottom us off every false rest, until only that which cannot be shaken shall remain.

One of the most impressive sermons I ever heard was preached by a sweet-faced old Quaker lady, who rose in the stillness and said, "Yesterday Sister Tabitha broke all to pieces my best china teapot, but the Lord, whom I trust, kept my soul in perfect peace, and enabled me not to utter a single word of reproach." That was all; the sermon ended; but into every heart there entered a sense of what it would mean to be kept in the immovable kingdom of the love of God.

And this kingdom may be our home, if we will but submit to the shakings of God, and will learn to rest only and always on Him.

May He hasten the day for each one of us!

Chapter 12: A Word To The Wavering Ones

*"But let him ask in faith, nothing wavering. For he that wavereth is
like a wave of the sea driven with the wind and tossed. For let not that
man think that he shall receive anything of the Lord."*

It would be difficult to find any one thing that produces more discomfort in the religious life than does a wavering faith. The figure given us by the Apostle James exactly describes it—"a wave of the sea driven by the wind and tossed." And just as it is impossible for a traveler to reach his destination by advancing one day, and retracing his steps the next, so is it equally impossible for the wavering soul, while it wavers, to reach any place of settled peace.

In our last chapter we considered the shakings of God; and it might be thought that our waverings would be akin to His shakings. But God's shakings are caused by His love, and are for our blessing, and always lead to rest and peace; while our waverings are caused by our want of faith, and always lead to discomfort and turmoil.

A wavering Christian is a Christian who trusts in the love of God one day and doubts it the next, and who is alternately happy or miserable accordingly. He mounts to the hilltop of joy at one time, only to descend at another time into the valley of despair. He is driven to and fro by every wind of doctrine, is always striving and never attaining, and is a prey to each changing influence, caused by his state of health, or by the influences around him, or even by the state of the weather.

You would suppose that even the most ignorant child of God would know without telling that this sort of experience is all wrong, and that to waver in one's faith after such a fashion is one of the things most dishonoring to the Lord, whose truth and faithfulness it so impugns. But as a fact, there are many Christians whose eyes are so blinded in the matter, that they actually think this tendency to waver is a tribute to the humility of their spirits, and who exalt every fresh attack of doubt into a secret and most pious virtue. A wavering Christian will say complacently, "Oh, but I know myself to be so unworthy, that I am sure it is right for me to doubt," and they will imply by their tone of superiority, that their hearer, if truly humble, would doubt also.

In fact, I knew one really devoted Christian, whose religious life was one long torment of doubt, who said to me once in solemn earnestness, after I had been urging him to have more faith, "My dear friend, if once I should be so presumptuous as to feel sure that God loved me, I should be certain I was on the direct road to hell." He thought, no doubt, that such an assurance could only arise from a feeling that he was good enough to be worthy of God's love, and that to feel this would be presumption. And in this he would have been right, for to think ourselves good enough to be worthy of God's love would be presumption indeed. But the ground for our assurance is not to come from our own goodness, but from the goodness of God; and while we never can be and never ought to be satisfied with the first, there cannot possibly be any question to one who believes the Bible as to the all-sufficiency of the last.

To see the absurdity, not to call it by any harsher name, of the position of doubt taken up by this dear Christian, it is only necessary to consider how it would work with any of our human relations in life. Try to imagine what it would be in the marriage relation, or in the relation of children to a parent, both of which relations are used by the Lord as figures of our relation to Himself. Suppose either wife or husband should have a wavering experience of confidence in the other, one day trusting, and the next day doubting; would this be considered a sign of true humility on the doubter's part, and therefore a thing to be cherished as a virtue? Or, similarly, if children should waver in their confidence toward their earthly parents, as Christians seem to feel at liberty to do with their heavenly Parent, what name could be found severe enough by which to call such unofficial conduct? Of course in earthly relations such wavering might come from the fact that one of the parties concerned was unworthy of confidence, and in this case it could be excused. But in the case of God there could not possibly be any such excuse; although the wavering faith of some of His children may, I am afraid, sometimes lead outsiders to conclude that He cannot be worthy of much confidence, or their faith would be more steadfast.

We would shrink in horror from being the cause of any such imputation on the character of God; but I think, if we are honest with ourselves, we will be forced to acknowledge that our wavering faith is calculated to convey just such an impression; and that it really is, therefore, in its essence disloyalty to a trustworthy God, and should be mourned over as a grievous sin. The truth is, although we may not know it, our wavering comes, not from humility, but from a subtle and often unconscious form of pride. True humility accepts the love that is bestowed upon it, and the gifts of that love, with a meek and happy thankfulness, while pride shrinks from accepting gifts and kindnesses, and is afraid to believe in the disinterested goodness of the one who bestows them. Were we truly humble, we would accept God's love with thankful meekness, and, while acknowledging our own unworthiness, would only think of it as enhancing His grace and goodness in choosing us as the recipients of such blessings.

A wavering faith is not only disloyal to God, but it is a source of untold misery to ourselves, and cannot in any way advance our spiritual interests, but must always under all circumstances hinder and upset them. The Apostle tells us that we are made partakers of Christ if we "hold the beginning of our confidence steadfast unto the end." To be steadfast is the exact contrary of wavering, and to expect the results of steadfastness as the outcome of wavering is as foolish as it would be to expect to reach the top of a mountain by alternately climbing two steps and sliding back three. And yet many people expect this very thing. They make a "beginning of confidence," and for a little time, while the freshness of it lasts, are full of joy and triumph. Then trials come, and temptations; and doubts begin to intrude; and instead of treating these doubts as enemies to be resisted and driven away, they receive them as friends, and give them entertainment; and sooner or later they begin to waver in their faith and in their allegiance, and from that moment all settled peace is gone. When skies are bright and all goes well with them, their faith revives, and they are happy; but when skies are dark and things go wrong doubts triumph, and they waver again.

I was having a conversation with a very eminent clergyman on the possibility of a religious life of abiding peace and rest, and he told me frankly that he did not believe it was possible, and that he thought most Christian experience was like his own. "Now I," he said, "when I want to write my sermons, I get up on the mountaintop by prayer and by climbing. I put my foot first on one promise and then on another, and so, by hard climbing and much praying, I reach the summit, and can begin my sermon. All goes swimmingly for a little while, and then suddenly an interruption comes, some trouble with my children, or some domestic upset in the house, or some quarrel with a neighbor, and down I tumble from the mountaintop, and can only get back again by another wearisome climb. "Sometimes," he said, "I stay on the summit for two or three days, and once in a great while, even for two or three weeks. But as to there being any possibility of being seated in heavenly places in Christ, and abiding there continually, I cannot believe it."

I am sure this will describe the experience of many of God's children, who are hungering and thirsting for the peace and rest Christ has promised them, but who seem unable to attain to it for more than a few moments at a time. They may get now and then a faint glimmer of faith, and peace seems to be coming, and then all the old doubts spring up again with tenfold power. "Look at your heart," they say; "see how cold it is, how indifferent. How can you for a moment believe that God can love such a poor, unworthy creature as you are?" And it all sounds so reasonable that they are plunged into darkness again.

The whole trouble arises from a want of faith. It seems commonplace to say it, for I have to say it so often, but in the spiritual life it is to us always, *always*, ALWAYS according to our faith. This is a spiritual law that can neither be neglected nor evaded. It is not an arbitrary law which we might hope could be repealed in our own especial case, but it is inherent in the very nature of things, and is therefore unalterable. And equally inherent in the nature of things is its converse, that if it is to be to us according to our faith, so will it also be to us according to our doubts.

The whole root and cause then of our wavering experience is not, as we may have thought, our sins, but is simply and only our doubts. Doubts create an impassable gulf between our souls and the Lord, just as inevitably as they do between us and our earthly friends; and no amount of fervor or earnestness can bridge this gulf in one case any more than in the other. "Let not that man that wavereth think that he shall receive anything of the Lord." This is not because God is angry, and visits His displeasure in this way on the man who doubts, but it is because of that inherent nature of things that makes it impossible for doubt and confidence to exist together, whether in earthly relations or heavenly, and which neither God nor man can alter. "To whom sware he that they should not enter into his rest but to them that believed not. So we see they could not enter in because of unbelief." It was not that God would not allow them to enter in as a punishment for their unbelief, but they simply could not. It was an impossibility. Faith is the only door into the kingdom of Heaven, and there is no other. If we will not go in by that door, we cannot get in at all, for there is no other way.

God's salvation is not a purchase to be made, nor wages to be earned, nor a summit to be climbed, nor a task to be accomplished; but it is simply and only a gift to be accepted, and can only be accepted by faith. Faith is a necessary element in the acceptance of any gift, whether earthly or heavenly. My friends may put their gifts upon my table, or even place them in my lap, but unless I believe in their friendliness and honesty of purpose enough to accept these gifts, they can never become really mine.

It is plain, therefore, that the Bible is simply announcing, as it always does, the nature of things, when it declares that "according to your faith" it shall be unto you. And the sooner we settle down to this the better. All our wavering comes from the fact that we do not believe in this law. We acknowledge, of course, that it is in the Bible, but we think it cannot really mean what it says, and that there must be some additions made to it; for instance, as "according to our fervency it shall be unto us," or "according to our importunity," or "according to our worthiness." And, if the whole truth were told, we are inclined to think that these additions of ours are, if anything, by far the most important part of the whole matter. As a consequence of this, our attention is mostly directed to getting these matters settled, and we watch our own frames and feelings, and search into our own worthiness or unworthiness with so much assiduity that we overlook almost altogether the one fundamental principle of faith, without which nothing whatever can be done. Moreover, as our disposition and feelings are the most variable things in the universe, and our sense of worthiness or unworthiness changes with our changing feelings, our experience cannot but waver; and the possibility of a steadfast faith recedes farther and farther into the background. We in short make the faithfulness of God, and the truth of His Word, depend upon the state of our feelings.

I am very certain that if any of our friends should treat us in this doubting fashion, we would be wounded and indignant beyond measure; and no feeling of unworthiness on their part could excuse them in our eyes for such a wavering of their confidence in us. In fact, we would far rather our friends should even sin against us than doubt us. No form of sinfulness ever hindered the Lord Jesus while on earth from doing His mighty works. The only thing that hindered Him was unbelief. In His own town, and among His own neighbors and friends, where naturally He would have liked to have performed some of His miracles, we are told that, "He did not many mighty works there because of their unbelief." It was not that He would not, but simply that He could not. And He cannot in our case, any more than in theirs.

But I am afraid some of you may think I am making a mistake, and that, in spite of what God has said, the man whose faith wavers can after all, if he is only fervent and earnest enough, receive something from the Lord. That means that you do not believe that God understands the laws of His Kingdom as well as you yourself do, and that it is safer to follow your own ideas rather than His Word. And yet you must know that hitherto your doubts have brought you nothing but darkness and misery. Recall the days, and weeks, and even perhaps months and years of a halting, stumbling, uncomfortable, religious life, and ask yourself honestly whereto the cause of it all has not been your wavering faith. If you believe one day that God loves you and is favorable to you, and the next day doubt His love, and fear He is angry with you, does it not stand to reason that you must waver in your experience from joy to misery; and that only a steadfast faith in His love and care could give you an unwavering experience?

The one question, therefore, for all whose faith wavers is how to put an end at once and forever to their wavering. And here I am thankful to say that I know of a perfect remedy The only thing you have to do is to *give it up*. Your wavering is caused by your doubting, and by nothing else. Give up your doubting, and your wavering will stop. Keep on with your doubting, and your wavering will continue. The whole matter is as simple as daylight; and the choice is in your own hands.

Perhaps you may think this is an extreme statement, for it has probably never entered your heads that you could give up doubting altogether. But I assert that you can. You can simply refuse to doubt. You can shut the door against every suggestion of doubt that comes, and can by faith declare exactly the opposite. Your doubt says, "God does not forgive my sins." Your faith must say, "He does forgive me; He says He does, and I choose to believe Him. I am His forgiven child." And you must assert this steadfastly, until all your doubts vanish. You have no more right to say that you are of such a doubting nature that you cannot help doubting, than to say you are of such a thieving nature that you cannot help thieving. One is as easily controlled as the other. You must give up your doubting just as you would give up your thieving. You must treat the temptation to doubt exactly as a drunkard must treat the temptation to drink; you must take a pledge against it.

The process I believe to be the most effectual is to lay our doubts, just as we lay our other sins, upon God's altar, and make a total surrender of them. We must give up all liberty to doubt, and must consecrate our power of believing to Him, and must trust Him to keep us trusting. We must make our faith in His Word as inevitable and necessary a thing as is our obedience to His will. We must be as loyal to our heavenly Friend as we are to our earthly friends, and must refuse to recognize the possibility of such thing as any questioning or doubting of His love or His faithfulness, or of any wavering in our absolute faith in His Word.

Of course temptations to waver will come, and it will sometimes look to us impossible that the Lord can love such disagreeable, unworthy beings as we feel ourselves to be. But we must turn as deaf an ear to these insinuations against the love of God as we would to any insinuations against the love of our dearest friend. The fight to do this may sometimes be very severe, and may even at times seem almost unendurable. But our unchanging declaration must continually be, "though he slay me, yet will I trust in him." Our steadfast faith will unfailingly bring us, sooner or later, a glorious victory.

Probably it will often seem to us as if it would be a righteous thing, in view of our many shortcomings, and only what a truly humble soul would do, to waver in our faith and to question whether the salvation of the Lord Jesus can be meant for us. But if we at all understand what the salvation of the Lord Jesus Christ is, we cannot fail to recognize that all this is only temptation; and that what we must do is to lift up the shield of faith persistently against it; for the shield of faith always does and always will quench every fiery dart of the enemy.

The Spirit of God never under any circumstance could suggest a doubt of the love of God. Wherever doubts come from, one thing is certain, they do not come from Heaven. All doubts are from an evil source, and they must always be treated as the suggestions of an enemy. We cannot, it is true, prevent the suggestions of doubt making themselves heard in our hearts, any more than we can prevent our ears from hearing the oaths of wicked men in the streets. But just as we can refuse to approve of or join in the oaths of these men, so can we refuse to pay any attention to these suggestions of doubt. The cases are exactly similar. But while in the case of the oaths, we know without any question that it would be wicked to join in with them, in the case of the doubts we have a lurking feeling that, after all, doubts may have something pious in them, and ought to be encouraged. But I believe one is as displeasing to God as the other.

Again I would repeat that the only way to treat the doubts that make you waver is to give them up. An absolute surrender is the only remedy. It is like the drunkard with his drink, half measures are of no manner of use. Total abstinence is the only hope.

The most practical way of doing this is not only to make the interior surrender, but to meet, as I have said, each doubt with a flat denial; and to carry the war into the enemy's country, as it were, by an emphatic assertion of faith in direct opposition to the doubt. For instance, if the doubt arises as to whether God can love anyone so sinful and unfaithful as you feel yourself to be, you must at once assert in definite words in your own heart, and if possible aloud to someone, that God does love you; that He says He does, and that His Word is a million times more trustworthy than any of your feelings, no matter how well founded they may seem to you to be. If you cannot find anyone to whom to say this, then write it in a letter, or else say it aloud to yourself and to God. Be very definite about it.

If in anything you have had a "beginning of confidence," if you have ever laid hold of any promise or declaration of the Lord's, hold on steadfastly to that promise or declaration without wavering, let come what may. There can be no middle ground. If it was true once, it is true still, for God is unchangeable. The only thing that can deprive you of it is your unbelief. While you believe, you have it. "Whatsoever things ye desire when ye pray, believe that ye receive them and ye shall have them."

Let nothing shake your faith. Should even sin unhappily overtake you, you must not let it make you doubt. At once, on the discovery of any sin, take I John 1:9 and act on it. "If we confess our sins, he is faithful and just to forgive us our sins, and to cleanse us from all unrighteousness." Confess your sin, therefore, immediately upon the discovery of it, and believe at once that God does forgive it, as He declares, and does again cleanse you from all unrighteousness. No sin, however grievous, can separate us from God for one moment, after it has been treated in this fashion. To allow sin to cause your faith to waver is only to add a new sin to the one already committed. Return at once to God in the way the Bible teaches, and let your faith hold steadfastly to His Word. Believe it, not because you feel it, or see it, but because He says it. Believe it, even when it seems to you that you are believing a lie. Believe it actively and steadfastly, through dark and through light, through ups and through downs, through times of comfort and through times of despair, and I can promise you, without a fear, that your wavering experience will be ended.

"Therefore, beloved brethren, be ye steadfast, immovable, always abounding in the work of the Lord, forasmuch as ye know that your labor is not in vain in the Lord." To be "immovable" in one's religious life is the exact opposite of wavering. In the Forty-sixth Psalm we can see what it is. The earth may be removed, and the mountains may be carried into the midst of the sea, our whole universe may seem to be in ruins, but while we trust in the Lord we "shall not be moved."

The man who wavers in his faith is upset by the smallest trifles; the man who is steadfast in his faith can look on calmly at the ruin of all his universe.

To be thus immovable in one's religious life is a boon most ardently to be desired, and it may be ours if we will only hold the beginning of our confidence steadfast to the end.

> Faith is sweetest of worships to him who so loves
> His unbearable splendors in darkness to hide;
> And to trust in Thy Word, dearest Lord, is true love,
> For those prayers are most granted which seem most denied.
> And faith throws her arms around all Thou hast told her,
> And able to hold as much more, can but grieve;
> She could hold Thy grand self, Lord! if Thou wouldst reveal it.
> And love makes her long to have more to believe.

Chapter 13: Discouragement

"The soul of the people was much discouraged because of the way."

The Church of Christ abounds with people who are "discouraged because of the way." Either inwardly or outwardly, and oftentimes both, things look all wrong, and there seems no hope of escape. Their souls faint in them, and their religious lives are full of discomfort and misery. There is nothing that so paralyzes effort as discouragement, and nothing that more continually and successfully invites defeat. The secret of failure or success in any matter lies far more in the soul's interior attitude than in any other cause or causes. It is a law of our being, which is only now beginning to be discovered, that the inward man counts for far more in every conflict than anything the outward man do or may possess.

And nowhere is this truer than in the spiritual life. Again I must repeat what I find it necessary to say so continually, that the Bible declares from beginning to end that faith is the law of the spiritual life, and that according to our faith it always shall be and always will be unto us. Then, since faith and discouragement cannot, in the very nature of things, exist together, it is perfectly manifest that discouragement must be an absolute barrier to faith. And that where discouragement rules, the converse to the law of faith must rule also, and it shall be to us, not according to our faith, but according to our discouragement.

In fact, just as courage is faith in good, so discouragement is faith in evil; and, while courage opens the door to good, discouragement opens it to evil.

An allegory that I heard very early in my Christian life has always remained in my memory as one of those warnings to motorists that we often see at the top of hills on country roads, "This hill is dangerous"; and it has many a time warned me away from the dangerous descent of discouragement.

The allegory declared that once upon a time Satan, who desired to entrap a devoted Christian worker, allied a council of his helpers to decide on the best way of doing it, and to ask for volunteers. After the case had been explained, an imp[2] offered himself to do the work.

"How will you do it?" asked Satan.

"Oh," replied the imp, "I will paint to him the delights and pleasures of a life of sin in such glowing colors that he will be eager to enter upon it."

"That will not do," said Satan, shaking his head. "The man has tried sin, and he knows better. He knows it leads to misery and ruin, and he will not listen to you."

Then another imp offered himself, and again Satan asked, "What will you do to win the man over?"

"I will picture to him the trials and the self-denials of a righteous life, and will make him eager to escape from them."

"Ah, that will not do either," said Satan, "for he has tried righteousness, and he knows that its paths are paths of peace and happiness."

Then a third imp started up and declared that he was sure he could bring the man over.

"Why, what will you do," asked Satan, "that you are so sure?"

"I will discourage his soul," replied the imp triumphantly.

"That will do, that will do," exclaimed Satan, "you will be successful. Go and bring back your victim."

An old Quaker has this saying, "All discouragement is from the Devil"; and I believe he stated a far deeper and more universal truth than we have yet fully understood. Discouragement cannot have its source in God. The religion of the Lord Jesus Christ is a religion of faith, of good cheer, of courage, of hope that maketh not ashamed. "Be discouraged," says our lower nature, "for the world is a place of temptation and sin." "Be of good cheer," says Christ, "for I have overcome the world." There cannot possibly be any room for discouragement in a world which Christ has overcome.

---

[2] A small evil spirit.

We must settle it then, once for all, that discouragement comes from an evil source, only and always. I know this is not the general idea, at least in the spiritual region of things. In temporal things, perhaps, we have more or less learned that discouragement is foolish, and even wrong; but, when it comes to spiritual things, we are apt to reverse the order, and make that commendable in one case, which is reprehensible in the other; and we even succeed in persuading ourselves that to be discouraged is a very pious state of mind, and an evidence of true humility.

The causes for our discouragement seem so legitimate, that to be discouraged seems to our short-sightedness the only right and proper state of mind to cultivate. The first and perhaps the most common of these causes is the fact of our own incapacity. It is right for us to be cast down, we think, because we know ourselves to be such poor, miserable, good-for-nothing creatures. It would be presumption, in the face of such incapacity, to be anything but discouraged.

Moses is an illustration of this. The Lord had called him to lead the children of Israel out of the land of Egypt; and Moses, looking at this own natural infirmities and weaknesses, was discouraged, and tried to excuse himself: "I am not eloquent, but I am slow of speech and of a slow tongue. They will not believe me nor hearken unto my voice." Naturally, one would think that Moses had plenty of cause for discouragement, and for discouragement very similar to that which is likely to assail us, when, because of our distrust in our own eloquence, or our own power to convince those to whom we are to be sent, we shrink from the work to which the Lord may be calling us. But notice how the Lord answered Moses, for in the same way I am convinced does He answer us. He did not do, what no doubt Moses would have liked best, try to convince him that he really was eloquent, or that his tongue was not slow of speech. He passed all this by as being of no account whatever, and simply called attention to the fact that, since He had made man's mouth and would Himself be with the mouth He had made, there could not possibly be any cause for discouragement, even if Moses did have all the infirmities of speech of which he had complained. "And the Lord said unto him, Who hath made man's mouth? or who maketh the dumb, or deaf, or the seeing, or the blind? Have not I, the Lord? Now therefore go, and I will be with thy mouth, and teach thee what thou shalt say."

When the word of the Lord came to Jeremiah telling him that He had organized him to be a prophet to the nations, Jeremiah felt himself to be entirely unequal to such a work, and said: "Ah, Lord God, behold, I cannot speak, for I am a child." But the Lord answered: "Say not, I am a child; for thou shalt go to all that I shall send thee, and whatever I say to thee, thou shalt speak. Be not afraid of their faces, for I am with thee to deliver thee, saith the Lord."

Gideon is another illustration. The Lord had called him to undertake the deliverance of His people from the oppression of the Midianites, and had said to him: "Go in this thy might, and thou shalt save Israel from the hands of the Midianites: have I not sent thee?" This ought to have been enough for Gideon, but he was a poor unknown man, of no family or position, and no apparent fitness for such a great mission; and, looking at himself and his own deficiencies, he naturally became discouraged, and said: "Wherewith shall I save Israel? Behold, my family is poor in Manasseh, and I am the least in my father's house." Other men, he felt, who had power and influence, might perhaps accomplish this great work, but not one so poor and insignificant as himself. How familiar this sort of talk must sound to the victims of discouragement among my readers, and how sensible and reasonable it seems! But what did the Lord think of it? "And the Lord said unto him,

Surely I will be with thee, and thou shalt smite the Midianites as one man"—simply and only the promise, "Surely I will be with thee." Not one word of encouragement did He give Gideon, nor does He give us as to our own capacities or fitness for the work required, but merely the bare statement of the fact of being sufficient for all possible needs, "I will be with thee." To all words of discouragement in the Bible this is the invariable answer, "I will be with thee"; and it is an answer that precludes all possibility of argument or of any further discouragement. I thy Creator and thy Redeemer, I thy strength and thy wisdom, I thy omnipresent and omniscient God, I will be with thee, and will protect thee through everything; no enemy shall hurt thee, no strife of tongues shall disturb thee; My presence shall be thy safety and thy sure defense.

One would think that in the face of such assertions as these not even the most fainthearted among us could find any loophole for discouragement. But discouragement comes in many subtle forms, and our spiritual enemies attack us in many disguises. Our own especial make-up or temperament is one of the most common and insidious of our enemies. Other people, who are made differently, can be cheerful and courageous, we think, but it is right that we should be discouraged when we see the sort of people we are, how foolish, how helpless, how unfit to grapple with any enemies! And there would indeed be ample cause for discouragement if we were to be called upon to fight our battles ourselves. We would be right in thinking we could not do it. But if the Lord is to fight them for us, it puts an entirely different complexion on the matter, and our want of ability to fight becomes an advantage instead of a disadvantage. We can only be strong in Him when we are weak in ourselves, and our weakness, therefore, is in reality our greatest strength.

The children of Israel can give us a warning lesson here. After the Lord had delivered them out of Egypt, and had brought them to the borders of the promised land, Moses urged them to go up and possess it. "Behold," he said, "the Lord thy God hath set the land before thee; go up and possess it, as the Lord God of thy fathers hath said unto thee; fear not, neither be discouraged." But the circumstances were so discouraging, and they felt themselves to be so helpless, that they could not believe God would really do all He had said; and they murmured in their tents, and declared that it must be because the Lord hated them that He had brought them out of Egypt in order to deliver them into the hands of their enemies. "And they said, Whither shall we go up? Our brethren have discouraged our heart, saying, The people is greater and taller than we; the cities are great and walled up to heaven; and moreover we have seen the sons of the Anakims there."

When we read the report of the spies we cannot be surprised at their discouragement; and we can even believe they would have felt that courage under such circumstances would be only foolhardiness. "The land through which we have gone to search it," the spies declared, "is a land that eateth up the inhabitants thereof: and all the men that we saw in it are men of a great stature. And there we saw the giants, the sons of Anak, which come of the giants: and we were in our own sight as grasshoppers, and so we were in their sight." Nothing could have seemed humbler than for them to look upon themselves as poor, good-for-nothing grasshoppers; and true humility would have seemed to teach that it would be the height of presumption for grasshoppers to try to conquer giants. We also often feel ourselves to be but grasshoppers in the face of the giants of temptation and trouble that assail us, and we think ourselves justified in being discouraged. But the question is not, whether we are grasshoppers, but whether God is; for it is not we who have to fight these giants, but God.

In vain, Moses reminded the Israelites of this. In vain he assured them that they had no need to be afraid of even the sons of the Anakims, for the Lord their God would fight for them. He even reminded them of past deliverances, and asked them if they did not remember how that "in the wilderness the Lord thy God bear thee as a man doth bear his son in all the way that ye went"; but they were still too discouraged to believe. And the result was that not one of that "evil generation" was allowed to see the Promised Land, except only Caleb and Joshua, who had steadfastly believed that God could and would lead them in.

Such are the fruits of giving way to discouragement, and such is the reward of a steadfast faith.

The Apostle in commenting on this story in Hebrews says: "And to whom sware he that they should not enter into his rest, but to them that believed not? So we see that they could not enter in because of unbelief."

Is there no parallel in all this to our case? Do we not look at our weakness instead of looking at the Lord's strength; and have we not sometimes become so discouraged as to sink into such "anguish of spirit," that we cannot even hearken to the Lord's own declarations that He will fight for us and will give us the victory? Our souls long to enter into the rest the Lord has promised; but giants and cities great and walled up to Heaven seem to stand in our pathway, and we are afraid to believe. So we too, like the Israelites, cannot enter in because of unbelief.

How different it would be if we only had faith enough to say with the Psalmist: "Though an host should encamp against me, my heart shall not fear; though war should rise against me, in this will I be confident... For in the time of trouble he shall hide me in his pavilion: in the secret of his tabernacle he shall hide me. He shall set me up upon a rock." How joyfully and triumphantly would we be able to enter into rest, if this were our language!

Another very subtle cause for discouragement is to be found in what is called the fear of man. There seems to exist in this world a company of beings called "they" who lord it over life with an iron hand of control. What will "they" say? What will "they" think? are among the most frequent questions that assail the timid soul when it seeks to work for the Lord. At every turn this omnipotent and ubiquitous "they" stands in our way to discourage us and make us afraid. This form of discouragement is apt to come under the subtle disguise of a due consideration for the opinion of others; but it is especially dangerous, because it exalts this "they" into the place of God, and esteems "their" opinions above His promises. The only remedy here, as in all other forms of discouragement, is simply the reiteration of the fact that God is with us. "Be not afraid of their faces; for I am with thee to deliver thee, saith the Lord." "For he hath said, I will never leave thee nor forsake thee. So that we may boldly say, Thy Lord is my helper, and I will not fear what man shall do unto me." How can any heart, however timid, dare to indulge in discouragement in the face of such assertions as these?

There is, however, one sort of discouragement that is very common, and that seems as if it must be right, even though in all other cases it may be wrong, and that is the discouragement that arises from our own failures. It was from this sort of discouragement that the children of Israel suffered after their defeat at Ai. They had "committed a trespass in the accursed thing," and "therefore they could not stand before their enemies"; and so great was their discouragement that it is said, "wherefore the hearts of the people melted and became as water," and "Joshua rent his clothes, and fell to the earth upon his face before the ark of the Lord, until the eventide, he and all the elders of Israel, and put dust upon their heads." When God's own people "turn their backs before their enemies" one might well think they ought indeed to "lie on their faces," and "put dust on their heads," because of the dishonor they have brought upon His great name. Discouragement and despair would seem the only proper and safe condition after such failures. But evidently the Lord thought otherwise, for He said to Joshua, "Get thee up; wherefore liest thou upon thy face?" The proper thing to do after a failure is not to abandon ourselves to utter discouragement, humble as this may appear; but at once to face the evil, and get rid of it, and afresh and immediately to consecrate ourselves again to the Lord. "Up, sanctify yourselves," is always God's command. "Lie down and be discouraged" is always our temptation.

But you may ask whether a sense of sin produced by the convictions of the Holy Spirit ought not to cause discouragement. If I see myself to be a sinner, how can I help being discouraged? To this I answer that the Holy Spirit does not convict us of sin in order to discourage us, but to encourage us. His work is to show us our sin, not that we may lie down in despair under its power, but that we may get rid of it. A good mother points out the faults of her children for the purpose of helping them correct those faults; and the convictions of the Holy Spirit are in truth one of our greatest privileges, if we only had the sense to see it; for they mean, not that we are to give up in discouragement, but that we are to be encouraged to believe that deliverance is coming.

The good housewife discovers the stains on her table linen, not in order that she may have it thrown aside as no longer fit for use, but in order that she may have it cleansed for future use; and, if she has a good laundress, she will not be discouraged by the worst of stains. Surely then when God says to us, "Though your sins be as scarlet, they shall be as white as snow," it is pure unbelief on our part to allow ourselves to be discouraged at even the worst of our failures, for God's "washing of regeneration" must be at least as effectual as the washing of any human laundress could possibly be.

Fenelon says concerning this: "It is of great importance to guard against discouragement on account of our faults. Discouragement is not a fruit of humility, but of pride, and nothing can be worse. It springs from a secret love of our own excellence. We are hurt at feeling what we are. If we become discouraged we are the more enfeebled, and from our reflections on our own imperfections, a chagrin arises that is often worse than the imperfection itself. Poor nature longs from self-love to behold itself perfect; it is vexed that it is not so, it is impatient, haughty, and out of temper with itself and with everybody else. Sad state; as though the work of God could be accomplished by our ill-humor. As though the peace of God could be attained by our interior restlessness."

Discouragement, from whatever source it may come, produces many sad results. One of its very worst is that it leads people to "murmur," and to "speak against God." When the children of Israel were "discouraged because of the way," we are told that they "spake against God," and asked all sorts of God-dishonoring questions. And I believe, if we could examine the causes of the rebelling and murmuring thoughts that sometimes beset us, we could find that they always begin in discouragement. The truth is that discouragement is really, in its essence, a "speaking against God," for it necessarily implies some sort of a failure on His part to come up to that which His promises have led us to expect of Him. The Psalmist recognizes this, and says concerning the discouraging questions His people asked in the days of their wilderness wandering, "Yes, they 'spake against God'; they said, 'Can God furnish a table in the wilderness?'" It appears, therefore, that even our questions as to God's power or willingness to help us, which perhaps seem to us so reasonable and even so humble, are really a "speaking against God," and are displeasing to Him, because they reveal the sad fact that we "believe not in him, and trust not in his salvation."

Another grievous quality in discouragement is its contagiousness. Nothing is more catching than discouragement. When the spies sent out by Moses brought up, as we have seen, and "evil report of the promised land," and told of the giants there, they so "discouraged the hearts of their brethren," that the people "lifted up their voices and cried," and utterly refused to go into the very land which the Lord had given them, and which they had started out to possess.

The "evil report" that so many Christians bring of their failures and their disappointments in the Christian life is one of the most discouraging things in our intercourse with one another. The hearts of many young Christians are, I believe, far too often thus discouraged by their older brethren, who have but little idea of the harm they are doing by their doleful accounts of the trials of the way.

I can never look back without shame to a time in my own life when I "discouraged the heart" of a young Christian friend, by the "evil report" I gave her of the "giants" of doubt and difficulty I had met with in my Christian pathway. And afterward, when a stronger faith in God had delivered me from all fear of these giants, I found that my former evil report had so effectually "discouraged her heart" that it was a long time before I could induce her to hearken to the good report I had then to bring.

So important did the Lord feel it to be that no one should discourage the heart of another that when Moses was giving to the Israelites God's laws concerning their methods of warfare, he said: "And the officers shall speak further unto the people, and they shall say, What man is there that is fearful and fainthearted? let him go and return unto his house, lest his brethren's heart faint as well as his heart."

Discouraged people, if they must be discouraged, ought at least to keep their discouragements to themselves, hidden away in the privacy of their own bosoms lest they should discourage the hearts of their brethren. We know from experience that courage is contagious, and that one really brave soul in moments of danger can save a crowd from a panic. But we too often fail to remember that the converse of this is true, and that one fainthearted man or woman can infect a whole crowd with fear. We consequently think nothing of expressing with the utmost freedom the foolish and wicked discouragements that are paralyzing all our own courage. We even sometimes, strange to say, sing our discouragements in our hymns at church or in prayer meeting.

> *Where is the blessedness I knew*
> *When first I saw the Lord?*
> *Where is that soul-refreshing view*
> *Of Jesus and His Word?*
> *What peaceful hours I then enjoyed,*
> *How sweet their memory still;*
> *But now I find an aching void,*
> *The world can never fill.*

Or this:

> *And shall we then forever live*
> *At this poor dying rate,*

> *Our love so faint, so cold to thee,*
> *And Thine to us so great?*
> *In vain we tune our formal songs,*
> *In vain we strive to rise;*
> *Hosannas languish on our tongues,*
> *And our devotion dies.*

To sing such hymns seems to me the greatest travesty on the worship of God that could well be conceived of. If there are "aching voids" in our experience, if our "love is cold and faint," and if we are living at a "poor, dying rate," at least let us keep it to ourselves. Because "hosannas languish on our tongues" is no reason why complainings and murmurings should be exalted into their place. Surely we cannot think it can be pleasing to God to hear them. What would we think of wives who should meet together to sing such things about their relation to their husbands? I do not believe they would be tolerated in society a single day.

If the Church of Christ would only expurgate all the hymns of discouragement from its hymn books, and would allow none but hymns of courage and good cheer to be sung by its members, I believe the faith of Christians would go up with a mighty bound. "Be of good cheer" is the command of the Lord for His disciples, always and under all circumstances; and He founded this command on the tremendous fact that He had overcome the world, and that therefore there was nothing left for us to be discouraged about. As I have said before, if we only understood what it means that Christ has overcome the world, I believe we would be aghast at the very idea of any one of His followers ever being discouraged again.

If you had been an Israelite in those days, which would you rather have been, dear reader, the spies who brought an evil report of the land, and so discouraged the hearts of their brethren as to bring upon them the dreary forty years of wilderness wandering, or Caleb and Joshua, who "stilled the people before Moses, and said, Let us go up at once and possess the land; for we are well able to overcome it"?

Which will you be now?

In the divine review of this episode, Moses spoke of Caleb as one who had "wholly followed" the Lord; and this "wholly following" consisted simply and only in the fact that Caleb had given his brethren a good report of land, and, when his colleagues had made the heart of the people to melt by their evil report, had encouraged them to go up and possess it.

I hardly think that this is the general interpretation of what "wholly following" means; and I fear that many otherwise really devoted Christians fail in this essential point and seem to make it almost the principal mission of their lives to discourage the hearts of their brethren by the doleful and despairing reports they bring of the difficulties and dangers of the way.

How different it would be if discouragement were looked upon in its true light as a "speaking against God," and only encouraging words were permitted among Christians and encouraging reports heard! How many times would the children of Israel have failed in conquering their enemies had there been no men of faith among them to encourage and cheer them? And, on the other hand, who can tell how many spiritual defeats and disasters your discouragements, dear reader, may have brought about in your own life, and in the lives of those around you?

In one of Isaiah's prophecies which begins with, "Comfort ye, comfort ye my people, saith your God," he gives us a wonderful description of God as the ground of comfort, and then sets forth what His people ought to be; and says in the course of the latter: "They helped everyone his neighbor, and everyone said to his brother, Be of good courage. So the carpenter encouraged the goldsmith, and he that smootheth with the hammer him that smote the anvil."

Shall we follow their example, and from henceforth encourage one another instead of discouraging?

If I am asked how we are to get rid of discouragements, I can only say, as I have had to say of so many other wrong spiritual habits, we must give them up. It is never worth while to argue against discouragement. There is only one argument that can meet it, and that is the argument of God. When David was in the midst of what were perhaps the most discouraging moments of his life, when he had found his city burned, and his wives stolen, and he and the men with him had wept until they had no more power to weep; and when his men, exasperated at their misfortunes, spake of stoning him, then we are told, "But David encouraged himself in the Lord his God"; and the result was a magnificent victory, in which all that they had lost was more than restored to them. This always will be, and always must be the result of a courageous faith, because faith lays hold of the omnipotence of God.

Over and over the Psalmist asks himself this question: "Why art thou cast down, O my soul, and why art thou disquieted within me?" And each time he answers himself with the argument of God: "Hope thou in God; for I shall yet praise him, who is the health of my countenance, and my God." He does not analyze his disquietude, or try to argue it away, but he turns at once to the Lord and by faith begins to praise Him.

It is the only way. Discouragement flies where faith appears; and, *vice versa*, faith flies when discouragement appears. We must choose between them, for they will not mix.

Chapter 14: The Shout Of Faith

*"And when ye hear the sound of the trumpet, all the people shall
shout with a great shout; and the wall of the city shall fall down flat,
and the people shall ascend up, every man straight before him."*

The shout of a steadfast faith is an experience that is in direct contrast to the moans of a wavering faith, and to the wails of discouraged hearts, both of which we have been considering in our last two chapters. In the history of the children of Israel there were many occasions when they indulged in these moanings and wailings and always to their sad undoing; but on one occasion at least they gave a magnificent shout of steadfast faith that brought them a glorious victory. And among the many "secrets of the Lord" that are discovered by the soul in its onward progress, I do not know of any that is more practically valuable than the secret of this shout of faith.

The occasion when it took place was at the time when the Israelites had just crossed the River Jordan, and were about to take possession of the Promised Land. God had said to Joshua, just before they crossed: "Now therefore arise, go over this Jordan, thou, and all this people, unto the land which I do give to them, even to the children of Israel. Every place that the sole of your foot shall tread upon, that have I given unto you, as I said unto Moses."

With this warrant they had crossed the river and entered into the land, no doubt expecting to get immediate possession. But at once upon their entrance they were brought face to face with one of those "cities great and walled up to heaven" that had so discouraged the heart of the spies forty years before. Well might they be appalled at the sight of it. To the eye of sense there seemed no possibility that they could ever conquer Jericho. They had no engines of warfare with which to attack it; and one can easily imagine the despair that must have seized upon them when they found themselves confronted with the walls and fortresses of such a city.

But the Lord had said to Joshua: "See, I have given into thine hand Jericho, and the king thereof, and the mighty men of valor." He had not said, "I will give," but, "I have given." It belonged to them already; but now they were called upon to take possession of it. It was as if a king should bestow an estate upon a courtier who was away in a foreign land, and this courtier should come back to take possession of it.

But the great question was, How? It looked impossible. But the Lord declared His plan; and after a few directions as to the order of their march, and blowing of their trumpets, He closed with these strange words: "And it shall come to pass, that when they make a long blast with the ram's horn, and when ye hear the sound of the trumpet, all the people shall shout with a great shout; and the wall of the city shall fall down flat, and the people shall ascend up, every man straight before him" (Joshua 6:5).

Strange words but true, for it came to pass just as the Lord had said. On the seventh day, when the priests blew with the trumpets, Joshua said to the people, "Shout, for the Lord hath given you the city." "And it came to pass, when the people heard the sound of the trumpet, and the people shouted with a great shout, that the walls fell down flat, so that the people went up into the city, every man straight before him, and they took the city."

Now, no one can suppose for a moment that this shout caused the walls to fall. And yet the secret of their victory lay in just this shout. For it was the shout of a faith which dared, on the authority of God's Word alone, to claim a promised victory while as yet there were no signs of this victory being accomplished. And according to their faith God did unto them; so that, when they shouted, He made the walls to fall.

God had declared that He had given them the city, and faith reckoned this to be true. Unbelief might well have said, "It would be better not to shout until the walls do actually fall, for, should there be any failure about it, the men of Jericho will triumph, and we shall bring dishonor on the name of our God." But faith laughed at all such prudential considerations, and, confidently resting on God's Word, gave a shout of victory while yet to the eye of sense that victory seemed impossible. And long centuries afterward the Holy Ghost thus records this triumph of faith in Hebrews: "By faith the walls of Jericho fell down, after they were compassed about seven days."

> *Faith, mighty faith, the promise sees*
> *And looks at that alone;*
> *Laughs at impossibilities,*
> *And cries, It shall be done.*

Jehoshaphat is another example of this shout of faith. He was told that a great multitude was coming up against him from beyond the sea, and he realized that he and his people had "no might" against them, and he could not tell "what to do." He did not waste his time and his energies in trying to prepare engines of warfare or in arranging plans for a battle, but he at once "set himself to seek the Lord." He stood in the congregation of the people, and said: "O Lord God of our fathers, art not thou God in heaven? and rulest not thou over all the kingdoms of the heathen? And in thine hand is there not power and might, so that none is able to withstand thee? Art not thou our God, who didst drive out the inhabitants of this land before thy people Israel, and gavest it to the seed of Abraham, thy friend, forever?... And now behold, the children of Ammon and Moab and Mount Seir... come to cast us out of thy possession, which thou hast given us to inherit. O our God, wilt thou not judge them? For we have no might against this great company that cometh against us; neither know we what to do: but our eyes are upon thee."

To this appeal the Lord answered through the mouth of His prophet in the following words: "Thus saith the Lord unto you, Be not afraid nor dismayed by reason of this great multitude, for the battle is not yours but God's... Ye shall not need to fight in this battle; set yourselves, stand ye still, and see the salvation of the Lord with you. O Judah and Jerusalem, fear not, nor be dismayed; tomorrow go out against them; for the Lord will be with you."

Without a thought of doubt Jehoshaphat and the children of Israel believed the Word of the Lord and began at once to praise Him beforehand for the victory that they were sure was coming. The next morning they rose early and went out to meet their enemy; and Jehoshaphat, instead of exhorting them as an ordinary general would have done to look to their arms and to be brave in battle, simply called upon them to have a courageous faith. "Hear me, O Judah, and ye inhabitants of Jerusalem," he said, "believe in the Lord your God, so shall ye be established; believe his prophets, so shall ye prosper."

Jehoshaphat then consulted with the people; and as their faith proved equal to his own, they appointed singers to go out before the army to sing praises as they went forward to meet the enemy. And it came to pass that when they began to sing and to praise, the Lord began to set ambushments against the enemy, so that they smote one another; and when the children of Israel came to a watchtower in the wilderness, from which they could see the great multitude that had come up against them, "behold, they were dead bodies fallen to the earth, and none escaped."

By this wonderful method of warfare they were made even "more than conquerors"; for they were "three days in gathering the spoil, it was so much."

David's fight with Goliath is another example of this method of victory. To the eye of sense David had no chance whatever of conquering the mighty giant, who had been defying the armies of Israel. But David, looking with the eye of faith, could see the unseen divine forces that were fighting on his side, and when Saul said to him: "Thou art not able to go against this Philistine to fight with him, for thou art but a youth, and he a man of war from his youth," David stood firm in his faith; and, after recounting some of his past deliverances, said calmly: "The Lord that delivered me out of the paw of the lion, and out of the paw of the bear, he will deliver me out of the hand of this Philistine." Saul, partly convinced by this strong faith, said, "Go, and the Lord be with thee." He could not, however, quite give up all trust in his own accustomed armor, and he armed David with a helmet of brass, and a coat of mail, and his own powerful sword, and David "assayed to go." But David soon found that he would not be able to fight in this sort of armor, and he put it off, and took instead the simple weapons that the Lord had blessed before—his staff, and his sling, and five smooth stones out of the brook; and thus equipped, he drew near to the giant.

When the giant saw the stripling who had come to fight him, he disdained him, and said contemptuously: "Come to me, and I will give thy flesh to the fowls of the air and the beasts of the field." And truly to the eye of the sense it looked as though this must necessarily be the end of such an apparently unequal battle. But David's faith triumphed, and he shouted a shout of victory before even the battle had begun. "Thou comest to me," he said, "with a sword, and with a spear, and with a shield; but I come to thee in the name of the Lord of hosts, the God of the armies of Israel, whom thou defiest. This day will the Lord deliver thee into mine hand, and I will smite thee, and take thy head from thee... that all the earth may know that there is a God in Israel. And all this assembly shall know that the Lord saveth not with sword and spear: for the battle is the Lord's, and he will give you into our hands."

In the face of such faith as this, what could even a giant do? Every word of that triumphant shout of victory was fulfilled; and the mighty enemy was delivered into the hands of the stripling he had disdained.

And so it will always be. Nothing can withstand the triumphant faith that links itself to omnipotence. For "this is the victory that overcometh the world, even our faith."

The secret of all successful warfare lies in this shout of faith. It is a secret incomprehensible to those who know nothing of the unseen divine power that waits on the demands of faith; a secret that must always seem, to those who do not understand it, the height of folly and imprudence.

We are all called to be "good soldiers of Jesus Christ," and to fight the "good fight of faith" against worse enemies than those which attacked the Israelites. Our enemies are interior, and the giant that defies us is the strength of our temptations and the powerlessness of our own strength to resist. It is a hard, and often a very discouraging fight, and many of God's children are weighed down under a dreary sense of apparently hopeless failure. They have sinned and repented again, so often, that they can see no hope of victory, and are ready to despair. They hate sin, and they love righteousness, and they long for victory, but the good that they would they do not, and the evil that they would not that they do. In the language of the Apostle they find a law in their members warring against the law of their mind, and bringing them into captivity to the law of sin that is in their members. They know they ought to conquer, but they do not know how. And it is for these that this chapter is written. If they can but discover the secret of this shout of faith they will know how, for it is absolutely certain that it never fails to bring victory.

In John 16:33 our Lord reveals the ground of this triumphant shout of faith. "Be of good cheer," He says, "for I have overcome the world." Not "I will overcome," but "I have overcome." It is already done; and nothing remains but for us to enter into the power of it. Joshua did not say to the people, "Shout, for the Lord will give you the city," but "Shout, for he hath given it." It has always seemed to me that it must have drained all Joshua's will power to his lips to render it possible for him to make such a statement, in face of the fact that the walls of the city were at that very minute standing up as massive and as impregnable as ever. But God was a reality to Joshua, and he was not afraid to proclaim the victory that had been promised, even before it was accomplished.

There is a great difference between saying, "The Lord will give," and "The Lord hath given." A victory promised in the future may be hindered or prevented by a thousand contingencies, but a victory already accomplished cannot be gainsaid. And when our Lord assures us, not that He will overcome the world, but that He has already done so, He gives an assured foundation for a shout of the most triumphant victory. Henceforward the forces of sin are a defeated and demoralized foe; and, if we believe the words of Christ, we can meet them without fear, since we have been made more than conquerors through Him who loves us.

It is a well-known fact that as long as a defeated army can keep its defeat a secret, it can still make some show of resistance. But the moment it finds out that its defeat is known, it loses all heart and becomes utterly demoralized, and has no resource left but to retreat.

The secret then lies in this that we must meet sin, not as a foe that has yet to be conquered, but as one that has already been conquered. When Rahab helped the spies who had been sent by Joshua to escape from the king of Jericho, she made this confession: "I know that the Lord hath given you the land, and that your terror is fallen upon us, and that all the inhabitants of the land faint because of you." If we were gifted with eyes that could see the unseen kingdom of evil, I believe we also should find that a terror and faintness has fallen upon all the forces of that unknown region, and that they see in every man and woman of faith a sure and triumphant conqueror.

It is because we do not know this secret that we meet our spiritual enemies with such fear and trembling, and suffer such disastrous defeats.

A Christian I know, who had been fearfully beset by temptation against which she had seemed to struggle in vain, was told this secret by one who had discovered it. It brought conviction at once, and she went forth to a fresh battle with the assurance of an already accomplished victory. It is needless to say that she was victorious; and she said afterward that it seemed to her as if she could almost hear the voice of the tempter saying as he slunk away, "Alas! it is all up with me now. She had found out the secret. She knows that I am an already conquered foe, and I am afraid I shall never be able to overcome her again!"

We are told that "for this purpose the Son of God was manifested, that he might destroy the works of the devil"; and again: "Ye know that he was manifested to take away our sins; and in him is no sin"; and again: "Now once in the end of the world hath he appeared to put away sin by the sacrifice of himself." We must accept it as a fact, therefore, that sin is for us a conquered foe. And if our faith will only lay hold of this fact, reckoning sin to be dead to us, and ourselves to be dead to sin; and will dare, when we come in sight of temptation, to raise the shout of victory, we shall surely find as the Israelites did that every wall will fall down flat, and that a pathway will be opened straight before us to take the city!

Our enemies are giants now just as truly as they were in Israel's day; and cities as great as Jericho, with walls as high, confront us in our heavenly pathway. Like the Israelites of old, we have no human weapons with which to conquer them. Our armor, like theirs, must be the "armor of God." Our shield is the same invisible shield of faith that protected them; and our sword must be, as theirs was, the sword of the Spirit which is the Word, that is, the promises and declarations of God. When our faith puts on this "armor of God," and lays hold of this "sword of the Spirit," and we confront our enemy with a shout of undaunted faith, we cannot fail to conquer the mightiest giant, or to take the strongest city.

But alas! how different is the usual method of our Christian warfare. Instead of a triumphant shout of victory, we meet our temptations with feeble resolutions, or with futile arguments, or with halfhearted self-upbraiding, or, failing all else, with despairing prayers. "O Lord, save me!" we cry; "O Lord, deliver me!" And when no deliverance has come, and the temptation has swept aside all our arguments and all our resolutions, and we have been grievously defeated, then we have cried out in our despair that God has failed us, and that there is for us no truth in the Apostle's declaration that with every temptation there is a way of escape that we may be able to bear it. This is the usual and the unsuccessful way of meeting temptation, as many of us know to our cost. But what we ought to do is very different. We must recognize it as a fact that sin is a conquered foe, and must meet it, therefore, with a shout of victory instead of with a cry for help. Where we prayed that the Lord would save us, we must make now the assertion that He does save us, and that he saves us now. We must add the little letter *s* to the word save, and make it the present instead of the future tense.

The walls may look as high and as immovable as ever; and prudence may say it is not safe to shout until the victory is actually won. But the faith that can shout in the midst of the sorest stress of temptation, "Jesus saves me; He saves me now!" such a faith will be sure to win a glorious and a speedy victory. Many of God's children have tried this plan, and have found it to work far beyond even their expectations. Temptations have come in upon them like a flood—temptations to irritability, or to wicked thoughts, or to bitterness of spirit, or to a thousand other things, and they have seen their danger; and their fears and their feelings have declared that there was no hope of escape. But their faith has laid hold of this grand fact that Christ has conquered; and they have fixed their gaze on the unseen power of God's salvation, and have given their shout of victory, "The Lord saves! He saves me now! I am more than conqueror through Him that loves me!" And the result is always a glorious victory.

It may sometimes seem so impossible that the Lord can or does save that the words will not say themselves inside, but have to be said aloud, forcing one's lips to utter them over and over, shutting one's eyes and closing one's ears against every suggestion of doubt no matter how plausible it may seem. These declarations of faith often seem untrue at first, so apparently real are the seen reasons for doubt and discouragement. But the unseen facts are truer than the seen, and if the faith that lays hold of them is steadfastly persisted in, they never fail in the end to prove themselves to be the very truth of God. "According to our faith" it always must be unto us, sooner or later, and when we shout the shout of faith, the Lord invariably gives the victory of faith.

I knew a Christian man who had entered upon this life of faith. He had naturally a violent temper and went about his work among his ungodly companions was sorely beset with temptations to give way to it. He knew it was wrong, and he struggled valiantly against it, but all in vain. Finally, one morning on his way to work he called in despair at the house of his Christian teacher and told him his difficulties. After explaining the suddenness of the temptations that came upon him, and the lack of time even to pray for help before he was overcome, he said, "Now can you tell me of any short road to victory; something that I can lay hold of just at the needed moment?"

"Yes," replied the minister; "when the temptation comes, at once lift up your heart to the Lord, and by faith claim the promised victory. Shout the shout of faith, and the temptation will flee before you."

After a little explanation of the glorious fact that sin is an already conquered foe, the man seemed to understand and went on his way to take his place in the ranks with his fellow men at the station where they were engaged in hauling freight. As usual he was met by taunts and sneers; and in addition he found that they had jostled him out of his rightful place in the ranks. The temptation to anger was almost overwhelming, but, folding his arms, he said inwardly over and over, "Jesus saves me; He saves me now!" At once his heart was filled with peace, and the victory was complete. Again he was tried; a heavy box was so rolled as to fall on his foot badly injuring him, and again he folded his arms and repeated his shout of victory, and at once all was calm. And so the day passed on. Trials and temptations abounded, but his triumphant shout carried him safely through them all, and the fiery darts of the enemy were all quenched by the shield of faith which he continually lifted up. Nighttime found him more than conqueror through Him who loved him; and even his fellow carmen were forced to own the reality and the beauty of a religion that could so triumph over their aggravating assaults.

The Psalmist, after telling of the enemies who were daily trying to swallow him up, declared triumphantly: "When I cry unto thee, then shall mine enemies turn back: this I know; for God is for me."

Dear reader, do you know what the Psalmist knew? Do you know that God is for you, and that He will cause your enemies to turn back? If you do, then go out to meet your temptations, singing a song of triumph as you go. Meet your very next temptation in this way. At this first approach begin to give thanks for the victory. Claim continually that you are more than conqueror through Him that loves you, and refuse to be daunted by any foe. Shout the shout of faith with Joshua, and Jehoshaphat, and David, and Paul; and I can assure you that when you shout, the Lord will "set ambushments," and all your enemies shall fall down dead before you.

Chapter 15: Thanksgiving Versus Complaining

*"In everything give thanks, for this is the will of God
in Christ Jesus concerning you."*

Thanksgiving or complaining—these words express two contrastive attitudes of the souls of God's children in regard to His dealings with them; and they are more powerful than we are inclined to believe in furthering or frustrating His purposes of comfort and peace toward us. The soul that gives thanks can find comfort in everything; the soul that complains can find comfort in nothing.

God's command is "In everything give thanks"; and the command is emphasized by the declaration, "for this is the will of God in Christ Jesus concerning you." It is an actual positive command; and if we want to obey God, we have simply got to give thanks in everything. There is no getting around it.

But a great many Christians have never realized this; and, although they may be familiar with the command, they have always looked upon it as a sort of counsel of perfection to which mere flesh and blood could never be expected to attain. And they, unconsciously to themselves perhaps, change the wording of the passage to make it say "be resigned" instead of "give thanks," and "in a few things" instead of "in everything," and they leave out altogether the words, "for this is the will of God in Christ Jesus concerning you."

If brought face to face with the actual wording of the command, such Christians will say, "Oh, but it is an impossible command. If everything came direct from God, one might do it perhaps, but most things come through human sources, and often are the result of sin, and it would not be possible to give thanks for these." To this I answer that it is true we cannot always give thanks for the things themselves, but we can always give thanks for God's love and care in the things. He may not have ordered them, but He is in them somewhere, and He is in them to compel, even the most grievous, to work together for our good.

The "second causes" of the wrong may be full of malice and wickedness, but faith never sees second causes. It sees only the hand of God behind the second causes. They are all under His control, and not one of them can touch us except with His knowledge and permission. The thing itself that happens cannot perhaps be said to be the will of God, but by the time its effects reach us they have become God's will for us, and must be accepted as from His hands.

The story of Joseph is an illustration of this. Nothing could have seemed more entirely an act of sin, nor more utterly contrary to the will of God than his being sold to the Ishmaelites by his wicked brethren; and it would not have seemed possible for Joseph, when he was being carried off into slavery in Egypt, to give thanks. And yet, if he had known the end from the beginning, he would have been filled with thanksgiving. The fact of his having been sold into slavery was the direct doorway to the greatest triumphs and blessings of his life. And, at the end, Joseph himself could say to his wicked brethren: "As for you, ye thought evil against me, but God meant it unto good." To the eye of sense it was Joseph's wicked brethren who had sent him into Egypt, but Joseph, looking at it with the eye of faith, said, "God did send me."

We can all remember, I think, similar instances in our own lives when God has made the wrath of man to praise Him, and has caused even the hardest trails to work together for our greatest good. I recollect once in my own life when a trial was brought upon me by another person, at which I was filled with bitter rebellion and could not see in it from beginning to end anything to be thankful for. But, as it was in the case of Joseph, that very trial worked out for me the richest blessings and the greatest triumphs of my whole life; and in the end I was filled with thanksgiving for the very things that had caused me such bitter rebellion before. If only I had had faith enough to give thanks at first, how much sorrow would have been spared me.

But I am afraid that the greatest heights to which most Christians in their shortsightedness seem able to rise is to strive after resignation to things they cannot alter, and to seek for patience to endure them. And the result is that thanksgiving is almost an unknown exercise among the children of God; and, instead of giving thanks in everything, many of them hardly give thanks in anything. If the truth were told, Christians as a body must be acknowledged to be but a thankless set. It is considered in the world a very discourteous thing for one man to receive benefits from another man and fail to thank him, and I cannot see why it is not just as discourteous a thing not to thank God. And yet we find people who would not for the world omit an immediate note of thanks upon the reception of any gift, however trifling, from a human friend, but who have never given God real thanks for any one of the innumerable benefits He has been showering upon them all their long lives.

Moreover, I am afraid a great many not only fail to give thanks, but they do exactly the opposite, and allow themselves instead to complain and murmur about God's dealings with them. Instead of looking out for His goodness, they seem to delight in picking out His shortcomings, and think they show a spirit of discernment in criticizing His laws and His ways. We are told that "when the people complained, it displeased the Lord"; but we are tempted to think that our special complaining, because it is spiritual complaining, cannot displease Him since it is a pious sort of complaining, and is a sign of greater zeal on our part, and of deeper spiritual insight than is possessed by the ordinary Christian.

But complaining is always alike, whether it is on the temporal or the spiritual plane. It always has in it the element of fault-finding. Webster says to complain means to make a charge or an accusation. It is not merely disliking the thing we have to bear, but it contains the element of finding fault with the agency that lies behind it. And if we will carefully examine the true inwardness of our complainings, I think we shall generally find they are founded on a subtle fault-finding with God. We secretly feel as if He were to blame somehow; and, almost unconsciously to ourselves, we make mental charges against Him.

On the other hand, thanksgiving always involves praise of the giver. Have you ever noticed how much we are urged in the Bible to "praise the Lord"? It seemed to be almost the principal part of the worship of the Israelites. "Praise ye the Lord, for the Lord is good: sing praises to his name, for it is pleasant." This is the continual refrain of everything all through the Bible. I believe, if we should count up, we would find that there are more commands given and more examples set for the giving of thanks "always for all things" than for the doing or the leaving undone of anything else.

It is very evident from the whole teaching of Scripture that the Lord loves to be thanked and praised just as much as we like it. I am sure that it gives Him real downright pleasure, just as it does us; and that our failure to thank Him for His "good and perfect gifts" wounds His loving heart, just as our hearts are wounded when our loved ones fail to appreciate the benefits we have so enjoyed bestowing upon them. What a joy it is to us to receive from our friends an acknowledgment of their thanksgiving for our gifts, and is it no likely that it is a joy to the Lord also?

When the Apostle is exhorting the Ephesian Christians to be "followers of God as dear children," one of the exhortations he gives in connection with being filled with the Spirit is this: "Giving thanks always for all things unto God and the Father, in the name of our Lord Jesus Christ." "Always for all things" is a very sweeping expression, and it is impossible to suppose it can be whittled down to mean only the few and scanty thanks, which seem all that many Christians manage to give. It must mean, I am sure, that there can be nothing in our lives which has not in it somewhere a cause for thanksgiving, and that, no mater who or what may be the channel to convey it, everything contains for us a hidden blessing from God.

The Apostle tells us that "every creature of God is good, and nothing to be refused, if it be received with thanksgiving." But it is very hard for us to believe things are good when they do not look so. Often the things God sends into our lives look like curses instead of blessings; and those who have no eyes that can see below surfaces judge by the outward seemings only and never see the blessed realities beneath.

How many "good and perfect gifts" we must have had during our lives, which we have looked upon only as curses, and for which we have never returned one thought of thanks! And for how many gifts also, which we have even acknowledged to be good, have we thanked ourselves, or our friends, or our circumstances, without once looking behind the earthly givers to thank the Heavenly Giver, from whom in reality they all come! It is as if we should thank the messengers who bring us our friends' gifts, but should never send any word of thanks to our friends themselves.

But, even when we realize that things come directly from God, we find it very hard to give thanks for what hurts us. Do we not, however, all know what it is to thank a skillful physician for his treatment of our diseases, even though that treatment may have been very severe. And surely we should no less give thanks to our Divine Physician, when He is obliged to give us bitter medicine to cure our spiritual diseases, or to perform a painful operation to rid us of something that harms.

But instead of thanking Him we complain against Him; although we generally direct our complaints, not against the Divine Physician himself who has ordered our medicine, but against the "bottle" in which He has sent it. This "bottle" is usually some human being, whose unkindness or carelessness, or neglect, or cruelty has caused our suffering; but who has been after all only the instrumentality or "second cause" that God has used for our healing.

Good common sense tells us that it would be folly to rail against the bottles in which the medicines, prescribed by our earthy physicians, come to us; and it is equal folly to rail against the "second causes" that are meant to teach us the lessons our souls need to learn.

When the children of Israel found themselves wandering in the wilderness, they "murmured against Moses and Aaron," and complained that they had brought them forth into the wilderness to kill them with hunger. But in reality their complaining was against God, for it was really He who had brought them there, and not Moses and Aaron, who were only the "second causes." And the Psalmist in recounting the story afterward called this murmuring against Moses and Aaron a "speaking against God." Divine history takes no account of second causes, but goes directly to the real cause behind them.

We may settle it, therefore, that all complaining is at the bottom "speaking against God," whether we are conscious of it or not. We may think, as the Israelites did, that our discomforts and deprivations have come from human hands only, and may therefore feel at liberty to "murmur against" the second causes which have, we may think, brought about our trials. But God is the great Cause behind all second causes. The second causes are only the instrumentalities that He uses; and when we murmur against these, we are really murmuring, not against the instrumentalities, but against God Himself. Second causes are powerless to act, except by God's permission; and what He permits becomes really His arranging. The Psalmist tells us that when the Lord heard the complainings of His people "He was wroth," and His anger came up against them "because they believed not in God, and trusted not in his salvation." And, at the bottom, all complainings mean just this, that we do not believe in God, and do not trust in His salvation.

The Psalmist says: "I will praise the name of God with a song, and magnify him with thanksgiving. This also shall please the Lord better than an ox or bullock that hath horns and hoofs." A great many people seem quite ready and willing to offer up an "ox or a bullock," or some great sacrifice to the Lord, but never seem to have realized that a little genuine praise and thanksgiving offered to Him now and then would "please him better" than all their great sacrifices made in His cause.

As I said before, the Bible is full of this thought from beginning to end. Over and over it is called a "sacrifice of thanksgiving," showing that it is as really an act of religious worship, as is any other religious act. In fact, the "sacrifice of thanksgiving" was one of the regular sacrifices ordained by God in the Book of Leviticus. "Oh that men would praise the Lord for his goodness, and for his wonderful works to the children of men! And let them sacrifice the sacrifices of thanksgiving, and declare his works with rejoicing." By

Him, therefore, let us offer the sacrifice of praise to God continually, that is, the fruit of our lips, giving thanks to His name.

It is such an easy thing to offer the "sacrifice of thanksgiving," that one would suppose everybody would be keen to do it. But somehow the contrary seems to be the case; and if the prayers of Christians were all to be noted down for any one single day, I fear it would be found that with them, as it was with the ten lepers who had been cleansed, nine out of every ten had offered no genuine thanks at all. Our Lord Himself was grieved at these ungrateful lepers, and said: "Were there not ten cleansed? But where are the nine? There are not found that returned to give glory to God, save this stranger." Will He have to ask the same question regarding any of us? We have often, it may be, wondered at the ingratitude of those nine cleansed lepers; but what about our own ingratitude? Do we not continually pass by blessings innumerable without notice, and instead fix our eyes on what we feel to be our trials and our losses, and think and talk about these, until our whole horizon is filled with them, and we almost begin to think we have no blessings at all?

We can judge of how this must grieve the Lord by our own feelings. A child who complains about the provision the parent has made wounds that parent's heart often beyond words. Some people are always complaining, nothing ever pleases them, and no kindness seems ever to be appreciated. We know how uncomfortable the society of such people makes us; and we know, on the contrary, how life is brightened by the presence of one who never complains, but who finds something to be pleased with in all that comes. I believe far more misery than we imagine is caused in human hearts by the grumblings of those they love; and I believe also that woundings we never dream of, are given to the heart of our Father in Heaven by the continual murmuring of His children.

How often is it despairingly said of fretful, complaining spirits upon whom every care and attention has been lavished, "Will nothing ever satisfy them?" And how often must God turn away, grieved by our complainings, when His love has been lavished upon us in untold blessings. I have sometimes thought that if we could but realize this, we would check our inordinate grief over even the trials that come from the death of those we love, and would try, for His dear sake, to be cheerful and content even in our lonely and bereft condition.

I remember hearing of a dear girl who was obliged to undergo a serious and very painful treatment for some disease, and the doctors had dreaded the thought of her groans and outcries. But to their amazement not even a moan escaped her lips, and all the time she smiled at her father who was present, and uttered only words of love and tenderness. The doctors could not understand it, and when the worst was over one of them asked how it could have been. "Ah," she said, "I knew how much my father loved me, and I knew how he would suffer if he saw that I suffered, so I tried to hide my suffering; and I smiled to make him think I did not mind."

Can any of us do this for our heavenly Father?

Job was a great complainer; and we may perhaps think, as we read his story, that if ever anyone had good cause for complaining, he had. His circumstances seemed to be full of hopeless misery. "My soul is weary of my life; I will leave my complaint upon myself; I will speak in the bitterness of my soul. I will say unto God, Do not condemn me; show me wherefore thou contendest with me. Is it good unto thee that thou shouldest oppress, that thou shouldest despise the work of thine hands?"

We can hardly wonder at Job's complaint. And yet could he but have seen the divine side of all his troubles, he would have known that they were permitted in the tenderest love, and were to bring him a revelation of God such as he could have had by no other means. Could he have seen that this was to be the outcome he would not have uttered a single complaint, but would have given triumphant thanks for the trials which were to bring him such a glorious fruition. And could we but see, in our heaviest trials, the end from the beginning, I am sure that thanksgiving would take the place of complaining in every case.

The children of Israel were always complaining about something. They complained because they had no water; and when water was supplied they complained that it was bitter to their taste. And we likewise complain because the spiritual water we have to drink seems bitter to our taste. Our souls are athirst, and we do not like the supply that seems to be provided. Our experiences do not quench our thirst, our religious exercises seem dull and unsatisfying; we feel ourselves to be in a dry and thirsty land where no water is. We have turned from the "Fountain of living waters," and then we complain because the cisterns we have hewed out for ourselves hold no water.

The Israelites complained about their food. They had so little confidence in God that they were afraid they would die of starvation; and then when the heavenly manna was provided they complained again because they "loathed such light food." And we also complain about our spiritual food. Like the Israelites, we have so little confidence in God that we are always afraid we shall die of spiritual starvation. We complain because our preacher does not feed us, or because our religious privileges are very scanty, or because we are not supplied with the same spiritual fare as others are, who seem to us more highly favored; and we covet their circumstances or their experiences. We have asked God to feed us, and then our souls "loathe" the food He gives, and we think it is too "light" to sustain or strengthen us. We have asked for bread, and we complain that He has given a stone.

But, if we only knew it, the provision our divine Master has made of spiritual drink and spiritual food is just that which is best for us, and is that for which we would be the most thankful if we knew. The amazing thing is that we cannot believe now, without waiting for the end, that the Shepherd knows what pasture is best for His sheep. Surely if we did, our hearts would be filled with thanksgiving and our mouths with praise even in the wilderness.

Jonah was a wonderful illustration of this. His prayer of thanksgiving out of the "belly of hell" is a tremendous lesson. "I have cried by reason of mine affliction unto the Lord, and he heard me; out of the belly of hell cried I, and thou heardest my voice. For thou hadst cast me into the deep, in the midst of the sea: and the floods compassed me about; all thy billows and thy waves passed over me... But I will sacrifice unto thee with a voice of thanksgiving; I will pay that I have vowed. Salvation is of the Lord."

No depth of misery, not even the "belly of hell," is too great for the sacrifice of thanksgiving. We cannot, it is true, give thanks for the misery, but we can give thanks to the Lord in the misery, just as Jonah did. No matter what our trouble, the Lord is in it somewhere; and, of course, being there, He is there to help and bless us. Therefore, when our "souls faint within us" because of our troubles, we have only to remember this, and to thank Him for His presence and His love.

It is not because things are good that we are to thank the Lord, but because He is good. We are not wise enough to judge as to things, whether they are really, in their essence, joys or sorrows. But we always know that the Lord is good, and that His goodness makes it absolutely certain that everything He provides or permits must be good; and must therefore be something for which we would be heartily thankful, if only we could see it with His eyes.

In a little tract called "Mrs. Pickett's Missionary Box," a poor woman, who had never done anything but complain all her life long, and who, consequently, had got to thinking that she had no benefits for which to give thanks, received a missionary box with the words written on it: "What shall I render unto the Lord for all His benefits toward me?" And she was asked by her niece, who believed in being thankful, to put a penny into the box for every benefit she could discover in her life. I will let her tell her own story.

"'Great benefits I have!' says I, standing with my arms akimbo, an' lookin' that box all over. 'Guess the heathen won't get much out of me at that rate.' An' I jest made up my mind I would keep count, jest to show myself how little I did have. 'Them few pennies won't break me,' I thought, and I really seemed to kinder enjoy thinkin' over the hard times I had.

"Well, the box sat there all that week, an' I used to say it must be kinder lonesome with nothin' in it; for not a penny went into it until next missionary meetin' day. I was sittin' on the back steps gettin' a breath of fresh air, when Mary came home, an' sat down alongside o' me an' began to tell me about the meetin', an' it was all about Injy an' the widders there, poor creturs, an' they bein' abused, an' starved, an' not let to think for themselves—you know all about it better'n I do!—an' before I thought I up an' said—

"'Well, if I be a widder, I'm thankful I'm where I kin earn my own livin', an' no thanks to nobody, an' no one to interfere!'

"Then Mary, she laughed an' said there was my fust benefit. Well, that sorter tickled me, for I thought a woman must be pretty hard up for benefits when she had to go clear off to Injy to find them, an' I dropped in one penny, an' it rattled round a few days without any company. I used to shake it every time I passed the shelf, an' the thought of them poor things in Injy kep' a comin' up before me, an' I really was glad when I got a new boarder for me best room, an' felt as if I'd oughter put in another. An' next meetin', Mary she told me about China, an' I thought about that till I put in another because I warn't a Chinese. An' all the while I felt kinder proud of how little there was in that box. Then one day, when I got a chance to turn a little penny sellin' eggs, which I warn't in the habit of, Mary brought the box in, where I was countin' of my money, and says—

"'A penny for your benefit, Aunt Mirandy.'

"An' I says, 'This ain't the Lord's benefit.'

"An' she answered, 'If 'tain't His, whose is it?' An' she begun to hum over somethin' out of one of the poetry books that she was always a readin' of—

> 'God's grace is the only grace,
>   And all grace is the grace of God.'

"Well, I dropped in my penny, an' them words kep' ringin' in my ears, till I couldn't help puttin' more to it, on account of some other things I never thought of callin' the Lord's benefits before. An' by that time, what with Mary's tellin' me about them meetin's, an' me most always findin' somethin' to put in a penny for, to be thankful that I warn't it, an' what with gettin' interested about it all, and sorter searchin' round a little now and then to think of somethin' or other to put a penny in for, there really come to be quite a few pennies in the box, an' it didn't ralle near so much when I shook it."

There is a psalm which I call our Benefit Psalm. It is Psalm 103, and it recounts some of the benefits the Lord has bestowed upon us, and urges us not to forget them. "Bless the Lord, O my soul, and forget not all his benefit." Our dear sister's Benefit Box had taught her something of the meaning of this psalm. All her life she had been forgetting the benefits the Lord had bestowed upon her, but now she was beginning to remember them.

Have we begun to remember ours?

If during the past year we had kept count of those benefits for which we had actually given thanks, how many pennies, I wonder, would our boxes have contained?

We sometimes sing at mission meetings a hymn of thanksgiving, with the chorus, "Count your many blessings, name them one by one, and it will surprise you what the Lord has done." And sometimes I have wondered whether any of us who were singing it so heartily had ever kept the slightest record of our blessings, or even in fact knew that we had any.

For the trouble is that very often God's gifts come to us wrapped up in such rough coverings that we are tempted to reject them as worthless; or the messengers who bring them come in the guise of enemies, and we want to shut the door against them, and not give them entrance. But we lose far more than we know when we reject even the most unlikely.

> *Evil is only the slave of good,*
> *And sorrow the servant of joy:*
> *And the soul is mad that refuses food*
> *From the meanest in God's employ.*

We are commanded to enter into His gates with thanksgiving, and into His courts with praise, and I am convinced that the giving of thanks is the key that opens these gates more quickly than anything else. Try it, dear reader. The next time you feel dead, cold, and low-spirited begin to praise and thank the Lord. Enumerate to yourself the benefits He has bestowed upon you, thank Him heartily for each one, and see if your spirits do not begin to rise, and your heart get warmed up.

Sometimes it may be that you feel too disheartened to pray; then try giving thanks instead; and, before you know it, you will find yourself "glad" in the multitude of His loving-kindnesses and His tender mercies.

One of my friends told me that her little boy one night flatly refused to say his prayers. He said there was not a single thing in all the world he wanted, and he did not see what was the good of asking for things that he did not want. A happy thought came to his mother as she said, "Well, Charlie, suppose then we give thanks for all the things you have got." The idea pleased the child, and he very willingly knelt down and began to give thanks. He thanked God for his marbles, and for a new top that had just been given him, and for his strong legs that could run so fast, and that he was not blind like a little boy he knew, and for his kind father and mother, and for his nice bed, and for one after another of his blessings, until the list grew so long that at last he said he believed he would never get done. And when finally they rose from their knees, he said to his mother, with his face shining with happiness, "Oh, Mother, I never knew before how perfectly splendid God is!" And I believe, if we sometimes followed the example of this little boy, we too would find out, as never before, the goodness of our God.

It is very striking to notice how much thanksgiving had to do with the building of the Temple. When they had collected the treasures for the Temple. When they had collected the treasures for the Temple, David gave thanks to the Lord for enabling them to do it. When the Temple was finished, they gave thanks again. And then a wonderful thing happened, for it came to pass as the trumpeters and singers were as one to make one sound to be heard in praising and thanking the Lord... that then the house was filled with a cloud, even the house of the Lord, so that the priests could not stand to minister by reason of the cloud; for the glory of the Lord had filled the house of God. When the people praised and gave thanks, then the house was filled with the glory of the Lord. And we may be sure that the reason our hearts are not oftener filled with the "glory of the Lord" is because we do not often enough make our voices to be heard in praising and thanking Him.

If the giving of thanks is the way to open the gates of the Lord, complaining on the other hand closes these gates. Jude quotes a prophecy of Enoch's concerning murmurers: "The Lord cometh," he says, "to execute judgment upon all, and to convince all that are ungodly among them... of all their hard speeches which ungodly sinners have spoken against him. These are murmurers, complainers, walking after their own lusts."

People who are "murmurers" and "complainers" make in their complainings more "hard speeches" against the Lord than they would like to own, or than they will care at the last day to face. And it is not to be wondered that the judgment of God, instead of the "glory of God," is the result.

I wish I had room to quote all the passages in the Bible about giving thanks and praises to the Lord. It is safe to say that there are hundreds and hundreds of them; and it is an amazing thing how they can have been so persistently ignored. I beg of you to read the last seven psalms, and see what you think. They are simply full to overflowing with a list of the things for which the Psalmist calls upon us to give thanks; all of them are things relating to the character and the ways of God, which we dare not dispute. They are not for the most part private blessings of our own, but are the common blessings that belong to all humanity, and that contain within themselves every private blessing we can possibly need. But they are blessings which we continually forget, because we take them for granted, hardly noticing their existence, and never give thanks for them.

But the Psalmist knew how to count his many blessings and name them one by one, and he would have us to do likewise. Try it, dear reader, and you will indeed be surprised to see what the Lord has done. Go over these psalms verse by verse, and blessing by blessing, and see if, like the little boy of our story, you are not made to confess that you never knew before "how perfectly splendid God is."

The last verse of the Book of Psalms, taken in connection with the vision of John in the Book of Revelation, is very significant. The Psalmist says, "Let everything that hath breath praise the Lord." And in the Book of Revelation, John, who declares himself to be our brother and our companion in tribulation, tells us that he heard this being done. "And every creature which is in heaven, and on the earth, and under the earth, and such as are in the sea, and all that are in them, heard I saying, Blessing, and honor, and glory and power, be unto him that sitteth upon the throne, and unto the Lamb, forever and ever."

The time for universal praise is sure to come some day. Let us begin to do our part now.

I heard once of a discontented, complaining man who, to the great surprise of his friends, became bright, and happy, and full of thanksgiving. After watching him for a little while, and being convinced that the change was permanent, they asked him what had happened. "Oh," he replied, "I have changed my residence. I used to live in Grumbling Lane, but now I have moved into Thanksgiving Square, and I find that I am so rich in blessings that I am always happy."

Shall we each one make this move now?

Chapter 16: Conformed To The Image Of Christ

"For whom he did foreknow, he also did predestinate to be conformed to the image of his Son, that he might be the firstborn among many brethren."

God's ultimate purpose in our creation was that we should finally be "conformed to the image of Christ." Christ was to be the firstborn among many brethren, and His brethren were to be like Him. All the discipline and training of our lives is with this end in view; and God has implanted in every human heart a longing, however unformed and unexpressed, after the best and highest it knows.

When God said in the beginning, "Let us make man in our image, after our likeness," we cannot for a moment suppose that He meant we were to be made in the image or likeness of His body. He must have meant that man was to be made in the image or likeness of His nature and character. Neither could He have meant that man, when first created, was to be created full fledged in this image, but only that he was to be begun, as all adult life is begun, in helpless ignorant babyhood. It is just as an architect could say of a great building, when as yet only the foundation-stones were in place, "This is a cathedral," so could God say of man, "This is My image," although as yet only the foundation-stones of this image were laid; for we are told that "the first man is of the earth earthy."

That it was only the foundation-stones of what was God's final purpose for man which were laid at the moment of man's first creation, is plain from the fact that man then had no knowledge of the difference be tween right and wrong, and was therefore, as babies are, in a very undeveloped state, and could not by any possibility be said, at least in this respect, to be in the likeness of God. But the embryo of God's image was in man, and God's purpose in regard to him began to be accomplished then, and it has gone on, in a grand process of evolution, ever since, both in the individual and in the race.

Christ is the pattern of what each one of us is to be when finished. We are "predestinated" to be conformed to His image, in order that He might be the firstborn among many brethren. We are to be "partakers of the divine nature" with Christ; we are to be filled with the spirit of Christ; we are to share His resurrection life, and to walk as He walked. We are to be one with Him, as He is one with the Father; and the glory God gave to Him, He is to give to us. And when all this is brought to pass, then, and not until then, will God's purpose in our creation be fully accomplished, and we stand forth "in his image and after his likeness."

Our likeness to His image is an accomplished fact in the mind of God, but we are, so to speak, in the manufactory as yet, and the great Master Workman is at work upon us. "It doth not yet appear what we shall be: but we know that, when he shall appear, we shall be like him; for we shall see him as he is."

And so it is written: "The first man Adam was made a living soul; the last Adam was made a quickening spirit. Howbeit that was not first which is spiritual, but that which is natural; and afterward that which is spiritual. The first man is of the earth, earthy; the second man is the Lord from heaven. As is the earthly, such are they also that are earthy; and as is the heavenly, such are they also that are heavenly. And as we have borne the image of the earthly, we shall also bear the image of the heavenly."

The grand process of Christian evolution is set forth here. "The first man Adam was made a living soul." This expression "living soul" means in the Hebrew, according to Cruden's Concordance, the same thing as "living creature," which was the description given of the animal kingdom; and man, therefore, when first created, was simply a perfect animal, "of the earth earthy," since he had no conscience, nor any knowledge of the difference between right and wrong.

Then we have given to us in an allegory an account of the first step in the evolution, by which the first Adam, i.e. the natural or animal man, was to be developed into the last Adam, i.e. the spiritual man. The serpent tempted man to eat of the tree of the know ledge of good and evil, and said, "For God doth know that in the day ye eat thereof, then your eyes shall be opened; and ye shall be as gods, knowing good and evil." And, after Adam and Eve had eaten of the tree, the Lord confirmed this, and said, "Behold, the man is become as one of us, to know good and evil."

Instead of this being a fall out of a higher state into a lower, as is so often thought, it really was a step upward out of a lower stage of development into a higher. It surely was a great advance for man when God could say of him, "Behold, the man is become as one of us, knowing good and evil." "As one of us."— this could not have been said of him before; and it marked a distinct step upward in his development. The baby's ignorant innocence, that knows no difference between right and wrong, may be a beautiful thing in its place, but it becomes imbecility when it continues on into manhood. And man, who was destined to "grow up into Christ in all things," needed first of all to become acquainted with the difference between right and wrong. No progress was possible until this took place. We cannot wonder, therefore, that St. Augustine calls it "felix culpa," the "happy fall."

The first step, therefore, in man's evolution had now been taken. Man had discovered the difference between right and wrong, and had begun to develop a spiritual nature, a nature which God Himself declared was akin to His own. And from henceforth the conflict between the spiritual man and the animal or natural man has never ceased to be carried on. "For the flesh lusteth against the spirit and the spirit against the flesh, and these are contrary the one to the other; so that you cannot do the things that ye would." "For they that are after the flesh do mind the things of the flesh; but they that are after the spirit, the things of the spirit. For to be carnally minded is death; but to be spiritually minded is life and peace; because the carnal mind is enmity against God; for it is not subject to the law of God, neither indeed can be."

Whatever we may think of natural evolution as taught by Darwin, we must all believe in this spiritual evolution as taught by Paul. A late writer has said, "God is gradually developing higher forms of life out of lower forms; the spiritual and the intellectual, out of the animal and the sensuous; and it is in this process of evolution that sin shows itself, sin being simply the supremacy of the lower over the higher." What might be right in a monkey is wrong in a man, and what might be excusable in our lower nature, becomes sin in our higher. What we must do then, in order to co-operate with God in our evolution, is, as Tennyson has said, to "move upwards, working out the beast, and let the ape and tiger die." Every time we conquer the "beast" in us, we help forward our evolution, and every time we let the "beast" conquer us, we hinder it.

It is deeply interesting to see that this process, which was begun in Genesis, is declared to be completed in Revelation, where the "one like unto the Son of man" gave to John this significant message to the overcomers: "Him that overcometh will I make a pillar in the temple of my God; and he shall go no more out: and I will write upon him the name of my God, and the name of the city of my God which is new Jerusalem, which cometh down out of heaven from my God: and I will write upon him my new name." Since *name* always means character in the Bible, this message can only mean that at last God's purpose is accomplished, and the spiritual evolution of man is completed—he has been made, what God intended from the first, so truly into His likeness and image, as to merit having written upon him the name of God!

Words fail before such a glorious destiny as this! But our Lord foreshadows it in His wonderful prayer when He asks for His brethren that "they all may be one; as thou, Father, art in me, and I in thee, that they also may be one in us: that the world may believe that thou hast sent me. And the glory which thou gavest me I have given them: that they may be one even as we are one. I in them, and thou in me, that they may be made perfect in one." Could oneness be closer or more complete?

Paul also foreshadows this glorious consummation when he declares that if we suffer with Christ we shall also be glorified together with Him, and when he asserts that the "sufferings of this present time are not worthy to be compared with the glory that shall be revealed in us." The whole Creation waits for the revealing of this glory, for Paul goes on to say that the "earnest expectation of the creature waiteth for the manifestation of the sons of God." And he adds finally: "And not only they, but ourselves also, which have the first fruits of the Spirit, even we ourselves groan within ourselves, waiting for the adoption, to wit, the redemption of our body."

In view of such a glorious destiny, at which I dare not do more than hint, shall we not cheerfully welcome the processes, however painful they may be, by which we are to reach it? And shall we not strive eagerly and earnestly to be "laborers together with God" in helping to bring it about? He is the great master Builder, but He wants our co-operation in building up the fabric of our characters, and He exhorts us to take heed how we build. We are all of us at every moment of our lives engaged in this building. Sometimes we build with gold, and silver, and precious stones, and sometimes we build with wood, and hay, and stubble. And we are solemnly warned that every man's work is to be made manifest, "for the day shall declare it, because it shall be revealed by fire." There is no escaping this. We cannot hope, when that day comes, to conceal our wood, and hay, and stubble, however successfully we may have managed to do so beforehand.

To my mind there is no more solemn passage in the whole Bible than the one in Galatians which says: "Be not deceived: God is not mocked: for whatsoever a man soweth, that shall he also reap. For he that soweth to the flesh shall of the flesh reap corruption; but he that soweth to the Spirit, shall of the Spirit reap life everlasting." It is the awful inevitableness of this that is so awe-inspiring. It is far worse than any arbitrary punishment; for punishment can sometimes be averted, but there is no possibility of altering the working of a natural law such as this.

In a Catechism I saw were the following questions and answers:

Q. What is the reward for generosity?

A. More generosity.

Q. What is the punishment for meanness?

A. More meanness.

No Catechism ever spoke more truly. We all of us know it for ourselves. In the parable of the talents our Lord illustrates this inevitable law. The condemnation on the unfaithful servant may have sometimes seemed to us unfair, but it was only the reaping of what that servant had sowed. "Take therefore the talent from him and give it unto him which hath ten talents. For unto every one that hath shall be given, and he shall have abundance: but from him that hath not, shall be taken away even that which he hath." This is no arbitrary pronouncement, but is simply a revelation of the inherent nature of things from which none of us can escape.

But in order to be laborers together with God, we must not only build with His materials but also by His processes, and of these we are often very ignorant. Our idea of building is of hard laborious work done in the sweat of our brow; but God's idea is far different. Paul tells us what it is. "We all," he says, "with open face beholding as in a glass the glory of the Lord, are changed into the same image from glory to glory, even as by the Spirit of the Lord." Our work is to "behold," and as we behold the Lord effects the marvelous transformation, and we are "changed into the same image by the Spirit of the Lord." This means, of course, to behold not in our earthly sense of merely looking at a thing, but in the divine sense of really seeing the thing. We are to behold with our spiritual eyes the glory of the Lord, and are to continue beholding it. The glory of the Lord does not mean, however, a great shine or halo. The real glory of the Lord is the glory of what He is and of what He does—the glory of character. And it is this we are to behold.

Let me give an illustration. Someone offends me, and I am tempted to get angry and retaliate. But I look at Christ and think of what He would have done, and dwell upon the thought of His gentleness and meekness and His love for the offending one; and, as I look, I begin to want to be like Him, and I ask in faith that I may be made a "partaker of his nature," and anger and revenge die out of my heart, and I love my enemy and long to serve him.

It is by this sort of beholding Christ that we are to be changed into His image; and the nearer we keep to Him the more rapid the change will be.

I have heard of a wonderful mirror known to science, which is called the parabolic mirror. It is a hollow cone lined with a mirror all over its inside surface. It possesses the power of focusing rays of light in different degrees of intensity in proportion to the increasing nearness to its meeting point at the top end of the cone, the power being more and more intense as the terminal point is approached. It has been discovered by science that at a certain stage in this advance toward the interior point where all the sides of the mirror meet in absolute oneness, the power of the focus concentrates all the light-giving properties of the sun's rays into such an intense brilliancy, as to make visible things never before discerned by the human eye, rendering even flesh transparent, and enabling us to see through the outer covering of our bodies to the inner operations beneath.

Advancing a little farther into the interior of our mirror, the heat properties of the sun's rays are so concentrated as to generate a heat sufficient to melt iron in sixteen seconds, and to dissipate in fourteen seconds the alloy of gold, leaving only the solid globule of the pure metal.

Advancing farther still, the photographing properties of the sunlight are so concentrated as to impress an ineffaceable image of the mirror upon anything that is passed for only one second through the focus.

Advancing still farther, nearly to the point of oneness, the magnetizing powers of light are so concentrated that anything exposed to it for a single instant becomes a powerful magnet, drawing afterward all things to itself.

Whether all this is scientifically correct or not, I am not enough of a scientist to know, but at least it will serve as an allegory to show the progress of the soul as it is changed from glory to glory in its evolution "into his image."

First, as we behold as in a mirror the glory of the Lord, we come to the light focus, which reveals our sinfulness and our need. "Then spake Jesus again unto them, saying, I am the light of the world; he that followeth me shall not walk in darkness, but shall have the light of life."

Second, as we draw closer, we reach the heat focus, where all our dross and reprobate silver is burned up. For He is like a refiner's fire, and like fuller's soap: and "he shall sit as a refiner and purifier of silver; and he shall purify the sons of Levi, and purge them as gold and silver, that they may offer unto the Lord an offering in righteousness."

Third, as we draw closer still, we come to the photographing focus, where the image of Christ is indelibly impressed upon our souls, and we are made like Him because we see Him as He is. "We know that when he shall appear, we shall be like him, for we shall see him as he is."

Fourth and finally, as we come to the point of oneness, we reach the magnetic focus, where our character is so conformed to Christ, that men seeing it will be irresistibly drawn to glorify our Father which is in Heaven.

If we would be conformed to the image of Christ, then we must live closer and ever closer to Him. We must become better and better acquainted with His character and His ways; we must look at things through His eyes, and judge all things by His standards.

It is not by effort or by wrestling that this conformity is to be accomplished; it is by assimilation. According to a natural law, we grow like those with whom we associate, and the stronger character always exercises the controlling influence. And, as divine law is all one with natural law, only working in a higher sphere and with more unhindered power, it need not seem mysterious to us that we should become like Christ by a spiritual union with Him.

But again I must repeat that this union with Christ cannot come by our own efforts, no matter how strenuous they may be. Christ is to "dwell in our hearts by faith," and He can dwell there in no other way. Paul, when he tells us that he was crucified with Christ, says: "Nevertheless I live: yet not I but Christ liveth in me: and the life that I now live, I live by the faith of the Son of God who loved me, and gave himself for me."

"Christ liveth in me," this is the transforming secret. If Christ liveth in me, His life must, in the very nature of things, be manifested in my mortal flesh, and I cannot fail to be changed from glory to glory into His image.

Our Lord's teaching about this is very emphatic. "Abide in me," He says, "and I in you. As the branch cannot bear fruit of itself except it abide in the vine; no more can ye, except ye abide in me. I am the vine, ye are the branches. He that abideth in me, and I in him, the same bringeth forth much fruit; for without me ye can do nothing."

This is literally true. If we abide in Him, and He in us, we can no more help bring forth fruit than can the branches of a flourishing vine. In the very nature of things the fruit must come.

But we cannot take the "old man" into Christ. We must put off the old man with his deeds before we can "put on the Lord Jesus Christ." And the Apostle, in writing to the Colossians, bases his exhortations to holiness of life on the fact that they had done this. "Lie not one to another," he says, "seeing that ye have put off the old man with his deeds, and have put on the new man, which is renewed in knowledge after the image of him that created him."

Sin must disappear at the incoming of Christ; and no soul that is not prepared to surrender all that is contrary to His will can hope to welcome Him. The "old man" must be put off if the new man is to reign. But both the putting off and the putting on must be done by faith. There is no other way. As I have tried to explain elsewhere, we must move our personality, our ego, our will out of self and into Christ. We must reckon ourselves to be dead to self, and alive only to God. "Reckon ye also yourselves to be dead indeed unto sin, but alive unto God through Jesus Christ our Lord." "Neither yield ye your members as instruments of unrighteousness unto sin; but yield yourselves unto God as those that are alive from the dead, and your members as instruments of righteousness unto God."

The same kind of reckoning of faith, which brings the forgiveness of sins within our grasp, brings also this union with Christ. To those who do not understand the law of faith, this will no doubt be as great a mystery as the secrets of gravitation were before the law of gravitation was discovered; but, to those who understand it, the law of faith works as unerringly and as definitely as the law of gravitation, and produces its results as certainly. No one can read the seventh chapter of Hebrews and fail to see that faith is an all-conquering force. I believe myself it is the creative force of the universe. It is the higher law that controls all the lower laws beneath it; and what looks like a miracle is simply the working of this higher controlling law.

Faith is, as I say, the law of Creation— "Through faith we understand that the worlds were framed by the word of God, so that things which are seen were not made of things which are seen were not made of things which do appear." We are told that "God spake and it was done, he commanded and it stood fast." And our Lord tells us that if we have faith we can do the same. "And Jesus answering saith unto them, Have faith in God. For verily I say unto you, That whosoever shall say unto this mountain, Be thou removed, and be thou cast into the sea, and shall not doubt in his heart, but shall believe that those things which he saith shall come to pass, he shall have whatsoever he saith. Therefore I say unto you, What things soever ye desire when ye pray, believe that ye receive them, and ye shall have them."

Faith, we are told, calls those things which be not as though they were; and, in so calling them, brings them into being. Therefore, although we cannot see any tangible sign of change when by faith we put off the old man, which is corrupt according to the deceitful lusts, and by faith put on the new man which after God is created in righteousness and true holiness, yet nevertheless, it has really been done, and faith has accomplished it. I cannot explain this theologically, but I can fearlessly assert that it is a tremendous practical reality; and that those souls who abandon the self-life, and give themselves up the Lord to be fully possessed by Him, do find that He takes possession of the inner springs of their being, and works there to will and to do of His good pleasure.

Paul prayed for the Ephesians that "Christ might dwell in their hearts by faith," and this is the whole secret of being conformed to His image. If Christ is dwelling in my heart I must necessarily be Christlike. I cannot be unkind, or irritable, or self-seeking, or dishonest; but His gentleness, and sweetness, and tender compassion, and loving submission to the will of His Father must be manifested in my daily walk and conversation.

We shall not be fully changed into the image of Christ until He shall appear, and we shall "see him as he is." But meanwhile, according to our measure, the life of Jesus is to be made "manifest in our mortal flesh." Is it made manifest in ours? Are we so "conformed to the image" of Christ that men in seeing us see a glimpse of Him also?

A Methodist minister's wife told me that at one time, when they had moved to a new place, her little boy came in after the first afternoon of play, and exclaimed joyfully, "Oh, Mother, I have found such a lovely, good little girl to play with, that I never want to go away again."

"I am very glad, darling," said the loving mother, happy over her child's happiness. "What is the little girl's name?"

"Oh," replied the child, with a sudden solemnity, "I think her name is Jesus."

"Why, Frank!" exclaimed the horrified mother, "what do you mean?"

"Well, Mother," he said deprecatingly, "she was so lovely that I did not know what she could be called but Jesus."

Are our lives so Christlike that anyone could have such a thought of us? Is it patent to all around us that we have been with Jesus? Is it not, alas, often just the contrary? Are not some of us so cross and uncomfortable in our living that exactly the opposite thing would have to be said about us?

Paul says we are to be "epistles of Christ," known and read of all men, "written, not with ink, but with the Spirit of the living God, not in tables of stone, but in fleshy tables of the heart." I firmly believe that if every child of God, all the world over, would begin from this day onward to be an "epistle of Christ," living a truly Christlike life at home and abroad, it would not be a month before the churches would all be crowded with inquirers, coming in to see what was the religion that could so transform human nature into something divine.

The world is full of unbelievers in the reality of the Christian religion, and nothing will convince them but facts which they cannot disprove. We must meet them with transformed lives. If they see that whereas once we were cross, now we are sweet; once we were proud, now we are humble; once we were fretful, now we are patient and calm; and if we are able to testify that it is the religion of Christ that has wrought this change, they cannot help but be impressed.

A Christian man who, on account of his earnest work, had gained a great reputation for piety, had unfortunately gained an equally great reputation for a bad temper and a sharp tongue. But at last, for some reason which no one could understand, a change seemed to come over him, and his temper and his tongue became as sweet and as gentle as they had before been violent and sharp. His friends watched and wondered, and at last one of them approached him on the subject, and asked him if he had changed his religion. "No," replied the man, "I have not changed my religion, but I have at last let my religion change me."

How much has our religion changed us?

It is very easy to have a church religion, or a prayer meeting religion, or a Christian-work religion; but it is altogether a different thing to have an everyday religion. To "show piety at home" is one of the most vital parts of Christianity, but it is also one far too rare; and it is not at all an uncommon thing to find Christians who "do their righteousness" before outsiders "to be seen of men," but who fail lamentably in showing their piety at home. I knew a father of a family who was so powerful in prayer at the weekly prayer meeting, and so impressive in exhortation that the whole church was much edified by his piety; but who, when he went home after the meetings, was so cross and ugly that his wife and family were afraid to say a word in his presence.

"And when thou prayest, thou shalt not be as the hypocrites are; for they love to pray standing in the synagogues and in the corners of the streets, that they may be seen of men. Verily I say unto you, They have their reward." These words, "They have their reward," seem to me among the most solemn in the Bible. What we do to be seen of men is seen of men, and that is all there is to it. There is no conformity to the image of Christ in this sort of righteousness that bears everyday trials cheerfully, and is patient under home provocations; that returns good for evil, and meets all the homely friction of daily life with sweetness and gentleness; that suffereth long and is kind; that envieth not; that flaunteth not itself; that is not puffed up; that seeketh not its own; is not easily provoked; and thinketh no evil; that beareth all things, believeth all things, hopeth all things, endureth all things. This is what it means to be conformed to the image of Christ! Do we know anything of such righteousness as this?

We sometimes talk about performing what we call our "religious duties," meaning by this expression our church services, or our stated seasons of devotion, or our Christian work of one sort or another; and we never dream that it is far more our "religious duty" to be Christlike in our daily walk and conversation than to be faithful even in these other things, desirable as they may be in themselves.

The righteousness of the Scribes and Pharisees was a righteousness of words and phrases and of ceremonial observances, and this is often very impressive to outsiders. But, because it was nothing more, our Lord condemns it in unmeasured terms: "Woe unto you, Scribes and Pharisees, hypocrites! For ye pay tithe of mint and anise, and cumin, and have omitted the weightier matters of the law, judgment, mercy, and faith: these ought ye to have done, and not to leave the other undone. Woe unto you, Scribes and Pharisees, hypocrites! For ye are like unto whited sepulchers, which indeed appear beautiful outward, but are within full of dead men's bones, and of all uncleanness." And He adds: "Even so ye also outwardly appear righteous unto men, but within ye are full of hypocrisy and iniquity."

It is very easy to say beautiful things about the religious life, but to *be* what we say is an altogether different matter. I know a Sunday school teacher who had been teaching her scholars a great deal about casting all your cares on the Lord, and trusting Him in times of trial; and they had been very much impressed. But at last a trouble came into the life of this teacher, and some of her scholars saw her in her own home while it lasted. To their amazement and distress they saw her fretting, and chafing, and worrying, and complaining, acting, in short, just as if there was no God to trust, or as if His ways were not ways of love and goodness. It was all "object lesson" to those children that undid all the good which that teacher's previous teaching had seemed likely to accomplish; and one of them, who was very observant, said to me triumphantly, "I thought it could not be true while Miss _____ was telling us about how we might trust the Lord for everything; and now I see it was only goody talk, for she doesn't do it herself."

A cross Christian, or an anxious one, a discouraged gloomy Christian, a doubting Christian, a complaining Christian, an exacting Christian, a selfish, cruel, hardhearted Christian, a self-indulgent Christian, a Christian with a sharp tongue or a bitter spirit; a Christian, in short, who is not Christlike may preach to the winds with as much hope of success, as to preach to his own family or friends, who see him as he is. There is no escape from this inevitable law of things, and we may as well recognize it at once. If we want our loved ones to trust the Lord, volumes of talk about it will not be one-thousandth part as convincing to them as the sight of a little real trust on our own part in the time of need. The longest prayer and the loudest preaching are of no avail in any family circle, however they may do in the pulpit, unless there is on the part of the preacher a living out of the things preached.

Some Christians seem to think that the fruits which the Bible calls for are some form of outward religious work, such as holding meetings, visiting the poor, conduction charitable institutions, and so forth. Whereas the fact is that the Bible scarcely mentions these at all as fruits of the Spirit, but declares that the fruit of the Spirit is love, joy, peace, long-suffering, gentleness, goodness, faith, meekness, temperance. A Christlike character must necessarily be the fruit of Christ's indwelling. Other things will no doubt be the outcome of this character; but first and foremost comes the character, or all the rest is but a hollow sham. A late writer has said: "A man can never be more than his character makes him. A man can never do more nor better than deliver or embody that which his character. Nothing valuable can come out of a man that is not first in the man. Character must stand behind and back up everything—the sermon, the poem, the picture, the book. None of them is worth a straw without it."

In order to become conformed to the image of Christ, we must of necessity be made "partakers of the divine nature." And, where this is the case, that divine nature must necessarily manifest itself. Our tastes, our wishes, our purposes will become like Christ's tastes, and wishes, and purposes; we shall change eyes with Him, and see things as He sees them. This is inevitable; for where the divine nature is, its fruits cannot fail to be manifest; and, where they are not manifest, we are forced to conclude that that individual, no matter how loud his professions, has not yet been made a partaker of the divine nature.

I can hear someone asking, But do you really mean to say that, in order to be made partakers of the divine nature, we must cease from our own efforts entirely, and must simply by faith put on Christ, and must let Him live in us and work in us to will and to do of His good pleasure? And do you believe He will then actually do it?

To this I answer most emphatically, Yes, I mean just that. I mean that if we abandon ourselves entirely to Him, He comes to abide in us, and is Himself our life. We must commit our whole lives to Him, our thoughts, our words, our daily walk, our downsittings, our uprisings. By faith we must abandon ourselves, and, as it were, move over into Christ, and abide in Him. By faith we must put off the old man, and by faith we must put on the new man. By faith we must reckon ourselves dead unto sin, and alive unto God; as truly dead as alive. By faith we must realize that our daily life is Christ living in us; and, ceasing from our own works, we must suffer Him to work in us to will and to do of His good pleasure. It is no longer truth about Him that must fill our hearts, but it is Himself—the living, loving, glorious Christ—who will, if we let Him, in very deed make us His dwelling place, and who will reign and rule within us, and "subdue all things unto himself." "Therefore if any man be in Christ, he is a new creature; old things are passed away; behold, all things are become new."

It was no mere figure of speech when our Lord in that wonderful Sermon on the Mount said to His disciples: "Be ye therefore perfect even as your Father in heaven is perfect." He meant, of course, according to our measure, but He meant that reality of being conformed to His image to which we have been predestined. And in the Epistle to the Hebrews we are shown how it is to be brought about. "Now the God of peace, that brought again from the dead our Lord Jesus, that great Shepherd of the sheep, through the blood of the everlasting covenant, make you perfect in every good work to do his will; working in you that which is well pleasing in His sight, through Jesus Christ: to whom be glory forever and ever. Amen."

It is to be by His working in us, and not by our working in ourselves, that this purpose of God in our creation is to be accomplished; and if it should look as regards some of us that we are too far removed from any conformity to the image of Christ for such a transformation ever to be wrought, we must remember that our Maker is not finished making us yet. The day will come, if we do not hinder, when the work begun in Genesis shall be finished in Revelation, and the whole Creation, as well as ourselves, shall be delivered from the bondage of corruption into the glorious liberty of the children of God.

"For we know that the whole creation groaneth and travaileth in pain together until now. And not only they, but ourselves also, which have the first fruits of the Spirit, even we ourselves groan within ourselves, waiting for the adoption, to wit the redemption of our body."

> 'Tis, shall Thy will be done for me? or mine,
> And I be made a thing, not after Thine;
> My own, and full of paltriest pretense?
> Shall I be born of God, or of mere man?
> Be made like Christ, or on some other plan?
> What though Thy work in me transcends my sense,
> Too fine, too high for me to understand.
> I trust entirely. Oh, Lord, with Thy labor grand!
> I have not knowledge, wisdom, insight, thought,
> Nor understanding fit to justify
> Thee in Thy work, O Perfect. Thou hast brought
> Me up to this, and lo! what thou hast wrought
> I cannot call it good. But I can cry
> "O enemy, the Maker hath not done;
> One day thou shalt behold, and from the sight wilt run."

Chapter 17: God Is Enough

*"My soul wait thou only upon God, for my expectation is from him.
He only is my rock and my salvation; he is my defense; I shall not be
moved. In God is my salvation, and my glory: the rock of my strength
and my refuge is in God."*

The last and greatest lesson that the soul has to learn is the fact that God, and God alone, is enough for all its needs. This is the lesson that all His dealings with us are meant to teach; and this is the crowning discovery of our whole Christian life. *God is enough!*

We have been considering in this book some aspects of the character and the ways of God as revealed to us in the Lord Jesus Christ; and also some of the mistakes which prevent us from appropriating the fullness that is ours in Him. And now in conclusion I want to tell, as best I can, what seems to me the outcome of the whole matter.

If God is what He would seem to be from the revealings we have been considering; if He is indeed the "God of all comfort," as we have seen; if He is our Shepherd; if He is really and truly our Father; if, in short, all the many aspects we have been studying of His character and His ways are actually true, then we must, it seems to me, come to the positive conviction that He is, in Himself alone, enough for all our possible needs, and that we may safely rest in Him absolutely and forever.

Most Christians have, I suppose, sung more often than they could count, these words in one of our most familiar hymns:

*Thou, O Christ, art all I want,
More than all in Thee I find.*

But I doubt whether all of us could honestly say that the words have expressed any reality in our own experience. Christ has not been all we want. We have wanted a great many things besides Him. We have wanted fervent feelings about Him, or realizations of His presence with us, or an interior revelation of His love; or else we have demanded satisfactory schemes of doctrine, or successful Christian work, or something of one sort or another, besides Himself, that will constitute a personal claim upon Him. Just Christ Himself, Christ alone, without the addition of any of our experiences concerning Him, has not been enough for us in spite of all our singing; and we do not even see how it is possible that He could be enough.

The Psalmist said in those old days: "My soul, wait thou only upon God: for my expectation is from him." But now the Christian says, "My soul, wait thou upon my sound doctrines, for my expectation is from them"; or, "My soul, wait thou on my good disposition and feelings, or upon my righteous works, or upon my fervent prayers, or upon my earnest striving, for my expectation is from these." To wait upon God only seems one of the unsafest things they can do, and to have their expectation from Him alone is like building on the sand. They reach out on every side for something to depend on, and, not until everything else fails, will they put their trust in God alone. George Macdonald says: "We look upon God as our last and feeblest resource. We only go to Him when we have nowhere else to go. And then we learn that the storms of life have driven us, not upon the rocks, but into the desired haven."

No soul can be really at rest until it has given up all dependence on everything else and has been forced to depend on the Lord alone. As long as our expectation is from other things, nothing but disappointment awaits us. Feelings may change, and will change with our changing circumstances; doctrines and dogmas may be upset; Christian work may come to naught; prayers may seem to lose their fervency; promises may seem to fail; everything that we have believed in or depended upon may seem to be swept away, and only God is left, just God, the bare God, if I may be allowed the expression; simply and only God.

We say sometimes, "If I could only find a promise to fit my case, I could then be at rest." But promises may be misunderstood or misapplied, and, at the moment when we are leaning all our weight upon them, they may seem utterly to fail us. But the Promiser, who is behind His promises, and is infinitely more than His promises, can never fail nor change. The little child does not need to have any promises from its mother to make it content; it has its mother herself, and she is enough. Its mother is better than a thousand promises. In our highest ideal of love or friendship, promises do not enter. One party may love to make promises, just as our Lord does, but the other party does not need them; the personality of lover or friend is better than all their promises. And should every promise be wiped out of the Bible, we would still have God left, and God would be enough. Again I repeat it, only God, He Himself, just as He is, without the addition of anything on our part, whether it be disposition or feelings, or experiences, or good works, or sound doctrines, or any other thing either outward or inward. "God only is my rock and my salvation; he is my defense: I shall not be moved."

I do not mean by this that we are not to have feelings, or experiences, or revelations, or good works, or sound doctrines. We may have all of these, but they must be the result of salvation, and never the procuring cause; and they can never be depended upon as being any indication of our spiritual condition. They are all things that come and go, and are dependent often upon the state of our health, or the condition of our surroundings, or even sometimes upon the quarter of the wind. Some people, for instance, can never believe that God loves them when the wind is in slightest degree as the groundwork for our confidence or our joy, we are sure to come to grief. What I do mean is that we are to hold ourselves absolutely independent of them all, resting in only the grand, magnificent fact that God is, and that He is our Savior; our inner life prospers just as well and is just as triumphant without these personal experiences or personal doings as it is with them. We are to find God, the fact of God, sufficient for all our spiritual needs, whether we feel ourselves to be in a desert or in a fertile valley. We are to say with the prophet: "Although the fig-tree shall not blossom, neither shall fruit be in the vines; the labor of the olive shall fail, and the field shall yield no meat, the flock shall be cut off from the fold, and there shall be no herd in the stall; yet I will rejoice in the Lord, I will joy in the God of my salvation."

The soul is made for this, and can never find rest short of it. All God's dealings with us, therefore, are shaped to this end; and He is often obliged to deprive us of all joy in everything else in order that He may force us to find our joy only and altogether in Himself. It is all very well, perhaps, to rejoice in His promises, or to rejoice in the revelations He may have granted us, or in the experiences we may have realized; but to rejoice in the Promiser Himself—Himself alone—without promises, or experiences, or revelations, this is crowning point of Christian life; and this is the only place where we can know the peace which passes all understanding, and which nothing can disturb.

It is difficult to explain just what I mean. We have so accustomed ourselves to consider all these accompaniments of the spiritual life as being the spiritual life itself that it is hard to detach ourselves from them. We cannot think that the Lord can be anything to us unless we find in ourselves something to assure us of His love and His care. And when we talk about finding our all in Him, we generally mean that we find it in our feelings or our views about Him. If, for instance, we feel a glow of love toward Him, then we can say heartily that He is enough; but when this glow fails, as sooner or later it is almost sure to do, then we no longer feel that we have found our all in Him. The truth is that what satisfies us is not the Lord, but our own feelings about the Lord. But we are not conscious of this; and consequently when our feelings fail we think it is the Lord who has failed, and we are plunged into darkness.

Of course, all this is very foolish, but it is such a common experience that very few can see how foolish it is. Perhaps an illustration may help us to clearer vision. Let us think of a man accused of a crime, standing before a judge. Which would be the thing of moment for that man: his own feelings toward the judge, or the judge's feelings toward him? Would he spend his time watching his own emotions, and trying to see whether he felt that the judge was favorable to him or would he watch the judge and try to discover from his looks or his words whether or not to expect a favorable judgment? Of course we will say at once that the man's own feelings are not of the slightest account in the matter, and that only the opinions and feelings of the judge are worth a moment's thought. The man might have all the "glows" and all the "experiences" conceivable, but these would avail absolutely nothing. Upon the judge only would everything depend.

This is what we would call a self-evident fact.

In the same way, if we will only bring our common sense to bear upon the subject, we cannot help seeing that the only really vital thing in our relations with the Lord is, not what are our feelings toward Him, but what are His feelings toward us. The man who is being tried must find in the judge all he needs, if he is to find it at all. His sufficiency cannot possibly be of himself, but it must be of the one upon whom his fate depends. And our sufficiency, the Apostle says, is not of ourselves but of God.

This, then, is what I mean by God being enough. It is that we find in Him, in the fact of His existence, and of His character, all that we can possibly want for everything. *God is,* must be our answer to every question and every cry of need. If there is any lack in the One who has undertaken to save us, nothing supplementary we can do will avail to make it up; and if there is no lack in Him, then He, of Himself and in Himself, is enough.

I wish it were possible to make my meaning plain, for I believe it is the secret of permanent deliverance from all the discomfort and unrest of every Christian life. Your discomfort and unrest arise from your strenuous but useless efforts to get up some satisfactory basis of confidence within yourselves; such, for instance, as what you consider to be the proper feelings, or the right amount of fervor or earnestness, or at least, if nothing else, a sufficient degree of interest in spiritual matters. And because none of these things are ever satisfactory (and, I may tell you, never will be), it is impossible for your religious life to be anything but uncomfortable.

But if we see that all our salvation from beginning to end depends on the Lord alone; and if we have learned that He is able and willing to do for us "exceeding abundantly above all we can ask or think," then peace and comfort cannot fail to reign supreme. Everything depends upon whether the Lord, in and of Himself, is enough for our salvation, or whether other things must be added on our part to make Him sufficient.

The thing that helped me personally more than anything else to come to a conviction that God was really enough for me was an experience I had some years ago. It was at a time in my religious life when I was passing through a great deal of questioning and perplexity, and I felt that no Christian had ever had such peculiar difficulties as mine before. There happened to be staying near me just then for a few weeks a lady who was considered to be a deeply spiritual Christian, and to whom I had been advised to apply for spiritual help. I summoned up my courage, therefore, one afternoon and went to see her, pouring out my troubles; I expected of course that she would take a deep interest in me, and would be at great pains to do all she could to help me.

She listened patiently enough, and did not interrupt me; but when I had finished my story, and had paused, expecting sympathy and consideration, she simply said, "Yes, all you say may be very true, but then, in spite of it all, there is God." I waited a few minutes for something more, but nothing came, and my friend and teacher had the air of having said all that was necessary.

"But," I continued, "surely you did not understand how very serious and perplexing my difficulties are."

"Oh, yes, I did," replied my friend, "but then, as I tell you, there is God." And I could not induce her to make any other answer. It seemed to me most disappointing and unsatisfactory. I felt that my peculiar and really harrowing experiences could not be met by anything so simple as merely the statement, "Yes, but there is God." I knew God was there, of course, but I felt I needed something more than just God; and I came to the conclusion that my friend, for all her great reputation as a spiritual teacher, was at any rate not able to grapple with a peculiar case such as mine was.

However, my need was so great that I did not give up with my first trial, but went to her again and again, always with the hope that she would sometime begin to understand the importance of my difficulties and would give me adequate help. It was of no avail. I was never able to draw forth any other answer. Always to everything would come the simple reply, with an air of entirely dismissing the subject, "Yes, I know; but there is God." And at last by dint of her continual repetition I became convinced that my friend really and truly believed that the mere fact of the existence of God, as the Creator and Redeemer of mankind, and of me as a member of the race, was an all-sufficient answer to every possible need of His creatures. And at last, because she said it so often and seemed so sure, I began dimly to wonder whether after all God might not be enough, even for my need, overwhelming and secular as I felt it to be. From wondering I came gradually to believing, that, being my Creator and Redeemer, He must be enough; and at last a conviction burst upon me that He really was enough, and my eyes were opened to the fact of the absolute and utter all-sufficiency of God.

My troubles disappeared like magic, and I did nothing but wonder how I could ever have been such an idiot as to be troubled by them, when all the while there was God, the Almighty and all-seeing God, the God who had created me, and was therefore on my side, and eager to care for me and help me. I had found out that God was enough and my soul was at rest.

The all-sufficiency of God ought to be as complete to the child of God as the all-sufficiency of a good mother is to the child of that mother. We all know the utter rest of the little child in the mother's presence and the mother's love. That its mother is there is enough to make all fears and all troubles disappear. It does not need the mother to make any promises; she herself, just as she is, without promises and without explanations, is all that the child needs.

356 Hannah Whitall Smith

My own experience as a child taught me this, beyond any possibility of question. My mother was the remedy for all my own ills, and, I fully believed, for the ills of the whole world, if only they could be brought to her. And when anyone expressed doubts as to her capacity to remedy everything, I remembered with what fine scorn I used to annihilate them, by saying, "Ah! but you don't know my mother."

And now, when any tempest-tossed soul fails to see that God is enough, I feel like saying, not with scorn, but with infinite pity, "Ah, dear friend, you do not know God! Did you know Him, you could not help seeing that He is the remedy for every need of your soul, and that He is an all-sufficient remedy. God is enough, even though no promise may seem to fit your case, nor any inward assurance give you confidence. The Promiser is more than His promises; and His existence is a surer ground of confidence than the most fervent inward feelings."

> Oh, utter but the name of God
>   Down in the heart of hearts,
> And see how from the soul at once
>   All anxious fear departs.

But someone may say, "All this is no doubt true, and I could easily believe it, if I could only be sure it applied to me. But I am so good-for-nothing and so full of sin, that I do not feel as if I had any claim to such riches of grace."

All the more, if you are good-for-nothing and full of sin, have you a claim on the all-sufficiency of God. Your very good-for-nothingness and sinfulness are your loudest claims. As someone has said, it is only the sinner that wants salvation who stands in the Savior's path. And the Bible declares that Christ Jesus came into the world to save sinners; not to save the righteous, not to save the fervent, not to save the earnest workers, but simply and only to save sinners. Why then should we spend our time and energies in trying to create a claim, which after all is no claim, but only a hindrance.

As long as our attention is turned upon ourselves and our own experiences, just so long is it turned away from the Lord. This is plain common sense. As I have said elsewhere, we can only see the thing we look at, and while we are looking at ourselves, we simply cannot "behold God." It is not that He hides Himself; He is always there in full view of all who look unto Him; but if we are looking in another direction, we cannot expect to see Him.

Heretofore, it may be, our eyes have been so fixed upon ourselves that all our interior questioning has been simply and only as regarded our own condition. Is my love for God warm enough? Am I enough in earnest? Are my feeling toward Him what they ought to be? Have I enough zeal? Do I feel my need as I ought? And we have been miserable because we have never been able to answer these questions satisfactorily. Although we do not know it, it has been a mercy we never could answer them satisfactorily, for, if we had, the self in us would have been exalted, and we should have been filled with self-congratulation and pride.

If we want to see God, our interior questioning must be, not about ourselves, but about Him. How does God feel toward me? Is His love for me warm enough? Has He enough zeal? Does He feel my need deeply enough? Is He sufficiently in earnest? Although these questions may seem irreverent to some, they simply embody the doubts and fears of a great many doubting hearts, and they only need to be asked in order to prove the fact that these doubts and fears are in themselves the real irreverence. We all know what would be the triumphant answers to such questions. No doubts could withstand their testimony; and the soul that asks and answers them honestly will be shut up to a profound and absolute conviction that God is and must be enough.

"All things are yours," declares the Apostle, "whether Paul, or Apollos, or Cephas, or the world, or life, or death, or things present, or things to come; all are yours; and ye are Christ's; and Christ is God's." It would be impossible for any statement to be more all-embracing. And all things are yours because you belong to Christ, not because you are so good and so worthy, but simply and only because you belong to Christ. All things we need are part of our inheritance in Him, and they only await our claiming. Let our needs and difficulties be as great as they may, there is in these "all things" a supply exceeding abundantly above all we can ask or think.

Because He is, all must go right for us. Because the mother is, all must go right, up to the measure of her ability, for her children; and infinitely more must this be true of the Lord. To the child there is, behind all that changes and can change, the one unchangeable fact of the mother's existence. While the mother lives, the child must be cared for; and, while God lives, His children must be cared for as well. What else could He do, being what He is? Neglect, indifference, forgetfulness, ignorance are all impossible to Him. He knows everything, He cares about everything, He can manage everything, and He loves us. What more could we ask?

God's saints in all ages have known this, and have realized that God was enough for them. Job said out of the depths of sorrows and trials, which few can equal, "Though he slay me, yet will I trust in him." David could say in the moment of his keenest anguish, "yea, though I walk through the valley of the shadow of death," yet "I will fear no evil, for thou art with me." And again he could say: "God is our refuge and strength, a very present help in trouble. Therefore will not we fear though the earth be removed, and though the mountains be carried into the midst of the sea; though the waters thereof roar and be troubled; though the mountains shake with the swelling thereof... God is in the midst of her; she shall not be moved; God shall help her, and that right early."

Paul could say triumphantly in the midst of many and grievous trials: "For I am persuaded that neither death, nor life, nor angels, nor principalities, nor powers, nor things present, nor things to come, nor height, nor depth, nor any other creature, shall be able to separate us from the love of God, which is in Christ Jesus our Lord."

Therefore, O doubting and sorrowful Christian hearts, in the face of all we have learned concerning the God of all comfort, cannot your realize with Job, and David, and Paul, and the saints of all ages that nothing else is needed to quiet all your fears, but just this, that *God is*. His simple existence is all the warrant your need requires for its certain relieving. Nothing can separate you from His love, absolutely nothing, neither death nor life, nor angels, nor principalities, nor powers, nor things present, nor things to come, nor height, nor depth, nor any other creature. Every possible contingency is provided for here; and not one of them can separate you from the love of God which is in Christ Jesus our Lord.

After such a declaration as this, how can any of us dare to question or doubt God's love? And, since He loves us, He cannot exist and fail to help us. Do we not know by our own experience what an imperative necessity it is for love to pour itself out in blessing on the ones it loves; and can we not understand that God, who is love, who is, if I may say so, made out of love, simply cannot help blessing us. We do not need to beg Him to bless us, He simply cannot help it.

Therefore God is enough! God is enough for time, God is enough for eternity. *God is ENOUGH!*

> *Only to sit and think of God,*
> *Oh, what a joy it is!*
> *To think the thought, to breathe the Name*
> *Earth has no higher bliss.*

Other Books on Reliance

And there are also many other things which Jesus did, the which, if they should be written every one, I suppose that even the world itself could not contain the books that should be written. Amen. — John 21:25

Andrew Murray Four Book Treasury
(ISBN 9781640322318)

Christian Omnibus Vol. 1 - Eight Books on Prayer
(ISBN 9781640323087)

Christian Omnibus Vol. 2 - Six Books on Victorious Living
(ISBN 9781640323100)

Following Christ: Losing Your Life for His Sake by Charles H. Spurgeon

In His Steps: What Would Jesus Do? by Charles M. Sheldon
(ISBN 9781640322493)

My Life in Christ by St John of Kronstadt

Treatise on the Love of God by De Sales, St Francis

Way Into the Holiest by F. B. Meyer

www.ingramcontent.com/pod-product-compliance
Lightning Source LLC
Chambersburg PA
CBHW072337090426

42741CB00012B/2822